MW00998419

Inferences during Reading

Inferencing is defined as "the act of deriving logical conclusions from premises known or assumed to be true," and it is one of the most important processes necessary for successful comprehension during reading. This volume features contributions by distinguished researchers in cognitive psychology, educational psychology, and neuroscience on topics central to our understanding of the inferential process during reading. The chapters cover aspects of inferencing that range from the fundamental bottom-up processes that form the basis for an inference to occur, to the more strategic processes that transpire when a reader is engaged in literary understanding of a text. Basic activation mechanisms, word-level inferencing, methodological considerations, inference validation, causal inferencing, emotion, development of inferences processes as a skill, embodiment, contributions from neuroscience, and applications to naturalistic text are all covered as well as expository text and online learning materials, and literary immersion.

EDWARD J. O'BRIEN is Professor of Psychology at the University of New Hampshire.

ANNE E. COOK is Professor of Educational Psychology at the University of Utah.

ROBERT F. LORCH, JR., is Professor of Psychology at the University of Kentucky.

Inferences during Reading

Edited by

Edward J. O'Brien
University of New Hampshire

Anne E. Cook
University of Utah

Robert F. Lorch, Jr.
University of Kentucky

CAMBRIDGE
UNIVERSITY PRESS

CAMBRIDGE
UNIVERSITY PRESS

University Printing House, Cambridge CB2 8BS, United Kingdom

Cambridge University Press is part of the University of Cambridge.

It furthers the University's mission by disseminating knowledge in the pursuit of education, learning, and research at the highest international levels of excellence.

www.cambridge.org
Information on this title: www.cambridge.org/9781107049796

© Cambridge University Press 2015

First published 2015

A catalogue record for this publication is available from the British Library

Library of Congress Cataloguing in Publication data

O'Brien, Edward J.
Inferences during reading / Edward J. O'Brien, University of New Hampshire,
Anne E. Cook, University of Utah, Robert F. Lorch, Jr., University of
Kentucky. – First Edition.
    pages   cm
Includes bibliographical references and index.
ISBN 978-1-107-04979-6 (Hardback)
1. Inference.   2. Cognitive psychology.   I. Cook, Anne E.   II. Lorch,
Robert F.   III. Title.
BF442.O27 2015
418'.4019–dc23   2014044901

ISBN 978-1-107-04979-6 Hardback

Contents

Figures

Tables

Boxes

Contributors

KATINKA BEKER Brain and Education Laboratory, Leiden University

CANDICE BURKETT Learning Sciences Research Institute, University of Illinois – Chicago

KIRSTEN R. BUTCHER Department of Educational Psychology, University of Utah

KATE CAIN Department of Psychology, Lancaster University

ANNE E. COOK Department of Educational Psychology, University of Utah

REINIER COZIJN Tilberg Center for Communication and Cognition, Tilburg University

SARAH DAVIES Department of Educational Psychology, University of Utah

MANUEL DE VEGA Department of Psychology, University of La Laguna

SHI FENG Department of Psychology, University of Memphis

EVELYN C. FERSTL IIG/Cognitive Science, University of Freiburg

STEFAN FRANK Centre for Language Studies, Radboud University Nijmegen

RICHARD J. GERRIG Department of Psychology, State University of New York – Stony Brook

CHRISTELLE GILLIOZ Department of Psychology, University of California – San Diego

SUSAN R. GOLDMAN Department of Psychology, University of Illinois – Chicago

ARTHUR C. GRAESSER Department of Psychology, University of Memphis

PASCAL GYGAX Department of Psychology, University of Fribourg

PANAYIOTA KENDEOU Department of Educational Psychology, University of Minnesota

HAIYING LI Department of Psychology, University of Memphis

ROBERT F. LORCH, JR. Department of Psychology, University of Kentucky

DIANA MCCARTHY Department of Theoretical and Applied Linguistics, University of Cambridge

KATHRYN S. MCCARTHY Department of Psychology, University of Illinois – Chicago

GAIL MCKOON Department of Psychology, The Ohio State University

LEO NOORDMAN Tilberg Center for Communication and Cognition, Tilburg University

JANE OAKHILL School of Psychology, University of Sussex

EDWARD J. O'BRIEN Department of Psychology, University of New Hampshire

MARJA OUDEGA Brain and Education Laboratory, Leiden University

CHARLES A. PERFETTI Learning Research and Development Center, University of Pittsburgh

CHANTEL S. PRAT Institute for Learning and Brain Sciences, University of Washington

ROGER RATCLIFF Department of Psychology, The Ohio State University

MURRAY SINGER Department of Psychology, University of Manitoba

JOSEPH Z. STAFURA Learning Research and Development Center, University of Pittsburgh

PAUL VAN DEN BROEK Department of Educational Studies, Leiden University

WIETSKE VONK Max Planck Institute for Psycholinguistics and Centre for Language Studies, Radboud University Nijmegen

WILLIAM G. WENZEL Department of Psychology, State University of New York – Stony Brook

BRIANNA L. YAMASAKI Department of Psychology, University of Washington

Preface

Research in the area of reading comprehension has made enormous progress during the last thirty or more years. There are numerous books, research articles, and journals devoted solely to work done on increasing our understanding of the comprehension process. Because reading comprehension is so complex, even today, there are no models of the complete process; instead, models are designed to address various subcomponents of the complete comprehension process. Perhaps one of the most important processes necessary for successful comprehension during reading is that of inferencing. Over the last twenty-five years, research on inference generation during reading has advanced to the point that it has become a relatively "mature" area. We know a great deal about this critical comprehension process. In fact, across disciplines (e.g., education, psychology) and perspectives, there has been a good deal of convergence in terms of theoretical accounts and understanding of both the reader and text characteristics that promote the types of inferential processes that facilitate comprehension. Despite this high level of convergence, there is no centralized resource that captures it. Our goal was to bring together a set of chapters that capture this convergence while also providing a unified resource for interested readers who want to learn about the current state of the field's understanding of the inference process. The present book contains chapters by many distinguished researchers on topics central to our understanding of the inferential process during reading. These chapters cover aspects of inferencing that range from the fundamental bottom-up processes that form the basis for an inference to occur to the more strategic processes that occur when a reader is engaged in literary understanding of a text. Within this range, a wide variety of topics are covered that include basic activation mechanisms, word-level inferencing, methodological considerations, inference validation, causal inferencing, emotion, development of inference processes as a skill, embodiment, contributions from neuroscience, as well as applications to naturalistic, expository text, online learning materials, and literary immersion. We have used this progression from lower-level to higher-level processing as the organizing framework for the sequence of chapters in the volume.

The topics in this volume are grounded in research that comes from a wide variety of perspectives, including basic cognitive psychology, applied educational psychology, and neuroscience. This interdisciplinary coverage is apparent throughout the volume; many chapters touched on different levels or topics in inferencing; and many topics were covered by chapters from a variety of different perspectives. Within this interdisciplinary mingle two fundamental principles emerged. First, there are some basic cognitive mechanisms (i.e., passive memory activation) that drive inference generation, regardless of whether the inference occurs at a very basic word level or at a higher level of literary interpretation. Second, when inferences are encoded, the exact nature of what is encoded affects ultimate comprehension, memory, and learning. This is true regardless of whether the inference occurs during reading of narrative text, expository text, or during the encoding of multimedia materials for academic purposes.

Challenges and directions for future work also emerge from this volume. It is clear that a better understanding of the active, strategic processes involved in the production of inferences is needed, such as those that include literary interpretation, or integrating content across several texts. Much of the research and theory presented in these chapters stopped short of providing any serious model of inference production that can explain and/or predict active, strategic processes on the part of the reader. It is clear that the next major step – and likely the most difficult step – in our understanding of the inference process will occur with the development of testable models of active inference production. Such a model would surely deepen our understanding of the inference process, as well as define where current models of inferencing succeed in explaining research findings, and, more important, where they fail.

We are indebted to the contributors to this volume for their efforts in writing chapters that captured the current state of research into inference processing. Each chapter contributes to this understanding in ways that are unique to each author's line of work, but also overlapping with other authors to the extent that the field has indeed begun to converge on a high level of understanding of the inference process. The chapters are ordered – roughly – in terms of the issues addressed, beginning with those that address the more bottom-up aspects of the inference process to those that address the interaction of both bottom-up and top-down processes, and finally to those chapters that raise the most interesting and still least understood aspects of inferencing during reading.

Edward J. O'Brien
Anne E. Cook
Robert F. Lorch

1   Comprehending implicit meanings in text without making inferences

Charles A. Perfetti Joseph Z. Stafura

There are two thin lines that separate descriptions of text comprehension. The first is the line between what a text says (i.e., its explicit or literal meaning) and what is inferable from the text (i.e., its implicit meaning). The second thin line is one that separates two kinds of implicit meaning processes. On one side of this line is what text researchers refer to as inferences. Although these inferences can be further sorted into various types (e.g., Graesser, Singer, and Trabasso, 1994), they have in common the idea that the meaning that is obtained is not in the words and syntax of the text but is constructed by the reader based on knowledge that is largely independent of that particular text. On the other side of the line are implicit meaning processes that are closely bound to the language of the text, the meanings of words, and the grammar of the language. These lines are "thin" because they divide meaning processes only approximately and are subject to encroachment in difficult cases. There is good company for such thin lines in closely related distinctions in linguistic descriptions, especially semantics versus pragmatics and meaning versus interpretation.

In text comprehension research, attention has been diffusely distributed across both lines, treating inferences as a set of differentiated types that contrast with literal meaning. Indeed, analyses of the variety of inferences have led to taxonomies that differentiate among nine different types (Pressley and Afflerbach, 1995) and even thirteen or fourteen types (Graesser et al., 1994). These multiple varieties cross various dimensions of mixed types, some reflecting linguistic devices in the text (thematic role assignment, referential anaphora), but most lacking linguistic sources, dependent on reader knowledge (e.g., character emotion, causal consequence) or coherence strategies (e.g., causal coherence). Taxonomies are of limited value when they are not well defined according to some classification hierarchy, however. A mature taxonomy, for example, a biological taxonomy, serves long-lasting functions (in between modification) because it is organized hierarchically around structural or functional principles (e.g., biological

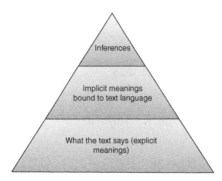

Figure 1.1 A hierarchical instrinsicalist view of explicit and implicit meaning. Texts are assumed to express explicit meanings constrained by the grammar of the language in combination with the meanings of words. Implicit meanings vary with how closely they depend on the text meanings. At the top level of the hierarchy are inferences that are not bound to the text language.

principles). Inference taxonomies have tended to reflect the earliest observational stages of classification, sorting observed cases into categories according to appearances, with emerging (ad hoc), incomplete hierarchical structures. Moreover, the processes that serve inferences appear to be highly general, functioning without specific guidance from the type of inference required (Myers and O'Brien, 1998).

A simpler approach is to capture the coarse-grain differences among the three types of thinly contrasting text meaning we referred to above: the literal; the linguistically constrained implicit meaning; and the linguistically independent, reader-constructed implicit meaning. This three-way classification assumes, not uncontroversially, that texts do contain some degree of intrinsic meaning, constrained by grammar and conventional word meanings. Figure 1.1 captures this approach in a hierarchical structure that puts the explicit meaning of the text at the foundation. Building directly on what the text says, the second level captures implicit meanings that a reader derives from the words and syntax of the currently read segment of text. The third level adds a range of implicit meanings that are heavily knowledge-dependent and cannot be made only by knowledge of words and syntax.

The triangle of Figure 1.1 is consistent with some proposals that try to capture broad, two-way distinctions in implicit meaning. Examples include text-connecting versus knowledge-based (Graesser et al., 1994); inter-sentence versus gap-filling (Cain and Oakhill, 1998); and automatic versus strategic (McKoon and Ratcliff, 1992). Such distinctions might correspond to the difference between level 2 and level 3 in Figure 1.1. However, some broad distinctions that are important in text comprehension, e.g., local vs. global (Graesser et al., 1994) seem less clearly reflected in the hierarchy without further assumptions about the role of the linguistic text in each case.

The hierarchical model is descriptive, referring to the levels of meaning from a text perspective rather than from the comprehension processes that produce meanings. Its value is to organize observations about text processes that can then be linked to comprehension processes. For example, one can see that much of the research interest in inferential comprehension is at the top of the pyramid, especially when questions concern comprehension skill. Thus, much of the work that locates poor inference making as a source of comprehension failure is at this level, where the application of knowledge or strategies beyond routine text comprehension is critical (e.g., Cain, Oakhill, Barnes, and Bryant, 2001; Oakhill, Cain, and Bryant, 2003).

In what follows, we take a closer look at the intermediate level, illustrating a kind of implicit meaning process that is often considered a lower-level automatic process. This intermediate level is below the level of which inference processing is typically examined.

The intermediate level: close-to-the-text inferences

One class of close-to-the-text inferences that has attracted some research attention is the syntactically triggered inference that secures coreference (e.g., Gordon and Hendrick, 1997). Simple pronoun binding is a nearly invisible process that ordinarily must be automatic. For example, in "John bought himself a present," "himself" is automatically linked to "John" because of the morphological trigger of the reflexive pronoun. This same fact of English morphosyntax prevents "him" from referring to John in "John bought him a present."

Other cases show complexities that demonstrate an implicit knowledge of syntax is what is responsible. For example, in the following sentences, readers bind a pronoun with a coreferential noun in accordance with a syntactic-binding principle. Thus, readers interpret "Bill" and "he" as coreferential in both (1a) and (1b), even though the main clause contains the proper noun in one case and a pronoun in the other.

1.   a. If **Bill** does well on the exam, **he** will pass the course.
        b. **Bill** will pass the course, if **he** does well on the exam.

However, in 2a and 2b readers show a sharp difference in making a coreferential interpretation.

2.   a. If **he** does well on the exam, **Bill** will pass the course.
        b. **He** will pass the course, if **Bill** does well on the exam.

Gordon and Hendrick (1997) confirmed that readers find only (2a) as an acceptable sentence for understanding "he" as referring to Bill. The general point, which covers a wide range of linguistic structures, is that an implicit knowledge of the language itself guides coreferential meaning processes so readily that one might be reluctant to consider them inferences at all.

However, not all text-dependent coreferential processes are triggered automatically by implicit syntactic knowledge. Below we consider coreferential processes that depend on word knowledge, which is less deterministic than syntactic knowledge and thus perhaps more variable in its use.

Word-to-text integration as an intermediate-level inference

Word-to-text integration is a second kind of close to the-text "inference" process that we have examined in research on reading comprehension. The quotes indicate that we have not heretofore referred to these processes as inferences and, indeed, one can question whether they are. However, what we have in previous work referred to as "word-to-text" integration (Perfetti and Stafura, 2014; Perfetti, Yang, and Schmalhofer, 2008) involves close-to-the-text meaning processes that seem to have some of the features of inferences. Moreover, part of our general claim in this chapter is that the borders that separate kinds of meaning processes may be permeable and it seems useful to think about a borderline case.

Word-to-text integration (WTI) is a recurring process in language comprehension. In its broadest sense it can include parsing processes, in which a syntactically coded word is fit to a partially constructed syntactic structure (phrase, clause, or sentence) in memory. Such a process must occur on virtually every word as it is encountered. However, in its more typical sense within text comprehension, WTI is the fitting of a word into a meaning representation that has been constructed, based on the reading of the text to that point.

Exactly what this meaning representation is could be a matter of some uncertainty. We assume, for now, that the relevant meaning representation is a mental model – a representation of what the text says – its basic linguistic meaning that is updated by WTI processes. However, the relevant representation could be simply a propositional level meaning representation. In fact, the two are so closely related during immediate memory-limited processing that separating them goes beyond what we can address in our research so far. For now, we assume that at the point a word is read, a motivated reader is constructing a mental model (Johnson-Laird, 1980) of what the text is about (a "situation model," (van Dijk and Kintsch, 1983) that is based primarily on the linguistic information in the text with some limited influences of extra-text knowledge. Considerations of working memory are relevant here. During text reading – at the moment a word is encountered – processing is occupied at the local text level by reading this single word and configuring it into syntactic structures and meaning relations that are active in working memory. Although in the long run, both syntactic and propositional information may fade, such information is prominent temporarily within a resource-limited processing system.

We illustrate WTI, on the assumption that it involves a connection to a working mental model of the text, with two slightly different texts, which are based on experiments by Stafura and Perfetti (in revision).

3.   a. While Cathy was riding her bike in the park, dark clouds began to gather, and it started to storm.

By the end of this sentence, we assume that the reader's mental model represents meaning information that includes referents and events, rather than the literal text. At the top level, the model is decomposable into two substructures: *Situation + Event:*

<SITUATION: Cathy on bike, in the park, dark clouds>
<EVENT: Storm>

The reader's text memory provides access to the situation, which can be updated through events described in the text. In this case, the situation is updated immediately by the storm event, as illustrated below with the updated element in italics.

<SITUATION: *Storm*, Cathy on bike in park>

Suppose the next sentence adds to text (3a) as repeated below in (3b):

3.   b. While Cathy was riding her bike in the park, dark clouds began to gather, and it started to storm. The rain ruined her beautiful sweater.

The new information from the second sentence – that the rain ruined the sweater – can be added to the situation model, introducing the result of the recently comprehended event, the ruination of a sweater.

<SITUATION: *rain-ruined sweater*, Cathy, storm>

But comprehension proceeds not only sentence by sentence but also word by word. The noun phrase that begins the new sentence – *The rain* – is understood immediately in relation to the situation model. The immediacy of this connection of word reading to text understanding is enabled by encoding and memory processes that are sensitive to conceptual/featural overlap (Kintsch, 1988; Myers and O'Brien, 1998). The reader understands "the rain" to refer to (and augment) the storm event and integrates it into the situation model.

Studying WTI through ERPs

These word-level integration processes can be observed through various reading measures that are sensitive to the word-by-word time course of processing, including event-related potential (ERP) methods and eye tracking. ERP measures allow for the observation of this integration as it occurs – a comprehension process rather than a comprehension product. Our experiments, using short texts such as (3) above, measure ERPs initiated by a target word that appears at the beginning of a new sentence, across a sentence boundary from the text that allows integration of "rain" in the current example. When the target word appears, the N400 component, an indicator of the fit between the word and its context (Kutas and Federmeier, 2000), is reduced in amplitude, indicating word-to-text integration (Yang, Perfetti, and Schmalhofer, 2007). This reduction is relative to a baseline condition, illustrated in text (4) below.

4.   When Cathy saw there were no dark clouds in the sky, she took her bike for a ride in the park. The rain that was predicted never occurred.

In text (4) there is no antecedent event for "rain." Reflecting the difficulty the reader has in integrating "rain" into the mental model, the N400 on the word "rain" has a more pronounced negative deflection. To describe this in more traditional psycholinguistic terms, coreferencing is not achieved because the prior sentence has no clear antecedent for "the rain."

Thus, text (4) is a baseline condition against which N400 reductions produced by text manipulations (paraphrase, inference, and explicit mention) are compared. Important is the fact that the second sentence of text (4) – and thus, the whole of text (4) – is perfectly comprehensible. However, the reader's situation model is different from that in (3) – there is no storm. So, when the word "rain" is encountered, there is no rapid integration process that adds "rain" to the situation model. Instead a new mental structure is built around "the rain" and (finally) its nonoccurrence.

The fact that text (4) is sensible is important, because in most research that uses the N400 as an indicator of semantic processing, something that is sensible is compared with something that is anomalous, or non-sensible. For example, in a classic N400 study, an ERP is recorded on the final word of a sentence that makes it sensible, e.g., "The pizza was too hot to eat"; and this is compared with a version in which the final word makes the sentence anomalous, e.g., "... too hot to drink" (Kutas and Hillyard, 1980). In these situations, the N400 differences are dramatic and appear amenable to explanations based on expectancy violations (Federmeier, 2007; Lau, Almeida, Hines, and Poeppel, 2009). The N400 is assumed to be sensitive to poor fit (failures of expectations to be met, or failures to make sense of what occurs). However, in our case, a comparison is made across sensible texts. The texts differ only in the degree to which they invite an immediate word-to-text integration process. Moreover, the critical word is across a sentence boundary from the relevant antecedent in the first sentence. Taken together, these two features of our experiments are more compatible with a post-lexical integration process (Brown and Hagoort, 1993) than with an expectancy explanation. It is difficult to imagine what word a reader might predict as the first word (or the head of the first noun phrase) across a sentence boundary; nearly any grammatical sentence beginning can continue on with coherent ties to the preceding sentence.[1]

The paraphrase effect. We have referred to the fact that the word "rain" is better integrated (immediately) with text (3) than with text (4) as the *paraphrase effect*. The ordinary sense of paraphrase, expressing an idea in words different from its original expression, does not apply very well to our use of "paraphrase." A well-written text does not use different words in a new sentence to express the same idea as in the previous sentence, as if avoiding repetition were the goal. Instead, paraphrase is about the text moving the situation model a bit forward while maintaining coherence. Thus, in text (3), "rain" is *not* another way of saying "storm." Rather, the text moves the mental model forward in a baby step by referring to a correlate or consequence of the storm with the word "rain." Perhaps reserving the concept of "updating" a mental model for more substantial semantic changes (O'Brien, Rizzella, Albrecht, and Halleran, 1998), we can refer to these paraphrase-induced changes as

[1] Several studies have examined the influence of message-level factors on word-level processing across sentences (e.g., Kuperberg, Paczynski, and Ditman, 2011; Otten and van Berkum, 2008). These studies suggest that multiple levels of linguistic information can influence word-level processing, consistent with the idea that N400 amplitudes are sensitive to both expectancy and fit (i.e., integration).

"fine tuning" the mental model, an updating of individual referents and events that are part of the mental model that does not involve removing a semantic contradiction.

Thus, the paraphrase effect reflects online comprehension – a sensitivity to moment-by-moment tuning of the mental model. We discovered in these experiments that skilled comprehenders showed the paraphrase effect more robustly than less-skilled comprehenders did (Perfetti et al., 2008; Stafura and Perfetti, unpublished). We suggested that less-skilled comprehenders were showing *sluggish* word-to-text integration. Such sluggishness may result in difficulty maintaining coherence across sentences, considering the largely incremental processes involved in comprehension (Just and Carpenter, 1980; Tyler and Marslen-Wilson, 1977).

Explicit meaning process or inference?

If, as suggested by Figure 1.1, meaning processes can be approximately ordered along three levels of text constraint, one might ask whether the paraphrase effect is an explicit text process or a kind of inference.[2] We address this question by referring again to our *storm – rain* example. Referring to "rain" after "storm" as a paraphrase is, as we suggested, a small update, a fine-tuning in the mental model that maintains coherence. However, the text could also leap forward with a giant step, as it would if instead of (3) we had (5).

5.   While Cathy was riding her bike in the park, dark clouds began to gather. The rain ruined her beautiful sweater.

Here, when the reader encounters "rain" there is no explicitly stated storm event in the mental model; so there is nothing to which "rain" gets attached, and no event or proposition to modify. Instead, the reader constructs a new event: rain. It's not a big stretch, given the dark clouds, to infer a rain event. And to keep the text coherent, this bridging inference (e.g., Graesser et al., 1994; Singer and Halldorson, 1996) is readily made, although with some detectable cost to processing efficiency. Yang et al. (2007) observed that for texts of this type, the N400 amplitude was nonsignificantly different from baseline. Reading "The rain ..." in

---

[2] If so, one might be tempted to argue that the result that skilled comprehenders show a stronger paraphrase effect than less skilled comprehenders is another example of less skilled comprehenders being poor at inference generation relative to more skilled comprehenders. We would counter such an argument by insisting the lexical basis of this problem points to something other than some generalized deficit in inferential processes.

sentence (5) was similar to reading "The rain ..." in sentence (4). Neither case provided an immediate integration opportunity, although we assume that most readers make the bridging inference in (5), provided they have a sufficiently high standard for coherence (van den Broek, Risden, and Husebye-Hartmann, 1995).

Instead of being stuck with a bridging inference at the second sentence of (3), the reader might make a forward or predictive inference during the first sentence. Such an inference would be generated while reading the clause "dark clouds began to gather" (i.e., a prediction that it will rain). But such an inference has little warrant. Maybe rain would be the next event, and maybe it wouldn't. Certainly the comprehension of the dark clouds in the first sentence allows a readiness to understand "the rain" when it does appear in the next sentence (hence, the N400 to (5) is not more negative than in (4)), but this does not compel a forward inference. Predictive inferences are variable, probabilistic, and generally less compelling than inferences that are needed to support coherence (Graesser et al., 1994; McKoon and Ratcliff, 1992). In reading, there is little or no clear evidence that such inferences are made immediately so that their effects can be measured upon reading on a single word – as opposed to later, when a new text segment affirms the event. The N400 results of Yang et al. (2007) suggest that the forward inference was not made consistently on the first word where such an inference becomes possible, and thus readers had to make a more costly bridging inference when they came to the word "rain" in the second sentence.

To locate bridging and forward inferences in the hierarchical model of Figure 1.1, the predictive inference is at the top of the pyramid, dependent on the reader's knowledge and perhaps on a level of engagement high enough to motivate prediction efforts. Bridging is a bit more difficult to place. While a bridging inference depends specifically on a linguistic gap in the text – it is triggered by a coherence break in the text – it also relies heavily on the reader's knowledge and on a standard of coherence, both of which are outside the narrow scope of the text language.

Returning to the paraphrase effect, we locate the effect at the intermediate level of the meaning processes model of Figure 1.1. There are two important elements in the meaning processes captured by the paraphrase effect and by WTI in general. One is the meaning of the word currently being read. The other is the preceding text – either the text itself, including a specific linguistic unit (a phrase or a full clause), or a mental model of the text with referents and events rather than linguistic units. In either case, the process is one of referential binding, in which the meaning of the currently read word is connected to an antecedent, a linguistic phrase, or a referent based on that phrase. To choose tentatively the mental model description: The meaning process triggered by the paraphrase word is a coreferential process that updates the mental model in a modest way. Referring to text (3), the word "rain" fine-tunes the event referred to by "started to storm." (This fine-tuning allows more substantial updating with the new information about the ruined sweater.) So the two aspects of WTI are the meaning of the word and the meaning of an immediately preceding (available in memory) stretch of text. The integration process selects the referential meaning of the word that is congruent with the meaning of the text and adds new information to the text representation.

To summarize, research on the paraphrase effect exemplifies important integration processes that occur routinely during reading. These processes are quite general, continuously applied to linguistic structures of various kinds – not just single words. In fact, the general case requires noun phrases, which are needed to establish referents, and clauses (or phrasal modifiers), which are needed to establish events. Comprehension depends in part on local word-to-text integration processes that may be said to include inferencing, but are heavily dependent on the use of word meanings. It is knowledge of word meanings and the ability to integrate their context appropriate meaning into a mental model that is critical at this level, which is intermediate to mainly intrinsically text-constrained meaning processes and unconstrained knowledge-rich and strategic processes.

Mechanisms of word-to-text integration

Readers obtain the critical intermediate levels of meaning through mechanisms that retrieve word meanings and their morphosyntactic information, integrating the results of these retrievals into the representation(s) of the text. (These include syntactic representations, which we are not addressing here.) We can ask more specifically about the nature of the processes that bring about the WTI exemplified through the paraphrase effect. The general picture is of interleaved processes of word meaning retrieval and memory resonance that produce a fit between the word and the text representation.

To illustrate, we repeat the brief text of (3b), which shows a text integration process that can occur at the word "rain" in the second sentence.

3   b. While Cathy was riding her bike in the park, dark clouds began to gather, and it started to storm. The rain ruined her beautiful sweater.

The critical word is "rain," where we observe ERP indicators of word-to-text integration – an N400 reduction compared with a baseline sentence

Table 1.1 *Passages showing manipulation of lexical association in the paraphrase effect (from Stafura and Perfetti, unpublished)*

Text condition	Sample passage
Strongly associated paraphrase	While Cathy was riding her bike in the park, dark clouds began to gather, and it started to storm. The **rain** ruined her beautiful sweater.
Weakly associated paraphrase	While Cathy was riding her bike in the park, dark clouds began to gather, and it started to shower. The **rain** ruined her beautiful sweater.
Baseline	When Cathy saw there were no dark clouds in the sky, she took her bike for a ride in the park. The **rain** that was predicted never occurred.

in which there is no storm event mentioned in sentence (1). The general question for such effects is whether they are message driven or lexically driven. This amounts to asking whether an association between the word "storm" and the word "rain" in the reader's lexicon is sufficient to produce the paraphrase effect. The answer to this question should be no to the extent that text comprehension relies on meaning processes beyond word association (assuming the N400 can detect a comprehension event as well as a purely lexical priming event). We tested this assumption by comparing texts in which there was a strong forward association between an antecedent word in the first sentence and a critical paraphrase word in the second sentence (Stafura and Perfetti, unpublished). This manipulation is shown in Table 1.1, where "the rain" is preceded by either a strong forward associate (*storm-rain*) or a weaker associate (*shower-rain*), as determined by both association norms and latent semantic analysis.[3] In a meaning judgment task using these words, a word preceded by a strong associate produced a larger N400 reduction than a word preceded by a weaker associate. This reflects a direct effect of lexical association on word meaning judgments. However, in the text reading task (Table 1.1), the strong and weak association conditions produced equivalent reductions in the N400 relative to the baseline. Figure 1.2 shows the mean amplitude of the N400 across parietal electrodes for the three conditions. The data show a clear and comparable reduction in negativity for strongly and weakly associated words.

This result clarifies the interpretation of the paraphrase effect reported in Yang et al. (2007). The processes must use some representation of the

---

[3] Note that latent semantic analysis does not provide information on the *direction* of association strength.

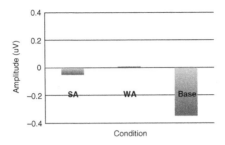

Figure 1.2 Average amplitude over parietal electrodes between 300 and 600 ms. following onset of critical word (e.g., "rain"). (SA = strong associate; WA = weak associate; Base = baseline). Relative to baseline, strongly and weakly associated words produced equivalent positive shifts. See Table 1.1 for materials.

meaning of the preceding text, in addition to the words of the text. More generally, WTI processes are the interaction of a word's meaning features stored in memory with the reader's representation of the text. The result is a context-sensitive meaning process that leads to referential binding to previous information, when that is possible; when that is not possible, a new information structure is begun, as proposed by Gernsbacher (1990). Reading the word activates its meaning features and its links to related words, initiating WTI. This initial process is partly captured by the construction phase of the construction-integration model (Kintsch, 1988) and depends on the accessibility of text information in memory, a foundation for memory-based theories of text comprehension (McKoon, Gerrig, and Greene, 1996; Myers and O'Brien, 1998). However, the effects of this activation are short-lived, as integration processes continue by selecting a more referential and context-relevant word meaning, integrating it into the text representation. These processes accomplish the critical component of text comprehension: to establish coreference and maintain coherence.

Finally, we emphasize an important component of WTI that is only implicit in what we have described so far. For the message level to influence how a word is processed (and thus integrated into the text representation), memory processes are critical. Working memory is usually invoked in describing comprehension, and while a limited capacity holding system for what was just read is important, a process that can retrieve information from both recent and more distant memory needs to be considered. Effortful retrieval and other coherence-saving moves (e.g., re-reading) may be a last-resort fallback for when the text is not making sense and when iterations of passive memory activation have failed to solve the problem. However, for the WTI process to proceed smoothly, a noneffortful, more passive memory process is usually sufficient: a resonance mechanism that automatically offers links to the word being read from what is accessible in memory (Myers and O'Brien, 1998). Integrative processes may be facilitated when an encountered word activates its associations, which then resonate with the memory of a word (or referent) recently encountered in the text. If so, backward association strength (*from* the word being read, rather than *to* it), which would capture some of this process, may turn out to be more important than forward association strength. Indeed, although forward association strength between words across a sentence boundary may not play a big role (Stafura and Perfetti, unpublished), backward association between the word being read and a preceding word in the text *does* affect early ERP indicators (at 200 ms) of the paraphrase effect (Stafura, Rickles, and Perfetti, unpublished). An example is shown in (6), where the critical word "rage" has a stronger directional association to the antecedent "anger" than vice versa.

6.   When the bear was awakened by the wandering chipmunk, he was filled
        with anger. His rage was intense and he chased the scared critter out of
        the cave.

In texts such as (6), the currently read word may activate a memory of the recently encountered word through a resonance process that supports the selection of the context-relevant meaning of the currently read word, and thus the WTI of that word.

Individual differences

WTI processes are potentially important as causal factors that produce individual differences in comprehension skill. Processes that depend on word meanings, as WTI processes do, are especially likely to show individual differences, because knowledge and use of word meanings are highly variable across individuals. There is evidence for comprehension skill differences among college readers in the paraphrase effect (Perfetti et al., 2008; Stafura and Perfetti, unpublished), although more research is needed to confirm the robustness of such differences and inform their explanation.

The reading systems framework (Perfetti and Stafura, 2014), which places the components of reading within a language-cognitive architecture from visual processing through higher-level comprehension, allows hypotheses about comprehension skill to be specific about the sources of comprehension difficulty. Within this theoretical framework, a leading candidate to explain individual differences in WTI is lexical knowledge, either vocabulary size (in a familiarity or passive knowledge sense) or more finely tuned word knowledge that supports the use of words in specific contexts, e.g., lexical quality (Perfetti, 2007). Beyond lexical knowledge are cognitive architecture factors, including working memory limitations (Just and Carpenter, 1992) and differences in executive functioning (e.g., Cutting, Materek, Cole, Levine, and Mahone, 2009). The latter can lead to differences in the effective inhibition of irrelevant word-level semantic information (Gernsbacher, 1990).

However, recent research by Van Dyke and Kukona (in press) casts doubt on conclusions that attribute causal status to differences in working memory and, instead, draws attention to the role of word knowledge in retrieval processes that occur during reading. The logic of the research rests on this well-established fact: When a memory load is introduced prior to sentence reading, the linguistic features of the memory-load words cause specific linguistic interference with the semantic-syntactic processing of the sentence that is beyond mere memory load (Gordon, Hendrick, Johnson, and Lee, 2006; Van Dyke and McElree, 2006). In their study, Van Dyke and Kukona presented a syntactically complex (embedded relative clause) cleft sentences such as (7):

7.   It was the boat that the guy who lived by the sea fixed in two sunny days.

Prior to reading sentence (7) the linguistically interfering memory load words (which participants were to remember) were *table-sink-truck*. Their linguistic potential for interference lies in the fact that *table, sink*, and *truck* refer to objects that one can fix. Thus, having to hold these words in memory can interfere with the processing of the main clause of the sentence, which contains a "fixed"-object construction (*the guy fixed the boat*) that has to be extracted from the sentence. In a noninterfering control condition, the verb of sentence (7) was *sailed* instead of *fixed*, and because *table, sink*, and *truck* do not refer to sailable objects, the linguistic basis for interference is eliminated, although the memory load remains the same. The critical result was that reading times for sentence (7) in the critical region containing "fixed," were slowed compared with the control sentence containing "sailed." Moreover, reading times were slowed more for low-comprehension than for high-comprehension participants (other measures also produced this skill contrast). Using a wide variety of assessments, Van Dyke and Kukona found that working memory had no explanatory power once IQ and other reading-related measures were accounted for. Instead, receptive vocabulary was the unique predictor of comprehension.

From their study, Van Johns and Kukona (2014) suggest that retrieval interference is a major threat to comprehension and that differences in comprehension skill may best be characterized in terms of susceptibility to interference rather than to the size of working memory. This account is consistent with an implication of the lexical quality hypothesis (Perfetti, 2007). The interference effect arises because underspecified features of words are encoded so that similarity among words (e.g., *boat, table, sink, truck*) is functionally increased, leading to greater interference. There is more to be learned about the generality of this interference mechanism and its dependency on word knowledge and the encoding of word meanings in context.

Conclusion: implicit meaning processes in comprehension skill

We have drawn attention to a framing of text meaning processes that allows explicit and implicit meaning processes to be viewed together from two perspectives, one from the perspective of the text language and the other from the perspective of the meaning processes that are used by readers in comprehension. The first of these, the view from the text, is represented in Figure 1.1. Much of our discussion has been from the view of reading processes, and we now add a representation of this view as part of Figure 1.3.

Figure 1.3 illustrates the complementarity of reading processes and the text-based hierarchy by adding a processing surface to form a pyramidal interface. Processes intrinsic to knowledge of a language are dominant in obtaining the explicit meaning of a text. (The right-side processing surface of the pyramid somewhat distorts the foundational role of word meaning and parsing processes, the latter are not labeled in Figure 1.3.)

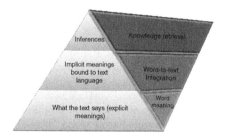

Figure 1.3 The mirrored pyramid view of text meaning processes. Descriptions of text meaning on the left face. Processes corresponding to these descriptions on the right face.

Processes primarily dependent on the reader's knowledge dominate the top level of inference making. Here, there are very important differences related to expertise concerning the interpretations readers obtain from texts. The ideas captured in this representation seem consistent with previous observations that divide inference making along lines of knowledge versus text dominance (e.g., Graesser et al., 1994) or automatic (minimal) and nonautomatic inferences (McKoon and Ratcliff, 1992). However, we do not assume that the different process descriptions correspond to independent mental operations. A recurring role for resonant memory activation during reading, as argued by Myers and O'Brien (1998) is likely to be part of all meaning processing, the explicit as well as the implicit.

Because it seems a bit neglected within the text research community, we have emphasized the importance of the intermediate level, where integration processes bind the products of word identification with those of text representation. This level captures the many examples in which the meaning is implicit, yet closely bound to the language of the text and in which words, as they are being read, are integrated with the reader's continuously tuned understanding of the text. Whether these WTI processes are called inferences or something else may matter for some purposes, but what they are called is of little consequence if the lines between implicit and explicit meaning processes are truly thin, as we suggested. However, these processes are consequential for comprehension, because they are critical for maintaining coherence by managing the routine fine-tuning of the reader's mental model.

REFERENCES

Brown, C., & Hagoort, P. (1993). The processing nature of the N400: evidence from masked priming. *Journal of Cognitive Neuroscience*, 5(1), 34–44.

Cain, K., & Oakhill, J. (eds.), (2008). *Children's Comprehension Problems in Oral and Written Language: A Cognitive Perspective*. New York: Guilford Press.

Cain, K., Oakhill, J. V., Barnes, M. A., & Bryant, P. E. (2001). Comprehension skill, inference-making ability, and their relation to knowledge. *Memory & Cognition*, 29(6), 850–9.

Cutting, L. E., Materek, A., Cole, C. A., Levine, T. M., & Mahone, E. M. (2009). Effects of fluency, oral language, and executive function on reading comprehension performance. *Annals of Dyslexia*, 59(1), 34–54.

Federmeier, K. D. (2007). Thinking ahead: the role and roots of prediction in language comprehension. *Psychophysiology*, 44(4), 491–505.

Gernsbacher, M. A. (1990). *Language Comprehension as Structure Building*. Hillsdale, NJ: Erlbaum.

Gernsbacher, M. A., & Faust, M. E. (1991). The mechanism of suppression: a component of general comprehension skill. *Journal of Experimental Psychology: Learning, Memory, and Cognition, 17*(2), 245–62.

Gordon, P. C., & Hendrick, R. (1997). Intuitive knowledge of linguistic co-reference. *Cognition, 62*(3), 325–70.

Gordon, P. C., Hendrick, R., Johnson, M., & Lee, Y. (2006). Similarity-based interference during language comprehension: evidence from eye tracking during reading. *Journal of Experimental Psychology: Learning, Memory, and Cognition, 32*(6), 1304–21.

Graesser, A. C., Singer, M., & Trabasso, T. (1994). Constructing inferences during narrative text comprehension. *Psychological Review, 101*(3), 371–95.

Johnson-Laird, P. N. (1980). Mental models in cognitive science. *Cognitive Science, 4*(1), 71–115.

Just, M. A., & Carpenter, P. A. (1980). A theory of reading: from eye fixations to comprehension. *Psychological review, 87,* 329–54.

(1992). A capacity theory of comprehension: individual differences in working memory. *Psychological Review, 99,* 122–49.

Kintsch, W. (1988). The role of knowledge in discourse comprehension: a construction-integration model. *Psychological Review, 95,* 163–82.

Kuperberg, G. R., Paczynski, M., & Ditman, T. (2011). Establishing causal coherence across sentences: an ERP study. *Journal of Cognitive Neuroscience, 23*(5), 1230–46.

Kutas, M., & Federmeier, K. D. (2000). Electrophysiology reveals semantic memory use in language comprehension. *Trends in Cognitive Sciences, 4*(12), 463–70.

Kutas, M., & Hillyard, S. A. (1980). Reading senseless sentences: brain potentials reflect semantic incongruity. *Science, 207*(4427), 203–5.

Lau, E., Almeida, D., Hines, P. C., & Poeppel, D. (2009). A lexical basis for N400 context effects: evidence from MEG. *Brain and Language, 111*(3), 161–72.

McKoon, G., Gerrig, R. J., & Greene, S. B. (1996). Pronoun resolution without pronouns: some consequences of memory-based text processing. *Journal of Experimental Psychology: Learning, Memory, and Cognition, 22*(4), 919.

McKoon, G., & Ratcliff, R. (1992). Inference during reading. *Psychological Review, 99*(3), 440–66.

Myers, J. L., & O'Brien, E. J. (1998). Accessing the discourse representation during reading. *Discourse Processes, 26*(2–3), 131–57.

Oakhill, J. V., Cain, K., & Bryant, P. E. (2003). The dissociation of word reading and text comprehension: evidence from component skills. *Language and Cognitive Processes, 18*(4), 443–68.

O'Brien, E. J., Rizzella, M. L., Albrecht, J. E., & Halleran, J. G. (1998). Updating a situation model: a memory-based text processing view. *Journal of Experimental Psychology: Learning, Memory, and Cognition, 24*(5), 1200–10.

Otten, M., & van Berkum, J. J. (2008). Discourse-based word anticipation during language processing: prediction or priming? *Discourse Processes, 45*(6), 464–96.

Perfetti, C. (2007). Reading ability: lexical quality to comprehension. *Scientific Studies of Reading*, *11*(4), 357–83.

Perfetti, C., & Stafura, J. (2014). Word knowledge in a theory of reading comprehension. *Scientific Studies of Reading*, *18*(1), 22–37.

Perfetti, C., Yang, C. L. and Schmalhofer, F. 2008. Comprehension skill and word-to-text integration processes. *Applied Cognitive Psychology*, *22*, 303–18. [CrossRef], [Web of Science ®]

Pressley, M., & Afflerbach, P. (1995). *Verbal Protocols of Reading: The Nature of Constructively Responsive Reading*. London: Routledge.

Singer, M., & Halldorson, M. (1996). Constructing and validating motive bridging inferences. *Cognitive Psychology*, *30*(1), 1–38.

Stafura, J., & Perfetti, C. A. (2014). Word-to-text integration: message level and lexical level influence in ERPs. *Neuropsychologia*, *64*, 41–53.

Stafura, J. Rickles, B., & Perfetti, C. A. (unpublished). ERP indicators of memory resonance processes in word-to-text integration.

Tyler, L. K., & Marslen-Wilson, W. D. (1977). The online effects of semantic context on syntactic processing. *Journal of Verbal Learning and Verbal Behavior*, *16*(6), 683–92.

Van den Broek, P., Risden, K., & Husebye-Hartmann, E. (1995). The role of readers' standards for coherence in the generation of inferences during reading. In R. F. Lorch and E. J. O'Brien (eds.), *Sources of Coherence in Reading* (pp. 353–73). Mahwah, NJ: Erlbaum.

Van Dijk, T. A., & Kintsch, W. (1983). Strategies of discourse, ed. T. A. Van Dijk & W. Kintsch, *Strategies of Discourse Comprehension*. New York: Academic Press.

Van Dyke, J. A., & McElree, B. (2006). Retrieval interference in sentence comprehension. *Journal of Memory and Language*, *55*(2), 157–66.

Van Dyke, J. A., Johns, C. L., & Kukona, A. (2014). Low working memory capacity is only spuriously related to poor reading comprehension. *Cognition*, *131*, 373–403.

Yang, C. L., Perfetti, C. A., & Schmalhofer, F. (2007). Event-related potential indicators of text integration across sentence boundaries. *Journal of Experimental Psychology: Learning, Memory, and Cognition*, *33*(1), 55–89.

Acknowledgment

Research that informed this chapter was supported by NIH award No. 1R01HD058566-01A1 (C. Perfetti, PI) to the University of Pittsburgh.

2   Passive activation and instantiation of inferences during reading

Anne E. Cook Edward J. O'Brien

The prominent position within early theories of discourse comprehension was that coherence required that each of the basic ideas contained in a text must be connected by either coreference (e.g., Kintsch and van Dijk, 1978), co-occurrence (e.g., Fletcher and Bloom, 1988), or causality (e.g., Trabasso and Sperry, 1985). When none of these factors are explicitly present in a text, the reader must provide those connections between disparate pieces of information in a text and/or fill in gaps left by the writer – that is, nearly all texts require some level of inference on the part of the reader. The underlying processes involved in inferencing fall into one of two broad categories: those that become available to the reader through passive activation of inferential information (Gerrig and O'Brien, 2005; McKoon and Ratcliff, 1992); and those that become available to the reader through the initiation of active, strategic processing to generate inferential content (e.g., Graesser and Kreuz, 1993; Graesser, Singer, and Trabasso, 1994; Singer, Graesser, and Trabasso, 1994). Because passive activation is considered a fundamental cognitive process that occurs below the reader's conscious control, it is likely to contribute to the availability of information that becomes part of an overall inference, even when active, strategic processes play a prominent and/or dominant role. Thus, it is important to gain a full understanding of this fundamental component of inferencing. With an understanding of the passive activation process in place, it then becomes a more manageable task to begin to parse out the important contributions of active, strategic processes in building a complete model of the inference process. In this chapter we will focus solely on the passive activation process that contributes to inference activation and to describe and discuss the factors that govern this process.

The passive activation process that contributes to inference activation is completely interwoven within the memory-based view of text processes (e.g., Gerrig and McKoon, 1998; McKoon and Ratcliff, 1992). Within this view, incoming information – as well as information already residing in active memory – serves as a signal to all of long-term memory, including both the inactive portion of the discourse representation as well as general world knowledge. These inactive concepts resonate in response to this signal to the extent that they share features in common with the information from which the signal emanated. Those concepts that resonate the most are incorporated into working memory and have the potential to become part of the overall representation of a text in memory (e.g., Myers and O'Brien, 1998; O'Brien, 1995; O'Brien and Myers, 1999). Two critical aspects of this resonance process with respect to inferences are that it is both unrestricted and dumb. The unrestricted nature of the mechanism refers to the idea that information may be reactivated from either the episodic discourse representation or from general world knowledge stored in semantic memory. Activation is "dumb" in the sense that any related information that resonates sufficiently is returned to working memory, independent of its relevance or appropriateness to the active portion of the discourse model.

Based on these assumptions, inferences would be viewed just as any other type of information that has the potential to be passively reactivated from memory (see Gerrig and O'Brien, 2005). The likelihood of activating any inference is a function of the degree to which the potential inference shares featural overlap with information currently in working memory. This is regardless of whether the inference in question is necessary for local coherence or just elaborates on information explicitly stated in the text (Garrod, O'Brien, Morris, and Rayner, 1990; McKoon and Ratcliff, 1986, 1992; O'Brien, Shank, Myers, and Rayner, 1988). That is, within the memory-based view, both the "necessity" of the inference for coherence and the goal-meeting properties of the inference are irrelevant (at least with respect to initial activation); if the inference in question is strongly related to information in working memory, it has the potential to be activated. In this chapter, we first describe evidence for this view from several investigations of necessary and elaborative inferences. Following this, we discuss the fate of activated information by considering questions about integration, instantiation, and validation.

Evidence for passive inference activation

"Necessary" inferences

Perhaps one of the most common types of inference is that in which the reader is required to connect a pronoun, noun, or referential phrase to information presented earlier in the text – an *anaphoric inference*. Because the word or phrase used to represent an anaphor may differ from that used to represent its antecedent, either lexically, semantically, or both, readers must make the connection between the two. When the anaphor is a pronoun, its antecedent typically occurs within the same sentence or the preceding sentence. This is because pronouns carry little semantic content that allow for a signal to activate appropriate antecedents (c.f. Greene et al., 1994). However, there is no such standard for nominal or noun phrase anaphora; in studies of these types of anaphoric inferences, anaphors and their antecedents are often separated by several sentences of text. This raises the following questions: When an antecedent for a given anaphor is not currently active, what is the process by which that antecedent is reactivated? What are the factors that influence this process?

McKoon and Ratcliff (1980; O'Brien, Duffy, and Myers, 1986) demonstrated that upon encountering an anaphor, antecedents are passively activated from long-term memory, as well as related information, even when the related information is not relevant (e.g., Dell, McKoon, and Ratcliff, 1983). As the lexical and semantic overlap between an anaphor and its antecedent increases, so do both the probability of access and the speed with which access occurs (Garrod and Sanford, 1977; O'Brien, Raney, Albrecht, and Rayner, 1997). In a study that laid the initial groundwork for the resonance model, O'Brien (1987) provided evidence that antecedents are reactivated via a backward parallel search process, in which more recently encountered antecedents tend to be accessed more quickly than those that are further back in the surface structure of the text (see O'Brien, 1995, for a review of resonance and its application to activation processes during reading). Subsequent work showed that these distance effects can be overridden by increases in causal connections or elaboration, such that more causally connected and/or more elaborated antecedents are reactivated faster, regardless of position in the text (O'Brien, Albrecht, Hakala, and Rizzella, 1995; O'Brien and Myers, 1987; O'Brien, Plewes, and Albrecht, 1990). Thus, the interconnectedness of the antecedent in memory strongly influences the likelihood and rate at which it will be accessed; and interconnectedness is a stronger predictor of accessibility than simple linear distance (Albrecht and O'Brien, 1991; O'Brien et al., 1990; 1995; 1997).

Within the memory-based view (and a resonance framework in particular), reactivation of antecedents occurs via a process that is not only passive, but also "dumb." When an anaphor is encountered, any related concepts in memory may be reactivated, even if they are not the correct antecedent (Corbett and Chang, 1983; O'Brien et al., 1995; see also Klin, Guzmán, Weingartner, and Ralano, 2006; Klin, Weingartner, Guzmán, and Levine, 2004; Levine, Guzmán, and Klin, 2000). For example, O'Brien and Albrecht (1991) used passages such as the example in Box 2.1, in which the contexts varied with respect to whether they supported an explicitly mentioned antecedent (e.g., cat) or an unmentioned concept (e.g., skunk). This was followed by a sentence containing an anaphoric phrase (e.g., what had run in front of her car). O'Brien and Albrecht then presented naming probes for either the correct antecedent (e.g., cat), or the unnamed concept (e.g., skunk). They found that "skunk" was activated in memory, even when the text contained an explicit reference to "cat." Moreover, if the context supporting the unnamed concept was sufficiently high, the unnamed concept was actually instantiated in place of the correct antecedent.

Similarly, Cook, Myers, and O'Brien (2005) found that readers reactivated concepts that were explicitly negated as possible antecedents (e.g., She decided not to buy the cello) just as quickly as nonnegated concepts (e.g., She decided to buy the cello), because both shared the same degree of featural overlap with the anaphoric phrase (e.g., Her friend asked her what instrument she bought). In combination, these two studies demonstrate how the unrestricted nature of the activation process results in reactivation of information from both the episodic memory trace (e.g., Cook et al.) and general world knowledge (O'Brien and Albrecht, 1991).

Box 2.1   Example from O'Brien and Albrecht (1991)

HIGH CONTEXT

Mary was driving in the country one day when she smelled a terrific odor. Suddenly, a small black cat with a white stripe down its back ran in front of her car.

LOW CONTEXT

Mary was driving in the country one day and she gazed at the setting sun as she drove. Suddenly, a small black cat with a long furry tail ran in front of her car.

FILLER

Mary knew she couldn't stop in time. However, she hoped she had managed to miss the animal and continued on her way. After a while she noticed she was low on gas.

REINSTATEMENT LINE

While at the gas station, the attendant asked her *what had run in front of her car.*
Antecedent Probe: CAT
Unmentioned Concept Probe: SKUNK

Although anaphoric inferences were previously thought to be necessary for coherence to be maintained, recent evidence has challenged this assumption. Klin and colleagues (Klin et al., 2004, 2006; Levine et al., 2000) presented evidence that when there is a strong distractor to an antecedent (i.e., an antecedent that shares many features in common with the correct antecedent), the correct antecedent may not be fully activated. Instead, they argued that activation is split between the distractor and the antecedent, such that only partial activation of the antecedent may occur (see also O'Brien et al., 1990; 1995). Similarly, Cook (2014) found that full activation of an antecedent is not available until after readers have moved past the anaphor in the text (see also Duffy and Rayner, 1990). In combination, these findings are inconsistent with the view that resolving an anaphor is necessary for comprehension to proceed.

Another type of necessary inference is one in which readers must infer a link between an event in the text and its causal antecedent. This type of inference is commonly called a backward *causal bridging inference*. Keenan, Baillett, and Brown (1984; see also Albrecht and O'Brien, 1995; Myers, Shinjo, and Duffy, 1987) demonstrated that ease of generating these inferences was predicted by the degree of causal relatedness between a consequence and its causal antecedent. In the example below, reading times for the target sentence increased as its causal relatedness to the preceding sentence decreased:

High: Joey's big brother punched him again and again.
Medium: Racing down the hill, Joey fell off his bike.
Low: Joey's crazy mother became furiously angry with him.
Unrelated: Joey went to a neighbor's house to play.
Target Sentence: The next day his body was covered with bruises.

This research was extended by Singer and colleagues (Singer, 1993; Singer and Ferreira, 1983; Singer and Halldorson, 1996; Singer, Halldorson, Lear, and Andrusiak, 1992), who provided evidence that causal bridging inferences are activated, even when the events are separated by several sentences of text. Moreover, Rizzella and O'Brien (1996) found that the activation of distant causal antecedents occurs even when there is a sufficient causal antecedent available in active memory. Consistent with the assumptions of a passive inference activation process, Rizzella and O'Brien argued that activation of causal information was driven by the same memory-based factors that drive the activation of nominal antecedents (e.g., distance and elaboration), rather than sufficiency (see also Albrecht and Myers, 1995; 1998; Myers, Cook, Kambe, Mason, and O'Brien, 2000).

As with anaphoric inferences, the degree to which causal bridging inferences are *necessary* for comprehension is questionable. Millis and Graesser (1994; see also Singer and Gagnon, 1999) used relatively easy expository texts and found evidence that causal bridging inferences are activated online. However, with more difficult technical expository texts, this is not always the case. Wiley and Myers (2003) presented readers with scientific texts designed to elicit causal bridging inferences and found that these inferences were activated only when all information related to the inference was immediately available in the text. Similarly, Noordman, Vonk, and Kempff (1992) found that backward causal inferences were only activated in expository texts when the inferences were relevant to specific task goals. Presumably, readers in both studies lacked the rich, interconnected network of background knowledge necessary to allow for the passive activation of these causal inferences. The findings from Noordman et al. demonstrated that attentional focus (through the use of task goals) can serve to "boost" activation of information that is in the network in memory, but may be somewhat impoverished (see Noordman, Vonk, Cozijn, and Frank, this volume, for an excellent review of the factors governing backward causal inferences).

The studies described in this section focused on "necessary" inferences – those that, when left unresolved, would presumably result in a break in local coherence. The evidence described indicates that in most cases, these inferences are activated online during reading. Whether they are activated, and how quickly they are activated, can be explained based primarily on memory-based factors (e.g., featural overlap, referential distance, causal relations, elaboration within the text, amount of supporting information in general world knowledge that has the potential to become available). We now consider the role of these same variables in the activation of "elaborative" inferences – those that are not assumed to be required for coherence to be maintained.

"Elaborative" inferences

In contrast to "necessary" inferences, "elaborative" inferences are not required for comprehension to proceed. Instead, they provide additional information beyond that which is explicitly stated in the text; this additional information is derived from the activation of general world knowledge (Cook and Guéraud, 2005). A common misconception among reading researchers in the 1990s was that these inferences were not passively activated during reading. As noted by Gerrig and O'Brien (2005), this misconception stemmed from the belief that readers have access to a limited amount of information from memory (e.g., Singer et al., 1994) and activation of certain categories of inferences does not occur unless the reader engages in strategic processing. However, as noted earlier, a passive resonance process that operates during normal comprehension can make a great deal of information "readily available" to the reader, regardless of whether it originated within the episodic representation of the text or general world knowledge, and whether it is required to maintain local coherence. Research on elaborative inferences has enabled a better understanding of the types of inferences that may be activated via this passive mechanism, as well as the factors that may limit inference activation.

O'Brien et al. (1988; see also Garrod et al., 1990) provided one of the first demonstrations that elaborative inferences can be passively activated during reading. They monitored participants' eye movements as they read passages in which the context provided either high or low support for a specific category exemplar that was either explicitly mentioned in the passage or merely implied. See Box 2.2 for an example. In the high context condition, a couple is enjoying a picnic when an army of tiny black bugs marches toward their food. In the low content condition, the couple are having a great afternoon outdoors, playing with a Frisbee and drinking wine. The text then either explicitly mentioned "ants" or, in the implicit condition, "bugs." Most important, in the implicit condition, it was not necessary for the maintenance of local coherence for the reader to elaborate on the "bugs" and infer that they were ants. A subsequent sentence in the text then made an anaphoric reference to the "ants." O'Brien et al. found that readers' gaze durations on this anaphoric reference were equivalent in both the high-context explicit and high-context implicit conditions, suggesting that readers had inferred and encoded "ants" in the high context condition, regardless of whether it had been explicitly mentioned or not. It is important to clarify that this inference had been activated before they reached the anaphoric reference – that is, before it was ever required for comprehension.

The demonstration that, under some conditions, elaborative inferences may be passively activated led to several studies focused on specific types of elaborative inferences. For example, Lea (1995) investigated whether readers activated *propositional logic inferences* online. He used texts in which *or-elimination* (p or q; not p/therefore q), and *modus ponens* inferences (if p then q; p/therefore q) were supported by information in the text, but they were not required for comprehension. Across several experiments, he demonstrated that these inferences were activated during reading. This was true independent of whether the inference activated was affirmative (e.g., p or q; not p/therefore q) or negated

---

Box 2.2   Example from O'Brien, Shank, Myers, and Rayner (1988)

It was a perfect afternoon for an outing.

High Context (Explicit/Implicit):
Eve and Mike were enjoying a pleasant picnic with lots of delicious food when an army of tiny black (ants/bugs) began marching across the blanket toward the goodies.
Low Context (Explicit/Implicit):
Eve and Mike were celebrating the afternoon by tossing a Frisbee and drinking lots of delicious wine when they were attacked by a bunch of tiny (ants/bugs) gathering all around them.
Filler: This always seemed to happen when they went out.
Reinstatement Sentence: The *ants* had managed to ruin in the outing.

(e.g., not both p and q; p/therefore not q) (Lea and Mulligan, 2002), or whether the inference was actually warranted or not given the premises provided (Rader and Sloutsky, 2002). However, such inferences appear to be activated only if both premises required for the inference are readily available (i.e., either immediately preceding the inference-evoking sentence or reinstated with a contextual cue; see Lea, Mulligan, and Walton, 2005).

Another type of elaborative inference concerns activating an unmentioned instrument (e.g., broom) in response to reading about an action or event (e.g., the boy cleared the snow from the stairs; Singer, 1979). Early research on these *instrumental inferences* suggested that they were typically not activated during reading but that readers were certainly capable of activating them if instructed to do so (Corbett and Dosher, 1978; Dosher and Corbett, 1982). Further, most evidence for the activation of instrumental inferences tended to be a result of backwards integration from the probe reflecting the inference to the text that elicited it (e.g., Singer, 1979). That is, readers' response times corresponded to the ease with which the probe could be integrated with the immediately preceding text – not the activation level of the probed concept at the time of test. In contrast, McKoon and Ratcliff (1981; see also Lucas, Tanenhaus, and Carlson, 1990) demonstrated that some instrumental inferences were activated and encoded during reading, but this was true only for instruments that were highly related to the action described in the text and had been explicitly mentioned earlier.

More recent research has shed light on the controversy over whether and when instrumental inferences are actually activated online.

Harmon-Vukić, Guéraud, Lassonde, and O'Brien (2009) presented readers with texts that were designed to evoke an instrumental inference (e.g., Carol focused on sewing each stitch very carefully). When the context supporting the inference was minimal, naming times to a probe word reflecting the inference (e.g., needle) were not facilitated; however, reading times on a target sentence that contradicted the inference were disrupted (e.g., The job would be easier if Carol had a needle). Harmon-Vukić et al. interpreted this finding as evidence that at least partial information about the instrument was activated during reading (e.g., McKoon and Ratcliff, 1986). This partial information may not have been specific enough to facilitate naming of a specific lexical item, but it was sufficient to disrupt reading times. In a subsequent experiment, Harmon-Vukić et al. found that when the context supporting the inference was enhanced, more information about the specific instrument was activated, and naming times to the probe word that represented the specific instrument were facilitated. Interestingly, though, across experiments, Harmon-Vukić et al. found that the instrumental inference was encoded in memory regardless of whether the context supporting the inference was high or low. But, the specificity of the information activated and encoded depended on whether the instrument had been explicitly mentioned in the text or on the degree of contextual support for the inference. Thus, as with some of the "necessary" inferences discussed in the previous section, the degree to which instrumental inferences or propositional logic inferences (Lea, 1995; Lea et al., 2005; Lea and Mulligan, 2002) are activated during reading depends on the strength of the relation between the inference-evoking context and the to-be-activated content.

The type of elaborative inference that has perhaps received the most attention in the literature (and therefore the most attention here) is the *predictive inference* – an inference in which "what comes next" in a narrative is activated. Because activation of such predictions is considered "optional" for comprehension, many researchers argued that these inferences are less likely to occur online; indeed if incorrect predictions are made and encoded, and subsequent text refutes them, it could lead to a later disruption in comprehension (e.g., O'Brien et al., 1988). However, in a landmark study that laid the foundation for much of what we know about predictive inferences, McKoon and Ratcliff (1986) began to unpack the conditions necessary for the activation of predictive inferences. For example, consider their classic example:

The director and the cameraman were ready to shoot close-ups when suddenly the actress fell from the 14th story.

Responses to recognition probes reflecting the inference concept (e.g., dead) immediately after the sentence ended were slower and less accurate than in a control condition. After delay, this was only true when the predictive context explicitly stated that the actress died. On the basis of these results, McKoon and Ratcliff argued that the predictive context primed the inference concept, but that this inference was only "minimally encoded" in the discourse representation. That is, some features of the concept of "dead" received some activation, but the overall inferential information that was available to the reader was broader and more general (e.g., something bad happened).

In a subsequent study, Potts, Keenan, and Golding (1988) found evidence for the activation of contextually supported predictive inferences, but this only tended to occur when binary response (e.g., lexical decision or recognition) probes were used, and not when naming times were recorded (see also Whitney, Ritchie, and Crane, 1992). Potts et al. cautioned that when testing for activation of predictive inferences, it is important to ensure that any facilitation is not due to context checking that occurred when the probe was presented. Murray, Klin, and Myers (1993) later confirmed and extended the findings of Potts et al. by also showing that it is important that the probe for inference activation be presented immediately after activation is presumed to occur rather than after a delay as small as one sentence (see also Keefe and McDaniel, 1993). They also provided readers with markedly stronger contexts than those that had been used in previous studies. For example:

Carol was fed up with her job waiting on tables. Customers were rude, the chef was impossibly demanding, and the manager had just made a pass at her that day. The last straw came when a rude man at one of her tables complained that the spaghetti she had just served was cold. As he became louder and nastier, she felt herself losing control. Without thinking of the consequences, she picked up the plate of spaghetti and raised it above the rude man's head.

When predictive contexts such as this were followed by a naming probe reflecting the inference (e.g., "dump"), response times were facilitated compared to a control condition. This study, and that of Keefe and McDaniel (1993), confirmed the findings and claims initially provided by McKoon and Ratcliff (1986): with sufficient contextual support, predictive inferences are passively activated during reading.

Studies on predictive inferencing then turned to the nature of the context necessary to support the activation of a predictive inference. In the studies just cited, both the context that supported the activation of a predictive inference and the inference-evoking sentence that was designed to evoke the predictive inference (e.g., "Without thinking of the consequences, she picked up the plate of spaghetti and raised it above the rude man's head") immediately preceded the point at which activation was measured. Cook, Limber, and O'Brien (2001) argued that predictive inferences are not simply primed by the immediately preceding context or the inference-evoking sentence, but by a combination of activation derived from the overall context, and the inference-evoking sentence, which in turn converges on inferential information in general world knowledge (see Cook and Guéraud, 2005). Moreover, because this convergence happens via passive memory activation processes, predictive inferences may be activated regardless of whether the context and inference-evoking sentence are adjacent in the text. To test these ideas, Cook et al. presented readers with passages in which context supporting a later predictive inference was either strong or weak. In the example in Box 2.3, Jimmy and his friends were throwing rocks at a target (high context condition), or they were throwing Nerf balls (low context condition). After several filler sentences, a sentence that evoked the inference was presented: "He missed, though, and he accidentally hit the door of a new car." Naming times to a probe word reflecting the inference concept (e.g., dent) were facilitated in the high context condition compared to the low context condition (see Calvo, 2000, for a similar finding). Thus, in the Cook et al. study, even though the context and the inference-evoking sentence were separated by several sentences of text, when the inference-evoking sentence was encountered, related information from the text was reactivated, which in turn activated other related information from general world knowledge – the inference.

The degree of contextual constraint in the text also affects the specificity of the activated information. In support of McKoon and Ratcliff's (1986) argument concerning minimal encoding of predictive inferences, Cook et al. (2001) argued that in most cases, the reader does not infer or encode a specific lexical item, but something much more general; that is, instead of the activation of a specific lexical item "dent," more general information regarding damaging outcomes that could be captured by a variety of probes representing "something bad happening" is likely activated and then instantiated. Lassonde and O'Brien (2009) extended this claim by arguing that the degree of inferential specificity was directly tied to the degree of contextual support; as contextual support increased, the degree of inferential specificity should increase. Lassonde and O'Brien confirmed this by showing that in the Cook et al. materials, the predicted inference could be captured by more than one lexical item (e.g., "dent" or "damage"). However, in a subsequent experiment, they altered the context supporting the inference to increase the support for a more specific prediction (e.g., They showed Jimmy their family's brand new car that didn't have any scratches or blemishes. They had to be

---

Box 2.3   Example from Cook et al. (2001)

INTRODUCTION

Jimmy was the new kid on the block. Although his parents urged him to go meet the other kids in the neighborhood, he was shy and hadn't made any new friends. One Saturday morning, his mom asked him to go to the store for her. While he was walking back home, Jimmy ran into some of the kids from the neighborhood. They asked him if he wanted to play with them. Jimmy was delighted and ran across the street to play with them.

HIGH CONTEXT CONDITION

They taught him a fun game that involved throwing rocks at a target to get points.

LOW CONTEXT CONDITION

They taught him a fun game that involved throwing Nerf balls at a target to get points.

FILLER

Jimmy and his friends were having a great time. Jimmy even won the game once or twice. He stepped up to take his turn and aimed at the target.
Inference-Evoking Sentence
He missed, though, and he accidentally hit the door of a new car.
Baseline Sentence
A dog came racing across the street and distracted Jimmy from his throw.
Target dent

---

careful when playing near it because its very soft metal would bend without much pressure). When the context was constrained in this manner, activation of the predictive inference was also more constrained, such that it was captured only by the more specific lexical item (e.g., "dent" was activated but "damage" was not).

The demonstration that predictive inferences result from the combination of the overall context and the inference-evoking sentence led to several investigations of how these two factors interact to influence inference activation. For example, Peracchi and O'Brien (2004) adapted passages from Murray et al. (1993) to create conditions in which the characteristics of the protagonist were either consistent, inconsistent, or neutral with respect to a predicted event. In the sample passage in

Box 2.4   Example from Peracchi and O'Brien (2004) and Guéraud, Tapiero, and O'Brien (2008)

PERACCHI AND O'BRIEN (2004) CONSISTENT CONDITION

Carol was known for her short temper and her tendency to act without thinking. She never thought about the consequences of her actions, so she often suffered negative repercussions. She refused to let people walk all over her. In fact, she had just gotten a ticket for road rage. She decided she would never put up with anyone that was not nice to her.

PERACCHI AND O'BRIEN (2004) INCONSISTENT CONDITION

Carol was known for her ability to settle any confrontation peacefully. She would never even think to solve her problems with physical violence. She taught her students and her own children how to solve problems through conversation. She believed this was an effective way to stop the increasing violence in the schools. Carol also helped other parents learn to deal with their anger.

GUÉRAUD, TAPIERO, AND O'BRIEN (2008) ALTERNATIVE TRAIT CONDITION

Carol had just come back to work after having had shoulder surgery. She needed to be careful whenever raising anything from a customer's table. Every time she did it, it would hurt so much that she thought she might faint. If she raised something too high, she was extremely uncomfortable all night. But, usually, she asked for help when she needed to clear a table.

Filler: One particular night, Carol had an extremely rude customer. He complained about his spaghetti and yelled at Carol as if it were her fault.
Inference-Evoking Sentence: Carol lifted the spaghetti above his head.
Baseline Sentence: She lifted the spaghetti and walked away.

Box 2.4, Carol is described as either ill-tempered and quick to act (consistent condition), or as a peaceful individual opposed to physical violence (inconsistent condition). The text then continues with a description of an event (e.g., a rude customer complains about his food), and the reader is presented with either a sentence that evokes an inference or a baseline sentence. In the example, the inference-evoking sentence "Carol lifted the spaghetti above his head" should yield the inference "dump" but only when the preceding context also supports that inference. Consistent with this prediction, Peracchi and O'Brien found activation of the predictive inference only when it was consistent with the character profile (see also Rapp, Gerrig, and Prentice, 2001). In a clever extension, Guéraud, Tapiero, and O'Brien (2008) demonstrated that the same inference-evoking sentence, when combined with different contexts, could yield completely different inferences. For example, consistent with Peracchi and O'Brien's findings, when Carol was described as ill-tempered and violence-prone and then lifted the plate of spaghetti over a rude customer's head, the inference "dump" was activated. However, if Carol was described as having shoulder problems (see Box 2.4) and then lifted the plate of spaghetti, the inference "pain" was facilitated (and "dump" was not activated).

Given the findings just described, it may be tempting to assume that the reader considers the relevance of the preceding context to the information in the inference-evoking sentence during the inference activation process. However, recall that the reactivation process that drives inference activation is assumed to be dumb. Thus, the activation obtained in these earlier studies should still occur even if the preceding context has been outdated so that it is no longer relevant. Cook, Lassonde, Splinter, Guéraud, Stiegler-Balfour and O'Brien (2014) used passages similar to those used by Peracchi and O'Brien (2004), but added a condition in which the protagonist characteristics in the consistent condition were clearly outdated (see also, O'Brien, Cook, and Guéraud, 2010; O'Brien, Cook, and Peracchi, 2004). For example, Carol is described as once having been ill-tempered and prone to act rashly, *but not anymore*. Cook et al. found that the inference that Carol dumped the spaghetti on the rude customer when the characteristics were described as outdated was just as likely to occur as when the same characteristics were presented as currently true. These findings corroborate the earlier demonstrations that predictive inferences result from the convergence of activation from the context and the inference-evoking sentence. Moreover, they provide evidence that the reactivation mechanism responsible for inference activation is "dumb."

Activation versus instantiation. As demonstrated by Keefe and McDaniel (1993), activation of predictive inferences in memory is fleeting. They found very little evidence for continued activation of predictive inferences after a brief delay (see also Cook et al., 2001; McKoon and Ratcliff, 1986; Potts et al., 1988). A logical question then is, once activated, what is the fate of predictive inferences in memory? Are predictive inferences encoded into the discourse representation in memory, and if so, what is the process by which this occurs? McKoon and Ratcliff found that although there was no evidence for activation of predictive inferences (e.g., dead) after a delay, a word representing the inferred concept served as an effective recall cue in both immediate and delayed tests. They interpreted this as indicating that the inference was "minimally encoded." That is, instead of encoding that the actress died, the reader may have encoded that "something bad happened." Several researchers have demonstrated that predictive inferences are not merely activated but are indeed encoded in memory (Fincher-Kiefer, 1995; Klin, Guzmán, and Levine, 1999; Klin, Murray, Levine, and Guzmán, 1999; Peracchi and O'Brien, 2004). More important, consistent with McKoon and Ratcliff's idea of minimal encoding, Cook et al. found that what is instantiated is more abstract in nature than a specific lexical item (see also Campion, 2004; Casteel, 2007; Fincher-Kiefer, 1993; 1996; McDaniel, Schmalhofer, and Keefe, 2001).

What is less clear from the literature, though, is *how* encoding, or instantiation, of inferences occurs. Researchers have for the most part focused on *whether* inferences are activated or instantiated, without any detailed discussion of the process by which inference instantiation occurs. Recent work conducted in our labs may shed light on this issue. Recall that Cook et al. (2014) found activation of predictive inferences (e.g., dump) regardless of whether the context supporting them was current (Carol was ill-tempered and violence-prone) or not (Carol used to be ill-tempered but not anymore), demonstrating the dumb nature of the activation process. We also questioned whether the instantiation process was just as dumb, or whether the inappropriate inferences (i.e., those that were based on out-dated information) would somehow be "pruned out" in the instantiation process. We continued the passage after the inference-evoking or baseline sentences with two to three backgrounding sentences, and then presented a target sentence that referenced the inference (e.g., She had dumped the plate on the customer.). If instantiation occurred after activation, reading times on the later-appearing target sentence should be faster in the inference-evoking condition than in the baseline condition. Our data supported this prediction but only in the consistent condition. When the contextual information supporting the inference was outdated, there was no evidence for instantiation. This suggests that the integration process that is presumed to follow activation (Kintsch, 1988) must involve some evaluative component that considers the link between activated content and the ongoing discourse model in terms of its relevance to the ongoing story, and general world knowledge (Long and Lea, 2005).

A framework for activation and instantiation of inferred information

The previous sections described ample evidence that a memory activation mechanism that is passive, dumb, and unrestricted (e.g., resonance; Myers and O'Brien, 1998; O'Brien and Myers, 1999) can account for activation of a wide variety of inferences. As Gerrig and O'Brien (2005) put it, these inferences are activated when the information supporting them is "readily available" (McKoon and Ratcliff, 1992), regardless of whether the inferences themselves fall into the categories of "necessary" or "elaborative."

Most current models of discourse processing incorporate this passive activation mechanism as the first phase of processing, to be followed by an integration phase that links activated information to the information currently being processed (Cook and Myers, 2004; Kintsch, 1998; Long and Lea, 2005; Sanford and Garrod, 1989, 2005). The integration phase in these models typically involves linking relevant information from the first phase to the ongoing discourse representation, while irrelevant information is dropped from memory. *How* the integration phase determines information relevance, though, has differed among these models. Some models, such as Kintsch's (1988) construction-integration model, have integration occurring via a passive convergence mechanism, whereas others suggest that attentional processing (Gerrig and O'Brien, 2005) or more strategic evaluation (Long and Lea, 2005) may be involved in integration.

We have recently proposed a three-stage model of discourse processing that we believe can account for the range of inferences described in this chapter, as well as differences in instantiation of activated content, such as the findings observed by Cook et al. (2014). Consistent with the two-stage models of discourse processing described in the previous paragraph, Cook and O'Brien (2014) argued that information is reactivated during reading via a passive activation mechanism, and then quickly linked with the contents of working memory. In a third stage, those linkages are then validated against information in memory. We adopted the resonance model (Myers and O'Brien, 1998; O'Brien and Myers, 1999) as the mechanism driving the activation stage (R). This is followed by the information-linking, or integration, stage (I), and then by the linkage validation stage (Val) – the RI-Val model of comprehension. Importantly, we assume that these three stages represent parallel, asynchronous processes that once begun, run to completion.

Within the RI-Val view, in the first stage (R), information must be activated above some minimum threshold to influence later stages of comprehension. Thus, if there is not enough information in a reader's general world knowledge to support a causal bridging inference, that inference may not be activated above threshold (e.g., see Noordman et al., this volume). Or if the retrieval signal is split among several distractor antecedents, no single antecedent may be activated above the minimum threshold (e.g., Klin et al., 2004; 2006; Levine et al., 2000; O'Brien et al., 1995). In those instances in which inferences are activated above threshold in memory, they are then integrated with the contents of working memory (I). Whether or not these linkages are instantiated into the ongoing discourse model may depend on what occurs during the validation (Val) stage, where linkages are compared against general world knowledge and the discourse representation. If linkages formed in the second stage are deemed relevant to the ongoing discourse model, they should be instantiated into memory. If they are deemed irrelevant during the validation stage, such as the inappropriately activated inferences observed by Cook et al. (2014), they would not be instantiated into memory; our findings were consistent with this assumption.

The passive information retrieval mechanism (R) assumed in our RI-Val view has been well researched. Future work should delve deeper into the mechanisms that drive the integration (I) and validation (Val) stages, as well as the factors that influence each stage. Interestingly, Steele, Bernat, van den Broek, Collins, Patrick, and Marsolek (2012) recently presented ERP evidence in which they identified multiple sequential processes underlying the N400 response to inference-evoking texts. These sequential effects referred to information activation, integration, and post-integration phenomena associated with inferences. Whether or not the processes identified in their study correspond to the processing stages assumed in the RI-Val model is an open question.

One factor that we assume influences the precision of the validation stage is the reader's standard of coherence (van den Broek, Risden, and Husbye-Hartman, 1995) for a given task. This may influence how long readers will wait for all three processes to run to completion, thereby maximizing or minimizing comprehension. For example, van den Broek, Lorch, Linderholm, and Gustafson (2001) found that the degree to which readers produced and instantiated elaborative inferences varied according to whether their standards of coherence were high (as in a studying context) or low (as in a reading-for-pleasure context; see also Linderholm and van den Broek, 2002; Narvaez, van den Broek, and Ruiz, 1999). What other variables influence the precision and timing of the validation stage is a ripe topic for future research.

Conclusion

In the preceding sections, we have established three main points. First, the necessary/elaborative inference distinction becomes blurred if activation of both types of inferences is governed by the same factors. Activation or nonactivation of these inferences is dependent on the amount of available information supporting the inference, the strength of the signal emanating from active memory, and the conceptual overlap between the inference-evoking information and the context supporting the inference. Second, although the inference activation process appears to be "dumb," the instantiation process is more evaluative in nature, such that it takes into account the relevance of the activated information to the ongoing discourse model. Third, the RI-Val view (Cook and O'Brien, 2014) can explain the activation, integration, and validation processes that are involved in inference activation and instantiation. Future work on inferencing should focus on the last two stages in this model.

In conclusion, this chapter focused on the passive processes involved in inference activation and instantiation. Because these fundamental passive processes are likely to influence and interact with the information that is made available via readers' more controlled, strategic processes, we argue that passive processes can be viewed as an essential building block for comprehension. To develop a complete model of inferencing, one would need to account for the independent and interactive contributions of the foundational passive processes described here, as well as the more strategic, constructive processes that encompass reader strategies.

REFERENCES

Albrecht, J. E., & Myers, J. L. (1995). Role of context in accessing distant information during reading. *Journal of Experimental Psychology: Learning, Memory, and Cognition, 21*(6), 1459–68.

(1998). Accessing distant text information during reading: effects of contextual cues. *Discourse Processes, 26*(2–3), 87–107.

Albrecht, J. E., & O'Brien, E. J. (1991). Effects of centrality on retrieval of text-based concepts. *Journal of Experimental Psychology: Learning, Memory, and Cognition, 17*(5), 932–39.

(1995). Goal processing and the maintenance of global coherence. In R. F. Lorch & E. J. O'Brien (eds.) *Sources of Coherence in Reading*, (pp. 263–78). Mahwah, NJ: Erlbaum.

Calvo, M. G. (2000). The time course of predictive inferences depends on contextual constraints. *Language and Cognitive Processes, 15*(3), 293–319.

Campion, N. (2004). Predictive inferences are represented as hypothetical facts. *Journal of Memory and Language, 50*(2), 149–64.

Casteel, M. A. (2007). Contextual support and predictive inferences: what do readers generate and keep available for use? *Discourse Processes, 44*(1), 51–72.

Cook, A. E. (2014). Processing anomalous anaphors. *Memory & Cognition, 42*, 1171–85.

Cook, A. E., & Guéraud, S. (2005). What have we been missing? The role of general world knowledge in discourse processing. *Discourse Processes, 39*(2–3), 265–78.

Cook, A. E., Lassonde, K. A., Splinter, A. F., Guéraud, S., Stiegler-Balfour, J. J., & O'Brien, E. J. (2014). The role of relevance in activation and instantiation of predictive inferences. *Language, Cognition, and Neuroscience, 29,* 244–57.

Cook, A. E., Limber, J. E., & O'Brien, E. J. (2001). Situation-based context and the availability of predictive inferences. *Journal of Memory and Language, 44*(2), 220–34.

Cook, A. E., & Myers, J. L. (2004). Processing discourse roles in scripted narratives: the influences of context and world knowledge. *Journal of Memory and Language, 50*(3), 268–88.

Cook, A. E., Myers, J. L., & O'Brien, E. J. (2005). Processing an anaphor when there is no antecedent. *Discourse Processes, 39*(1), 101–20.

Cook, A. E., & O'Brien, E. J. (2014). Knowledge activation, integration, and validation during narrative text comprehension. *Discourse Processes, 51,* 26–49.

Corbett, A. T., & Chang, F. R. (1983). Pronoun disambiguation: accessing potential antecedents. *Memory & Cognition, 11*(3), 283–94.

Corbett, A. T., & Dosher, B. A. (1978). Instrument inferences in sentence encoding. *Journal of Verbal Learning and Verbal Behavior, 17*(4), 479–91.

Dell, G. S., McKoon, G., & Ratcliff, R. (1983). The activation of antecedent information during the processing of anaphoric reference in reading. *Journal of Verbal Learning and Verbal Behavior, 22*(1), 121–32.

Dosher, B. A., & Corbett, A. T. (1982). Instrument inferences and verb schemata. *Memory & Cognition, 10*(6), 531–39.

Duffy, S. A., & Rayner, K. (1990). Eye movements and anaphor resolution: effects of antecedent typicality and distance. *Language and Speech, 33*(2), 103–19.

Fincher-Kiefer, R. (1993). The role of predictive inferences in situation model construction. *Discourse Processes, 16*(1–2), 99–124.

(1995). Relative inhibition following the encoding of bridging and predictive inferences. *Journal of Experimental Psychology: Learning, Memory, and Cognition, 21*(4), 981–95.

(1996). Encoding differences between bridging and predictive inferences. *Discourse Processes, 22*(3), 225–46.

Fletcher, C. R., & Bloom, C. P. (1988). Causal reasoning in the comprehension of simple narrative texts. *Journal of Memory and language, 27*(3), 235–44.

Garrod, S., O'Brien, E. J., Morris, R. K., & Rayner, K. (1990). Elaborative inferencing as an active or passive process. *Journal of Experimental Psychology: Learning, Memory, and Cognition, 16*(2), 250–57.

Garrod, S., & Sanford, A. (1977). Interpreting anaphoric relations: the integration of semantic information while reading. *Journal of Verbal Learning and Verbal Behavior, 16*(1), 77–90.

Gerrig, R. J., & McKoon, G. (1998). The readiness is all: the functionality of memory-based text processing. *Discourse Processes, 26*(2–3), 67–86.

Gerrig, R. J., & O'Brien, E. J. (2005). The scope of memory-based processing. *Discourse Processes, 39*(2–3), 225–42.

Graesser, A. C., & Kreutz, R. J. (1993). A theory of inference generation during text comprehension. *Discourse Processes, 16*(1–2), 145–60.

Graesser, A. C., Singer, M., & Trabasso, T. (1994). Constructing inferences during narrative text comprehension. *Psychological Review, 101*(3), 371–95.

Greene, S. B., Gerrig, R. J., McKoon, G., & Ratcliff, R. (1994). Unheralded pronouns and management by common ground. *Journal of Memory and Language, 33*(4), 511–26.

Guéraud, S., Tapiero, I., & O'Brien, E. J. (2008). Context and the activation of predictive inferences. *Psychonomic Bulletin & Review, 15*(2), 351–56.

Harmon-Vukić, M., Guéraud, S., Lassonde, K. A., & O'Brien, E. J. (2009). The activation and instantiation of instrumental inferences. *Discourse Processes, 46*(5), 467–90.

Keefe, D. E., & McDaniel, M. A. (1993). The time course and durability of predictive inferences. *Journal of Memory and Language, 32*(4), 446–63.

Keenan, J. M., Baillet, S. D., & Brown, P. (1984). The effects of causal cohesion on comprehension and memory. *Journal of Verbal Learning and Verbal Behavior, 23*(2), 115–26.

Kintsch, W. (1988). The role of knowledge in discourse comprehension: a construction-integration model. *Psychological Review, 95*(2), 163–82.

(1998). *Comprehension: A Paradigm for Cognition.* Cambridge University Press.

Kintsch, W., & Van Dijk, T. A. (1978). Toward a model of text comprehension and production. *Psychological Review, 85*(5), 363–94.

Klin, C. M., Guzmán, A. E., & Levine, W. H. (1999). Prevalence and persistence of predictive inferences. *Journal of Memory and Language, 40*(4), 593–604.

Klin, C. M., Guzmán, A. E., Weingartner, K. M., & Ralano, A. S. (2006). When anaphor resolution fails: partial encoding of anaphoric inferences. *Journal of Memory and Language, 54*(1), 131–43.

Klin, C. M., Murray, J. D., Levine, W. H., & Guzmán, A. E. (1999). Forward inferences: from activation to long-term memory. *Discourse Processes, 27*(3), 241–60.

Klin, C. M., Weingartner, K. M., Guzmán, A. E., & Levine, W. H. (2004). Readers' sensitivity to linguistic cues in narratives: how salience influences anaphor resolution. *Memory & Cognition, 32*(3), 511–22.

Lassonde, K. A., & O'Brien, E. J. (2009). Contextual specificity in the activation of predictive inferences. *Discourse Processes, 46*(5), 426–38.

Lea, R. B. (1995). Online evidence for elaborative logical inferences in text. *Journal of Experimental Psychology: Learning, Memory, and Cognition, 21*(6), 1469–82.

Lea, R. B., & Mulligan, E. J. (2002). The effect of negation on deductive inferences. *Journal of Experimental Psychology: Learning, Memory, and Cognition, 28*(2), 303–17.

Lea, R. B., Mulligan, E. J., & Walton, J. L. (2005). Accessing distant premise information: how memory feeds reasoning. *Journal of Experimental Psychology: Learning, Memory, and Cognition, 31*(3), 387–95.

Levine, W. H., Guzmán, A. E., & Klin, C. M. (2000). When anaphor resolution fails. *Journal of Memory and Language*, 43(4), 594–617.

Linderholm, T., & van den Broek, P. (2002). The effects of reading purpose and working memory capacity on the processing of expository text. *Journal of Educational Psychology*, 94(4), 778–84.

Long, D. L., & Lea, R. B. (2005). Have we been searching for meaning in all the wrong places? Defining the "search after meaning" principle in comprehension. *Discourse Processes*, 39(2–3), 279–98.

Lucas, M. M., Tanenhaus, M. K., & Carlson, G. N. (1990). Levels of representation in the interpretation of anaphoric reference and instrument inference. *Memory & Cognition*, 18(6), 611–31.

McDaniel, M. A., Schmalhofer, F., & Keefe, D. E. (2001). What is minimal about predictive inferences? *Psychonomic Bulletin & Review*, 8(4), 840–46.

McKoon, G., & Ratcliff, R. (1980). The comprehension processes and memory structures involved in anaphoric reference. *Journal of Verbal Learning and Verbal Behavior*, 19(6), 668–82.

(1981). The comprehension processes and memory structures involved in instrumental inference. *Journal of Verbal Learning and Verbal Behavior*, 20(6), 671–82.

(1986). Inferences about predictable events. *Journal of Experimental Psychology: Learning, Memory, and Cognition*, 12(1), 82–91.

(1992). Inference during reading. *Psychological Review*, 99(3), 440–66.

Millis, K. K., & Graesser, A. C. (1994). The time-course of constructing knowledge-based inferences for scientific texts. *Journal of Memory and Language*, 33(5), 583–99.

Murray, J. D., Klin, C. M., & Myers, J. L. (1993). Forward inferences in narrative text. *Journal of Memory and Language*, 32(4), 464–73.

Myers, J. L., Cook, A. E., Kambe, G., Mason, R. A., & O'Brien, E. J. (2000). Semantic and episodic effects on bridging inferences. *Discourse Processes*, 29(3), 179–99.

Myers, J. L., & O'Brien, E. J. (1998). Accessing the discourse representation during reading. *Discourse Processes*, 26(2–3), 131–57.

Myers, J. L., Shinjo, M., & Duffy, S. A. (1987). Degree of causal relatedness and memory. *Journal of Memory and Language*, 26(4), 453–65.

Narvaez, D., van den Broek, P., & Ruiz, A. B. (1999). The influence of reading purpose on inference generation and comprehension in reading. *Journal of Educational Psychology*, 91(3), 488–96.

Noordman, L. G., Vonk, W., Cozjin, R., & Frank, S. (2014, this volume). Causal inferences and world knowledge. In E. J. O'Brien, A. E. Cook, & R. F. Lorch (eds.). *Inferences during Reading*. Cambridge University Press.

Noordman, L. G., Vonk, W., & Kempff, H. J. (1992). Causal inferences during the reading of expository texts. *Journal of Memory and Language*, 31(5), 573–90.

O'Brien, E. J. (1987). Antecedent search processes and the structure of text. *Journal of Experimental Psychology: Learning, Memory, and Cognition*, 13(2), 278–90.

(1995). Automatic components of discourse comprehension. In R. F. Lorch & E. J. O'Brien (eds.) *Sources of Coherence in Reading* (pp. 159–76). Mahwah, NJ: Erlbaum.

O'Brien, E. J., & Albrecht, J. E. (1991). The role of context in accessing antecedents in text. *Journal of Experimental Psychology: Learning, Memory, and Cognition, 17*(1), 94–102.

O'Brien, E. J., Albrecht, J. E., Hakala, C. M., & Rizzella, M. L. (1995). Activation and suppression of antecedents during reinstatement. *Journal of Experimental Psychology: Learning, Memory, and Cognition, 21*(3), 626–34.

O'Brien, E. J., Cook, A. E., & Guéraud, S. (2010). Accessibility of outdated information. *Journal of Experimental Psychology: Learning, Memory, and Cognition, 36*, 979–91.

O'Brien, E. J., Cook, A. E., & Peracchi, K. A. (2004). Updating situation models: a reply to Zwaan and Madden. *Journal of Experimental Psychology: Learning, Memory, and Cognition, 30*, 289–91.

O'Brien, E. J., Duffy, S. A., & Myers, J. L. (1986). Anaphoric inference during reading. *Journal of Experimental Psychology: Learning, Memory, and Cognition, 12*(3), 346–52.

O'Brien, E. J., & Myers, J. L. (1987). The role of causal connections in the retrieval of text. *Memory & Cognition, 15*(5), 419–27.

(1999). Text comprehension: a view from the bottom up. In S. R. Goldman, A. C. Graesser, & P. van den Broek (eds.) *Narrative Comprehension, Causality, and Coherence: Essays in Honor of Tom Trabasso*, 35–53. Mahwah, NJ: Erlbaum.

O'Brien, E. J., Plewes, P. S., & Albrecht, J. E. (1990). Antecedent retrieval processes. *Journal of Experimental Psychology: Learning, Memory, and Cognition, 16*(2), 241–9.

O'Brien, E. J., Raney, G. E., Albrecht, J. E., & Rayner, K. (1997). Processes involved in the resolution of explicit anaphors. *Discourse Processes, 23*(1), 1–24.

O'Brien, E. J., Shank, D. M., Myers, J. L., & Rayner, K. (1988). Elaborative inferences during reading: do they occur online? *Journal of Experimental Psychology: Learning, Memory, and Cognition, 14*(3), 410–20.

Peracchi, K. A., & O'Brien, E. J. (2004). Character profiles and the activation of predictive inferences. *Memory & Cognition, 32*(7), 1044–52.

Potts, G. R., Keenan, J. M., & Golding, J. M. (1988). Assessing the occurrence of elaborative inferences: lexical decision versus naming. *Journal of Memory and Language, 27*(4), 399–415.

Rader, A. W., & Sloutsky, V. M. (2002). Processing of logically valid and logically invalid conditional inferences in discourse comprehension. *Journal of Experimental Psychology: Learning, Memory, and Cognition, 28*(1), 59–68.

Rapp, D. N., Gerrig, R. J., & Prentice, D. A. (2001). Readers' trait-based models of characters in narrative comprehension. *Journal of Memory and Language, 45*(4), 737–50.

Rizzella, M. L., & O'Brien, E. J. (1996). Accessing global causes during reading. *Journal of Experimental Psychology: Learning, Memory, and Cognition, 22*(5), 1208–18.

Sanford, A. J., & Garrod, S. C. (1989). What, when, and how? Questions of immediacy in anaphoric reference resolution. *Language and Cognitive Processes*, 4(3–4), SI235–62.

(2005). Memory-based approaches and beyond. *Discourse Processes*, 39(2–3), 205–24.

Singer, M. (1979). Processes of inference during sentence encoding. *Memory & Cognition*, 7(3), 192–200.

(1993). Causal bridging inferences: validating consistent and inconsistent sequences. *Canadian Journal of Experimental Psychology/Revue canadienne de psychologie experimentale*, 47(2), 340–59.

Singer, M., & Ferreira, F. (1983). Inferring consequences in story comprehension. *Journal of Verbal Learning and Verbal Behavior*, 22(4), 437–48.

Singer, M., & Gagnon, N. (1999). Detecting causal inconsistencies in scientific text. In S. R. Goldman, A. C. Graesser, & P. van den Broek (eds.) *Narrative Comprehension, Causality, and Coherence: Essays in Honor of Tom Trabasso* (pp. 179–94).Mahwah, NJ: Erlbaum.

Singer, M., Graesser, A. C., & Trabasso, T. (1994). Minimal or global inference during reading. *Journal of Memory and Language*, 33(4), 421–41.

Singer, M., & Halldorson, M. (1996). Constructing and validating motive bridging inferences. *Cognitive Psychology*, 30(1), 1–38.

Singer, M., Halldorson, M., Lear, J. C., & Andrusiak, P. (1992). Validation of causal bridging inferences in discourse understanding. *Journal of Memory and Language*, 31(4), 507–24.

Steele, V. R., Bernat, E. M., van den Broek, P., Collins, P. F., Patrick, C. J., & Marsolek, C. J. (2012). Separable processes before, during, and after the N400 elicited by previously inferred and new information: evidence from time-frequency decompositions. *Brain Research*, 1492, 92–107.

Trabasso, T., & Sperry, L. L. (1985). Causal relatedness and importance of story events. *Journal of Memory and Language*, 24(5), 595–611.

Van den Broek, P., Lorch, R. F., Linderholm, T., & Gustafson, M. (2001). The effects of readers' goals on inference generation and memory for texts. *Memory & Cognition*, 29(8), 1081–87.

Van den Broek, P., Risden, K., & Husebye-Hartmann, E. (1995). The role of readers' standards for coherence in the generation of inferences during reading. In R. F. Lorch & E. J. O'Brien (eds.) *Sources of Coherence in Reading*, (pp. 353–73). Mahwah, NJ: Erlbaum.

Whitney, P., Ritchie, B. G., & Crane, R. S. (1992). The effect of foregrounding on readers' use of predictive inferences. *Memory & Cognition*, 20(4), 424–32.

Wiley, J., & Myers, J. L. (2003). Availability and accessibility of information and causal inferences from scientific text. *Discourse Processes*, 36(2), 109–29.

3 Cognitive theories in discourse-processing research

Gail McKoon and Roger Ratcliff

Much has been learned in the past decades about how readers comprehend discourse. In large part, advances have come about because empirical methods were developed in the 1980s that allow the examination and separation of online processes, off-line processes, and the memory representations that result from these processes. This chapter reviews these methods and shows what can be interpreted from them. We begin with several general points, continue with a discussion of particular methods, and then review new methodologies that have been developed in the last several years. In the course of these discussions, we use examples from our own research, but many others (including all the authors of the other chapters in this book) have provided similar examples.

1. The first general point is that cognitive processes can be separated into those that occur quickly and automatically and those that occur more slowly and strategically (Posner, 1978). For example, for the sentence "The janitor swept the classroom," a reader might infer that the janitor used a broom, and do so automatically or strategically. Usually, in the field of discourse research, interest has focused on what a reader understands without special, strategic effort. However, in other fields, such as education, it might be strategic effects that are of most interest.

2. The second general point concerns the process by which information is retrieved from memory automatically. Theories over the past several decades have described the process as "resonance" (beginning with Lockhart, Craik, and Jacoby, 1976, and Ratcliff, 1978; first applied in discourse-processing research as the "minimalist hypothesis" by McKoon and Ratcliff, e.g., 1986; 1992).

   The notion of resonance is that information retrieval is a fast, passive process (i.e., an automatic one) by which cues in short-term memory interact with all the information in long-term memory in parallel. This fast, easy process accesses all the information in memory, but the degree to which any specific cue in short-term memory evokes any specific piece of information in long-term memory depends on the strength of the association between them in memory. This strength determines the degree to which the information is evoked. In its essence, fast, passive, parallel retrieval provides information "for free."

For discourse processing research, it is important to stress that resonance-type retrieval can operate both during reading and during memory tests. For the janitor sentence, the contents of short-term memory during reading would be the words of the sentence and their meanings, including the words "swept" and "janitor" and their meanings. The degree to which "broom" became available during reading (and possibly encoded) would depend on the strength of the associations among "broom," "swept," "janitor," and their meanings.

The fact that an item in short-term memory can match information in long-term memory to varying degrees has an important implication for investigations of whether and what kinds of inferences are automatically encoded during reading. In early discourse processing research, questions about inference encoding were almost always phrased in an all-or-none manner. With resonance models, this is no longer appropriate.

The application of the resonance view to memory tests can again be illustrated with the "janitor" sentence. The word "broom" might be tested in single-word recognition, where subjects decide whether test words are old or new according to whether they had appeared in a previously read sentence. If "broom" were presented as a test word, it would make available "The janitor swept the classroom" sentence to the degree that "broom" was encoded as part of its meaning during reading. If "broom" was encoded during reading to a sufficiently high degree, then subjects might respond, in error, that the word "broom" had actually appeared as part of the janitor sentence.

Resonance theories make no distinction between a lexicon of information about words and memory for other kinds of information; a cue evokes all kinds of information at once. In contrast, in research prior to about 1990, it was often said that the processes that identify a word, for lexical decision, for example, can be divided into "pre-lexical" processes and "post-lexical" processes (e.g., Forster, 1981). Pre-lexical processes determine the information about a word that is available from the lexicon and post-lexical processes determine whether and how that information is relevant to whatever language comprehension task is at hand. The moment at which information from the lexicon became available to post-lexical processing was labeled "the magic moment" (Balota, 1990). In this view, the effects of some variable on pre-lexical processes occur independently of effects on comprehension. For example, the word "swept" in the janitor sentence might facilitate lexical access for "broom" but this would indicate nothing about whether "broom" is inferred as the instrument of "swept."

3. The third general point is that retrieval from long-term memory is context dependent (Tulving, 1974): Memory can never be assessed without taking into account the environment of other cues in which a particular cue to memory is tested. The environment includes other information in short-term memory at the time of the memory test, and it also includes general characteristics of the test situation as a whole. The assumption of context-dependent retrieval has been incorporated into all current models of memory. A correlate of it is that it is never possible to know that some piece of information has not been encoded into memory; there always might be some test environment in which it is (to some degree) retrieved.

4. The fourth general point is that the combination of resonance retrieval and context-dependent retrieval provides an interpretation of priming effects that is quite different from the traditional spreading activation interpretation (but see ACT*, Anderson, 1983). In text processing research, priming has been examined between words, phrases, and sentences, for example, "dog" and "cat" in lexical decision. Ratcliff and McKoon (1988) explain findings like this with a compound-cue model, a model that is an implementation of context-dependent retrieval into global retrieval models (e.g., Gillund and Shiffrin, 1984). In the model, all the contents of short-term memory are combined to match against long-term memory. For "dog" and "cat," responses to "cat" are facilitated because the compound cue "dog cat" makes available the associations between them in long-term memory. The model explains priming data both qualitatively and quantitatively.

The import of Ratcliff and McKoon's model lies, in part, in its sharp contrast with traditional spreading activation accounts of priming by which the prime activates the target before the target itself is presented – "dog" as a test item immediately activates "cat" and so responses to "cat" as a test item are facilitated. In the compound-cue model, there is no advance effect of "dog;" the association can affect performance only when "dog" and "cat" are together in short-term memory.

In discourse research, the compound-cue model applies in three situations. In one, subjects are given a list of texts to read followed by a recognition test, where the tested items can be single words, phrases, or sentences. To the extent that the prime and target are associated in the encoded representation of a text, their compound should facilitate "old" responses to the target. For the sentence "The janitor swept the classroom," the memory test might be recognition of single words.

Responses to "janitor" immediately preceded by "classroom" would be facilitated to the extent that they were encoded together when the sentence was read. Likewise, if "broom" was encoded during reading, then "janitor" or "classroom" should facilitate "old" responses (i.e., incorrect responses) to "broom."

The second situation in which the compound-cue model applies is that, during reading, the words of a text form compounds of the words and their meanings, and these compounds are matched against memory. For the janitor sentence, the compound would be made up of: "janitor" and its meanings, "swept" and its meanings, "classroom" and its meanings, the meanings evoked by all the pairs ("janitor-swept," "janitor-classroom," and "swept-classroom"), and the meanings evoked by the triple "janitor-swept-classroom." Comprehension of this sentence would be facilitated to the extent that general knowledge provided pre-existing associations among parts of the compound.

The third situation occurs when items (words, phrases, or sentences) are tested "online," that is, during reading or immediately after it. In this procedure, the test item forms a compound with the text information preceding it. From the compound-cue point of view, information from the text does not activate information in memory about the test item before the test item is presented, again in sharp contrast to a traditional spreading activation mechanism.

Measuring comprehension and memory

There are many empirical paradigms that have been used in the discourse-processing literature, and they vary in the interpretations of data that are possible from them. Here we discuss five of the most popular paradigms.

1. In cued and free recall, subjects are asked to produce all the information that they remember from a text. The first issue with these methods is that subjects' responses may reflect information that was encoded during reading or information that was constructed at the time of the memory test (and in either case, processing might be automatic or strategic). For example, if "The janitor swept the classroom" was a to-be-remembered sentence and the test of memory was cued recall, subjects might produce "broom" in response to "janitor."

This response might be due to "broom" being inferred when the sentence was read and encoded into memory as part of the representation of the sentence, or it might be that subjects connect "broom" to the janitor sentence only when "janitor" is presented as a cue.

In an early demonstration of this problem, Corbett and Dosher (1978) gave subjects lists of sentences to read and remember, and followed them with cues for recall. They found that "hammer" was an equally good cue for the sentence "John pounded the nail with a rock" as for the sentence "John pounded the nail." Either "hammer" was not encoded with "John pounded the nail" or it was encoded with both "John pounded the nail" and "John pounded the nail with a rock." Either way, it cannot be argued that "hammer" was encoded during reading as the instrument of pound.

The second issue with cued and free recall is that subjects can edit their responses, perhaps to make them seem more coherent. Suppose, for example, they recall that something happened, but not to whom it happened. They might attempt to make their recall more coherent by deleting the "something happened" information from it or they might attempt to make their recall more coherent by generating new information that was not part of the to-be-remembered information.

A third issue is that subjects' performance in recall tasks presents a classic case of an item-selection artifact: The subject, not the experimenter, selects what responses to make. A subject might have a perfect verbatim representation of a to-be-remembered text, but still produce only partial information at test (perhaps because responding with full information would require too much time). A subject might remember, for example, everything from a multisentence text but decide to produce only the highlights.

2. Several paradigms have the same problems as cued and free recall. In a "topicality" experiment, subjects are asked to generate a topic sentence for a text they have read, in a multiple-choice experiment, they are given several possible choices to answer a test question, and in a question-answering experiment, they are given open-ended questions. In all three of these paradigms, subjects' responses are likely to reflect information constructed at the time of the test. Also, subjects are usually given as much time as they want to make their responses and that may encourage them to adopt special strategies.

Two other paradigms have an additional problem. In a "close" experiment, subjects are given sentences with blanks in them and for each, they are asked to fill in the blank with a word appropriate to the sentence. Subjects in a "think-aloud" experiment are asked to talk about what they are thinking as they read through a text. For these paradigms, responses are at least as likely to reflect constructed information as automatically encoded information, and highly likely to reflect special strategies. The additional problem is that they are disruptive to normal reading.

Subjects cannot decide what to say aloud or what to fill into a blank without, at least temporarily and to some extent, losing track of what they are reading.

Finally, empirical measures must have bases in theory, but for none of these paradigms are there well-understood models for how responses are produced. What determines what information subjects produce when they "think aloud"? What are the processes by which a word is generated to fill in a blank? Of all the information from a text that is available in memory, how does a subject pick which to report? One implication of this problem – the lack of theoretical understanding of response mechanisms – is that there is no way to know what to do when the methods give different results. If subjects produce the correct referent of a pronoun when they think aloud but not when they are asked an open-ended question, how can it be decided whether the referent was encoded automatically during reading? This is in strong contrast to the highly developed models for retrieval in paradigms for which responses are fast and automatic.

3. In online tests, a subject's task is usually single-word recognition or lexical decision. Online tests are essential to investigations of reading. They show the information that is available to a subject at particular points in time. However, there are two important issues for the interpretations of online data that are sometimes overlooked. One is that online tests can show what information is available during reading but they cannot show what is encoded into memory. "Broom" might be available during reading, because it is evoked by "The janitor swept the classroom," but not encoded into the representation of the sentence in memory. Knowing what was encoded into memory requires an off-line task. The second issue, mentioned above, is that online tests tap only the interactions of the test item with the text being read; there is no way to separate out the contribution of the test item alone.

To illustrate misconstruals of online data we give three examples, two for lexical decision and one for naming latencies. First, in a classic study, Onifer and Swinney (1981) presented sentences like the two below auditorily. Somewhere during each sentence a string of letters for lexical decision appeared visually. The items of interest were ambiguous words such as "bug." Test words that matched one or the other of the word's meanings ("insect" or "spy") appeared either immediately after the ambiguous word or several words later. Onifer and Swinney's finding was that response times (RTs) for both words were shorter than control test words at immediate test, but at the later test, RTs were shorter only for the word appropriate to the context of the sentence. In other words, for both sentences below, RTs for both "insect" and "spy" were speeded immediately after "bug," but at the later test, only "spy" was speeded for the first sentence and only "insect" for the second.

> For several weeks following the exterminator's visit, they did not find a single bug anywhere in the apartment.

> For several weeks following the discovery that they were being watched by the CIA, they kept checking the phone for a bug or a hidden video camera.

The standard and highly influential interpretation of this result was that both meanings of an ambiguous word are activated immediately; context does not operate quickly enough to activate only the appropriate meaning. However, the view that interactions between test word and context determine RTs gives a different interpretation: Responses to "spy" and "insect" are fast with immediate test because they are in short-term memory in a compound cue with "bug." Responses for the inappropriate word are slow later because "bug" is no longer in short-term memory.

In another study with online lexical decision, Nicol and Swinney (1989) examined whether readers understand the implicit objects of verbs. In "the police stopped the boy that the crowd at the party accused of the crime," the object of "accused" is "boy." They found what they took to be a very surprising result – responses to "girl," a strong associate of "boy," were speeded, relative to a control, immediately after "accused" compared to immediately before. They attributed this to readers filling in "boy" as the implicit object. However, again, consideration of interactions between test word and context gives a different interpretation, one demonstrated by McKoon and Ratcliff (1994) with the sentence "The crowd at the party accused the boy," for which responses to "girl" were speeded from before to after "accused" even though "boy" was not an implicit object.

In addition to recognition and lexical decision, naming latencies have often been used to test for the availability of words during reading. For example, for the "bug" sentence, "insect" and "spy" and their control words would be presented just as for lexical decision except that the readers' task would be to name the words as quickly as possible. If naming latencies showed no difference between "insect" and "spy" relative to their controls at either of the two test positions, then it would have been concluded that readers did not comprehend the context relevance of one of "bug's" meanings over the other. This conclusion is incorrect because of the scaling problem that naming latencies are much shorter than lexical decision or recognition latencies. This means that effects that are significant in the latter two cases may not be significant for naming latencies. In other words, if an experimental variable does not affect naming latencies, it cannot be concluded that that variable is not effective in comprehension.

4. In off-line tests, some amount of unrelated material is presented between the text to be remembered and the test items. The test is usually recognition, for which the test items might again be single words, phrases, or sentences. Typically, subjects are asked to respond as quickly and accurately as possible. If off-line recognition is to be used to investigate automatic processes, then two requirements must be met to rule out strategic processes: One is that responses must be faster than the amount of time that would be needed for strategic processes, which has been shown in a number of studies to be around 700 ms (e.g., McKoon and Ratcliff, 1989a), and the other is that the probability with which the test items of interest occur must be low so that subjects do not guess the purpose of the experiment and adopt special strategies for it.

Off-line tests are appealing for several reasons. One is that the experimenter chooses the items to be tested; there is no item-selection artifact. Another is that they show what was actually encoded during reading, not just what was available. Still another is that the experimenter can choose what combinations of items to test. For the janitor sentence, the experimenter might want to look at memory for the individual words and so the test would be single-word recognition. The experimenter could also choose conjunctions of words, and so the test would be recognition of phrases or whole sentences.

McKoon and Ratcliff (1986) were the first to demonstrate how off-line recognition could be used to investigate encoded inferences, specifically inferences about what would happen next in a discourse. For example, for the sentence "The cameraman was ready to shoot close-ups when the actress fell from the 14th story," "dead" would be what happened next. The aim of the experiment was to show that "dead" was encoded as an inference when the sentence was read. McKoon and Ratcliff's paradigm met the conditions necessary for testing automatic processes: The experimental test words occurred with a low probability and responses were faster than 700 ms.

There were four conditions in the experiment, two versions of the sentence and two test contexts. One version of the sentence was the one given above. The other was "Suddenly the director fell upon the cameraman, demanding that he get a close-up of the actress on the 14th story," which provides an essential control. It uses words from the sentence that predicts "dead" that might be pre-experimentally related to "dead," but rearranges them into a sentence that does not predict "dead." With this control, it cannot be the case that responses to "dead" reflect pre-experimental associations instead of inferences that were encoded during reading.

The compound-cue view suggests that automatic retrieval for sentences such as the actress one will depend on the context in which the "dead" test words are presented. McKoon and Ratcliff used two contexts; the test words were immediately preceded by a prime from their sentence, "actress" for "dead," or the word "ready" (as a neutral prime).

What McKoon and Ratcliff found was that responses to "dead" were more likely to be "old" (an error) when the prime was "actress" than when it was "ready." It was this retrieval context effect that led us to describe the "dead" inference as "minimal" (McKoon and Ratcliff, 1992).

Soon after McKoon and Ratcliff's (1986) paper, Potts, Keenan, and Golding (1988) proposed a different mechanism to explain the "actress dead" result. Their idea was that the prime "actress" activates its sentence and then when "dead" is presented, it is checked against the sentence for compatibility. Since "dead" is compatible with the predicting sentence, responses to it tend to be errors. With the neutral prime "ready," the sentence is not activated, and so there are fewer errors.

However, there are two reasons to think that Potts et al.'s hypothesis is not correct. One is that there was not sufficient time in McKoon and Ratcliff's experiment for compatibility checking – the SOA between the prime and the test word was only 200 ms, and subjects were instructed to respond within 600 ms of onset of the test word. The second reason stems from other experiments by McKoon and Ratcliff (1989a). With the same paradigm as McKoon and Ratcliff (1986), they used sentences that should evoke a member of a category, sentences such as "The young attorney wanted to make sure she had fresh juice for breakfast so she squeezed the fruit herself." Responses to "oranges" tended to be errors to the same degree with "ready" as a prime as with "attorney." Because "ready" could not provide access to the "attorney" sentence, Potts et al.'s hypothesis can be rejected.

5. It is often claimed that the time it takes subjects to read a word, sentence, or text gives insight into what they understand from the

sentence. Sometimes reading times are measured by subjects control-ling the amount of time they spend reading each word, phrase, or sentence, and sometimes they are measured by eye movements, looking at first-pass reading times, total reading times, and probabil-ities of regression.

However, reading times do not show unambiguously how readers comprehend texts. Reading times can show "glitches" in processing but not the results of them. The problem is that reading times are subject to speed/accuracy trade-offs. Slowdowns in reading can occur because a subject, facing some difficulty in comprehension, takes the time to understand the textual information fully and correctly, or because the subject slows down enough to appreciate the difficulty but not enough to fully resolve it (McKoon and Ratcliff, 1992, were the first to discuss this issue). Failing to resolve difficulties encountered during reading is prob-ably a characteristic of most everyday reading.

The view that comprehension is often incomplete is nicely illustrated by the "Moses illusion" (Erickson and Mattson, 1981). When asked how many animals of each kind Moses took on the Ark, most subjects easily answer "two," not noticing that the sentence has evoked incorrect information.

The Moses illusion also illustrates another point: The absence of a slowdown does not mean that there was no difficulty in processing. The assumption that all possible comprehension difficulties are reflected in reading time is an assumption that is, and must be, incorrect.

Another issue with reading times is that when they slow for one set of sentences but not a comparison set, then it cannot be determined whether comprehension of one set was facilitated relative to the other or one set was inhibited relative to the other. For the two texts below, Sanford and Garrod (1981) found slower reading times for the "control the class" sentence for the first compared to the second text. They attributed this to inhibition: The "on his way to school" sentence gener-ated the inference that John was a schoolboy, and the mismatch between this inference and John controlling the class was thought to be respon-sible for the slower reading times. Instead it could be that no inference was generated about John being a schoolboy from the "on his way to school" sentence. Instead, reading times were faster with the second text because comprehension of "control the class" was facilitated by its good match with John teaching math.

> *John was on his way to school. The bus trundled slowly along the road. He hoped he could control the class today.*
> *John was not looking forward to teaching math. The bus trundled slowly along the road. He hoped he could control the class today.*

Questions about comprehension and memory

Our argument in this chapter is that reading comprehension and memory can be fruitfully investigated only when the methods used to investigate them are based on an explicit conceptualization of retrieval processes: Fast automatic processes can be separated from slower strategic ones and, when retrieval is automatic, it is a resonance-type process by which cues in short-term memory are matched passively against all the information in long-term memory in parallel in a context-dependent fashion. In the next sections, we illustrate the impact of this conceptualization of retrieval with a series of examples from our own research, although all of the same points can be made with the research of many others. All of the examples represent inferences of one sort or another: Simple ones such as the referent of a pronoun and more complex ones such as what will happen next in a story.

Available and encoded. If a reader can be said to have understood an inference, then the required information must have been available during reading and the inference must be encoded into memory. McKoon and Ratcliff (1980) and Dell, McKoon, and Ratcliff (1983) showed both for nominal anaphors. They used four-sentence texts, such as the one to follow, in two conditions. In the first, the fourth sentence begins with an anaphor that refers to an entity mentioned in the first sentence. For the following text, readers should infer that "the criminal" refers to the burglar mentioned in the first sentence. In the second condition, the fourth sentence begins with an entity not previously mentioned, "dog."

> The burglar surveyed the garage.
> The banker and his wife were on vacation. Newspapers were piled
>   at the curb.
> The criminal OR a dog slipped away from the streetlamp.

Dell et al. (1983) used an online single-word recognition paradigm. The words of a text were presented one at a time for 250 ms per word (about normal reading time for college students). At any point during a text, a test word could be presented instead of the next word of the text. For the burglar text, for example, "burglar" was presented as a test word immediately after "the criminal" in the first condition and immediately after "a dog" in the second condition. Dell et al.'s hypothesis was that the relation between the criminal and the burglar would lead to facilitation of responses to "burglar," and this is what they found.

Dell et al. also tested the word "vacation" immediately after "the criminal" and "a dog." It was possible that something other than the relation between "the criminal" and "the burglar" was responsible for the facilitation of "burglar" in the "criminal" condition. Perhaps, for example, "a dog" might have been more difficult to understand for some reason than "the criminal." Counter this possibility, Dell et al. found that RTs for "vacation" did not differ between the two conditions.

Dell et al. also tested the word "garage" immediately after "the criminal" and "a dog" to show that faster responses for "burglar" after "the criminal" were not due solely to the a priori semantic relatedness of "criminal" and "burglar." Connecting "the criminal" to "burglar" when "the criminal" is read should have made not only "burglar" more available but also words directly related to "burglar," such as "garage," and Dell et al. found that it did.

We stress again that facilitation for "burglar" and "garage" does not mean that the connections among "burglar," "criminal," and "garage" were encoded into memory when the criminal sentence was read, only that they became more available when "the criminal" text was read than when "the dog" text was read.

To look at what connections are encoded into memory, McKoon and Ratcliff (1980) used off line single word recognition. For the burglar text, the test word "streetlamp" was immediately preceded by the test word "burglar." If the inference that "the criminal" referred to "the burglar" and was encoded when "the criminal" was read, then responses to "streetlamp" should be facilitated in the first condition compared to the second and, again, this is the result that was found.

Available but not relevant. When, during reading, the words and meanings of a text evoke strongly associated information from long-term memory, then that information can be irrelevant to the meaning of the text as a whole. To show the immediate availability of such information, McKoon and Ratcliff (1989b) used the same paradigm as Dell et al., with single-sentence texts of the three kinds shown below. In each case, the test word was "sit," for which the correct response was "new," and it was presented immediately after the final words of the sentences.

1. *After shopping for hours, the grandmother headed for her favorite chair.*
2. *After shopping for hours, the grandmother headed for her favorite store.*
3. *After shopping for hours, the grandmother found the perfect chair.*

Responses to "sit" were slower and less accurate after the first sentence than the second, indicating that it was only the final word, "chair," of the first sentence that evoked "sit." The more interesting finding was that responses to "sit" were as slow and inaccurate after the third sentence as after the first. Consistent with a compound cue, the relation between "chair" and "sit" affected responses even when "sit" was irrelevant to the text.

Connections among the elements of a text. Of all the types of inferences that have been investigated in discourse research, the most common are inferences that connect the elements of a text. The key to predictions about such connections is that the elements of a text that are currently being read evoke other information via resonance-type retrieval.

Consider the text below, used in experiments by McKoon and Ratcliff (1980).

Early French settlements in North America were strung so thinly along major waterways that land ownership was not a problem. The Frenchmen were fur traders, and, by necessity, the fur traders were nomads. Towns were few, forts and trading posts were many. Little wonder that the successful fur trader learned to live, act, and think like an Indian. Circulation among the Indians was vital to the economic survival of the traders.

To fully comprehend this text, a reader needs to infer the connection between "circulation among the Indians was vital" and "the fur traders were nomads." This connection is not explicit in the text – it is left unsaid that it was the fur traders for whom circulation was vital. However, if readers do infer this, then "circulation among the Indians was vital to the fur traders" should evoke earlier-mentioned information about the fur traders, for example, that they were nomads. In contrast, "land owner-ship was not a problem" should not directly evoke earlier information about the fur traders because the land ownership information is a general fact about early settlements.

To test whether readers infer the connection between "circulation among the Indians was vital" and "the fur traders were nomads," McKoon and Ratcliff used an off-line test. The test items were phrases from the text and for each, subjects were asked to decide whether it was true or false according to a previously read text. The manipulation was one of priming. The target test item was "the fur traders were nomads." If the test item that immediately preceded it was "circulation among the Indians was vital," responses were faster and more accurate than if the preceding test item was "land ownership was not a problem." This result is especially noteworthy because the French settlements text is fairly complex, yet the combination of inferred information and resonance-type retrieval leads to the encoding of appropriate connections.

Pronoun resolution without pronouns. Perhaps the most powerful of the demonstrations of resonance-type retrieval during reading has been provided in studies by Gerrig and McKoon and colleagues (Gerrig and McKoon, 1998; 2001; Greene, Gerrig, McKoon, and Ratcliff, 1994; Love and McKoon, 2011; McKoon, Gerrig, and Greene, 1996). In these studies, we have used texts such as the one below that has three parts:

INTRODUCTION MENTIONS THREE CHARACTERS

Jane was dreading dinner with her cousin, Marilyn. She complained loudly to her roommate, Gloria. "Every time I go to dinner at my cousin's I get sick. Gloria asked, "Why did you agree to go?" Jane said, "Because I'm too wimpy to say no." Jane went off to have dinner.

MIDDLE PART DOES NOT MENTION COUSIN MARILYN OR JANE

Gloria decided to cook something nice for herself for dinner. "As long as I'm alone," she thought, "I'll eat well." Gloria searched her refrigerator for ingredients. She found enough eggs to make a quiche.

CONCLUSION

Gloria was still up when Jane arrive home about midnight. Gloria asked Jane, "Did she make the evening unbearable?"

We labeled the first sentence of the conclusion the "reunion" sentence. The idea was that information in this sentence would evoke, via resonance-type retrieval, information from the introduction sentences. In the example above, "Gloria was still up when Jane arrived home about midnight" would evoke the information that Jane and Gloria were roommates, that Jane had a cousin named Marilyn, that Jane was going to dinner with her cousin, and so on. The hypothesis was that evoking this information would increase the availability of "cousin Marilyn." To demonstrate this, Gerrig et al. used an online, single-word recognition paradigm. The test word "cousin" was presented immediately before or immediately after the reunion sentence. The result was a speed-up in RTs from the first of these test points to the second, relative to a control condition. Moreover, when "cousin" was tested immediately after the sentence with the pronoun ("Did she make ..."), there was no further decrease in RTs. It is this finding that we labeled "pronoun resolution without pronouns."

One important comment about Gerrig et al.'s experiments is that, almost certainly, the idea to look for pronoun resolution without pronouns would not have happened without the resonance-based retrieval framework. Previously, it had been assumed that pronouns find their antecedents by searching backward through a text. The resonance view eliminated backward search as the main process by which referents of pronouns are automatically found.

The results of Gerrig et al.'s experiments are an especially compelling use of the resonance-based framework. The reunion sentence evoked "cousin" via a fast, passive process, and an explicit pronoun did not further increase "cousin's" availability. The configuration of cues at the test point immediately after the reunion sentence (the information in the reunion sentence and the test word "cousin") served to draw together appropriate portions of the text; the pronoun in the second sentence of the conclusion was not essential.

Integrating text information and general knowledge. Connections among text elements can also depend on information that is evoked from long-term memory about general knowledge of the world. Allbritton, McKoon, and Gerrig (1995) provided a demonstration of this with narratives that evoked common metaphor-based schemas. The two narratives below illustrate the two conditions of the experiment. The hypothesis was that in the first narrative, "the city's crime epidemic" would evoke a schema for "epidemic" as a metaphor. The final sentence, "public officials desperately looked for a cure," is consistent with this metaphor, and so it should be closely connected to "the city's crime epidemic." In the second narrative, "the city's crime epidemic" would still evoke the epidemic-as-metaphor schema, but the intervening information between this and the final sentence moves the narrative to a nonmetaphoric use of "cure" in the final sentence.

In Allbritton et al.'s experiment, the paradigm was a priming manipulation with test statements presented for true/false judgments. "Public officials desperately looked for a cure" was the target test statement, and it was immediately preceded by "The city's crime epidemic was raging out of control." Consistent with the hypothesis, "true" responses to the target were faster for the schema-matching version than the mismatching version.

METAPHOR-MATCHING
The most recent crime statistics confirmed what New Yorkers had suspected. All major categories had increased significantly from last year. The city's crime epidemic was raging out of control. Extra police patrols had been ordered, but they had little effect. If anything, they seemed to aggravate the problem. Patrols in problem areas only inflicted more violence on neighboring areas. Soon, the violence began to infect even "safe" neighborhoods. Public officials desperately looked for a cure.

METAPHOR-MISMATCHING
The most recent crime statistics confirmed what New Yorkers had suspected. All major categories had increased significantly from last year. The city's crime epidemic was raging out of control. Though badly needed, police patrols in the city could not be increased. A new and virulent strain of pneumonia was plaguing the force. Almost a third of the department was infected already. The disease had struck at the worst possible time. Public officials desperately looked for a cure.

In another experiment that looked at the interactions among textual information and real-world knowledge, McKoon, Ratcliff, and Seifert (1989) used narratives that expressed schemas such as "going to the beach," "going to a restaurant," and "going shopping." The two narratives below both instantiate "going to the beach."

1. *Linda decided to skip work on Thursday and go to the beach. At the beach, Linda found the parking lot to be surprisingly full for a weekday, but she eventually found a spot. The beach, too, was crowded, but Linda was still able to spread her towel in a dry place close to the water. Not wanting to get a sunburn, Linda put on some sunscreen. After lying on her towel for some time, Linda was getting hot so she decided to take a dip, and dove into the refreshing water. Although she usually enjoyed the power of her executive secretary position, today she was happy not to be at work. After a short swim, Linda toweled off and packed up her things for the long walk to the car.*

2. *Because the sun was shining so brightly, Nancy decided to spend the day by the sea. When she had gotten to her favorite seaside spot, Nancy parked her car under a tree. Nancy walked quickly over the hot sand until she found an empty space where she could lay her blanket. Hoping to add some color to her pale skin, Nancy splashed on some baby oil. The sun was very strong, so Nancy decided to get up and go for a swim. Nancy slowly strolled out into the cool ocean. Her hobby was bird-watching, so she watched the cliffs above her for nesting swallows. When she finally felt water logged, she headed back to her blanket. She dried off for a while in the warm sun and then dressed for the trip home.*

In McKoon et al.'s experiment, subjects were given forty-two narratives to read, and among them (widely separated in the list of forty-two) were two narratives for each of twenty-one schemas. After the forty-two stories, there was a list of 216 test phrases given for true/false judgments. There were three conditions of interest:

1. SAME SCHEMA, SAME NARRATIVE
    found an empty space for her blanket
    slowly strolled out into the ocean
2. SAME SCHEMA, DIFFERENT NARRATIVE
    spread her towel in a dry place
    slowly strolled out into the ocean
3. DIFFERENT SCHEMA, DIFFERENT NARRATIVE
    looked over the wine list and ordered chablis (from a restaurant-schema narrative)
    slowly strolled out into the ocean

The hypothesis for the experiment was that schema-related information in one narrative would evoke schema-related information in another narrative when the two narratives shared the same schema. Consistent with this, responses to "slowly strolled out into the ocean" were faster in the second condition than the third. In fact, responses in the second condition were just as fast as in the first. The conclusion is that information in the narratives evoked general knowledge about a relevant schema, and when two narratives evoked the same schema, they became associated in memory.

Degrees of availability. In the resonance retrieval framework and the memory models from which it was derived, pieces of information evoke each other to varying degrees. Some pieces of information may be so strongly evoked that they become encoded into the representation of a text, and others so weakly evoked that they play no part at all in comprehension.

This view of memory suggests that the referents of anaphors may not be uniquely identified during reading. A pronoun, for example, might be uniquely identified only if the referent it evoked was higher in strength than any other possible referents. Greene, McKoon, and Ratcliff (1992) showed how this might occur with simple texts such as the one below.

Mary and John were doing dishes after dinner. One of them was washing while the other dried. Mary accidentally scratched John with a knife and then she dropped it on the counter.

At the end of this text, Mary and John have both been explicitly mentioned twice and so they may be equally salient (with perhaps a slight edge to Mary as the subject of the last sentence). Greene et al. used the same paradigm as the Dell et al. (1983) study described above. The test words of interest were the two possible referents of the pronoun in the last sentence plus another word from the text that was not connected directly to the two characters. For the text above, these words were "Mary," "John," and "dishes." When these test words were presented at the end of the final sentence, responses to "Mary" and "John" were faster than responses to "dishes," but they themselves were equally fast. The interpretation of this result is that, at the time of the test, Mary and John were equally salient and so "she" did not differentially evoke Mary over John. A crucial feature of the design of this experiment is the use of the test word "dishes." Without it, the failure to find a difference between "Mary" and "John" would be simply a null hypothesis.

If information is evoked during reading to varying degrees, then the natural question is what variables can make some entity in a text more or less available than another. One such variable is the syntactic position of a concept in a discourse. As an example, consider "John smeared the wall with paint" and "John smeared paint on the wall." "Wall" is said to be more salient in direct-object position than object-of-preposition position and so, it is hypothesized, "John smeared the wall with paint" implies that the whole wall was affected by the painting activity whereas "John smeared paint on the wall" allows the wall to be only partially painted.

To obtain empirical evidence about how syntactic positions affect saliency, McKoon, Ratcliff, Ward, and Sproat (1993) used texts with two versions:

The librarian was furious when she got to work today. Somebody had inserted some magazines inside some newspapers late last night.

OR

The librarian was furious when she got to work today. Somebody had inserted some newspapers inside some magazines late last night.

In an off-line, single-word recognition experiment, responses to "magazines" were faster when it was in direct object position than when it was in object-of-preposition position.

Concepts in a text can also be made more salient by their relations to general knowledge. A narrative from McKoon and Ratcliff (1992) had the two versions below. The hypothesis was that "picking a flower for someone" is particularly salient because it corresponds to well-known schemas about gifts (e.g., the giver seeks to please the receiver, the receiver will likely thank the giver, etc.). "Smelling a flower for a moment" does not correspond to a well-known schema.

A girl was enjoying the warm spring weather. She walked up to the entrance of a park and bent down to an ornamental display to pick a flower for her sister.

OR

bent down to an ornamental display to smell a flower for a moment.

Then she walked into the park and down to a small stream where some ducks were feeding. She smiled to see seven tiny ducklings trailing behind their mother."

McKoon and Ratcliff (1992) tested the hypothesis with an online, single word recognition test in which a test word appeared at the end of the text (immediately after "mother" for the text above). There were two possible test words, "flower" and "display." For "flower," responses were faster with the "picking flower" text than with the "smelling flower" text, indicating that "flower" was indeed more salient when it was picked. Responses to "display" were also faster with the "picking" version than the "smelling" version, indicating that the "picking" version brought not only "flower" into increased salience but also information connected to it.

Glenberg et al. (1987) gave a different interpretation of the result for "flower." Our texts were modifications of the ones they used. For the "flower" text, the words "to an ornamental display" were words that we added. Glenberg et al. claimed that shorter RTs for "flower" were the result of readers encoding a complete, real-life model of the situation described by the text, a model in which the flower would still be in possession of the girl at the end of the "picking" version but not the "smelling" version. However, this interpretation is ruled out by McKoon and Ratcliff's finding that "display" also had faster responses after the "picking" version.

Finally, we mention one more demonstration of the effect salience can have on the degree of match between a test word and textual information. Gerrig, Love, and McKoon (2009) hypothesized that small mysteries about an entity in a text could make the entity more salient. If, for example, a text mentioned a person named "Judy" but did not specify anything about her role in the narrative, then the identity of Judy would present a small mystery to the reader. Supporting Gerrig et al.'s suggestion, responses to "Judy" as a test word in an online, single-word recognition experiment were faster when her role was not explained than when it was ("the principal Judy"). In another chapter of this volume, Gerrig and Wenzel give a complete discussion of the importance of small mysteries like "Judy."

Retrieval context. One demonstration of the power of context was provided by McKoon and Ratcliff (1995) in a lexical decision experiment. They showed that the standard priming effect between highly associated words such as "close far" could be eliminated by context. Priming was observed when the other pairs in a list had the same relation, opposites, as "close far" (e.g., "broad narrow") but not when the other pairs had a different relation (e.g., "cold snow," "sour lemon," "blue sky"). We conclude from this that even such strong associates as "close far" can be overridden by context.

In discourse research, context effects are well-appreciated. For example, in the McKoon and Ratcliff (1986) study described above, the most important finding was a context effect – subjects tended to make more errors when the to-be-inferred word was tested with a prime from its sentence than when the prime was "ready."

A similar result was obtained for interactions of general knowledge with textual information (McKoon and Ratcliff, 1988). The sentences "The still life would require great accuracy. The painter searched many days to find the color most suited to use in the painting" are more about tomatoes being red than round. Full understanding of the text should include the "red" information but, as with the "dead" inference, we found that the "red" information was encoded only minimally. When test sentences that were consistent with the meaning of a text, like "tomatoes are red," were given for off-line true/false judgments, responses were facilitated only when the test sentence was immediately preceded in the test list by other information from the same text (e.g., "The still life would require great accuracy").

Summary. Overall, the general cognitive principles listed at the beginning of this chapter and their application to methodologies designed to investigate discourse processing have led to many intriguing findings that might otherwise have gone unnoticed. We have illustrated this here with findings that were surprising when they were introduced to the field, for example, pronoun resolution without pronouns, schema-related connections from one otherwise unrelated narrative to another, subtle effects of syntactic salience, and the context effects that are inter-preted as reflecting minimal encoding.

New directions

Reading comprehension research such as that reviewed here has focused mainly on college students, but reading comprehension is a highly important issue for other populations. Older adults need to understand, for example, medical and legal information, and high-school dropouts need to understand the information on GED tests. The general question is whether and how discourse processing differs between those popula-tions and college students. We first describe a method, a computational model, for comparing data between populations and then apply that method to inferences of the "actress-dead" kind. The studies we review compared older adults (sixty-five to seventy-five year olds) to college students (McKoon and Ratcliff, 2013).

Comparisons of performance between old and young face two crucial problems. One is that older adults often set more conservative speed/accuracy criteria than young adults, that is, they are more concerned to avoid errors. The second is that older and young adults have different baseline levels of performance: older adults' RTs tend to be considerably slower. These two differences mean that older adults' and young adults' performance cannot be directly compared. For example, suppose "robin" was presented for lexical decision. Older adults' accuracy might be better than young adults' because their lexical knowledge for "robin" is better, or their knowledge might be worse and their higher accuracy the result only of more conservative speed/accuracy criteria. For RTs, older adults might be slower than young adults because their knowledge is worse or because their criteria are more conservative.

When subjects make two-choice recognition decisions or lexical deci-sions, the question of interest is often whether the information on which older adults base their decisions (e.g., lexical information about "robin") is of the same, better, or worse quality than that of young adults. To answer this question requires a computational model that can separate out speed/accuracy differences from quality-of-information differences.

The model we have used is Ratcliff's diffusion model (1978; Ratcliff and McKoon, 2008). With the model, we have found that in some (although not all) memory and perceptual tasks, the quality of the older adults' information is as good young adults'. The reason older adults are slower is usually due to more conservative speed/accuracy criteria (and also to slowdowns in processes outside those of interest, such as encoding a stimulus or executing a response). In the next section, we explain how the diffusion model separates information quality from speed/accuracy criteria.

The diffusion model

In the model, evidence about a stimulus accumulates over time from a starting point (z) to one or the other of two criterial amounts, or boundaries, one for each choice. The higher the quality of the evidence, the higher the rate at which it is accumulated. The rate of accumulation is called drift rate, v. Stimuli that differ in difficulty (e.g., in lexical decision, low frequency versus high-frequency words) differ in drift rates. A response is executed when the amount of accumulated evidence reaches a boundary, either zero for a negative response or a for a positive response. The processes outside the decision process (e.g., encoding, response execution) are combined into a single parameter of the model that has mean duration Ter ms. Noise (within-trial variability) in the accumulation of evidence from the starting point to the boundaries results in processes with the same mean drift rate terminating at different times (producing RT distributions) and sometimes terminating at the wrong criterion (producing errors).

The values of drift rates, the nondecision component, and the boundaries are assumed to vary from trial to trial. The assumption of across-trial variability is required if participants cannot accurately set these parameters at the same values from trial to trial. Across-trial variability in drift rate is assumed to be normally distributed with SD η, across-trial variability in the nondecision component is assumed to be uniformly distributed with range st, and across-trial variability in the starting point is assumed to be uniformly distributed with range sz.

The diffusion model is designed to explain all the aspects of two-choice data – accuracy, mean correct and mean error RTs, the shapes and locations of RT distributions, and the relative speeds of correct and error responses. Explaining all of these data simultaneously puts powerful constraints on the model. The model also can reconcile seemingly contradictory results for accuracy and RTs. For example, item recognition data show large increases in RTs with age coupled with small changes in accuracy or no changes in accuracy at all. The RT data suggest large decrements with age, whereas the accuracy data suggest only small decrements. The diffusion model reconciles these seemingly inconsistent results by mapping the two dependent variables onto the same underlying decision process.

Associations. To illustrate application of the diffusion model, we review a comparison (McKoon and Ratcliff, 2012) of two ways of measuring the strength of the association between two items in long-term memory. In McKoon and Ratcliff's study, older and young subjects were given pairs of words to learn. Sometimes the test items were single words presented for recognition and the strength of the association between the two words of a pair was measured by priming (one member of a pair immediately preceding the other). Other times, to test associative recognition, the test items were pairs of words and subjects were asked to decide whether the words had been studied in the same or different pairs (all the words in a pairs test list had been on the list of to-be-learned pairs). The degree to which same-pair responses were facilitated over different-pair responses was the measure of associative strength. This study was the first to address the question of whether priming in single-word recognition depends on the same information in memory as associative recognition.

Performance on associative recognition has usually been measured in terms of accuracy, and priming effects in item recognition have usually been measured in terms of RTs. This is because the effects of priming on accuracy tend to be small and the effects on RTs tend to be large, whereas for associative recognition, the same-versus different-pair effects are large in accuracy and small in RTs.

Accuracy and RTs for the single-word and pairs-recognition tasks cannot be directly compared because they are measured on different scales, accuracy on a probability-correct scale and RTs on a time scale. Neither RT nor accuracy can be used alone as the basis of a model of performance. A model built solely on accuracy data would almost surely be invalidated by RT data, and a model built solely on RTs would almost surely be invalidated by accuracy data. Using the diffusion model allows accuracy and RTs to be mapped onto the same metrics: drift rates, speed/accuracy criteria, and nondecision times. Another difference between the two tasks is that in single-word recognition, the correct response to both primed and unprimed test words is "yes," but in associative recognition, the correct response to same-pair tests is different from the correct response to different-pair tests. Just as with accuracy and RTs, the model allows the different responses to be measured on the same metric.

McKoon and Ratcliff's (2012) application of the diffusion model showed that associative recognition and priming in single-word recognition depend on the same information in memory and that this is true for both older and young subjects. This is a conclusion that could not have been drawn without the model. The findings were, first, that there were significant correlations between associative-recognition drift rates and priming drift rates, for both older and young adults; second, that drift rates for priming and drift rates for associative recognition tracked each other as a function of age; and third, that drift rates for priming and associative recognition tracked each other as a function of subjects' IQ. The significant correlations between drift rates for the two tasks show that subjects who do well on one of the tasks also do well on the other, which supports the hypothesis that they rely, at least to some extent, on the same information in memory. The correlations with IQ are what would be expected: higher IQ subjects remember information better.

In the discourse processing literature, same-different pair recognition has not been used. However, it offers a new way to measure the connections encoded between pieces of text information, and this measure can be compared to priming. The question is whether the two measures lead to the same conclusions about discourse processing, or different ones. If they are different, then empirical explorations of the differences may provide new, strong tests of what is going on in discourse processing.

Actress-dead inferences. To show application of the diffusion model to discourse processing research, we replicated McKoon and Ratcliff's 1986 experiment with actress-dead kinds of inferences and off-line single-word recognition, and we compared older adults' performance (ages sixty-five to ninety) to college students' (McKoon and Ratcliff, 2013). For the "dead" test words, we found that the students were considerably faster than the older subjects, but not more accurate. As previously described, with these data alone, there are several possible interpretations: The older subjects were slower because the quality of the evidence about "dead" on which they based their decisions was worse, because they set more conservative speed/accuracy criteria, because they had shorter nondecision times, or some combination of these. They might have been equally accurate because the quality of their information was as good, because they set their criteria more conservatively, because their nondecision processes were the same as young subjects', or some combination of these.

When we used the model to explain the data, there was a clear and compelling result: The quality of the information about the actress being dead (drift rate in the model) was just as good for the older adult's as for the young. In other words, they understood what would happen to the actress just as well as the young adults. The older adults were slower only because they set their speed/accuracy criteria farther apart and their nondecision times were longer.

Conclusion

All of the theories described in this chapter have led to interpretations of empirical methods and results that have defined discourse processing research since the early 1980s. It is from this foundation that we can ask new questions about what readers understand from discourse, questions such as the fascinating ones raised and illustrated by Gerrig and Wenzel in their chapter.

We especially appreciate the new issues that can be addressed by computational modeling. To our knowledge, the McKoon and Ratcliff (2013) experiment described here is the first application of a sequential sampling model to investigations of language comprehension for older adults. In a similar manner, we are currently extending the model to adults who are learning to read. We firmly believe that using the model will, in the near future, allow investigations of the degree to which many other populations understand and remember all sorts of textual information.

REFERENCES

Allbritton, D. W., McKoon, G., & Gerrig, R. (1995). Metaphor-based schemas and text representations: making connections through conceptual metaphors. *Journal of Experimental Psychology: Learning, Memory, and Cognition, 21*, 612–25.

Anderson, J. R. (1983). *The Architecture of Cognition*. Cambridge: Harvard University Press.

Balota, D. A. (1990). The role of meaning in word recognition. In D. A. Balota, G. B. Flores d'Arcais, & K. Rayner (eds.), *Comprehension Processes in Reading* (pp. 9–32). Mahwah, NJ: Erlbaum.

Corbett, A. T., & Dosher, B. A. (1978). Instrument inferences in sentence encoding. *Journal of Verbal Learning and Verbal Behavior, 17*, 479–91.

Dell, G. S., McKoon, G., & Ratcliff, R. (1983). The activation of antecedent information during the processing of anaphoric reference in reading. *Journal of Verbal Learning and Verbal Behavior, 22*, 121–32.

Erickson, T. D., & Mattson, M. E. (1981). From words to meaning: a semantic illusion. *Journal of Verbal Learning and Verbal Behavior, 20*, 540–51.

Forster, K. I. (1981). Frequency blocking and lexical access: one mental lexicon or two? *Journal of Verbal Learning and Verbal Behavior, 20*, 190–203.

Gerrig, R. J., Love, J., & McKoon, G. (2009). Waiting for Brandon: how readers respond to small mysteries. *Journal of Memory and Language, 60,* 144–53.

Gerrig, R., & McKoon, G. (1998). The readiness is all: the functionality of memory-based text processing. Invited article, *Discourse Processes, 26,* 67–86.

(2001). Memory processes and experiential continuity. *Psychological Science, 12,* 81–5.

Gillund, G., & Shiffrin, R .M. (1984). A retrieval model for both recognition and recall. *Psychological Review, 91,* 1–67.

Glenberg, A. M., Meyer, M., & Lindem, K. (1987). Mental models contribute to foregrounding during text comprehension. *Journal of Memory and Language, 26,* 69–83.

Greene, S. B., Gerrig, R. J., McKoon, G., & Ratcliff, R. (1994). Unheralded pronouns and the management of common ground. *Journal of Memory and Language, 33,* 511–26.

Greene, S. B., McKoon, G., & Ratcliff, R. (1992). Pronoun resolution and discourse models. *Journal of Experimental Psychology: Learning, Memory, and Cognition, 18,* 266–83.

Lockhart, R. S., Craik, F .I. M., & Jacoby, L. (1976). In J. Brown (ed.), *Recall and Recognition.* London: Wiley.

Love, J., & McKoon, G. (2011). Rules of engagement. incomplete and complete pronoun resolution. *Journal of Experimental Psychology: Learning, Memory, and Cognition, 37,* 874–87.

McKoon, G., Gerrig, R. J., & Greene, S. B. (1996). Pronoun resolution without pronouns: some consequences of memory based text processing. *Journal of Experimental Psychology: Learning, Memory, and Cognition, 22,* 919–32.

McKoon, G., & Ratcliff, R. (1980). The comprehension processes and memory structures involved in anaphoric reference. *Journal of Verbal Learning and Verbal Behavior, 19,* 668–82.

(1986). Inferences about predictable events. *Journal of Experimental Psychology: Learning, Memory, and Cognition, 12,* 82–91.

(1988). Contextually relevant aspects of meaning. *Journal of Experimental Psychology: Learning, Memory, and Cognition, 14,* 331–43.

(1989a). Inferences about contextually defined categories. *Journal of Experimental Psychology: Learning, Memory, and Cognition, 15,* 1134–46.

(1989b). Assessing the occurrence of elaborative inference with recognition: compatibility checking vs. compound cue theory. *Journal of Memory and Language, 28,* 547–63.

(1992). Inference during reading. *Psychological Review, 99,* 440–66.

(1994). Sentential context and online lexical decision. *Journal of Experimental Psychology: Learning, Memory, and Cognition, 20,* 1239–43.

(1995). Conceptual combinations and relational contexts in free association and in priming in lexical decision. *Psychonomic Bulletin & Review, 2,* 527–33.

(2012). Aging and IQ effects on associative recognition and priming in item recognition. *Journal of Memory and Language, 66,* 416–37.

(2013). Aging and predicting inferences: a diffusion model analysis. *Journal of Memory and Language, 68,* 240–54.

McKoon, G., Ratcliff, R., & Seifert, C. (1989). Making the connection: generalized knowledge structures in story understanding. *Journal of Memory and Language*, *28*, 711–34.

McKoon, G., Ratcliff, R., Ward, G., & Sproat, R. (1993). Syntactic prominence effects on discourse processes. *Journal of Memory and Language*, *32*, 593–607.

Nicol, J., & Swinney, D. (1989). The role of structure in coreference assignment during sentence comprehension. *Journal of Psycholinguistic Research*, *18*, 5–20.

Onifer, W., & Swinney, D. A. (1981). Accessing lexical ambiguities during sentence comprehension: effects of frequency of meaning and contextual bias. *Memory & Cognition*, *9*, 225–36.

Posner, M. I. (1978). *Chronometric Explorations of Mind*. Mahwah, NJ: Erlbaum.

Potts, G. R., Keenan, J. M., & Golding, J. M. (1988). Assessing the occurrence of elaborative inference: lexical decision versus naming. *Journal of Memory and Language*, *27*, 399–415.

Ratcliff, R. (1978). A theory of memory retrieval. *Psychological Review*, *85*, 59–108.

Ratcliff, R., & McKoon, G. (1988). A retrieval theory of priming in memory. *Psychological Review*, *95*, 305–108.

(2008). The diffusion decision model: theory and data for two-choice decision tasks. *Neural Computation*, *20*, 873–922.

Sanford, A. J., & Garrod, S. C. (1981). *Understanding Written Language*. New York: Wiley.

Tulving, E. (1974). Cue-dependent forgetting. *American Scientist*, *62*, 74–82.

4   Validation of text and discourse inferences – and explicit content

Murray Singer

From the beginning of contemporary language processing research, it has been recognized that comprehension is extensively inferential (Bransford, Barclay, and Franks, 1972). This is aptly captured by this dialogue from the movie *Shadowlands* (Attenborough and Nicholson, 1993):

JACK: I'm not lying, why should I be?
JOY: It's just that you don't say it all, do you?
JACK: Well, one can't say it all, it would take too long.

The exchange succinctly captures the dilemma of the speaker or writer. If one had to specify every detail of the context of an event, one would never get to "the point." Douglas Adams (1985, pp. 130–1) demonstrated that satirically. Rather than simply state that his character went to bed, he elaborated that idea, and considerably more, with the following prose: "[Arthur] went up the stairs, all fifteen of them, opened the door, went into his room, took off his shoes and socks and then all the rest of his clothes one by one and left them in a neatly crumpled heap on the floor ..."

Among the discourse ideas that are frequently unstated are those that link the current constituent to its antecedents. The sequence, *The patient was examined. The doctor made some notes* only implies that it was the doctor who examined the patient. Likewise, from *The lightning struck. The hut collapsed*, the reader detects that the first event caused the second, even in the absence of a causal connective (e.g., Keenan and Kintsch, 1974). These regularities were accommodated by the given-new analysis of *bridging inferences* (Haviland and Clark, 1974). From that perspective, syntactic and semantic cues indicate that *The doctor made some notes* designates "doctor" as information that the reader is assumed to already know about (given), and the making of notes as new information. Therefore, upon reading the second sentence of *The patient was examined. The doctor made some notes*, the reader must find an antecedent of *doctor*

68

although one has not been explicitly stated. This problem was posited to be solved by the application of the ordinary world knowledge that *doctor* is the likely agent of the first sentence.

The given-new analysis highlighted the fact that bridging inferences are critical to comprehension: In their absence, discourse coherence would be lost. Evidence from both memory and online measures favored the encoding of bridging inferences during the course of comprehension. Thus, sentences that afford a strong inferential bridge, such as *The cat leapt up on the table, Fred picked up the cat and put it outside*, are effective recall cues for one another (Black and Bern, 1981). Reading time for a sentence increases with its causal-semantic distance from its antecedent (Keenan, Baillet, and Brown, 1984; Myers, Shinjo, and Duffy, 1987), an outcome interpreted to reflect the difficulty of constructing the bridge. Both inferences answer time (Singer, 1980) and the time needed to name a displayed word representing an inference ("naming time"; Potts, Keenan, and Golding, 1988) are similar to corresponding measures for explicit text ideas.

Many bridging inferences make reference to mundane knowledge, such as *patients are examined by doctors*. Therefore, bridging-inference evidence raised the question of how that knowledge interacts with discourse ideas during comprehension. This chapter is largely devoted to that issue.

Inference validation

Many coordinations of discourse ideas strongly suggest that they must be bridged. However, this does not guarantee that the tentative bridge is compatible with the reader's knowledge. The problem is illustrated by an ordinary sequence, such as *The bright sun lit the field. Al's snowman began to melt.* Insofar as the sentences share no content words, the reader must *assume* that they are related, consistent with the principle that the writer is being cooperative (Grice, 1975). This readily suggests the bridging inference that the first event caused the second. Consider, however, contrasting sequences, such as *The bright moon lit the field. Al's snowman began to melt* and *The bright sun lit the field. Al's snowman began to freeze.* Both sequences describe circumstances less usual than sun melting a snowman. However, their juxtaposition invites bridging neither more nor less than the original *sun/melt* sequence. However, in attempting to bridge the *moonlight/melt* sequence, for example, the reader might find it slightly odd. What processes could account for this reaction?

Russell Revlin and I first addressed this puzzle with reference to a different construction: namely, *Sue is a surgeon. Mary is a doctor, too* (see Figure 4.1A). The conjunctive adjunct *too* signals that someone else must be a doctor, but no prior doctor has been mentioned. We proposed that such sequences initiate the bridging processes illustrated in Figure 4.1B. For *Mary is a doctor, too* to make sense, Sue must likewise be a doctor. That places the reader in a situation analogous to a deductive reasoner faced with a syllogism with a missing premise (called an enthymeme). Figure 4.1B shows that the reader can tacitly construct a mediating fact that solves the enthymeme, such as *A surgeon is a doctor*. However, only in confirming that the mediating fact is consistent with world knowledge has the reader validated the tentative bridge (Figure 4.1C). Without this last step, *Sue is a logger. Mary is a doctor, too* would seem as agreeable as the *surgeon* sequence.

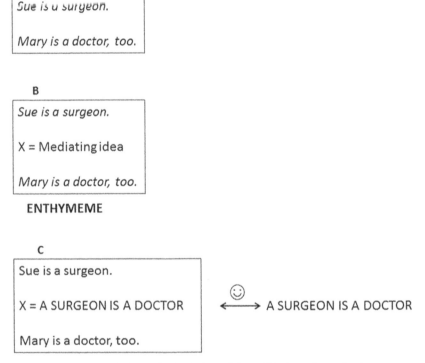

Figure 4.1 Schematic depiction of the validation of anaphoric resolution signaled by the conjunctive adjective, too.

In an initial test of these hypotheses, we predicted that *Sue is a surgeon. Mary is a doctor* would prime relevant world knowledge more with than without the adjunct, *too*. Consistent with this prediction, people answered a subsequent question, *Is a surgeon a doctor?* faster when the preceding sentence had included the adjunct (Singer, Revlin, and Halldorson, 1990). Similarly, people correctly answered "no" to *Is a waiter a doctor?* more quickly after reading *Al is a waiter. Bill is a doctor, however,* than after *Al is a waiter. Bill is a doctor.* These advances offered the opportunity to scrutinize the processes of bridging inference concerning other discourse relations.

Validating causal bridging inferences

Examination of *causal inferences* is particularly demanded by the central role of causation in numerous text genres. Physical causation is especially relevant to expositions. The comprehension of narratives, in contrast, hinges on understanding the interrelations among people's motives and goals, and the actions that they initiate (Graesser, 1981; Schank and Abelson, 1977; Trabasso, van den Broek, and Suh, 1989). This section first considers studies that examined several interrelated hypotheses pertaining to narrative readers' validation both of physical and motivational causes. Then, issues specific to expository text are considered.

Validating narrative causal bridges

The enthymeme analysis of Figure 4.1 generalized readily to causal bridges. The sequence *The bright sun lit the field. Al's snowman began to melt* requires a mediating fact that, coupled with the antecedent event, accounts for the outcome. The mediating fact, such as SUN MELTS SNOW, must be reconciled with one's world knowledge in order that the tentative bridging inference be validated.

Physical causation. Extensive tests of the validation model focused on materials such as set (1).

1.   a. The confused clerk unplugged the electrical cord. (causal)
        a'. The confused clerk plugged in the electrical cord. (temporal)
        b. The computer screen went blank.
        c. Do computers run on electricity?

In the most basic experiment, subjects read either the causal sequence (1a)–(1b) or the control "temporal" sequence (1a')–(1b). Immediately after either, they answered question (1c). The validation model entails that understanding the causal sequence will engage the knowledge that computers use electricity. Consistent with this analysis, the subjects correctly answered question (1c) faster after reading the causal than the temporal sequence (Singer, Halldorson, Lear, and Andrusiak, 1992).

It is also noteworthy that reading time for sentence (1b) was lower in the causal than in the temporal condition. This reflected that (1b) was causally closer to (1a) than (1a') and replicated important prior findings (Keenan et al., 1984; Myers et al., 1987).

In contrast with (1a)–(1b), (1a')–(1b) describes a temporal sequence of events that could plausibly occur but that either was not causal or at least involved causes different from (1a)–(1b) (cf. Black and Bern, 1981). In addition, the similarity of the content words of sentences (1a) and (1a') was one protection against the possibility that facilitation of (1c) stemmed simply from the specific words in (1a)–(1b) (McKoon and Ratcliff, 1986).

In another important control condition, it was observed that when (1c) was preceded by either (1a) or (1a') alone (i.e., without 1b), no answer time difference emerged (Singer and Halldorson, 1996; Singer et al., 1992). This indicated that it was the need to reconcile (1b) with its antecedent that initiated a bridging inference and thus the hypothetical validation processes that the inference demands.

Related effects. Further implications of the validation model were explored using a variety of manipulations. Consider the sequence, *The confused clerk tripped over the electrical cord. The computer screen went blank.* It implies rather than states that the cord was disconnected from the electrical source. Nevertheless, validating this sequence should engage the same knowledge as causal sequence (1a)–(1b) because the cause of the screen going blank is ultimately the same in both cases. Consistent with this analysis, *Do computers run on electricity?* was answered equally quickly after people read either the *tripped over* sequence or sequence (1a)–(1b), and faster than after the temporal sequence (Singer et al., 1992, Experiment 3). Furthermore, reading time for sentence (1b) in this "far cause" sequence was intermediate to the near-cause and temporal conditions, consistent with the aforementioned causal-distance effect (Myers et al., 1987).

Likewise, consider that the chronological order of events is reversed in *Al's snowman began to melt. The bright sun lit the field.* Nevertheless, readers readily detect that it was the second event that caused the first. As a result, validating reversed causal sequences should activate the same knowledge as chronological ones. Consistent with this proposal, answer time to *Does sun melt snow?* was about equal following chronological and reversed causal sequences and was greater in a contrasting temporal condition (Singer et al., 1992, Experiment 4).

The latter results corroborated and refined the validation analysis. However, it was another series of experiments that arguably most illuminated the model (Singer, 1993). The critical new condition is illustrated by set (2).

2.   a. Dorothy poured water on the bonfire.
        b. The fire grew hotter.

Sequence (2; see Figure 4.2a) describes an unusual outcome, but the reader cannot know this without validating the inference. Figure 4.2b shows that, as for the more usual *Dorothy poured water on the bonfire. The fire went out*, the reader of (2a)–(2b) tacitly hypothesizes that (2a) and (2b) are causally related. Therefore, a mediating fact is constructed that would account for the fire growing hotter, such as *Water feeds fire*. At Figure 4.2c, evaluating this fact against world knowledge reveals a blatant mismatch. This inconsistency would likely appreciably inflate reading-comprehension time for sentence (2b) (O'Brien and Albrecht, 1992). It is noteworthy that these processes access the knowledge that WATER EXTINGUISHES FIRE, exactly the same idea that would be invoked for a consistent outcome such as *The fire went out*. This, perhaps counterintuitively, suggested that answer time for *Does water extinguish fire?* would be faster after the inconsistent *hotter* sequence than a control sequence. Using materials illustrated in Box 4.1, both the reading-time and answer-time predictions were supported (Singer, 1993). These results emphasize that readers cannot know a priori whether text ideas mesh with their discourse context. Congruence can be established only by validation processing.

Box 4.1   Sample materials for comparing causal consistent, causal inconsistent, and temporal-control conditions (Singer, 1993)

Dorothy poured the bucket of water on the bonfire. The fire went out. (Consistent)
Dorothy poured the bucket of water on the bonfire. The fire grew hotter. (Inconsistent)
Dorothy placed the bucket of water by the bonfire. The fire grew hotter. (Temporal control)
Does water extinguish fire? (question)

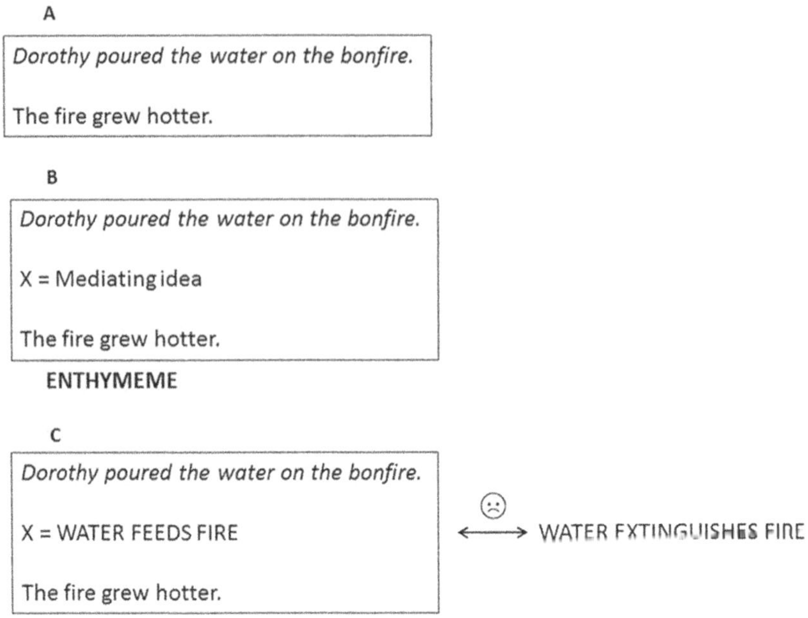

A

> Dorothy poured the water on the bonfire.
>
> The fire grew hotter.

B

> Dorothy poured the water on the bonfire.
>
> X = Mediating idea
>
> The fire grew hotter.

ENTHYMEME

C

> Dorothy poured the water on the bonfire.
>
> X = WATER FEEDS FIRE
>
> The fire grew hotter.

☹
←——→ WATER EXTINGUISHES FIRE

Figure 4.2 Schematic depiction of validating a causal bridging inference.

It is emphasized that the inconsistent *fire grew hotter* sequence is simply unusual and not anomalous. Higher outcome-sentence reading times for inconsistent than consistent sequences likely result in part from people's active reasoning about the inconsistency, such as that the bonfire in question might have been huge.

Motivational causation. Narrative comprehension rests extensively on understanding the interrelation among people's motives, plans, goals, and actions. In the following text, for example, why the son will try to save his father and carry a knife are obvious to any reader.

A wilderness tiger carried (the woodcutter) off in its mouth. The woodcutter's son saw his father's danger, and ran to save him if possible. He carried a long knife. (di Prima, 1960, p. 117)

There is a close analogy between physical effects causing outcomes and people's motives causing their actions (Schank and Abelson, 1977; Trabasso et al., 1989). This suggested that the validation of motivational inferences might closely resemble that for physical cause. Consider set (3):

3.   a. Laurie left early for the birthday party. (motive antecedent)
         a'. Laurie left the birthday party early. (control antecedent)
         b. She headed north on the freeway. (intervening)
         c. She exited at Antelope Drive. (intervening)
         d. She spent an hour shopping at the mall. (outcome)
         e. Do birthday parties involve presents? (validating world knowledge)

Disregarding the "intervening" sentences for the moment, the validation model posits that, upon reading sequence (3a)–(3d), the reader constructs a mediating idea such as that Laurie needed to shop for a birthday present. Consistent with this analysis, answer times to questions about the hypothetically validating knowledge (e.g., 3e) were lower after sequence (3a)–(3d) than after control sequence, (3a')–(3d) (Singer and Halldorson, 1996).

In the scrutiny of motive-inference validation, new hypotheses were evaluated. First, validation processes were monitored over moderate text differences. In one experiment, sentences (3a)–(3d) were separated by either two (as in set 3) or four intervening sentences that otherwise preserved local coherence. As with consecutive sentences, questions about the validating knowledge were answered more quickly after these more distant motive-inference sequences than in equivalent control conditions (Singer and Halldorson, 1996, Experiment 2). This is consistent with the coherence assumption of constructionism (Graesser, Singer, and Trabasso, 1994), according to which readers monitor situational coherence (e.g., spatial, motivational) across moderate text distances.

Another motive-inference study examined the interrelations, in long-term representations of text meaning, among the ideas posited to participate in validation processing (Halldorson and Singer, 2002). This study used a priming procedure (McKoon and Ratcliff, 1988), in which subjects read sets of three passages. After each set, they answered intermixed questions about the details of those three passages and the world-knowledge posited to validate text inferences. Questions about the motivational antecedents and world knowledge (e.g., questions based on 3a and 3e) mutually facilitated one another more than did control antecedents and world knowledge. Likewise, narrative outcomes (e.g., 3d) were primed more by the relevant knowledge (3e) when they had appeared in motive than in control sequences. These results indicate that the knowledge that is recruited to validate a bridging inference becomes integrated with the content of the inference.

Unlike in the physical-cause studies (e.g., Singer et al., 1992), reading time for motivational outcomes such as (3d) was not lower in the motive-inference condition than in the control condition; rather, the two were approximately equal (Halldorson and Singer, 2002; Singer and Halldorson, 1996). This was interpreted to indicate, for example, that regardless of whether Laurie goes shopping before or after a birthday party, it takes about the same amount of time to detect *a reason* for her doing so. Of course, those reasons differ between the motive and control conditions, resulting in faster *answer times* for questions about the knowledge posited to validate a particular motive inference.

Validating expository causal bridges

Expository text is instrumental in presenting new ideas to the reader. Expositions are found in myriad varieties, including textbook chapters, scientific journal papers, and articles in popular magazines.

The heavy reliance of expositions, such as narratives, on causal relations might suggest that inference validation would be similar in the two. However, at least four differences between those genres question the matter. First, expositions use abstract structures, such as mechanisms and descriptions, not common to narratives. One type of *mechanism* captures the relations between a motive and its contributing actions. Unlike narrative episodes, however, they particularly refer to equipment or machines (Black, 1985). For example, the motive of moving goods along shallow rivers can be accomplished with *barges*, which must protect the cargo from the elements and which are propelled by tugboats. *Descriptions* identify some of the defining and characteristic properties of a concept. Thus, porcupines overcome their short limbs with protective spines and represent two families evolved from unrelated ancestors. Mechanisms and descriptions, in turn, comprise other abstract structures, such as lists, hierarchies, and rhetorical structures (Black, 1985; Seely and Long, 1994).

Second, readers are less familiar with these structures than with prototypical story schemas (e.g., Mandler and Johnson, 1977; Thorndyke, 1977). This renders the evolving form of expositions less predictable than narratives. Third, readers are generally much less familiar with the *content* of expositions than narratives, as suggested by the instructional purpose of many expositions. Unfamiliar domain knowledge fosters less detailed text representations (McNamara, Kintsch, Songer, and Kintsch, 1996), impedes detecting the higher-level organization of the text (Spilich, Vesonder, Chiesi, and Voss, 1979), and in general permits less automatic text processing than is afforded by relevant knowledge (Haenggi and Perfetti, 1994; Kintsch, 1994; McKoon and Ratcliff, 1992). Fourth, readers likely approach expositions with systematically different goals than for narratives, such as studying, learning, and memorizing. These characteristic-orienting tasks (Zwaan, 1994) might promote distinct inference processing.

In spite of these differences, Kieras (1985) noted that readers must be able to learn from expository text. He proposed, therefore, that they have robust inferential procedures for extracting new information even from the unfamiliar content of expositions. These assertions prompted us to compare expository and narrative inference validation.

The application of the validation model to expository comprehension was relatively straightforward. A prototype example in our studies has been *Some fireworks emit crimson flames because they contain calcium salt.* The conjunction *because* in this sequence demands that there be some mediating fact, which, combined with some fireworks containing calcium salt, accounts for their producing crimson flames. We posited that readers can construct the mediating idea, CALCIUM SALT BURNS WITH A CRIMSON FLAME; even in the absence of knowledge about chemistry.

We explored these issues using materials derived from ordinary science encyclopedias, such as set (4) (Singer, Harkness, and Stewart, 1997).

4.   a. The making of fireworks developed as an art whose secrets were passed down from generation to generation. (leading)
        b. Calcium salt produces a red flame. (explicit; *OPTIONAL*)
        c. Some fireworks emit crimson flames because they contain calcium salt. (target)
        d. The manufacture of fireworks is done with elaborate safety precautions owing to the hazards involved. (final)
        e. Do calcium salts emit crimson flames? (experimental question)

Sentence (4c) would, on its own, require the construction and validation of a causal bridge between its clauses. However, in our experiments, the passage appeared either with (explicit) or without (implicit) sentence (4b), which directly states the posited mediating fact.

If readers *do not validate* expository bridging inferences, there would be no reason for the reading time for target (4c) to differ in the presence versus absence of (4b). In that event, however, answer time to question (4e) ought to be greater in the implicit than the explicit condition. Conversely, if expository inferences are validated, then reading time for (4c) in the implicit condition would exceed the explicit condition: Without (4b), the reader of (4c) would have to engage in complex inferential processing. In that event, however, answer time for (4e) might be similar in the two conditions. Table 4.1 shows that Singer et al.'s (1997, Experiment 4) data matched the latter pattern both for reading time and answer time, that is, the pattern associated with expository inference validation.

Table 4.1 *Mean target reading times and experimental question answer times (in milliseconds [ms]) of Singer, Harkness, and Stewart (1997, Experiment 4) as a function of relation (explicit, implicit)*

	Relation	
Measure	Explicit	Implicit
Reading time*	4,630	4,940
Answer time◆	2,771	2,849

* $p < .05$.
◆ Not significant.

These findings were congruent with readers' bridging of expository outcomes to their implied goals (Graesser and Bertus, 1998). Further studies refined our understanding of expository-inference validation. Readers detect inconsistencies between explicit text statements and ideas that they could know only as a result of having validated preceding inferential sequences (Singer and Gagnon, 1999). Another study (Singer and O'Connell, 2003) indicated that connectives are critical to the detection of expository causal inferences, in contrast with comparable narratives sequences (Singer, 1986). Detection of tentative inferences, in turn, is necessary for validation. More specifically, most readers do not grasp the underlying causation of *Some fireworks emit crimson flames. They contain calcium salt* in the absence of the conjunction *because*. This is due to their lack of knowledge about obscure scientific facts. Singer and O'Connell also documented the validation of science inferences (a) that are embedded in longer passages (*mean* = 9.3 sentences) that preserved more of their encyclopedic entries; and (2) regardless of the position of the inference sequence in the passage (early, middle, late). It is noteworthy, however, that validation appears to be impeded for sequences of excessive complexity and/or length, such as *We find the first stages of coal development in stagnant water because coal development requires an oxygen poor environment* (Noordman, Vonk, and Kempff, 1992).

Indirect evidence of inference validation: consistency effects

Evidence of people's sensitivity to inferential congruence pervades the study of text comprehension. Many related findings pertain to the reader's monitoring of situational coherence. Text situation models (van Dijk and Kintsch, 1983) comprise numerous dimensions, including those of cause, motivation, location, time, and narrative-protagonist (Zwaan, Magliano, and Graesser, 1995; Zwaan and Radvansky, 1998).

Some early findings concerning situational bridging inferences were alluded to earlier: Consider passages such as (5) and (6).

5.   Tony's friend suddenly pushed him into a pond. He walked home, soaking wet, to change his clothes.

6.   Tony met his friend near a pond in the park. He walked home, soaking wet, to change his clothes.

Rating data indicated that the identical, second sentence of these sequences is causally further from the first sentence of (6) than (5). Concomitantly, reading time for the second sentence is greater in sequence (6) than (5) (Keenan et al., 1984; Myers et al., 1987). Reading time would be equal in these conditions if the reader did not monitor the relevant causal inferences. I characterize these findings as *indirect* evidence for validation only because the researchers did not experimentally probe validating knowledge such as *ponds contain water* and *water is wet*.

Parallel findings of readers' sensitivity to discourse congruence appear on most if not all situational dimensions. On the spatial dimension, for example, reading time is greater for the second sentence of *Jane waited outside the door of her health club, waiting for the instructor. The instructor came in* than when the first sentence has placed Jane *inside* the club (O'Brien and Albrecht, 1992). Reading time is typically likewise inflated by infelicities of time (e.g., *Claudia's train arrived in Dresden on time after Markus's train. She was already waiting for him when he got off the train*; Rinck, Hahnel, and Becker, 2001) and motivation (e.g., a vegetarian ordering a cheeseburger; Albrecht and O'Brien, 1993). These effects could emerge only if the reader were attentive to the congruence, with reference to relevant knowledge, between the current discourse and its antecedents (Cook and Guéraud, 2005).

Demonstrations of consistency effects have enabled the refinement of our understanding text situational representations. For example, the initiation and completion of *temporal episodes* are guided by cues as ostensively minor as verb tense and verb aspect (Gernsbacher, 1990; Magliano and Schleich, 2000; Radvansky, Zwaan, Federico, and Franklin, 1998). The encoding of the spatial information, *standing under the bridge*, varies according to its importance, such as whether the bridge is blocking moonlight or rain (Radvansky and Copeland, 2000). Motive inferences depend on subtleties ranging from the prior completion of contributing subgoals (Lutz and Radvansky, 1997; Suh and Trabasso, 1993) to the interplay among different narrative characters' subgoals (Richards and Singer, 2001). Such exquisite effects could not emerge without the application of relevant world knowledge to the evolving discourse representation.

Validation of explicit text content

It stands to reason that if readers validate candidate inferences, they likewise monitor the congruence of explicit text content. Many research programs offer evidence that converges on the latter conclusion. This brief treatment mainly emphasizes validation with reference to the discourse context and to relevant world knowledge, rather than lower-level syntactic and semantic felicity.

Central to some influential formulations, in fact, is the premise that discourse validation coincides with rather than follows lower-level evaluations (Ferreira, Bailey, and Ferraro, 2002; Nieuwland and Kuperberg, 2008). I have proposed that, although researchers' explicit focus on language validation is currently expanding (e.g., Schroeder, Richter, and Hoever, 2008), some candidate general principles of validation are already emerging (Singer, 2013). It is worthwhile to briefly consider them.

Principles of language validation

Immediacy. Each discourse word has been proposed to be interpreted, at all levels of analysis, immediately upon its presentation, within about one-fourth to one-third of a second (Just and Carpenter, 1980). Event-related potentials (ERPs), in which electrophysiological scalp signals (EEGs) are measured after the appearance of a critical stimulus (the "event"), have provided relevant evidence. Thus, a negative ERP voltage deflection at about 400 ms (the N400) indicates that people detect knowledge-based inconsistencies (*Dutch trains are white* when they are actually yellow) as quickly as semantic inconsistencies (*Dutch trains are sour*; van Berkum, Hagoort, and Brown, 1999). In a reading-time study, subjects encountered one of the two versions of sentences such as *Donna used the hose to wash her filthy (car [plausible]/hair [implausible]) after returning from the beach*. Reading time was immediately inflated at the less plausible word, *hair* (Matsuki et al., 2011).

Comparable effects obtain when sentences such as *Jenny heard/saw the mountain lion pacing in its cage* are encountered in more complex messages. The researchers observed that there is a transient anomaly in *Jenny heard the mountain* … because one cannot hear a mountain. In fact, eye tracking for this sequence revealed inflated reading time at *mountain* relative to the nonanomalous, *saw,* version (Staub, Rayner, Pollatsek, Hyona, and Majewski, 2007).

Evaluating the immediacy of validation is challenging. Considerable behavioral evidence indicates that passive, automatic mechanisms within the first 250 ms of processing yield erroneous or spurious computations in disambiguation, anaphoric resolution, and inferencing (Dell, McKoon, and Ratcliff, 1983; Ratcliff and McKoon, 1989; Swinney, 1979; Till, Mross, and Kintsch, 1988). This is suggestive of two stages of comprehension processing. Indeed, the psycholinguistic alternative to immediacy has been the two-step view that syntactic and lower-level semantic analyses precede integration with the discourse context and world knowledge (see discussions of Ferreira et al., 2002; Nieuwland and Kuperberg, 2008). However, whether successive stages of automatic and controlled processing (Neely, 1977) map to a sequence of sentential versus context analysis is debatable. Furthermore, some ERP and eye-tracking studies suggest that complex semantic factors such as statement truth either overwhelm (Nieuwland and Martin, 2012) or interact with (Boudewyn, Gordon, Long, Polse, and Swaab, 2012) automatic associative retrieval; even within 250 ms of stimulus presentation. Thus, the status of immediate validation will demand continued scrutiny.

Validation is routine. This principle states that the scrutiny of congruence is part of readers' typical orientation to text and does not require special strategies. Isberner and Richter (2013) applied a Stroop-like task to this analysis. Subjects encountered sentences such as *Frank had a broken pipe. He called the plumber/doctor* under an unusual orienting instruction: namely, to respond "yes" if the last word of the sentence changed the font color and "no" otherwise. The researchers predicted that if validation persists in this task, congruity effects would emerge: namely, faster "yes" than "no" answers for plausible sentences and vice versa for implausible ones. The data supported this analysis even though the task did not require that the subject monitor sentence meaning.

However, certain conditions do seem to disengage validation. In one study, we asked subjects to monitor spelling accuracy in texts with sequences such as the aforementioned, *Laurie left early for the birthday party, She spent an hour shopping at the mall.* With this orientation, the usual inference-validation profile of faster judgments of relevant knowledge in the inference condition than a control condition disappeared (Singer and Halldorson, 1996; see also Singer, 2006, Experiment 3). In conclusion, comprehension validation seems quite resistant to disruption (Isberner and Richter, 2013) but may be thwarted in shallow-orientation tasks.

Validation enables representational updating. The updating of discourse representations is of central interest and debate in contemporary research (e.g., O'Brien, Cook, and Peracchi, 2004; Zwaan and Madden, 2004). In this regard, validation has been characterized as epistemic gatekeeping: Only if the current text is determined to be congruent with the discourse should it promote situation model updating (Schroeder, Richter, and Hoever, 2008). In one pertinent study, we measured people's ERP responses to stories bearing sequences such as (7) (Ferretti, Singer, and Harwood, 2013).

7.   a. Ken and his brother (ate oranges/ate apples/ate) while they cycled to practice.
         b. The coach established that it was oranges that Ken ate.

In the stories, three locally coherent sentences intervened between (7a) and (7b). Only when (7a) did not specify what was eaten (viz. *ate while they cycled*) was there a *positive* ERP response about 1 second after the word "oranges" in (7b). This signature has been associated with situation-model updating (Burkhardt, 2006). The outcome is consistent with the sensible notion that a representation ought to be updated when the reader encounters believable novel information (viz. "oranges").

Manipulating factors such as subtleties of discourse causation (Rapp and Kendeou, 2009) and the denial of prior text ideas (O'Brien, Rizzella, Albrecht, and Halleran, 1998) generates complex profiles of representational updating. The bearing of discourse validation on updating will likely receive considerable scrutiny in the future.

Validation memory processes resemble intentional retrieval. The memory-based text processing analysis states that comprehension depends on the passive resonance of antecedent ideas to the current discourse constituent (e.g., Greene, Gerrig, McKoon, and Ratcliff, 1994; O'Brien and Albrecht, 1991; O'Brien, Lorch, and Myers, 1998). Validating a text constituent against its discourse context, of course, requires the retrieval of relevant antecedents. Because readers are not typically intending to remember the preceding text, these retrieval processes would be passive in nature. At the same time, I hypothesized that validation memory processes resemble those underlying *intentional* discourse-retrieval tasks, such as question answering (Singer, 2006; 2009; see also Knoeferle, Urbach, and Kutas, 2011). This claim assumes that some fundamental mechanisms of memory retrieval do not vary as a function of one's strategy.

In a behavioral study bearing on these issues (see also Ferretti et al.'s, 2013, aforementioned ERP experiment), subjects read sequences such as *The boys ate oranges/apples while they cycled to practice . . . The coach*

established that it (was/wasn't) oranges that the boys ate. Additional text
intervened between the two sentences. The *reading time* patterns for the
second sentence (i.e., *The coach established* ...) resembled *intentional
verification times* for ordinary sentences such as *Two (is/is not) (even/odd)*
(Wason and Jones, 1963). Differences between those patterns were
analyzed to stem from subtle pragmatic cues of the discourse (Singer,
2006; see also Ferretti, Singer, and Patterson, 2008; Knoeferle et al.,
2011). These results supported the main hypothesis.

Other candidate principles. Some potential discourse-validation
principles are arguably entailed by those considered above. For example,
immediate validation has been generally equated with the *parallel* evaluation of congruence at both lower (syntactic, semantic) and higher
(discourse context, world knowledge) levels of analysis. Parallel validation would be consistent with connectionist principles of constraint
satisfaction, according to which high-level and low-level representations
mutually influence one another in parallel (Rumelhart and McClelland,
1986).

It is tempting to consider that routine, nonstrategic validation implies
that validation is automatic (Ferguson and Zayas, 2009; Wiswede, Koranyi, Müller, Langner, and Rothermund, 2012). However, whether
validation has yet been assessed against well-defined criteria of cognitive
automaticity seems uncertain (cf. Bargh, 1994; Rawson, 2004; Singer,
Graesser, and Trabasso, 1994). Finally, validation seems almost certain
to exhibit appreciable individual differences (Just and Carpenter, 1992;
Long, Oppy, and Seely, 1994). Investigators have already begun to
inspect this issue (Knoeferle et al., 2011; Singer and Doering, 2014).

Comparing explicit and implicit validation

The initial inventory of validation principles included the notion that
validation applies to discourse implications as well as explicit content
(Singer, 2013). Here, that proposal might seem superfluous: Much of the
compelling evidence of readers' sensitivity to text congruence has originated from inference-processes research. In particular, readers' detection
of inconsistencies on all situational dimensions (e.g., causal, temporal,
spatial) arises appreciably from their computation of *implied* discourse
relations. Detecting inconsistencies, in turn, reflects ongoing validation.
These findings are complemented by the more direct evidence of inference validation that has been considered here.

However, do principles of validation of *explicit text ideas* generalize
to inference validation? It seems likely that they do. Virtually all demonstrations that people are sensitive to implied situational incongruence

originate from *routine* comprehension tasks, without subjects being asked to adopt special strategies (cf. Isberner and Richter, 2013; Singer, 2006, Experiment 3; Singer and Halldorson, 1996). Attentiveness to inferential inconsistency appears *immediate*, as indexed by online tasks. In this regard, reading times reveal that the implied motivational inconsistency of a vegetarian ordering a cheeseburger is detected immediately (Stewart, Kidd, and Haigh 2009).

Likewise, the similarity of the memory processes of validation and intentional retrieval receives extensive support in the inferential domain. The memory-based text-processing claim that antecedent text ideas passively resonate to the current segment, discussed earlier, originates in basic-memory research (e.g., Ratcliff, 1978). This analysis suggests that factors such as similarity, distinctiveness, and degree of elaboration will enhance access to those antecedents whereas cue-antecedent distance will impede it. Consider the similarity between the current constituent and its antecedent. In one study, reading that Mary went to bed inflated reading time when subjects had previously learned that she was supposed to book a flight before midnight. However, that was only the case when the critical sentence mentioned the leather sofa on which Mary had sat earlier, thereby increasing its *similarity* to the antecedent (Albrecht and Myers, 1995; see also Albrecht and Myers, 1998; O'Brien and Albrecht, 1991; O'Brien, Albrecht, Hakala, and Rizzella, 1995). Existing evidence thus favors the relevance of validation principles to explicit and implicit text ideas alike.

Validation failures

Contrary to readers' systematic validation of text is extensive evidence of people's tendency to overlook text consistencies. Readers can neglect conspicuous contradictions, such as a character making sandwiches in the absence of bread (Cohen, 1979). Furthermore, readers can be unaware of such misunderstandings of text: Their comprehension monitoring can be deficient (Glenberg, Wilkinson, and Epstein, 1982; Maki and Berry, 1984).

A complete treatment must therefore accommodate validation deficiencies. Jenkins's (1980) scheme of considering the stimulus, individual, and task factors that regulate behavior is useful in this regard (Singer, 2006; 2013). Consider first *message* variables (i.e., the stimulus). Certainly, texts of high complexity may stymie validation. As discussed earlier, readers seem able to validate the inferences underlying *Some fireworks emit crimson flames because they contain calcium salt* (Singer et al., 1997) but not those of more complex sequences of the same general nature (Noordman et al., 1992). Text distance affects validation: Complex motivational inferences expose inconsistencies less when the relevant antecedent is distant rather than close in the text (Albrecht and Myers, 1995). Sentence topical structure contributes to the familiar "Moses illusion" that causes people to spuriously answer "two" to *How many animals of each kind did Moses take on the ark?* even though it was Noah who sailed the ark. That is, the failure to correctly validate *Moses* likely results from its embedding in a presupposed rather than a focused phrase of the sentence (Glenberg et al., 1982).

One *reader* characteristic that impacts inference validation is working memory capacity, indexed by the reading span task (Daneman and Carpenter, 1980). Thus, older readers tend to miss the aforementioned anomaly of making sandwiches without bread more than do younger readers, an outcome that likely reflects working memory differences (Cohen, 1979). Likewise, low reading span coupled with below-average access of relevant knowledge results in deficient activation of the ideas that validate bridging inferences. Readers with these qualities do not exhibit facilitation of COFFEE CAN KEEP YOU AWAKE upon reading *Garry was about to start all-night duty at the hospital ... He drank a cup of coffee in the cafeteria* (Singer and Ritchot, 1996).

Finally, the intentional or tacit goals associated with one's reading *task* will likely affect validation. In the extreme, reading while the conditions of distraction or mind-wandering will impede text validation (McKoon and Ratcliff, 1992; Smallwood, McSpadden, and Schooler, 2008). Even tasks that emphasize discourse form over meaning might do the same. As discussed earlier, however, there is conflicting evidence on the latter point. That is, whereas proofreading for spelling errors appeared to disrupt inference validation (Singer and Halldorson, 1996), the validation of explicit text context persisted under a Stroop orientation (Isberner and Richter (2013). Thus, fully gauging the impact of the reader's goals on validation is a task that lies ahead.

Language validation and theories of comprehension

It is unlikely that readers strictly succeed or fail in validating text meaning. Rather, the challenge will be to determine how regularities of inferential and explicit validation mesh theories of comprehension. In this regard, it is noteworthy that construction-integration (CI) theory (Kintsch, 1988; 1998) posits that each text segment first promotes the *construction* of a tentative network of explicit, implied, and associated discourse ideas. Many of these ideas are likely accessed, by passive memory processes, from the antecedent text and the reader's world knowledge (Greene et al., 1994; O'Brien, Lorch, and Myers, 1998). Although central to many aspects of comprehension, passive retrieval might also set the stage for validation.

At the *integration* stage of CI, activation is settled in the constructed network, effectively eliminating less relevant ideas. Validation processes would likely be a determinant of the degree of congruence or harmony (Britton and Eisenhart, 1993) of the resulting representation. Then, the *updating* of these representations would, as discussed earlier, be contingent on validation. Updating would be associated with the CI integration stage (Ferretti et al., 2013). Lexical, semantic, and contextual validation would be executed in parallel (e.g., van Berkum et al., 1999). An important caveat, discussed earlier, is that mapping lexical and contextual analyses with hypothetical stages of construction and integration is an ongoing challenge.

Certain theoretical formulations are particularly predicated on the validation *deficiencies* of those doing the understanding. Thus, according to the scenario mapping analysis (Sanford and Garrod, 1998), a reader's focus on global coherence might obscure the local anomaly of phrases such as *where to bury the SURVIVING DEAD* (nb. one cannot both survive and be dead). The "good-enough" framework posits that comprehension regularly results in partial or erroneous representations (Ferreira et al., 2002), including those that comprise inadequate validation.

In any theoretical framework, validation deficiencies must reflect general cognitive mechanisms. Thus, deficits of working memory resources and of reading skill might underlie the local-global competition proposals of scenario mapping. Interestingly, such deficits have alternatively been posited to favor local representations (Long, Oppy, and Seely, 1997) or global ones (Hannon and Daneman, 2004). We recently conjectured that this discrepancy might reflect differing *degrees* of reader deficits (Singer and Doering, 2014).

Other validation failures have likewise been related to cognitive regularities. Ferreira et al. (2002) proposed that comprehension immediacy may be demanded by the rapid forgetting of the verbatim message (Jarvella, 1971). However, immediacy increases the risk of inaccuracy. Likewise, even simple sentences afford syntactic and semantic ambiguities and so offer a multiplicity of interpretations. Sanford and Graesser (2006) observed that deriving all of these interpretations would overwhelm cognitive resources but ignoring some of them might favor erroneous or anomalous alternatives.

In conclusion, contemporary research converges on myriad validation phenomena, at both the inferential and explicit level of discourse interpretation. Some of these phenomena are readily addressed by existing analyses, and others will likely guide further theory refinement.

REFERENCES

Adams, D. (1985). *So Long, and Thanks for All the Fish*. London: Pan Books.

Albrecht, J. E., & Myers, J. L. (1995). The role of context in accessing distant information during reading. *Journal of Experimental Psychology: Learning, Memory & Cognition, 21*, 1459–68.

(1998). Accessing distant text information during reading: effects of contextual cues. *Discourse Processes, 26*, 87–108.

Albrecht, J. E. & O'Brien, E. J. (1993). Updating a mental model: maintaining both local and global coherence. *Journal of Experimental Psychology: Learning, Memory, and Cognition, 19*, 1061–70.

Attenborough, R. (Producer/Director), & Nicholson, W. (Writer). (1993). *Shadowlands [motion picture]*. United States: HBO Studios.

Bargh, J. A. (1994). The four horsemen of automaticity: awareness, efficiency, intention, and control in social cognition. In R. Wyer, Jr., & T. Srull (eds.), *Handbook of Social Cognition* (2nd ed.). (pp. 1–40). Mahwah, NJ: Erlbaum.

Black, J. B. (1985). An exposition on understanding expository text. In B. Britton & J. Black (eds.), *Understanding Expository Text* (pp. 249–67). Mahwah, NJ: Erlbaum.

Black, J. B., & Bern, H. (1981). Causal inference and memory for events in narratives. *Journal of Verbal Learning and Verbal Behavior, 20*, 267–75.

Boudewyn, M. A., Gordon, P. C., Long, D. L., Polse, L., & Swaab, T. Y. (2012). Does discourse congruence influence spoken language comprehension before lexical association? Evidence from event-related potentials. *Language and Cognitive Processes, 27*, 698–733.

Bransford, J. D., Barclay, J. R., & Franks, J. J. (1972). Semantic memory: a constructive versus interpretive approach. *Cognitive Psychology, 3*, 193–209.

Britton, B. K., & Eisenhart, F. J. (1993). Expertise, text coherence, and constraint satisfaction: effects on harmony and settling rate. *Proceedings of the Fifteenth Annual Conference of the Cognitive Science Society*. Mahwah, NJ: Erlbaum.

Burkhardt, P. (2006). Inferential bridging relations reveal distinct neural mechanisms: evidence from event-related brain potentials. *Brain and Language, 98*, 159–68.

Cohen, G. (1979). Language comprehension in old age. *Cognitive Psychology, 11*, 412–29.

Cook, A. E., & Guéraud, S. (2005). What have we been missing? The role of general world knowledge in discourse processing. *Discourse Processes, 39*, 365–78.

Daneman, M., & Carpenter, P. A. (1980). Individual differences in working memory and reading. *Journal of Verbal Learning and Verbal Behavior, 19*, 450–66.

Dell, G. S., McKoon, G., & Ratcliff, R. (1983). The activation of antecedent information during the processing of anaphoric reference in reading. *Journal of Verbal Learning and Verbal Behavior*, *22*, 121–32.

di Prima, D. (1960). *Various Fables from Various Places*. New York: Putnam.

Ferguson, M. J., & Zayas, V. (2009). Automatic evaluation. *Current Directions in Psychological Science*, *18*, 362–66.

Ferreira, F., Bailey, K. G. B., & Ferraro, V. (2002). Good-enough representations in language comprehension. *Current Directions in Psychological Science*, *11*, 11–15.

Ferretti, T. R., Singer, M., & Harwood, J. (2013). Processes of discourse integration: evidence from event-related brain potentials. *Discourse Processes*, *50*, 165–86.

Ferretti, T. R., Singer, M., & Patterson, C. (2008). Electrophysiological evidence for the time-course of verifying text ideas. *Cognition*, *108*, 881–88.

Gernsbacher, M. A. (1990). *Language Comprehension as Structure Building*. Mahwah, NJ: Erlbaum.

Glenberg, A. M., Wilkinson, A. C., & Epstein, W. (1982). The illusion of knowing: failure in the self-assessment of comprehension. *Memory & Cognition*, *10*, 597–602.

Graesser, A. C. (1981). *Prose Comprehension beyond the Word*. New York: Springer-Verlag.

Graesser, A. C., & Bertus, E. L. (1998). The construction of causal inferences while reading expository texts on science and technology. *Scientific Studies of Reading*, *2*, 247–69.

Graesser, A. C., Singer, M., & Trabasso, T. (1994). Constructing inferences during narrative text comprehension. *Psychological Review*, *101*, 371–95.

Greene, S. B., Gerrig, R. J., McKoon, G., & Ratcliff, R. (1994). Unheralded pronouns and management by common ground. *Journal of Memory and Language*, *35*, 511–26.

Grice, H. P. (1975). In P. Cole and J. Morgan (eds.), *Syntax and Semantics (Vol. III): Speech Acts* (pp. 41–58). New York: Seminar Press.

Haenggi, D., & Perfetti, C. A. (1994). Processing components of college-level reading. *Discourse Processes*, *17*, 83–104.

Halldorson, M., & Singer, M. (2002). Inference processes: integrating relevant knowledge and text information. *Discourse Processes*, *34*, 145–62.

Hannon, B., & Daneman, M. (2004). Shallow semantic processing of text: an individual-differences account. *Discourse Processes*, *37*(3), 187–204.

Haviland, S. E., & Clark, H. H. (1974). What's new? Acquiring new information as a process in comprehension. *Journal of Verbal Learning and Verbal Behavior*, *13*, 512–21.

Isberner, M. B., & Richter, T. (2013). Can readers ignore implausibility? Evidence for nonstrategic monitoring of event-based plausibility in language comprehension. *Acta Psychologica*, *142*, 15–22.

Jarvella, R. J. (1971). Immediate memory and discourse processing. In Gordon H. Bower (ed.), *The Psychology of Learning and Motivation* (Vol. *XIII*, pp. 379–421). New York: Academic Press.

Jenkins, J. J. (1980). Can we have a fruitful cognitive psychology? *Nebraska Symposium on Motivation, 28,* 211–38.

Just, M. A., & Carpenter, P. A. (1980). A theory of reading: from eye fixations to comprehension. *Psychological Review, 87,* 329–54.

(1992). A capacity theory of comprehension: individual differences in working memory. *Psychological Review, 99,* 122–49.

Keenan, J. M., Baillet, S. D., & Brown, P. (1984). The effects of causal cohesion on comprehension and memory. *Journal of Verbal Learning and Verbal Behavior, 23,* 115–26.

Kieras, D. E. (1985). Thematic processes in the comprehension of technical prose. In B. Britton & J. Black (eds.), *Understanding Expository Prose* (pp. 89–107). Mahwah, NJ:Erlbaum.

Kintsch, W. (1988). The role of knowledge in discourse comprehension: a construction-integration model. *Psychological Review, 95,* 163–82.

(1994). Text comprehension, learning, and memory. *American Psychologist, 49,* 294–303.

(1998). *Comprehension: A Paradigm for Cognition.* New York: Cambridge University Press.

Knoeferle, P., Urbach, T. P., & Kutas, M. (2011). Comprehending how visual context influences incremental sentence processing: insights from ERPs and picture-sentence verification. *Psychophysiology, 48,* 495–506.

Long, D. L. Oppy, B. J., & Seely, M. R. (1994) Individual differences in the time course of inferential processing. *Journal of Experimental Psychology: Learning, Memory, and Cognition, 20,* 1456–70.

(1997). Individual differences in readers' sentence- and text-level representations. *Journal of Memory and Language, 36,* 129–45.

Lutz, M. F., & Radvansky, G. A. (1997). The fate of completed goal information. *Journal of Memory and Language, 36,* 293–310.

Magliano, J. P., & Schleich, M. C. (2000). Verb aspect and situation models. *Discourse Processes, 29,* 83–112.

Maki, R. H., & Berry, (1984). Metacomprehension of text material. *Journal of Experimental Psychology: Learning, Memory, and Cognition, 10,* 663–79.

Mandler, J. M., & Johnson, N. S. (1977). Remembrance of things parsed: story structure and recall. *Cognitive Psychology, 9,* 111–51.

Matsuki, K., Chow, T., Hare, M., Elman, J. L., Scheepers, C., & McRae, K. (2011). Event-based plausibility immediately influences online language comprehension. *Journal of Experimental Psychology: Learning, Memory, and Cognition, 37,* 913–34.

McKoon, G., & Ratcliff, R. (1986). Inferences about predictable events. *Journal of Experimental Psychology: Learning, Memory, and Cognition, 12,* 82–91.

(1988). Contextually relevant aspects of meaning. *Journal of Experimental Psychology: Learning, Memory, and Cognition, 14,* 331–43.

(1992). Inference during reading. *Psychological Review, 99,* 440–66.

McNamara, D. S., & Kintsch, W. (1996). Learning from texts: effects of prior knowledge and text coherence. *Discourse Processes, 22,* 247–88.

McNamara, D. S., Kintsch, E., Songer, N. B., & Kintsch, W. (1996). Are good texts always better? Interactions of text coherence, background knowledge, and levels of understanding in learning from text. *Cognition and Instruction, 14,*–43.

Myers, J. L., Shinjo, M., & Duffy, S. A. (1987). Degree of causal relatedness and memory. *Journal of Verbal Learning and Verbal Behavior, 26,* 453–65.

Neely, J. H. (1977). Semantic priming and retrieval from lexical memory: roles of inhibitionless spreading activation and limited-capacity attention. *Journal of Experimental Psychology: General, 106,* 226–54.

Nieuwland, M. S., & Kuperberg, G. R., (2008). When the truth is not too hard to handle. *Psychological Science, 19,* 1213–18.

Nieuwland, M. S., & Martin, A. E. (2012). If the real world were irrelevant, so to speak: the role of propositional truth value in counterfactual sentence comprehension. *Cognition, 122,* 102–9.

Noordman, G. M., Vonk, W., & Kempff, H. J. (1992). Causal inferences during the reading of expository texts. *Journal of Memory and Language, 31,* 573–90.

O'Brien, E. J., & Albrecht, J. E. (1991). The role of context in accessing antecedents in text. *Journal of Experimental Psychology: Learning, Memory, and Cognition, 17,* 94–102.

(1992). Comprehension strategies in the development of a mental model. *Journal of Experimental Psychology: Learning, Memory, and Cognition, 18,* 777–84.

O'Brien, E. J., Albrecht, J. E., Hakala, C. M., & Rizzella, M. L. (1995). Activation and suppression of antecedents during reinstatement. *Journal of Experimental Psychology: Learning, Memory, and Cognition, 21,* 626–34.

O'Brien, E. J., Cook, A. E., & Peracchi, K. A. (2004). Updating situation models: Reply to Zwaan and Madden. *Journal of Experimental Psychology: Learning, Memory, and Cognition, 30,* 289–91.

O'Brien, E. J., Lorch, R. F., & Myers, J. L. (1998). Memory-based text processing [Special issue]. *Discourse Processes, 26* (2–3).

O'Brien, E. J., Rizzella, M. L., Albrecht, J. E., & Halleran, J. G. (1998). Updating a situation model: a memory based test processing review. *Journal of Experimental Psychology: Learning, Memory, and Cognition, 24,* 1200–10.

Potts, G. R., Keenan, J. M., & Golding, J. M. (1988). Assessing the occurrence of elaborative inferences: lexical decision versus naming. *Journal of Memory and Language, 27,* 399–415.

Radvansky, G. A., & Copeland, D. E. (2000). Functionality and spatial relations in memory and language. *Memory & Cognition, 28,* 987–92.

Radvansky, G. A., Zwaan, R. A., Federico, T., & Franklin, N. (1998). Retrieval from temporally organized situation models. *Journal of Experimental Psychology: Learning, Memory, and Cognition, 24,* 1224–37.

Rapp, D. N., & Kendeou, P. (2009). Noticing and revising discrepancies as texts unfold. *Discourse Processes, 46,* 1–24.

Ratcliff, R. (1978). A theory of memory retrieval. *Psychological Review, 85,* 59–108.

Ratcliff, R., & McKoon, G. (1989). Similarity information versus relational information: differences in the time course of retrieval. *Cognitive Psychology, 21,* 139–55.

Rawson, K. A. (2004). Exploring automaticity in text processing: syntactic ambiguity as a test case. *Cognitive Psychology, 49,* 333–69.

Richards, E., & Singer, M. (2001). Representation of complex goal structures in narrative comprehension. *Discourse Processes*, *31*, 111–35.

Rinck, M., Hahnel, A., & Becker, G. (2001). Using temporal information to construct, update, and retrieval situation models of narratives. *Journal of Experimental Psychology: Learning, Memory, and Cognition*, *27*, 67–80.

Rumelhart, D. E., McClelland, J. L., and the PDP Research Group. (1986). *Parallel Distributed Processing: Explorations in the Microstructure of Cognition (Vol. I)*. Cambridge, MA: Bradford Books.

Sanford, A. J., & Garrod, S. (1998). The role of scenario mapping in text comprehension. *Discourse Processes*, *26*, 159–90.

Sanford, A. J., & Graesser, A. C. (2006). Shallow processing and underspecification. *Discourse Processes*, *42*, 99–108.

Schank, R. C., & Abelson, R. P. (1977). *Scripts, Plans, Goals, and Understanding*. Mahwah, NJ: Erlbaum.

Schroeder, S., Richter, T., & Hoever, I. (2008). Getting a picture that is both accurate and stable: situation models and epistemic validation. *Journal of Memory and Language*, *59*, 237–59.

Seely, M. R., & Long, D. L. (1994). The use of generalized knowledge structures in processing television news items. In H. van Oostendorp & R. Zwaan (eds.), *Naturalistic Prose Comprehension* (pp. 149–63). Norwood, NJ: Ablex.

Singer, M. (1980). The role of case-filling inferences in the coherence of brief passages. *Discourse Processes*, *3*, 185–201.

(1986). Answering yes-no questions about causes. *Memory & Cognition*, *14*, 55–63.

(1993). Causal bridging inferences: validating consistent and inconsistent sequences. *Canadian Journal of Experimental Psychology*, *47*, 340–59.

(2006). Verification of text ideas during reading. *Journal of Memory and Language*, *54*, 574–91.

(2009). Tacit verification of determinate and indeterminate text ideas. *Canadian Journal of Experimental Psychology*, *63*, 185–92.

(2013). Validation in reading comprehension. *Current Directions in Psychological Science*, *22*, 361–66.

Singer, M., & Doering, J. C. (2014). Exploring individual differences in language validation. *Discourse Processes*, *51*, 167–88.

Singer, M., & Gagnon, N. (1999). Detecting causal inconsistencies in scientific text. In S. Goldman, A. Graesser, & P. van den Broek (eds.), *Narrative Comprehension, Causality, and Coherence: Essays in Honor of Tom Trabasso* (pp. 179–94). Mahwah, NJ: Erlbaum.

Singer, M., Graesser, A. C., & Trabasso, T. (1994). Minimal or global inference in reading. *Journal of Memory and Language*, *33*, 421–41.

Singer, M., & Halldorson, M. (1996). Constructing and validating motive bridging inferences. *Cognitive Psychology*, *30*, 1–38.

Singer, M., Halldorson, M., Lear, J. C., & Andrusiak, P. (1992). Validation of causal bridging inferences. *Journal of Memory and Language*, *31*, 507–24.

Singer, M., Harkness, D., & Stewart, S. T. (1997). Constructing inferences in expository text comprehension. *Discourse Processes*, *24*, 199–228.

Singer, M., & O'Connell, G. (2003). Robust inference processes in expository text comprehension. *European Journal of Cognitive Psychology*, *15*, 607–31.

Singer, M., Revlin, R., & Halldorson, M. (1990). Bridging-inferences and enthymeme. In A. C. Graesser and G. H. Bower. (eds.), *The Psychology of Learning and Motivation* (Vol. *XXV*, pp. 35–51). New York: Academic Press.

Singer, M., & Ritchot, K. (1996). Individual differences in inference validation. *Memory & Cognition*, *24*, 733–43.

Smallwood, J., McSpadden, M., & Schooler, J. W. (2008). When attention matters: the curious incident of the wandering mind. *Memory & Cognition*, *36*, 1144–50.

Spilich, G. J., Vesonder, G. T., Chiesi, H. L., & Voss, J. F. (1979). Text processing of domain-related information for individuals with high and low domain knowledge. *Journal of Verbal Learning and Verbal Behavior*, *18*, 275–90.

Staub, A., Rayner, K., Pollatsek, A., Hyona, J., & Majewski, H. (2007). The time course of plausibility effects on eye movements in reading: evidence from noun-noun compounds. *Journal Experimental Psychology: Learning Memory and Cognition*, *33*, 1162–69.

Stewart, A. J., Kidd, E., & Haigh, M. (2009). Early sensitivity to discourse-level anomalies: evidence from self-paced reading. *Discourse Processes*, *46*, 46–69.

Suh, S., & Trabasso, T. (1993). Inferences during reading: converging evidence from discourse analysis, talk-aloud protocols and recognition priming. *Journal of Memory and Language*, *32*, 279–300.

Swinney, D. A. (1979). Lexical access during sentence comprehension: (re) consideration of context effects. *Journal of Verbal Learning and Verbal Behavior*, *18*, 545–69.

Thorndyke, P. W. (1977). Cognitive structures in comprehension and memory of narrative discourse. *Cognitive Psychology*, *9*, 77–110.

Till, R. E., Mross, E. F., & Kintsch, W. (1988). Time course of priming for associate and inference words in a discourse context. *Memory & Cognition*, *16*, 283–98.

Trabasso, T., van den Broek, P., & Suh, S. Y. (1989). Logical necessity and transitivity of causal relations in stories. *Discourse Processes*, *12*, 1–25.

van Berkum, J. J. A., Hagoort, P., & Brown, C. M. (1999). Semantic integration of sentences and discourse: evidence from the N400. *Journal of Cognitive Neuroscience*, *11*, 657–71.

van Dijk, T. A., & Kintsch, W. (1983). *Strategies of Discourse Comprehension*. New York: Academic Press.

Wason, P. C., & Jones, S. (1963). Negatives: denotation and connotation. *British Journal of Psychology*, *54*, 299–307.

Wiswede, D., Koranyi, N., Müller, F., Langner, O., & Rothermund, K. (2012). Validating the truth of propositions: behavioral and ERP indicators of truth evaluation processes. *Social Cognitive and Affective Neuroscience*. Advance access, published April 17, 2012.

Yang, C. L., Perfetti, C. A., & Schmalhofer, F. (2007). Event-related potential indicators of text integration across sentence boundaries. *Journal of Experimental Psychology: Learning, Memory, and Cognition*, *33*, 55–89.

Zwaan, R.A., (1994). Effect of genre expectations on text comprehension. *Journal of Experimental Psychology: Learning, Memory, and Cognition, 20,* 920–33.

Zwaan, R. A., & Madden, C. J. (2004). Updating situation models. *Journal of Experimental Psychology: Learning, Memory, and Cognition, 30,* 283–88.

Zwaan, R. A., Magliano, J. P., & Graesser, A. C. (1995). Dimensions of situation-model construction in narrative comprehension. *Journal of Experimental Psychology: Learning, Memory, and Cognition, 21,* 386–97.

Zwaan, R. A., & Radvansky, G. A. (1998). Situation models in language comprehension and memory. *Psychological Bulletin, 123,* 162–85.

5   Inference generation in text comprehension: automatic and strategic processes in the construction of a mental representation

Paul van den Broek, Katinka Beker, and Marja Oudega

Automatic and strategic processes in inference generation and text comprehension

Inferences are essential to the comprehension of a text or other discourse. Through inferences the reader connects parts of the text and, in doing so, creates coherence beyond the individual text units (e.g., sentences, clauses). Given their central role to text comprehension, inferences feature prominently in cognitive models of reading and comprehension. In this paper, we review central aspects of inferences in text generation and comprehension, in three sections organized around three aspects of inference making: (1) What inferences are made during reading and what are the processes involved (online)? (2) What role do inferences play in a mental representation of the text once reading has been completed (off-line)? (3) How do the moment-by-moment inferential processes during reading (online) result in the gradual emergence of the mental representation the reader has at completion of the reading (off-line)? In the final section we briefly review extensions to the study of the development of reading skills, and to the study of neurological processes involved in text comprehension.

Different types of semantic relations can be inferred by readers. In this chapter, we focus on those relations that most directly contribute to comprehension and a coherent representation of the text, namely referential and causal/logical relations (Sanders and Spooren, 2007; Singer, 1994; van den Broek, 1994). Referential relations establish the identity of an object or person in one part of the text to that in another part (e.g., the anaphoric 'she' in one sentence refers to 'Amanda' in an earlier sentence; 'the building' in one sentence refers to a factory mentioned in an earlier portion of the text). Causal/logical relations establish the explanation or logical antecedents of events or information in one sentence by connecting them to events or information in another sentence (e.g., the glass breaking in one sentence is explained by a protagonist dropping the glass in an earlier sentence; the fact that a particular region is described as a desert in one sentence implies that the ground is dry in another sentence).

Most research on inference generation has been conducted on comprehension of narrative texts, which revolve around structures of physical and motivational causality (Schank and Abelson, 1977; Trabasso, Secco, and van den Broek, 1984). In contrast, much less research has been conducted on informational texts, in which logical relations tend to be more prevalent. As a result, most theoretical models of inference generation focus on causal rather than on logical relations (in addition to referential relations). However, the results that are available on informational texts suggest that the processes involved in generating causal relations in narratives generalize *mutatis mutandis* to the generation of logical relations (Linderholm and van den Broek, 2002; van den Broek and Kendeou, 2008; van den Broek, Lorch, Linderholm, and Gustafson, 2001; Wiley and Myers, 2003).

Inferential processes during reading

As readers proceed through a text, they engage in various types of inferential processes, resulting in different kinds of inferences. Some of the processes are automatic, others are strategic;[1] some occur frequently, others occur only infrequently. The most important of these inferences and underlying processes have been investigated in considerable detail by various researchers. The results of the various investigations are combined and integrated in the Landscape model of reading comprehension, which provides a comprehensive model of the inferential processes that take place during reading (McNamara and Magliano, 2009; van den Broek, Risden, Fletcher, and Thurlow, 1996; van den Broek, Rapp, and Kendeou, 2005; for a computational implementation of the model, see Tzeng, van den Broek, Kendeou, and Lee, 2005).

In the Landscape model and other models of text comprehension, inferential processes occur in cycles, with each new text input triggering a new combination of processes (Kintsch, 1988; McNamara and Magliano, 2009; van den Broek, 1990; 1994).[2] Some processes occur at virtually every cycle, whereas others occur only at some cycles. As a consequence, over the course of reading a text the particular

---

[1] Here, we use 'automatic' to indicate that a process is outside the reader's active control; we use 'strategic' to indicate optional processes that are actively initiated by the reader.

[2] The text unit of investigation varies between researchers. Most adopt the main clause or sentence. In this chapter we use the main clause as a unit of analysis, but the description of inferential processes applies regardless of the unit.

combinations of processes and the resulting types of inferences fluctuate. We will return to this point later; we first consider the inferential processes as they take place for an individual input cycle.

Automatic and strategic processes in inference generation. A direct relation can be inferred between two pieces of information if the two pieces are simultaneously active in the reader's working memory or focus of attention (Kintsch, 1988; Sanford, Sanford, Molle, and Emmot, 2006; van den Broek and Kendeou, 2008; van den Broek, Risden et al., 1996). The activation pattern at any particular cycle is strongly determined, of course, by the newly read text as well as by activation carried over from the immediately preceding processing cycle (e.g., Kintsch and van Dijk, 1978). As a result, concepts in the current input and those still in working memory from the preceding cycle are prime candidates for being connected through inferences.

In addition, each newly read concept may activate other concepts through automatic and through strategic inferential processes. One set of automatic processes that is particularly important to comprehension consists of associative processes by which the concepts in the current input activate other concepts that, for a particular reader, are semantically associated to the input concepts. Such automatic activation processes (variously called 'cohort activation', 'resonance', 'spreading activation') occur in the reader's memory representation of the preceding parts of the text (i.e., episodic memory; Myers and O'Brien, 1998; O'Brien, Plewes, and Albrecht, 1990) but also in the reader's prior knowledge (semantic memory; van den Broek, 1990; Wiley and Myers, 2003). The degree of activation of concepts through memory-based processes at a particular input cycle is a function of: (1) the strength of each candidate concept's semantic relation to concepts in the current clause (Albrecht and O'Brien, 1993; Kintsch, 1988; O'Brien, Raney, Albrecht, and Rayner, 1997; Perfetti, 2007; Perfetti and Hart 2002), (2) the strength of each candidate concept's representation in memory (e.g., concepts that have been elaborated in the earlier text are more strongly represented and, hence, more readily available than nonelaborated concepts [O'Brien, Rizzella, Albrecht, and Halleran, 1998]; concepts in familiar scenarios are produced more reliably and through different neural mechanisms than those in less familiar scenarios [Sundermeier, Virtue, Marsolek, and van den Broek, 2005]), and (3) the presence/absence of other concepts in the memory representation that compete for activation with the candidate concept (e.g., Kendeou and O'Brien, 2014; Tzeng et al., 2005; van den Broek, Young, Tzeng, and Linderholm, 1999). Finally, it is conceivable that the degree of activation depends on (4) the source for the candidate concept: It is possible that text representation and background knowledge are accessed in parallel and with equal activation parameters, but it also may be the case that one source has an inherent advantage over the other (even when equal on the three preceding factors).

In summary, concepts in the current input cycle resonate with concepts in the reader's memory for the text and in his or her background knowledge (Myers and O'Brien 1998; O'Brien et al., 1998; van den Broek, 1990; van den Broek, Young et al., 1999). As a result, each concept in the current input automatically activates a cohort of strongly associated concepts from memory which, in turn, enable the generation of inferences (van den Broek et al., 2005; van den Broek, Risden et al., 1996).

In addition to the automatic activation processes, information may be activated and inferences may be generated through strategic processes by which the reader attempts to create coherence in his or her representation of the text. These strategic, coherence-based processes are particularly likely to occur if the automatic processes do not establish adequate coherence for the reader (van den Broek, 1994). They include search and retrieval from the same memory sources that are accessed through the automatic resonance processes: Information that has been stored as part of comprehension of the text read so far can be reinstated and prior knowledge can be activated through elaborative inferences that add information not explicitly mentioned in the text (Hyönä, Lorch, and Rinck, 2003; Magliano, Trabasso, and Graesser, 1999; Sundermeier, van den Broek, and Zwaan, 2005).

Strategic processes also include physical searches in the prior text (e.g., looking back in the text to find the referent for a character in the current input cycle), accessing other information sources such as other texts, searching the internet, and so on (Bråten, Britt, Strømsø, and Rouet, 2011). Strategic processes are initiated by the reader and, by definition, are not automatic. However, they may be triggered by text properties (e.g., text signals such as headers; Lorch, LeMarié, and Grant, 2011) and, moreover, they may become automatized with repeated practice (Ackermann, 1988; Laberge and Samuels, 1974; Pearson and Hamm, 2005). As we discuss later, there are considerable individual and developmental differences in the 'toolbox' of strategies that readers have available.

In addition to these inferences aimed at understanding the current clause, automatic and strategic processes may elicit forward or predictive inferences about following, as-yet-unread, text. Forward inferences may anticipate the occurrence of specific or general upcoming events or facts (Cook, Limber, and O'Brien, 2001; Linderholm, 2002; Linderholm and van den Broek, 2002; van Berkum, Brown, Zwitserlood, Kooijman, and Hagoort, 2005; Whitney, Ritchie, and Crane, 1992) or the assumed role of currently active information for the future texts (e.g., readers frequently give preferential status to statements about protagonists' goals and keep them activated into subsequent cycles in anticipation of future relevance [Fletcher and Bloom, 1988; Fletcher, Chrysler, van den Broek, Deaton, and Bloom, 1995]).

Combining automatic and strategic processes: standards of coherence and validation of inferences. The occurrence of automatic and strategic processes raises the question of what determines the balance between them. As mentioned, during reading the automatic processes occur continually and automatically but strategic processes only occur if, in the perception of the reader, the automatic processes do not yield adequate coherence (van den Broek, 1994; van den Broek, 2005). This raises the question of what determines 'adequacy' of coherence and, hence, when strategic processes will and will not take place during reading. Whether the coherence that results from the automatic processes is adequate depends on the reader's *standards of coherence* (van den Broek, Bohn-Gettler, Kendeou, Carlson, and White, 2011; van den Broek, Risden, and Husebye-Hartmann, 1995). Standards of coherence reflect the types and strength of coherence a reader aims to achieve in a particular reading situation. Although a reader's standards may be explicit, in many reading situations they are implicit and the reader may not be aware of them. With regard to types of coherence, in most reading situations readers attempt to establish referential coherence and causal/logical coherence, but they may also adopt standards of other types of coherence, such as spatial, emotional, and so on. Moreover, each standard may be adopted to various degrees of strength. For example, while reading *The Brothers Karamazov* a reader may find it sufficient to know that 'he' on page 463 refers to one of the several brothers mentioned earlier or may want to know exactly which brother. While reading an expository text, a reader may be satisfied to understand the general point in the text or may want to know the details of the arguments.

The standards of coherence in a particular reading situation are a joint function of characteristics of the reading situation (e.g., the reading task, instructions, presence of distractors), of the reader (e.g., reading goals, motivation, working memory capacity), and of the text (e.g., presence of text signals such as headers and connectives, text genre, perceived source credibility). For reviews, see van den Broek, Risden et al. (1995), and van den Broek, Bohn-Gettler et al. (2011).

If, at any cycle, the concepts activated through the automatic processes yield enough coherence to meet a reader's standards of coherence, then strategic processes are not needed and are unlikely to be initiated, and the reader continues through the text. However, if the standards are not met, for instance if referential or causal/logical coherence is lacking or retrieved information is inconsistent with the current text input, then strategic processes are likely to be initiated. As mentioned, these processes may take place under conscious guidance of the reader, or implicitly, for instance, because they have become automatized through repeated experience.

Underlying the Landscape model's integration of memory-based and coherence-based processes is the assumption that the information that is activated through these processes is evaluated against the reader's current standards of coherence. Recently there has been considerable interest in *validation*, the mechanisms by which readers check the correctness and completeness of inferences they generate against information in earlier parts of the text and against their background knowledge (Cook and O'Brien, 2014; Singer, 2006; Singer, 2013). For example, Richter and colleagues (Isberner and Richter, 2014; Richter, 2011) have proposed that coherence is continually monitored by validating textual information against prior knowledge. They propose a two-component process similar to that posited by the Landscape model, with automatic and strategic components. As long as incoming text information is plausible or consistent with prior knowledge, automatic processes will predominate (Isberner and Richter, 2014; cf. Long and Lea, 2005; van den Broek, 1994). To validate text information against prior knowledge, this knowledge needs to be sufficiently accessible by the automatic processes. Accessibility is a function of factors similar to those proposed in the Standards for Coherence framework. For example, parts of a text that are more elaborated, more recently read, or more typical members of a semantic category are more accessible (Barnes, Dennis, and Haefele-Kalvaitis, 1996; Myers, Cook, Kambe, Mason, and O'Brien, 2000). The influence of these automatic, memory-based plausibility checks is demonstrated in slowdowns in reading (Albrecht and O'Brien, 1993; Singer, 2006), longer fixations (Cook and Myers, 2004), and more look-backs and rereads (Braze, Shankweiler, Ni, and Palumbo, 2002) when reading implausible or inconsistent information. In this view, when incoming information is implausible or inconsistent, the automatic validation process can be supplemented by a strategic validation process aimed at trying to resolve or explain the violation by making more elaborate judgments about the plausibility of the information. This two-stage description of the comprehension process is similar to the stages described in the Landscape model. The two approaches focus on complementary aspects of the comprehension processes. Whereas the

Landscape model focuses on specifying properties of and influences on standards of coherence – the benchmarks for plausibility and coherence – and assumes validation processes, the Validation model described by Isberner and Richter (2014; Richter, 2011) focuses on the validation processes and assumes the existence of benchmarks against which to validate.

Causal inference in the comprehension of texts. Causal-logical inferences are essential to a reader's text comprehension as they allow the reader to identify how the events and facts in one sentence lead to the events and facts in another sentence. As a result, the reader can construct a causally and semantically integrated representation of the text as a whole, instead of a simple list of individual sentences or clauses. Causal inferences are generated through the processes described above. Which of these processes take place at any particular point in the text and, hence, which of all possible causal relations are established depend on the reader's standards of causal coherence. These standards can be described in terms of *necessity* and *sufficiency*. An individual piece of activated information becomes causally connected to the events and facts in the focal statement if, in the perception of the reader, it is *necessary* for the focal events/fact to occur. If the causal relations identified in this manner together provide *sufficient* causal explanation for the current focal statement, then processing stops and the reader continues to the next sentence. Even if additional causal relations are possible, they likely are not detected by the reader because her or his standards do not require them. If, however, the causal explanation provided by these processes does not meet the reader's standards for causal coherence, then (add-itional) cohesion-based processes will take place. These cohesion-based processes recruit additional concepts from background knowledge and earlier reading cycles, to establish the lacking necessity and sufficiency. They will continue until adequate coherence is established or the reader gives up and continues. The degree of attained causal coherence can be expressed in terms of the sufficiency of explanation provided by the activated information for the events and/or facts in the focal statement (Einhorn and Hogarth, 1986, Trabasso, van den Broek, and Suh, 1989): The extent to which the activated information makes it likely that, in the general circumstances described in the text, the focal event or fact would follow.

A reader's standards of causal coherence determine how much suffi-ciency is enough for the reader to continue to the next sentence. As with any type of standards of coherence, standards of causal coherence are in the *perception of the reader.* They vary between individuals and, within an indi-vidual, from reading situation to reading situation, depending on properties

Table 5.1 *Causally relevant inferences*

Category of inferences	Type of inference	Description
Backward causal inferences	Bridging or connecting inferences	Causal antecedent is still active in WM from preceding reading cycle
	Reinstatement inferences	Causal antecedent is not currently active in WM but is reread or reactivated from preceding text
	Explanatory inferences	Causal antecedent is not currently active in WM but is reactivated from background knowledge
Forward causal inferences	Predictive inferences	Future consequent is predicted because of high sufficiency of the focal event (based on background knowledge and/or prior text)
Other	Elaborative inferences	Associated information that is not relevant for the explanation or logical structure is activated, but could influence coherence at later cycles
	Multiple texts/ documents inferences	Inferences (described above) involving multiple texts or documents instead of single texts

of the text (e.g., genre, text signals), of the individual (e.g., motivation, reading goal, background knowledge), and of contextual factors (e.g., reading task, distractions). If comprehension is successful relative to the reader's standards, the causal relations that are established through these processes together provide adequate causal explanation for the events and facts in the focal statement in the perception of the reader.

Through the automatic and strategic processes, modulated by the reader's standards of causal coherence, several types of causal inferences may be established (Table 5.1). Some of these primarily involve connecting the current input to parts of the prior text.[3] One such inference concerns *bridging* or *connecting* inferences. These occur when a relation is inferred between the focal sentence and the events or facts that are still activated from the immediately preceding reading cycle (Kintsch, 1988; Myers et al., 2000; Perfetti and Stafura, 2013; Perfetti, Yang, and Schmalhofer, 2008). *Reinstatement inferences* occur when the current input is connected to prior textual information that is no longer in working memory or attentional focus. Reinstating inferences require

---

[3] We use the term 'primarily' here because all inferences will involve both textual and background knowledge. For instance, to connect two parts of text the reader inevitably recruits some background knowledge (Kintsch, 1988; Perfetti, 2007).

reactivation of the prior and deactivated information from memory by the processes described above or by rereading (part of) the preceding text. There is ample evidence that reinstatements are frequently made by readers to establish causal coherence. For example, results from probe recognition and reading time studies show that when readers encounter a protagonist's action in a narrative text they reinstate information about a protagonist's goal that motivates the action from earlier sections of the text (Huitema, Dopkins, Klin, and Myers, 1993), and the greater the distance between the focal statement and the to-be-reinstated goal, the more time the reinstatement takes (Bloom, Fletcher, van den Broek, Reitz, and Shapiro, 1990). Likewise, when encountering a break in causal coherence in narrative or expository texts, readers reactivate concepts from the earlier text that provide an explanation for the apparent break (Klin, 1995; Sundermeier, van den Broek et al., 2005; Wiley and Myers, 2003), including spatial information if causally relevant (Sundermeier, van den Broek et al., 2005). Evidence for reactivation from prior text comes from the finding that such earlier text information is automatically reactivated even when it has been outdated by subsequent information – provided that the outdating is not extensive (Kendeou, Smith, and O'Brien, 2013).

Other types of inferences primarily involve activation of concepts from the reader's background knowledge. The resulting inferences fall into three subgroups. *Explanatory inferences* occur when activated semantic (background) knowledge provides causal antecedent(s) for the events or facts in the current input. Such inferences add to the sufficiency of causal explanation for the focal event and to the likelihood of attaining the reader's standards of causal coherence. There is ample evidence that readers construct such inferences based on background knowledge. For example, when reading a sentence pair such as 'Mary poured the water on the bonfire. The fire went out,' readers routinely infer that the fire went out *because* of the water and, to do so, retrieve background knowledge that water extinguishes fire (Cook and O'Brien, 2014; Richter, Schroeder, and Wöhrmann, 2009; Singer and Halldorson, 1996; Singer, Halldorson, Lear, and Andrusiak, 1992). A second example comes from findings that reading about actions elicits generation of inferences about the instruments typically used in those actions (O'Brien, Shank, Myers, and Rayner, 1988).

Predictive inferences occur when the current input and background knowledge combine to foreshadow what will occur next in the text. They may take various forms. Predictive inferences about specific events in the upcoming text are the most frequently investigated. For example, a text containing a sentence 'He angrily threw the porcelain vase against the wall' may elicit a predictive inference that the vase will break (McKoon and Ratcliff, 1986). The results of studies using probing techniques, reading times, electrophysiological measures of reading of continuation sentences, and so on have shown that readers do generate predictive inferences about specific upcoming events, albeit less reliably and less frequently than the inferences about explanations or causal antecedents that we described above (Keefe and McDaniel, 1993; Klin, Guzmán, and Levine, 1999).

Whether a predictive inference will be made depends on properties of the text, of the reader, and of the particular reading situation. For example, an important factor concerns the semantic constraints that the combination of textual information and the reader's background knowledge provides towards a candidate predictive inference: The stronger the semantic constraints, the more likely it is that the candidate inference will be generated (Cook et al., 2001; Lassonde and O'Brien, 2009; Linderholm, 2002; Linderholm and van den Broek, 2002; Murray, Klin, and Myers, 1993; Peracchi and O'Brien, 2004; van Berkum et al., 2005; van den Broek, 1990, 1994; Virtue, van den Broek, and Linderholm, 2006; Whitney et al., 1992). Also, the reader's purpose for reading affects the degree to which predictive inferences are generated (Linderholm and van den Broek, 2002; McCrudden, Magliano, and Schraw, 2010; Narvaez, van den Broek, and Barrón Ruiz, 1999; van den Broek et al., 2001), as does the reader's working memory capacity – often in interaction with reading goals and textual constraints (Linderholm and van den Broek, 2002; Virtue et al., 2006). As a final example, the tasks or instructions that readers are given (e.g., by teacher or experimenter) for reading a text may influence the goals the reader sets for reading and, hence, his or her processing (Linderholm and van den Broek, 2002; McCrudden et al., 2010). With regard to predictive inferences, as with other inferences, both memory-based and coherence-based processes may influence their generation.

Other types of predictive inferences have been investigated less extensively. For example, it is conceivable that a reader generates inferences about general rather than specific events (e.g., 'something bad will happen'; Lassonde and O'Brien, 2009; van den Broek, 1990). There has been little investigation of such inferences although research focusing only on inferences about specific events underestimates the occurrence of predictive inferences. Another type of predictive inference is the anticipation of continued relevance of a particular piece of information. For example, Fletcher, Bloom and colleagues have shown that while reading narratives, readers frequently give preferential status to goal statements or events that have not yet had consequences and continue to activate these goals or events into subsequent cycles in anticipation of future relevance (Fletcher and Bloom, 1988; Fletcher et al., 1995). Likewise, linguistic cues such as the implicit causality of verbs may lead the reader to anticipate a particular character to become the lead protagonist in the subsequent clause (e.g., 'David praised Linda because *she* ...'; Koornneef and van Berkum, 2006). Finally, readers may make predictions based on the unfolding text structure (e.g., based on knowledge about the genre or structure of the text at hand; Lea, Kayser, Mulligan, and Myers, 2002).

Elaborative inferences concern the activation of concepts from memory that are not necessary for explanation or logical structure. Elaborative inferences involve activation of information that is associated with components of the current input. Information can be associated with content presented in previous parts of the text ('the protagonists both like dogs') or with background knowledge ('I like dogs too'). Elaborative inferences are influenced by the context. The more constraining the context is towards a particular elaborative inference, the higher the likelihood that the inference is made (O'Brien et al., 1988). Although not necessary for establishing coherence at the current cycle, their activation may influence coherence at later cycles. For example, elaborative inferences at one cycle may increase the availability of information that *will* be causally relevant and become part of an explanatory inference at a later cycle. One instance of this concerns *instrument inferences*, by which the reader infers the instrument to a described action or event. For example, inferring 'hammer' after reading 'Bobby pounded the boards' (McKoon and Ratcliff, 1981), this instrument may unexpectedly become relevant later in the narrative.

At any reading cycle any combination of the described processes can take place. The various inferential processes and the resulting types of causal inferences are summarized in the Causal Inference Maker model (see Figure 5.1, adapted from van den Broek, 1994). When one considers the text as a whole, the processes and inferences fluctuate dynamically from one cycle to the next. Moreover, the processing at one cycle may interact with the processing at a subsequent cycle (e.g., the activations during processing of the first affects the availability of information for the processing of the second). The Landscape model captures the inferential processes as they unfold over the course of reading a text as well as the fluctuating patterns of processes and resulting inferences (van den Broek, Risden et al., 1996; Linderholm, Virtue, Tzeng, and van den Broek, 2004; McNamara and Magliano, 2009).

In this brief review we have focused on inferences within a single text. Inferences may occur in other situations as well. For example, inferences

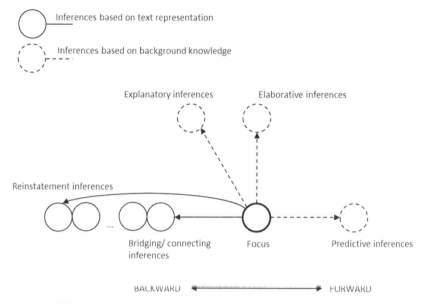

Figure 5.1 The causal inference maker (adapted from van den Broek, 1994). Nodes represent concepts or events, arrows reflect the direction of the inference.

may be generated to establish coherence across different documents (Goldman, 2004; Perfetti, Rouet, and Britt, 1999) or informational sources from different media. Different sources of information require within-text-inferences as well as across-text-inferences. Contrasting views held by authors of multiple documents can make these processes very hard (Bråten et al., 2011). These fall outside the scope of this chapter. However, the processes and constraints as described here could be extended and adapted to apply in those situations as well.

Individual differences. It is important to note that individuals differ in their inference making. A detailed review of the sources for such differences is beyond the scope of this chapter, but a summary may be useful (for more extensive discussions, see Helder, van den Broek, van Leijenhorst, and Beker, 2013; McNamara and Kendeou, 2011; van den Broek and Espin, 2012). We already mentioned several factors such as working memory and background knowledge. Factors that contribute to such individual differences generally fall into three categories: general cognitive characteristics of the reader, general comprehension skills, and reading comprehension skills (Helder et al., 2013; van den Broek and Espin, 2012).

One category of factors contributing to individual differences in inference generation concerns *general cognitive reader characteristics*. Readers with a larger working memory capacity differ from readers with a smaller working memory capacity with respect to several types of inferences (Cain, Oakhill, and Bryant, 2004; Linderholm, 2002). For example, they generate predictive inferences faster (Estevez and Calvo, 2000), generate fewer elaborative inferences (Whitney, Ritchie, and Clark, 1991) and are better able to ignore irrelevant details than readers with smaller working memory capacity (Sanchez and Wiley, 2006).

Inferences involving semantic memory are also influenced by the amount of background knowledge that the reader possesses on the topic in the text (Adams, Bell, and Perfetti, 1995; Britton, Stimson, Stennett, and Gülgöz, 1998; Pearson, Hansen, and Gordon, 1979; Rawson and Kintsch, 2002) and by the depth and breadth of concept/vocabulary knowledge on the concepts in the text (Ouellette, 2006; Perfetti et al., 2008; Strasser and del Río, 2014). A third general cognitive reader characteristic that has been implicated concerns the reader's strength of executive functions. Because a reader's information-processing capacity is limited, inhibition of irrelevant parts of the texts and shifting attention between them are essential components of reading. Indeed, the ability to inhibit responses and the ability to shift attention both contribute to reading comprehension (Kieffer, Vukovic, and Berry, 2013).

A second category of factors contributing to individual differences in inference generation concerns the efficacy of the reader's general *comprehension processes/skills*. These factors influence comprehension in general (in texts but also other media), and include a person's inference-generation skills, ability to allocate attention to central information, and knowledge and application of appropriate standards of coherence (Gernsbacher, Varner, and Faust, 1990; Kendeou, Bohn-Gettler, White, and van den Broek, 2008).

A third category of factors contributing to individual differences in inference generation concerns *reading comprehension skills*. Individual differences in inferential processes during reading occur as a result of differences in basic reading skills (e.g., the ability to decode the words in the text; Perfetti, Landi, and Oakhill, 2005) and of higher-order factors. The latter include differences in reading-specific comprehension strategies, in motivation, and in knowledge about texts (e.g., in knowledge about text genres, about the use of text signals, etc.; Lorch et al., 2004; Lorch, Diemer et al., 1999; Lorch, Sanchez et al., 1999; Oakhill and Cain, 2012; Pressley and McCormick, 1995).

Together, these three sets of factors modulate the inferential processes summarized above. They may do so alone or in interaction. For example, readers generally adjust their processing of a text to fit their reading purpose, but when reading for study purposes, readers with smaller working-memory capacity do so less effectively than readers with larger capacity (Linderholm and van den Broek, 2002).

The role of causal inferences in the mental representation of a text

Causal inferences play a central role in readers' representations of text after they have finished reading. The more causal relations a text has, the more coherent it is and the better readers' memory for the text is (e.g., Graesser, McNamara, Louwerse, and Cai, 2004; Sanders and Noordman, 2000; Trabasso et al., 1984). Within a text, events with many connections are recalled (Trabasso et al., 1984; van den Broek, Rohleder, and Narvaez, 1996), included in summaries (Trabasso and van den Broek, 1985; van den Broek and Trabasso, 1986), and rated as important more often than events with few connections (O'Brien and Myers, 1987; Trabasso and Sperry, 1985; Trabasso and van den Broek, 1985; van den Broek, 1989). When the number of causal relations of statements is increased by editing the context, their importance and inclusion in summaries increase (van den Broek, 1988). Similar results have been observed concerning events that are part of the causal chain that runs through a narrative: They are more strongly represented than statements that are not part of the chain (Black and Bower, 1980; Wolman, van den Broek, and Lorch, 1997).

Results from studies using cued recall and priming show that individual relations are included in the representation of the text stored in long-term memory. For example, after reading a text, readers recognize a textual event more quickly when it is preceded by a causally related event from the text than when it is preceded by a nonrelated event – even if the latter event was much closer to the target event in the surface structure of the text (van den Broek and Lorch, 1993). Likewise, when presented with questions after reading a text, readers appear to trace a path of causal relations to the answer in their representation of the text (O'Brien and Myers, 1987).

These results suggest that the mental representation of a text resembles a *network* of (causally) connected nodes. The nodes represent events, facts, and concepts identified from the text and from background knowledge and the connections represent semantic relations that the reader has constructed between the nodes (Graesser and Clark, 1985; Kintsch and van Dijk, 1978; Trabasso et al., 1984). Thus, the representation includes more than just the events and facts in the text; it captures the situation that is described by the text – hence it is often referred to as *situation model* (Kintsch, 1988; Zwaan, Magliano, and Graesser, 1995).

There are, of course, considerable individual differences in the representation that readers construct of a text. Many of the factors described above with respect to individual differences in inferential processes during reading have been found to affect the memory representation of a text as well, resulting in individual differences in readers' *sensitivity to structural centrality* in terms of their representation of the text (McNamara and Kendeou, 2011; Miller and Keenan, 2009; van den Broek, Helder, and van Lijenhorst., 2013).[4]

Connecting inference generation during reading and the construction of a mental representation of a text – the Landscape model

The causal and other coherence-building inferences that are generated as the reader proceeds through a text (online) lead to the gradual emergence of the reader's mental representation of the text (off-line). The relation between the online and off-line aspects of comprehension is reciprocal: On the one hand, the processes at a particular cycle are in part determined by the mental representation of the text that has been built in the preceding reading cycles; on the other hand, the processes result in an update of the episodic memory representation of the text read so far. The Landscape model captures the dynamic and reciprocal interplay between online processes and the emerging representation (van den Broek and Gustafson, 1999; van den Broek, Risden et al., 1996; van den Broek, Young et al., 1999).

The processes elicited by individual sentences combine to create a 'landscape' of fluctuating processes and activations, influenced by text, reader, and reading context properties. These fluctuating processes and activations lead to an updating of the episodic memory representation by each new cycle: New events and facts and new semantic relations are added to the existing representation, and the memory traces of existing

---

[4] It is important to note that most research on the mental representation of texts has used memory tasks to assess the representation. Successful off-line comprehension of a text entails more than just memory, however, including the 'learning' of textual information by incorporating it into one's background knowledge, the ability to apply the information, to compare it to information in other texts, and so on (van den Broek and Espin, 2012; Pressley and McCormick, 1995). Recent research on the extent to which different types of text are able to modify a reader's misconceptions is a good example of extending memory-focused reading research to a broader range of comprehension situations (Kendeou, and van den Broek, 2007; Tippett, 2010).

nodes and relations are modified. The updating is a function of the co-activation of the individual events and facts in the reading cycle (Kendeou and O'Brien, 2014 ; Kintsch and van Dijk, 1978; Linderholm et al., 2004; van den Broek and Kendeou, 2008): The more strongly two co-occurring concepts are activated, the more strongly the concepts and their relation are included or strengthened in the representation. The specifics of these updating processes currently are the focus of considerable research.

Extending research on inferential processes during reading

The development of inference making during reading. The models of the cognitive processes and inferences involved in reading comprehension have been developed primarily in the context of adult readers (usually college students). There also is a considerable body of research literature on the development of reading comprehension and inferential skills (for reviews, see Oakhill and Cain, 2007; van den Broek et al., 2013; van den Broek, White, Kendeou, and Carlson, 2009). With age, children develop all of the components that were described above concerning individual differences (Lynch et al., 2008; Oakhill and Cain, 2012; Tilstra, McMaster, van den Broek, Kendeou, and Rapp, 2009). General cognitive skills such as the capacity and/or efficiency of working memory and executive functions, including the ability to focus on relevant and ignore irrelevant information, become stronger. In addition, background knowledge on a wide range of topics increases – although the famous studies by Chi and others (Chi and Koeske, 1983) on children's knowledge of dinosaurs have shown that even very young children can have extensive knowledge in a specialized area and, as a result, may make sophisticated inferences. Likewise, with maturation, experience, and schooling, both general and reading-specific comprehension skills improve. This, together with increased knowledge of text structure, genres, text devices, and so on, contributes to a steady increase in the ability to process and store texts.

   The development of comprehension skills starts before reading age. In the toddler years, infants already identify causal relations between simple events they witness (Bauer, 2013). Preschool children identify causal and other coherence relations between narrative events they see on-screen or hear through parents or others who read to them, and construct network representations (van den Broek, Kendeou, Lousberg, and Visser, 2011; van den Broek, Lorch, and Thurlow, 1996). This development extends in the reading domain once children start reading independently (Lynch et al., 2008; Pearson, Moje, and Greenleaf, 2010; Williams, 1993). As a result of the developments in the components outlined in the preceding paragraph, on average the networks become richer and more focused on the structurally important units in the text: Children become more sensitive to structural centrality (Lynch and van den Broek, 2007; Oakhill and Cain, 2012; van den Broek, Lynch, Naslund, Ievers-Landis, and Verduin, 2003; van den Broek et al., 2013). In addition, they become increasingly able to identify relations that are abstract, cover large distances in the surface structure of the text, combine multiple antecedents, and/or cross boundaries of units within the text (e.g., paragraphs or sections), between texts, and between media.

The results of recent longitudinal investigations show that comprehension and inference-generation skills at an early age predict reading comprehension at a later age (Kendeou, van den Broek, White, and Lynch, 2007; Oakhill and Cain, 2012). Comprehension and basic, code-related language skills represent distinct clusters of skills, which develop relatively independently and come together when the child begins to read for comprehension (Gough and Tunmer, 1986; Kendeou, Savage, and van den Broek, 2009; Tilstra et al., 2009; Whitehurst and Lonigan, 1998). This contribution is independent from the contribution of basic language skills such as decoding, phonological awareness, and the like.

The neurological basis of inferences-making and comprehension. Investigations of the neural bases of inference making and comprehension of text are beginning to provide insight into the brain structures involved in the processing of text – although much still is unknown. One line of research uses divided visual field and fMRI techniques to explore the possibility that the brain's hemispheres differ in their roles in the comprehension of text. The results of these studies suggest that, at least in right-handed readers, the left hemisphere is more involved in the activation of concepts and inferences that are relatively strongly constrained by the text or the reader's background knowledge, whereas the right hemisphere is more involved in activating concepts and inferences that are less constrained by text and background knowledge (Beeman, Bowden, and Gernsbacher, 2000; Sundermeier, Virtue et al., 2005; cf. Long and Baynes, 2002). The two hemispheres thus may complement each other in neurological functionality. Furthermore, there is some indication that the right hemisphere may be recruited when the inferential task is too demanding for the left hemisphere alone (Prat, Mason, and Just, 2011).

A second line of neuroimaging research focuses on identifying the neural circuitry that is involved in text comprehension. To make causal inferences between two sentences, a large ensemble of brain structures is recruited. These structures are bilateral and include both prefrontal and temporal areas, possibly reflecting the various stages of activation of information, retrieval, and integration of that information (cf. Kuperberg, Lakshmanan, Caplan, and Holcomb, 2006). When comprehension of multi-sentence texts are considered, the finding of involvement of multiple brain structures is replicated. Although different investigations yield somewhat different combinations of neural structures, they also roughly overlap, resulting in the notion that there is an 'extended language network' of brain structures that supports reading comprehension (Ferstl, Neumann, Bogler, and Von Cramon, 2008; Mason and Just, 2006; Perfetti and Frishkoff, 2008). Ongoing neurological investigations will fill in many details in the above general picture of the role of various neural structures in text comprehension, and increasingly connect components of text processing to specific brain structures and functions.

Conclusion

Inferences are essential to successful understanding of texts, whether in books or in digital forms. Readers construct such inferences through a combination of fast/automatic and slow/strategic processes (cf. Kahneman, 2011). The automatic processes often are adequate to provide a degree of coherence that meets the reader's standards, but strategic processes may supplement them when the coherence achieved by automatic processes alone is inadequate. In this context, 'strategic' does not necessarily refer to very consciously selected and extensive strategies, but rather to (sometimes automated) actions that fit the moment-to-moment situation. Thus, they often resemble more closely the strategic actions by an athlete who sees the ball appear and in a flash recognizes the opportunity to score than the conscious and thoughtful reflections, for example, about implications of winning or losing the game for the standings in the competition.

These online inferential processes, influenced by the reader's standards for coherence, lead to the gradual emergence of a memory representation of the text. Understanding inferential processes and how they affect children's and adults' comprehension requires investigation of both the automatic and strategic components, and of the translation into a memory representation. Insights gained from such investigations elucidate how the human mind comprehends what it read, but also how the necessary skills develop and how their development may be fostered through educational intervention.

REFERENCES

Ackermann, P. (1988). Determinants of individual differences during skill acquisition: Cognitive abilities and informational processing. *Journal of Experimental Psychology: General*, *117*, 288–318.

Adams, B. C., Bell, L. C., & Perfetti, C. A. (1995). A trading relationship between reading skill and domain knowledge in children's text comprehension. *Discourse Processes*, *20*, 307–23.

Albrecht, J. E., & O'Brien, E. J. (1993). Updating a mental model: maintaining both local and global coherence. *Journal of Experimental Psychology: Learning, Memory, and Cognition*, *19*, 1061–70.

Barnes, M. A., Dennis, M., & Haefele-Kalvaitis, J. (1996). The effects of knowledge availability and knowledge accessibility on coherence and elaborative inferencing in children from six to fifteen years of age. *Journal of Experimental Child Psychology*, *61*, 216–41.

Bauer, P. J. (2013). Theory and processes in memory development: infancy and early childhood. In R. E. Holliday & T. A. Marche (eds.). *Child Forensic Psychology* (pp. 9–38). New York: Palgrave Macmillan.

Beeman, M. J., Bowden, E. M., & Gernsbacher, M. A. (2000). Right and left hemisphere cooperation for drawing predictive and coherence inferences during normal story comprehension. *Brain and Language*, *71*, 310–336.

Black, J. B., & Bower, G. H. (1980). Story understanding as problem-solving. *Poetics*, *9*, 223–50.

Bloom, C. P., Fletcher, C. R., van den Broek, P., Reitz, L., & Shapiro, B. P. (1990). An online assessment of causal reasoning during comprehension. *Memory & Cognition*, *18*, 65–71.

Bråten, I., Britt, M. A., Strømsø, H. I., & Rouet, J.-F. (2011). The role of epistemic beliefs in the comprehension of multiple expository texts: toward an integrated model. *Educational Psychologist*, *46*, 48–70.

Braze, D., Shankweiler, D., Ni, W., & Palumbo, L. C. (2002). Readers' eye movements distinguish anomalies of form and content. *Journal of Psycholinguistic Research*, *31*, 25–44.

Britton, B. K., Stimson, M., Stennett, B., & Gülgöz, S. (1998). Learning from instructional text: test of an individual-differences model. *Journal of Educational Psychology*, *90*, 476–91.

Cain, K., Oakhill, J., & Bryant, P. (2004). Children's reading comprehension ability: concurrent prediction by working memory, verbal ability, and component skills. *Journal of Educational Psychology*, *96*, 31–42.

Chi, M. T., & Koeske, R. D. (1983). Network representation of a child's dinosaur knowledge. *Developmental Psychology*, *19*, 29–39.

Cook, A. E., Limber, J. E., & O'Brien, E. J. (2001). Situation-based context and the availability of predictive inferences. *Journal of Memory and Language*, *44*, 220–34.

Cook, A. E., & Myers, J. L. (2004). Processing discourse roles in scripted narratives: the influences of context and world knowledge. *Journal of Memory and Language*, *50*, 268–88.

Cook, A. E., & O'Brien, E. J. (2014). Knowledge activation, integration, and validation during narrative text comprehension. *Discourse Processes, 51*, 26–49.

Einhorn, H. J., & Hogarth, R. M. (1986). Judging probable cause. *Psychological Bulletin, 99*, 3–19.

Estevez, A., & Calvo, M. G. (2000). Working memory capacity and time course of predictive inferences. *Memory, 8*, 51–61.

Ferstl, E. C., Neumann, J., Bogler, C., & Von Cramon, D. Y. (2008). The extended language network: a meta-analysis of neuroimaging studies on text comprehension. *Human Brain Mapping, 29*, 581–93.

Fletcher, C. R., & Bloom, C. P. (1988). Causal reasoning in the comprehension of simple narrative texts. *Journal of Memory and Language, 27*, 235–44.

Fletcher, C. R., Chrysler, S. T., van den Broek, P., Deaton, J. A., & Bloom, C. P. (1995). The role of co-occurrence, coreference, and causality in the coherence of conjoined sentences. In R. F. Lorch & E. J. O'Brien (eds.), *Sources of Coherence in Reading* (pp. 203–18). Mahwah, NJ: Erlbaum.

Gernsbacher, M. A., Varner, K. R., & Faust, M. E. (1990). Investigating differences in general comprehension skill. *Journal of Experimental Psychology: Learning, Memory, and Cognition, 16*, 430–45.

Goldman, S. R. (2004). Cognitive aspects of constructing meaning through and across multiple texts. In N. Shuart-Faris & D. Bloome (eds.), *Uses of Intertextuality in Classroom and Educational Research* (pp. 317–52). Greenwich, CT: Information Age Publishing.

Gough, P. B., & Tunmer, W. E. (1986). Decoding, reading, and reading disability. *Remedial and Special Education, 7*, 6–10.

Graesser, A. C., & Clark, L. F. (1985). *Structures and Procedures of Implicit Knowledge*. Norwood, NJ: Ablex.

Graesser, A. C., McNamara, D. S., Louwerse, M. M., & Cai, Z. (2004). Coh-Metrix: analysis of text on cohesion and language. *Behavior Research Methods, Instruments, and Computers, 36*, 193–202.

Helder, A., van den Broek, P., Van Leijenhorst, L., & Beker, K. (2013). Sources of comprehension problems during reading. In B. Miller, L. Cutting, & P. McCardle (eds.), *Unraveling Reading Comprehension: Behavioral, Neurobiological, and Genetic Components* (pp. 43–53). Baltimore, MD: Paul H. Brookes Publishing.

Huitema, J. S., Dopkins, S., Klin, C. M., & Myers, J. L. (1993). Connecting goals and actions during reading. *Journal of Experimental Psychology: Learning, Memory, and Cognition, 19*, 1053–60.

Hyönä, J., Lorch, R. F., Jr., & Rinck, M. (2003). Eye movement measures to study global text processing. In J. Hyönä, R. Radach, & H. Deubel (eds.), *The Mind's Eye: Cognitive and Applied Aspects of Eye Movement Research* (pp. 313–34). Amsterdam: Elsevier.

Isberner, M. B., & Richter, T. (2014). Comprehension and validation: separable stages of information processing? A case for epistemic monitoring in language comprehension. In D. N. Rapp & J. L. G. Braasch (eds.), *Processing Inaccurate Information: Theoretical and Applied Perspectives from Cognitive Science and the Educational Sciences* (pp. 245–76). Cambridge, MA: MIT Press.

Kahneman, D. (2011). *Thinking, Fast and Slow*. New York: Farrar, Strauss and Giroux.

Keefe, D. E., & McDaniel, M. A. (1993). The time course and durability of predictive inferences. *Journal of Memory and Language, 32*, 446–63.

Kendeou, P., Bohn-Gettler, C., White, M. J., & van den Broek, P. (2008). Children's inference generation across different media. *Journal of Research in Reading, 31*, 259–72.

Kendeou, P., & O'Brien, E. J. (2014). The knowledge revision components (KReC) framework: processes and mechanisms. In D. N. Rapp & J. L. G. Braasch (eds.), *Processing Inaccurate Information: Theoretical and Applied Perspectives from Cognitive Science and the Educational Sciences* (pp. 353–77). Cambridge, MA: MIT Press.

Kendeou, P., Savage, R., & van den Broek, P. (2009). Revisiting the simple view of reading. *British Journal of Educational Psychology, 79*, 353–70.

Kendeou, P., Smith, E. R., & O'Brien, E. J. (2013). Updating during reading comprehension: Why causality matters. *Journal of Experimental Psychology: Learning, Memory, and Cognition, 39*, 854–65.

Kendeou, P., & van den Broek, P. (2007). The effects of prior knowledge and text structure on comprehension processes during reading of scientific texts. *Memory & Cognition, 35*, 1567–77.

Kendeou, P., van den Broek, P., White, M. J., & Lynch, J. S. (2007). Comprehension in preschool and early elementary children: skill development and strategy interventions. In D. S. McNamara (ed.), *Reading Comprehension Strategies: Theories, Interventions, and Technologies* (pp. 27–45). Mahwah, NJ: Erlbaum.

Kieffer, M. J., Vukovic, R. K., & Berry, D., (2013). Roles of attention shifting and inhibitory control in fourth-grade reading comprehension. *Reading Research Quarterly, 48*, 333–48.

Kintsch, W. (1988). The role of knowledge in discourse comprehension: A construction integration model. *Psychological Review, 95*, 163–82.

Kintsch, W., & Van Dijk, T. A. (1978). Toward a model of text comprehension and production. *Psychological Review, 85*, 363–94.

Klin, C. M. (1995). Causal inferences in reading: from immediate activation to long-term memory. *Journal of Experimental Psychology: Learning, Memory, and Cognition, 21*, 1483–94.

Klin, C. M., Guzmán, A. E., & Levine, W. H. (1999). Prevalence and persistence of predictive inferences. *Journal of Memory and Language, 40*, 593–604.

Koornneef, A. W., & van Berkum, J. J. (2006). On the use of verb-based implicit causality in sentence comprehension: evidence from self-paced reading and eye tracking. *Journal of Memory and Language, 54*, 445–65.

Kuperberg, G. R., Lakshmanan, B. M., Caplan, D. N., & Holcomb, P. J. (2006). Making sense of discourse: an fMRI study of causal inferencing across sentences. *Neuroimage, 33*, 343–61.

LaBerge, D., & Samuels, S. J. (1974). Toward a theory of automatic information processing in reading. *Cognitive Psychology, 6*, 293–323.

Lassonde, K. A., & O'Brien, E. J. (2009). Contextual specificity in the activation of predictive inferences. *Discourse Processes, 46*, 426–38.

Lea, R. B., Kayser, P. A., Mulligan, E. J., & Myers, J. L. (2002). Do readers make inferences about conversational topics? *Memory & Cognition, 30,* 945–57.

Linderholm, T. (2002). Predictive inference generation as a function of working memory capacity and causal text constraints. *Discourse Processes, 34,* 259–80.

Linderholm, T., & van den Broek, P. (2002). The effects of reading purpose and working memory capacity on the processing of expository text. *Journal of Educational Psychology, 94,* 778–84.

Linderholm, T., Virtue, S., Tzeng, Y., & van den Broek, P. (2004). Fluctuations in the availability of information during reading: capturing cognitive processes using the Landscape model. *Discourse Processes, 37,* 165–86.

Long, D. L., & Baynes, K. (2002). Discourse representation in the two cerebral hemispheres. *Journal of Cognitive Neuroscience, 14,* 228–42.

Long, D. L., & Lea, R. B. (2005). Have we been searching for meaning in all the wrong places? Defining the 'search after meaning' principle in comprehension. *Discourse Processes, 39,* 279–98.

Lorch, E. P., Diener, M. B., Sanchez, R. P., Milich, R., Welsh, R., & van den Broek, P. (1999). The effects of story structure on the recall of stories in children with attention deficit hyperactivity disorder. *Journal of Educational Psychology, 91,* 213–83.

Lorch, E. P., Eastham, D., Milich, R., Lemberger, C. C., Polley Sanchez, R., Welsh, R., & van den Broek, P. (2004). Difficulties in comprehending causal relations among children with ADHD: the role of cognitive engagement. *Journal of Abnormal Psychology, 113,* 56–63.

Lorch, R., LeMarié, J., & Grant, R. (2011). Signaling hierarchical and sequential organization in expository text. *Scientific Studies of Reading, 15,* 267–84.

Lorch, E. P., Sanchez, R. P., van den Broek, P., Milich, R., Murphy, E. L., Lorch Jr, R. F., & Welsh, R. (1999). The relation of story structure properties to recall of television stories in young children with attention-deficit hyperactivity disorder and nonreferred peers. *Journal of Abnormal Child Psychology, 27,* 293–309.

Lynch, J. S., & van den Broek, P. (2007). Understanding the glue of narrative structure: Children's on- and off-line inferences about characters' goals. *Cognitive Development, 22,* 323–40.

Lynch, J. S., van den Broek, P., Kremer, K. E., Kendeou, P., White, M. J., & Lorch, E. P. (2008). The development of narrative comprehension and its relation to other early reading skills. *Reading Psychology, 29,* 327–65.

Magliano, J. P., Trabasso, T., & Graesser, A. C. (1999). Strategic processing during comprehension. *Journal of Educational Psychology, 91,* 615–29.

Mason, R. A., & Just, M. A. (2006). Neuroimaging contributions to the understanding of discourse processes. In M. Traxler & M. A. Gernsbacher (eds.), *Handbook of Psycholinguistics* (pp. 765–99). Amsterdam: Elsevier.

McCrudden, M. T., Magliano, J. P., & Schraw, G. (2010). Exploring how relevance instructions affect personal reading intentions, reading goals and text processing: a mixed methods study. *Contemporary Educational Psychology, 35,* 229–41.

McKoon, G., & Ratcliff, R. (1981). The comprehension processes and memory structures involved in instrumental inference. *Journal of Verbal Learning and Verbal Behavior, 20,* 671–82.

(1986). Inferences about predictable events. *Journal of Experimental Psychology: Learning, Memory, and Cognition, 12,* 82–91.

McNamara, D. S., & Kendeou, P. (2011). Translating advances in reading comprehension research to educational practice. *International Electronic Journal of Elementary Education, 4,* 33–46.

McNamara, D. S., & Magliano, J. (2009). Toward a comprehensive model of comprehension. *Psychology of Learning and Motivation, 51,* 297–384.

Miller, A. C., & Keenan, J. M. (2009). How word decoding skill impacts text memory: the centrality deficit and how domain knowledge can compensate. *Annals of Dyslexia, 59,* 99–113.

Murray, J. D., Klin, C. M., & Myers, J. L. (1993). Forward inferences in narrative text. *Journal of Memory and Language, 32,* 464–73.

Myers, J. L., Cook, A. E., Kambe, G., Mason, R. A., & O'Brien, E. J. (2000). Semantic and episodic effects on bridging inferences. *Discourse Processes, 29,* 179–99.

Myers, J. L., & O'Brien, E. J. (1998). Accessing the discourse representation during reading. *Discourse Processes, 26,* 131–57.

Narvaez, D., van den Broek, P., & Barrón Ruiz, A. B. (1999). The influence of reading purpose on inference generation and comprehension in reading. *Journal of Educational Psychology, 91,* 488–96.

Oakhill, J., & Cain, K. (2007). Introduction to comprehension development. In K. Cain & J. Oakhill (eds.), *Children's Comprehension Problems in Oral and Written Language: A Cognitive Perspective* (pp. 3–40). New York: Guilford Press.

(2012). The precursors of reading ability in young readers: evidence from a four-year longitudinal study. *Scientific Studies of Reading, 16,* 91–121.

O'Brien, E. J., & Myers, J. L. (1987). The role of causal connections in retrieval of text. *Memory & Cognition, 15,* 419–27.

O'Brien, E. J., Plewes, P. S., & Albrecht, J. E. (1990). Antecedent retrieval processes. *Journal of Experimental Psychology: Learning, Memory, and Cognition, 16,* 241–49.

O'Brien, E. J., Raney, G. E., Albrecht, J. E., & Rayner, K. (1997). Processes involved in the resolution of explicit anaphors. *Discourse Processes, 23,* 1–24.

O'Brien, E. J., Rizzella, M. L., Albrecht, J. E., & Halleran, J. G. (1998). Updating a situation model: a memory-based text processing view. *Journal of Experimental Psychology: Learning, Memory, and Cognition, 24,* 1200–10.

O'Brien, E. J., Shank, D. M., Myers, J. L., & Rayner, K. (1988). Elaborative inferences during reading: Do they occur online? *Journal of Experimental Psychology: Learning, Memory, and Cognition, 14,* 410–20.

Ouellette, G.P. (2006). What's meaning got to do with it: the role of vocabulary in word reading and reading comprehension. *Journal of Educational Psychology, 98,* 554–66.

Pearson, P. D., & Hamm, D. N. (2005). The assessment of reading comprehension: a review of practices-past, present, and future. In

S. G. Paris & S. A. Stahl (eds.), *Children's Reading Comprehension and Assessment* (pp. 13–70). Mahwah, NJ: Erlbaum.

Pearson, P. D., Hansen, J., & Gordon, C. (1979). The effect of background knowledge on young children's comprehension of explicit and implicit information. *Journal of Literacy Research, 11*, 201–9.

Pearson, P. D., Moje, E., & Greenleaf, C. (2010). Literacy and science: each in the service of the other. *Science, 328*, 459–63.

Peracchi, K. A., & O'Brien, E. J. (2004). Character profiles and the activation of predictive inferences. *Memory & Cognition, 32*, 1044–52.

Perfetti, C. (2007). Reading ability: lexical quality to comprehension. *Scientific Studies of Reading, 11*, 357–83.

Perfetti, C., & Frishkoff, G. A. (2008).The neural bases of text and discourse processing. In B. Stemmer & H. A. Whitaker (eds.), *Handbook of the Neuroscience of Language* (pp. 165–74). Cambridge, MA: Elsevier.

Perfetti, C. A., & Hart, L. (2002). The lexical quality hypothesis. In L. Verhoeven, C. Elbro, & P. Reitsma (eds.), *Precursors of Functional Literacy* (pp. 189–213). Amsterdam/Philadelphia: John Benjamins.

Perfetti, C. A., Landi, N., & Oakhill, J. (2005). The acquisition of reading comprehension skill. In M. J. Snowling & C. Hulme (eds.), *The Science of Reading: A Handbook* (pp. 227–47). Oxford, UK: Blackwell.

Perfetti, C. A., Rouet, J.-F., & Britt, M. A. (1999). Towards a theory of documents representation. In H. van Oostendorp & S. R. Goldman (eds.), *The Construction of Mental Representations during Reading* (pp. 99–122). Mahwah, NJ: Erlbaum.

Perfetti, C., & Stafura, J. (2013). Word knowledge in a theory of reading comprehension. *Scientific Studies of Reading, 18*, 1–16.

Perfetti, C., Yang, C. L., & Schmalhofer, F. (2008). Comprehension skill and word-to-text integration processes. *Applied Cognitive Psychology, 22*, 303–18.

Prat, C. S., Mason, R. A., & Just, M. A. (2011). Individual differences in the neural basis of causal inferencing. *Brain and Language, 116*, 1–13.

Pressley, M., & McCormick, C. B. (1995). *Advanced Educational Psychology for Educators, Researchers, and Policymakers*. New York: HarperCollins.

Rawson, K. A., & Kintsch, W. (2002). How does background information improve memory for text content? *Memory & Cognition, 30*, 768–78.

Richter, T. (2011). Cognitive flexibility and epistemic validation in learning from multiple texts. In J. Elen, E. Stahl, R. Bromme, & G. Clarebout (eds.), *Links between Beliefs and Cognitive Flexibility* (pp. 125–40). Berlin: Springer.

Richter, T., Schroeder, S., & Wöhrmann, B. (2009). You don't have to believe everything you read: background knowledge permits fast and efficient validation of information. *Journal of Personality and Social Psychology, 96*, 538–58.

Sanchez, C. A., & Wiley, J. (2006). An examination of the seductive details effect in terms of working memory capacity. *Memory & Cognition, 34*, 344–55.

Sanders, T. J. M., & Noordman, L. G. M. (2000). The role of coherence relations and their linguistic markers in text processing. *Discourse Processes, 29*, 37–60.

Sanders, T., & Spooren, W. (2007). Discourse and text structure. In D. Geeraerts & H. Cuykens (eds.), *Handbook of Cognitive Linguistics* (pp. 916–43). Oxford University Press.

Sanford, A. J., Sanford, A. J., Molle, J., & Emmott, C. (2006). Shallow processing and attention capture in written and spoken discourse. *Discourse Processes*, *42*, 109–30.

Schank, R., & Abelson, R. (1977). *Scripts, Plans, Goals and Understanding: An Inquiry into Human Knowledge Structures*. Mahwah, NJ: Erlbaum.

Singer, M. (1994). Discourse inference processes. In M. A. Gernsbacher (ed.), *Handbook of Psycholinguistics* (pp. 479–515). San Diego, CA: Academic Press.

  (2006). Verification of text ideas during reading. *Journal of Memory and Language*, *54*, 574–91.

  (2013). Validation in reading comprehension. *Current Directions in Psychological Science*, *22*, 361–66.

Singer, M., & Halldorson, M. (1996). Constructing and validating motive bridging inferences. *Cognitive Psychology*, *30*, 1–38.

Singer, M., Halldorson, M., Lear, J. C., & Andrusiak, P. (1992). Validation of causal bridging inferences in discourse understanding. *Journal of Memory and Language*, *31*, 507–24.

Strasser, K., & del Rio, F. (2014). The role of comprehension monitoring, theory of mind, and vocabulary depth in predicting story comprehension and recall of kindergarten children. *Reading Research Quarterly*, *49*, 169–87.

Sundermeier, B. A., van den Broek, P., & Zwaan, R. A. (2005). Causal coherence and the availability of locations and objects during narrative comprehension. *Memory & Cognition*, *33*, 462–70.

Sundermeier, B. A., Virtue, S. M., Marsolek, C. J., & van den Broek, P. (2005). Evidence for dissociable neural mechanisms underlying inference generation in familiar and less-familiar scenarios. *Brain and Language*, *95*, 402–13.

Tilstra, J., McMaster, K., van den Broek, P., Kendeou, P., & Rapp, D. N. (2009). Simple but complex: Components of the simple view of reading across grade levels. *Journal of Research in Reading*, *32*, 383–401.

Tippett, C. D. (2010). Refutation text in science education: a review of two decades of research. *International Journal of Science and Mathematics Education*, *8*, 951–70.

Trabasso, T., Secco, T., & van den Broek, P. W. (1984). Causal cohesion and story coherence. In H. Mandl, N. L. Stein, & T. Trabasso (eds.), *Learning and Comprehension of Text* (pp. 83–111). Mahwah, NJ: Erlbaum.

Trabasso, T., & Sperry, L. (1985). Causal relatedness and importance of story events. *Journal of Memory and Language*, *24*, 595–611.

Trabasso T., & van den Broek, P. W. (1985). Causal thinking and the representation of narrative events. *Journal of Memory and Language*, *24*, 612–30.

Trabasso, T., van den Broek, P., & Suh, S. Y. (1989). Logical necessity and transitivity of causal relations in stories. *Discourse Processes*, *12*, 1–25.

Tzeng, Y., van den Broek, P., Kendeou, P., & Lee, C. (2005). The computational implementation of the Landscape model: modeling inferential processes and memory representations of text comprehension. *Behavior Research Methods*, *37*, 277–86.

Van Berkum, J. J., Brown, C. M., Zwitserlood, P., Kooijman, V., & Hagoort, P. (2005). Anticipating upcoming words in discourse: evidence from ERPs and reading times. *Journal of Experimental Psychology: Learning, Memory, and Cognition*, *31*, 443–67.

Van den Broek, P. W. (1988). The effects of causal relations and hierarchical position on the importance of story statements. *Journal of Memory and Language*, *27*, 1–22.

(1989). Causal reasoning and inference making in judging the importance of story statements. *Child Development*, *60*, 286–97.

(1990). Causal inferences in the comprehension of narrative texts. In A. C. Graesser & G. H. Bower (eds.), *Psychology of Learning and Motivation: Inferences and Text Comprehension* (pp. 175–96). New York: Academic Press.

(1994). Comprehension and memory of narrative texts: inferences and coherence. In M. A. Gernsbacher (ed.), *Handbook of Psycholinguistics* (pp. 539–88). New York: Academic Press.

(2005). Integrating memory-based and constructionist processes in accounts of reading comprehension. *Discourse Processes*, *39*, 299–316.

Van den Broek, P., Bohn-Gettler, C., Kendeou, P., Carlson, S., & White, M. J. (2011). When a reader meets a text: the role of standards of coherence in reading comprehension. In M. T. McCrudden, J. P. Magliano, & G. Schraw (eds.), *Text Relevance and Learning from Text* (pp. 123–40). Greenwich, CT: Information Age Publishing.

Van den Broek, P., & Espin, C. A. (2012). Connecting cognitive theory and assessment: Measuring individual differences in reading comprehension. *School Psychology Review*, *41*, 315–25.

Van den Broek, P., & Gustafson, M. (1999). Comprehension and memory for texts: three generations of research. In S. R. Goldman, A. C. Graesser & P. van den Broek (eds.), *Narrative Comprehension, Causality, and Coherence: Essays in Honor of Tom Trabasso* (pp. 15–34). Mahwah, NJ: Erlbaum.

Van den Broek, P. W., Helder, A., & van Leijenhorst, L. (2013). Sensitivity to structural centrality: developmental and individual differences in reading comprehension skills. In M. A. Britt, S. R. Goldman, & J-F Rouet (eds.), *Reading: From Words to Multiple Texts* (pp. 132–46). New York: Routledge.

Van den Broek, P., & Kendeou, P. (2008). Cognitive processes in comprehension of science texts: the role of co-activation in confronting misconceptions. *Applied Cognitive Psychology*, *22*, 335–51.

Van den Broek, P., Kendeou, P., Lousberg, S., & Visser, G. (2011). Preparing for reading comprehension: fostering text comprehension skills in preschool and early elementary school children. *International Electronic Journal of Elementary Education*, *4*, 259–68.

Van den Broek, P., & Lorch, Jr., R. F. (1993). Network representations of causal relations in memory for narrative texts: evidence from primed recognition. *Discourse Processes*, *16*, 75–98.

Van den Broek, P., Lorch, Jr., R. F., Linderholm, T., & Gustafson, M. (2001). The effects of readers' goals on inference generation and memory for texts. *Memory & Cognition*, *29*, 1081–7.

Van den Broek, P., Lorch, E. P., & Thurlow, R. (1996). Children's and adults' memory for television stories: the role of causal factors, story-grammar categories, and hierarchical level. *Child Development*, *67*, 3010–28.

Van den Broek, P., Lynch, J. S., Naslund, J., Ievers-Landis, C. E., & Verduin, K. (2003). The development of comprehension of main ideas in narratives: evidence from the selection of titles. *Journal of Educational Psychology*, *95*, 707–18.

Van den Broek, P., Rapp, D., & Kendeou, P. (2005). Integrating memory-based and constructionist processes in accounts of reading comprehension. *Discourse Processes*, *39*, 299–316.

Van den Broek, P. W., Risden, K., Fletcher, C. R., & Thurlow, R. (1996) A 'landscape' view of reading: fluctuating patterns of activation and the construction of a stable memory representation. In B. K. Britton & A. C. Graesser (eds.), *Models of Understanding Text* (pp. 165–87). Mahwah , NJ: Erlbaum.

Van den Broek, P., Risden, K., & Husebye-Hartmann, E. (1995). The role of reader's standards of coherence in the generation of inferences during reading. In E. P. Lorch & E. J. O'Brien (eds.), *Sources of Coherence in Reading* (pp. 353–74). Mahwah, NJ: Erlbaum.

Van den Broek, P., Rohleder, L., & Narváez, D. (1996). Causal inferences in the comprehension of literary texts. In R. J. Kreuz & M. S. MacNealy (eds.), *Empirical Approaches to Literature and Aesthetics* (pp. 179–200). Norwood, NJ: Ablex.

Van den Broek, P. W., & Trabasso, T. (1986). Causal networks versus goal hierarchies in summarizing text. *Discourse Processes*, *9*, 1–15.

Van den Broek, P., White, M. J., Kendeou, P., & Carlson, S. (2009). Reading between the lines: developmental and individual differences in cognitive processes in reading comprehension. In R. Wagner, C. Schatschneider, & C. Phythian-Sence (eds.), *Beyond Decoding: The Behavioral and Biological Foundations of Reading Comprehension* (pp. 107–23). New York: Guilford Press.

Van den Broek, P., Young, M., Tzeng, Y., & Linderholm, T. (1999). The Landscape model of reading: inferences and the online construction of a memory representation. In H. van Oostendorp & S. R. Goldman (eds.), *The Construction of Mental Representations during Reading* (pp. 71–98). Mahwah, NJ: Erlbaum.

Virtue, S., van den Broek, P., & Linderholm, T. (2006). Hemispheric processing of inferences: the effects of textual constraint and working memory capacity. *Memory & Cognition*, *34*, 1341–54.

Whitehurst, G. J., & Lonigan, C. J. (1998). Child development and emergent literacy. *Child Development*, *69*, 848–72.

Whitney, P., Ritchie, B. G., & Clark, M. B. (1991). Working-memory capacity and the use of elaborative inferences in text comprehension. *Discourse Processes*, *14*, 133–45.

Whitney, P., Ritchie, B. G., & Crane, R. S. (1992). The effect of foregrounding on readers' use of predictive inferences. *Memory & Cognition, 20,* 424–32.

Wiley, J., & Myers, J. L. (2003): Availability and accessibility of information and causal inferences from scientific text. *Discourse Processes, 36,* 109–29.

Williams, J. P. (1993). Comprehension of students with and without learning disabilities: Identification of narrative themes and idiosyncratic text representations. *Journal of Educational Psychology, 85,* 631–41.

Wolman, C., van den Broek, P. W., & Lorch, R. F. (1997). Effects of causal structure on immediate and delayed story recall by children with mild mental retardation, children with learning disabilities, and children without disabilities. *Journal of Special Education, 30,* 439–55.

Zwaan, R. A., Magliano, J. P., & Graesser, A. C. (1995). Dimensions of situation model construction in narrative comprehension. *Journal of Experimental Psychology: Learning, Memory, and Cognition, 21,* 386–97.

6   Emotion inferences during reading: going beyond the tip of the iceberg

Pascal Gygax and Christelle Gillioz

Introduction

At Hornsgatan she happened to glance towards Kaffebar and saw Blomkvist coming out with Berger in tow. He said something, and she laughed, putting her arm around his waist and kissing his cheek. They turned down Brannkyrkagatan in the direction of Bellmansgatan. Their body language left no room for misinterpretations – it was obvious what they had in mind. The pain was so immediate and so fierce that Lisbeth stopped in mid-stride, incapable of movement. Part of her wanted to rush after them. She wanted to take the metal sign and use the sharp edge to cleave Berger's head in two. She did nothing as thoughts swirled through her mind. Analysis of consequences. Finally she calmed down. 'What a pathetic fool you are, Salander,' she said out loud.   (Laarson, 2011, pp. 589–90)

Though Swedish author Stieg Laarson's true literary intentions may never be known to us, his award-winning series, as illustrated by this passage, conveys a large amount of affective information. From Michael Blomkvist and Erika Berger's apparent happiness to Lisbeth Sallander's despair and anger, this passage suggests a rather large panel of possible emotions felt by the protagonists. It may seem quite tricky to monitor all possible emotions while reading, yet research presented in this chapter seems to indicate that readers encode the emotions of the main protagonist quite readily.[1]

Interestingly, some authors have argued that the affective status of the (main) protagonist (explicit or implied) could guide our reading (e.g., Miall, 1989) (1) by giving us a self-referential context to attribute specific meanings to text, (2) by providing us with relevant information to better link different elements of the text or (3) to anticipate the protagonists' future actions. Though this idea is rather undisputed, the exact processes that enable readers to construct a representation of the main protagonist's emotional status are still unclear.

---

[1] Surprisingly, very little has been done to investigate emotion inferences associated with multiple protagonists.

In this chapter, we intend to follow the path that has guided the literature on this topic, gradually shifting from a mostly psycholinguistic focus to a broader interdisciplinary scope.

Grounding work

In 1992, Morton Ann Gernsbacher, Hill Goldsmith, and Rachel Robertson conducted a study soon to be considered as the most prominent one in the field. In their study, composed of three experiments, they investigated readers' propensity to infer emotions that are not explicitly mentioned in the text. To investigate this issue, they presented participants with short narratives such as:

John, who always made good grades, had just transferred to a new school. He wished he had a hobby to occupy his time, or something to keep him busy in the afternoons until he made more friends. After all, his new school was simply not very much of a challenge. And today was no different. As he walked home, he thought about another afternoon, just sitting around watching stupid reruns on TV.

In this particular narrative, the authors were interested in the possibility that readers integrate the emotion *boredom* into their mental representation of the situation. Interestingly, like most other authors in the field, they have very broadly considered the notion of *emotion*, as illustrated by the inclusion of *boredom* here as a possible emotion. In their first experiment, the authors presented target sentences with either a matching emotion (e.g., *It didn't take an expert to see the boredom written all over his face*) or a mismatching one (e.g., *It didn't take an expert to see the curiosity written all over his face*). Self-paced reading times were recorded on these target sentences, and the results showed that participants were faster to read sentences that comprised a matching emotion than those with a mismatching emotion. After the authors ran analyses to dismiss a pure surprise effect, these results constituted a strong indication that readers had inferred the main protagonist's emotion when reading the narrative. In their second experiment, instead of merely comparing emotions that could be considered as semantically opposite, they contrasted emotions that shared valence but were different (e.g., *boredom* vs. *anger*). Their idea was to see whether readers were only inferring something that would resemble *valence* (i.e., *feel good* vs. *feel bad*), signalling a rather superficial representation of emotions. This was not the case: the difference between the matching and the mismatching sentences was still reliable, though slightly smaller. In their final experiment, the authors shifted to a somewhat more online measure, a naming task, to rule out any effects that could be merely imputed to a forced activation due to the presence of target sentences comprising emotion terms. The results showed a reliable difference in the naming speed of target emotions between matching and mismatching terms. In a different study, Gernsbacher and Robertson (1992) confirmed that the differences in reading times between matching and mismatching target sentences were not merely dependent on the ease with which incoming target sentences were mapped but also on the activation of relevant emotion knowledge during reading. Gernsbacher and colleagues showed that readers do infer emotions during reading, and that these emotions go beyond simple valence.

Follow-up studies based on these conclusions were quite numerous and revealed a wide range of processes. For instance, deVega, Leon, and Diaz (1996) showed that readers readily update their representation of characters' emotions if needed. In their first experiment, they presented participants with two-part narratives, where the second part of each narrative either reinforced the emotion presented in the first part (i.e., *cumulative* context), or deviated from it (i.e., *shifting* context). For example, in one of the narratives, a character is presented as feeling *insecure*, and in the second part, something happens to make him fell *flattered*. The authors were interested in examining whether a *match vs. mismatch* effect in a target sentence presented after the first part of the narrative would be any different than one in a target sentence presented after the second part of the narrative, especially in the shifting context. deVega et al. (1996) found that when the second part of the narrative reinforced the emotion presented in the first part, the mismatch effect after the second part was even stronger than after the first part. Importantly, in the shifting context, the mismatch effect after the second part depended on the emotion presented in the second part (and not in the first part), suggesting that readers had updated their mental representations of emotion. Still, the authors argued that the emotion in the first part could just have faded away as readers process the second (shifting context) part of the narrative. In their second experiment, the authors ruled out this possibility. They simply extended the length of the narratives by adding neutral information to them and examined mismatching effects at the end of these extended narratives. Results showed similar mismatching effects at the end of these extended narratives, supporting the idea that the representation of the main character's emotions remains activated beyond local context.

In another series of experiments, deVega, Diaz and Leon (1997) showed that readers' representation of the main character's emotion was bound to the main character's knowledge of the situation portrayed in the text. In their first experiment,[2] participants were presented with

---

[2] The other two experiments examined different ways to measure emotion inferences and go beyond the scope of this brief presentation of the authors' work.

narratives containing information of which the main character was aware, as well as information only available to readers that could contradict the main character's emotional reaction. For example, in one narrative, a girlfriend is suggested as feeling sympathetic for her boyfriend because he has to work long hours and is late. In fact, he is just engrossed in a poker match. Results indicated that when the main character was ignorant of the information provided to readers (i.e., the boyfriend is engrossed in a poker match), they seemed to disregard it when constructing a representation of the main character's emotion (i.e., the emotion sympathetic is encoded).

Gernsbacher, Hallada and Robertson (1998) showed that the processes by which readers build these mental representations of emotion were rather *automatic*. In a series of experiments, they examined mismatch effects when participants had to perform different interfering tasks while reading narratives such as those presented earlier. They showed that the mismatch effects found in earlier studies were always present, even when the interfering task was highly demanding (i.e., remembering four randomly presented consonants whilst reading an entire narrative), suggesting that emotion inferences are rather effortless and automatic.

Although these studies provided us with invaluable insight into our understanding of emotion inferences, one important question remained: What exactly do readers encode when making emotion inferences? Gygax, Oakhill and Garnham (2003) addressed this issue, taking a somewhat indirect approach. Instead of trying to assess the information in readers' mental representations directly, they tried to assess if emotion inferences were specific enough to lead to representations containing particular and precise emotion terms. In their experiment, they used the same methodology as Gernsbacher et al.'s (1992) first and second experiments. However, instead of contrasting semantically opposite emotions, Gygax et al. compared target sentences containing emotions that shared several semantic features (i.e., more than just valence). For example, they compared target sentences containing *bored* and *curious* (as in Gernsbacher et al., 1992), as well as sentences containing synonym emotions (e.g., *unchallenged*) and similar emotions (e.g., *lonely*). The latter comparisons were the most interesting ones. Even though they clearly differed from the primary matching emotions tested in previous studies, they were still possible continuations. Results indicated a clear *match vs. mismatch* effect (e.g., *curious* was difficult to integrate), yet there were no differences between all matching emotions (primary, synonym and similar). Though the authors did not directly access the information included in readers' mental representations, they concluded that this information was *at least* broad enough to encompass a wide range of possible emotions, dismissing previous (implicit or explicit)[3] claims that readers' representations of emotions were specific. In fact, this conclusion echoed research on predictive inferences. As contextual support increases for a particular predictive inference, the specificity of this inference also increases (e.g., Lassonde and O'Brien, 2009), meaning that the number of lexical items possible for an inference decreases. We will come back to this issue later in the chapter.

Although these results were quite informative, two important issues remained unresolved. First, the exact content of readers' mental representations of emotion was still unclear; and the conditions that could facilitate a more specific representation were unspecified. If the latter issue seemed more accessible, and unsurprisingly has generated more empirical work (as presented later), the former is far more complicated. Gygax, Tapiero and Carruzzo (2007) attempted to access this information by grounding their study on the widely accepted idea that emotions are composed of different components (e.g., Ellsworth, 1991; Frijda, 1986; Scherer, 2005) and that readers may only integrate part of the emotion construct into their mental representations of emotions (i.e., the *pars pro toto* [the part for the whole] principle from Hermann, 1982). Gygax et al. (2007) suggested that one of the most prominent *parts* that may constitute a good candidate could be *behavioural information*. Briefly, they argued that when readers process a narrative about a character that, for example, may feel *sad*, they are more likely to infer *cry* (or a related behaviour) than *sad* per se (see Box 6.1 for an example). To test this idea, they simply contrasted target sentences containing matching and mismatching emotion terms to target sentences containing matching and mismatching behaviours. Interestingly, they found that self-paced reading time differences were much larger when the target sentences contained matching versus mismatching behaviours than when they contained emotion terms. These results were important in three ways. First, they provided us with some explanation of the lack of specificity found earlier (Gygax et al., 2003). Second, they addressed the content of readers' mental representations more precisely by suggesting some *pars pro toto* principles, whereby the information in readers' mental representations may constitute only part of what one would call an emotion inference. Finally, they signalled the need for psycholinguists interested in this topic to better address and understand the way emotional inferences are

---

[3] For example, Gernsbacher et al. (1992) stated that "readers' representations of characters' emotional states are very explicit; readers do not simply represent that an outcome was positive or negative" (p. 108).

constructed. This final issue is most crucial, and we will come back to it in detail. Before entering the heart of this matter, let us consider several empirical attempts at identifying the conditions facilitating emotion inferences in general as well as emotion inferences that are more specific and complex.

Gygax, Garnham and Oakhill (2004) suggested that one of the problems in previous research (including their own) was that the narratives that had been used did not carry enough information to grant adequate resources to build complex or specific representations of emotions. To explain the processes underlying their suggestion, they introduced the notion that, as emotions may be constructed from a set of components (e.g., Alvarado, 1998; Clore and Ortony, 1988; Ortony and Clore, 1989; Ortony and Turner, 1990), such as valence; a specific emotion can only be reached if all necessary components are present in the narratives and appraised appropriately. They therefore expanded previously used narratives to ensure that more emotion information was provided and identifiable; however, they did not precisely control the exact number of components present in the narratives (and this will be discussed later). Basically, they presented participants with experimental narratives that were twice as long as the narratives used previously and conveyed more information pertaining to the main protagonist's emotion status (see Box 6.2 for an example). In the first experiment, participants were presented with the extended narratives along with four emotions. One emotion (Matching) had been tested in previous experiments (including that of Gernsbacher et al., 1992), one was a

---

Box 6.1   Example of an experimental narrative used in Gygax et al. (2007)

NARRATIVE

Suzanne came back from her regular visit to the nursing home. She walked slowly from the nursing home to her place. She thought of the days with her grandmother with a heavy heart. She had trouble holding back her tears when thinking of her grandmother alone in her room.

TARGET SENTENCES

Matching emotion: As you could expect, Suzanne was feeling sad.
Mismatching emotion: As you could expect, Suzanne was feeling happy.
Matching behaviour: She sat on her sofa, wrapped in a blanket.
Mismatching behaviour: She danced all night, as she was always the one to show others how to party.

Box 6.2   Example of an extended narrative used in Gygax et al. (2004)

SHORT VERSION OF THE NARRATIVE (FROM GYGAX ET AL., 2003)

For Trevor, this had to be the best week of his 18-year life. Tonight he would be graduating first in his high school class. Just yesterday he received a formal acceptance letter from Harvard. And he had just hung up the phone after talking with someone very special who had said that she'd go with him to the graduation party.

EXTENDED VERSION OF THE NARRATIVE

It was Friday afternoon. For Trevor, this had to be the best week of his 18-year life. Tonight he would be graduating first in his high school class. Just yesterday he received a formal acceptance letter from Harvard. Harvard had been Trevor's first choice. He had worked very hard for it, and finally he'd been accepted. The acceptance letter also mentioned that he could apply for a scholarship. That scholarship would help him a lot. And he had just hung up the phone after talking with someone very special who had said that she'd go with him to the graduation party.

TARGET SENTENCES

Matching: happy
Matching synonym: pleased
Matching similar: proud
Mismatching: depressed

synonym of it, one was similar to but not synonymous with it, and finally one was simply a mismatching emotion. When explicitly asked to choose the best-suited emotion out of the four for each narrative (Experiment 1), participants chose the Matching one more often, implying a specific representation. However, when those emotions were embedded in target sentences in a self-paced reading experiment (Experiment 2), there was no sign of specificity. The reading times of target sentences containing matching, synonymous and similar emotions were all equivalent, and all three were different from the reading times of target sentences containing mismatching emotions. In the same paper (Experiments 3 and 4), the authors also tried to force the use of extra cognitive resources by making the emotion inferences needed for comprehension (i.e., readers *had* to infer the emotion). The narratives were constructed to convey ambiguous information (see Box 6.3 for an example) that could be resolved by inferring the main character's emotional state. Again, the results, at least online, were not different from those of previous experiments, implying that the processes at stake were quite impermeable to the content of the experimental narratives, and that they were quite constant across experiments.

Gillioz, Gygax and Tapiero (2012) questioned this conclusion by suggesting that most research on emotion inferences may have missed important individual differences, and that results found so far, especially those addressing the specificity of emotion inferences, could just be due

---

**Box 6.3   Example of an ambiguous narrative
used in Gygax et al. (2004) focused on the emotion of sad.
In the ambiguous version, the ambiguous part is in italics.**

SHORT VERSION OF THE NARRATIVE (FROM GYGAX ET AL., 2003)

Pam had just returned from her regular Tuesday visit to the nursing home. Today, there had been several problems. One elderly patient had died. Another had fallen and broken her hip. And all the faces had looked wrinkled, withered, and neglected. The sheer magnitude of the problems simply overcame Pam. When she had wanted to see the patient with the broken hip, she was told that the patient had been transferred to the city hospital. The injury was more serious than initially thought. Pam entered the empty room. She knew the patient well. Pam used to bring that patient fresh flowers every Tuesday morning. She always enjoyed having a chat with her. Now Pam was sitting on the patient's bed. A tear ran slowly down her cheek.

AMBIGUOUS VERSION OF THE NARRATIVE

Pam was working for an organisation helping the elderly. The organisation was in close contact with different nursing homes. Today, Pam was visiting one of the nursing homes. She was sitting on an empty bed. For a while, she looked at her hands. It was Pam's regular Tuesday visit to the nursing home. Today, there had been several problems. One elderly patient had died. Another had fallen and broken her hip. And all the faces had looked wrinkled, withered, and neglected. The sheer magnitude of the problems had simply overcome Pam. When she had wanted to see the patient with the broken hip, she was told that the patient had been transferred to the city hospital. The injury was more serious than initially thought. Pam had entered the empty room. She knew the patient well. Pam used to bring that patient fresh flowers every Tuesday morning. She always enjoyed having a chat with her.

to some confounding factor. Attempts to consider individual differences had been quite sparse in the literature, yet Komeda and Kusumi (2006) made a very good attempt at addressing this issue. In their study, the participants were asked to read emotional narratives describing relief- or worry-related situations. In half of the narratives, a shift related to the described emotion appeared in the middle of the text (e.g., a protagonist is anxious about an exam as he has not studied at all, yet when receiving the exam, he notices that the questions are easy) whereas in the other half the whole narratives were consistent with the described emotion. After each narrative, the participants were asked to rate how personally similar to and empathic towards the protagonist they felt. Results showed that readers who were highly engaged in the narratives (i.e., high empathy and high personal similarity) were more sensitive to shifts in the text. In all, Komeda and Kusumi (2006) showed that high-empathy readers may have better dispositions to attribute emotions to protagonists. Following the same line of research, and based on Gygax et al. (2007), Gillioz et al. (2012) investigated (1) general working memory, (2) spatial working memory, (3) empathy and (4) simulation as possible factors influencing emotion inferences. Working memory was evaluated with Daneman and Carpenter's (1980) French version of the Reading Span Test (RST) (Delaloye, Ludwig, Borella, Chicherio and de Ribaupierre, 2007) as well as with a standardized version of the Corsi Block-Tapping Task (Kessels, van Zandvoort, Postma, Kappelle and de Haan, 2000). Empathy was assessed with a French version of the Interpersonal Reactivity Index (IRI) by Davis (1980; 1983) and finally, simulation was examined by explicitly asking (in the second part of the experiment) participants to simulate the situation portrayed in the text. Out of these different factors, only spatial working memory was a determinant, especially in the prevalence of behavioral elements included in readers' mental representations.

Intermediate conclusions

Globally, these studies seemed to indicate that readers do infer the main protagonist's emotional status when reading narratives in a rather spontaneous way (they even update their representations if needed), yet none of them managed to clearly identify the exact information that may be integrated in readers' mental representations. Early work on the topic seemed to indicate rather specific representations (e.g., Gernsbacher et al., 1992) yet later work signaled rather general representations (e.g., Gygax et al., 2004), inasmuch as the content of readers' representations seemed in line with a relatively large panel of possible emotions.

Though the term "superficial" was actually used to define readers' mental representations of emotions (e.g., Gygax et al., 2004), it may have been misleading as it gave the feeling that readers were not able (or were not sufficiently proficient) to reach more complex and specific emotion representations. As recently argued (Gillioz and Gygax, 2013), this is probably not true, even to the point that readers may actually be quite good at adapting their representations to the quality and quantity of information given in the narratives, following the *good enough representations* principle (Sanford and Graesser, 2006) or even the *granularity* hypothesis (Sanford and Garrod, 2005). Though the latter hypothesis has been mostly cited in conjunction with predictive inferences, its core assumption – at a "crude" level of granularity, the representation is rather general and can be captured by different lexical items – is highly relevant to the idea of un-specificity of emotion inferences.

A new way to consider emotion narratives

Gillioz and Gygax (2013) suggested that two main problems may have led researchers to make slightly inaccurate conclusions about emotion inferences. First, they argued that most researchers have underestimated the very construct of emotions when generating their experimental narratives; and second, they argued that the habitual *match versus mismatch* paradigm (used in most studies on the topic) was not giving access to finely tuned inference processes.

The former issue directly addressed the way researchers created their experimental materials and how much control they had over the emotional content of their experimental narratives. In fact, they argued that, habitually, only a small amount of information was provided as to the exact emotional content of these narratives. In most cases, researchers wrote their materials and pretested them to ensure appropriate relevancy, both in terms of possible target emotions and topic. However, Gillioz and Gygax (2013) argued that by doing so, researchers most likely missed some important emotion information that might enable readers to construct more complex or specific representations of emotions. To avoid missing such information, they suggested that emotion narratives should be based on the very components of emotion (e.g., appraisal, physiological reaction, action tendency) thoroughly described in emotion research as constitutive elements of emotional experiences (e.g., Ekman, 1977; Frijda, 1986; Scherer, 2005). To Gillioz and Gygax (2013), the work of Klaus Scherer and colleagues (e.g., Fontaine, Scherer, Roesch and Ellsworth, 2007; Fontaine, Scherer and Soriano, 2013; Scherer, 2005) was particularly appropriate for this, as it precisely outlined the semantic field of emotions. Based on the componential theories of emotion (e.g., Ellsworth and Scherer, 2003; Ortony, Clore and Collins, 1988; Scherer, 1984; 2005), Scherer and colleagues identified the most relevant emotion features of five grounding components: (1) the Cognitive, (2) the Neurophysiological, (3) the Motivational, (4) the Motor Expression and (5) the Subjective Feeling components. These features constitute semantic elements that define the components of any given emotion. For example, the feature *to smile* is constitutive of the Motor Expression component and strongly characteristic of the emotion *happy*. Very importantly, through the GRID instrument (the description of which goes beyond the scope of this chapter) Fontaine et al. (2007) defined not only all the features constitutive of emotion experiences, but also their weight, in terms of relatedness, associated to a set of twenty-four emotions.

Gillioz and Gygax (2013) constructed experimental emotional narratives based on Fontaine et al.'s (2007) components profiles of twenty-four emotions. By doing this, they ensured that the emotion construct present in the narratives was as relevant as possible. In addition, they varied the degree of congruency of the emotion context provided in the narratives (see Box 6.4 for an example), by including either all components of emotion experiences or only three components. Manipulating the number of emotion components in the narratives enabled them to address the second issue, namely the overreliance in previous research on the *match versus mismatch* paradigm. By manipulating the number of features presented in the experimental narratives, they were able to keep the same target sentences across conditions. For example, a target sentence evaluating the emotion *happy* (i.e., *John felt happy*) was preceded by a high saliency context in one condition – all defining components being present and described by their most salient features (e.g., *to smile* for the Expression component) – and was preceded by a moderate yet still congruent saliency context in another condition – three out of five components being present and described by their most salient features. Consequently, only matching emotions, that differed in their saliency (e.g., *high* vs. *moderate*), were tested, enabling a more finely tuned look at the processes at stake.

Gillioz and Gygax (2013) expected faster reading times of target sentences in the high saliency condition, compared to target sentences in the lesser salient conditions. However, the effects were quite the opposite. Participants' reading times were significantly longer for target sentences that were preceded by high saliency contexts. These results forced the authors to consider alternative interpretations of self-paced reading times, at least alternative to the habitual *faster* = *more likely to have been previously integrated* interpretation, that were actually heavily based

---

Box 6.4   Example of an emotional narrative used in Gillioz and Gygax (2013) in two saliency conditions. The optimal condition has all components of emotion experiences and the moderate version has only three components (in italics are the filler sentences replacing the two removed component sentences)

OPTIMAL VERSION

As she was arguing with her best friend, Emily did not agree with her and could not help shouting at her. As soon as she heard what she said, Emily fell silent. At the same time, she felt a knot in her stomach. Emily knew she could have avoided this situation. She really wanted to disappear. At that moment, Emily felt bad. Emily felt guilty (target sentence).

MODERATE VERSION

As she was arguing with her best friend, Emily did not agree with her and could not help shouting at her. *The two friends were at Emily's place. They were talking about what had happened that day.* Emily knew she could have avoided this situation. She really wanted to disappear. At that moment, Emily felt bad. Emily felt guilty (target sentence).

---

on the mismatching condition. Among these alternative interpretations, one seemed of particular interest; it differentiated information *integration* from shallower information *mapping*. In sum, information that readers deem necessary for integration into their mental representations (i.e., highly specific and relevant information) requires more attention resources, and hence takes longer to process.

Besides suggesting that readers' representations can be specific when given the appropriate emotional content, this interpretation suggests that reading times (here self-paced and eye-movement monitoring) may have to be considered more cautiously. In fact, a closer look at the data from the three matching conditions in Gygax et al. (2004) suggests that their results leaned towards a similar trend; their lack of specificity might have been triggered by the presence of the mismatching condition, undermining differences between matching conditions.

Difficult issues and theoretical perspectives

From all the studies presented so far, the complexity of emotion inferences is quite apparent. In summary, we believe that the difficulty of defining the content of readers' mental representations of emotion, or even the major difficulty in defining emotions, may have deterred researchers from investigating emotion inferences and their applied perspectives. Compared to research on different types of inferences, which may actually share similar inferential processes (e.g., predictive inferences), research on this topic is rather sparse. One important additional difficulty, which has never really been directly addressed within the psycholinguistic realm, is whether readers need to actually *feel* emotions (i.e., by some kind of self-referential experience) to understand characters' emotional states or whether the main protagonist's emotional state can be *deduced* by some logical mental process (e.g., O'Rorke and Ortony, 1994, suggested that reasoning about emotions takes the form of *abduction*). As such, the most drastic consequence to this particular issue is that implicit measures, such as those used in mental imagery to investigate the functional neuroanatomy linked to the construction of situation models including the protagonist's emotion, are very difficult to assess (as illustrated by the work of Ferstl and colleagues; Ferstl, Rinck and von Cramon, 2005; Ferstl and von Cramon, 2007). One would have a rather large panel of mental processes to address when looking at emotion inferences. This is especially true when considering more complex emotions (e.g., anxiety, confusion) for which context may be even more important.

However, we suggest that researchers should actually consider these seemingly problematic issues as true empirical questions. The difficulty of distinguishing experiential mapping from more straightforward (so to speak) reasoning processes may actually be challenging to psycholinguists and others because emotion inferences, as with other inferences necessary for comprehension, most likely consist of a network of cross-modal representations. In this sense, the embodied cognition framework provides a particularly pertinent background for future studies on emotion inferences. Given that emotions are embodied by nature (e.g., Niedenthal, Barsalou, Ric and Krauth-Gruber, 2005) and that mental models are perceptual (e.g., Barsalou, 1999; Glenberg, 1999; Glenberg, Meyer and Lindem, 1987; Zwaan, 2004), researchers interested in emotion inferences may well consider embodiment both in terms of theoretical as well as methodological background. To illustrate a potential strength from broadening classical emotion inference research to adjacent fields, Niedenthal, Winkielman, Mondillon and Vermeulen (2009) showed that blocking the activation of facial muscle characteristics of given emotions impaired the comprehension of related emotion words. Havas, Glenberg and Rinck (2007) demonstrated a similar interference effect on the comprehension of emotion sentences when blocking facial muscles. Along the same line of thinking, Havas, Glenberg, Gutowski, Lucarelli and Davidson (2010) showed that patients treated with botulinum toxin-A (i.e., a substance that paralyzes muscles) were slower to comprehend anger sentences (the content of which would require the paralysed muscles for full comprehension), yet were equally as fast to comprehend happy or sad sentences as nonpatients. Further targeting simulation processes at the discourse level will undeniably add valuable insights into the comprehension and construction of emotion inferences.

Applied perspectives

The apparent complexity that has accompanied studies on emotion inferences has made research into the potential applications of our understanding of emotion inferential processes quite difficult. In a sense, this is unfortunate, as one can easily see how understanding the way readers process affective information in text may prove to be invaluable, both in terms of the identification of early emotion comprehension difficulties (or more global comprehension difficulties) as well as the propensity of some of the population to be better at representing emotions. As a matter of fact, Gygax, Wagner-Egger, Parris, Seiler and Hauert (2008) did address the latter issue by showing that elite football players (from the highest professional division in Switzerland) as well as low-level players (from the lowest amateur division in Switzerland) were more inclined to build mental representations of emotion when reading football situations than mid-level football players (from the semi-professional division). The latter were more inclined to include information about the *position of others*. The authors argued that in football, emotions (i.e., emotion inferences) were dependent on players' expertise. More precisely, they argued that high-level football players used emotions to complement their skills, low-level football players used them to compensate for their skills, and that mid-level players needed to inhibit this information to make sure it was not detrimental to the development of their technical skills.

To our knowledge very little attention has been devoted to the identification of early emotion comprehension difficulties. One exception is Blanc (2010), who investigated children aged five to seven and a possible developmental trend in the reliance on emotion inferences to guide comprehension. In her experiment, children were orally presented with three tales, and after each tale, they had to judge whether a series of fourteen statements were compliant or not with the tale (half were true and half were false). Six of the statements (three true and three false) were related to the main character's emotional state. The other

statements were related to causality and space. Even when her participants seemed to show more accurate responses on causality and spatial
statements, five-year-olds were particularly attentive to behavioural
expressions of emotions, whereas older children were also attentive to
other emotional dimensions. The author argued that younger children's
sensitivity to behavioural expressions of emotions is corroborated by a
number of studies showing the importance of facial expression in the
early development of emotion understanding (e.g., Harris, 2000).

These two examples, of course, do not constitute the only areas where
emotion inferences could prove to be valuable assets to our understanding of the mental processes involved. In fact, there is a plethora of
possible domains that may benefit from research on emotion inferences.
One good example is the understanding of bilingualism, or more generally, multilingualism, and its relation to emotion inferences or, more
broadly put, emotion understanding. In this sense, emotion inferences
would not only constitute interesting markers of language proficiency,
but also interesting indicators of the social representation shifts that
readers and speakers of different languages may readily undergo.

Concluding comment

In this chapter, we raised different issues with the investigation of emotion inferences from text. First, and paralleling research on predictive
inferences, we argued that spontaneous emotion inferences might be
quite general, especially if the context does not grant specific emotion
representations. Second, and related to the first issue, we suggest that
more attention to research on the very construct of emotions may enable
us to identify more precisely the contextual parameters needed for
readers to build more specific (and maybe more complex) representations of emotions. Third and finally, we argued that the difficulties
associated with the study of emotion inferences might be challenging,
especially to those researchers interested in, or even attracted by, interdisciplinary approaches to reading comprehension.

REFERENCES

Alvarado, N. (1998). A reconsideration of the structure of the emotion lexicon.
    Motivation and Emotion, 22, 329–44.
Barsalou, L. W. (1999). Language comprehension: archival memory or
    preparation for situated action? *Discourse Processes*, 28, 61–80.
Blanc, N. (2010). The comprehension of stories between 5 and 7 years: what
    representation of emotional information? *Canadian Journal of Experimental
    Psychology*, 64, 256–65.

Clore, G. L., & Ortony, A. (1988). The semantics of the affective lexicon. In V. Hamilton, G. H. Bower, & N. H. Frijda (eds.), *Cognitive Perspectives on Emotion and Motivation*. Amsterdam: Springer.

Daneman, M., & Carpenter, P. A. (1980). Individual differences in working memory and reading. *Journal of Verbal Learning and Verbal Behavior, 19*, 450–66.

Davis, M. H. (1980). A multidimensional approach to individual differences in empathy. *JSAS Catalog of Selected Documents in Psychology, 10*, 85.

(1983). Measuring individual differences in empathy: evidence for a multidimensional approach. *Journal of Personality and Social Psychology, 44*, 113–26.

de Vega, M., Diaz, J. M. & Leon, I. (1997). To know or not to know: comprehending protagonists' beliefs and their emotional consequences. *Discourse Processes, 23*, 169–92.

de Vega, M., Leon, I. & Diaz, J. M. (1996). The representation of changing emotions in reading comprehension. *Cognition and Emotion, 10*, 303–22.

Delaloye, C., Ludwig, C., Borella, E., Chicherio, C. & de Ribaupierre, A. (2008). The Reading Span as a measure of working memory capacity: norms based on a French speaking population of 775 younger and older adults. *Revue européenne de psychologie appliquée, 58*, 89–103.

(2007). L'empan de Lecture comme épreuve mesurant la capacité de mémoire de travail: Normes basées sur une population francophone de 775 adultes jeunes et âgés. *Revue Européenne de Psychologie Appliquée, 58*(2), 89–103.

Ekman, P. (1977). Biological and cultural contributions to body and facial movement. In J. Blacking (ed.), *The Anthropology of the Body* (pp. 34–84). London: Academic Press.

Ellsworth, P. C. (1991). Some implications of cognitive appraisal theories of emotion. In K. T. Strongman (ed.), *International Review of Studies on Emotion* (pp. 143–61). New York: Wiley.

Ellsworth, P. C., & Scherer, K. R. (2003). Appraisal processes in emotion. In R. J. Davidson, K. R. Scherer & H. H. Goldsmith (eds.), *Handbook of Affective Sciences* (pp. 572–95). New York: Oxford University Press.

Ferstl, E. C., Rinck, M., & Cramon, D. Y. (2005). Emotional and temporal aspects of situation model processing during text comprehension: an event-related fMRI study. *Journal of Cognitive Neuroscience, 17*, 724–39.

Ferstl, E. C., & Von Cramon, D. Y. (2007). Time, space and emotion: fMRI reveals content-specific activation during text comprehension. *Neuroscience Letters, 427*(3), 159–64.

Fontaine, J. R., Scherer, K. R., Roesch, E. B. & Ellsworth, P. (2007). The world of emotion is not two-dimensional. *Psychological Science, 18*, 1050–7.

Fontaine, J., Scherer, K. R. & Soriano, C. (eds.), (2013). *Components of Emotional Meaning: A Sourcebook*. Oxford University Press.

Frijda, N. H. (1986). *The Emotions*. Cambridge University Press.

Gernsbacher, M. A., Goldsmith, H. H. & Robertson, R. R. W. (1992). Do readers mentally represent characters' emotional states? *Cognition and Emotion, 6*, 89–111.

Gernsbacher, M. A., Hallada, B. M. & Robertson, R. R. W. (1998). How automatically do readers infer fictional characters' emotional states? *Scientific Studies of Reading*, *2*, 271–300.

Gernsbacher, M. A., & Robertson, R. R. (1992). Knowledge activation versus sentence mapping when representing fictional characters' emotional states. *Language and Cognitive Processes*, *7*, 353–71.

Gillioz. C., & Gygax, P. M. (2013). Going beyond the simple match-mismatch effect might be complex, but more insightful: a study on emotional inferences. Paper presented at the 22nd Meeting of the Society for Text and Discourse, July, Montreal, Canada.

Gillioz, C., Gygax, P. & Tapiero, I. (2012). Individual differences and emotion inferences during reading comprehension. *Canadian Journal of Experimental Psychology/Revue canadienne de psychologie expérimentale*, *66*, 239–50.

Glenberg, A. (1999). Why mental models must be embodied. In G. Rickheit & C. Habel (eds.), *Mental Models in Discourse Processing and Reasoning*. Amsterdam: Elsevier.

Glenberg, A. M., Meyer, M. & Lindem, K. (1987). Mental models contribute to foregrounding during text comprehension. *Journal of Memory and Language*, *26*, 69–83.

Gygax, P. M., Garnham, A., & Oakhill, J. (2004). Inferring characters' emotional states: can readers infer specific emotions? *Language and Cognitive Processes*, *19*, 613–38.

Gygax, P. M., Oakhill, J., & Garnham, A. (2003). The representation of characters' emotional responses: do readers infer specific emotions? *Cognition and Emotion*, *17*, 413–28.

Gygax, P., Tapiero, I. & Carruzzo, E. (2007). Emotion inferences during reading comprehension: what evidence can the self-pace reading paradigm provide? *Discourse Processes*, *44*, 33–50.

Gygax, P., Wagner-Egger, P., Parris, B., Seiler, R. & Hauert, C.-A. (2008). A psycholinguistic investigation of football players' mental representations of game situations: does expertise count? *Swiss Journal of Psychology*, *67*, 85–95.

Harris, P. L. (2000). Understanding emotion. In M. Lewis & J. Haviland-Jones (eds.), *Handbook of Emotions* (2nd edn., pp. 281–92). New York: Guilford Press.

Havas, D. A., Glenberg, A. M., Gutowski, K. A., Lucarelli, M. J. & Davidson, R. J. (2010). Cosmetic use of botulinum toxin-A affects processing of emotional language. *Psychological Science*, *21*, 895–900.

Havas, D. A., Glenberg, A. M. & Rinck, M. (2007). Emotion simulation during language comprehension. *Psychonomic Bulletin & Review*, *14*, 436–41.

Herrmann, T. (1982). Language and situation: the pars pro toto principle. In C. Frazer & K. Scherer (eds.), *Advances in the Social Psychology of Language* (pp.123–58). Cambridge University Press.

Kessels, R. P. C., van Zandvoort, M. J. E., Postma, A., Kappelle, L. J. & de Haan, E. H. F. (2000). The Corsi block-tapping task: standardization and normative data. *Applied Neuropsychology*, *7*, 252–58.

Komeda, H., & Kusumi, T. (2006). The effect of a protagonist's emotional shift on situation model construction. *Memory & Cognition*, *34*, 1548–56.

Larsson, S. (2011). *The girl with the Dragon Tattoo*. London: Quercus.

Lassonde, K. A., & O'Brien, E. J. (2009). Contextual specificity in the activation of predictive inferences. *Discourse Processes*, *46*, 426–38.

Miall, D. S. (1989). Beyond the schema given: affective comprehension of literary narratives. *Cognition & Emotion*, *3*, 55–78.

Niedenthal, P. M., Barsalou, L. W., Ric, F. & Krauth-Gruber, S. (2005). Embodiment in the acquisition and use of emotion knowledge. In L. Feldman Barrett, P. M. Niedenthal, & P. Winkielman (eds.), *Emotion and Consciousness* (pp. 21–50). New York: Guilford Press.

Niedenthal, P. M., Winkielman, P., Mondillon, L. & Vermeulen, N. (2009). Embodiment of emotion concepts. *Journal of Personality and Social Psychology*, *96*, 1120–36.

O'Rorke, P., & Ortony, A. (1994). Explaining emotions. *Cognitive Science*, *18*, 283–323.

Ortony, A., & Clore, G. L. (1989). Emotions, moods and conscious awareness. *Cognition and Emotion*, *3*, 125–37.

Ortony, A., Clore, G. L. & Collins, A. (1988). *The Cognitive Structure of Emotions*. New York: Cambridge University Press.

Ortony, A., & Turner, T. J. (1990). What's basic about basic emotions? *Psychological Review*, *97*, 315–29.

Sanford, A. J., & Garrod, S. C. (2005). Memory-based approaches and beyond. *Discourse Processes*, *39*, 205–24.

Sanford, A. J., & Graesser, A. C. (2006). Shallow processing and underspecification. *Discourse Processes*, *42*, 99–108.

Scherer, K. R. (1984). On the nature and function of emotion: a component process approach. In K. R. Scherer & P. Ekman (eds.), *Approaches to Emotion* (pp. 293–317). Mahwah, NJ: Erlbaum.
  (2005). What are emotions? And how can they be measured? *Social Science Information*, *44*, 695–729.

Winkielman, P., Niedenthal, P. & Oberman, L. (2008). The embodied emotional mind. In G. R. Semin & E. R. Smith (eds.), *Embodied Grounding: Social, Cognitive Affective and Neuroscientific Approaches* (pp. 263–88). New York: Cambridge University Press.

Zwaan, R. A. (2004). The immersed experiencer: toward an embodied theory of language comprehension. In B. H. Ross (ed.), *The Psychology of Learning and Motivation: Advances in Research and Theory* (Vol. XLIV, pp. 35–62). New York: Academic Press.

7   Inference processing in children:
     the contributions of depth and breadth
     of vocabulary knowledge

Jane Oakhill, Kate Cain, and Diana McCarthy

Introduction

It is clear that effective reading comprehension depends on sound knowledge of the meanings of the words in a text. Even if the words can be decoded to sound, comprehension cannot occur unless the meanings of most of the words are known to the reader. But even though word decoding and vocabulary knowledge are crucial to text comprehension, we have previously argued that these word-level skills are necessary but not sufficient to support comprehension, and that other ("higher-level") processes, such as inference skills and comprehension monitoring, are crucial, too (see Cain and Oakhill, 2007, for an overview of these ideas and supporting research). However, more recently, we have been conducting research that provides a rapprochement between these different perspectives on reading comprehension: those that focus on "higher-level" processes and those that focus on "lower-level" (in this instance, lexical) processes, and it is on this work that we focus in the present chapter.

Skilled reading is complex. It requires the coordination of a range of skills and rapid access to text-relevant knowledge. Words must be decoded and their meanings retrieved, the individual sentences need to be parsed and understood, the information in the text needs to be integrated across sentences, and inferences need to be made to fill in any gaps in the text. Thus, a number of different skills and abilities – inference making, comprehension monitoring, and understanding of text structure in particular – have been shown to be linked to children's reading comprehension, both within and across time (Oakhill, Cain, and Bryant, 2003; Oakhill and Cain, 2012).

It has long been known that there is a strong relation between vocabulary and reading comprehension across a wide age range (Carroll, 1993), but the main question we address in this chapter is whether there is a relation between different *aspects of vocabulary knowledge,* and *specific component skills* of reading comprehension. Furthermore, we examine whether it is having the vocabulary knowledge or speed of access to that knowledge that is more important for good comprehension.

140

Perfetti's *lexical quality hypothesis* provides the basis for hypotheses about what it is about word knowledge, and the quality of that knowledge, that might limit comprehension skill. That is, lexical quality is not only concerned with the quality of the representations of individual words, but also the way in which that quality (or lack of it) might affect reading comprehension. The basic idea is that if the reader has high-quality word codes, and can retrieve semantic information about individual words with ease, then that, in turn, will facilitate comprehension (e.g., Perfetti, 2007; Perfetti and Hart, 2001; Perfetti, Wlotko, and Hart, 2005). Lexical quality includes different aspects of knowledge about word forms (phonology, orthography, grammatical class) and meaning. It is the last of these – the quality of the meaning representation – on which we focus here.

As outlined above, it is clear that knowledge of word meanings will be fundamentally important for reading comprehension. However, the relation between vocabulary and reading comprehension is likely to be more complex than a simple causal one in which a large (broad) vocabulary results in successful reading comprehension. To better understand the possible relations between vocabulary and comprehension, we first need to consider in more detail what is meant by vocabulary knowledge, and the ways in which it might influence understanding.

Receptive vocabulary assessments such as the Peabody Picture Vocabulary Test (PPVT: Dunn and Dunn, 2007: in the United Kingdom, the British Picture Vocabulary Scale, [BPVS]: Dunn, Dunn, Whetton, and Pintillie, 1992) operate on the assumption that people either "know" a word or not. However, there are degrees to which one can know the meaning of a word, which can be illustrated simply by the differential difficulty of matching a spoken word to a choice of pictures (as in the BPVS), or providing a definition of that word. The former task can often be completed successfully with only a fairly rudimentary knowledge of a word's meaning, which may be facilitated by being able to rule out some of the distractors, whereas providing a definition requires a much more secure knowledge of the meaning, rather than just a "ballpark" approximation to it.

The measures of receptive vocabulary described above (PPVT and BPVS) assess *breadth* of vocabulary knowledge: the number of words known. In contrast, the amount of knowledge about a word is referred to as *depth* of knowledge. For example, you might have heard the word "nautilus," and you might know that it is some sort of animal. But what else do you know about the nautilus? Slightly more in-depth knowledge might be that it is a creature that lives in the sea, and that it has a spiral external shell. More in-depth still would be knowledge that the nautilus lives in the pelagic zone (i.e., in deeper waters) and that it is a cephalopod (i.e., in the same family as squid, cuttlefish, and octopi) so, like other cephalopods, it has tentacles. In fact, it is the only cephalopod that has an exterior shell. Recently, research has demonstrated the importance of depth of knowledge (i.e., detailed knowledge about the meanings of words) relative to the vocabulary breadth (i.e., the number of words known, Ouellette, 2006). This work has shown that assessments of vocabulary depth (such as producing word definitions or selecting synonyms) are better predictors of reading comprehension than are measures of breadth of vocabulary.

The relation between vocabulary semantic skills and reading comprehension

The relations between reading comprehension and vocabulary knowledge are complex. We have evidence (Cain, Oakhill, and Lemmon, 2004; Cain, Oakhill, and Elbro, 2003) that level of reading comprehension and inference ability are associated with the ability to derive new vocabulary meanings from context. More generally, inference skills can predict vocabulary development (Cain and Oakhill, 2011). Thus, it is likely that reading comprehension ability and, in particular, inference skills, are linked to one's ability to understand, and refine one's understanding of, the meanings of words. However, there are also likely to be links in the opposite direction. Thus, the associative links between words, which are the product of having a rich vocabulary, will support reading comprehension through the support of inference making. In particular, depth of vocabulary knowledge is likely to be more important in inference making because the rich and well-connected semantic representations of words will permit the rapid activation not only of the word's meaning but also of related concepts, which can provide the basis for many of the inferences that are crucial for the construction of a coherent representation of a text. Returning briefly to the nautilus example above, if you have an in-depth knowledge about this creature, then you would easily be able to make links in a text that referred to the animal's shell or tentacles (even though this is a very unusual combination of characteristics in the animal kingdom). In this chapter we report new findings on the relation between aspects of vocabulary knowledge and reading comprehension in children.

It is widely agreed that readers (and listeners) go beyond the literal information laid out in a text and construct a representation of the state of affairs described in the text that incorporates relevant information from prior knowledge. This sort of representation is referred to as a Mental Model (Johnson-Laird, 1983) or a Situation Model (Kintsch, 1998). Such models should both be locally cohesive and globally coherent (van den Broek, Risden, and Huseby-Hartman, 1995), so that they are an integrated representation of the ideas in the text and are also made coherent by the incorporation of inferences from background knowledge. Although there are many different taxonomies of inference types, for our research the most relevant distinction is between local cohesion inferences and global coherence inferences, also referred to as text-connecting (or bridging) and gap-filling inferences previously (Baker and Stein, 1981; Cain and Oakhill, 1999; Elbro and Buch-Iversen, 2013; Graesser, Singer, and Trabasso, 1994).

Inferences to support local cohesion enable the reader to establish connections between different propositions in the text. There are individual differences in this ability to connect up ideas in text both in children and in adults (e.g., Cain and Oakhill, 1999; Long and Chong, 2001; Oakhill, 1982). Sometimes the need for these linkages is signaled explicitly in the text, for instance, by anaphors or definite references, but very often the need for such links is not explicitly cued and depends on the reader identifying links between word meanings (e.g., synonymous words, or instance-category pairings) such as: *she tried to flag down the car, but the driver of the vehicle seemed oblivious to her presence.* The successful integration of clauses or sentences in such examples requires an inference that draws on vocabulary and background knowledge, as well as integrative processing. Children who are good reading comprehenders are more likely to make these local cohesion inferences than children who are poorer comprehenders (Cain and Oakhill, 1999). Many of these inferences depend on the activation of the meanings of single words or phrases.

Global coherence inferences, as the name suggests, are important in understanding the gist of the text more broadly. An example of this sort of inference might be to derive the moral of the story, or work out the location or period in history when a story takes place. Very frequently, such information is not stated explicitly in the text but needs to be inferred by the reader, in conjunction with the reader's background knowledge. Such inferences differ from the local cohesion inferences discussed above in that they are not signaled by a single word or phrase in the text and do not simply involve the integration of two clauses or sentences. Indeed it would be possible for readers or listeners to construct an integrated representation of a text without ever generating these types of inference, but that representation would tend to be vague and under specified. Thus, global coherence inferences are generally considered necessary in text comprehension (Graesser et al., 1994). In comparison with good comprehenders, children with comprehension problems are less likely to make these global coherence inferences

(Cain and Oakhill, 1999; Oakhill, 1984). The poor comprehenders' difficulties with such inferences are not related to their lack of knowledge; they have the relevant background knowledge but fail to activate and apply it during text comprehension (Cain and Oakhill, 1999; Cain, Oakhill, Barnes, and Bryant, 2001).

We already have some evidence that good comprehenders are more likely than poor comprehenders to activate semantic associates of words, even when the task does not require them to do so. This evidence comes from a study by Weekes, Hamilton, Oakhill, and Holliday (2008), which used a false memory task (The DRM paradigm: Deese, 1959; Roediger and McDermott, 1995) to assess children's memory for word lists. The findings showed that good comprehenders made more errors than poor comprehenders in falsely recognising so-called theme words. These were words that captured the gist of a list. So, for instance, if the list to be remembered was comprised of the words "sit," "legs," "seat," "couch," "desk," "sofa," "wood," "cushion," "swivel," "stool," "sitting," "rocking," "bench," the theme word would be "chair," and the good comprehenders were more likely to falsely state that they had heard such words. In the second study reported below we used a variant of this task to explore the relation between gist memory and children's ability to activate aspects of lexical knowledge.

The analysis above suggests that the link from vocabulary to comprehension has at least three potential bases: detailed knowledge of words' meanings; activation of the relevant aspects of a word's meaning (and semantic associates); and use of that information to support comprehension. The analysis of different types of inference processing, and their different demands, leads to the hypothesis that vocabulary depth may be a more important predictor of inference skill than vocabulary breadth and, more specifically, that depth of vocabulary knowledge may be more important for global coherence inferences than for local cohesion inferences, because rich detailed and precise semantic representation of the word will make it more likely that thematically related words will come into mind to support the making of global coherence inferences. Because such inferences are not cued by specific words such as anaphors, they are likely to be more dependent on such activation processes.

Study one: the relation between aspects of vocabulary knowledge and different types of inferences

In this first study (Cain and Oakhill, unpublished), we consider the role of both breadth and depth of vocabulary in relation to literal understanding and to different types of inferences in children.

Previous studies of the relation between aspects of vocabulary and children's reading comprehension have, unfortunately, assessed vocabulary depth and vocabulary breadth in different ways: specifically, the ability to provide word definitions has been used as a measure of breadth by Tannenbaum, Torgesen, and Wagner (2006) but as a measure of depth by Ouellette (2006). We prefer the latter's judgment that word definitions require depth of knowledge and use that classification in the present study. Both the above studies showed that an individual's ability to provide word definitions is more strongly related to measures of reading comprehension than are other assessments of vocabulary knowledge, although vocabulary in general is predictive of comprehension level. What has not been investigated thus far is how these different aspects of vocabulary knowledge are related to inference skill.

In the first study presented here, we have analyzed data that were collected as part of a longitudinal investigation (see Oakhill and Cain, 2012). At age ten to eleven, the children in that study completed assessments of vocabulary that tapped into both breadth and depth of knowledge, plus an experimental assessment of comprehension in which the children read stories and then answered questions to assess three different levels of comprehension: memory for literal details, ability to make local cohesion inferences, and ability to make global coherence inferences. We predicted that vocabulary knowledge would be related to inference skill in general (but not so much to the ability to answer literal questions), but that depth of vocabulary would be most strongly related to the ability to answer the global coherence inference questions. This is because such questions typically rely on making (sometimes subtle) semantic links across the text as a whole, and require the ability to link information in the text to background knowledge.

In the present study, the sample of eighty-three ten- to eleven-year-olds (all of whom spoke English as their first language, and none of whom had reported behavioral, emotional, or learning difficulties) were administered a comprehension assessment, two vocabulary assessments, and the experimental comprehension task described above. The assessments were as follows.

Ability assessments and procedure

Reading ability. All children completed the *Neale Analysis of Reading Ability: Revised* (NARA-R: Neale, 1989), which consists of a series of graded passages, each followed by a set of open-ended questions (a mixture of literal and inferential questions). At the end of the assessment, two scores are available: one for word reading accuracy (based on number of words read aloud correctly) and one for comprehension ability (based on number of questions answered correctly). For the purposes of this study, we used the word reading accuracy scores only, which are based on the number of word reading errors made.

Vocabulary. The *British Picture Vocabulary Scales (BPVS*: Dunn et al., 1992) was used as a measure of vocabulary breadth. This task is a British version of the PPVT (Dunn and Dunn, 2007). The task is to select one picture, out of a choice of four, that represents the meaning of a word spoken by the experimenter. Testing stops when a prescribed number of errors have been made. There were two assessments of vocabulary depth from the *Wechsler Intelligence Test for Children – III (WISC-III*: UK edition, Wechsler 1992), the Vocabulary and Similarities subtests. The Vocabulary subtest of the WISC-III requires participants to define words that increase in difficulty, for example, "alphabet," "island," "precise," and the Similarities subtest requires participants to identify how two things are similar, for example, "wheel" and "ball" (easy item) and "first – last" (more difficult item). Because the two subtests to assess depth contained a different number of items, we calculated the percentage correct of the total possible score for each one and summed these to create a single score.

Inference and integration task. We developed a measure of inference skill to assess different aspects of text comprehension: memory for literal information, integration of premises within the text (i.e., local cohesion inferences), and integration of textual premises with general knowledge and across the text more broadly (i.e., global coherence). The children were required to read three short passages out loud, and were then asked open-ended questions after each one. There were two questions for each question type, and responses were scored using a rubric of correct and incorrect answers. One point was awarded for each question (the maximum score was 6 for each question type: literal, local cohesion inferences, global coherence inferences). There were too few items to obtain a reliable measure of internal consistency for each question type.

The relations between breadth and depth of vocabulary and comprehension for different types of information

First, we explored the relations between the vocabulary measures and performance on the different types of comprehension questions. None of the vocabulary measures was associated with recall of literal information from the texts, and were only weakly correlated with local cohesion inferences (breadth, $r =.23$, $p <. 05$; depth $r =.21$, ns). The relation between the vocabulary measures and the children's ability to answer the global coherence inferences was, however, much stronger (breadth $r = .48$, $p < .001$; depth r = .52, $p < .001$).

To test the more specific predictions, we performed three pairs of multiple regression analyses, with performance on either the literal questions, local cohesion inferences, or global coherence inferences as the outcome variables. Because the measure of inference making required children to read the texts themselves, rather than listen to them, in the first step of each analysis, word reading accuracy was entered to control for differences in word reading ability. Age was also entered at that step. In each of the analyses, vocabulary depth was entered at the second step, and vocabulary breadth was entered at the third step. In the complementary analysis of the pair, the order of vocabulary depth and breadth was reversed. In this way, we could test whether each aspect of vocabulary knowledge (breadth vs. depth) predicted unique variance in performance on the different aspects of comprehension skill. In the case of literal memory, very little variance was accounted for by the measures of vocabulary once word reading accuracy and age had been controlled for, so these results will not be considered further. The out comes of the analyses with the two different types of inference skill as outcome variables can be seen in Figure 7.1.

These analyses showed that both breadth and depth of vocabulary knowledge accounted for variance in performance on the local cohesion inferences when entered at the second step, but neither predicted additional variance when entered at the third step (i.e., following the other vocabulary measure). The pattern of results when performance on the global coherence inferences was the outcome measure was rather different, however. In this case, vocabulary depth accounted for additional

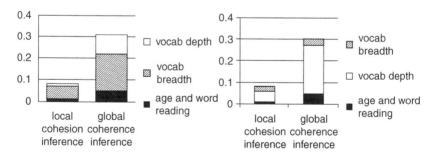

Figure 7.1 Study 1: Prediction of the two inference types by age and word reading (step 1) and vocabulary breadth and depth (steps 2 and 3). The values represent $\Delta R2$ for each successive step, with the first step at the bottom of the column and the final step at the top.

variance in performance on these questions, even when entered after vocabulary breadth. A comparison of the standardized beta coefficients showed that vocabulary breadth was the stronger predictor of local cohesion inferences, whereas vocabulary depth was the stronger predictor of the global coherence inferences. Thus, these findings support our prediction that, although vocabulary is important for both types of inference, the measure of vocabulary depth in particular is a strong predictor of performance on the global coherence inferences.

In the correlational analyses, it was also evident that literal memory for the text was significantly related to the ability to answer local cohesion inference questions ($r = .38$, $p < .001$) but only weakly related ($r = .20$, ns) to performance on the global coherence inferences. We therefore carried out some further analyses to explore the relations between the two types of inference skill and vocabulary when performance on the literal questions was controlled. In these analyses, performance on the literal questions was entered in the second step (after age and word-reading accuracy) and the two vocabulary measures were entered together in the third and final step. The results showed that literal memory accounted for a significant portion of variance (14 percent) in performance on local cohesion inferences and vocabulary did not make a significant contribution when entered at the final step. In contrast, literal memory accounted for a much smaller portion of variance (5 percent) of performance on global coherence inferences, and vocabulary continued to be an important determinant of performance on this type of inference.

Conclusions from Study 1

These findings further our understanding of the relations between vocabulary knowledge and text understanding in children in two ways. First, the results demonstrate that vocabulary knowledge is considerably more important for inference making than for understanding of a text at a more literal level. Second, the results show that different aspects of vocabulary knowledge are differentially important for inference making. More specifically, depth of vocabulary knowledge is the more critical factor in accounting for performance on global coherence inferences (even after literal memory for the text is taken into account), whereas breadth of knowledge is more likely to be related to ability to make local cohesion inferences (though this relation does not hold once literal memory for the text had been controlled for).

In the case of global coherence inferences, the picture is rather different. In this case, the relation between literal memory and performance on the inference questions was weak, and depth of vocabulary knowledge remained a strong predictor of performance on these questions, even when literal memory had been taken into account. This is probably because good performance on these sorts of inference requires the reader to interrelate words in the text that are associated by a common setting, theme, or character. Hence, they are more reliant on the reader having a rich semantic network of meanings, which is tapped into by measures of depth of vocabulary.

We suggest that different types of inference may be more or less heavily dependent on different types of vocabulary knowledge. In particular, depth of knowledge, which likely enhances the reader's ability to see inter-relations between words in a text, is strongly related to performance on global coherence inferences. One of the depth measures used in the present study was a definitions task, as used by Ouellette (2006) and, in agreement with his findings, we also found that the breadth measure we used was more strongly correlated with decoding skill than with vocabulary depth. Thus, our pattern of results is consistent with earlier findings.

The strong relation between literal memory for the text and ability to make local coherence inferences may arise because these types of inferences require that the reader has an accurate representation of the propositions in the text, in order to establish links between them. However, it is somewhat surprising that neither measure of vocabulary accounted for variance in local cohesion inferences once literal memory had been taken into account, because this inference type often requires knowledge of words' meanings and the links between them. However, in the present study, the vocabulary tasks were untimed, and this might help to account for the rather weak relation between vocabulary and this type of inference. Recent work has shown that both accuracy of word knowledge and speed of retrieval make independent contributions to text comprehension in children (Richter, Isberner, Naumann, and Neeb, 2013), which might suggest that the two measures pick up on different aspects of lexical quality and that, perhaps in young readers in particular, speed of access to semantic information might be more important than accuracy. It is to this issue that we turn in the second study reported here.

Study 2: Depth of vocabulary knowledge and comprehension skill: considerations of accuracy and speed

The study just described demonstrates that the quality of word meanings has an important influence on young children's reading comprehension, specifically their global coherence inference making. In addition to the quality of knowledge about individual word meanings, the speed with which word meanings can be retrieved needs to be considered. Reading comprehension occurs in real time, so fast and accurate access to word meanings (and, indeed, other sorts of knowledge) is crucial. There are many models of reading that emphasize the importance of fluency and automaticity of access to word meanings (e.g., Laberge and Samuels, 1974; Perfetti and Lesgold, 1977) although training studies have failed to provide evidence for a direct causal relation between speed of word access and reading comprehension – perhaps because automatic and fluent access to word meanings is necessary, but not sufficient, to ensure skilled comprehension. Similarly, some training studies have succeeded in improving vocabulary knowledge (e.g., Beck, Perfetti, and McKeown, 1982; Jenkins, Pany, and Schreck, 1978; Tuinman and Brady, 1974), but few have shown concomitant increases in comprehension skill. This lack of transfer may well be related to the finding that just because a reader knows the meaning of a word, that knowledge does not guarantee that that meaning will be activated and used during comprehension. For instance, we have shown previously that children may possess relevant background knowledge but do not necessarily activate it and use it to make inferences during comprehension (Cain and Oakhill, 1999; Cain et al., 2001).

To address these issues, in the second study reported below, we assessed not only children's knowledge about word meanings, but also the speed with which they could access that knowledge. Because in the first study depth of vocabulary knowledge was found to be a more reliable predictor of comprehension skill and global coherence inferences in particular, we focus on depth of vocabulary knowledge in the second study.

Fifty-seven nine- and ten-year-olds were assessed on a series of tasks intended to tap depth of vocabulary. They were asked to both produce and understand synonyms and hypernyms (superordinate terms) and to make speeded judgments about whether pairs of words had a particular relation to each other (synonyms or not; hypernyms or not). The relation between both accuracy and speed on these tasks and reading ability (both word reading and comprehension) was explored. In addition, in light of the results from Study 1 showing a strong relation between assessment of vocabulary depth and global coherence inferences, we gave the children a modified version of the DRM task used by Weekes et al. (2008) to assess their gist memory for information (in this case, lists of thematically related words).

Ability assessments and procedure

Reading ability. The same assessment of reading ability: the *Neale Analysis of Reading Ability: Revised* (NARA-R: Neale, 1989) was also used in Study 2. This test was described above.

Judgment tasks. To assess comprehension of written synonyms and hypernyms, the children performed judgment tasks in which words pairs of words were presented on a computer screen and accuracy and response times recorded. The children performed the synonym task first, then the hypernym task. The tasks were explained to the children as follows. In the case of the synonyms they were told to press the *yes* button if the words "mean the same," otherwise to press the *no* button. In the case of the hypernyms, they were told to press yes if the first word "was a type of" the second word. In both cases they were given an example ("loud" and "noisy" mean the same, "is lemonade a sort of drink?") and were given four practice items before each task. They then went on to complete ten experimental items for each task, which were randomly intermixed with an equal number of distractor items, which should have elicited a no response (e.g., Do "feather" and "light" mean the same? "Is cheese a sort of meat?"). As a control measure for response times, the children also did a same/different (identity matching) task for word pairs (same or different). This task was included so that we could take into account the speed with which children could respond when they were making simple visual matching judgments about words, rather than semantic judgments. The data from this task were included in the regression analyses to control for speed of response per se.

Production tasks. There were two production tasks: one to assess knowledge of synonyms and one to assess knowledge of hypernyms. The children performed the synonym task first, then the hypernym task. In the synonym production task, the children were told that the experimenter would read out a word and they should think of another word that meant the same thing. They were given a series of ten words (e.g., "quick," "begin") and their responses to each word were noted. In the hypernym production task, they were reminded of the computer task they had recently completed ("lemonade is a type of drink") and were told they should answer "type of" questions about a set of words (e.g., "What is a pineapple a type of?").

The tasks were presented in the order described above because we were concerned about carry-over effects from one task to another. In particular, we thought that the computerized tasks (in which word pairs were presented) would help sensitize the children to what was required in the production tasks (though, of course, different words were used in the two types of task, judgment vs. comprehension). Within each task, the order of presentation of words (or word pairs) was randomized separately for each child. The synonym and hypernym productions were scored by two independent raters, and any disagreements were resolved by a third rater. Usually, productions received either two, one, or zero points, with two points awarded for the target answer (e.g., *skirt – clothing*), one point awarded for a partially correct (typically a more inclusive category as in the case of hypernyms, e.g., *pineapple – food*, or a word closely related in the case of synonyms, e.g., *rescue – help*), and zero points for error responses or no response (e.g., in the hypernym task: *tennis-ball*, and in the synonym task: *enormous-small*). In rare cases where a more specific category was produced, a score of three was awarded (e.g., *trumpet – brass instrument*, where two points were awarded for the more common response – *musical instrument*).

Theme word task. In this task, we adapted the DRM task used by Weekes et al. (2008), so that the theme words were more directly elicited, in line with the more direct nature of the other word-level tasks. The children were required to think of one word that best represented the theme of a set of words that were read to them. The instructions, as presented to the child, were as follows: "I am going to read you a list of words, all the words in the list will be clues to what I am thinking about; listen carefully to the list and then I would like you to guess what I am thinking about."

They were given some examples, such as:

> *teacher, friends, play, learn, book, maths* – target *school*
> *type, keyboard, internet, email, printer, mouse* – target *computer*

and if they did not produce the correct answer it was provided for them. They were then presented with a series of seven additional lists and were required to come up with a single word as the theme. The children's responses were given a score from two (for a target word as produced by an adult sample), one (for a response that captured the theme but was not the intended target and which was, typically, slightly less specific), and zero (for an incorrect or no answer). For example, for the list: "rest, bed, tired, dream, snooze, blanket," the target word was "sleep," but one point was awarded for the responses "night" or "nighttime."

Exploring the relations between accuracy and speed of access to depth of vocabulary and reading comprehension

The purpose of the analyses below was to investigate the extent to which any relation between vocabulary knowledge (as measured by the production tasks) and reading comprehension was mediated by speed of access to word meanings, and by speed of response times per se (i.e., performance on an analogous word-matching task that did not require any semantic judgments). We analyzed performance on the synonym and hypernym tasks separately because, although performance on the judgment tasks (both accuracy and times) was significantly inter-correlated, the synonym and hypernym production tasks were not (the correlation was zero). Finally, we assessed the relation between the various measures of vocabulary depth, and children's ability to link words to determine the theme of a word list. We regard the theme words task as a measure of gist extraction.

First, we explored the relation between the various assessments of depth of vocabulary knowledge and reading comprehension. Performance on both the synonym and hypernym tasks (judgment times and accuracy) was correlated with reading comprehension, as was performance on the "theme words" task (all correlations were moderate: between .35 and .60). The synonym and hypernym production tasks were also significantly correlated with comprehension skill (.27 and .39, respectively). Moreover, in this sample, Neale reading comprehension and word reading were significantly correlated (.63) and word reading was also significantly correlated with the synonym and hypernym judgment tasks (correlations between .46 and .67) but not with the theme word task.

Because both reading comprehension and word reading correlated with the variables of interest, we conducted a series of multiple regression analyses in which we controlled for level of word reading ability. Furthermore, we also controlled for synonym and hypernym production ability in the regression model, because it is likely that children who have a more secure knowledge of synonyms and hypernyms (as exhibited in the production tasks) would also be more accurate, and faster, in the judgment tasks.

In the first two regression models, the outcome variable was reading comprehension, and the variables entered were word reading accuracy, judgment times in the control task, score on the relevant production task (as a control for knowledge of synonyms and hypernyms), and times to make correct judgments in the synonym and hypernym judgment tasks. The outcomes of these analyses are shown in Figure 7.2 (for the synonym and hypernym data separately). As can be seen from this figure, in both cases (synonyms and hypernyms), time to make the judgments added substantially (and significantly) to the prediction of Neale reading comprehension, even after word reading ability, performance on the relevant production task and speed of responding in an analogous word matching task had been controlled.

We then explored the relation between performance on the theme words task, the vocabulary assessments, and reading comprehension. Performance on the theme words task was significantly correlated with reading comprehension (though not with single word reading accuracy) and moderately (though not always significantly) correlated with the synonym and hypernym judgment tasks. To explore whether the relation

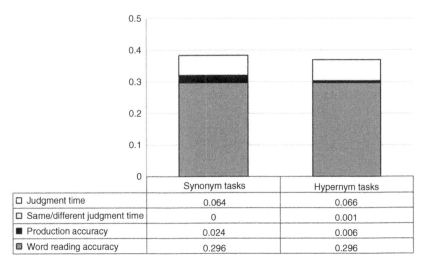

	Synonym tasks	Hypernym tasks
☐ Judgment time	0.064	0.066
☐ Same/different judgment time	0	0.001
■ Production accuracy	0.024	0.006
▨ Word reading accuracy	0.296	0.296

Figure 7.2 Study 2: Synonym and hypernym tasks as predictors of reading comprehension skill. The values represent ΔR2 for each successive step, with the first step at the bottom of the column and the final step at the top.

between the theme word tasks and reading comprehension was mediated by performance on the word judgment tasks, we conducted two sets of regression analyses, one in which we entered synonym performance and one in which we entered hypernym performance, to explore whether performance on these tasks mediated the relation between performance on the theme word task and comprehension skill.

The results of these analyses are shown in Figure 7.3. In summary, even after the effects of synonym judgment accuracy and response times had been taken into account, the theme word task accounted for significant additional variance in comprehension skill (6 percent). When the equivalent analyses were conducted including performance on the hypernym tasks, the theme words task predicted a nonsignificant portion of additional variance in comprehension skill (3 percent). Thus, the relation was not entirely mediated by word-level knowledge in a straightforward manner. From these data, we cannot conclude that hypernym knowledge is more important than synonym knowledge in linking the ability to derive gist (as measured by the theme word task) and comprehension skill (as measured by the Neale Analysis) because the additional predictive power of the theme word task was small in both cases (3 vs. 6 percent) and differed by only 3 percent in the two cases. Of course, we do not mean to imply from these results that extraction of the gist of a text (or indeed

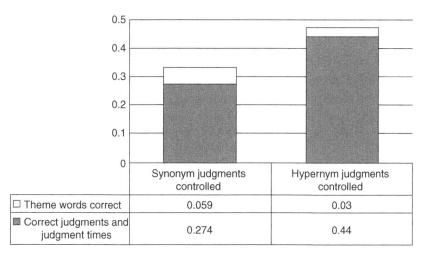

Figure 7.3 Study 2: Theme words as predictors of reading comprehension with synonym judgment performance controlled (left-hand side) and hypernym judgment performance controlled (right-hand side). The values represent ΔR2 for each successive step, with the first step at the bottom of the column and the final step at the top.

the related process of making inferences from a text) is dependent specifically on the reader's ability to derive synonyms and hypernyms, but to be more broadly based on assessments of their vocabulary depth, of which these are intended as representative measures.

Conclusions and future directions

These are, as far as we know, the first studies to explore the relation between different aspects of vocabulary knowledge and different dimensions of text comprehension. In the first study, we found that depth of vocabulary knowledge was an important predictor of one type of inference in particular – global coherence inferences – even when word reading skill and literal memory for the text had been taken into account. There are many studies in the literature that emphasize the importance of vocabulary for reading comprehension, but our studies provide evidence for much more specific links: that is, that a particular aspect of vocabulary (depth) is related to a specific component skill of comprehension (the ability to make global coherence inferences). Thus, the findings from this study suggest that, in order to further understanding of the links between vocabulary and comprehension, it is important to consider vocabulary and comprehension not as monolithic constructs, but to look in more detail at the processes that contribute to effective comprehension, and to consider how they are related to different aspects of vocabulary. In the second study, we found a strong and specific link between speed of semantic access in vocabulary tasks (synonym and hypernym judgment tasks) and reading comprehension. The link was not entirely mediated by word reading skill, or by knowledge about words (measured in a production task), and was not related to an association between comprehension skill and generally faster response times in a nonsemantic judgment task. These findings suggest that it is not sufficient to "know" the meanings of words in a text, but that the facility with which the semantic representations of words can be accessed is also important for comprehension. As discussed above, the speed of access to a word's semantics is likely to be important for efficient comprehension because comprehension happens in real time and, if appropriate meanings and associations of words are not accessed very rapidly, the reader will have moved on to the next word, or the next sentence, and the opportunity for semantic information to support inference and integration of the text will have been missed.

Furthermore, in this second study, we hypothesized that access to vocabulary knowledge, and depth of knowledge in particular, would be related to children's ability to make inferential links to derive gist (in this case, from word lists). We based our hypothesis on previous evidence that shows that children who were good comprehenders were *more* likely than poor comprehenders to exhibit false memories for words that captured the theme of a list they had been asked to remember, but which had not actually been presented (Weeks et al., 2008). The present results replicate the link between comprehension skill and gist memory, using a variant of that task, and provide some evidence that the relation between gist memory and reading comprehension is substantially, though not entirely, mediated by the speed and accuracy of activation of word-level knowledge.

The results we have reported suggest that the child's depth of vocabulary knowledge might underpin his or her ability to make global coherence inferences from a text, in particular. We end by considering in more detail how this might work. First, read the following snippet of text (an extract from a longer story):

Today was the big match, the last game of the season. There was only a minute of the game left and neither team had scored yet. The crowd watched in silence as Jake took the penalty shot. The goalkeeper missed the ball and the crowd cheered and roared. Jake had scored the winning goal. His teammates were very happy.

Then answer the question, "What sport was Jake playing?" To answer that question, the reader needs to appreciate that several words taken together (*match, game, team, penalty shot, goalkeeper, ball, winning goal,* and *teammates*) indicate that Jake is playing in a football (soccer) match. If the reader can make associations between the meanings of different words in the text quickly and easily, he or she will very easily be able to infer what is going on in the story, and the question will be trivially easy.

Although the studies we have presented are relatively small-scale investigations, the results suggest that further exploration of the ways in which depth of vocabulary knowledge mediates aspects of text comprehension would be fruitful. In particular, the data we have presented are correlational. In order to inform teaching and interventions, it would be important to ascertain whether there is a causal link developmentally between depth of vocabulary knowledge and reading comprehension and inference skill, or whether it is level of reading comprehension that drives the learning of, and increasing depth of knowledge of, word meanings. We already have some evidence from other studies which indicates that reading comprehension level and inference skills appear to be critically associated with the ability to derive the meanings of new words from context (Cain et al., 2003; Cain et al., 2004) and predict vocabulary development (Cain and Oakhill, 2011) and Verhoeven, van Leeuwe, and Vermeer (2011) provide evidence of reciprocity between reading comprehension and vocabulary development during the early school years.

REFERENCES

Baker, L., & Stein, N. (1981). The development of prose comprehension skills. In C. M. Santa & B. L. Hayes (eds.), *Children's Prose Comprehension: Research and Practice.* Newark, DE: International Reading Association.

Beck, I. L., Perfetti, C. A., & McKeown, M. G. (1982). Effects of long-term vocabulary instruction on lexical access and reading comprehension. *Journal of Educational Psychology, 74*(4), 506–21.

Cain, K., & Oakhill, J. V. (1999). Inference making ability and its relation to comprehension failure in young children. *Reading and Writing. An Interdisciplinary Journal, 11*(5–6), 489–503.

(2007). *Children's Comprehension Problems in Oral and Written Language: A Cognitive Perspective.* New York: Guilford Press.

(2011). Matthew effects in young readers' reading comprehension and reading experience aid vocabulary development. *Journal of Learning Disabilities, 44* (5), 431–43.

(unpublished). Reading comprehension and vocabulary: is vocabulary more important for some aspects of comprehension? *L'année Psychologique/Topics in Cognitive Psychology.*

Cain, K., Oakhill, J. V., Barnes, M. A., & Bryant, P. E. (2001). Comprehension skill, inference-making ability, and their relation to knowledge. *Memory & Cognition, 29*(6), 850–59.

Cain, K., Oakhill, J. V., & Elbro, C. (2003). The ability to learn new word meanings from context by school-age children with and without language comprehension difficulties. *Journal of Child Language*, *30*(3), 681–94.

Cain, K., Oakhill, J. V., & Lemmon, K. (2004). Individual differences in the inference of word meanings from context: the influence of reading comprehension, vocabulary knowledge, and memory capacity. *Journal of Educational Psychology*, *96*(4), 671–81.

Carroll, J. B. (1993). *Human Cognitive Abilities: A Survey of Factor-Analytic Studies*. New York: Cambridge University Press.

Deese, J. (1959). On the prediction of occurrence of particular verbal intrusions in immediate recall. *Journal of Experimental Psychology: Learning, Memory, and Cognition*, *58*(1), 17–22.

Dunn, L. M., & Dunn, D. M. (2007). *Peabody Picture Vocabulary Test*, (PPVT-4). Minneapolis, MN: Pearson Assessments.

Dunn, L. M., Dunn, L. M., Whetton, C., & Pintillie, D. (1992). *British Picture Vocabulary Scale*. Windsor, UK: NFER-Nelson.

Elbro, C., & Buch-Iverson, I. (2013). Activation of background knowledge for inference making: effects on reading comprehension. *Scientific Studies of Reading*, *17*(6), 1–18.

Graesser, A. C., Singer, M., & Trabasso, T. (1994). Constructing inferences during narrative text comprehension. *Psychological Review*, *101*(3), 371–95.

Jenkins, J., Pany, D., & Schreck, J. (1978). *Vocabulary and Reading Comprehension: Instructional Effects*. Champaign, IL: University of Illinois, Center for the Study of Reading.

Johnson-Laird, P. N. (1983). *Mental Models: Towards a Cognitive Science of Language, Inference, and Consciousness*. Cambridge University Press.

Kintsch, W. (1998). *Comprehension: A Paradigm for Cognition*. New York: Cambridge University Press.

LaBerge, D., & Samuels, S. J. (1974). Toward a theory of automatic information processing in reading. *Cognitive Psychology*, *6*(2), 293–323.

Long, D. L., & Chong, J. L. (2001). Comprehension skill and global coherence: a paradoxical picture of poor comprehenders' abilities. *Journal of Experimental Psychology: Learning, Memory, and Cognition*, *27*(6), 1424–29.

Neale, M. D. (1989). *The Neale Analysis of Reading Ability – revised*. Windsor, UK: NFER.

Oakhill, J. V. (1982). Constructive processes in skilled and less-skilled comprehenders' memory for sentences. *British Journal of Psychology*, *73*(1), 13–20.

  (1984). Inferential and memory skills in children's comprehension of stories. *British Journal of Educational Psychology*, *54*(1), 31–9.

Oakhill, J. V., & Cain, K. (2012). The precursors of reading ability in young readers: evidence from a four-year longitudinal study. *Scientific Studies of Reading*, *16*(2), 91–121.

Oakhill, J. V., Cain, K., & Bryant, P. E. (2003). The dissociation of word reading and text comprehension: evidence from component skills. *Language and Cognitive Processes*, *18*(4), 443–68.

Ouellette, G. P. (2006). What's meaning got to do with it: the role of vocabulary in word reading and reading comprehension. *Journal of Educational Psychology*, *98*(3), 554–66.

Perfetti, C. A. (2007). Reading ability: lexical quality to comprehension. *Scientific Studies of Reading*, *11*(4), 357–83.

Perfetti, C. A., & Hart, L. (2001). The lexical basis of comprehension skill. In D. S. Gorfein (ed.), *On the Consequences of Meaning Selection: Perspectives on Resolving Lexical Ambiguity* (pp. 67–86). Washington, DC: APA.

Perfetti, C. A., & Lesgold, A. M. (1977). Discourse comprehension and sources of individual differences. In M. A. Just & P. A. Carpenter (eds.), *Cognitive Processes in Comprehension*. Mahwah, NJ: Erlbaum.

Perfetti, C. A., Wlotko, E. W., & Hart, L. A. (2005). Word learning and individual differences in word learning reflected in event-related potentials. *Journal of Experimental Psychology: Learning, Memory, and Cognition*, *31*(6), 1281–92.

Richter, T., Isberner, M. B., Naumann, J., & Neeb, Y. (2013). Lexical quality and reading comprehension in primary school children. *Scientific Studies of Reading*, *17*(6), 415–34.

Roediger, H. L., & McDermott, K. B. (1995). Creating false memories: remembering words not presented in lists. *Journal of Experimental Psychology: Learning, Memory, and Cognition*, *21*(4), 803–14.

Tannenbaum, K. R., Torgesen, J. K., & Wagner, R. K. (2006). Relationships between word knowledge and reading comprehension in third-grade children. *Scientific Studies of Reading*, *10*(4), 381–98.

Tuinman, J. J., & Brady, M. E. (1974). How does vocabulary account for variance on reading comprehension tests? A preliminary instructional analysis. In P. Nacke (ed.), *Twenty-third National Reading Conference Yearbook*. Clemson, SC: National Reading Conference.

van den Broek, P. W., Risden, K., & Husebye-Hartman, E. (1995). The role of readers' standards for coherence in the generation of inferences during reading. In R. F. Lorch & E. J. O'Brien (eds.), *Sources of Coherence in Reading* (pp. 353–73). Mahwah, NJ: Erlbaum.

Verhoeven, L., van Leeuwe, J., & Vermeer, A. (2011). Vocabulary growth and reading development across the elementary school years. *Scientific Studies of Reading*, *15*(1), 8–25.

Wechsler, D. (1992) *Wechsler Intelligence Scale for Children – 3rd edition*. London: Psychological Corporation, Harcourt Brace.

Weekes, B. S., Hamilton, S., Oakhill, J., & Holliday, R. E. (2008). False recollection in children with reading comprehension difficulties. *Cognition*, *106*(1), 222–33.

8   A general inference skill

Panayiota Kendeou

Introduction

What does it mean to be a competent reader in the twenty-first century? The fields of education and psychology have been dominated by the persistent efforts of state and national agencies, researchers and educators to build a comprehensive understanding of reading comprehension and its development (Alexander, 2012; Common Core State Standards Initiative, 2010). Despite varying, and often conflicting, perspectives on the nature and definition of reading, the ability to draw inferences remains the cornerstone of reading comprehension. Indeed, inference ability has emerged as one of the unique and significant predictors of reading comprehension in longitudinal studies for both children and adults (Cain, Oakhill, Barnes, and Bryant, 2001; Cromley and Azevedo, 2007; Hannon and Daneman, 1998; Kendeou, Bohn-Gettler, White, and van den Broek, 2008; Kendeou, van den Broek, White, and Lynch, 2007, 2009; Oakhill and Cain, 2012).

My goal in this theoretical contribution is to present a case for a *general inference skill* – that is, a skill that depends on the core, fundamental processes of activation and integration of information and generalizes across contexts. In building my case, first I draw on the discourse processes literature to define inference skill and review the types of inferences studied in the fields of education and psychology. Next, I discuss developmental data from the areas of event comprehension and discourse processes that provide evidence for a general inference ability that transfers across different media in young children. Finally, I discuss the implications of a general inference skill for the instruction and assessment of inferencing, and future directions for research in this area.

Inference skill: a higher–order skill with low and high boundaries

Reading comprehension is among the most complex human activities. This complexity demands a theoretical model to describe the cognitive and linguistic processes involved, as well as their development. Currently, there are a number of models[1] depicting the development of various processes and skills relating to reading comprehension. These models are concerned primarily with the mental representation the reader constructs in the process of understanding words, sentences, and their respective relations (for a review of these models, see McNamara and Magliano, 2009). These models and theories emphasize the importance of different skills and processes that are relevant to reading comprehension. These processes, lower and higher level, dynamically interact and are necessary for a complete account of reading comprehension. With respect to lower-level skills, there is general consensus that comprehension of text depends heavily on word identification (e.g., Ehri, 2005; Gough and Tunmer, 1986; Perfetti, 2007; Stafura and Perfetti, 2014), fluency (e.g., Fuchs, Fuchs, Hosp, and Jenkins, 2001; LaBerge and Samuels, 1974), and vocabulary knowledge (e.g., Anderson and Freebody, 1981; Beck, Perfetti, and McKeown, 1982; Nagy, Herman, and Anderson, 1985; RAND, 2002; Stanovich, 1986; Tannenbaum, Torgesen, and Wagner, 2006; Torgensen, Wagner, Rashotte, Burgess, and Hecht, 1997). With respect to higher-order skills, research has consistently highlighted the critical role of inference generation (e.g., Cain and Oakhill, 1999; Graesser, Singer, and Trabasso, 1994; Kintsch, 1998; van den Broek, 1990; 1997) in addition to comprehension monitoring (Baker, 1984; Oakhill, Hartt, and Samols, 2005) and working memory (Baddeley, 2003; Cowan, 2010; Daneman and Carpenter, 1980; Swanson and O'Connor, 2009).

What is an inference?

In the context of reading comprehension, an inference is information that is retrieved or generated during reading to *fill in* information that is left implicit in a text (Elbro and Buch-Iversen, 2013; Kintsch, 1998; McNamara and Magliano, 2009; Oakhill, 1984). Typically, the process of generating an inference is assumed to be two-staged, in which reading current information in the text first activates and reinstates into working memory previously acquired information (from prior text or long-term

---

[1] These models include the construction-integration model (Kintsch and Van Dijk, 1978), the landscape model (Tzeng, van den Broek, Kendeou, and Lee, 2005; van den Broek, Young, Tzeng, and Linderholm, 1999), the structure building model (Gernsbacher, 1990), the resonance model (O'Brien and Myers, 1999; Myers and O'Brien, 1998), the event-indexing model (Zwaan, Langston, and Graesser, 1995), the causal network model (Trabasso, van den Broek, and Suh, 1989), and the constructionist model (Graesser, Singer, and Trabasso, 1994).

memory); then, the current information gets integrated with the newly activated content (McKoon and Ratcliff, 1992). This two-stage process highlights the important difference between *activation* and *integration* of information in inference generation. Indeed, the activation of information can occur independently of its integration with current text, and activation cannot guarantee integration (Blanc, Kendeou, van den Broek, and Brouillet, 2008; Cook, Halleran, and O'Brien, 1998; Kendeou, Smith, and O'Brien, 2013; Long and Chong, 2001; O'Brien, Cook, and Guéraud, 2010; O'Brien, Cook, and Peracchi, 2004). Most important, the activation and integration processes are asynchronous, parallel processes with the onset of activation preceding the onset of integration (Cook and O'Brien, 2014). Thus, the conceptualization of inference generation as a two-stage process is guided primarily by the onset of the two core processes involved rather than because they are discrete processes. Indeed, activation and integration are often perceived as continuous and overlapping because they run in parallel (Kintsch, 1998).

With respect to the activation stage, there is consensus in the literature that the activation of information from memory is a passive process (e.g., Resonance; Myers and O'Brien, 1998; O'Brien and Myers, 1999); thus, it is beyond the intention or the control of the reader. Furthermore, information is activated on the basis of featural overlap, independent of whether it is appropriate or relevant to the specific reading situation (Cook, Lassonde, Splinter, Guéraud, Stiegler-Balfour, and O'Brien, 2013). The integration process is also perceived as a passive process that depends to a large extent on activation but has the potential to be influenced by attentional, strategic processes. In turn, the execution of these two parallel, asynchronous processes is influenced by the readers' standards of coherence. Standards of coherence refer to a set of implicit or explicit criteria for comprehension that readers employ during reading (van den Broek, Bohn-Gettler, Kendeou, Carlson, and White, 2011; van den Broek, Lorch, Linderholm, and Gustafson, 2001; van den Broek, Risden, and Husebye-Hartmann, 1995). These criteria vary between individuals, as well as within an individual across reading situations. These standards are influenced directly by various aspects of the reader, the text, and the reading task. It is, therefore, assumed that these factors (reader characteristics, text characteristics, and task demands) exert their influence on inference generation directly but also indirectly via the reader's standards of coherence.

By conceptualizing the activation and integration of information as distinct, parallel, and asynchronous processes that support inference generation we can determine more precisely when and under what conditions inferences are generated. For example, factors that can influence the activation and integration processes, such as individual differences, task demands, and text characteristics, can influence inference generation. This conceptualization also has implications for identifying potential sources of failure in inference generation. One source pertains to whether there is activation of relevant information, whereas a second source pertains to whether there is integration of that information. As mentioned above, the mere activation of relevant information is not sufficient to ensure integration, and thus, inference generation. For example, there is evidence that even if the amount of available relevant information is equal, readers differ in the extent to which they generate inferences (Cain et al., 2001). Furthermore, difficulties in the activation of relevant information are detrimental to the inference process. Such difficulties may be the result of encoding failures in the context of the current text, lack of knowledge, lack of knowledge accesibility, or any combination of these. The activation of the relevant information is also constrained by working memory in at least two important ways. Working memory influences the quantity of the information that can be retrieved, and the efficiency of the retrieval process from long-term memory (Daneman and Carpenter, 1980; Engle and Conway, 1998). Thus, there are several factors that have the potential to influence this two-stage process and put at risk the successful generation of inferences.

Taxonomies of inferences

The conceptualization of inference as the process of *activation* and *integration* of information can contribute to a better understanding of the various taxonomies of inferences proposed in the literature. With respect to the source of the information necessary to be activated for the inference, inferences may depend exclusively on textual information or depend on both textual information and general world knowledge. For example, inferences that depend exlusively on textual information have often been termed in the literature as *text-connecting* (Graesser et al., 1994; Kintsch and Kintsch, 2005), *intersentence* (Cain and Oakhill, 1999), *text-to-text* (Cromley and Azevedo, 2007), *bridging* (Singer and Ritchot, 1996; van den Broek, 1990) or *coherence* inferences (Bowyer-Crane and Snowling, 2005). Inferences that depend on both textual information and general world knowledge have often been termed in the literature as *knowledge-based or extratextual* (Graesser et al.,1994; Kintsch and Kintsch, 2005), *elaborative* (Bowyer-Crane and Snowling, 2005; Kintsch, 1998; O'Brien, 1987; O'Brien, Shank, Myers, and Rayner, 1988; van den Broek, 1990), or *gap-filling* (Cain and Oakhill, 1999).

Another distinction that has been made is between *local* and *global* inferences (Albrecht and O'Brien, 1993; Graesser et al., 1994; O'Brien and Albrecht, 1992). Local inferences involve connecting current text information with the immediately preceding context (i.e., information in working memory, generally the previous one to three sentences), whereas global inferences involve connecting current text with relevant information presented previously in the text but no longer available in working memory. Local inferences typically involve coherence inferences and bridging inferences, whereas global inferences often involve inferences about the goal, theme, or main point of the text.

Perhaps the most controversial distinction that has been made in the literature is that of the nature of the inferential process itself that centered around *automatic* versus *strategic or controlled* types of inferences (Graesser et al., 1994; Kintsch, 1993; McKoon and Ratcliff, 1992). On the one hand, the minimalist view (McKoon and Ratcliff, 1992) supports that only those inferences that are necessary for coherence or are supported by available information will be encoded during reading, and the reader generates those automatically. On the other hand, the constructionist view (Graesser et al., 1994) supports that readers routinely draw inferences to achieve coherence and do so strategically in a "search after meaning" fashion. The field has now reached a consensus: the minimalist and the constructionist views describe different and legitimate points of the inference generation process on a continuum (Kintsch and Kinstch, 2005; van den Broek, Rapp, and Kendeou, 2005). The minimalist view focuses on the lower boundary of the inferential process (effortless, passive, and automatic), whereas the constructionist view focuses on the higher boundary of the inferential process (effortful, active, and strategic).

Related to the aforementioned is the distinction between *online* and *off-line* inferences (Graesser et al., 1994; Long, Oppy, and Seely, 1994). Online inferences are those that are normally generated during the course of reading, whereas off-line inferences are generated after reading is complete, often during a retrieval task. Even though there has been some debate as to what types of inferences are generated online, there is consensus that context influences what will or will not be inferred (Albrecht and O'Brien, 1993; Lassonde and O'Brien, 2009; Lea, Kayser, Mulligan, and Myers, 2002; McKoon and Ratcliff, 1992; O'Brien and Albrecht, 1992; Peracchi and O'Brien, 2004). For example, the minimalist view suggests that only inferences based on readily available information or those required for coherence are encoded during reading, unless a reader adopts special goals or strategies. The constructionist view suggests that superordinate goals, causal antecedents, and theme inferences are encoded online in most cases but not under all conditions of reading. Thus, with reading being highly contextual and dynamic, the distinction between online and off-line inferences is a rather trivial one.

A more general classification of inferences comes from the work on logic and reasoning in reading comprehension. In the context of this work, a distinction has been made between *inductive* and *deductive* inferences (Singer and Lea, 2012). Inductive inferences are based on our general understanding of the world and are probabilistic in nature, whereas deductive inferences are certain to be true if the premises they are based on are true. Thus, the inductive inference category likely includes most of the aforementioned types of inferences. The deductive inferences category, though, includes only inferences that are generated following the rules of logic (Lea, 1995; 1998).

Above and beyond what inferences readers routinely generate over the course of reading, it is also important to consider what inferences *can* potentially be generated. A number of elegant studies using verbal protocols and in-depth content analyses have resulted in extensive lists of the different types of inferences that could be encoded over the course of various reading situations. One notable example is the taxonomy by van den Broek, Fletcher, and Risden (1993). Van den Broek et al. developed this taxonomy by focusing on (1) the function of each type of inference in terms of maintaining coherence, and (2) the source of the information that is being activated. This taxonomy includes backward inferences (e.g., anaphoric inferences), connecting inferences, reinstatements, backward elaborations, orthogonal elaborations, forward elaborations, and associations. It is important to reemphasize that these studies focused on revealing the repertoires of inferences that children or adults can generate, not necessarily what individuals do generate during typical reading experiences.

Gerrig and O'Brien (2005), however, argued that creating a taxonomy of inferences has limited value because the initial basic process of inference activation is the same, independent of inference type. They argued that inferential information becomes available to the extent that information in active memory makes contact with information from earlier in the text, from prior knowledge, or both. Nevertheless, given the manner in which information is organized in memory, some types of inferences may have a higher likelihood of being generated than others (e.g., causal inferences are typically and routinely generated), but the basic activation process that leads to the activation of any type of inference is the same. Thus, perhaps the importance of taxonomies of inferences becomes important only when considering the text characteristics that might favor or constrain the generation of one type of inference over another.

This brief review highlights the variability, the complexity, and the mixed findings for the types and occurrences of inferences in the literature. This research, however, also has led to a number of issues on which the scientific community has reached consensus. Specifically, previous research has yielded a large body of empirical findings suggesting that inferencing is a two-stage process involving both the activation and integration of information in memory. There is also consensus that inference ability or skill is perceived as a higher-order skill (as opposed to lower-level) that can be best conceptualized as a continuum with low and high boundaries. At the low end of the continuum, the inference process is described as effortless, passive, and automatic. At the high end of the continuum, the inference process is described as effortful, active, and strategic. The interesting question is the nature of the development of this skill. I turn to this issue next.

Developmental patterns in inference skill

How do we develop the ability to make inferences? This higher-order skill must be acquired, and it warrants instructional attention in its own right. Its acquisition follows the developmental stages of any cognitive skill development. These stages involve a cognitive stage that leads to the initial encoding of the skill; an associative stage during which initial errors in skill execution are corrected; and finally, an autonomous stage during which the skill continues to expand and its execution is improved (Anderson, 1982). Most important, by conceptualizing inference skill as the activation and integration of information, we can also identify *what develops* in inference skill. As argued above, the activation and integration of information are distinct, parallel, and asynchronous processes. Because the activation process is passive, its development likely asymptotes very quickly and early and therefore plays a very minor role in what develops in inference skill. What likely develops is the integration process because it has the potential to be influenced by attentional and strategic processes. Specifically, the integration process develops and improves as attentional focus and executive functions develop and improve (Diamond, 2013; Liu, Reichle, and Gao, 2013). That said, the factor that likely explains the most variance in the development of inference skill is neither the activation nor the integration process, but the reader's general world knowledge. That is because the development of readers' prior knowledge (in terms of richness and interconnectedness), influences directly the product of the activation process and, thus, the integration process. In fact, when attentional focus is held relatively constant, then any variability in inference skill will be dominated by prior knowledge.

The developmental literature provides evidence consistent with this view that inference skill is directly linked primarily to knowledge acquisition. Specifically, inference skill follows a systematic developmental progression (e.g., van den Broek, 1989; 1990; 1997) that is consistent with the acquisition of general world knowledge via implicit and explicit learning experiences. This progression starts with inferences that involve concrete physical relations that occur close together. Next are inferences that involve concrete physical relations between distant events. Next are causal inferences involving characters' goals and emotions or other internal states. The next level involves inferences for hierarchical and thematic relations between clusters of events. The final, and the highest, level is inferences that involve a moral or a main idea. It is important to note that even very young children *can* generate all of these types of inferences, but they generally need the inferences involved to be highly constrained by the text or prior knowledge (van den Broek et al., 2005).

A number of developmental studies on inference skill also show that young readers are able to generate different types of inferences if they are provided with specific instructions or assistance (Cain, Oakhill, and Elbro, 2003;Cain, Oakhill, and Lemmon, 2004; Oakhill, Cain, and Bryant, 2003). For example, young readers are likely to make inferences when they are encouraged to elaborate on the text (Paris, Lindauer and Cox, 1977), when they are being questioned (Basche, 2001; Omanson, Warren, and Trabasso, 1978; Paris and Lindauer, 1976), or when inferences are necessary to establish coherence (Casteel, 1993; Casteel and Simpson, 1991; van den Broek, 1990). Most important, training studies that aim to teach children directly how to generate inferences do so with the use of directed questioning techniques (McGee and Johnson, 2003; McMaster et al., 2012; van den Broek, Kendeou, Lousberg, and Visser, 2011; Yuill and Oakhill, 1988). Following the conceptualization of inference skill as the activation and integration of information, the aforementioned instructional and scaffolding approaches are likely effective because (1) they provide appropriate cues to general world knowledge, thereby influencing the product of the activation process, and (2) they direct attentional focus to the relevant information in the text, thereby influencing the integration process.

Evidence for a general inference skill

The underlying assumption that supports the view of a general inference skill stems from the conceptualization of inference generation as a two-stage process that involves the execution of the parallel and asynchronous processes of activation and integration. In this section, I will discuss evidence that demonstrates the generalizability of inference skill across different media. This evidence takes the form of processing similarities for event sequences that require *fill-in* information, independent of the medium in which they are presented (e.g., written text, oral instructions, televised show). It is important to note that this does not mean that there are no processing differences between different media. In fact, there is long-standing evidence in the literature that different media differ in fundamental ways (Bus and Neuman, 2009; Magliano, Dijkstra, and Zwann, 1996; Magliano, Loschy, Clinton, and Larson, 2013). The important point here is that the actual processes by which inferences are generated across different media are the same.

Positive transfer of inference skills across media is plausible for at least two additional reasons. First, understanding texts presented using different media (via television, aurally, written) requires many of the same cognitive processes (e.g., sequencing events, connecting events, activating and integrating background knowledge, monitoring comprehension). In fact, a number of theorists in the field of discourse processes have already argued that models of reading comprehension can extend to other media as well (Gernsbacher, 1990; Kintsch, 1998; Magliano et al., 2013; Magliano, Radvansky, and Copeland, 2007; McNamara and Magliano, 2009). Second, research indicates that the same structural factors (e.g., number of causal connections, explicitness of goals, event boundaries) predict what individuals remember from televised, oral, or written narratives (Kendeou, White, and Lorch, 2008; Lorch and Sanchez, 1997; Lynch and van den Broek, 2007; Lynch, van den Broek, Kremer, Magliano, Kopp, McNerney, Radvansky, and Zacks, 2012; O'Brien and Myers, 1987; van den Broek, Helder, and Van Leijenhorst, 2013).

Important to the argument for a general inference skill is evidence for inference generation that has been observed in nonreading contexts and well before children become conventional readers (Moshman, 2004). For example, there is evidence that two-year-old children can infer causal relations between sequences of events (Bauer, 2007; Bauer and Lukowski, 2010); four-year-old children can generate deductive inferences in various settings and contexts (Lynch and van den Broek, 2007; Wenner, 2004), as well as causal inferences of the events they experience (van den Broek, Lorch, and Thurlow, 1996). Similar findings have been reported when six-year-old children listen to aurally presented stories (Trabasso and Nickels, 1992).Thus, even very young children engage in inferential processes to comprehend the events they experience in their everyday lives. Notably, these inferential processes are grounded in causality.

Further evidence for the generalization of inference skill comes from the work of Kendeou et al. (2008). Kendeou et al. investigated the degree to which children's inference generation ability generalized across different media and predicted comprehension over and above other important precursors to reading comprehension, such as basic language skills and vocabulary. They followed two cohorts of children aged four and six as they turned six and eight years old, respectively. At each time point they assessed children's inference and narrative comprehension skills using aural, televised, and written stories. The findings showed that children generated a variety of inferences across the different media. These inferences included character goals, actions, causal antecedents, causal consequences, character states, and emotions. Not all types of inferences, though, contributed equally to narrative comprehension. There was a clear developmental pattern, with goal inferences contributing to comprehension as early as four years of age and continuing strong at ages six and eight. Causal inferences (antecedents and consequences) significantly contributed to comprehension at ages six and eight. Character actions and emotions significantly contributed to comprehension only at age eight. Most important, this pattern was *independent of media factors* and it was consistent with the developmental hierarchy of inferences reported in the extant literature (e.g., Bourg, Bauer and van den Broek, 1997; Neuman, 1988; Trabasso and Nickels, 1992; van den Broek, 1997) demonstrating children's increased sensitivity to the centrality of the causal structure of narratives as they grow older (Goldman and Varnhagen, 1986; van den Broek, 1989; 1990; van den Broek et al., 2013).

A legitimate question is whether there is evidence in the literature that supports the idea that the ability to generate inferences does *not* generalize across media. The answer is yes. However, the evidence for an inference skill that is *medium-specific* is very limited (Pezdek, Lehrer, and Simon, 1984) compared to the evidence that has accumulated and supports common, core inference processes across different media (Kendeou et al., 2008; 2009; Lorch and Sanchez, 1997; Lynch and van den Broek, 2007; Lynch et al., 2008; Magliano et al., 1996; 2012; 2013; van den Broek et al., 1996; 2013). Furthermore, the general inference view can account for media-specific influences on inference generation as well. For example, some media provide multiple connections to general world knowledge and, therefore, increased access and activation of both relevant and irrelevant information. Relevant information can facilitate inference generation, whereas irrelevant information will likely hinder inference generation. Thus, different media, depending on the patterns of activation they produce, will act as facilitators or as obstacles for inference generation and comprehension.

Implications for early assessment and interventions

Having made the case for inference as a skill that generalizes across different media, I now argue that this view has important implications for early assessment, diagnosis, and intervention of reading comprehension difficulties in the early years. Indeed, a significant group of children who are proficient in lower-level reading skills (such as decoding) but have difficulties in reading comprehension struggle because of failures in inference generation (Cain et al., 2001; Cain and Oakhill, 2006; Kendeou et al., 2009; McKeown, Beck, and Blake, 2009). The typical profile of these children is intact word reading but poor reading comprehension. This description characterizes typical struggling readers in school settings, who make up approximately 10 percent of school-age children (Nation, 2005).

The first implication of the general inference view relates to the assessment of inference skill in young children even before the beginning of formal reading instruction. That a child's inference skill generalizes across different media allows for the use of nonreading contexts, for example via aural or televised stories, to assess one's ability to generate different types of inferences. Thus, such assessment might be used for early identification of students who experience difficulties in inference generation early on, so that this ability can be subsequently and appropriately developed through targeted interventions. To assess inference skill in young children we have developed a methodology that is based on our longitudinal work on narrative comprehension (Kendeou et al., 2005; 2007; 2008; 2009; van den Broek et al., 2005; 2011). In this methodology, children first watch television narratives or listen to aurally presented narratives. Children are then asked questions aimed at different levels of inference making related to the causal structure of the narrative. These questions target causal inferences, character action inferences, character emotion inferences, character goal inferences, and theme inferences. The emphasis in this assessment approach is on the patterns of question answering, rather than just on the amount.

A second implication relates to the types of strategy interventions that might be used with young children to build inference skill. There are ample examples in the literature with questioning-based interventions or focused book-reading activities that encourage children to be actively involved before, during, and after reading. These interventions are used to develop and foster language comprehension skills in young children by focusing specifically on inference generation (e.g., Berkeley, Scruggs, and Mastropieri, 2010; Fricke, Bowyer-Crane, Haley, Hulme, and Snowling, 2013; McGee and Johnson, 2003; McKeown et al., 2009;

McMaster et al., 2012; Pressley, Graham, and Harris, 2006; Yuill and Oakhill, 1988). These inference-focused interventions could be used with young children during listening to a story or watching a televised story and with questioning activities focused on the important events as indicated by the causal structure of the story (van den Broek et al., 2013).

In the context of the general inference view, these targeted questions have the potential to influence inference generation because they (1) 'cue' the activation of the relevant information needed, and (2) explicitly facilitate the integration of that information because integration is necessary for providing a correct answer to the question. As children's representations develop in breadth and depth, the number and types of questions answered correctly will increase. For example, while children still have impoverished representations (either because they are low-skill or because they are still young; Ericsson and Kintsch, 1995), focused questioning targeting highly constrained inferences at the local level will contribute to the development of better representations. These better representations will subsequently make it possible to answer questions at a global level (and, thus generate global inferences). These global inferences will also contribute to the development of even better representations, which in turn, will make it possible for children to answer questions focused at higher levels of inference making, and so on. Ultimately, the aim would be for children to internalize and transfer this inference skill from nonreading to reading contexts.

Future directions

Assuming a general inference skill that depends on fundamental memory processes and generalizes across different media raises a number of questions that warrant further exploration. One issue is the extent to which the convergence observed in inference generation across different media is limited to narrative prose or whether it generalizes to expository prose. Narrative prose (e.g., novels, short stories) tends to follow a familiar and often common structure. Indeed, most narratives have a beginning, a middle, and an end; they also typically contain settings, characters, and a plot. More important, narratives have a close correspondence to everyday experiences (Kintsch, 1998). Expository prose (e.g., textbooks, encyclopedias), in contrast, tends to present information following various, and not always familiar, structures (Duke, 2004; Williams et al., 2005). Common structures include sequence, problem-solution, compare-contrast, cause-effect, and refutation. Although I have argued that the actual processes by which inferences are generated across media are the same, the evidence in support of this claim has accumulated from research with narrative prose. It will be important to address this issue in the context of expository prose in future research.

A second issue that warrants further investigation pertains to the factors that influence individual differences in inference skill across different media. A number of factors have been reported in the literature and are known to influence individual differences in inference generation during reading; among those, readers' prior knowledge (Kendeou and van den Broek, 2005; Kintsch, 1988; McNamara, 2001; McNamara, Kintsch, Songer, and Kintsch, 1996), working memory capacity (Cain et al., 2004; Linderholm and van den Broek, 2002), standards of coherence (van den Broek et al., 1995; 2001; 2011), and reading skill (Cain and Oakhill, 1999; Cain et al., 2001) are considered particularly influential. Do the same factors that predict individual differences in inference generation in texts also account for individual differences in visual media? Or are there medium-specific factors that exert direct influences on inference generation? It will be important to address this issue in future research as well.

A final issue pertains to the conditions that can result in comprehension benefits, rather than difficulties, in the use of different media to foster inference generation. For example, a media approach to inference generation training potentially can improve comprehension, if it increases the attention a child can devote to the relevant information in the story (Kendeou, van den Broek, Helder, and Karlsson, 2014). If it does not increase attention to the to-be-inferred information, then it will have no benefit or it may even have a detrimental effect (van den Broek et al., 2011). For example, when narratives are presented in televised format, young children will likely focus on loud and flashy, but unimportant, events as compared to the same narratives presented in auditory form (van den Broek et al., 1996; Wenner, 2004). This problem frequently is compounded when multimedia are used to motivate or increase interest in the comprehender rather than to present opportunities for strategy or skill instruction (van den Broek, Kendeou, and White, 2009). Thus, understanding the conditions and features that can facilitate inference generation is important for the design of effective, educational (multi)media.

Concluding remarks

The ability to draw inferences is considered the cornerstone of reading comprehension. My goal in this theoretical contribution is to present a case for the existence of a *general inference skill*. In doing so, I drew on literatures in discourse processes and event comprehension and provided evidence that inference generation is an acquired skill that depends on the activation and integration of information; it follows a systematic developmental progression in which what develops is in an ever-increasing knowledge base; and it generalizes across different media. The conceptualization of inference ability as a general skill opens up the possibility for the development of assessment and instructional approaches that can support the acquisition of the skill in one medium and its transfer in another medium. At the same time, such conceptualization opens up the possibility for identifying the sources of failures in inference generation, which can, in turn, inform the design of targeted interventions.

REFERENCES

Ackerman, B. P. (1986). Referential and causal coherence in the story comprehension of children and adults. *Journal of Experimental Child Psychology*, *41*, 336–66.
  (1988). Reason inferences in the story comprehension of children and adults. *Child Development*, *59*, 1426–42.
Albrecht, J. E., & O'Brien, E. J. (1993). Updating a mental model: maintaining both local and global coherence. *Journal of Experimental Psychology: Learning, Memory, and Cognition*, *19*, 1061–70.
  (1995). Goal processing and the maintenance of global coherence. In R. F. Lorch & E. J. O'Brien (eds.) *Sources of Coherence in Reading* (pp. 159–76). Mahwah, NJ: Erlbaum.
Alexander, P. A., & The Disciplined Reading and Learning Research Laboratory (2012). Reading into the future: competence for the 21st century. *Educational Psychologist*, *47*, 259–80.
Anderson, J. R. (1982). Acquisition of cognitive skill. *Psychological Review*, *89*, 369–406.
Anderson, R. C., & Freebody, P. (1981). Vocabulary knowledge. In J. Guthrie (ed.), *Comprehension and Teaching: Research Reviews* (pp. 77–117). Newark, DE: International Reading Association.
Baddeley, A. (2003). Working memory and language: an overview. *Journal of Communication Disorders*, *36*(3), 189–208.
Baker, L. (1984). Children's effective use of multiple standards for evaluating their comprehension. *Journal of Educational Psychology*, *76*, 588–97.
Barnes, M. A., Dennis, M., & Haefele-Kalvaitis, J. (1996). The effects of knowledge availability and knowledge accessibility on coherence and elaborative inferencing in children from six to fifteen years of age. *Journal of Experimental Child Psychology*, *61*, 216–41.
Basche, P. (2001). Inferential questioning: effects on comprehension of narrative texts as a function of grade and timing. *Journal of Educational Psychology*, *93*, 521–29.
Bauer, P. J. (2007). Recall in infancy: a neurodevelopmental account. *Current Directions in Psychological Science*, *16*, 142–46.

Bauer, P. J., & Lukowski, A. F. (2010). The memory is in the details: relations between memory for the specific features of events and long-term recall in infancy. *Journal of Experimental Child Psychology, 107*, 1–14.

Beck, I. L., Perfetti, C. A., & McKeown, M. G. (1982). Effects of long-term vocabulary instruction on lexical access and reading comprehension. *Journal of Educational Psychology, 74*, 506–20.

Berkeley, S., Scruggs, T. E., & Mastropieri, M. A. (2010). Reading comprehension instruction for students with learning disabilities, 1995–2006: a meta-analysis. *Remedial and Special Education, 31*, 423–36.

Blanc, N., Kendeou, P., van den Broek, P., & Brouillet, D. (2008). Updating situation models: empirical data and simulations. *Discourse Processes, 45*, 103–21.

Bourg, T., Bauer, P., & van den Broek, P. (1997). Building the bridges: the development of event comprehension and representation. In P. van den Broek, P. Bauer, & T. Bourg (eds.), *Developmental Spans in Event Comprehension and Representation: Bridging Fictional and Actual Events* (pp. 385–407). Mahwah, NJ: Erlbaum.

Bowyer-Crane, C., & Snowling, M. J. (2005). Assessing children's inference generation: what do tests of reading comprehension measure? *British Journal of Educational Psychology, 75*, 189–201.

Bus, A. G., & Neuman, S. B. (2009). *Multimedia and Literacy Development: Improving Achievement for Young Learners*. New York: Routledge.

Cain, K., & Oakhill, J. V. (1999). Inference making ability and its relation to comprehension failure in young children. *Reading and Writing, 11*(5–6), 489–503.

(2006). Profiles of children with specific reading comprehension difficulties. *The British Journal of Educational Psychology, 76*(4), 683–96.

Cain, K. Oakhill, J. V., Barnes, M. A., & Bryant, P. E. (2001). Comprehension skill, inference making ability, and the relation to knowledge. *Memory & Cognition, 29*, 850–9.

Cain, K., Oakhill, J. V., & Elbro, C. (2003). The ability to learn new word meanings from context by school-age children with and without language comprehension difficulties. *Journal of Child Language, 30*(3), 681–94.

Cain, K., Oakhill, J., & Lemmon, K. (2004). Individual differences in the inference of word meanings from context: the influence of reading comprehension, vocabulary knowledge, and memory capacity. *Journal of Educational Psychology, 96*, 671–81.

Casteel, M. A. (1993). Effects of inference necessity and reading goal on children's inferential generation. *Developmental Psychology, 29*, 346–57.

Casteel, M. A., & Simpson, G. B. (1991). Textual coherence and the development of inferential generation skills. *Journal of Research in Reading, 14*, 116–29.

Common Core State Standards Initiative. (2010). *Common core state standards for English language arts and literacy in history/social studies, science, and technical subjects*. Washington, DC: Council of Chief State School Officers and National Governors Association. Retrieved from www.corestandards.org/

Cook, A. E., Halleran, J. G., & O'Brien, E. J. (1998). What is readily available during reading? A memory-based view of text processing. *Discourse Processes*, *26*(2&3), 109–29.

Cook, A. E., Lassonde, K. A., Splinter, A., Guéraud, S., Stiegler-Balfour, J. J., & O'Brien, E. J. (2013). The role of relevance in the activation and instantiation of predictive inferences. *Language and Cognitive Processes*, *29*, 244–57.

Cook, A. E., & O'Brien, E. J. (2014). Knowledge activation, integration, and validation during narrative text comprehension. *Discourse Processes*, *51*, 26–49.

Cowan, N. (2010). Multiple concurrent thoughts: the meaning and developmental neuropsychology of working memory. *Developmental Neuropsychology*, *35*(5), 447–74.

Cromley, J., & Azevedo, R. (2007). Testing and refining the Direct and Inferential Mediation Model of reading comprehension. *Journal of Educational Psychology*, *99*, 311–25.

Daneman, M., & Carpenter, P. A. (1980). Individual differences in working memory and reading. *Journal of Verbal Learning and Verbal Behavior*, *19*, 450–66.

Diamond, A. (2013). Executive functions. *Annual Review of Psychology*, *64*, 135–68.

Duke, N. K. (2004). The case for informational text. *Educational Leadership*, *61*(6), 40–5.

Ehri, L. (2005). Learning to read words: theory, findings and issues. *Scientific Studies of Reading*, *9*, 167–88.

Elbro C., & Buch-Iversen, I. (2013). Activation of background knowledge for inference making: effects on reading comprehension. *Scientific Studies of Reading*, *17*, 435–52.

Engle, R. W., & Conway, A. R. A. (1998). Working memory and comprehension. In R. H. Logie & K. J. Gilhooly (eds.), *Working Memory and Thinking* (pp. 67–92). East Sussex, UK: Psychology Press.

Ericsson, K. A., & Kintsch, W. (1995). Long-term working memory. *Psychological Review*, *102*, 211–45.

Fricke, S., Bowyer-Crane, C. A., Haley, A. J., Hulme, C., & Snowling, M. (2013). Efficacy of language intervention in the early years. *Journal of Child Psychology and Psychiatry*, *54*(3), 280–90.

Fuchs, L. S., Fuchs, D., Hosp, M. K., & Jenkins, J. R. (2001). Oral reading fluency as an indicator of reading competence: a theoretical, empirical, and historical analysis. *Scientific Studies of Reading*, *5*(3), 239–56.

Gernsbacher, M. A. (1990). *Language Comprehension as Structure Building*. Mahwah, NJ: Erlbaum.

Gerrig, R. J., & O'Brien, E. J. (2005). The scope of memory-based processing. *Discourse Processes*, *39*, 225–42.

Goldman, S. R., & Varnhagen, C. K. (1986). Memory for embedded and sequential episodes in stories. *Journal of Memory and Language*, *25*, 401–18.

Gough, P. B., & Tunmer, W. E. (1986). Decoding, reading, and reading disability. *Remedial and Special Education*, *7*(1), 6–10.

Graesser, A., Singer, M., & Trabasso, T. (1994). Constructing inferences during narrative comprehension. *Psychological Review, 101*, 371–95.

Hannon, B., & Daneman, M. (1998). Facilitating knowledge-based inferences in less-skilled readers. *Contemporary Educational Psychology, 23*, 149–72.

Kendeou, P., Bohn-Gettler, C., White, M. J., & van den Broek, P. (2008). Children's inference generation across different media. *Journal of Research in Reading, 31*(3), 259–72.

Kendeou, P., Lynch, J., Broek, P., Espin, C., White, M., & Kremer, K. (2005). Developing successful readers: building early comprehension skills through television viewing and listening. *Early Childhood Education Journal, 33*(2), 91–8.

Kendeou, P., Smith, E. R., & O'Brien, E. J. (2013). Updating during reading comprehension: why causality matters. *Journal of Experimental Psychology: Learning, Memory, and Cognition, 39*, 854–65.

Kendeou, P., & van den Broek, P. (2005). The effects of readers' misconceptions on comprehension of scientific text. *Journal of Educational Psychology, 97*, 235–45.

(2007). The effects of prior knowledge and text structure on comprehension processes during reading of scientific texts. *Memory & Cognition, 35*(7), 1567–77.

Kendeou, P., van den Broek, P., Helder, A., & Karlsson, A. K. J. (2014). A cognitive view of reading comprehension: implications for reading difficulties. *Learning Disabilities Research & Practice, 29*(1), 10–16.

Kendeou, P., van den Broek, P., White, M., & Lynch, J. (2007). Preschool and early elementary comprehension: skill development and strategy interventions. In D. S. McNamara (ed.), *Reading Comprehension Strategies: Theories, Interventions, and Technologies.* (pp. 27–45). Mahwah, NJ: Erlbaum.

(2009). Predicting reading comprehension in early elementary school: the independent contributions of oral language and decoding skills. *Journal of Educational Psychology, 101*(4), 765–78.

Kintsch, W. (1988). The role of knowledge in discourse comprehension: a construction-integration model. *Psychological Review, 95*(2), 163–82.

(1993). Information accretion and reduction in text processing: inferences. Special issue: Inference generation during text comprehension. *Discourse Processes, 161*–2, 193–202.

(1998). *Comprehension: A Paradigm for Cognition.* New York: Cambridge University Press.

Kintsch W., & Kintsch, E. (2005). Comprehension. In S. G. Paris and S. A. Stahl (eds.), *Current Issues in Reading Comprehension and Assessment* (pp. 71–92). Mahwah, NJ: Erlbaum.

LaBerge, D., & Samuels, S. J. (1974). Toward a theory of automatic information processing in reading. *Cognitive Psychology, 6*(2), 293–323.

Lassonde, K. A., & O'Brien, E. J. (2009). Contextual specificity in the activation of predictive inferences. *Discourse Processes, 46*, 426–38.

(2013). Occupational stereotypes: activation of male bias in a gender neutral world. *Journal of Applied Social Psychology, 43*, 387–96.

Lea, R. B. (1995). Online evidence for elaborative logical inferences in text. *Journal of Experimental Psychology: Learning, Memory, and Cognition, 21,* 1469–82.

(1998). Logical inference and comprehension: how mental logic and text processing theories need each other. In M. D. S. Braine & D. P. O'Brien (eds.), *Mental Logic* (pp. 63–78). Mahwah, NJ: Erlbaum.

Lea, R. B., Kayser, P., Mulligan, E. J., & Myers, J. (2002) Do readers make inferences about conversational topics? *Memory & Cognition, 30,* 945–57.

Linderholm, T., & van den Broek, P. (2002). The effects of reading purpose and working memory capacity on the processing of expository text. *Journal of Educational Psychology, 94*(4), 778–84.

Liu, Y., Reichle, E. D., & Gao, D. - G. (2013). Using reinforcement learning to examine dynamic attention allocation during reading. *Cognitive Science, 37,* 1507–40.

Long, D. L., & Chong, J. L. (2001). Comprehension skill and global coherence: A paradoxical picture of poor comprehenders' abilities. *Journal of Experimental Psychology: Learning, Memory, and Cognition, 27*(6), 1424–29.

Long, D. L., Oppy, B. J., & Seely, M. R. (1994). Individual differences in the time course of inferential processing. *Journal of Experimental Psychology: Learning, Memory, and Cognition, 20*(6), 1456–70.

Lorch, E. P., & Sanchez, R. P. (1997). Children's memory for televised events. In P. W. van den Broek, P. J. Bauer & T. Bourg (eds.), *Developmental Spans in Event Comprehension and Representation: Bridging Fictional and Actual Events.* (pp. 271–91). Mahwah, NJ: Erlbaum.

Lynch, J. S., & van den Broek, P. (2007). Understanding the glue of narrative structure: children's on- and off-line inferences about characters' goals. *Cognitive Development, 22,* 323–40.

Lynch, J. S., van den Broek, P., Kremer, K. E., Kendeou, P., White, M. J., & Lorch, E. (2008). The development of narrative comprehension and its relation to other early reading skills. *Reading Psychology, 29,* 327–65.

Magliano, J. P., Dijkstra, K., & Zwaan, R. (1996). Generating predictive inferences while viewing a movie. *Discourse Processes, 22,* 199–224.

Magliano, J. P., Kopp, K., McNerney, M. W., Radvansky, G. A., & Zacks, J. M. (2012). Aging and perceived event structure as a function of modality. *Aging, Neuropsychology, and Cognition, 19,* 264–82.

Magliano, J. P., Loschky, L. C., Clinton, J., & Larson, A. M. (2013). Is reading the same as viewing? An exploration of the similarities and differences between processing text- and visually based narratives. In B. Miller, L. Cutting, and P. McCardle (eds.), *Unraveling the Behavioral, Neurobiological, and Genetic Components of Reading Comprehension* (pp. 78–90). Baltimore, MD: Brookes Publishing.

Magliano, J. P., Radvansky, G. A., & Copeland, D. E. (2007). Beyond language comprehension: situation models as a form or autobiographical memory. In F. Schmalhofer & C. Perfetti (eds.), *Higher Level Language Processes in the Brain: Inference and Comprehension Processes* (pp. 379–91). Mahwah, NJ: Erlbaum.

McGee, A., & Johnson, H. (2003). The effect of inference training on skilled and less skilled comprehenders. *Educational Psychology, 23,* 49–59.

McKeown, M. G., Beck, I. L., & Blake, R. G. K. (2009). Rethinking reading comprehension instruction: a comparison of instruction for strategies and content approaches. *Reading Research Quarterly*, *44*(3), 218–53.

McKoon G., & Ratcliff, R. (1992). Inference during reading. *Psychological Review*, *99*, 440–66.

McMaster, K. L., van den Broek, P., Espin, C. A., White, M. J., Rapp, D. N., Kendeou, P., Bohn-Gettler, C. M., & Carlson, S. (2012). Making the right connections: differential effects of reading intervention for subgroups of comprehenders. *Learning and Individual Differences*, *22*(1), 100–11.

McNamara, D.S. (2001). Reading both high-coherence and low-coherence texts: effects of text sequence and prior knowledge. *Canadian Journal of Experimental Psychology*, *55*, 51–62.

McNamara, D. S., Kintsch, E., Songer, N. B., & Kintsch, W. (1996). Are good texts always better? Interactions of text coherence, background knowledge, and levels of understanding in learning from text. *Cognition and Instruction*, *14*, 1–43.

McNamara, D. S., & Magliano, J. (2009). Toward a comprehensive model of comprehension. In B. Ross (ed.), *The Psychology of Learning and Motivation* (pp. 297–384). New York: Elsevier.

Moshman, D. (2004). From inference to reasoning: the construction of rationality. *Thinking & Reasoning*, *10*, 221–39.

Myers, J. L., & O'Brien, E. J. (1998). Accessing the discourse representation during reading. *Discourse Processes*, *26*(2–3), 131–57.

Nagy, W. E., Herman, P. A., & Anderson, R. C. (1985). Learning words from context. *Reading Research Quarterly*, *20*(2), 233–53.

Nation, K. (2005). Children's reading comprehension difficulties. In M. Snowling & C. Hulme (eds.), *The Science of Reading: A Handbook* (pp. 248–65). Oxford: Blackwell.

Neuman, S. B. (1988). The displacement effect: assessing the relation between television viewing and reading performance. *Reading Research Quarterly*, *23*, 414–40.

Oakhill, J. (1984). Inferential and memory skills in children's comprehension of stories. *British Journal of Educational Psychology*, *54*, 31–39.

Oakhill, J. V., & Cain, K. (2012). The precursors of reading ability in young readers: Evidence from a four-year longitudinal study. *Scientific Studies of Reading*, *16*, 91–121.

Oakhill, J., Cain, K., & Bryant, P. E. (2003). The dissociation of word reading and text comprehension: evidence from component skills. *Language and Cognitive Processes*, *18*(4), 443–68.

Oakhill, J., Hartt, J., & Samols, D. (2005). Levels of comprehension monitoring and working memory in good and poor comprehenders. *Reading and Writing*, *18*(7–9), 657–86.

O'Brien, E. J. (1987). Antecedent search processes and the structure of text. *Journal of Experimental Psychology: Learning, Memory, and Cognition*, *13*, 278–90.

O'Brien, E. J., & Albrecht, J. E., (1992). Comprehension strategies in the development of a mental model. *Journal of Experimental Psychology: Learning, Memory, and Cognition*, *18*, 777–84.

O'Brien, E. J., Cook, A. E., & Guéraud, S., (2010). Accessibility of outdated information. *Journal of Experimental Psychology: Learning, Memory, and Cognition, 36*, 979–91.

O'Brien, E. J., Cook, A. E., & Peracchi, K. A. (2004). Updating a situation model: a reply to Zwaan and Madden (2004). *Journal of Experimental Psychology: Learning, Memory, and Cognition, 30*, 289–91.

O'Brien, E. J., & Myers, J. L. (1987). The role of causal connections in the retrieval of text. *Memory & Cognition, 15*, 419–27.

(1999). Text comprehension: a view from the bottom up. In S. R. Goldman, A. C. Graesser, & P. van den Broek (eds.), *Narrative Comprehension, Causality, and Coherence: Essays in Honor of Tom Trabasso* (pp. 36–53). Mahwah, NJ: Erlbaum.

O'Brien, E. J., Shank, D. A., Myers, J. L., & Rayner, K. (1988). Elaborative inferences during reading: do they occur online? *Journal of Experimental Psychology: Learning, Memory, and Cognition, 14*, 410–20.

Omanson, R. C., Warren, W. H., & Trabasso, T. (1978). Goals, inferential comprehension, and recall of stories by children. *Discourse Processes, 1*, 337–54.

Paris, S. G., & Lindauer, B. K. (1976). The role of inference in children's comprehension and memory for sentences. *Cognitive Psychology, 8*, 217–27.

Paris, S. G., Lindauer, B. K., & Cox, G. (1977). The development of inferential comprehension. *Child Development, 48*, 1728–33.

Paris, S. G., & Upton, L. R. (1976). Children's memory for inferential relationships in prose. *Child Development, 47*, 660–8.

Peracchi, K. A., & O'Brien, E. J. (2004). Character profiles and the activation of predictive inferences. *Memory & Cognition, 32*, 1044–52.

Perfetti, C. (2007). Reading ability: lexical quality to comprehension. *Scientific Studies of Reading, 11*, 357–83

Perfetti, C., & Stafura, J. (2014). Word knowledge in a theory of reading comprehension. *Scientific Studies of Reading, 18*, 22–37.

Pezdek, K., Lehrer, A., & Simon, S. (1984). The relationship between reading and cognitive processing of television and radio. *Child Development, 55*, 2072–82.

Pressley, M., Graham, S., & Harris, K. (2006). The state of educational intervention research as viewed through the lens of literacy intervention. *British Journal of Educational Psychology, 76*(1), 1–19.

RAND Reading Study Group. (2002). *Reading for Understanding: Toward a Research and Development Program in Reading Comprehension*. Santa Monica, CA: RAND.

Rapp, D. N., van den Broek, P., McMaster, K. L., Kendeou, P., & Espin, C. A. (2007). Higher-order comprehension processes in struggling readers: a perspective for research and intervention. *Scientific Studies of Reading, 11*, 289–312.

St. George, M., Mannes, S., & Hoffman, J. E. (1997). Individual differences in inference generation: An ERP analysis. *Journal of Cognitive Neuroscience, 9*(6), 776–87.

Singer, M., & Lea, R. B. (2012) Inference and reasoning in discourse comprehension. In H.-J. Schmid and D. Geeraerts (eds.), *Handbook of Cognitive Pragmatics* (pp. 85–119). Berlin: Mouton de Gruyter.

Singer, M., & Ritchot, K. (1996). Individual differences in inference validation. *Memory & Cognition, 24*, 733–43.

Stafura, J. Z., & Perfetti, C. A. (2014). Word-to-text integration: message level and lexical level influences in ERPs. *Neuropsychologia, 64*, 41–53.

Stanovich, K. (1986). Matthew effects in reading: some consequences of individual differences in the acquisition of literacy. *Reading Research Quarterly, 21*(4), 360–407.

Swanson, H. L., & O'Connor, R. (2009). The role of working memory and fluency practice on the reading comprehension of students who are dysfluent readers. *Journal of Learning Disabilities, 42*(6), 548–75.

Tannenbaum, K. R., Torgesen, J. K., & Wagner, R. K. (2006). Relationships between word knowledge and reading comprehension in third-grade children. *Scientific Studies of Reading, 10*, 381–98.

Torgesen, J. K., Wagner, R. K., Rashotte, C. A., Burgess, S., & Hecht, S. (1997). Contributions of phonological awareness and rapid automatic naming ability to the growth of word-reading skills in second to fifth grade children. *Scientific Studies of Reading, 1*, 161–85.

Trabasso, T., & Nickels, M. (1992). The development of goal plans of action in the narration of a picture story. *Discourse Processes, 15*(3), 249–75.

Van den Broek, P. (1997). Discovering the cement of the universe: the development of event comprehension from childhood to adulthood. In P. van den Broek, P. W. Bauer, & T. Bourg (eds.), *Developmental Spans in Event Comprehension and Representation* (pp. 321–42). Mahwah, NJ: Erlbaum.

Van den Broek, P., Bohn-Gettler, C., Kendeou, P., Carlson, S., & White, M. J. (2011). When a reader meets a text: the role of standards of coherence in reading comprehension. In M. T. McCrudden, J. Magliano, & G. Schraw (eds.), *Relevance Instructions and Goal-Focusing in Text Learning* (pp. 123–40). Greenwich, CT: Information Age Publishing.

Van den Broek, P., Fletcher, C. R., & Risden, K. (1993). Investigations of inferential processes in reading: a theoretical and methodological integration. *Discourse Processes, 16*, 169–80.

Van den Broek, P., Kendeou, P., Kremer, K., Lynch, J. S., Butler, J., White, M. J., & Lorch, E. P. (2005). Assessment of comprehension abilities in young children. In S. Paris & S. Stahl (eds.), *Children's Reading Comprehension and Assessment* (pp. 107–30). Mahwah, NJ: Erlbaum.

Van den Broek, P., Kendeou, P., & White, M. J. (2009). Cognitive processes during reading: implications for the use of multimedia to foster reading comprehension. In A. G. Bus & S. B. Neuman (eds.), *Multimedia and Literacy Development: Improving Achievement for Young Learners* (pp. 57–73). New York: Routledge.

Van den Broek, P., Lorch, R., Linderholm, T., & Gustafson, M. (2001). The effects of readers' goals on inference generation and memory for texts. *Memory & Cognition, 29*(8), 1081–7.

Van den Broek, P., Lorch, E.P., & Thurlow, R. (1996). Children's and adults' memory for television stories: the role of causal factors, story-grammar categories, and hierarchical level. *Child Development*, *67*, 3010–28.

Van den Broek, P., Rapp, D. N., & Kendeou, P. (2005). Integrating memory-based and constructionist approaches in accounts of reading comprehension. *Discourse Processes*, *39*, 299–316.

Van den Broek, P., Risden, K., & Husebye-Hartmann, E. (1995). The role of readers' standards for coherence in the generation of inferences during reading. In R. F. Lorch & E. J. O'Brien (eds.), *Sources of Coherence in Text Comprehension* (pp. 353–73). Mahwah, NJ: Erlbaum.

Van den Broek, P. W. (1989). Causal reasoning and inference making in judging the importance of story statements. *Child Development*, *60*, 286–97.

  (1990). The causal inference maker: towards a process model of inference generation in text comprehension. In D. A. Balota, G. B. Flores d'Arcais & K. Rayner (eds.), *Comprehension Processes in Reading* (pp. 423–46). Mahwah, NJ: Erlbaum.

  (1997). Discovering the cement of the universe: the development of event comprehension from childhood to adulthood. In P. W. van den Broek, P. J. Bauer & T. Bourg (eds.), *Developmental Spans in Event Comprehension and Representation: Bridging Fictional and Actual Events* (pp. 321–42). Mahwah, NJ. Erlbaum.

Van den Broek, P. W., Helder, A., & Van Leijenhorst, L. (2013). Sensitivity to structural centrality: developmental and individual differences in reading comprehension skills. In M. A. Britt, S. R. Goldman & J.-F. Rouet (eds.), *Reading: From Words to Multiple Texts* (pp. 132–46). New York: Routledge, Taylor & Francis Group.

Van den Broek, P. W., Kendeou, P., Lousberg, S., & Visser, G. (2011). Preparing for reading comprehension: fostering text comprehension skills in preschool and early elementary school children. *International Electronic Journal of Elementary Education*, *4*(1), 259–68.

Wenner, J. (2004). Preschoolers' comprehension of goal structure in narratives. *Memory*, *12*(2), 192–202.

Williams, J. P., Hall, K. M., Lauer, K. D., Stafford, K. B., DeSisto, L. A., & deCani, J. S. (2005). Expository text comprehension in the primary grade classroom. *Journal of Educational Psychology*, *97*(4), 538–50.

Yuill, N., & Oakhill, J. (1988). Effects of inference awareness training on poor reading comprehension. *Applied Cognitive Psychology*, *2*, 33–45.

9   Toward an embodied approach to inferences
      in comprehension: the case of action language

Manuel de Vega

In this chapter I propose that the embodied cognition approach provides a plausible psychological foundation for linguistic meaning, and
could shed light on the study of inferences in comprehension. The
chapter is organized as follows. First, I discuss how symbolist and
embodied approaches to meaning differ. Second, I present the functional advantages of embodied cognition to explain some linguistic and
nonlinguistic phenomena. Third, I deal with how embodied cognition
could underlie inferences in text comprehension. Fourth, I describe
some empirical support, from my own and others' laboratories, for
embodied meaning, relying not only on behavioral data, but also on
neurological data. This review of the literature focuses on action-related
language, which is a growing subject in the embodiment literature with
implications for inferences. Finally, I discuss how the embodied meaning proposal complements and enriches the classical findings in the
literature of inferences.

Symbolism versus embodiment

There are two general approaches to linguistic meaning: symbolist
theories and embodiment theories. The symbolist approach assumes that
words and sentences activate mental symbols, which are abstract, arbitrary, and amodal. From a pure symbolist perspective, comprehension
basically consists of a translation process from an external symbolic
language (words) into an internal symbolic language (mental symbols).
The symbolist doctrine has been very popular in cognitive sciences,
because it allowed computational analyses of language meaning in terms
of symbolic codes such as propositions, lists of features, semantic networks, semantic dimensions, and more recently, statistical co-occurrence
models. Also, symbolic theories have impressive capabilities to predict
psychological phenomena such as priming effects, word recognition,
combinatorial and compositional processes, ambiguity resolution, categorical judgments, anaphor resolution, and also knowledge-based

inferences. In fact, some theoretical approaches in the field of language comprehension either explicitly or implicitly assume a propositional-symbolist account of meaning and inferences (Britton, van Dussen, Glynn, and Hemphill 1990; Kintsch, 1998; McKoon and Ratcliff, 1992; van den Broek, 1990).

One problem with symbolism, however, is that language meaning lacks grounding in the world (de Vega, Glenberg, and Graesser, 2008; Harnad, 1990; Searle, 1980). Namely, words refer only to abstract symbols, associated with other symbols, which in turn are associated with other symbols, and so on. Thus, language meaning remains in a sort of "Chinese room," never interfacing with the world experience (Searle, 1980). The need for grounding in the world is evident in conversational settings, where speakers continuously refer to entities and events in the current environment and, thus, words have to be mapped into perception and action to be fully understood. But even when we refer to absent events we must be able to establish a correspondence between the linguistic utterances and the real world. For instance, in a route description task, it is useful for the addressee to build an embodied representation, which guides her to identify the described landmarks, and to produce the appropriate navigation (straight walks and turns) in the real environment (e.g., Denis, Daniel, Fontaine, and Pazzaglia, 2001). However, for traditional symbolic theories the grounding problem remains unsolved.

The embodiment approach to meaning considers that language is grounded in the world. This means that the same perceptual, motor, and emotional brain mechanisms used in real-world experiences are involved to some extent in the processing of linguistic meaning. According to the embodied approach, meaning consists of the mental simulation of the objects, events, and situations to which words refer. For instance, when people read or listen to the sentence "John hammered a nail on the wall," this would briefly activate in their mind visual, auditory, motor, and even emotional images of the scene. And if their brain activity was recorded, we could expect small activations in their visual, auditory, and motor cortex, overlapping the regions involved in the performance of hammering a nail. But is this true? Fortunately, the field of embodied cognition is now a well-established field and relies on behavioral and neurological evidence, as we will see in this chapter.

In principle, the embodiment approach is biologically well motivated. As happens in many other species' brains, the human brain devotes extensive neural networks to processing biologically relevant information online: perceiving stimuli in several modalities, planning and executing motor actions, or processing the emotional or affective value of events. It seems reasonable that the human language, a relatively new brain function, reutilizes by means of an exaptation process the sensorimotor brain networks for new functions such as representing and communicating meaning. Moreover, the reutilization of the sensorimotor networks to build linguistic meaning has functional advantages in comparison with an amodal and ungrounded representational system, as I will argue in the next section.

Functional advantages of embodiment

I already mentioned that symbolist theories (at least in their extreme version) are not able to solve the grounding problem, whereas embodied meaning is by definition grounded. Now I will discuss the functional advantages of embodied meaning in more detail, focusing on the functions of motor resonance in action-related language: (1) motor resonance facilitates the interface with the physical events, making the organism get ready for action (or inaction); (2) motor resonance facilitates communication between speakers providing a mechanism for common ground; and (3) motor resonance provides biological evaluation of the events.

Interface with the physical world

A functional advantage of embodied meaning is that it provides a better interface with the world than purely symbolist approaches. Embodied representations provide direct grounding of words in the world or, more accurately, in the perceptual and motor experience of the world, overcoming in this way the grounding problem of symbolism. Generally speaking, embodied representations are situational and they prepare agents for situated action, in contrast with symbolic representations that only provide categorical information (as in a dictionary or encyclopedia entry) and, thus, only prepare agents for retrieving associated symbols (e.g., Barsalou, Santos, Simmons, and Wilson, 2008).

The need of embodied/situated meaning is quite obvious in conversational settings, in which the speakers frequently refer to current events. Thus, the referents of pronouns (I, you, she) or demonstratives (this, that) demand a direct connection between words and ongoing perceptual and motor experiences (de Vega, 2008). A pragmatic function of human communication is to provide enough cues for the addressee to specify the particular object, event, or state referred to. Given that many word referents are perceptual, a perceptual-like meaning might be a more efficient interfacing system than an abstract amodal code. Embodied meaning has the advantage of using a common code with perceptual experience, and mapping from one to the other is thus potentially straightforward. For instance, if your interlocutor asks you "Is there a red book on the table?" you can build a visual representation of the sentence meaning that can be directly verified against your visual experience, because both the linguistic and the perceptual source use similar sensory (and brain) mechanisms. In contrast, specifying reference in a purely symbolic system may require transduction functions to map amodal symbols into perceptual experience or vice versa. In the previous example, you may start translating the sentence into a propositional representation: ON <BOOK, TABLE> and IS <BOOK, RED>. In turn, these amodal propositions should be linked to perceptual features in the environment to make the verification task possible. This two-way process may be computationally possible, in principle, but it seems less parsimonious than using embodied representations of meaning.[1]

Linguistic reference to online perceptual events is a genuine inferential phenomenon that has generally been neglected in the language comprehension literature, although it deserves attention. But even when conversations deal with events not in the current situation, the connection with world referents is necessary in many cases, as in route descriptions, working instructions, and the like. The idea that embodied meaning is an efficient "preparation for action" is also germane to the notion of meaning as affordances mobilization postulated by Glenberg and Kaschak (2002). Thus, nouns corresponding to objects would automatically activate motor affordances. For example, the word "paper" activates motor affordances, involving cover activations in your motor system, such as "getting," "tearing," "throwing," or "writing," depending on the particular context.

Communication

A primary function of language is communication, and successful communication needs alignment of the interlocutors' representations (e.g., Garrod and Pickering, 2004). In other words, we understand each other to the extent that we are able to build similar referents for words and sentences. Embodied representations seem to be an efficient way to do so, because the interlocutors use the same perceptual-motor machinery (shared by all individuals) to build embodied simulations. For instance, motor resonance would be similar in the speaker who says, "Give me the

---

[1] A third logical possibility is using amodal symbols (e.g., propositions) to encode both the visual experience and the language meaning, making them directly comparable. However, it seems quite paradoxical explaining visual perception, with its reach sensory quality, in terms of language-like, arbitrary, amodal symbols.

bottle" and the addressee who understands the request. Rizzolatti and Arbib (1998) proposed the mirror neurons system as a possible neural mechanism for the building of shared representations between interlocutors. Mirror neurons have the property of parity: they fire both in the agent and the observer, and this very property is necessary for shared meaning and successful communication.

Alternatively, we could also conceive that people share similar propositional-symbolic representations to guarantee efficient communication among interlocutors. However, whereas we know relatively well the perceptual, motor, and emotional processes taking place in the human brain, and we also know that we all share these basic processes, it is less clear how similar our propositional-symbolic representations actually are. To begin with, there are not neural implementations of symbolic theories. Although the classical Broca and Wernicke areas are involved in linguistic functions, such as encoding a word's forms or executing a word's articulatory programs, it is less clear that these structures are in charge of processing a word's meaning. Thus, the Wernicke's area could be responsible for the phonetic analysis and recognition of spoken words, and the Broca's area controls the motoric programs of speech (Pulvermüller, 2008). It is also possible that these areas have the capability of generating linguistic associations, based on sound similarity, root similarity, antonyms, synonyms, and more. (Barsalou et al., 2008). These all are important functions that contribute to speeded language processing (e.g., by creating lexical expectations during comprehension). However, according to Barsalou et al. (2008), they involve a relatively shallow processing that cannot be identified with meaning.

Furthermore, formal implementations with propositional representations utilized by symbolic approaches also have important drawbacks. They consist of applying certain rules and procedures. In many cases, these procedures are not performed by any independent algorithm, but they are applied by hand by trained collaborators. Only recently, algorithms have been created with certain capability to parse sentences automatically into propositions, and guide contextual meaning (see Kintsch, 2008 for a review). On the other hand, propositional codes show notable differences among researchers. For instance, let us consider the sentence "The boy petted and hugged the puppy." The Kintsch and van Dijk's (1978) propositional analysis labels predicates (main verbs, adjectives, adverbs) and arguments (nouns, pronouns) with English words, whereas the syntax is relatively underspecified and does not capture such formal distinctions as subject versus predicate phrases: (PETTED, PUPPY, BOY) and (HUGGED, PUPPY, BOY). By contrast, propositions in Anderson's (1983) ACT theory have a syntax that explicitly captures subject-predicate distinction, and makes an explicit distinction between conceptual tokens and types: (a * boy) and (b * puppy) and (a * pet OFb)) and (a * (hug OFb)). As a consequence of these different assumptions about representations, the structural properties of sentences differ quite a bit among propositional analyses, and the propositional approaches do not offer a solid foundation to explain pragmatic communication.

Evaluation

Embodied meaning allows a fast emotional assessment of the biological value of events. For instance, according to Damasio (1994), the primary emotional brain (e.g., the amygdala in the limbic system) evolved to ensure body survival, generating body physical responses to face biological risks and threats, such as predators' or competitors' proximity. When complex brains capable of thinking and talking evolved, connections between the frontal cortex and the limbic system emerged, allowing the assessment of cognitive and linguistic information with the same embodied markers (emotions) primarily used for survival. For this reason, language can trigger emotions that provide immediate information about the adaptive value of the message. Just think of the intensive emotions that good news, bad news, insults, or flatteries provoke on us, and how these kinds of linguistic information guide or modulate our behavior. Some experiments clearly showed that even understanding fictional stories with emotional content involves subliminal activation of expression-related muscles in the reader's face (Havas, Glenberg, and Rinck, 2007).

Embodied inferences

Before elaborating on the notion of embodied inferences, let us review a few definitions of inferences. "An inference is defined as any piece of information that is *not explicitly stated in the text*" (McKoon and Ratcliff, 1992, p. 440). "Knowledge-based inferences are critical building-blocks in the referential *situation model* that readers construct" (Graesser, Singer and Trabasso 1994, p. 372). "When comprehending a text, it is generally assumed that readers will use their general *world knowledge* to generate those inferences that 'fill the gaps' between what has been explicitly stated and what the 'fully filled-in' message was intended to convey" (Cook, Limber, and O'Brien, 2001, p. 220). Independently of the theoretical details assumed by the authors, there is an agreement that inferences are based on world-knowledge (including situation models), and they consist of adding pieces of information, which are not explicit in the text.

This minimal account of inferences serves as a starting point to consider whether or not embodied representations produce inferences. Namely, do the sensorimotor processes triggered by language add pieces of information to the discourse representation? To answer this question I will distinguish first between two possible levels of embodied representations: lexical and situational. Lexical embodied representations are obviously associated with individual words, involving the activation of sensorimotor properties of the objects or events referred to by these words. For instance, the word "tomato" could activate modal traces of color shape, tact, and taste depending on the linguistic context, or the task demands (Goldberg, Perfetti, and Schneider, 2006; McKoon and Ratcliff, 1988; Pecher, Zeelenberg, and Barsalou 2003), and the verb "to give" could activate visual or motoric activations of a transfer motion of the arms (Glenberg and Kaschak 2002; Glenberg, Sato, Cattaneo, Riggio, Palumbo, and Buccino, 2008; de Vega et al., 2013). These lexical-based embodied representations could be considered genuine inferences, because they add some pieces of information to the linguistic and conceptual features of words

But meaning involves higher-order representations that go beyond lexical representations. In extended language, comprehenders need to create sentence-level and text-level representations, which involve combinatorial processes of individual words' meanings. It is precisely in these higher-order representations where inferences could be more necessary to reach local and global coherence. Symbolic-propositional theories are quite efficient to deal with complex meaning, being able to combine conceptual units into individual propositions, and coreferent sets of propositions, according to their semantic relations in the text (e.g., Kintsch, 1998; Kintsch and van Dijk, 1978). Also schema-based theories (e.g., Rumelhart, 1980), and situation models theories (e.g., Zwaan and Radvansky, 1998) deal pretty well with complexity, supporting some inferential processes. To what extent do embodied representations, built up during ordinary reading, scale up to complex meaning? This is a question not entirely resolved, but some embodied cognition approaches explicitly deal with complex meaning. For instance, Barsalou's (1999) perceptual symbols theory postulates simulators as mechanisms to generate complex embodied representations, Glenberg and Kaschak's (2002) indexical hypothesis considers that high-order embodied representations are guided by grammar constructions, Zwaan's (2004) immersed experiencer theory proposed that combinatorial embodied simulations occur incrementally in the clause intonational units, and de Vega's (2008) reference specification proposal also considers the role of deixis and grammar in online, displaced and decoupled reference.

Behavioral studies on action language

Action compatibility effects (ACE) in simple sentences

One way to test whether action language involves a motor simulation is to use dual-task paradigms, in which the comprehension of action-related sentences overlaps or immediately precedes the performance of a related action. In the basic procedure, participants are asked to understand sentences describing motor events and to perform a motor task designed to match or mismatch the meaning of the sentences. The rationale is that when the action described by the sentence and the motor action match, a meaning-action interaction might be observed, indicating that both share motor processes. With this paradigm, a meaning-action facilitation effect was reported in some cases. That is, the meaning-action matching conditions produce faster responses than the mismatching conditions (Borreggine and Kaschak, 2006; Glenberg and Kaschak, 2002; Zwaan and Taylor, 2006). For example, Glenberg and Kaschak (2002) asked people to provide sensibility judgments for sentences describing a motion toward or away from them (e.g., "Andy delivered the pizza to you" or "You delivered the pizza to Andy") or nonsense sentences. For some participants the "yes" response involved a hand motion toward their body, and the "no" response was a hand motion away from their body; for other participants it was the other way around. The judgments for sensible sentences were faster for the matching conditions (e.g., sentences describing a transfer toward you, responding "yes" toward you) than for the mismatching conditions. Zwaan and Taylor (2006) obtained a similar meaning-action facilitation, using sentences describing actions, which usually involve a hand clockwise (e.g., "Louis sharpened the pencil") or counter-clockwise rotation (e.g., "Eric turned down the volume"). In their second experiment, participants were given each sentence aurally and made a speeded sensibility judgment, by turning a knob clockwise or counter-clockwise. As in the previous meaning-action effect experiments, they found faster sensibility judgments for the matching condition.

Other studies have found interference rather than facilitation for the meaning-action matching conditions (Buccino, Riggio, Melli, Binkofski, Gallese, and Rizzolatti, 2005; de Vega, Moreno, and Castillo, 2013). For instance, Buccino et al. (2005) gave participants hand-action sentences (e.g., "He took the cup"), foot-action sentences (e.g., "He kicked the ball"), or abstract sentences, and they had to respond if the sentence described an action, and refrain from responding otherwise. Hand responses were faster for foot-action than hand-action sentences, and foot responses were faster for hand-action than foot-action sentences. In other words, using the same effectors than those implicit in the sentence meaning interferes with rather than facilitates motor responses. In another experiment Buccino et al. (2005) sent single-pulse transcraneal magnetic stimulation (TMS) to participants' hand-motion brain areas or foot-motion brain areas synchronized with the motion verb of each sentence. They recorded the motor-evoked potentials (MEPs) of muscles related to hand motion and foot motion, and again found interference in the matching conditions; namely, decreasing MEP at hand sites for hand-motion sentences, and decreasing MEP at foot sites for foot-motion sentences.

Several factors could contribute to the discrepancy in the meaning-action effect results, for either facilitation or interference in the matching conditions. The experiments differ in the complexity of the linguistic materials (single words, single-clause sentences, or double-clause sentences), the semantic task (sensibility judgments, categorical judgments, lexical decision), the response paradigm (choice, go/no-go, self-paced reading), and the temporal overlap between the linguistic stimulus and the motor response.

To explore the role of meaning-action temporal overlap, de Vega et al. (2013) manipulated the temporal delay between the comprehension process and the production of the motor response. They used incomplete transfer sentences describing motions toward oneself or away from oneself (see Box 9.1), and they measured the motor responses at several delays following the transfer verb.[2] Each sentence was presented word by word automatically on the center of the screen, and the transfer verb (e.g., threw) was animated with a forward or backward motion that either matched or mismatched the sentence meaning. The interval between the verb presentation and its apparent motion was manipulated between-participants (100 vs. 200 vs. 350 ms) as to vary the temporal overlap between the transfer verb and the sensorimotor event. While reading, participants had their right-hand index finger on a resting key, and once they had identified the moving word direction, they had to press one of the two alternative keys placed ahead or behind the resting key, to match the direction of the word motion (motor task). At the end of the incomplete sentence, participants also performed a choice task between two alternative completion words, pressing either the "1" or "2" keys with their left-hand fingers (semantic task).

---

[2] Given the relative freedom of Spanish word order, we were able to use sentences in which the transferred object, the agent or receiver, and the direction of the transfer were mentioned before the transfer verb, before the end-of-sentence wrap-up processes.

Whereas in most ACE studies the motor and the semantic processes cannot be dissociated, the de Vega et al. (2013) procedure allows for a separate checking of the influence of action language on the concurrent motor task (response to the motion cue at the verb), and the influence of the motor task on comprehension (semantic choice at the end of the sentence). For short verb-action delays (100–200 ms) they found interference; namely slower responses in the matching conditions (e.g., transfer away/motion away) than in the mismatching condition (e.g., transfer toward/motion away). By contrast, when the motion cue was given with a delay of 350 ms after the transfer verb, there was facilitation in the matching conditions, indicating priming between meaning and action. These results were found both for the motor response times and for the semantic choice times, as Figure 9.1 illustrates.

The most interesting effect was the interference observed in the matching conditions, when the action verb and the motor response were temporally close. A possible explanation is that in this case neural competition for the same motor resources takes place. For instance, it might be the case that constructing a simulation of an away transfer motion during language comprehension requires the activation of some specific neurons in the motor cortex that are tuned to respond to planning or execution actions in that direction, and this causes a

---

Box 9.1   Examples of materials from the action compatibility effect experiments by de Vega et al. (2013)

Away transfer

La pelota / de tenis / se la **pasé** al contrario / sobre la

| 1. PORTERÍA | 2. RED |

Literal translation: The tennis ball I it **threw** to my rival over the
Canonical translation: I **threw** the tennis ball to my rival over the

| 1. GOAL | 2. NET |

Toward transfer

La pelota / de tenis / me la **pasó** el contrario / sobre la

| 1. PORTERÍA | 2. RED |

Literal translation: The tennis ball me it **threw** my rival over the
Canonical translation: My rival **threw** me the tennis ball over the

| 1. GOAL | 2. NET |

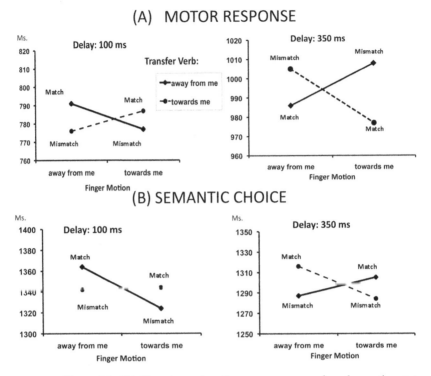

Figure 9.1 (A) Mean latencies of motor responses when the motion cue was presented 100 vs. 350 ms after the verb onset. (B) Mean latencies of semantic choices at the same motion cue delays (de Vega et al., 2013).

momentary competition for the same neuronal resources when the participant performs an away motion. However, it seems that the neural overload fades quite soon; because when the motion was delayed more than 200 ms the standard facilitation for meaning-action matching conditions was found. The early onset and short life of the motor effect fits well with neuroscience data that also demonstrate a fast and brief activation of action-related meaning, as we will see in the next section (Pulvermüller, Shtyrov, and Ilmoniemi, 2003). On the other hand, the meaning–action modulation was two-way: the comprehension of the sentences' meaning modulated the performance of a concurrent movement task and the movement task modified performance in comprehension of the sentences, suggesting that the motor component is a functional feature of action-related meaning rather than epiphenomenal.

Action compatibility effects in abstract language

The meaning-action effects occur also in abstract or metaphorical language. For instance, ACE was observed not only in literal sentences describing manual transfer of objects (e.g., "Mary gave you the present" or "You gave Mary the present"), but also in metaphorical sentences describing transfer of information (e.g., "Liz told you the story" or "You told Liz the story"), as reported in some studies (Glenberg and Kaschak, 2002; Glenberg et al., 2008). We also tested in our laboratory ACE for abstract sentences such as counterfactuals and metaphors (de Vega and Urrutia, 2011; Santana and de Vega, 2011).

People use counterfactuals to make conjectures about how past events might have been if just a relatively small change in the situation had occurred. For instance, "If I had studied last week, I would have passed the exam." Counterfactuals involve two meanings: a realistic meaning or how things really happened (I did not study nor pass the exam), and an alternative meaning of how things would have happened (I did study and pass the exam). The two meanings are necessary to fully produce or understand counterfactuals. In some experiments performed by de Vega and Urrutia (2011), participants listened to sentences including a transfer action either in counterfactual (e.g., "If my brother had been generous he would have lent me the Harry Potter novel"), or factual format (e.g., "Since my brother is generous he has lent me the Harry Potter novel"). At the moment of the transfer verb presentation (lent) participants received a visual cue prompting them to move their finger away from or toward themselves to press a given key. As in de Vega et al.'s (2013) study, the motor response was slower in the matching conditions, both in the factual and counterfactual sentences, suggesting that neural competition in the motor brain also occurs for the counterfactual meaning.

In the same vein, Santana and de Vega (2011) performed a study with orientational metaphors, such as those originally described by Lakoff and Johnson (1980), to test whether metaphorical meaning activates motor representations online. According to Lakoff and Johnson some metaphorical notions (good, virtue, happiness, consciousness, health, wealth, high status, power, etc.) are mapped onto the "up" pole of the vertical dimension, whereas the opposite notions (evil, vice, sadness, unconsciousness, illness, poverty, low status, etc.) are mapped onto the "down" pole of the vertical dimension. Santana and de Vega were interested to test whether understanding up/down orientational metaphors is associated with the corresponding movements. With this idea, they designed three types of sentences: concrete literal sentences (e.g.,

"The pressured gas made the balloon rise in the sky"), orientational metaphors (e.g., "Her talent for politics made her rise with victory") and abstract literal sentences (e.g., "His working capability made him succeed as a professional"). While reading each sentence, participants performed an upward or downward hand motion immediately following the motion verb that either matched or mismatched the direction conveyed by the sentence meaning. The latency of the motor response was collected, as well as the response time for a yes/no comprehension question that followed the sentence. In the experiments, the hand motion was prompted by a visual cue (upward or downward animation of the sentence verb, in Exp. 1, or a color change in the sentence verb in Exp. 2), and the results showed faster responses in the matching conditions for all three kinds of sentences. For instance, in the case of metaphors understanding "her talent for politics made her rise with victory" speeded upward motions, whereas understanding the metaphor "His multiple errors made him bury his hopes" speeded downward motions. Notably, similar effects were observed in abstract literal sentences, despite the fact that they included abstract verbs (e.g., to fail, to succeed) rather than motion verbs. This means that the motor processes are associated with the metaphorical conceptual organization, rather than with the lexicon of concrete verbs. Again, as in de Vega et al. (2013) the meaning-action effects are two-way: on the motor response latency, and on the comprehension task latency.

Conclusions

We can derive several conclusions from the ACE studies. First, motor processes can be activated (or inferred) when people understand action language. These motor processes are not purely lexical (e.g., exclusively associated with the verb meaning), but require phrase or clause integration. Thus, transference toward or away from oneself requires integrating several pieces of information, such as who is agent and who is the receptor (you vs. another person), and what is the object transferred.

Second, in some studies the action-meaning effects were two-way, providing evidence that motor processes are functional features of meaning (de Vega et al., 2013; Santana and de Vega, 2011). Specifically, the ACE observed in the motor task indicates that the sentence meaning modulates a subsequent body action, whereas the ACE obtained in the semantic task might offer information on the reverse process: how a previous body action modulates sentence comprehension. In other words, the two ACEs indicate a mutual influence between the meaning of action sentences and the corresponding actions. This mutual influence supports the idea that the motor simulation is a functional component of sentence meaning. In other words, a motor action temporally overlapping an action verb modulates the meaning-related motor simulation and thus impairs or facilitates comprehension.

Third, the motor activations occur not only in literal language, describing physical events or actions, but also in some kinds of abstract language. Specifically, we have mentioned how understanding sentences referred to transfer of information, and sentences describing hypothetical events (counterfactuals) modulated away-toward hand motions. Also orientational metaphors, and even abstract sentences describing success/failure events, modulated up-down hand motions.

The ACE studies are a fruitful approach to motor processes underlying language. However, they do not provide direct neurological evidence on motor processes. Moreover, the use of double task procedures could produce task demands very different from ordinary comprehension. In other words, the motor activations observed in language could be triggered by the concurrent motor task. In the next section we turn to the neurological studies that provide direct evidence of motor activations under ordinary comprehension demands.

Neurological studies on action language

The neuroanatomy of action language

In the last decade, many experiments on cognitive neuroscience have reinforced the notion that language comprehension could involve a mental simulation of embodied experience. Thus, Pulvermüller and his collaborators have studied the neural activity underlying the comprehension of action verbs (Pulvermüller, Hauk, Nikulin, and Ilmoniemi, 2005). In one experiment, participants listened to action verbs while their brain hemodynamic response was recorded by means of functional magnetic resonance imaging (fMRI). The verbs referred to motions either of the mouth (e.g., lick), the fingers and hands (e.g., pick), or the legs (e.g., kick). The same participants performed in another experimental session real motions of their mouths, hands, and legs. The results were clear: performing physical actions activated the expected somatotopic regions in the motor and premotor cortex. Thus, mouth motions produced specific activations in regions near the Sylvius fissure, finger and hand motions activated dorsolateral areas, and foot and leg motions showed activation in the vertex and inter-hemispheric sulcus. Most importantly, listening to action verbs caused partial activation of the same areas as executing the corresponding actions. Notice that participants just listened to the words passively; namely, they were not asked to perform any particular task with them or even to pay attention to them. In spite of this, the obtained somatotopic activation indicates that it was quite automatic, suggesting strongly established connections between the neurons responsible for word recognition and the specific motor areas in the brain.

Other experiments have shown that not only isolated action verbs, but also action-related sentences activate motor and premotor brain areas (Aziz-Zadeh, Wilson, Rizzolatti, and Iacoboni, 2006; Tettamanti, Manenti, Della Rosa, Falini, Perani, Cappa, and Moro, 2008). For instance, in their fMRI study Tettamanti et al. (2008) recorded brain activity while participants listened to sentences, which described motions of the mouth ("I bite the apple"), hands ("I grasp a knife"), or legs ("I kick the ball"). They also listened to abstract sentences as a control condition ("I appreciate the sincerity"). The results showed that all the action-related sentences, unlike control sentences, share activation in a specific subregion of the Broca area (*pars triangularis*) in the left inferior frontal gyrus. The role of the Broca area in the comprehension of action-related language is not surprising, because this is a genuine motor area, not only involved in the production of language, but also in the comprehension and execution of actions (e.g., Hamzei, Rijntjes, Dettmers, Glauche, Weiller, and Buëchel, 2003). Tettamanti and his collaborators also reported that the somatotopic regions, mentioned above, were selectively activated by mouth-, hands-, and legs-related sentences.

Even action language referring to hypothetical or nonoccurring events also activates motor regions in the brain. For instance, de Vega, León, Hernández, Valdés, Padrón, and Ferstl (2014) gave participants complex sentences involving each an antecedent and a consequent clause. The action sentences were written in three formats: factual, negation, or counterfactual, as shown in the next examples:

> Factual action: Given that it was my birthday/I *unwrapped the gifts.*
>
> Negation action: Given that it was not my birthday/I *didn't unwrap the gifts.*
>
> Counterfactual action: If it had been my birthday/I *would have unwrapped the gifts.*

In comparison with nonaction sentences, action sentences elicited stronger activations in the supplementary motor area, extending to the primary motor area, as well as in regions generally associated with the planning and understanding of actions (left superior temporal gyrus, left and right supramarginal gyri). Also, action sentences elicited stronger activations in the extrastriate body area, a region involved in the visual processing of human body movements. Interestingly, these action-related effects occurred not only in factuals, but also in negations and counterfactuals, suggesting that brain regions involved in action understanding and planning are activated by default even when the actions are described as hypothetical or as not happening. Moreover, some of these regions overlapped with those activated during the observation by the same participants of action videos, indicating that the act of understanding action language and that of observing real actions share neural networks, as Figure 9.2 shows. These results support the claim that embodied representations of linguistic meaning are important even in abstract linguistic contexts.

The neuronal overlap between performing actions and understanding action-sentences was also observed when action effort was manipulated. Moving a heavy object demands more physical effort and in some cases more planning than moving a light object. Not surprisingly, effort has a correlate in brain activity. Thus, motor and

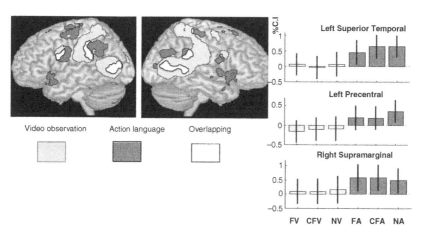

Figure 9.2 Left panel: Clusters of activation in the video observation task (light gray), in the action language task (dark gray), and regions that overlap between the two tasks (white). Right panel: percent change in the BOLD signal for the action language compared to visual language in three overlapping regions. Each bar represents one language condition: FV = factual-visual; CFV = counterfactual-visual; NV = negation-visual; FA = factual-action; CFA = counterfactual-action; and NA = negation-action. Action sentences, regardless of their grammatical structure, elicited more activation on these action-related regions than visual sentences (de Vega et al., 2014).

premotor areas in the brain are activated differentially according to the degree of physical effort necessary for the target action, as reported in some recent papers. For instance, producing different degrees of effort in a squeezing task correlated with the volume of activation in the contralateral sensory-motor cortex and the supplementary motor area (Cramer et al., 2002). More important to the purpose of this chapter, sentences describing actions with different degrees of effort also resulted in corresponding degrees of activation in motor areas of the brain. Thus, when people understand action-related sentences the implicit weight of the objects involved in the action plays a role in the embodied simulations of meaning. In an event-related fMRI study, Moody and Gennari (2010) recorded brain activity while participants read sentences describing actions toward objects differing in weight, and therefore demanding varying degrees of physical effort: high-effort (e.g., pushing the piano), low-effort (e.g., pushing the chair), and no-effort (e.g., remembering the piano). They also obtained functional regions of interest when the same participants performed a physical effort task (e.g., squeezing a ball). The results of the reading task indicated that motor and premotor regions, overlapping with those activated by the squeezing task, were sensitive to the degree of effort implicit in the action-related sentences. Thus the Broca area, among others, was specifically engaged in sentences describing high-effort actions, whereas the left inferior parietal lobe was sensitive to sentences describing both high- and low-effort actions. The observed sensitivity of the motor brain to the implicit effort of sentences demonstrated that language comprehension elicits action representations that are object-specific. In addition, these object-specific representations were built online, namely during the combinatorial process that integrates the verb and the noun meanings.

In another study, Urrutia, Gennari, and de Vega (2012) tested whether sentences describing hypothetical scenarios were also sensitive to the effort manipulation. They used counterfactual sentences describing low- and high-effort actions, such as "If Pedro had decided to paint the room, he would have moved the picture/sofa." Given that counterfactual sentences do not describe "real" events, but just imaginary events that did not happen, it may be unnecessary to activate embodied representations of counterfactual events because they do not have a real-world referent. In spite of this, Urrutia et al. reported more activation in high- than in low-effort counterfactuals in the left inferior parietal lobe, extending to the supramarginal gyrus, which is a motor region associated with action planning processes, including assessment of size, weight, and muscles involved in the action.

The neurophysiology of action language

The neuroimaging studies provide important insights on how the brain motor networks play a role in the comprehension of action-related language. However, the poor temporal resolution of this technique makes it convenient to use other complementary techniques, which allow accurate tracing of the temporal course of motor activation in the brain. Thus, Pulvermüller et al. (2003) used magnetoencephalography (MEG) to explore the temporal pattern of activation of brain regions, while participants listened to the same action verbs employed in the aforementioned neuroimaging experiment. They observed activations in the specific somatotopic brain areas as soon as 200 ms after the word onset, and only 30 ms after activation in the Broca area. These activations, however, were short-lived and faded very soon, confirming the automaticity of motor resonance also established by behavioral studies.

Another technique recently used to explore the time course of motor activation consists of analyzing brain rhythm changes associated with action-related language. Specifically, electroencephalography (EEG) studies have found that the mu rhythms are a good marker of motor processes in the brain. The mu rhythms have a frequency of 8–14 Hz, similar to the alpha band rhythms although differing in their distribution (central in mu and posterior in alpha) and their functionality. Particularly, mu rhythms are synchronized in resting states and become desynchronized when individuals perform actions, when they see others' actions, or when they imagine performing actions themselves (see review by Pineda, 2005). In a recent experiment Moreno, de Vega, and León (2013a) collected EEG data while participants listened to action sentences (I hammer a nail), abstract sentences (I trust in friendship), or they observed action-related videos. Resting periods between blocks of trials were used as a baseline condition. The EEG-induced activity was analyzed by computing the power in the mu band, and a significant desynchronization was observed for action-related sentences, as well as action observations in the central electrodes (C3, Cz, C4). By contrast, the mu activity was kept at the baseline level in the abstract sentences. Figure 9.3 illustrates these results. The modulation of mu rhythms by action-related language can be considered strong evidence of motor resonance, and when using time-frequency analysis of the EEG signal provides an accurate timing of the phenomenon.

Some recent papers also explored mu sensitivity to action sentences, using time-frequency analysis of the EEG signal. This technique allows revealing the time course of mu suppression across the sentence. For example, van Elk, van Schie, Zwaan, and Bekkering (2010) analyzed

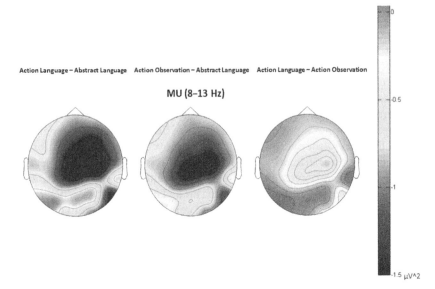

Figure 9.3 Scalp distribution of the mu oscillatory rhythms (8–13 Hz), calculated by subtracting the mean EEG power between pairs of conditions. The differences between Action language and Abstract language (leftward plot), and between Action observation and Abstract language (central plot), indicate mu suppression (negative values in the scale) in both action conditions. Instead, Action language and Action observation (rightward plot) do not show any difference in this oscillatory band.

changes in brain oscillatory rhythms while participants read action sentences with a human agent ("The woman is swimming in the pool") or an animal agent ("The duck is swimming in the pond"). They found EEG desynchronization in the mu and beta frequency rhythms, with respect to the resting baseline periods, associated with the action verbs. Notice, however, that the absence of nonaction sentences as a contrasting condition does not allow concluding that mu and beta rhythms are exclusively modulated by action language. On the other hand, they found larger desynchronization in the context of animal agents than in the context of human agents. According to the authors, a possible reason for this is that action verbs have higher cloze probability in animal contexts than in human contexts; for instance, "swimming" can be predicted more easily given "ducks" than given "woman." Still, it remains intriguing why the modulation of mu and beta occurs for sentences describing animal actions, which do not belong to the human motor repertoire.

More recently Moreno, de Vega, León, and Bastiaansen (2013b) contrasted action sentences (Cortarás el pastel de fresa/You will cut the strawberry cake), perceptual sentences (Mirarás los mensajes del email/ You will watch the email messages), and abstract sentences (Dudarás del precio del producto/You will doubt the product's price). They found that action sentences reduced mu power at the noun (pastel/cake) rather than the verb (cortarás/you will cut), suggesting that the readers need to integrate the sentence information to produce the motor simulation in the brain. Also, the sources estimation confirmed that the mu effects are associated with the supplementary motor areas in the brain, which fits pretty well with some of the neuroimaging results mentioned above.

Up to now we have collected some evidence that understanding action language elicits motor processes in the brain. But, to what extent are these motor activations functional for the construction of discourse meaning and inferences? Several studies manipulated motor compatibility of described actions to explore the functional consequences of motor representations. Performing motor actions is strongly constrained by the properties of our body as well as by temporal parameters. For instance, we can perform an almost infinite variety of manual actions at different moments, but we get into difficulty if we want to do two manual actions at once (e.g., cutting bread and opening a bottle), since many manual actions involve the use of both hands. This sensory-motor knowledge could penetrate the comprehension of action language. For instance, in a behavioral study, de Vega, Robertson, Glenberg, Kaschak, and Rinck (2004) created incongruent sentences violating embodied constraints, namely describing a character performing two actions with the same body effectors at once. In this condition they reported longer reading times than for sentences in which the same motor actions were described as consecutive, or were simultaneous but involved different body effectors. More recently, Santana and de Vega (2013) performed similar experiments using event-related potentials (ERPs). In their Exp. 1, participants read that a protagonist performed two actions either simultaneously or consecutively (e.g., While [After] cleaning the wound *he unrolled the bandage*), and they found, in the second action clause, specific brain responses for sentences with incompatible manual actions performed at once. In other words, there was an increase in the amplitude in the N400 component, a general brain signature for semantic incongruence, in comparison with sentences describing the same manual actions performed consecutively. This motor congruence effect could not be attributed to lexical factors, because the second clause, which was analyzed in the ERPs, was exactly the same across counterbalanced conditions in the compatible as in the incompatible sentences. Still, there is a possibility that the adverbs themselves produced the differences. Maybe *while*-sentences require more cognitive resources, independently of their content, than *after*-sentences simply because the semantics of simultaneity is cognitively more demanding, as it violates the temporal iconicity principle (Dowty, 1986; Zwaan, 1996). To rule out this explanation, another experiment was designed, including always sentences with the adverb *while* to establish the temporal relation between two actions, and making congruence dependent on their motor features. In the compatible condition, the first action was perceptual and the other one motor (e.g., While looking at the wound *he unrolled the bandage*), whereas in the incompatible condition both events were manual actions (e.g., While cleaning the wound *he unrolled the bandage*). The N400 effects for the former incompatible condition were replicated, again in the second-clause noun, as shown in Figure 9.4.

Notice that in both experiments the N400 was obtained in the noun that followed the second-clause verb (*bandage*), rather than in the verb itself (*unrolled*). This means that the brain detects the incompatibility only when the action information is completed, after integrating the action and the object that the action refers to, and after integrating such information with the previous context. In other words, the compatibility

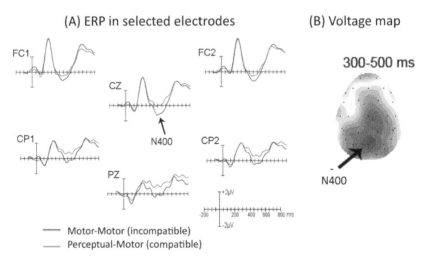

(A) ERP in selected electrodes   **(B) Voltage map**

——— Motor-Motor (incompatible)
——— Perceptual-Motor (compatible)

Figure 9.4 (A) Sentences describing incompatible actions performed at the same time enhanced the N400 component of the ERP, indicating a brain response to motor incoherence. (B) The distribution of the N400 component in the scalp is central-posterior (Santana and de Vega, 2013).

effect is not produced by a simple violation of verb lexical expectations. By contrast, it seems that action verbs alone are too indeterminate in some cases to represent the motor properties of actions; for instance, *to open* can lead to quite different motor programs depending on the specific object on which the action is performed (compare *he opened the umbrella* and *he opened the folder*). Consequently, the delayed N400 we found in the noun could reflect a global discourse integration process that allows readers to "discover" the unfeasibility of the actions. Moreover, these results suggest that action verbs embedded in sentences do not automatically trigger motor representations, but rather these representations are context-dependent. In our study, the N400 effects found on the noun, and not at the verb, could reflect that the brain motor areas are engaged only when sufficient information is given to appropriately represent the referred action.

The motor compatibility effects were also analyzed in an elegant ERP experiment using an ACE paradigm (Aravena, Hurtado, Riveros, Cardona, Manes, and Ibáñez, 2010). The authors reported an enhanced N400 component when participants were asked to perform a response with a hand shape mismatching the action sentence they had just listened to; for instance, pressing a button with the closed hand after hearing "The show was praiseworthy, so Rocío applauded." This N400 effect indicates, as in the previous study, a semantic incongruence effect, which was caused by motor incompatibility, in this case between action sentences and real motor actions. Moreover, they found in the mismatching conditions a modulation of another ERP component associated with the response, which indicated that the sentence meaning also modified the motor processes.

Conclusions

The neuroimaging studies of language confirmed and extended, at least in the case of action language, the embodiment account of meaning first proposed by experimental psychologists (e.g., Barsalou et al., 2008; de Vega et al., 2013; Glenberg and Kaschak, 2002; Zwaan and Taylor, 2006). These studies clearly revealed the activation of motor and premotor brain areas, typically involved in planning, executing, and controlling actions during the comprehension of action words, literal action sentences, action sentences describing hypothetical events, and even metaphorical sentences. The results reviewed in this section cannot be attributed to any special task demands associated with an artificial experimental paradigm, as was the case in the ACE studies. The neuroimaging studies, of course, have their own artificiality derived, for instance, from a noisy and uncomfortable experimental environment. But beyond these nuisances, young and well-motivated participants are capable of performing reading and comprehension tasks surprisingly well during the scanning sessions. In any case, the behavioral and neuroimaging results converge in that readers of action language routinely activate motor processes. On their side, electrophysiological studies provide a temporal high-resolution view of the comprehension processes. Especially promising are the experiments that analyze the brain dynamics associated with motor processes, particularly the study of mu oscillatory rhythms. This new approach already offers clear evidence that understanding action language has the same neurophysiological signatures as performing or observing real actions.

The neurological studies also converge with the behavioral studies in other aspects. They confirm that embodied representations can be either lexical or higher order, involving in some cases phrase-, sentence-, and text-level integration. Moreover, they show that embodied representations underlie abstract forms of language, such as negations or counterfactuals. Finally, they show that embodied representations are a fundamental aspect of meaning, as demonstrated by the motor compatibility studies.

Concluding remarks

The study of inferences in comprehension has been a popular topic in psycholinguistics during the last several decades. Researchers have described important features of inferences in comprehension, usually guided by dichotomous distinctions. For instance, they have empirically explored whether inferences are automatic or strategic, local or global, predictive or bridging, necessary or elaborative, world knowledge or text-based, occurring online or off-line, and so on. Also, researchers have paid attention to some contents that are privileged for inference making (e.g., causal, spatial, temporal, emotional), and the role inferences play in building discourse coherence. The cumulative advances in the topic have been impressive, and we know pretty well when and where we can expect inferences, what kind of inferences, and what their time course would be. However, our knowledge on the specific representational mechanisms underlying inferences is still limited, and it seems that understanding the mechanisms of inferences is inextricably associated with understanding the nature of meaning representation. In other words, inferences could be just collateral consequences of the normal functioning of our representational system during comprehension. The more we know of this representational system the better we will understand inferences.

On the other hand, embodied cognition has a growing influence, and it is becoming a well-established framework in cognitive sciences, with a strong empirical and theoretical foundation in the field of language comprehension. It is time, therefore, to establish a bridge between the study of inferences and the study of the embodied meaning, which could be fruitful for both scientific communities. This chapter was an effort in this direction, although I realize that it may not do justice either to the field of embodied cognition or the field of inferences.

We did not reflect here, for instance, the studies that showed embodied activations associated with visual, auditory, or olfactory modalities during language comprehension, or the studies revealing emotional and mentalizing processes activated during narrative comprehension. However, the focus on action language was appropriate as a representative subject in embodied cognition. The action system is primarily responsible for planning and executing motor programs aimed at moving our body in the environment or interacting with objects. I presented and discussed evidence that this action system also plays a functional role in language comprehension and inferences. Thus, when people understand action language they activate motor brain areas that partially overlap with those activated by performing actions. These activations are not just motor resonances at the lexical level; they are genuine inferences that require in many cases combinatorial processes within- and between-sentences, and go sometimes beyond the information explicitly stated in the text. These embodied inferences serve in some cases as predictive or elaborative. For instance, the activation of motor processes by language users is a sort of preparation for action, in conversational settings. Also embodied inferences could be backward or bridging inferences, as when the motor simulation allows for understanding of others' actions either in the real interaction with people, or while reading about fiction characters in narratives.

The embodied approach is not necessarily incompatible with other recent approaches to discourse and inferences processes, such as the memory-based theories (Cook et al., 2001; Myers and O'Brien, 1998), or the C-I theory (Kintsch, 1988). These theories emphasize the role played by the passive activation of pre-existing world knowledge or early portion of the texts. Given the associative nature of human memory, the time pressure of comprehension processes, and the limits of short-term working memory, it is very reasonable to think so. An embodied cognition approach could also accommodate the role of passive memory-based processes, but with additional constraints: memory-based processes involve not only word and conceptual traces but also sensory-motor traces triggered by words. Also, the combination of sensory-motor traces

into high-order representations would be constrained not only by words
and grammar, but also by our body functional features.

Acknowledgments

The preparation of this manuscript was funded by the Spanish Ministry
of Economy and Competitiveness (Grant SEJ2011-28679), the Canary
Agency for Research, Innovation, and the Information Society (NEU-
ROCOG Project), the Campus Atlántico Tricontinental, and the European Regional Development Funds.

REFERENCES

Anderson, J. R. (1983). *The Architecture of Cognition*. Cambridge, MA: Harvard
    University Press.
Aravena, P., Hurtado, E., Riveros, R., Cardona, J. F., Manes, F., & Ibáñez, A.
    (2010). Applauding with closed hands: neural signature of action-sentence
    compatibility effects. *PLoS ONE,*. 5, 1–14.
Azız-Zadeh, L., Wilson, S. M., Rizzolatti, G., & Iacoboni, M. (2006). Congruent
    embodied representations for visually presented actions and linguistic
    phrases describing actions. *Current Biology*, 16,1818–23.
Barsalou, L. (1999). Perceptual symbol system. *Behavioral and Brain Sciences*, 22,
    577–660.
Barsalou, L., Santos, A., & Simmons, W. K., & Wilson, C. D. (2008). Language
    and simulation in conceptual processing. In M. de Vega, A. Glenberg, & A.
    Graesser (eds.). *Symbols, and Embodiment. Debates on Meaning and Cognition*
    (pp. 245–84). New York: Oxford University Press.
Borreggine, K. L., & Kaschak, M. P. (2006). The action–sentence compatibility
    effect: it's all in the timing. *Cognitive Science*, 30, 1097–112.
Britton, B. K., van Dussen, L., Glynn, S. M., & Hemphill, D. (1990). The
    impact of inferences on instructional text. In A. C. Graesser & G. H. Bower
    (eds.). *Inferences and Text Comprehension*. San Diego: Academic Press.
Buccino, G., Riggio, L., Melli, G., Binkofski, F., Gallese, V., & Rizzolatti, G.
    (2005). Listening to action-related sentences modulates the activity of the
    motor system: a combined TMS and behavioural study. *Cognitive Brain
    Research*, 24, 355–63.
Cook, A. E., Limber, J. E., & O'Brien, E. J. (2001). Situation-based context and
    the availability of predictive Inferences. *Journal of Memory and Language*, 44,
    220–34.
Cramer, S. C., Weisskoff, R. M, Schaechter, J. D., Nelles, G., Foley, M.,
    Finklestein, S. P., & Rosen, B. R. (2002). Motor cortex activation is related
    to force of squeezing. *Human Brain Mapping*, 16(4): 197–205.
Damasio A. R. (1994). *Descartes' Error. Emotion, Reason and the Human Brain*.
    New York: Putnam's Sons.
Denis, M., Daniel, M. P., Fontaine, S., & Pazzaglia, F. (2001). Language, spatial
    cognition, and navigation. In M. Denis, R. H., Logie, C. Cornoldi, M. de

Vega, & J. Engelkamp (eds.). *Imagery, Language, and Visuo-spatial Thinking* (pp. 137–60). New York: Psychology Press.

de Vega, M. (2008). Levels of embodiment: from pointing to counterfactuals. In M. de Vega, A. M. Glenberg, & A. C. Graesser (eds.). *Symbols and Embodiment. Debates on Meaning and Cognition* (pp. 285–308). New York: Oxford University Press.

de Vega, M., Graesser, A., & Glenberg, A. (2008). Reflecting on the debate. In M. de Vega, A. Glenberg, & A. Graesser (eds.). *Symbols and Embodiment: Debates on Meaning and Cognition* (pp. 397–440). New York: Oxford University Press.

de Vega, M., León, I., Hernández, J.A., Valdés, M., Padrón, I., & Ferstl, E.C. (2014). Action sentences activate sensory-motor regions in the brain independently of their status of reality. *Journal of Cognitive Neuroscience*.

de Vega, M., Moreno, V., & Castillo, M. D. (2013). The comprehension of action-related sentences may cause interference rather than facilitation on matching actions. *Psychological Research, 77*, 20–30.

de Vega, M., Robertson, D. A., Glenberg, A. M., Kaschak, M. P., & Rinck, M. (2004). On doing two things at once: temporal constraints on actions in language comprehension. *Memory & Cognition, 32*, 1033–43.

de Vega, M., & Urrutia, M. (2011). Counterfactual sentences activate embodied meaning: an action-sentence compatibility effect study. *Journal of Cognitive Psychology, 23*, 962–73.

Dowty, D. (1986). The effects of aspectual class on the temporal structure of discourse: semantics or pragmatics? *Linguistic Philosophy, 9*, 37–61.

Garrod, S., & Pickering, M. J. (2004). Why is conversation so easy? *Trends in Cognitive Sciences, 8*, 8–11.

Glenberg, A. M., & Kaschak, M. P. (2002). Grounding language in action. *Psychonomic Bulletin & Review, 9*, 558–65.

Glenberg, A. M., Sato, M., Cattaneo, L., Riggio, L., Palumbo, D., & Buccino, G. (2008). Processing abstract language modulates motor system activity. *Quarterly Journal of Experimental Psychology, 61*, 905–19.

Goldberg, R., Perfetti, C., & Schneider, W. (2006). Perceptual knowledge retrieval activates sensory brain regions. *Journal of Neuroscience, 26*, 4917–21.

Graesser, A. C., Singer, M., & Trabasso, T. (1994). Constructing inferences during narrative text comprehension. *Psychological Review, 101*, 371–95.

Hamzei, F., Rijntjes, M., Dettmers, C., Glauche, V. Weiller, C., & Büchel, C (2003). The human action recognition system and its relationship to Broca's area: an fMRI study. *NeuroImage, 19*, 637–44.

Harnad, S. (1990). The symbol grounding problem. *Physica, 42*, 335–46.

Havas, D. A., Glenberg, A. M., & Rinck, M. (2007). Emotion simulation during language comprehension. *Psychonomic Bulletin & Review, 14*, 436–41.

Kintsch, W. (1988). The role of knowledge in discourse comprehension: a construction-integration model. *Psychological Review, 95*, 163–82.

(1998). *Comprehension: A Paradigm for Cognition*. New York: Cambridge University Press.

(2008). Symbol systems and perceptual representations. In M. de Vega, A. Glenberg, & A. Graesser (eds.). *Symbols and Embodiment: Debates on Meaning and Cognition* (pp. 397–440). New York: Oxford University Press.

Kintsch, W., & Van Dijk, T. A. (1978). Toward a model of text comprehension and production. *Psychological Review, 85,* 363–94.

Lakoff, G., & Johnson, M. (1980). *Metaphors We Live By.* University of Chicago Press.

McKoon, G., & Ratcliff, R. (1988). Contextually relevant aspects of meaning. *Journal of Experimental Psychology: Learning, Memory, and Cognition, 14,* 331–43.

(1992). Inference during reading. *Psychological Review, 99,* 440–66.

Moody, C. L., & Gennari, S. P. (2010). Effects of implied physical effort in sensory-motor and pre-frontal cortex during language comprehension. *NeuroImage, 49,* 782–93.

Moreno, I. Z., de Vega, M., & León, I. (2013a). Understanding action language modulates oscillatory mu and beta rhythms in the same way as observing actions. *Brain and Cognition, 82,* 236–42.

Moreno, I. Z., de Vega, M., León, I., & Bastiaansen, M. (2013b). The time course of motor resonance during the comprehension of action-sentences. A time-frequency analysis of mu rhythms modulation. *Unpublished manuscript.*

Myers, J. L., & O'Brien, E. J. (1998). Accessing the discourse representation during reading. *Discourse Processes, 26(2–3),* 131–57.

Pecher, D., Zeelenberg, R., & Barsalou, L. W. (2003). Verifying properties from different modalities for concepts produces switching costs. *Psychological Science, 14,* 119–24.

Pineda, J. (2005). The functional significance of mu rhythms: translating "seeing" and "hearing" into "doing". *Brain Research Reviews, 50,* 57–68.

Pulvermüller, F. (2008). Grounding language in the brain. In M. de Vega, A. M. Glenberg, & A. C. Graesser (eds.). *Symbols and Embodiment. Debates on Meaning and Cognition* (pp. 85–116). New York: Oxford University Press.

Pulvermüller, F., Hauk, O., Nikulin, V. V., & Ilmoniemi, R. J. (2005). Functional links between motor and language systems. *European Journal of Neuroscience, 21,* 793–97.

Pulvermüller, F., Shtyrov, Y., & Ilmoniemi, R. J. (2003). Spatiotemporal patterns of neural language processing: an MEG study using minimum-norm current estimates. *Neuroimage, 20,* 1020–5.

Rizzolatti, G., & Arbib, M. A. (1998). Language within our grasp. *Trends in Neuroscience, 21,* 188–94.

Rumelhart, D. E. (1980). Schemata: the building blocks of cognition. In R. Spiro et al. (eds.). *Theoretical Issues in Reading Comprehension.* Mahwah, NJ: Erlbaum.

Santana, E., & de Vega, M. (2011). Orientational metaphors are embodied … and so are their literal counterparts. *Frontiers in Psychology, 90(2),* 1–12.

(2013). An ERP study of motor compatibility effects in action language. *Brain Research, 1526,* 71–83.

Searle, J. R. (1980). Minds, brains, & programs. *Behavioral and Brain Sciences, 3*, 417–57.

Tettamanti, M., Manenti, R., Della Rosa, P. A., Falini, A., Perani, D., Cappa, S. F., & Moro, A. (2008). Negation in the brain: modulating action representations. *Neuroimage, 43*, 358–67.

Urrutia, M., Gennari, S. P., & de Vega, M. (2012). Counterfactuals in action: an fMRI study of counterfactual sentences describing physical effort. *Neuropsychologia, 50*, 3663–72.

Van den Broek, P. J. (1990). Causal inferences and the comprehension of narrative texts. In A. C. Graesser & G. H. Bower (eds.). *Inferences and Text Comprehension*. San Diego: Academic Press.

Van Elk, M., van Schie, H. T., Zwaan, R. A., & Bekkering, H. (2010). The functional role of motor resonance in language processing: motor-cortical oscillations support lexical-semantic retrieval. *Neuroimage, 50*, 665–77.

Zwaan, R. A. (1996). Processing narrative time shifts. *Journal of Experimental Psychology: Learning, Memory, and Cognition, 22*, 1196–207.

(2004). The immersed experiencer: toward an embodied theory of language comprehension. In B. H. Ross (ed.), *The Psychology of Learning and Motivation*. Vol. *XLIV* (pp. 35–62). New York: Academic Press.

Zwaan, R. A., & Radvansky, G. A. (1998). Situation models in language and memory. *Psychological Bulletin, 123*, 162–85.

Zwaan, R. A., & Taylor, L. J. (2006). Seeing, acting, understanding: motor resonance in language comprehension. *Journal of Experimental Psychology: General, 135*, 1–11.

10   The cognitive and neural correlates of
individual differences in inferential processes

Chantel S. Prat and Brianna L. Yamasaki

"For sale: Baby shoes, never worn."

Ernest Hemingway is rumored to have written these six words onto a napkin at a bar, winning a bet that he could write a story in under ten words. Whether or not this legend is true, the example of the short story nicely illustrates the power of inferential processes, which supported the economical writing style for which Hemingway was famous. For the purposes of this chapter, an inference will be defined as any information the reader brings to bear to bridge the gap between what a text explicitly states and the meaning a writer intends to convey. For the six words printed above to be considered a story, a reader must imagine various scenarios that could link the propositions in the text, resulting in the seemingly rare situation in which a pair of baby shoes that have never been worn end up for sale. Interestingly, the extent to which an individual will "read between the lines" to elaborate upon the information explicitly mentioned in a text varies widely from reader to reader.

Research over the past thirty years has demonstrated that the ability to generate such inferences is one of the hallmarks of skilled comprehension (e.g., Just and Carpenter, 1992; Long, Oppy, and Seely, 1994; 1997; Oakhill, 1983; 1984). Understanding the nature of individual differences in inferential abilities is essential not only for understanding high-level reading comprehension, but also for understanding how individuals reason about the world around them. This chapter will summarize the research on individual differences in inferential abilities, with an emphasis on more recent work investigating the neural bases of such differences.

Individual differences in inferential abilities result from a critical interaction between reader characteristics and text characteristics (e.g., Long, Seely, and Oppy, 1996; Prat, Mason, and Just, 2011). Readers vary in their ability to generate inferences and to integrate them into their mental models of what is happening in the story. At the same time, texts vary in the extent to which they require or invite inferences during comprehension, and the ease with which such inferences can be drawn. Undoubtedly, much of this book will focus on the characteristics of texts that influence inferential processes; however, it is worth mentioning here as well that inferences are generated under a variety of conditions and constraints, some of which magnify individual differences in comprehension (such as when inferences are elaborative or optional), and others of which diminish them (such as when inferences are necessary to maintain coherence in a text: St. George, Mannes, and Hoffman, 1997). We will revisit the relevance of different conditions under which inferences may be drawn in more detail at a later point in this chapter, when resource availability and processing demands are discussed.

With respect to the individual reader, at least two conditions must be met in order for an inference to be incorporated into a reader's understanding of a text: (a) he or she must have access to the relevant background knowledge necessary to generate the inference, and (b) he or she must have the available neurocognitive resources necessary for generating and integrating the inference into his or her mental model of the text being comprehended. These two conditions are not completely independent, as accessing the relevant background knowledge also draws upon mental resources. Research on the importance of background knowledge and resource availability for inferential processes is summarized in the subsequent sections.

The role of individual differences in background knowledge on inference generation

The integration of a reader's background knowledge with the ideas explicitly mentioned in a text (also called the propositional, or text-based representation) is necessary for building a discourse (or situation) model of the scenario unfolding in a text (Gernsbacher, Varner, and Faust 1990; Graesser, Singer, and Trabasso, 1994; Kintsch, 1988; McKoon and Ratcliff, 1992). To construct a discourse model, readers must engage in inferential processing to interpret and to organize text information in light of their prior understanding of the knowledge domain. Thus, the nature and richness of a reader's existing knowledge about relevant topics of the story can dramatically influence their ability to generate inferences and use them to organize and elaborate upon the information explicitly mentioned in the text.

It is not surprising then, that research has repeatedly demonstrated that background knowledge or expertise interacts with a reader's ability to comprehend and later remember the information presented in texts (Barry and Lazarte, 1998; Bransford and Johnson, 1972; Long, Prat, Johns, Morris, and Jonathan, 2008; Long, Wilson, Hurley, and Prat,

2006). Contemporary psycholinguistics research has further investigated the integration of such background knowledge into a reader's discourse model using a dual-process model of recognition memory (e.g., Jacoby and Dallas, 1981; Mandler, 1980; Yonelinas, 2002). Dual-process models emphasize that two factors contribute to an individual's ability to recognize information previously presented to them. The first factor involves an assessment of the *familiarity* of an item, and the second factor involves a more vivid, *recollective* experience. Thus, dual-process recognition paradigms (also called remember/know paradigms) first ask readers whether a particular item or sentence appeared in a text, and then ask them whether that item is familiar to them, or if they explicitly recall reading it. Using a Remember/Know paradigm, Long and colleagues examined how individual differences in domain expertise influence a reader's ultimate memory for the events that unfold during a story (Long and Prat, 2002; Long et al., 2006; 2008). Across three experiments, the authors examined readers' memories for information presented in texts. Consistent with previous research, they found that readers with greater relevant background knowledge (usually *"Star Trekspertise"*) were more likely to recognize information explicitly mentioned in the text. Using a *"Remember/ Know"* paradigm (Tulving, 1985) to further examine the nature of the memory traces, Long and colleagues found that individuals with greater background knowledge had recognition processes that were accompanied by a more vivid, "recollective" experience, rather than an increased general sense of familiarity (Long and Prat, 2002; Long et al., 2006; 2008).

Importantly for this chapter, readers with greater relevant expertise were also more likely to elaborate on the texts they read with inferences based on their background knowledge. The seamlessness with which experts integrate background knowledge and information explicitly mentioned in the texts into their discourse models is evidenced by the fact that experts are more likely to *misremember* inferential material as being explicitly mentioned in the texts than are novices (Long et al., 2008). Interestingly, even for these false memories, experts more frequently report a vivid, "recollective" experience rather than a general sense of "familiarity," when reflecting on their memories of inferred information. In other words, experts are more likely to report that they vividly remember reading a statement that mentions potentially inferred information, even though that information was never mentioned in the text. This effect did not generalize to all inferential material, however, as both groups also read scientific texts outside of their areas of expertise and showed no differences in false alarming to inferential materials.

In some cases, the relevant background information needed for generating inferences is provided previously in the text. In such conditions, a *bridging* (or *backward*) inference is typically required to link a new proposition to the information previously read. Research on individual differences in bridging inferences has shown that factors associated with the availability of the antecedents in memory predict the ease with which the inference can be generated in all individuals. For instance, the difficulty of generating bridging inferences increases with the distance between the relevant textual information and the coherence break that signals the need for an inference in all readers (e.g., Karasinski and Weismer, 2010). The increased demands placed by having to retrieve information presented longer ago in time do not affect all readers equally, however. For instance, individuals with higher working memory capacities, whom are generally assumed to have more "resources" available for processing texts (discussed in detail below), seem able to ameliorate the memory demands placed by such long-distance inferences. This effect typically results in an interaction between inference difficulty (as measured by the amount of time or information that elapses between the antecedent and the coherence break) and individual working memory capacity (e.g., Just and Carpenter, 1992; Karasinski and Weismer, 2010).

In summary, the first precondition of generating an inference is access to the relevant background knowledge necessary for doing so. Individual differences in the availability of background knowledge may stem from pre-existing differences in expertise on topics relevant to the situation unfolding in a text (e.g., Long et al., 2008). Alternatively, when pertinent knowledge is previously mentioned in a text, factors related to the ease with which an individual can access the relevant antecedents (such as working memory capacity) will relate to the likelihood that an inference may be drawn. In the next section on resource availability, the second precondition of inference generation, we will discuss the nature of capacity constraints on inferential processes by exploring working memory capacity in more detail.

The role of resource constraints on inferential processes

Discourse comprehension has been theorized to rely on a "pool" of neurocognitive resources that must support the multiple subcomponent processes (e.g., decoding, lexical access, and syntactic parsing), executed largely in parallel, during comprehension (e.g., Just and Carpenter, 1992).[1]

---

[1] There is an ongoing debate about the extent to which these subcomponent processes rely on shared (Just and Carpenter, 1992; Just, Carpenter, and Varma, 1999) versus distinct (e.g., Waters and Caplan, 1996) resource pools. Owing to space constraints and the focus of this chapter, we will not delve into that issue in detail here.

The likelihood that any particular process will have enough resources to support it depends critically on both the total amount of resources available to an individual, and on where in the "hierarchy of importance" that process lies for comprehension. This hierarchy can be constructed based on two factors: (a) the extent to which one type of processing relies on the output of another process, and (b) the extent to which a particular process is necessary for maintaining coherence between the incoming text and the reader's mental model of the story. Inferences lie near the top of this hierarchy, because to draw an inference, readers must first use word-level decoding and sentence-level parsing processes to build a propositional (or text-based) representation of the events explicitly mentioned in the text (Graesser et al., 1994; McKoon and Ratcliff, 1992). Thus, only readers with enough resources available after the propositional representations have been constructed will be able to use inferential processes to create an elaborated discourse model of the situation unfolding in the story (e.g., Long, Oppy, and Seely, 1994; 1997).

It is worth nothing that even within this hierarchy, not all inferences are created equally. For instance, numerous studies suggest that when a coherence break occurs in the story, bridging inferences are *required* to maintain continuity in the comprehension process (e.g., Haviland and Clark, 1974). In contrast, *predictive* (or forward) inferences are not required to maintain continuity in the comprehension process. Thus, bridging inferences can be viewed as having a higher priority in terms of resource consumption than do predictive, or other optional, elaborative inferences.

Given the competition for limited resources, it is not surprising that individual differences in reading skill are most obvious when measuring comprehension processes that lie at the top of the resource consumption hierarchy. In other words, when comparing the comprehension of passages that require bridging inferences to those that invite predictive inferences, individual differences are greater on the optional, predictive inferences than on the required, bridging ones (e.g., St. George et al., 1997).

But what determines the amount of resources accessible to an individual during comprehension? According to the seminal "Capacity Theory of Comprehension," (Just and Carpenter, 1992) resource availability maps onto two dissociable components: (1) the efficiency with which a reader can execute the various subcomponent processes of comprehension, and (2) the total size of the "resource pool" (or capacity) one has available for executing all comprehension processes. In their influential paper, Just and Carpenter (1992) extended the metaphor of energy consumption first discussed by Kahneman (1973) by stating that the amount of resources an individual has available is akin to the amount of amperes a home can draw on (with some neighbors having access to more energy than others), whereas the efficiency with which an individual can execute the component processes of comprehension can be viewed as an index of energy efficiency of the various appliances in the home. Given equal access to amperes, the household with the most efficient appliances will be able to accomplish more with the resources available to them.

Research on individual differences in reading ability has repeatedly demonstrated that both "efficiency" and "capacity" relate to individual differences in inferential processes (e.g., Calvo, Eztevez, and Dowens, 2003; Estevez and Calvo, 2000; Hannon and Daneman, 1998; Linderhom, 2002; Singer and Ritchot, 1996). Until recently, it was difficult to disentangle the relative roles of each on inferencing, as they are often correlated with one another (e.g., Singer, Andruslak, Reisdorf, and Black, 1992) or not independently considered. Contemporary individual differences research, however, has shown that indices of efficiency, which are typically predicted specifically by linguistic skill and experience (Maxwell, Fenwick, Fenton, and Dollimore, 1974), predict different patterns of performance than do indices of more general "capacity" (e.g., Calvo, 2005; Singer et al., 1992). Importantly, a number of recent neuroimaging investigations have demonstrated that individual differences in "efficiency" and "capacity" have distinct neural characterizations during reading comprehension under a variety of conditions (Prat, 2011; Prat and Just, 2011; Prat, Keller, and Just, 2007; Prat et al., 2011; Prat, Mason, and Just, 2012). This research, summarized below, has been used to generate an enriched understanding of the biological constraints on discourse comprehension in general, and on inferential processes specifically.

The neural correlates of skilled comprehension

To the best of our knowledge, only three published neuroimaging experiments to date have directly investigated the neural correlates of individual differences in inferential abilities (Prat et al., 2011; Virtue, Haberman, Clancy, Parrish, and Jung-Beeman, 2006; Virtue, Parrish, and Jung-Beeman, 2008). Although each of these papers provides valuable information about the neural correlates of inferential processes and how they vary in different contexts (e.g., as a function of causal relatedness: Prat et al., 2011, or predictability: Virtue et al., 2008) and across readers of different abilities (Prat et al., 2011; Virtue et al., 2006; 2008), variability in the methods used and in the classification of "skilled comprehension" makes it difficult to integrate the findings from the three investigations. For instance, Virtue and colleagues divided participants into two groups using a median split based on their verbal working memory capacity (Virtue et al., 2006; 2008), whereas Prat and colleagues (2011) correlated indices of neural activation with Nelson-Denny Reading Test (Brown, 1960) vocabulary scores. In addition, participants in both of Virtue's experiments listened to stories presented auditorally, while participants in Prat's experiments read stories presented visually (Prat et al., 2011; Virtue et al., 2006; 2008). Research on the effects of modality on language comprehension has shown that auditory comprehension involves greater recruitment of bilateral cortical circuitry than visual comprehension does (Buchweitz, Mason, Tomich, and Just, 2009). Because methodological variability makes it difficult to directly integrate the results of these three experiments, the subsequent sections will summarize the broader field of research investigating the neural characteristics of skilled reading comprehension ability. We will then use these characteristics to anchor our discussion on the neural bases of individual differences in inferential ability, revisiting the existing research on this topic.

Individual differences in reading skill and neural efficiency. One of the best understood links between brain function and individual differences in cognitive abilities is that more-skilled individuals generally accomplish a task more efficiently, using fewer neural resources, than less-skilled individuals (Haier, Siegel Nuechterlein, Hazlett, Wu, Paek, Browning, and Buchsbaum, 1988; Maxwell et al., 1974; Neubauer and Fink, 2009; Prat and Just, 2011; Prat et al., 2007; 2011; Reichle, Carpenter, and Just, 2000). The assumption behind efficiency research is that the amount of "mental resource consumption" that is required to effectively perform a task is reflected by the amount of brain activation observed during the task. Resource consumption can thus be measured either by the spread of activation in a defined region or set of regions (more focal activation patterns are more efficient), or by the intensity of activation in a defined region (less activation is more efficient).

With respect to reading comprehension ability, Maxwell and colleagues (1974) were the first to demonstrate that skilled comprehenders have more efficient neural processes. Using EEG recordings of fourteen-year-old boys, Maxwell and others found that good comprehenders had more efficient neural processes, as indicated by significantly lower power throughout the frequency bands than did poor comprehenders. The relation between increased neural efficiency and improved language comprehension abilities has subsequently been replicated in adults (Prat and Just, 2011; Prat et al., 2007; 2011; Reichle et al., 2000), and for more general individual differences in intelligence and reasoning abilities (for a review, see Neubauer and Fink, 2009).

One might ask whether neural efficiency is related to specific (e.g., linguistic) skills that can be refined with experience, or to more general processing capacities or traits, such as general intelligence. In the experiment conducted by Maxwell et al. (1974), individuals were not engaged in a cognitive task while EEGs were recorded (suggesting a more general effect of efficiency). However, when EEG recordings were taken from the participants while their eyes were closed, no reliable differences in efficiency were found. The authors surmised that the differences in efficiency were more obvious when information processing was occurring (in the eyes open condition), and would be greatest under conditions in which the subjects were engaged in comprehension processes, although this was not tested in the study.

Contemporary neuroimaging research has provided additional information about the generality of individual differences in neural efficiency, both by exploring the factors related to variability in efficiency and by examining the correspondence between regions where efficiency differences are observed and individual abilities. One excellent illustration of this can be seen in the results of Reichle et al. (2000), who conducted a neuroimaging investigation of a sentence-picture verification task. In their experiment, readers were asked to read sentences such as "It is not true that the star is above the plus" and then to answer true/false questions about whether a subsequent picture matched the information in the sentence (i.e., a + sign over the image of a star) or didn't match (i.e., a star depicted over a + sign) in one of two strategy conditions. In the verbal strategy condition, participants were asked to remember the words in the sentence. In the visual imagery condition, participants were asked to form a mental image of the information described in the sentence. Using an individual differences manipulation, the authors found that participants with higher verbal working memory capacities showed more efficient processing in typical left-lateralized language regions (e.g., Broca's area) than did participants with low capacities *when verbal strategies were used.* In contrast, individuals with higher visual-spatial skills showed more efficient processing in typical visual association regions (e.g., parietal cortex) than did individuals with lower visual-spatial skills *when spatial strategies were used.* In other words, the predictive power of skill in a particular domain (verbal versus visuo-spatial) was observed during conditions that evoked that particular type of processing, and in brain regions that subserved that type of process. These results are consistent with the view that neural efficiency is related to skill at a particular

Table 10.1 *Sample stimuli used in Prat, Mason, and Just (2011)*

Passage type	Context sentence	Manipulated sentence
Coherent/ Cohesive	Sandra walked barefoot on the littered beach.	*Consequently*, she had to clean out the wound on her foot.
Coherent/ Incohesive	Sandra walked barefoot on the littered beach.	She had to clean out the wound on her foot.
Less-Coherent/ Cohesive	Tom decided to run a marathon for charity.	*Consequently*, he had many visitors at the hospital.
Less-Coherent/ Incohesive	Tom decided to run a marathon for charity.	He had many visitors at the hospital.

task (or component thereof) and is manifest by a reduction in activation in the neural networks necessary for completing that task.

With respect to language comprehension tasks, Prat and colleagues (Prat et al., 2007; 2011; Prat and Just, 2011) have repeatedly found that increased reading skill (typically measured using standardized tests of reading comprehension such as the Nelson-Denny Reading Test) is correlated with increased neural efficiency (see Prat, 2011 for a review). In their investigation of individual differences in inference comprehension, Prat et al. (2011) also found that skilled readers had more efficient activation patterns than did less-skilled readers. In this experiment, individuals read two-sentence passages that varied in causal relatedness (coherence) and the presence or absence of clause connectives cueing relatedness (cohesion: See Table 10.1). Individual differences in neural efficiency were manifest both during baseline reading (when reading the context sentences), and during the portion of the passage that could invite an inference. This was primarily manifest by decreased activation in right hemisphere homologues of left hemisphere language regions. The relation between right hemisphere activation and reading skill during inference comprehension can be seen in Figure 10.1, reproduced with permission from Prat, Mason, and Just (2011).

When considering the individual differences in neural efficiency during inferential processes, however, one must keep in mind an important caveat. In order for efficiency comparisons to be valid, one must first establish that individuals are performing a task at the same level, using the same strategies. For instance, higher-working-memory-capacity individuals often have higher activation levels in relevant executive processing areas than do lower-capacity individuals when completing working memory tasks (e.g., McGettigan, Warren, Eisner, Marshall, Shanmugalingam, and Scott, 2011; Osaka, Osaka, Kondo, Morishita,

Increased Right Hemisphere Activation in Less-Skilled Readers during Passage Comprehension

(A)

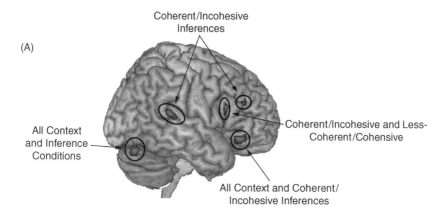

(B)

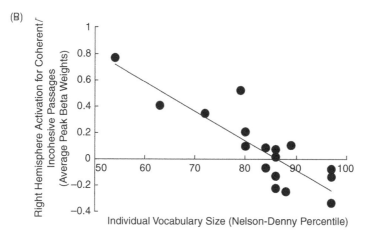

Figure 10.1 (A) Activation map depicting reliable negative correlations between vocabulary size and right hemisphere activation for all context sentences (in blue) and all inference conditions (overlap in white), for coherent/incohesive passages (in red), for coherent and for less-coherent/incohesive passages (in yellow). Overlap between coherent/incohesive and context is depicted in purple. Overlap between coherent and less-coherent/incohesive passages is depicted in dark yellow. (B) Scatterplot depicting the correlation between individual vocabulary size and RH activation during coherent/incohesive inferences.

Fukuyama, Aso, and Shibasaki, 2003). However, higher-capacity individuals also outperform lower-capacity individuals on such tasks (obviously), and thus it is difficult to know whether lower-capacity individuals have less activation because they are not engaging in the task as consistently (e.g., are "giving up" on difficult trials), because they are not employing some appropriate executive strategy (e.g., conflict monitoring), or because of any other number of explanations (e.g., poorer functioning of frontal-parietal networks). The same argument can be made for comprehension of passages that invite, but do not require, inferences. When comparing activation of good and poor comprehenders, one must remember that a plethora of behavioral investigations (such as those mentioned in the beginning of this chapter) have demonstrated that skilled readers are more likely to generate optional or elaborative inferences than are less-skilled readers. Thus, increased activation in skilled readers, such as those observed by Virtue and colleagues may reflect additional inferential processing (Virtue et al., 2006; 2008). In fact, Prat et al. (2011) found that less-skilled readers had greater activation in three out of four passage conditions, where cues for either cohesion or coherence were present (see Table 10.1). In the fourth, arguably most difficult condition, where the passages consisted of "distant" causally related sentences without clause connectives (no cohesion), skilled readers showed greater activation than did less-skilled readers. One limitation of all three neuroimaging investigations of individual differences is that there was no direct assessment of whether readers were generating inferences either online or later for the various passages. We see this as an important direction for future studies aimed at investigating the neural correlates of inferential processes in general, and at individual differences in inferential abilities specifically.

Taken together, the efficiency research discussed in this section suggests a possible explanation for differences in the amount of elaboration in which skilled and less-skilled readers engage in. Specifically, it is possible that increased neural efficiency in baseline comprehension processes results in greater availability of cortical resources in the language network for the execution of nonessential, elaborative comprehension processes that characterize skilled reading.

Individual differences in working memory capacity and neural adaptability. Where in the brain might the "pool of resources," first described by Just and Carpenter (1992) and referred to throughout this chapter, lie? The most obvious answer would be that higher-capacity individuals simply have more neurons (or bigger brains), which enable greater computational power. Although it is true that working memory and intelligence are positively correlated with brain size (e.g., Posthuma, Baaré, Pol, Hilleke, Kahn, Boomsma, and De Geus, 2003), the correlation is approximately 0.27, explaining roughly 7 percent of the variance. Thus, it is likely that some characteristic or characteristics of neural *functioning* also differ in higher- and lower-capacity individuals. One such characteristic that has been investigated is neural adaptability (Prat et al., 2007). Human cognition in general, and language comprehension in particular, are characterized by dynamic processing demands; thus a cortical network performing a complex task must be able to adapt to changing task requirements (e.g., Garlick, 2002; Schafer, 1982). With respect to language comprehension, adaptability can be conceived of as the dynamic recruitment of neural networks on an "as-needed" basis with changing task demands. Although a modal set of areas activates for any given task, additional resources and/or areas may be recruited to deal with changes in the level or type of demand. For example, dorsolateral prefrontal cortex becomes recruited when comprehension of a sentence requires problem-solving processes (Newman, Just, and Carpenter, 2002). Such cortical dynamics can be indexed by variation in activation levels within the same networks (e.g., Prat et al., 2007; Prat and Just, 2011) as well as by reconfiguration of networks to involve new regions (Newman et al., 2002).

It is worth noting that in both of Virtue et al.'s (2006, 2008) investigations of individual differences in inferential processes, the dependent variable reported was a larger *increase* in activation for passages that invited inferences *over* passages that explicitly mention all information required for comprehension in higher-capacity individuals than in lower-capacity individuals. However, whether activation differed as a function of working memory capacity independent of passage condition was not reported (Virtue et al., 2006; 2008). Thus the results described by Virtue and colleagues also demonstrate increased adaptability, or tighter coupling between changes in brain activation and changes in task demands, in higher-capacity than in lower-capacity individuals during inferential processes.

The research described in this section thus far has shown that variability in neural adaptability is related to individual differences in working memory capacity (e.g., Prat et al., 2007; Prat and Just, 2011; Virtue et al., 2006; 2008), but differences in adaptability have also been demonstrated as a function of individual differences in reading skill (Yeatman, Ben-Shachar, Glover, and Feldman, 2010). Thus, one might ask whether individual differences in adaptability arise purely due to differences in neural efficiency, as resource availability is a precondition for the recruitment of additional resources. Another possibility is that differences in adaptability arise from some property of brain function (e.g., better plasticity, improved function of control regions) that underpins cortical dynamics and is somewhat separable from resource availability. If the latter is true, then systematic differences in coupling between changes in the computational demands of a task and changes in cortical activation underpin individual differences in general mental function (e.g., Garlick, 2002). These two accounts are not mutually exclusive, as it is plausible that both efficient resource utilization and resource allocation mechanisms are necessary for fluent neural adaptability.

One experiment to date has directly examined the mechanism behind individual differences in neural adaptability. In a sentence comprehension paradigm, Prat and Just (2011) examined syntactic adaptability (changes in activation observed with changing syntactic complexity) under varying extrinsic working-memory demands. Individuals read syntactically simple two-clause conjoined sentences such as "The kitten licked the puppy and climbed the stairs" or syntactically complex object relative sentences such as "The kitten that the puppy licked climbed the stairs" either alone (No Load Condition), preceded by three to-be-remembered words (Low Load Condition), or preceded by three to-be-remembered pronounceable nonword strings (High Load Condition). They found that for all readers, syntactic adaptability decreased as the external working memory demands of the task increased, highlighting the importance of resource availability for neural adaptability. They also found that higher-working-memory-capacity individuals showed greater syntactic adaptability across all working memory loads than did lower-capacity individuals. Although these results support the notion that individual differences in adaptability are related to individual differences in efficiency, the results in this experiment cannot be fully explained by differences in resource availability. First, when vocabulary size and working memory capacity were allowed to compete for variance in a multiple regression analysis, the largest differences in neural efficiency were related to vocabulary size, whereas differences in neural adaptability were found only as a function of verbal working-memory capacity. In addition, the networks in which individual differences in efficiency and adaptability were observed were not overlapping. Thus, although resource availability is clearly a precondition for neural recruitment, these data suggest that another facet of brain function that systematically differs between individuals may contribute to individual differences in comprehension abilities.

The importance of flexible "control" during inference comprehension. To better understand the cognitive implications of improved neural adaptability, it is important to consider the functioning of the regions in which individual differences in adaptability are observed.

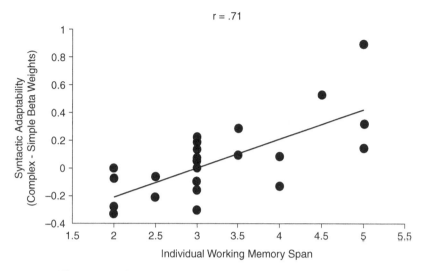

Figure 10.2 Scatterplot depicting the relation between average syntactic adaptability (mean complex – simple peak beta weights) and individual working memory capacity.

Across two neuroimaging investigations, increased working memory capacity was associated with increased adaptability in cognitive control structures, including the striatum and prefrontal cortex (Prat et al., 2007; Prat and Just, 2011). Interestingly, these regions were among the first implicated in functional neuroimaging investigations of working memory demands (Rypma, Prabhakaran, Desmond, Glover, and Gabrieli, 1999). In their seminal study, Rympa and colleagues asked the question, "Where is capacity?" by investigating regions where brain activation increased as a function of the number of letters individuals were asked to hold in memory. They found that across individuals, activation in medial and superior frontal regions as well as in the striatum increased as the working memory load increased. In two neuroimaging experiments of reading comprehension, Prat and colleagues also found that modulation of these regions varied significantly as a function of individual working memory capacity (Prat et al., 2007; Prat and Just, 2011). In fact, working memory capacity accounted for 50 percent of the variability in adaptability of this control network as depicted in Figure 10.2 (Prat and Just, 2011).

Even though it is uncontroversial that prefrontal cortical regions (including Broca's area and its right hemisphere homologue) play a critical role in language processes, the striatum (consisting of bilateral caudate nuclei and putamen) has recently received increasing attention for its involvement in linguistic "control" (Buchweitz and Prat, in press; Friederici, 2006; Prat and Just, 2011; Stocco, Yamasaki, Natalenko, and Prat, 2014). Prat and colleagues (Buchweitz and Prat, 2013; Prat and Just, 2011; Prat, 2012; Stocco et al., 2012) have capitalized on a computational model that describes striatal function as a gate, enabling flexible selection and routing of signals to the prefrontal cortex (e.g., Stocco, Lebiere, and Anderson, 2010) to understand the role of the striatum in skilled comprehension processes. Specifically, they propose that the ability to flexibly select the pertinent information (e.g., a semantic or propositional representation) for a given language task and to route it to the prefrontal cortex for further processing facilitates "skilled" comprehension. The capacity of the striatum to control which signals are eventually directed to the prefrontal cortex provides the critical link between striatal function, working memory capacity, neural adaptability, and skilled comprehension. Specifically, by altering the number and types of signals that are routed to prefrontal cortex, the striatum can strategically allocate the most relevant information to the appropriate prefrontal processing centers, much like an expert juggler can accommodate for more balls in his circle by strategically increasing each ball's airtime and reducing each ball's handling time. Although this research area is new and somewhat speculative at this point, converging results suggest that individual differences in working memory capacity during reading comprehension, in general, and during inferential processes, specifically, may arise due to the improved functioning of a neural circuit that allows for the flexible selection and transmission of signals to the prefrontal cortex. We see this as an exciting avenue for future research.

Summary and broader implications

The ability to generate inferences and integrate them with information explicitly mentioned in the text is necessary for creating a complete, coherent discourse model. As such, inferential abilities are considered to be one of the hallmarks of skilled comprehension processes, and have thus been widely investigated. One main focus of this chapter is on understanding the biological correlates of individual differences in comprehension ability, in general, and on inferential processes specifically. This research suggests that the ability to generate inferences is related, in part, to the efficiency with which a reader can execute more basic linguistic processes. Such efficiency is likely to improve with practice, consistent with the typical educational models. On the other hand, comprehension abilities are also reflected by the ability to adapt neurally as the conditions required of the task change. Such adaptability is related to working memory capacity, which has traditionally been viewed as a "static" or immutable reflection of an individual's fluid cognitive abilities. Recently, however, evidence for the ability to train working memory capacity is mounting (e.g., Jaeggi, Buschkuehl, Jonides, and Perrig, 2008; Jaeggi, Buschkuehl, Jonides, and Shah, 2011; Takeuchi et al., 2010). Thus, the future of education may include an emphasis on training more general cognitive mechanisms, with the goal of improving a broad array of skills (including inferencing) that rely upon flexible allocation of resources. Although very little of this work has looked specifically at individual differences in inferential abilities, we see this as a critical area for future research. Ultimately, a clearer understanding of the biological constraints on inferential processes will inform theories of the nature of skilled comprehension, and will have important implications for reading education.

REFERENCES

Barry, S., & Lazarte, A. A. (1998). Evidence for mental models: how do prior knowledge, syntactic complexity, and reading topic affect inference generation in a recall task for nonnative readers of Spanish? *The Modern Language Journal*, *82*(2), 176–93.

Bransford, J. D., & Johnson, M. K. (1972). Contextual prerequisites for understanding: some investigations of comprehension and recall. *Journal of Verbal Learning and Verbal Behavior*, *11*(6), 717–26.

Brown, J. I. (1960). The Nelson-Denny Reading Test.

Buchweitz, A., Mason, R. A., Tomitch, L., & Just, M. A. (2009). Brain activation for reading and listening comprehension: an fMRI study of modality effects and individual differences in language comprehension. *Psychology & Neuroscience*, *2*(2), 111–23.

Buchweitz, A., & Prat, C. (2013). The bilingual brain: flexibility and control in the human cortex. *Physics of Life Reviews*, *10*, 428–43.

Calvo, M. G. (2005). Relative contribution of vocabulary knowledge and working memory span to elaborative inferences in reading. *Learning and Individual Differences*, *15*(1), 53–65.

Calvo, M. G., Estevez, A., & Dowens, M. G. (2003). Time course of elaborative inferences in reading as a function of prior vocabulary knowledge. *Learning and Instruction*, *13*(6), 611–31.

Estevez, A., & Calvo, M. G. (2000). Working memory capacity and time course of predictive inferences. *Memory*, *8*(1), 51–61.

Friederici, A. D. (2006). What's in control of language? *Nature Neuroscience*, *9*(8), 991–2.

Garlick, D. (2002). Understanding the nature of the general factor of intelligence: the role of individual differences in neural plasticity as an explanatory mechanism. *Psychological Review, 109*(1), 116–36.

Gernsbacher, M. A., Varner, K. R., & Faust, M. E. (1990). Investigating differences in general comprehension skill. *Journal of Experimental Psychology: Learning, Memory, and Cognition, 16*(3), 430-45.

Gerrig, R. J., & O'Brien, E. J. (2005). The scope of memory-based processing. *Discourse Processes, 39*(2&3), 225–42.

Graesser, A. C., Singer, M., & Trabasso, T. (1994). Constructing inferences during narrative text comprehension. *Psychological Review, 101*(3), 371–95.

Haier, R. J., Siegel Jr, B. V., Nuechterlein, K. H., Hazlett, E., Wu, J. C., Paek, J., Browning, H. L., & Buchsbaum, M. S. (1988). Cortical glucose metabolic rate correlates of abstract reasoning and attention studied with positron emission tomography. *Intelligence, 12*(2), 199–217.

Hannon, B., & Daneman, M. (1998). Facilitating knowledge-based inferences in less-skilled readers. *Contemporary Educational Psychology, 23*(2), 149–72.

Haviland, S. E., & Clark, H. H. (1974). What's new? Acquiring new information as a process in comprehension. *Journal of Verbal Learning and Verbal Behavior, 13*(5), 512–21.

Hitch, G., & Baddeley, H. (1974). Working memory. *Recent Advances in Learning and Motivation, 41*–89.

Jacoby, L. L., & Dallas, M. (1981). On the relationship between autobiographical memory and perceptual learning. *Journal of Experimental Psychology: General, 110*(3), 306–40.

Jaeggi, S. M., Buschkuehl, M., Jonides, J., & Perrig, W. J. (2008). Improving fluid intelligence with training on working memory. *Proceedings of the National Academy of Sciences, 105*(19), 6829–33.

Jaeggi, S. M., Buschkuehl, M., Jonides, J., & Shah, P. (2011). Short- and long-term benefits of cognitive training. *Proceedings of the National Academy of Sciences, 108*(25), 10081–6.

Just, M. A., & Carpenter, P. A. (1992). A capacity theory of comprehension: individual differences in working memory. *Psychological Review, 99*, 122–49.

Just, M. A., Carpenter, P. A., & Varma, S. (1999). Computational modeling of high-level cognition and brain function. *Human Brain Mapping, 8*, 128–36.

Kahneman, D. (1973). *Attention and Effort*. Englewood Cliffs, NJ: Prentice Hall.

Karasinski, C., & Weismer, S. E. (2010). Comprehension of inferences in discourse processing by adolescents with and without language impairment. *Journal of Speech, Language and Hearing Research, 53*(5), 1268–79.

Kintsch, W. (1988). The role of knowledge in discourse comprehension: a construction-integration model. *Psychological Review, 95*(2), 163–82.

Linderholm, T. (2002). Predictive inference generation as a function of working memory capacity and causal text constraints. *Discourse Processes, 34*(3), 259–80.

Long, D. L., Oppy, B. J., & Seely, M. R. (1994). Individual differences in the time course of inferential processing. *Journal of Experimental Psychology: Learning, Memory, and Cognition, 20*(6), 1456–70.

(1997). Individual differences in readers' sentence- and text-level representations. *Journal of Memory and Language*, *36*(1), 129–45.

Long, D. L., & Prat, C. S. (2002). Memory for *Star Trek*: the role of prior knowledge in recognition revisited. *Journal of Experimental Psychology: Learning, Memory, and Cognition*, *28*(6), 1073–82.

Long, D. L., Prat, C., Johns, C., Morris, P., & Jonathan, E. (2008). The importance of knowledge in vivid text memory: an individual-differences investigation of recollection and familiarity. *Psychonomic Bulletin & Review*, *15*(3), 604–9.

Long, D. L., Seely, M. R., & Oppy, B. J. (1996). The availability of causal information during reading. *Discourse Processes*, *22*(2), 145–70.

Long, D. L., Wilson, J., Hurley, R., & Prat, C. S. (2006). Assessing text representations with recognition: the interaction of domain knowledge and text coherence. *Journal of Experimental Psychology: Learning, Memory, and Cognition*, *32*(4), 816–27.

Mandler, G. (1980). Recognizing: the judgment of previous occurrence. *Psychological Review*, *87*(3), 252–71.

Maxwell, A. E., Fenwick, P. B. C., Fenton, G. W., & Dollimore, J. (1974). Reading ability and brain function: a simple statistical model. *Psychological Medicine*, *4*(3), 274–80.

McGettigan, C., Warren, J. E., Eisner, F., Marshall, C. R., Shanmugalingam, P., & Scott, S. K. (2011). Neural correlates of sublexical processing in phonological working memory. *Journal of Cognitive Neuroscience*, *23*(4), 961–77.

McKoon, G., & Ratcliff, R. (1992). Inference during reading. *Psychological Review*, *99*(3), 440–66.

Neubauer, A. C., & Fink, A. (2009). Intelligence and neural efficiency. *Neuroscience & Biobehavioral Reviews*, *33*(7), 1004–23.

Newman, S. D., Just, M. A., & Carpenter, P. A. (2002). Synchronization of the human cortical working memory network. *Neuroimage*, *15*, 810–22.

Oakhill, J. (1983). Instantiation in skilled and less skilled comprehenders. *Quarterly Journal of Experimental Psychology*, *35*(3), 441–50.

(1984). Inferential and memory skills in children's comprehension of stories. *British Journal of Educational Psychology*, *54*(1), 31–9.

Osaka, M., Osaka, N., Kondo, H., Morishita, M., Fukuyama, H., Aso, T., & Shibasaki, H. (2003). The neural basis of individual differences in working memory capacity: an fMRI study. *NeuroImage*, *18*(3), 789–97.

Posthuma, D., Baaré, W. F., Pol, H., Hilleke, E., Kahn, R. S., Boomsma, D. I., & De Geus, E. J. (2003). Genetic correlations between brain volumes and the WAIS-III dimensions of verbal comprehension, working memory, perceptual organization, and processing speed. *Twin Research*, *6*(2), 131–39.

Prat, C. S. (2011). The brain basis of individual differences in language comprehension abilities. *Language and Linguistics Compass*, *5*(9), 635–49.

(2012). The neural basis of language faculties. In I. B. Weiner, R. J. Nelson, and S. Mizumori (eds.), *Handbook of Psychology, Volume III: Biological Psychology and Neuroscience* (pp. 595–619) Hoboken, NJ: Wiley.

Prat, C. S., & Just, M. A. (2011). Exploring the neural dynamics underpinning individual differences in sentence comprehension. *Cerebral Cortex*, *21*(8), 1747–60.

Prat, C. S., Keller, T. A., & Just, M. A. (2007). Individual differences in sentence comprehension: a functional magnetic resonance imaging investigation of syntactic and lexical processing demands. *Journal of Cognitive Neuroscience*, *19*(12), 1950–63.

Prat, C. S., Mason, R. A., & Just, M. A. (2011). Individual differences in the neural basis of causal inferencing. *Brain and Language*, *116*(1), 1–13.

(2012). An fMRI investigation of analogical mapping in metaphor comprehension: the influence of context and individual cognitive capacities on processing demands. *Journal of Experimental Psychology: Learning, Memory, and Cognition*, *38*, 282–94.

Reichle, E. D., Carpenter, P. A., & Just, M. A. (2000). The neural basis of strategy and skill in sentence-picture verification. *Cognitive Psychology*, *40*, 261–95.

Rypma, B., Prabhakaran, V., Desmond, J. E., Glover, G. H., & Gabrieli, J. D. (1999). Load-dependent roles of frontal brain regions in the maintenance of working memory. *Neuroimage*, *9*(2), 216–26.

Schafer, E. W. (1982). Neural adaptability: a biological determinant of behavioral intelligence. *International Journal of Neuroscience*, *17*(3), 183–91.

Singer, M., Andruslak, P., Reisdorf, P., & Black, N. L. (1992). Individual differences in bridging inference processes. *Memory & Cognition*, *20*(5), 539–48.

Singer, M., & Ritchot, K. F. (1996). The role of working memory capacity and knowledge access in text inference processing. *Memory & Cognition*, *24*(6), 733–43.

St. George, M. S., Mannes, S., & Hoffman, J. E. (1997). Individual differences in inference generation: an ERP analysis. *Journal of Cognitive Neuroscience*, *9*(6), 776–87.

Stocco, A., Lebiere, C., & Anderson, J. R. (2010). Conditional routing of information to the cortex: a model of the basal ganglia's role in cognitive coordination. *Psychological Review*, *117*(2), 541.

Stocco, A., Lebiere, C., O'Reilly, R. C., & Anderson, J. R. (2012). Distinct contributions of the caudate nucleus, rostral prefrontal cortex, and parietal cortex to the execution of instructed tasks. *Cognitive, Affective, & Behavioral Neuroscience*, *12*, 611–28.

Stocco, A., Yamasaki, B., Natalenko, R., & Prat, C. S. (2014). Bilingual brain training: a neurobiological framework of how bilingual experience improves executive function. *International Journal of Bilingualism*, *18*, 67–92.

Takeuchi, H., Sekiguchi, A., Taki, Y., Yokoyama, S., Yomogida, Y., Komuro, N., & Kawashima, R. (2010). Training of working memory impacts structural connectivity. *The Journal of Neuroscience*, *30*(9), 3297–303.

Tulving, E. (1985). Memory and consciousness. *Canadian Psychology/Psychologie Canadienne*, *26*(1), 1–12.

Virtue, S., Haberman, J., Clancy, Z., Parrish, T., & Jung-Beeman, M. J. (2006). Neural activity of inferences during story comprehension. *Brain Research*, *1084*(1), 104–14.

Virtue, S., Parrish, T., & Jung-Beeman, M. (2008). Inferences during story comprehension: cortical recruitment affected by predictability of events and working memory capacity. *Journal of Cognitive Neuroscience*, *20*(12), 2274–84.

Waters, G. S., & Caplan, D. (1996). The capacity theory of sentence comprehension: critique of Just and Carpenter (1992). *Psychological Review*, *103*(4), 761–72.

Yeatman, J. D., Ben-Shachar, M., Glover, G. H., & Feldman, H. M. (2010). Individual differences in auditory sentence comprehension in children: an exploratory event-related functional magnetic resonance imaging investigation. *Brain and Language*, *114*(2), 72–9.

Yonelinas, A. P. (2002). The nature of recollection and familiarity: a review of 30 years of research. *Journal of Memory and Language*, *46*(3), 441–517.

11 Inferences during text comprehension: what neuroscience can (or cannot) contribute

Evelyn C. Ferstl

Acknowledgments

I thank the editors of the present volume for the opportunity to contribute to this book. Ed O'Brien and Anne Cook provided insightful and constructive feedback that greatly improved the chapter.

It is unusual when a researcher is provided the opportunity to write on any topic solely based on their perspective rather than on the objective, irrefutable facts their research has produced. So, I welcomed the invitation to write a chapter on my own neuroscientific work on inference processes during reading, and do that from a rather personal point of view.

I will start out with the motivation to conduct neuroscientific studies on inference processes, briefly summarizing nonaphasic language deficits and a number of my own studies on this topic. In the second section, I will review the first neuroimaging studies on coherence building. I will then summarize the most important findings, sketch theoretical proposals, and point to further research questions. Throughout this chapter, I will focus on my own perspective. Thus, I apologize to all colleagues who work in this field for not including their work in sufficient detail.

In the chapter, some basic neuroanatomical knowledge is assumed. For easier reference, the anatomical labels used throughout are shown in Figures 11.1 and 11.2.

After having completed my dissertation on text comprehension in 1994, I started a postdoc at the Max Planck Institute for Cognitive Neuroscience in Leipzig, Germany. This was quite a move: from behavioral cognitive science to an environment in which laboratories with the latest methodological advances were being set up, combined with clinical applications as required at the associated Day Clinic for Cognitive Neurorehabilitation. Functional magnetic resonance imaging was just starting to be used with the goal of localizing subprocesses of language comprehension. Although the scanner was already available, the statistical analysis methods had yet to be developed to allow for sophisticated

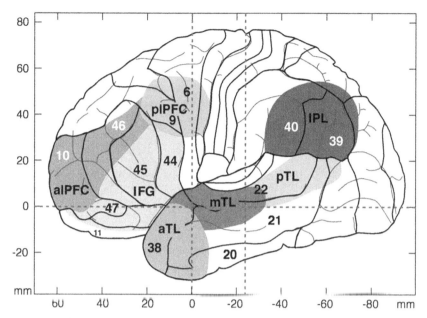

Figure 11.1 A left lateral view of the Talairach standard stereotaxic
brain. Overlaid and shaded are regions of interest that indicate the most
important brain regions for text comprehension in context (alPFC =
anterior lateral prefrontal cortex, plPFC = posterior lateral prefrontal
cortex, IFG = inferior frontal gyrus; aTL = anterior temporal lobe;
mTL = middle temporal lobe; pTL = posterior temporal lobe; IPL =
inferior parietal lobe). The numbers denote the cytoarchitectonic fields
as described by Brodmann (1909).

experimentation. Similarly, studies using event-related potentials
(ERPs), based on the electro-encephalogram (EEG), were beginning to
be conducted, with the promise to provide a fine-grained temporal
resolution of language comprehension. However, the issues of interest
were still rather basic, such as a dissociation of syntax and semantics.
That text comprehension or inferencing could be studied at all using
these methods was far from obvious – and it took a number of years until
sufficient experience with the methods had been accumulated to venture
into these "fuzzy" areas.

An area in which behavioral methods were readily applicable is the
communication deficits of patients with brain injuries. Patient studies
have been a rich source of neuroscienctific knowledge since the first
attempts to associate brain regions with cognitive functions. Interestingly, my knowledge of the psychology of text comprehension and

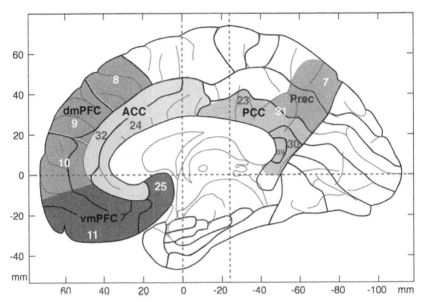

Figure 11.2 A right medial view of the Talairach standard stereotaxic brain. Once more, only those regions are shaded and labeled that are important for the present discussion (Prec = precuneus; PCC = posterior cingulate cortex, ACC = anterior cingulate cortex; dmPFC = dorso-medial prefrontal cortex; vmPFC = ventro-medial prefrontal cortex). The numbers denote the cytoarchitectonic regions described by Brodmann (1909).

discourse production seemed to be particularly useful for studying a special group of patients, those with nonaphasic communication deficits.

Nonaphasic language deficits

That lesions to the language cortex of the left hemisphere (LH) can lead to aphasic language deficits has been known since the late nineteenth century. The aphasias have been extensively studied and a number of diagnostic tests are available to estimate their severity and describe the individual's set of symptoms. Nonaphasic language deficits, on the other hand, have been less well studied. Coined by Prigatano, Roueche, and Fordyce (1986), this term describes disorders of communication in the absence of aphasic symptoms. The deficits are said to be on the level of pragmatics and discourse, rather than on the levels of phonology, semantics, or syntax.

One of the most noticeable symptoms in nonaphasic language deficit is the lack of coherence in language production. Patients with frontal lobe damage are described as hypo- or hyperphasic. This often manifests itself in patients by saying too little or too much, jumping from topic to topic, or failing to take into account the listeners' prior knowledge. The common theme is that they do not participate in establishing common ground. Collections of these symptoms include, but are not restricted to, problems with subtle semantic selection, the use of cues to turn taking, the structuring of dialogue, as well as unusual social behavior, such as using swear words or contextually inappropriate registers, or being too explicit. An obvious explanation for this type of deficit is a modality general problem with language-based inferences. If these patients have problems using background knowledge for filling in gaps during conversation, they respond inappropriately, and their discourse might seem incoherent or beside the point.

Another type of nonaphasic language disturbance is the right hemisphere syndrome (Brownell and Martino, 1998). Interestingly, the symptoms are very similar to language deficits after frontal lobe damage. In particular, the discourse production is incoherent, the patients exhibit inappropriate social behavior, and they have difficulties understanding subtle implications or nonliteral language.

Within a text comprehension framework, a plausible theoretical account for the frontal lobe communication deficits is rather easy to sketch. Problems with, in clinical neuropsychology terms, executive functions, or, in cognitive science terms, a variety of subprocesses (e.g., working memory, attention, problem solving, source memory, and structuring and planning ability), must lead to deficits in higher-level language use, in particular, text comprehension and discourse production. All of these components play a role in text comprehension models. For example, the construction-integration model (Kintsch, 1988) contains assumptions about a working memory buffer, activation of lexical and general world knowledge, and inhibition of inappropriate content based on a spreading activation process, among others – all of which could be postulated to require frontal lobe functionality.

Right hemisphere (RH) language, on the other hand, is much more difficult to grasp. In fact, the instruments provided by text comprehension theories in the cognitive science framework of the eighties and nineties of the twentieth century did not speak to this issue at all (see Beeman and Chiarello, 1998). The cognitive functions most likely to be impaired after RH lesion are visuo-spatial processes and possibly attention and vigilance. More subtle descriptions included emotional processes, such as the interpretation of affective prosody, or some working memory functions. It was generally agreed, however, that the RH has little or no role in linguistic processing proper (but see Zaidel, 1978), and that communication deficits were likely to be secondary to more general cognitive dysfunction or to impairments of social behavior.

Despite this lack of theoretical accounts, a large number of studies on inference processes have been conducted in patients after brain damage, and in particular, after right hemisphere damage (e.g., Beeman, Bowden, and Gernsbacher, 2000; Brownell, Potter, Bihrle, and Gardner, 1986; Lehman-Blake and Tompkins, 2001; Tompkins, Fassbinder, Lehman-Blake, Baumgärtner, and Jayaram, 2004). Many of the earlier studies were based on single case studies or on group studies without specific lesion information. Thus, as McDonald (1993) pointed out, many of the RH patients' lesions might have encroached upon frontal regions, preventing the researcher from a clear dissociation of frontal and right-sided symptoms.

Patient studies on inferencing

Our work on inference processes in patients with brain damage started from clinical observations of discourse production deficits. Rather than classifying patients according to the lesion location, we wanted to describe communication profiles across a variety of tasks. The working assumption was that nonaphasic deficits were not modality specific, but that they were caused by a general problem with executive functions that would be reflected in text comprehension deficits on similar levels. In particular, a hyperphasic profile (i.e., extensive flow of spontaneous speech) is characterized by too much detail information and a lack of global coherence. The patient jumps from topic to topic and cannot easily return to the global topic of the conversation. We hypothesized that patients with this type of discourse production would also have problems with deriving a macrostructure of longer discourse and with selecting context-appropriate inferences from unselectively activated associations. Conversely, patients with a hypophasic profile (i.e., with little self-generated spontaneous speech) were expected to fail to activate background knowledge necessary for bridging consecutive sentences. In a master's thesis, Florian Siebörger (1999) attempted to find evidence for these hypotheses in a series of single-case studies. Using a number of discourse production tasks and a corresponding set of text comprehension experiments, he attempted to identify characteristic patterns of text comprehension deficits corresponding to the discourse production profiles. Unfortunately, the results from five patients with nonaphasic language deficits did not provide evidence for such a correspondence – mostly because our patients performed

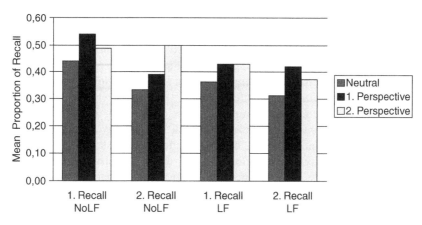

Figure 11.3 Recalled idea units in a replication of the Anderson and Pichert paradigm. Patients without left frontal lesions (NoLF) show the expected pattern: in the first recall attempt, the encoding perspective (1. Perspective) is recalled more easily. A change of perspective facilitates recall of an alternative contents (2. Perspective) in the second recall attempt. In contrast, patients with left frontal lesions (LF) did not use either the encoding or the recall perspective.

surprisingly well in the comprehension tasks. We concluded that the distinction of production subprofiles was too subtle, and that the single-case approach could only be successful if we knew more about the type and severity of comprehension impairments.

In the first of a number of group studies (Ferstl, Guthke, and von Cramon, 1999), we adopted a classical paradigm from the text comprehension literature. Based on the idea that frontal lobe damage would lead to impairments of deliberate, strategic use of knowledge during comprehension, we developed a version of the Anderson and Pichert (1978) task. In this experiment, a story including the description of a house is presented. Depending on the perspective taken during reading (e.g., burglar or real estate agent), different details in the story become more or less salient. Anderson and Pichert (1978) had shown that recall for relevant information was superior, and that a change to the less-relevant perspective improved recall performance of the less-relevant information in a second attempt. In our patient study we classified patients with brain lesions according to the presence or absence of left and right frontal lesions (LF vs. RF). As shown in Figure 11.3, analyses including both factors showed that the lateralization of the lesion was crucial: only the presence of left-sided lesions, but not right-sided ones, had consequences for the performance in the task. In contrast to patients without left frontal lesions, LF patients did not show effects of the perspective switch. In the second recall trial, they still focused on the encoding perspective and could not recall additional information. Thus, the use of a comprehension goal during encoding and the use of an appropriate strategy during retrieval required an intact left frontal lobe.

Applying this finding to inferencing, it seemed likely that nonautomatic, strategic inferences would be most difficult for LF patients. To test this hypothesis in an ecologically valid and easily comprehensible fashion, we designed a simple coherence judgment task. The psycholinguistic community had developed quite a few sophisticated methods for experimentally assessing inference processes, in particular, priming methods or cross-modal lexical decision or naming tasks (see Haberlandt, 1994; McKoon and Ratcliff, this volume, for review). However, these methods did not seem particularly apt for patient studies – and later neuroimaging experiments. First, they require specific target words that may or may not be consistent with an inference at a particular point during processing. Thus, the materials need to be constructed in a particularly careful way. Second, the results depend on reaction times. In special populations, and in particular in patients with brain lesions, the heterogeneity is very large. Reaction times might be prolonged due to other deficits, such as attention, visual impairments, or motor impairments, such as paresis or ataxia. Thus, we were looking for a paradigm in which error rates would be informative without the need for additional reaction time analyses. In addition, it was important that the task would be easily comprehensible without complicated instructions. Finally, we were looking for a simple, nonverbal response: it should require neither overt language production, nor complex decision-making processes.

To fit these criteria, we designed a coherence judgment task, in which participants simply had to decide whether two sentences "made sense together" or whether they were unrelated. For the coherent condition, 160 short scenarios were written, consisting of two sentences each. The sentences had simple syntactic structures, with one or two clauses only. Care was taken that the second sentence was related to the first via a knowledge-based inference, but not through simple word repetitions, associative relations, or cohesive ties, such as pronouns or conjunctions. The incoherent condition was then created by pairing scenarios in a way such that switching their context sentences would yield implausible, incoherent sentence pairs. Examples are provided in Table 11.1 (taken from Ferstl and von Cramon, 2002). Finally, all target sentences (the second sentences in each pair) were rewritten in a cohesive version by adding pronouns or conjunctions that gave explicit lexical cues to the

Table 11.1 *Example materials for the four conditions of the experiment*

Coherent	Incoherent
Incohesive	
Mary's exam was about to start.	Laura got a lot of mail today.
The palms were sweaty.	The palms were sweaty.
Laura got a lot of mail today.	Mary's exam was about to start.
Some friends has remembered the birthday.	Some friends has remembered the birthday.
Sometimes a truck drives by the house.	The lights have been on since last night.
The dishes start to rattle.	The dishes start to rattle.
The lights have been on since last night.	Sometimes a truck drives by the house.
The car doesn't start.	The car doesn't start.
Cohesive	
Mary's exam was about to start.	Laura got a lot of mail today.
Therefore, her palms were sweaty.	*Therefore, her* palms were sweaty.
Laura got a lot of mail today.	Mary's exam was about to start.
Her friends had remembered *her* birthday.	*Her* friends had remembered *her* birthday.
Sometimes a truck drives by the house	The lights have been on since last night.
That's when the dishes start to rattle.	*That's when* the dishes start to rattle.
The lights have been on since last night.	Sometimes a truck drives by the house.
That's why the car doesn't start.	*That's why* the car doesn't start.

Note. Items have been translated from the original German. Cohesive ties are italicized.

connection between the sentences. The hypothesis was that these lexical cues would aid inferencing for coherent sentence pairs only, but would render the detection of incoherent sentence pairs more difficult.

From a psycholinguistic point of view, these materials were not well controlled: We did not distinguish between inference or relation types (e.g., goal-directed, causal, temporal, spatial, etc.); we did not distinguish types of cohesion (pronouns vs. conjunctions); and we did not evaluate for which type of relationship the presence or absence of cohesive ties would be more or less effective. Also, there was no way to distinguish online inferences during reading from off-line reasoning during the response period, and we could not eliminate potential effects of response criteria or biases. However, from a neuroscientific point of view, the materials and task were perfect because they were intended to maximize the potential for uncovering effects. The experimental paradigm was considered merely a very first step before returning to more differentiated methodological requirements and picking up more sophisticated theoretical questions. At the time, I surely did not anticipate how powerful the paradigm would turn out to be.

In a first step, it was necessary to validate empirically the categorization of sentence pairs into coherent and incoherent scenarios, and to quantify the effects of cohesion on the ease of the coherence judgment. A control group of adults comparable to a brain-lesioned patient population was tested on an auditory version of the experiment (Ferstl, 2006). The participants' ages ranged from approximately twenty-five to sixty-five years and they represented a wide variety of educational levels and occupations. The most important finding was the almost perfect agreement in the coherence judgment task. Despite the often mentioned notion that finding coherence in these sentence pairs is not all-or-none but depends on the length of the inference chain and on individual preferences, only 5 percent of the responses differed from the prior classification. Nevertheless, the error rates showed the expected interaction between coherence and cohesion: Cohesion facilitated coherence building but made it more difficult to detect coherence gaps.

Similar to the Ferstl et al. (1999) experiment on perspective changes, the neuropsychological study used a lesion localization approach (Ferstl, Guthke, and von Cramon, 2002). Twenty-five patients of various etiologies, in particular, vascular and traumatic brain injury, were classified according to whether the lesion involved the frontal and temporal lobes, and whether the lesion was left or right lateralized. As shown in Figure 11.4, the patients performed as well as the control group, with only about 8 percent errors on average. In contrast to the previous study, there was no effect of cohesion. The most striking result was dramatically elevated error rates for patients with left frontal lesions in the coherent condition only; LF patients found about 25 percent of the coherent sentence pairs unrelated and could not find the content-based connection between them. Reaction times showed the same pattern. This dramatic failure to draw bridging inferences was not seen in patients with right hemisphere lesions, or in patients with nonfrontal lesions.

These findings implicated the left frontal lobe as the crucial region for knowledge-based inferences. Although this result seems clear-cut, it was not satisfying from a neuroanatomical level at all. To illustrate this, let's go into a bit of frontal lobe anatomy. The frontal lobe takes up a third of the human cortex. In fact, the evolution of structural properties of the frontal lobes in humans compared to other species (e.g., volume, white-to-gray matter ratio, or lateralization; Smaers, Steele, Case, Cowper, Amunts, and Zilles, 2011) is sometimes said to enable higher-level cognitive processes (Deacon, 1997). Thus, it is not surprising that the frontal lobes encompass subregions with decidedly different functionalities. A review of this goes beyond the scope of this chapter, but I would like to single out two subregions in the lateral frontal lobe. The

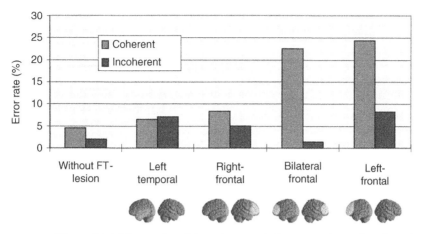

Figure 11.4 The results of the coherence judgment task as a function of lesion location and coherence of the sentence pair. The colored regions in the schematic brain images indicate the approximate regions affected, but most individual patients' lesions were smaller than the marked areas. The most striking result is the failure of patients with left frontal and bilateral frontal lesions to draw bridging inferences for the coherent sentence pairs (FT = fronto-temporal).

dorso-lateral prefrontal cortex (dlPFC) had been implicated in executive functions on one hand, and Broca's area, part of the inferior frontal gyrus (IFG), is known for its role in basic language processes. More specifically, I would like to bring attention to the area at the junction of the precentral and inferior frontal sulci that Brass and colleagues (Brass, Derrfuss, Forstmann, and Cramon, 2005; Derrfuss, Brass, von Cramon, Lohmann, and Amunts, 2009) have termed the frontal junction area. In Figure 11.1, this region is labeled pIPFC (BA 9/6), and it is activated in executive function paradigms, such as Stroop, dual tasks, or task switching. More generally, the region seems to be involved whenever task demands require flexible adjustments of task sets (Brass et al., 2005). In contrast, the posterior part of the inferior frontal gyrus (IFG, BA44, also Broca's area), just adjacent to the frontal junction area, is more likely to be engaged during language processing, and even more specifically, during syntactic processing, articulation, and the like. As mentioned, a review of the debate about the specificity for language and about the exact anatomical delineation is beyond the scope of this article (Uylings, Malofeeva, Bogolepova, Amunts, and Zilles, 1999). Patients with frontal lobe damage, in particular, patients with diffuse brain damage due to traumatic brain injury, rarely have lesions restricted to one or the other of these two adjacent regions. Thus, behavioral patient studies are usually not particularly appropriate for a fine-grained anatomical differentiation.

Coherence judgment: functional neuroimaging

Our next step was to conduct a neuroimaging study using the coherence judgment paradigm to pinpoint the anatomical localization of inference processes. Before summarizing the results of this first study, let us go back to when the study was planned and conducted and look at the imaging literature available in 1999 (see also Ferstl, 2007). In an extensive review of neuroimaging studies showing frontal lobe activations, Grady (1999) included only six studies on language, most of which used word-level tasks. The questions of interest were, for instance, to distinguish phonological from lexico-semantic or syntactic processes. The anatomical focus lay – in relation to aphasiology – on the left-sided perisylvian language regions (Broca's area and Wernicke's area in the posterior temporal lobe; in Figure 11.1 labeled as IFG, BA 44, and pTL, respectively). Language processing in context, and in particular, language interpretation, was not yet on the agenda. The most interesting results had been reported by Mazoyer, Tzourio, Frak, Syrota, Murayama, Levrier, Salamon, Dehaene, Cohen, and Mehler (1993). They used positron-emission tomography (PET) in a very small group of participants to compare word level, sentence level, and story processing. Interestingly, some of their results still hold today. Mazoyer et al. (1993) confirmed the involvement of the language regions but also showed that the anterior temporal lobes (aTLs) were engaged bilaterally whenever syntactic information on the phrase level was added. Most important, the only region specific for story comprehension was the left superior frontal gyrus, reaching into the dorso-medial prefrontal cortex (dmPFC, Figure 11.2). In contrast to the predictions from the neuropsychological patient literature, there was no evidence for right hemisphere activation besides the aTL. Figure 11.5 illustrates this general pattern, which I have termed the extended language network (Ferstl, Neumann, Bogler, and von Cramon, 2008), using a very similar result from one of our own studies (Ferstl and von Cramon, 2002).

In our first neuroimaging study, we used fMRI. In contrast to the then prevalent blocked design, in which trials of the same condition were presented in short blocks, we used an event-related design in which the conditions were mixed and the order of presentation was pseudo-randomized. The hypotheses for our coherence judgment paradigm were not very specific. The main question of interest was whether the inference demands would engage the language cortex proper, whether they

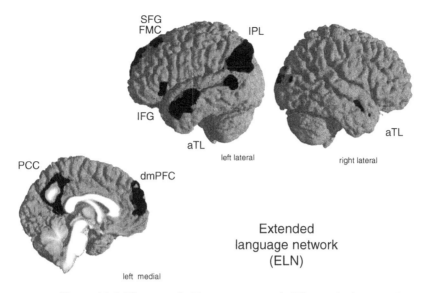

SFG
FMC   IPL

IFG
aTL

aTL

left lateral   right lateral

PCC

dmPFC

Extended
language network
(ELN)

left medial

Figure 11.5 The extended language network. The particular activation
patterns from a comparison of language stimuli to a baseline of
pronounceable jabberwocky sentences (Ferstl and von Cramon, 2002).

would lead to left dlPFC activation (relating to strategic task demands),
or whether the right hemisphere would be recruited during more holistic
contextual processing (cf. Jung-Beeman, 2005).

The results were very surprising indeed (Ferstl and von Cramon,
2001a). Processing incoherent sentence pairs – in comparison to coherent ones – did not lead to any specific activation. We had expected that
when faced with nonsensical sentence pairs, comprehenders would
actively search for a connection and engage in a strategic inference
process, which, in turn, would be reflected in left frontal or right hemispheric brain activation. This was obviously not the case. The floor effect
in the error rates for incoherent sentence pairs confirmed that the distinction between the two conditions was so clear-cut that no additional
processing ensued. In the reverse contrast, comparing coherent to incoherent scenarios, two medial regions emerged rather than the expected
dlPFC or RH activations. In coherent more than in incoherent trials, the
dmPFC already described by Mazoyer et al. (1993), and a region in the
posterior cingulate cortex, that is, the ventral precuneus (PCC/prec),
were active.

In fact, exactly the same two regions had been found in one of the very
few previous studies using language materials beyond the word level.

This study had been conducted for an altogether different purpose, however. Motivated by autism research, a group at the University College London had developed a story comprehension task targeting so-called Theory-of-Mind (ToM) processes. This concept had been introduced in developmental psychology and applied to account for the social communication deficits of autistic persons. In general, ToM is what enables individuals to make inferences about beliefs, intentions, and motivations of others to understand their behavior. Fletcher et al. (1995) used two story types in a PET study. In the ToM stories, for example, a burglar running away is stopped by a police officer who merely wants to return a lost glove. Questions probing the comprehension of the story required the inference that the burglar thought he had been caught and the police officer wanted to arrest him. In non-ToM control stories ("physical stories"), similarly complex questions were asked, but they did not tap ToM reasoning (such as a story about the influence of weather on an air raid). And just as the experiment was about the comprehension of social behavior, not about language, the results showed activations in regions not usually mentioned in the context of language processing: the same two medial regions found in our inference study; the dmPFC and the PCC/prec were more activated by ToM inferences than by physical inferences.

This finding was rather puzzling. Further research showed that the dmPFC was – and still is – a region stirring much debate. It was of interest to social psychologists, neurologists, and even philosophers, because its function seemed to be important for positioning oneself in a social environment, and for maintaining a sense of self and processing of self-relevant information. Such a function, even if defined in less fuzzy terms, surely did not have a place in the text comprehension models from a cognitivist tradition. Consequently, it was necessary to rethink what the task actually required and to reinterpret previous ideas about inference processes. One prerequisite for this was, however, to be confident about the results – which was not easy given the lack of experience with the rather complex fMRI analysis methods still being developed at the time. However, a follow-up study using auditory presentation of the sentence pairs replicated the coherence effect found in the reading experiment (Ferstl and von Cramon, 2001b).

The most parsimonious account consistent with a social neuroscience account as well as with the text comprehension framework was to postulate that the inferences in our task had ToM content, and thus, that the activations actually reflected social communication processes rather than linking utterances by knowledge-based inferences. Such an account would be perfectly compatible with theories of inferencing that singled out goal-directed or goal-oriented inferences as particularly important (e.g., Singer, Graesser, and Trabasso, 1994; Trabasso, van den Broek and Suh, 1989). More interesting, this explanation would lend support to a qualitative distinction of different inference types which had been postulated in text linguistics for some time. If inferences about the intentions of the story's protagonists were processed by different brain regions than, let's say, causal, elaborative, or predictive inferences, then it would become necessary to further refine models to provide specific mechanisms for these inference categories. An alternative account, which I found intuitively more likely, was that the ToM tasks used to study dmPFC functionality induced inference processes that were more demanding than in the respective control conditions. Rather than postulating a module for social communication (cf. Tooby and Cosmides for an evolutionary account), distinct from the rest of cognition, I hypothesized that both ToM reasoning and the processes induced by the types of sentence materials used in our studies shared a common inference component.

In a first step, we reevaluated the content of the sentence pairs used in the coherence judgment task. For a follow-up experiment (Ferstl and von Cramon, 2002), we then divided the materials into two halves: sixty sentence pairs explicitly mentioned people and contained some person-related information ("animate," such as the first two examples in Table 11.1: about Mary and Laura, resp.), whereas sixty others were about inanimate topics (e.g., a truck or dishes: the third and fourth examples in Table 11.1). Participants were scanned while conducting the same coherence judgment task as before for the inanimate sentence pairs. For the animate sentences, instructions stressing the ToM component were used: participants were asked to evaluate the intentions, motivations, and emotions of the people mentioned. The latter instructions led to increases in dmPFC activation, particularly for the incoherent animate sentence pairs. For the inanimate sentence pairs, a replication of the previous coherence effect was obtained: coherent sentence pairs engaged the dmPFC more strongly than incoherent trials. Thus, the inference process activated the region even in the absence of ToM content, and even in the absence of protagonists and their goals.

Although this result was consistent with the hypothesis of an overarching process encompassing both ToM and inferences, it still did not lead to a well-delineated definition of what exactly this process might be. In the meantime, a number of other imaging studies had been published in which fronto-medial activation was found. Some of these used language stimuli, but many did not. Common to these studies seemed to be that most of them required a self-guided judgment for which there was no predefined right or wrong answer, but for which the participants had to define their own criteria and draw on their prior knowledge. For example, Binder, Frost, Hammeke, Bellgowan, Rao, and Cox (1999) presented words for ad hoc semantic classification, Jacobsen, Schubotz, Höfel, and von Cramon (2006) asked to evaluate the aesthetics of visual patterns, and Zysset, Huber, Ferstl, and von Cramon (2002) asked participants to decide whether they agreed with a short statement. In this latter study, episodic ("I have been to Leipzig") or evaluative statements ("I like Leipzig") were compared to factual statements ("Leipzig is a city"). Evaluation engaged the dmPFC to a larger extent, while episodic memory retrieval led to increased PCC/prec activation. Thus, the co-activations of these two medial regions seemed to reflect two aspects of a knowledge-based, self-guided process.

This functional attribution of the dmPFC was consistent with the aforementioned findings from a variety of studies. At the same time, it did not readily provide concrete predictions for a given experiment. Consider the coherence judgment as a case in point: even if this process had been postulated before conducting the coherence judgment task, it would not have helped us to predict that the coherent sentence pairs rather than the incoherent ones would activate the dmPFC. Why should the comprehension of unrelated sentences not induce the same type of inference process as the coherent ones, even if unsuccessful?

To test the hypothesis that the inference process rather than the stimulus properties give rise to dmPFC engagement, Florian Siebörger conducted an additional fMRI study using the same materials with still another instruction (Sieörger, Ferstl, and von Cramon, 2007). To induce inference processes independent of the stimulus properties, participants were asked to rate sentence pairs on a four-point scale from totally unrelated to highly related. Examples were provided for creative but possible inference chains connecting seemingly unrelated sentences. The whole brain analysis was based on the individuals' responses rather than on the predefined coherence of the sentence pairs. And indeed, all four relatedness conditions elicited dmPFC activation, with shifts in the time course reflecting variable decision times. This experiment confirmed that the inference activity, rather than the stimulus properties, gave rise to the dmPFC activation. Further confirmation of the role of the dmPFC for coherence building was provided in a study on verbal humor (Sieörger, 2006), in which, among other text types, coherent and incoherent short stories were included. Coherent texts elicited more activation in dmPFC than incoherent control texts.

In the meantime, a number of other laboratories have conducted neuroimaging studies on inferencing during text comprehension (Chow,

Kaup, Raabe, and Greenlee, 2008; Friese, Rutschmann, Raabe, and Schmalhofer, 2008; Kuperberg, Lakshmanan, Caplan, Holcomb, 2006; Mason and Just, 2004; Virtue, Parrish, and Beeman, 2008; see Ferstl, 2010, for review.). In a computational meta-analysis, we confirmed that in contrasts comparing coherent to incoherent language (e.g., stories vs. unrelated sentences) the dmPFC and the PCC/prec were consistently co-activated (Ferstl et al., 2008). Thus, we can be confident that the dmPFC does play an important role during inferencing. Despite this convergence, making clear a priori predictions about the involvement of the fronto-medial cortex is still difficult. One precondition seems to be a deliberate decision or reasoning component. Studies that investigated inferences during on-going story comprehension (Virtue, Haberman, Clancy, Parrish, and Jung-Beeman, 2006; Virtue et al., 2008) or in the absence of an overt judgment task (e.g., Jin, Liu, Mo, Fang, Zhang, Lin, 2009) are more likely to report lateral frontal or temporal activations. On the other hand, it is perfectly clear that whenever dmPFC activation is reported in an imaging study, the specific inference demands of the task need to be analyzed. Or, put in other words, we can use the presence of dmPFC activation as clear indication for self-guided, strategic inference processes as outlined before. How this inference diagnostic can be applied is the topic of the next section.

dmPFC activation as diagnostic tool

Experimental psychologists are often skeptical when it comes to neuroimaging, because many studies yield unpredicted activations that need to be interpreted post hoc. This is done by collecting a number of studies showing similar activations and then attempting to find the overlap between the tasks used in these studies. However, knowledge about the functional neuroanatomy can be very informative and useful for dissociating qualitatively distinct processes. For example, activations in the dlPFC are evidence for flexible adjustment to task demands, as shown in executive function type tasks, while, as another example, orbito-frontal activations reflect evaluative processes in relation with emotion, reward, or decision making.

To illustrate this type of reasoning, let us consider a study on situation model processing (van Dijk and Kintsch, 1983). Although the general idea is that situation models are an integration of the language input with inferred information, there are separate research traditions. Our study was designed in collaboration with Mike Rinck, who had extensive prior experience with behavioral experiments on this topic (e.g., Rinck, Hähnel, and Becker, 2001). Using the inconsistency paradigm developed by O'Brien and colleagues (e.g., Albrecht and O'Brien, 1993; O'Brien and Albrecht, 1992), stories were written that contained a global inconsistency on the situation model level (e.g., a girl feeling sad at a successful, happy party, or a switch in the order of two events). The question of interest was whether neuroimaging could identify regions involved in detecting and processing the inconsistencies (in comparison to consistent control stories), and whether the different story contents (emotional vs. temporal) would elicit activation in domain-specific regions (e.g., the limbic system for emotion processing). The latter manipulation was intended as a test of the event-indexing model (Zwaan, Langston, and Graesser, 1995), and, more specifically, of an embodied approach to situation model building (Zwaan, 2004). The results for immediate detection of the inconsistencies in emotional stories confirmed this hypothesis by showing orbito-frontal and amygdala activations (Ferstl, Rinck, and von Cramon, 2005). However, when analyzing the period from the inconsistent word to the end of the story (i.e., the period in which the comprehenders try to "fix" the inconsistency by a repair process), unpredicted results were found. Only the temporal stories elicited lateral frontal activation (alPFC), possibly related to such a repair process. The emotional stories, in which the inconsistency could be reconciled by additional assumption (e.g., the girl might be sad because her friend did not show up) activated the dmPFC instead. We interpreted these results as reflecting an inference about the state of mind of the protagonists. This explanation was consistent both with a ToM account of dmPFC function, as well as with a strategic inference during reading. In any case, we were safe to conclude that the emotional inconsistencies elicited inference processes that were qualitatively different from those required to process the temporal inconsistencies.

Models of text comprehension

As noted previously, traditional models of text comprehension use quite a different terminology and conceptualization compared to neuroscientific theories. Predictions from cognitive models to neuroimaging are usually based on one process operationalization, rather than a more comprehensive theory. One exception is the attempt by J. R. Anderson and colleagues to derive neuroanatomical correspondences from their general purpose architecture ACT-R (Anderson, Bothell, Byrne, Douglass, Lebiere, and Qin, 2004). Given the gradual convergence of the findings of the last ten or fifteen years, it might be time to integrate the neuroscientific data with text comprehension theory.

Surprisingly, the attempts to do so are few and far between. My own reviews (Ferstl, 2007; 2010; Ferstl et al., 2008) have started out with the framework by van Dijk and Kintsch (1983; Kintsch 1988) – with some success and many failures. For instance, I have interpreted a dorsal precuneus activation in our situation model experiment (Ferstl, Rinck, and von Cramon, 2005) as reflecting reinstatement search, or more specifically, as a shift of attention from the local information to the prior global discourse context. To delineate the function of the anterior temporal lobes, I drew on the concept of propositionalization, or less formally, on the idea of phrasal idea units on the textbase level. In contrast, there is no obvious localization for construction versus integration, or for lexical activation versus inhibition within a text comprehension framework (although there have been suggestions drawing on lateralization, e.g., Jung-Beeman, 2005). Studies using methods with better temporal resolution are needed to further investigate these distinctions (such as ERP studies, e.g., Steele, Bernat, van den Broek, Collins, Patrick, and Marsolek, 2013; Yang, Perfetti, and Schmalhofer, 2007).

The most specific neuroscientifically motivated attempt at a compre hensive theory was presented by Mason and Just (2006). In their review chapter, they sketch a model assigning various brain regions different subprocesses of text comprehension. In addition to the left-sided language cortex, they postulate a coarse coding region in the right posterior temporal lobe. This region's function is to activate wide semantic fields needed for creative, unpredicted associations and inferences (Beeman, 1998; Jung-Beeman, 2005). Further components are a coherence monitoring network (bilateral dlPFC), a spatial imagery network (bilateral iPL), and, most important, the dmPFC as the "protagonist's perspective interpreter." Interestingly, the posterior cingulate cortex (pCC/prec) is not included.

Another approach is to conduct meta-analyses and interpret the components of the resulting networks. Mar (2011; see also 2004) used this method to compare social cognition and story comprehension, and to confirm the large overlap between these domains. Our own meta-analysis (Ferstl et al., 2008) was conducted to confirm the generalizability of the results from single neuroimaging studies. Once more, the interpretation proceeded along the lines of trying to interpret each region's function and to associate it with processes as postulated by psychological theories of text comprehension. The resulting extended language network (ELN) was remarkably similar to that already described by Mazoyer et al. (1993). However, it is important to stress that such a meta-analytic approach is descriptive and does not qualify as a process model. In particular, the goal of neuroimaging is to dissociate processes by describing differential patterns of brain activation. In contrast, fMRI and PET do not readily provide information on the flow of information, on the time course of the subprocesses, or on their interaction.

Last, but not least, I would like to mention the embodied cognition approach to text comprehension (Glenberg and Gallese, 2012; Zwaan, 2004; see also de Vega, this volume). This framework abandons the propositional text representation in favor of a perceptually grounded resonance of prior experience. Although this theory is not directly related to the strategic inference processes discussed in this chapter, it is a very influential development. Furthermore, the theory draws in part on neuroscientific findings, most notably the observation of motor resonance, that is, the activation of the motor or premotor cortex by words denoting actions (Pulvermüller, 2005). This idea has been taken to the level of sentence interpretation and inferencing). Although there is some debate about the status of embodied representations in nonliteral language, such as metaphors and idioms (e.g., Romero Lauro, Mattavelli, Papagno, and Tettamanti, 2013), there is evidence for domain-specific representations (e.g., Ferstl et al., 2005). For example, de Vega et al. (2014) have recently shown that complex sentences mentioning actions elicit activations overlapping with regions involved during action observation Another interesting empirical question directly following from this theory has not yet been studied in sufficient detail: namely the psychological relevance of a propositional – or more generally – of a verbal text representation. A better understanding of these issues requires combining results from text comprehension studies, whose focus is the final interpretation (i.e., the situation model level) with results from semantic and syntactic processing on the sentence level, whose focus is on the exact wording. Interesting theoretical accounts bridging these areas are, among others, Kuperberg (2007) and Hagoort (2013), exemplifying recent approaches to language comprehension and inferencing.

Other laboratories' approaches to inferencing

A thorough synthesis of recent studies on the neuroscience of inferencing is beyond the scope of this chapter, and a number of reviews are available (Bornkessel-Schlesewsky and Friederici, 2007;; Ferstl, 2007; 2010; Ferstl et al., 2008; Ferstl and Zacks, in press; Mar, 2004; 2011; Mason and Just, 2006). In addition, I would like to point the reader to exciting recent developments. Several lines of research are currently being pursued to further our understanding of higher-level language comprehension, and, in particular, of inference processes. Some of these approaches add theoretical concepts that traditionally have not been used in text linguistics, and others use different methodologies (cf. Ferstl, 2010).

Methodological developments to neuroimaging

A general development in neuroimaging research is to move from region-based localization to a network-based approach. Rather than using the subtraction method to identify single brain regions that are more active during one condition compared to another, connectivity studies have been conducted to describe networks of brain regions that are functionally connected, or to compare brain activation to anatomical connectivity maps (e.g., Chow et al., 2008; Buchweitz, Mason, Tomitch, and Just, 2009; Siebörger et al., 2007).

Another interesting approach is the use of localizers for sharpening hypotheses about brain activations. Rather than conducting a whole-brain analysis in which all brain regions are exploratorily included, a separate scan is used prior to the experiment of interest to localize in each individual a given region or set of regions. Fedorenko and Kanwisher (2009) propose that using this approach in language comprehension research will lead to more consistent results. Recently, de Vega et al. (2014) have successfully applied this method to study the relationship between action observation and comprehension of action related language.

Other methods

One important line of research is the use of event-related or evoked potentials (ERP). Based on the electroencephalogram (EEG), this method directly measures brain activity with very high temporal resolution, at the expense of spatial specificity. This method yields highly interesting data on discourse influences on syntactic disambiguation, on semantic integration, or on referential processes (van Berkum, 2004, for review). More generally, the paradigm has been successfully applied to the question of whether language comprehension involves prediction of upcoming words, an issue highly relevant to the question of whether inferences are drawn immediately during comprehension.

Other special populations

My neuropsychological studies summarized in the first part were based on a lesion approach. To study the necessity of a brain region for a certain function, neurological patients are identified whose acquired brain injury overlaps with this region of interest. This work will be continued and, hopefully, yield interesting results. In addition, other special populations have been studied as models for functional deficits. Persons with disorders of the autistic spectrum (ASD; including autism, Asperger syndrome, and pragmatic language deficit) have been studied to evaluate the relationship of language comprehension and ToM (e.g., Buchweitz et al., 2009). Furthermore, Gina Kuperberg and colleagues (see also Boudewyn, Carter, and Swaab, 2012) have begun to apply paradigms and findings from inference research to the study of schizophrenia. Patients affected exhibit unconnected and incoherent discourse production, and some findings suggest frontal lobe involvement (Kuperberg and Caplan, 2003). Consequently, it is of interest whether these individuals also have difficulties with coherence building during comprehension.

Other theoretical proposals

Traditionally, neurobiological models of language have focused on the word and sentence level, or on a distinction of lexico-semantic and syntactic processes. Hagoort (2013) has recently proposed a framework in which language is seen in a more holistic way, including communication beyond the sentence. In particular, he notes the need for including attentional and inferential processes over and above linguistics proper. The model conceptualizes language processing as involving memory processes for accessing word meanings and world knowledge (localized in temporoparietal areas), control processes for guiding the comprehension process (localized in dlPFC), and, most importantly, a unification component (a region in the IFG, overlapping with the upper portion of Broca's area and extending into more anterior IFG [BA 47], as well as the frontal junction area [BA6]). Unification is defined as "deriving new and complex meaning from the lexical building blocks," the latter being retrieved using the memory component in the left temporal lobe. In terms of the psycholinguistics of text comprehension, this definition might include inferencing as well as building idea units in the sense of propositionalization, functions that I would associate with the dmPFC and the aTL, respectively.

Largely compatible with this view is an approach grounded in linguistic theory. Pylkkänen, Brennan, and Bemis (2011) argue for a more thorough analysis of language materials used in neuroscientific studies. Using magnetoencephalography (MEG), they postulate functions for two key areas. An anterior midline field (similar to the dmPFC discussed here) is seen to be important for coercion, a process by which the meaning of a phrase is reinterpreted given the constraints of the sentence context. For example, in the sentence "The writer finished the book," the object noun phrase "the book" does not fill the required argument slot of the verb finish, and thus an event interpretation ("writing the book") is inferred. In contrast, Brennan, Nir, Hasson, Malach, Heeger, and Pylkkänen (2012) have shown that left aTL activation (not IFG activation) increases with syntactic complexity, and in particular, with semantic composition (e.g., processing a minimal phrase such as "red book").

Both proposals are perfectly in line with the more psychologically motiv-ated interpretations discussed earlier.

Both theories, the MUC approach and the linguistically grounded approach, provide testable hypothesis. The future will show how these approaches converge, and whether they can be productively merged with traditional theories of text comprehension.

Some answers

It is not possible here to give credit to all the other neuroscientific studies on inference processes and higher-level language processing. Neither is it feasible to discuss their differences and commonalities here. Instead, I would like to formulate explicitly – and succinctly – what I think the most important conclusions are from this research.

Inferencing during reading, and more generally, text comprehension, engages an extended language network (ELN; Ferstl et al., 2008). The regions most closely linked to inferencing are the dmPFC, the PCC/prec, and the bilateral anterior temporal lobes. Tentative functions for these regions include self-initiated cognitive processes, the updating of situ-ation models, and the packaging of phrasal or idea units, respectively. The dmPFC activation reflects strategic inference processes, in particu-lar those requiring an explicit stimulus evaluation, rather than more automatic associative or memory-resonance processes (O'Brien, Lorch, and Myers, 1998). The latter are reflected in lateral fronto-temporal activations, in particular, the left IFG and the middle right temporal lobe (cf. Virtue et al., 2008; see also Hagoort, 2013). Further research is needed to evaluate whether this distinction maps onto the more fine-grained analyses from behavioral research.

Inferences across the sentence boundary are qualitatively similar to inferences on the word or sentence level. The text length influences subprocesses such as memory retrieval or reinstatement only, but not associative lexico-semantic processes or self-guided strategic evaluation. Inferencing during reading is domain general, not language specific. All relevant regions, most notably the dmPFC, but also the right temporal lobe, subserve other, nonverbal functions as well. Inference processes similar to those during reading can be elicited in a variety of ways, for example, by pictorial stimuli or self-guided thinking. However, it cannot be excluded that people use verbal strategies for these tasks. Van Over-walle (2009) stressed the fact that verbal stimuli, in particular, short story–like materials, tend to involve the dmPFC more than similarly socially relevant visual stimuli. Inferencing during reading overlaps with Theory-of-Mind processing. Theory-of-Mind involves inferences about traits and intentions; reading involves inferences about the mind of others (protagonists, communication partners, writers, experimenters). Although the exact relationship between the two remains controversial (see next section), both are core components of communication.

Some open questions

The most puzzling open question is the role of the right hemisphere during language comprehension and inferencing. Although patient studies and clinical descriptions of deficits document inference deficits, the contribution of the right hemisphere is still a riddle. Even though there is some evidence for RH involvement, there are many other studies without (see Ferstl, 2007; 2010 for review). In our own laboratory, for example, we recently confirmed both activations of the dmPFC as well as the RH in a semantic integration task on the sentence level (Franzmeier et al., in preparation; cf. Baumgärtner, Weiller, and Büchel, 2002). In contrast, the results of a series of transcranial magnetic stimulation (TMS) experiments confirmed a causal contribution of the left temporal lobe, but did not yield a consistent pattern concerning the right hemisphere (Franzmeier, Hutton, and Ferstl, 2012). It is widely agreed that RH components play a role, but their specific function is a matter of debate. For example, in their model, Mason and Just (2006) included a coarse coding component in the right temporal lobe to accommodate their finding of RH activation during a classical inference task (Mason and Just, 2004). However, they also leave open the possibility that the right hemisphere unspecifically supports the left hemisphere whenever the latter's capacity overflows. Further research is needed to dissociate these and other alternative accounts of RH function.

A second important open question, despite the abundance of studies on social cognition (cf. van Overwalle, 2009), is the exact relationship between Theory-of-Mind and verbal communication. The comprehensive meta-analysis by Mar (2011), who distinguished between verbal and nonverbal ToM and compared both to narrative comprehension, yields large overlapping networks, but does not help much for elucidating the relationship between the two domains. And in fact, this is not surprising given the strong link between them. Attempts to disentangle them using the developmental trajectory are equally difficult and have not produced a clear-cut answer (see Ferstl, 2012; Malle, 2002). Similarly, autism or Asperger syndrome has been has been taken as a model for ToM deficits, but persons with this diagnosis also frequently have language deficits, in particular with pragmatics, narratives, or nonliteral language (Ferstl, 2012; Frith, 2003). It is likely that the two domains are so closely interwoven that a dissociation is impossible (cf. Malle, 2002).

Further research

From a text-linguistic point of view, many issues on inferencing have not yet been studied with neuroimaging methodology. Some of these are too subtle, some are not important enough to warrant the rather expensive experimentation, and some require a more fine-grained temporal resolution. Of the ones for which neuroimaging seems appropriate, I will single out a few examples. First, there are still only a few studies directly comparing different inference types (such as, causal, goal directed, elaborative, etc.), or different inference processes (e.g., deliberate vs. associative) in the same participants. While this work requires careful design and control of the materials to avoid confounds, the behavioral literature readily provides appropriate paradigms. Second, most of the research on inferencing uses narrative text. To disentangle contributions of social cognition and language comprehension, we need more work on other genres, such as expository or procedural texts. Such materials will also enable us to investigate the effects of text difficulty on inference processes, or to compare local bridging inferences to complex knowledge based inferences. Finally, in the behavioral literature, reading or comprehension skill has played an enormous role (e.g., (Gernsbacher, 1990; Perfetti, Yang, and Schmalhofer, 2008). Individual differences are important for diagnostics and to improve instructions. With more sophisticated analysis methods, correlative studies are now feasible, for example, to study the influence of working memory (cf. Virtue et al., 2008), vocabulary, or background knowledge, and many other factors.

Conclusions

In this chapter I summarized my own work on neuroimaging of inference processes to illustrate its contribution to text linguistics and the psychology of higher-level language comprehension. Of course, it is important to stress that this was a personal view. Other researchers might interpret these results in other ways, or they might evaluate the benefits and pitfalls of neuroscientific methods differently (cf. van Lancker-Sidtis, 2006). However, the opportunity to get a glimpse into brain function, in addition to behavioral data and computational models, has greatly influenced my thinking about language and communication.

In my opinion, one of the most important take-home messages from this work is that theories of higher-level language processing and inferencing need to move from pure psycholinguistics to a more holistic cognitive science approach. A strict separation of language, cognition, and social psychology is clearly too restrictive. Instead, communication needs to be treated in a holistic way, including and integrating linguistic, cognitive, affective, and social components. Of course, this has been acknowledged by text comprehension researchers as well (e.g., in studies on emotion in language comprehension, such as de Vega, 2010), but neuroscientific research has pushed these issues to the forefront more quickly.

Conversely, the fine-grained psycholinguistic distinctions as evidenced in a wealth of behavioral data need to be integrated with neuroscientific research. Clinically motivated research, and neurolinguistic theory in general, must include the text and discourse level (cf. Hagoort, 2013). Thorough knowledge of inference processes needs to be taken into account during experimental design and, particularly, during the interpretation of neuroimaging results. I am convinced that a combination of methods and theories will further our understanding of inference processes during reading.

REFERENCES

Albrecht, J. E., & O'Brien, E. J. (1993). Updating a mental model: maintaining both local and global coherence. *Journal of Experimental Psychology: Learning, Memory, and Cognition, 19*, 1061–70.

Anderson, J. R., Bothell, D., Byrne, M. D., Douglass, S., Lebiere, C., & Qin, Y. (2004). An integrated theory of the mind. *Psychological Review, 111*, 1036–60.

Anderson, R. C., & Pichert, J. W. 1978. Recall of previously unrecallable information following a shift in perspective. *Journal of Verbal Learning and Verbal Behavior, 17*, 1–12.

Baumgärtner, A., Weiller, C., & Büchel, C. (2002). Event-related fMRI reveals cortical sites involved in contextual sentence integration. *NeuroImage, 16*, 736–45.

Beeman, M. (1998). Coarse semantic coding and discourse comprehension. In M. Beeman and C. Chiarello (eds.), *Right Hemisphere Language Comprehension: Perspectives from Cognitive Neuroscience* (pp. 255–84). Mahwah, NJ: Erlbaum.

Beeman, M., Bowden, E. M., & Gernsbacher, M. A. (2000). Right and left hemisphere cooperation for drawing predictive and coherence inferences during normal story comprehension. *Brain and Language, 71*, 310–36.

Beeman, M., & Chiarello, C. (1998). *Right hemisphere language comprehension: Perspectives from cognitive neuroscience.* Mahwah, NJ: Erlbaum.

Binder, J. R., Frost, J. A., Hammeke, T. A., Bellgowan, P. S. F., Rao, S. M., & Cox, R. W. (1999). Conceptual processing during the conscious resting state: a functional MRI study. *Journal of Cognitive Neuroscience, 11*, 80–93.

Bornkessel-Schlesewsky, I., & Friederici, A. F. (2007). Neuroimaging studies of sentence and discourse comprehension. In M. G. Gaskell (ed.), *The Oxford Handbook of Psycholinguistics* (pp. 407–24). Oxford University Press.

Boudewyn, M. A., Carter, C., & Swaab, T. Y. (2012). Cognitive control and discourse comprehension in schizophrenia. *Schizophrenia Research and Treatment*, 1–7.

Brass, M., Derrfuss, J., Forstmann, B., & Cramon, D. Y. (2005). The role of the inferior frontal junction area in cognitive control. *Trends in Cognitive Sciences*, 9(7), 314–6.

Brennan, J., Nir, Y., Hasson, U., Malach, R., Heeger, D. J., & Pylkkänen, L. (2012). Syntactic structure building in the anterior temporal lobe during natural story listening. *Brain and Language*, *120*, 163–73.

Brodmann, K., (1909). Vergleichende Lokalisationslehre der Großhirnrindein ihren Prinzipien dargestellt auf Grund des Zellenbaues. Leipzig: Barth, JA.

Brownell H. H., Potter H. H., Bihrle A. M., & Gardner H. (1986). Inference deficits in right brain-damaged patients. *Brain and Language*, *27*, 310–21.

Brownell, H. H., & Martino, G. (1998). Deficits in inference and social cognition: the effects of right hemisphere brain damage on discourse. In M. Beeman & C. Chiarello (eds.), *Right Hemisphere Language Comprehension* (pp. 309–28). Mahwah, NJ: Erlbaum.

Buchweitz, A., Mason, R. A., Tomitch, L., & Just, M. A. (2009). Brain activation for reading and listening comprehension: an fMRI study of modality effects and individual differences in language comprehension. *Psychology & Neuroscience*, *2*, 111–23.

Chow, H. M., Kaup, B., Raabe, M., & Greenlee, M. W. (2008). Evidence of fronto-temporal interactions for strategic inference processes during language comprehension. *NeuroImage*, *40*, 940–54.

Deacon T. W. (1997). *The Symbolic Species*. New York: Norton.

Derrfuss, J., Brass, M., von Cramon, D. Y., Lohmann, G., & Amunts, K. (2009). Neural activations at the junction of the inferior frontal sulcus and the inferior precentral sulcus: interindividual variability, reliability, and association with sulcal morphology. *Human Brain Mapping*, *30*(1), 299–311.

de Vega, M. (2010). The representation of changing emotions in reading comprehension. *Cognition & Emotion*, *1*, 303–22.

de Vega, M., Leon, I., Hernandez, J. A., Valdes-Sosa, M., Padron, I., & Ferstl, E. C. (2014). Action sentences activate sensory-motor regions in the brain independently of their status of reality. *Journal of Cognitive Neuroscience*, *26*, 1363–76.

Fedorenko, E., & Kanwisher, N. (2009). Neuroimaging of language: why hasn't a clearer picture emerged? *Language and Linguistics Compass*, *3*/4, 839–65.

Ferstl, E. C. (2006). Text comprehension in middle-aged adults: is there anything wrong? *Aging, Neuropsychology and Cognition*, *13*(1), 62–85.

(2007). The functional neuroanatomy of text comprehension: what's the story so far? In F. Schmalhofer & C. A. Perfetti (eds.), *Higher Level Language Processes in the Brain: Inference and Comprehension Processes* (pp. 53–102). Mahwah, NJ: Erlbaum.

(2010). The neuroanatomy of discourse comprehension: where are we now? In V. Bambini (Hrsg.), *Neuropragmatics, Special Issue of Italian Journal of Linguistics*, *22*, 61–88.

(2012). Theory-of-Mind und kommunikation: zwei seiten der gleichen medaille? [Theory-of-Mind and communication: two sides of the same coin?]. In H. Förstl (ed.), *Theory of Mind: Neurobiologie und Psychologie sozialen Verhaltens* (2nd ed.). Heidelberg: Springer.

Ferstl, E. C., Guthke, T., & von Cramon, D. Y. (1999). Change of perspective in discourse comprehension: encoding and retrieval processes after brain injury. *Brain and Language, 70*, 385–420.

(2002). Text comprehension after brain injury: left prefrontal lesions affect inference processes. *Neuropsychology, 16*, 292–308.

Ferstl, E. C., Neumann, J., Bogler, C., & von Cramon, D. Y. (2008). The extended language network: a meta-analysis of neuroimaging studies on text comprehension. *Human Brain Mapping, 29*, 581–93.

Ferstl, E. C., Rinck, M., & von Cramon, D. Y. (2005). Emotional and temporal aspects of situation model processing during text comprehension: an event-related fMRI study. *Journal of Cognitive Neuroscience, 17*, 724–39.

Ferstl, E. C., & von Cramon, D. Y. (2001a). The role of coherence and cohesion in text comprehension: an event-related fMRI study. *Cognitive Brain Research, 11*, 325–40.

(2001b). Inference processes during text comprehension: is it the left hemisphere after all? *Journal of Cognitive Neuroscience (Supplement), 128.*

(2002). What does the fronto-median cortex contribute to language processing: coherence or theory of mind? *NeuroImage, 17*, 1599–1612.

Ferstl, E. C., & Zacks, J. M. (in press). Discourse comprehension. In S. L. Small & G. Hickok (eds.), *The Neurobiology of Language.* Amsterdam: Elsevier.

Fletcher, P. C., Happe, F., Frith, U., Baker, S. C., Dolan, R. J., Frackowiak, R. S. J., & Frith, C. D. 1995. Other minds in the brain: a functional imaging study of "theory of mind" in story comprehension. *Cognition, 57*, 109–28.

Franzmeier, I., Müller-Feldmeth, D., Mader, I., Weiller, C., & Ferstl, E. C. (2014). *Semantic processing in a sentence context relies on a bilateral network: evidence from an fMRI study.* Manuscript in preparation.

Franzmeier, I., Hutton, B. H., & Ferstl, E. C. (2012). The role of the right temporal lobe in contextual sentence integration: A TMS study. *Cognitive Neuroscience. 3*, 1–7.

Friese, U., Rutschmann, R., Raabe, M., & Schmalhofer, F. (2008). Neural indicators of inference processes in text comprehension: an event-related functional magnetic resonance imaging study. *Journal of Cognitive Neuroscience, 20*, 2110–24.

Frith, U. (2003) *Autism. Explaining the Enigma* (2nd edn.). Oxford, UK: Blackwell.

Gernsbacher, M. A. (1990). *Language as Structure Building.* Mahwah, NJ: Erlbaum.

Glenberg, A. M, & Gallese V. (2012). Action-based language: a theory of language acquisition, comprehension, and production. *Cortex, 48*(7), 905–22.

Grady, C. L. (1999). Neuroimaging and activation of the frontal lobes. In B. L. Miller & J. L. Cummings (eds.), *The Human Frontal Lobes: Functions and Disorders.* New York: Guilford.

Haberlandt, K. (1994). Methods in reading research. In M. A. Gernsbacher (ed.), *Handbook of Psycholinguistics* (pp. 1–25). San Diego: Academic Press.

Hagoort, P. (2013). MUC (memory, unification, control) and beyond. *Frontiers in Psychology, 4*, 1–13.

Jacobsen, T., Schubotz, R. I., Höfel, L., & von Cramon, D. Y. (2006). Brain correlates of aesthetic judgment of beauty. *NeuroImage, 29*, 276–85.

Jin, H., Liu, H.-L., Mo, L., Fang, S.-Y., Zhang, J. X.,& Lin, C.-D. 2009. Involvement of the left inferior frontal gyrus in predictive inference making. *International Journal of Psychophysiology, 71*, 142–8.

Jung-Beeman M. (2005). Bilateral brain processes for comprehending natural language. *Trends in Cognitive Science, 9*, 512–8.

Kintsch, W. (1988). The use of knowledge in discourse processing: a construction-integration model. *Psychological Review, 95*, 163–82.

Kuperberg, G. R. (2007). Neural mechanisms of language comprehension: challenges to syntax. *Brain Research, 1146*, 23–49.

Kuperberg, G. R., & Caplan, D. (2003). Language dysfunction in schizophrenia. In R. B. Schiffer, S. M. Rao, & B. S. Fogel (eds.), *Neuropsychiatry* (2nd ed., pp. 444–66). Philadelphia: Lippincott Williams and Wilkins.

Kuperberg, G. R., Lakshmanan, B. M., Caplan, D. N., & Holcomb, P. J.(2006). Making sense of discourse: an fMRI study of causal inferencing across sentences. *NeuroImage, 33*, 343–61.

Lehman-Blake M. T., & Tompkins C. A. (2001). Predictive inferencing in adults with right hemisphere brain damage. *Journal of Speech, Language, and Hearing Research, 44*, 639–54.

Malle B. F. (2002). The relation between language and theory of mind in development and evolution. In T. Givon & B. F. Malle (eds.), *The Evolution of Language out of Pre-language* (pp. 265–84). Amsterdam: Benjamins.

Mar, R. A. (2004). The neuropsychology of narrative: story comprehension, story production and their interrelation. *Neuropsychologia, 42*, 1414–34.

(2011). The neural bases of social cognition and story comprehension. *Annual Review of Psychology, 62*, 103–34.

Mason, R. A., & Just, M. A. (2004). How the brain processes causal inferences in text: a theoretical account of generation and integration component processes utilizing both cerebral hemispheres. *Psychological Science, 15*, 1–7.

(2006). Neuroimaging contributions to the understanding of discourse processes. In M. Traxler & M. A. Gernsbacher (eds.), *Handbook of Psycholinguistics* (pp. 765–99). Amsterdam: Elsevier.

Mason, R. A., Williams, D. L., Kana, R. K., Minshew, N., & Just, M. A. (2008). Theory of mind disruption and recruitment of the right hemisphere during narrative comprehension in autism. *Neuropsychologia, 46*, 269–80.

Mazoyer, B. M., Tzourio, N., Frak, V., Syrota, A., Murayama, N., Levrier, O., Salamon, G., Dehaene, S., Cohen, L., & Mehler, J. (1993). The cortical representation of speech. *Journal of Cognitive Neuroscience, 5*, 467–79.

McDonald, S. (1993). Viewing the brain sideways? Frontal versus right hemisphere explanation of nonaphasic language disorders. *Aphasiology, 7*, 535–49.

O'Brien, E. J., & Albrecht, J. E. (1992). Comprehension strategies in the development of a mental model. *Journal of Experimental Psychology: Learning, Memory, and Cognition, 18*, 777–84.

O'Brien, E. J., Lorch, R. F., & Myers, J. (1998). *Memory-based text processing.* Mahwah, NJ: Erlbaum.

Perfetti, C. A., Yang, C-L., & Schmalhofer, F. (2008). Comprehension skill and word-to-text processes. *Applied Cognitive Psychology, 22* (3), 303–18.

Prigatano, G. P., Roueche, J. R., & Fordyce, D. J. (1986). Nonaphasic language disturbances after brain injury. In G. P. Prigatano, D. J. Fordyce, H. K. Zeiner, J. R. Roueche, M. Pepping, & B. C. Wood (eds.), *Neuropsychological Rehabilitation after Brain Injury.* Baltimore: Johns Hopkins University Press.

Pulvermuüller, F. (2005). Brain mechanisms linking language and action. *Nature Reviews Neuroscience, 6*, 576–82.

Pylkkänen, L., Brennan J., & Bemis, D. K. (2011). Grounding the cognitive neuroscience of semantics in linguistic theory. *Language & Cognitive Processes, 26* (9), 1317–37.

Rinck, M., Hähnel, A., & Becker, G. (2001). Using temporal information to construct, update, and retrieve situation models of narratives. *Journal of Experimental Psychology: Learning, Memory, and Cognition, 27*, 67–80.

Romero Lauro L. J., Mattavelli, G., Papagno, C., & Tettamanti M. (2013). She runs, the road runs, my mind runs, bad blood runs between us: literal and figurative motion verbs: an fMRI study. *Neuroimage. 83, 361–71.*

Siebörger, F. T. (1999). *Profile von Textverstehen und Diskursproduktion nach Hirnschädigung.* Unpublished Master Thesis, University of Osnabrück, Germany.

(2006). *Funktionelle Neuroanatomie des Textverstehens: Kohärenzbildung bei Witzen und anderen ungewöhnlichen Texten.* Leipzig: MPI-Series in Human Cognitive and Brain Sciences (Vol. *LXXXIII*).

Siebörger, F. T., Ferstl, E. C.,& von Cramon, D. Y. (2007). Making sense of nonsense: an fMRI study of task induced inference processes during discourse comprehension. *Brain Research, 1166*, 77–91.

Singer, M., Graesser, A. C., & Trabasso, T. (1994). Minimal or global inference during reading. *Journal of Memory& Language, 33*, 421–41.

Smaers, J. B., Steele, V. R., Case, C. R., Cowper, A., Amunts, K., & Zilles, K. (2011). Primate prefrontal cortex evolution: human brains are the extreme of a lateralized ape trend. *Brain, Behavior and Evolution, 77*, 67–78.

Steele, V. R., Bernat, E. M., van den Broek, P., Collins, P. F., Patrick, C. J., & Marsolek, C. J. (2013). Separable processes before, during, and after the N400 elicited by previously inferred and new information: evidence from time-frequency decompositions. *Brain Research, 1492*, 92–107.

Tompkins C. A., Fassbinder W., Lehman-Blake M., Baumgärtner A., & Jayaram N. (2004). Inference generation during text comprehension by adults with right hemisphere brain damage: activation failure versus multiple activation. *Journal of Speech, Language, and Hearing Research, 47*, 1380–95.

Tooby, J., & Cosmides, L. (1995). The psychological foundations of culture. In J. H. Barkow, L. Cosmides, and J. Tooby (eds.), *The Adapted Mind:*

Evolutionary Psychology and the Generation of Culture (pp. 19–136). New York: Oxford University Press.

Trabasso, T., van den Broek, P., & Suh, S. (1989). Logical necessity and transitivity of causal relations in stories. *Discourse Processes, 12*, 1–25.

Uylings, H. B. M., Malofeeva, L. I., Bogolepova, I. N., Amunts, K., & Zilles, K. (1999). Broca's language area from a neuroanatomical and developmental perspective. In C. M. Brown & P. Hagoort (eds.), *The Neurocognition of Language* (pp. 319–36). Oxford University Press.

van Berkum, J. J. A. (2004). Sentence comprehension in a wider discourse: can we use ERPs to keep track of things? In M. Carreiras & C. Clifton, Jr. (eds.), *The Online Study of Sentence Comprehension: Eye Tracking, ERPs and Beyond* (pp. 229–70). New York: Psychology Press.

van Dijk, T. A., & Kintsch, W. (1983). *Strategies of Discourse Comprehension*. New York: Academic Press.

van Lancker Sidtis, D. (2006). Does functional neuroimaging solve the questions of neurolinguistics? *Brain and Language, 98*, 276–90.

van Overwalle, F. (2009). Social cognition and the brain: a meta-analysis. *Human Brain Mapping, 30*, 829–58.

Virtue S., Haberman J., Clancy Z., Parrish T., & Jung Beeman M. (2006). Neural activity of inferences during story comprehension. *Brain Research, 1084*, 104–14.

Virtue, S., Parrish, T., & Jung-Beeman, M. (2008). Inferences during story comprehension: cortical recruitment affected by predictability of events and working memory capacity. *Journal of Cognitive Neuroscience, 20*, 2274–84.

Yang C. L., Perfetti C. A., & Schmalhofer F. (2007). Event-related potential indicators of text integration across sentence boundaries. *Journal of Experimental Psychology: LMC, 33* (1), 55–89.

Zaidel, E. (1978). Lexical organization in the right hemisphere. In P. Buser & A. Rougeul-Buser (eds.), *Cerebral Correlates of Conscious Experience* (pp. 177–97). Amsterdam: Elsevier.

Zwaan, R. A. (2004). The immersed experiencer: toward an embodied theory of language comprehension. In B. H. Ross (ed.), *The Psychology of Learning and Motivation*, Vol. *XLIV* (pp. 35–62). Amsterdam: Elsevier.

Zwaan, R. A., Langston, M. C., & Graesser, A. C. (1995). The construction of situation models in narrative comprehension: an event-indexing model. *Psychological Science, 6*, 292–97.

Zysset, S., Huber, O., Ferstl, E. C., & von Cramon, D. Y. (2002). The anterior fronto-median cortex and evaluative judgment: an fMRI study. *NeuroImage, 15*, 983–91.

12   Causal inferences and world knowledge

Leo Noordman, Wietske Vonk, Reinier Cozijn,
and Stefan Frank

Theoretical background

Research on inferences in discourse processing has been characterized
for a long time by the question of what kinds of inference are likely made
online and what kinds of inference are not. Considering that in principle
an unlimited number of inferences can be made while the human processing capacity is limited, the question arises how the inferences are
controlled. In the 1970s and 1980s, one tried to answer this question by
classifying inferences, assuming that the different classes vary in the
likelihood of being made. The classifications were in general based on
textual characteristics, such as whether the inference is a forward or a
backward inference in the text; whether it is necessary for coherence or
just elaborative, whether it necessarily follows from the text or only
possibly. Inferences were also classified with respect to their content,
for instance, as inferences about instruments, causes, consequences,
goals, time, or place. There was some consensus that inferences that
are necessary for coherence, including backward bridging inferences, are
made online and other kinds of inference are not (Singer, 1994, 2007;
van den Broek, 1994). By then, however, it was already clear that that
conclusion fell short (Noordman, Vonk, and Kempff, 1992). Whether an
inference is made does not only depend on its function in the text, but
also on the availability of the required information and the reader's
knowledge. This has also been acknowledged in the two main views that
emerged in the 1990s: the minimalist view and the constructionist view.
According to the minimalist view (McKoon and Ratcliff, 1992), only two
classes of inferences are made during reading, those that are based on
easily available information and those that are required for local coherence. Crucial here is how to establish what "easily available information"
is. The constructionist view (Graesser, Singer, and Trabasso, 1994) is
characterized by a search (or effort) after meaning. Readers have a
particular goal in reading: construct a coherent meaning representation –
a mental model – and explain what is being read. In constructing such a

mental model, world knowledge is activated. The main issue in both the minimalist view and the constructionist view was the question of which inferences are made online. Inferences were still considered as a rather isolated phenomenon rather than as a component process in discourse comprehension.

In the last decade, research on inferences got embedded in a broader cognitive framework. It seemed to be promising to conceive inferences as a component process in discourse comprehension and to relate inferences to the readers' world knowledge (Vonk and Noordman, 2001). This has been proposed in the memory-based approach to text processing (Gerrig and McKoon, 1998). In this approach, an inference is a process that takes place in active memory and makes contact with information in long-term memory, which includes information from the previous discourse representation and world knowledge. Given that the controlling factor for inferences is "easily available information," some rapprochement between the minimalist and constructionist views on inferences emerges. Three observations may illustrate this rapprochement. First, since easily available information includes parts of the previous discourse (including knowledge about the goal of the protagonist) as well as world knowledge about the topic, it does not follow from "easily available information" that only a very restricted class of inferences is made (Noordman and Vonk, in press). Second, the experiments by O'Brien, Myers, and colleagues demonstrated that the claim that readers attend to only local coherence was too strong because global inferences about the protagonist were made even though the text was locally coherent (Albrecht and O'Brien, 1993). O'Brien and colleagues argued that even though global information concerning a protagonist did not remain "active" in memory (Myers, O'Brien, Albrecht, and Mason, 1994), such information was "readily available" through a fast-acting resonance process (see O'Brien, 1995, for a review). In fact, a characteristic of the protagonist can remain "available" even if it is mentioned quite a distance ago. This is because information in a discourse is not only linearly but also hierarchically structured (van Dijk and Kintsch, 1983). Third, even the role of goal-directed behavior, which is a characteristic of constructionism, is not altogether incompatible with minimalism and can be accommodated within memory-based processing: The reader's goal dictates what information the reader is after, which, in turn, determines what information is currently in focus and available.

The position we advocate is also nicely articulated by Gerrig and O'Brien (2005) in their discussion of memory-based processing. They argue that whether an inference is made or not does not depend on the

262   Leo Noordman, Wietske Vonk, Reinier Cozijn, and Stefan Frank

kind of inference, but on the activation of information in memory: "Inferences are encoded to the extent that information in active memory makes contact with relevant or necessary information from inactive portions of the discourse model and general world knowledge" (Gerrig and O'Brien, 2005, p. 236). They also acknowledge the role of the reader's goals in their approach. The crucial mechanism in their memory-based processing is "resonance" (Myers and O'Brien, 1998; Ratcliff, 1978): Inactive information of the previous discourse representation and world knowledge becomes activated in proportion to its match with the incoming text input.

We take memory-based processing as our framework. Both textual information and the world knowledge of the reader can be readily available information. According to memory-based processing, concepts from earlier in the discourse representation and world knowledge resonate with the incoming text. But the notion of memory-based processing allows for sources of activation other than just the incoming text. There are factors related to the reader that can increase the accessibility of information. For instance, the reader's goal can influence what information is in focus. Concepts in current focus get more attention, which increases their activation and accessibility. Furthermore, some information is intrinsically more available than other information. Specifically, human beings have the propensity to deal with causal relations (Noordman, 2005): Consecutive sentences are preferably interpreted in a causal way, supporting Levinson's (1983) principle of informativeness. According to Kant, causality is one of the conditions that we impose on our experience: "The empirical knowledge of phenomena is only possible by the fact that we subject the succession of phenomena ... to the law of causality" (Kant, 1781 B234). Causality is a preferred mode of interpretation and in that sense causal information is easily available.

In this paper we review our research that demonstrates how causal inferences depend on world knowledge. The first part addresses experimental studies on knowledge and inferences. The second part addresses the modeling of knowledge-based inferences. In the first part, world knowledge is manipulated in two different ways. In the first section of that part, we vary the familiarity of the causal relations expressed in the texts while keeping the population of readers constant. Results show that inferences of unfamiliar causal relations, even if they are marked by the conjunction *because*, are not made online. It will turn out that inferences of unfamiliar causal relations are made only if they are made more available under the influence of the reader's goal. Inferences that concern familiar causal relations, on the other hand, *are* made online. But a prerequisite is that the relations are marked by a conjunction, in our case by the conjunction *because*. In the second section of the experimental part, we vary the expertise of the readers in a particular domain, while keeping the texts constant. Experts and nonexperts in economics were compared while reading the same texts in the domain of economics. Results of these expert-versus-nonexpert studies support the conclusion from the experiments in which the familiarity of the causal relations is manipulated. Nonexperts in economics do not make the inferences about the causal relations online, although they are familiar with the concepts in the relations. Experts, on the other hand, do make the inferences. Interestingly, the experts made the inferences even in the absence of the conjunction *because*. Apparently, experts read texts that concern their expertise in a more careful way.

The second part of the paper deals with modeling knowledge-based inferences. We first review the role of world knowledge in models of discourse processing and inferencing. We then discuss a formal model that we developed earlier in which inferences are considered as world knowledge applications (Frank, Koppen, Noordman, and Vonk, 2003). The model simulates the process of causal inferences and explains a number of findings from the reading experiments, but it does not yet account for all the empirical data. We discuss how further extensions of the model might explain the findings from our reading experiments.

Experimental studies on knowledge and inferences

Manipulating knowledge: familiar and unfamiliar information

In the experiments presented in this section, we investigated the role of world knowledge by varying the familiarity of the information to be inferred. The inferences concerned causal relations that were unfamiliar to readers (Noordman, Vonk, and Kempff, 1992) or familiar to readers (Cozijn, Commandeur, Vonk, and Noordman, 2011; Cozijn, Noordman, and Vonk, 2011; Vonk and Noordman, 1990).

Unfamiliar relations are not inferred

Noordman et al. (1992) investigated whether backward causal inferences are made online during the processing of causal relations in text. Expository texts – with an average length of 7.6 sentences – contained a causal relation that was signaled by the causal connective *because*. The causal relations were unfamiliar to the readers, as was checked in a questionnaire. For example, in a text on spray cans, the causal relation read "Chlorine compounds make good propellants, because they react with almost no other substance." Based on the connective *because*, this sentence can be analyzed in terms of syllogistic reasoning. The sentence expresses the conclusion of the syllogism – chlorine compounds make good propellants – and the minor premise – they (i.e., chlorine compounds) react with no other substances. What is missing from the syllogism is the major premise: Propellants must not react with the product in the spray can. The connective *because* signals that the information of the major premise has to be inferred to justify the causal relation. This inference is backward and contributes to the coherence of the discourse.

To test whether the inference was made during reading, the causal relation sentence was either preceded or not preceded by a sentence explicitly stating the major premise. This explicitly mentioned premise was supposed to facilitate the inference. If the explicit information is not given, it should take more time to make the inference. This should lead to a longer reading time of the *because* sentence. After reading the text, participants had to verify a statement that contained the explicit information. Because the inference was expected to be made online in both the explicit and the implicit conditions, no difference was predicted for the verification times.

The results did not provide evidence for inferential processing during reading: Reading times did not differ between the explicit and the implicit conditions (see Table 12.1, line A1). Apparently, the explicit information did not activate the inferential relation between the concepts.

Table 12.1 *Mean reading and verification times (ms) in the causal relation experiments (the codes in the first column are for textual reference)*

	Task	Connective	Measure	Information Explicit	Implicit	
A1	Comprehension	*because*	Reading time	3807	3921	
A2			Verification time	2657	2955	⋆̲
B1	Topic-related question	*because*	Reading time	4700	5411	⋆̲
B2	Nontopic-related question		Reading time	4243	4014	
C1	Inconsistency judgment	*because*	Reading time	5478	6093	⋆̲
C2			Verification time	3594	3867	
D1	Comprehension	*but*	Reading time	1473	1536	⋆̲
D2			Verification time	2169	2198	

⋆ Significant difference

The explicit information, however, did help readers to verify the inference sentence after reading the text. Verification times were shorter in the explicit than in the implicit condition (see Table 12.1, line A2), suggesting that the inferences were made during verification. The combined set of results indicated that the causal inference was not made during reading, but, instead, after reading the text when the task required the readers to do so.

To obtain confirming evidence for this result, a follow-up experiment was conducted with similar materials. But in this experiment, the explicit sentence with the major premise was changed into its opposite. For example, for the causal sentence "Chlorine compounds make good propellants because they react with almost no other substance," the explicit sentence read "Propellants must combine with the product in the spray can," which contradicts the inference. Recall that the relations that had to be inferred were unfamiliar to the readers. In one condition, the participants were asked to read and check the texts for improvements. Seventy-six percent of the participants did not detect the inconsistency. In the other condition, participants were told that there might be an inconsistency in the text and, if so, that they had to correct it. Forty-five percent of the participants did not detect the inconsistency. This smaller percentage can be attributed to the effect of the instructed reading goal. But even in the latter case, a considerable percentage did not detect the inconsistency between the explicit information and the inference to be made, which is rather amazing. However, the fact that a substantial part of the participants did not make the inference online is consistent with the reading time results from the earlier experiment.

Conclusion: The results of the experiments with unfamiliar relations indicated that, unexpectedly, the inferences were not made during reading, even though the inferences would contribute to local coherence. These results suggest that the reader's knowledge controls inferences.

Unfamiliar relations are not inferred unless motivated
by the reader's goal

Although readers did not make the causal inference *during* reading, even when the conjunction *because* would allow them to do so, they did make the inference after reading when they were instructed to verify the information. Furthermore, when readers were instructed to improve the texts, the inferences were made, as was evidenced by the inconsistency detection. These two task-dependent effects suggest that online reading behavior may be affected by the reader's goal. The reader's goal can be defined in terms of the task demands, but also in terms of a specific topic.

In agreement with memory-based processing, the reader's topic goal may play a role in focusing the reader's attention to specific concepts and make these concepts more accessible. Both the goal in terms of task and in terms of topic were investigated in Noordman et al. (1992).

One experiment investigated whether the reader's topic-goal can motivate the reader to make inferences even if they are not familiar. As in the earlier experiments, participants read expository texts that dealt with unfamiliar causal relations. Participants had to give an oral answer to an explicit question about the text. The question was presented before reading the text. The texts had two types of question, but each participant was presented with only one question per text. The first type of question was about the causal relation. In case of the spray cans, the question was "How do spray cans work?" This question was intended to put the causal relation in current focus and thereby make it more accessible. Presumably, the causal relation is then more thoroughly processed and the inference made. The second type of question was about a different part of the text that occurred after the causal relation sentence. This question was not expected to elicit the causal inference during reading. The results supported the predictions: If the question was about the causal relation, the reading times on the causal relation sentences were shorter in the explicit condition than in the implicit condition (see Table 12.1, line B1). If the question was about a different part of the text, however, no difference between the conditions in the reading times on the causal relations sentences was observed (see Table 12.1, line B2). The interaction of text condition and type of question was significant. Apparently, having to answer a question about the causal relation urged the readers to make the inference online.

In another experiment, the reader's goal was defined by the task in which participants had to judge for each sentence whether it was consistent or inconsistent with its preceding context. To that end, one or more inconsistencies were inserted into the texts, but never into the causal relation sentence. The texts contained an explicit and implicit condition, as in the earlier experiments. Reading times of the *because* sentences were significantly shorter in the explicit condition than in the implicit condition and the verification times revealed no differences (see Table 12.1, lines C1 and C2), indicating that the task of checking sentences for inconsistencies elicited the inference to be made online.

Conclusion: These experiments showed that the goal of the reader is an important factor in determining whether inferences are made online. If the information to be inferred is unknown to the reader, the reader's goal can ensure that the inferences are made during reading. This has been demonstrated for the goal defined in terms of topic and task. This inference behavior is tantamount to learning: Readers infer knowledge that they did not have before.

Familiar relations are inferred

The assumption that inferences are made if they are familiar to the reader has been addressed in Vonk and Noordman (1990). In this study, narrative texts on familiar topics were presented that contained a causal–contrastive relation sentence marked with the connective *but*. An example is the sentence "The room was large, but one was not allowed to make music in the room" in a text about a girl who is looking for a room to rent. As with the aforementioned *because*-sentences, the readers could make an inference based on the conventional implication of the connective, in this case the contrastive *but*. In the context of having to evaluate the acceptability of the room, the readers may infer that a large room is attractive for the girl, which is rather obvious, and that not being able to make music is unattractive for the girl, which implies that the girl plays an instrument. This inferential information was either given in the prior context or not. In the explicit condition, the prior text contained the sentence "The girl wanted to make music in the room." In the implicit condition, this sentence was absent. After the text, a verification statement was presented that contained the information to be inferred from the text. If the inference was made online, the reading time on the *but* clause in the target sentence should be shorter in the explicit condition than in the implicit condition, and there should be no difference in the verification times. The results were in line with the predictions (see Table 12.1, lines D1 and D2), supporting the conclusion that the inference was made online. The availability of prior knowledge is an important factor in determining whether inferences are made online.

The role of available knowledge in the processing of causal relations was also investigated in a listening study (Cozijn, Commandeur, Vonk, and Noordman, 2011). In a visual world paradigm experiment, participants listened to sentences that contained an implicit causality verb, such as *to feel sorry for*: "The camel felt sorry for the octopus after the exam because he could not get a pass mark for the work." At the same time, their eye movements were monitored while they looked at a screen on which drawings of the two protagonists (camel and octopus) and a distractor item (a piece of paper with a pencil representing the exam) were presented (see Figure 12.1).

The aim of the study was to find out how quickly comprehenders assign a referent to the ambiguous pronoun *he* in the *because* clause and, more specifically, whether they use the information in the verb to

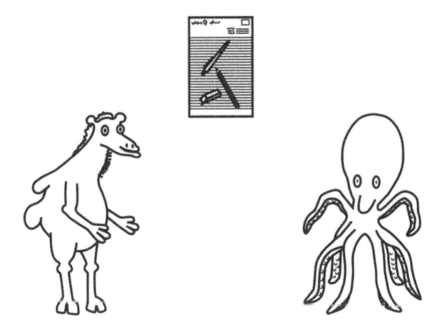

Figure 12.1 Example of a visual stimulus in the visual world paradigm experiment (vector traces of the original bitmap images). The three figures represent a camel, an octopus, and a piece of paper with pencils and an eraser representing the distractor "the exam" (Cozijn et al., 2011, p. 385).

make a preliminary interpretation as soon as (or even before) they hear the pronoun. The preliminary interpretation of *he* in the present example is that *he* refers to the octopus. For present purposes, however, we are interested in the definitive interpretation of the pronoun that can only be made at the end of the sentence. The participants had to point with their index finger to the referent of the pronoun on the screen. The interpretation of the pronoun requires an inference. As explained above, understanding the connective *because* involves a backward causal inference; in this case, "A person who cannot get a pass mark is felt sorry for." This inference is in line with our knowledge about exams (not getting a pass mark is a suitable reason for being felt sorry for by someone). In another condition, the pronoun had to be resolved by linking it to the other protagonist, the camel. For instance, "The camel felt sorry for the octopus after the exam, because he could not give a pass mark for the work." This pronoun resolution goes against the preliminary interpretation. The eye-movement data showed that the inference was made at the end of the sentence: When the second clause was "because he could not get a pass mark for the work," participants started looking at the correct referent at an earlier moment than when the second clause was "because he could not give a pass mark for the work," in which case world knowledge had to redress the preliminary pronoun assignment. With respect to the main question of the experiment, a preliminary interpretation of the pronoun was made very early, long before the disambiguating information was heard.

Conclusion: The results of the studies discussed in this section show that the availability of knowledge controls whether inferences are made during reading or listening. Inferences are made online only if their content is part of the reader's knowledge.

The causal inference process can be described in the framework of memory-based processing. Words in the text activate concepts in the reader's long-term memory. If the relations between the concepts are familiar to the reader (i.e., if they are stored in long-term memory), these relations are activated; they are checked against the reader's world knowledge and added to the text representation. The explicit information facilitates the inference by activating the causal relation. If the relation between the concepts is not familiar but is signaled in the text (e.g., by a causal conjunction), the relation can in principle be derived and added as new information to the text representation. The latter process is learning, as new information is then acquired from the text. Our results indicate that learning is not the normal mode in which readers process a text. Under normal reading circumstances, backward causal inferences, even if they are signaled by *because*, are not made during reading if they concern unfamiliar information. This result contrasts with our everyday belief that learning from text is self-evident and occurs all the time. Apparently, what is learned from text in normal reading depends on the reader's knowledge: Inferences about unfamiliar relations are not made. New information is learned only if readers are motivated to really understand the text.

Familiar relations are inferred only if supported by a conjunction

In the introduction, we claimed that humans have the propensity to interpret consecutive sentences in a causal way. The experiments showed that, for familiar relations, causal inferences were made online. How strong is this tendency to make causal inferences? Do the inferences depend on the presence of a conjunction such as *because*? This was investigated in Cozijn, Noordman, and Vonk (2011). Readers were presented with short narrative texts (seven sentences) on familiar topics

that contained a familiar causal relation either signaled by *because* or not
signaled. They processed causal relation sentences such as, "Mr. Smith
was delayed because there was a large traffic jam on the highway," while
their eye movements were monitored. As explained above, the inference
to be made when reading this sentence is the major premise of a syllogistic chain of reasoning. In this case, the inference is "A traffic jam causes
delay." This inference is part of the reader's knowledge. On the basis of
the previous experiments, this inference should be made in the presence
of the conjunction, leading to an increase in reading time. This will be
manifest at the end of the sentence when the reader has the information
to make the inference. If the inference depends on the presence of the
conjunction *because* (Singer and O'Connell, 2003), the reading time at
the end of the sentence should be shorter when the conjunction was
absent than when it was present. To test this prediction, half of the texts
did not contain the causal connective. The means of the regression path
reading times are shown in Table 12.2, line A.

The results showed that if the connective *because* was present, reading
times on the final words of the sentence were significantly longer than
If the connective was absent. This indicates that the inference was
made online only when the connective was present in the sentence.
To ascertain whether the reading time difference could indeed be
attributed to inferential processing, a second experiment with the
same materials was conducted with a verification task that addressed
the inferential information. Reading was self-paced. The results of the
reading times analysis were in line with those of the first experiment:
The reading times at the end of the sentence were longer if the connective was present than if it was absent (see Table 12.2, line B1).
Importantly, the verification times were shorter if the connective was
present in the text than if it was absent (see Table 12.2, line B2). This

Table 12.2 *Mean reading and verification times (ms) in the* because
experiments (the codes in the first column are for textual reference)

	Paradigm	Measure	Connective Present	Absent	
A	Eye tracking	Reading time	512	448	*
B1	Self-paced	Reading time	581	547	*
B2		Verification time	2,317	2,406	*

* Significant difference

is in line with the reading time results, because if the inference was made during reading, verifying a statement about that information is easier than when the inference was not made.

Conclusion: The results of these experiments suggest that the presence of the connective *because* is necessary for readers to make the causal inference online.

Manipulating knowledge: expert and nonexpert readers

In the preceding section, the effect of the reader's knowledge on inferences was investigated by varying the familiarity of the inferences. In the current section, the effect of the reader's knowledge on inferences is investigated by varying the knowledge of the readers. The aim is to show that inferences related to the reader's knowledge, and only those, are made during reading. This is achieved by having two groups of subjects, experts and nonexperts in a particular domain, read the same texts in that domain. Both the experts and the nonexperts should be familiar with the concepts that are used in the texts, but only the experts should be familiar with the causal relations between the concepts, because these relations constitute the inferences. We selected the field of economics as the domain of expertise. In two experiments, the knowledge of experts and nonexperts was elicited and represented in knowledge networks (Noordman, Vonk, and Simons, 2000; Simons, 1993).

Knowledge representation of experts and nonexperts

Participants were either experts or nonexperts in economics. The experts were advanced doctoral students in economics. The nonexperts were advanced doctoral students in disciplines not related to economics, such as psychology and linguistics. In the first experiment, ninety economic concepts were selected from the most frequent concepts that appeared during one month and a half in a Dutch quality newspaper. The experts and nonexperts were asked to freely associate to the economic concepts and to label relations between the concepts. The participants were requested to write down in one minute as many associations to the economic concepts as stimulus words as they could. In addition, they had to describe the relation between the stimulus word and the responses. Free associations were collected because the associations reflect the participant's knowledge representation (Graesser and Clark, 1985). The average number of word associations for experts (5.94) was significantly greater than for nonexperts (4.01). In describing the relations between the stimulus words and the responses, experts described significantly more associations (4.48) than nonexperts (2.65), and their associations were much more frequently described in terms of causal relations than those of the nonexperts.

In the second experiment, eighty different concepts from the previous experiment were put into 100 different pairs. Experts and nonexperts judged the familiarity of the eighty concepts on a seven-point scale. Subsequently, their knowledge about the relations between the 100 concept pairs was investigated: They were requested to judge the familiarity of the relations on a seven-point scale, to describe the nature of the relation, and, in particular to indicate whether the relation between the concepts was direct or indirect, whether a bidirectional or unidirectional influence existed between the two economic entities, and whether or not the relation was restricted to specific conditions. The familiarity of the concepts was significantly higher for experts (5.99) than for nonexperts (5.39). Similarly, the relations between the concepts were more familiar to the experts (6.16) than to the nonexperts (4.18). Seventy of the 100 relations were described as causal by the experts and only thirty-nine by the nonexperts.

On the basis of the relations between the concepts, semantic networks were constructed for the experts and the nonexperts. Parts of the networks are presented in Figures 12.2 and 12.3. The boxes (nodes) in the networks are the economic concepts. In the corners of the network, the concepts *consumer*, *producer*, *bank*, and *government* are added that give some ordering in the networks. The lines represent relations between the concepts. A relation between two concepts was assumed to exist only if that relation was formulated by at least 75 percent of the participants. The figures show whether the relations were causal or definitional, whether they were unidirectional or bidirectional, and whether there was a positive influence or a negative influence between the two concepts.

Experts were more familiar with the relations than were the nonexperts. The number of causal relations was much larger for the experts than for the nonexperts.

Parts of these networks were isolated as "knowledge schemes" to be used in the reading experiments. A knowledge scheme consisted of three concepts (A, B, and C) and two unidirectional relations between them (A-B; B-C). They can be expressed in one complex sentence, for example, "The increase in *inflation* (A) deteriorates the *competitive position* (B) and this leads to a decrease in the *exports* (C)." Based on such a knowledge scheme, the following sentence can be formulated: "The exports are decreasing because the inflation weakens the competitive position." On the basis of the elicited data, thirty knowledge schemes were identified that satisfied the following two criteria: The concepts in

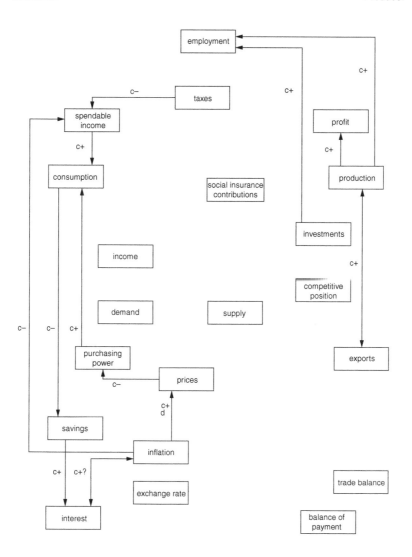

Figure 12.2 Knowledge representation of nonexperts (Noordman et al., 2000, p. 252).

274   Leo Noordman, Wietske Vonk, Reinier Cozijn, and Stefan Frank

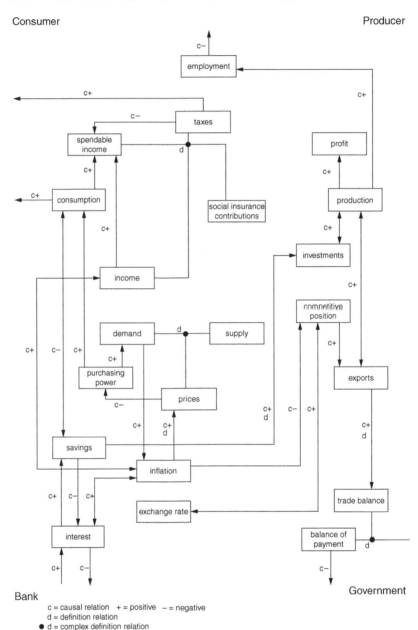

Figure 12.3 Knowledge representation of experts (Noordman et al., 2000, p. 253).

the scheme were familiar to both the experts and the nonexperts and the relations in that scheme were familiar only to the experts. Forty-one concepts were involved in these knowledge schemes. For the thirty knowledge schemes, the familiarity of the concepts was the same for experts (6.05) as for nonexperts (5.95), whereas the relations were significantly more familiar to the experts (6.22) than to the nonexperts (3.91).

Reading by experts and nonexperts

The knowledge schemes of the experts and nonexperts formed the basis for the reading materials. The length of the texts was on average nine sentences. An example of a causal sentence based on the earlier mentioned scheme is the sentence "The American exports have been suffering a decline in the last few months, because rising inflation impairs the competitive position of the United States" in a text on the American economy. This sentence expresses the relation between three economic concepts as it applies to the specific situation described by the text, schematically: "C, because A leads to B." The conjunction *because* triggers the major premise inference that a weakened competitive position decreases the exports. This inference concerns the direction of the causal relation between the concepts (B leads to C) as well as the sign of the relation (there is a positive correlation between B and C). It is assumed that the relation between "competitive position" and "exports" is activated only for the experts, because only for the experts is the relation familiar. This general relation is then applied to the American economic situation described by the text, and becomes part of the text representation of the experts. This constitutes the inference.

The inferences were measured by presenting the *because* sentence in two conditions, similarly to earlier experiments (Simons, 1993). In the explicit condition, the *because* sentence was preceded by a sentence that expresses the causal relation implied by the target sentence (B leads to C). An example is "Generally speaking, the competitive position of a country has a strong influence on the volume of its exports." In the implicit condition, the explicit information was not given. Experts are expected to make the inference and, therefore, the reading time for the target *because* sentence should be shorter in the explicit condition than in the implicit condition. This difference is predicted to occur during the reading of the *because* clause. It is unlikely that the inference is made during the reading of the main clause. For the nonexperts, the relation between the two concepts is not available and, therefore, it is expected that they do not make the inference, neither in the implicit nor in

276   Leo Noordman, Wietske Vonk, Reinier Cozijn, and Stefan Frank

Table 12.3 *Mean reading and verification times (ms) in the expert–nonexpert experiments (the codes in the first column are for textual reference)*

	Delay	Reader	Measure	Explicit	Implicit	
				Information		
A1		Expert	Reading time	3027	3449	*
A2		Nonexpert	Reading time	3734	3845	
A3		Expert	Verification time	4438	4901	*
A4		Nonexpert	Verification time	3948	4431	*
B1		Expert	Reading time	3942	4222	*
B2	Immediate	Expert	Verification time	4569	4919	*
B3	Delayed	Expert	Verification time	4656	5950	*

* Significant difference

the explicit condition. Consequently, there should be no reading time difference between the two conditions.

In addition to the reading task, a verification task was used. One statement referred to the inferred relation between competitive position and exports. This statement used the concepts of the target sentence. For the example above, this statement was "The impaired competitive position caused a decline of the exports." Because experts are expected to make the inference during reading in the implicit as well as in the explicit condition, there should be no difference in verification times between the explicit and implicit conditions. Nonexperts are expected not to make the inference during reading but at the moment they have to verify the relation between the two concepts. As in the earlier experiments, the effect of the explicit information for the nonexperts should be that the verification time is shorter in the explicit condition than in the implicit condition. For the experts, but not for the nonexperts, the reading times of the target subordinate clause were significantly longer in the implicit condition than in the explicit condition (see Table 12.3, lines A1 and A2).

The difference for the experts was significantly greater than for the nonexperts. The verification latencies were shorter in the explicit condition than in the implicit condition for the nonexperts, but also for the experts (lines A3 and A4). The reading times support the conclusion that the experts made the inference during reading and the nonexperts did not. The verification latencies for the nonexperts confirmed this interpretation: They made the inferences only if they were explicitly requested to do so. The verification latencies for the experts showed a nonpredicted difference between the explicit and implicit conditions. These data suggest that experts make the inference both during reading and at verification. How can this result be explained? A likely interpretation is that the verification task sets the goal for the experts. They take the verification task as a challenge to exploit their expertise in evaluating statements in their expertise domain. As we have seen earlier, the goal can lead to more thorough processing and to inferencing. This is true for an instructed goal as well as for a self-imposed goal. According to this interpretation, the inference is activated during reading but is not sufficiently encoded for the verification task. The experts compute the inference again at verification, and this is due to their motivation in evaluating a statement in their expertise domain. This motivation-explanation is strengthened by the fact that the verification times for the experts are longer than for the nonexperts: The experts become more critical in the verification task. In agreement with this interpretation is the fact that no verification difference was observed in the earlier experiments in which reading time differences indicated an inference; in those experiments expertise did not play a role.

This interpretation presupposes that inferred information is not robustly encoded and decays over time more so than explicit information. The interpretation reminds us of results found for predictive inferences: Keefe and McDaniel (1993) found decreasing activation for predictive inferences over time; Cook, Limber, and O'Brien (2001) observed that predictive inferences are not robustly encoded so that they have to be computed again. The coding of the inference after reading is no longer sufficiently activated for performing the verification task. This leads to the prediction that the verification time difference between the explicit and implicit condition is greater in delayed verification than in immediate verification.

Decay of inferences. In an experiment similar to the previous one, a verification task was administered immediately after the target sentence was read or after the whole text (Simons, 1993). If the activation of the inference decreases over time, one expects that the difference in verification times between the explicit and implicit conditions increases over time and is greater after reading the text than after reading the target sentence. The reading times for the target subordinate clause in the implicit condition were longer than in the explicit condition (see Table 12.3, line B1). The verification latencies were significantly longer in the implicit condition than in the explicit condition (see Table 12.3, lines B2 and B3). Crucially, this difference was greater in the delayed condition than in the immediate condition.

The finding of shorter reading times in the explicit condition replicates the earlier results and confirms the theory that inferences that correspond to available knowledge are made during reading. The significant inter-action between implicit versus explicit condition and the moment of verification confirms that the inference is made during reading, that the inferred information is available immediately after reading the target sentence, but that the information after a delay is less available than information that was expressed in the text. Indeed, in the explicit condi-tion there was no difference between the immediate and the delayed verification.

Conclusion: The results of the experiments in this paper are firm evidence for the conclusion that the knowledge of the reader controls the online inferences. This conclusion is based on experiments in which the availability of knowledge about the topic has been established in an empirical way. Difference in knowledge was operationalized by manipu-lating the familiarity of the text materials and by manipulating the expertise of the readers. Next, we turn to the issue of how such effects might be incorporated into a computational cognitive model.

Modeling knowledge-based inference

Knowledge and inferences in computational models

Computational simulations of inference for text comprehension can be highly valuable for uncovering the cognitive processes and representa-tions that underlie the relation between knowledge, reading goal, and inferences. Because the generation of inferences depends to a large extent on the reader's (or listener's) world knowledge, models of this process should incorporate a knowledge base and be able to apply the subset of knowledge required for understanding the particular text under consideration. The problem here is that people have access to a vast amount of knowledge, any part of which may turn out to be relevant. The human discourse-comprehension system rarely seems to experience any problem finding exactly the required knowledge. In computational modeling, however, this is still an unsolved problem: How can a very large knowledge base be implemented and efficiently accessed in a cog-nitively plausible manner?

Early approaches

Several early models of discourse comprehension (e.g., Golden and Rumelhart, 1993; Kintsch, 1988; van den Broek, Risden, Fletcher, and Thurlow, 1996) dealt with (or, rather, avoided) this problem by including the required piece(s) of knowledge and (if anything) not much more. As argued by Frank, Koppen, Noordman, and Vonk (2008), such an ad hoc approach results in models the predictive value of which cannot be properly evaluated. This is because the behavior of such a model is usually demonstrated by applying it to a single text from some experimental study. As a consequence, the outcome is merely anecdotal: There is no set of results whose statistical reliability can be assessed. However, even if the model is tested on a range of texts (from a single experimental study), the inference work for each text is essentially done by the modeler rather than the model. This is because each text requires a different subset of total world knowledge, which needs to be hand-selected before the model can run. In such cases, it remains unclear how the model would fare if it would have to find the knowledge that is relevant for a particular text itself.

An alternative approach arose from early work in artificial intelligence (AI): "Frames" and "scripts" (Charniak, 1977; Schank and Abelson, 1977) were conceived to organize human knowledge into discrete packages, each dealing with a particular type of event or situation (e.g., there could be different scripts for "going to a restaurant," "going to the cinema," etc.). The system would then be able to process all stories that depend only on knowledge within the implemented frames and scripts. Although such knowledge structures became much less popular for AI systems in later years, they have been applied more recently as well (Mueller, 2004; 2007). As Kintsch (1988) rightly argues, however, the problem with frames and scripts is that they cannot model both the creativity and precision of discourse comprehension: They either employ too much knowledge and reasoning power (making them too inflexible) or not enough (making them too unconstraining).

The "microworld" approach

The "microworld" method of knowledge implementation (Frank et al., 2008) is similar to the frames-and-scripts approach in that the knowledge base is reduced to a small, well-defined domain, and all knowledge of this domain is incorporated in the model. The difference is that frames and scripts select a realistic part of human knowledge and (erroneously) treat it as if it were isolated from all the rest. In contrast, the microworld approach is to select a smaller world rather than a small part of the real world. This yields a small, but unrealistic, knowledge base that can be fully included in a model. That is, rather than assuming that the unimplemented knowledge is irrelevant (as in the frames-and-scripts approach), the assumption is that there *is no* unimplemented knowledge.

In the microworld approach, there is no attempt to model a realistic language user and to simulate the processing of realistic texts. This may appear like a serious drawback, but it does away with the problem of frames and scripts because texts that require unimplemented knowledge can never occur in the microworld approach. Consequently, the microworld approach allows one to run many simulations without ad hoc adaptation of the implemented knowledge and, therefore, to statistically evaluate a model's general predictions. A quantitative comparison between numerical measures of model and human behavior is not possible because the two knowledge bases are incomparable (in size, but most likely also in content). However, as Frank et al. (2008) explained, the same problem plagues models that incorporate only text-specific knowledge. Moreover, *qualitative* comparisons between microworld-model predictions and experimental findings are both possible and valuable. In such a qualitative comparison, a parameter of the model (or of its input) is manipulated in a way that corresponds to the experimental manipulation. To the extent that the effect of the manipulation on the model mirrors that of a human experiment, the model simulation was successful. This is demonstrated, for example, by the distributed situation space (DSS) model (Frank et al., 2003), which will be discussed below.

Implementing realistic world knowledge

Needless to say, the microworld approach to knowledge implementation is not optimal. Ideally, *all* of a reader's knowledge would be implemented, so that model predictions can directly (and quantitatively) be evaluated against human experimental data. Currently, the only feasible method for implementing realistically sized knowledge bases is to extract them automatically from large text corpora. Techniques for extracting word meaning from corpora have been around for quite some time; the best known being latent semantic analysis (Landauer and Dumais, 1997) and hyperspace analogue to language (Lund and Burgess, 1996). However, access to lexical semantics clearly does not suffice for discourse comprehension because a *propositional* semantics is needed. There have been several suggestions for combining word-meaning representations to yield the meaning of phrases, sentence, or propositions (e.g., Grefenstette and Sadrzadeh, 2011; Kintsch, 2001; Mitchell and Lapata, 2010), but it remains to be seen whether such an approach can ever yield knowledge about the meaning of propositions. After all, a proposition's meaning (and, in particular, its relation to other propositions) cannot usually be derived from the meanings of its predicate and arguments.

For example, the fact that traffic jams can cause one to be late for work is a piece of world knowledge that is not inherent to the meaning of the words "traffic jam," "work," and "late." Hence, we are skeptical about claims that combining word-meaning representations can give rise to the type of world knowledge required for text comprehension (see Frank et al., 2008, for a further discussion of this issue). This is not to say that automatic extraction of propositional knowledge from texts is impossible. In fact, recent work on this problem has yielded promising first results (e.g., Kintsch and Mangalath, 2011; Padó, Crocker, and Keller, 2009), although it did not yet lead to models that simulate knowledge-based causal inferences.

The question remains whether it is even theoretically possible to extract a significant part of a person's world knowledge from corpora. According to Glenberg and Robertson (2000), language comprehension often relies on our embodied experiences with the real world – knowledge that cannot be extracted from mere texts. Hence, knowledge extraction from text corpora may need to be integrated with extraction from data sets in other modalities (Andrews, Frank, and Vigliocco, in press). As such work is still in its infancy, the best available current option seems to be the microworld approach.

The distributed situation space model

The distributed situation space (DSS) model (Frank et al., 2003) simulates the generation of inferences not as logical reasoning but as the result of pattern matching to knowledge of the microworld. This knowledge is divided into knowledge of possible states of the world and knowledge of causal/temporal relation between states. Because the model makes no distinction between temporal and causal relations, we will simply refer to this part of knowledge as causal. Hence, story situations are states in the microworld and causal knowledge relates the states at consecutive points in story time. The model does not make use of surface form or textbase representations: Everything takes place at the level of Kintsch and van Dijk's (1978) situation model. Recent evidence indeed suggests that readers represent causal relations at the situational level only (Mulder and Sanders, 2012).

Formally, the state of affairs at one moment in a story is represented as a vector in high-dimensional *situation space*. This space is organized such that it encodes the probabilistic relations between all possible microworld situations. For example, the vector representation of "Bob plays soccer" also represents the fact that (with very high probability) Bob is outside, because (in this microworld) soccer is only played outside. Likewise, the same vector represents that it is very unlikely that Bob is inside. Note that these relations indeed occur at the level of the situation model and not in the textbase: They are relations within the microworld, not within a text.

Knowledge about the causal relations between time-consecutive microworld situations is encoded in a matrix that relates all situation-space dimensions to each other. For example, this matrix contains the knowledge that if Bob plays soccer he is likely to be tired soon but unlikely to have been tired just before. Hence, the temporal sequence of story events "Bob plays soccer (and then) Bob is tired" is more coherent than "Bob is tired (and then) Bob plays soccer."

The DSS model simulates the process of causal inference as follows: First, the situations described by a story text (so far) are encoded as situation-space vectors. Next, these vectors adapt to the causal know-ledge matrix, such that they come to fit this knowledge more closely without contradicting the story statements. As a result, the represented sequence of microworld situations gradually changes, increasing the probability of particular states of affairs and decreasing the probability of others. This comes down to inferring (to a certain extent) what is (and what is not) the case at each point in story time. This process continues until the vectors' total rate of change drops below a threshold value, set by the *depth-of-processing* parameter. The larger this parameter's value, the lower the threshold, and hence the longer the inference process takes to halt. The required amount of time before the threshold is reached serves as the model's prediction of the time needed to compre-hend (i.e., read) the current story statement.

As explained above, the microworld approach makes it impossible to directly compare human behavioral data on experimental texts to model predictions on the same texts. Nevertheless, the DSS model has been able to explain a number of important findings from the discourse-comprehension literature. For example, a story statement is read faster if it is more causally coherent with the previous statement (Myers, Shinjo, and Duffy, 1987) and the same relation holds in the model (Frank et al., 2003). Also, an extension to the DSS model for resolving referential ambiguity (Frank, Koppen, Noordman, and Vonk, 2007) correctly predicted, among others, how implicit causality affects reading times and pronoun-resolution error rates, and how this relation depends on processing depth.

In short, the DSS model simulates knowledge-based inferences in discourse comprehension and explains a number of findings from read-ing experiments. This raises the question of whether the model can also account for some of the results presented earlier in this chapter. As will become clear, the DSS model "as is" does not explain these results. However, it seems likely that its general framework, with relatively minor changes, does allow for simulating the reading experiments and that the results will be consistent with the experimental findings.

Simulating the effect of reading goals

To some extent, the effect of reading goal is captured by the model's depth-of-processing parameter. Increasing its value increases both modeled processing time and amount of inference (Frank et al., 2003). Noordman, Vonk, and Kempff (1992) compared reading for comprehension to reading for consistency checking (which, supposedly, requires deeper processing) and indeed found that the latter condition resulted in slower reading and more inferences (see Table 12.1, lines A1 and C1).

When participants were asked to read a text with the goal of answering a particular question, this facilitated the drawing of inferences only for facts that were relevant to the question at hand. This question-dependent effect of inference cannot be modeled by varying the one-dimensional depth-of-processing parameter, as it will affect the overall level of inference. What seems to be required is a mechanism for dynamically adapting processing depth to the current content of the text, something that lies far beyond the model's scope.

Simulating the effect of the presence of a conjunction

We have seen that the presence of a conjunction slows down reading at the end of the sentence and reduces off-line verification time (see Table 12.2), indicating that it facilitates the drawing of an inference. In a sense, it is as if the conjunction signals to the reader that comprehension effort must be temporarily increased. As such, the presence of a conjunction can be simulated in the DSS model in the same manner as the occurrence of deep processing owing to a specific reading goal – by increasing the value of the depth-of-processing parameter. The only difference would be that the increase in processing depth would be short-lived, applying only to the statements linked by a conjunction.

Simulating the effect of a reader's knowledge

The differences between nonexperts' and experts' causal knowledge can be modeled in a relatively straightforward manner by varying the content of the causal knowledge matrix. Although this has not yet been attempted, the outcome is easy to predict. Recall that the model processes a statement more quickly if it is more coherent with the previous statement. If the text states that "Q because P," and there is indeed a positive causal relation from P to Q encoded in the matrix (i.e., it models an expert), simulated reading time will be shorter than if the causal relation is not present in the matrix (i.e., it models a nonexpert). This indeed corresponds to the experimental results (see Table 12.3, lines A1 and A2).

How about the effect of the presence of an explicit statement about the causal relation between P and Q? For experts, this statement is said to activate the causal knowledge. For nonexperts, the explicit statement may lead to new world knowledge. The DSS model was never intended to simulate the update of world knowledge due to text statements, and "knowledge activation" has no meaning within the model. Nevertheless, we can speculate about how these operations can be captured within the DSS framework.

First, note that in the experiment described under "reading by experts and nonexperts," the explicit statement mentioned that a causal relation from P to Q exists without including the direction of the effect. That is, the statement was ambiguous between "if P then Q" and "if P then not Q." In either case, the statement would lead to the selection of the situation space vectors representing world states P and Q. The causal knowledge matrix can then be updated such that the relation from P to Q is strengthened.[1] However, the two states are not yet linked in the knowledge matrix of a nonexpert and since the direction of the effect is absent from the explicit statement it is unknown whether the connections from P to Q should receive positive or negative values. Hence, the matrix cannot be updated. This problem does not occur in the expert knowledge matrix because P and Q are already linked, be it positively or negatively. The result is that only when simulating an expert does the explicit statement increase the coherence of the text "Q because P." Indeed, this is what the experiment showed: The explicit condition resulted in faster reading by experts but not by nonexperts (see Table 12.3, lines A1 and A2).

Conclusion: The experiments presented in this chapter indicate that inferences about causal relations are made during reading only if the relations are part of the reader's knowledge: Inferences depend on the availability of knowledge. How can we account for this role of world knowledge? The memory-based approach to discourse processing seems to offer a plausible framework, but a problem for this approach is to

---

[1] In much the same way, the matrix values are originally learned from many examples of consecutive microworld situations.

specify what available knowledge is. Available knowledge should be specified independently of the reading results; otherwise, one makes a circular argument. That is, if certain inferences are made during reading, for example, concerning a visit to a restaurant, the explanation is that the restaurant script is available, but if no instrumental inferences are made for stirring coffee, the explanation is that the instrument is not easily available. In the research we discussed in this paper, world knowledge was identified in an empirical way and independently of results of a reading task. World knowledge was manipulated in two ways: by varying the texts and by varying the reader's knowledge. In the first experiments, the familiarity of the inferences in the texts was manipulated. In the subsequent experiments, the knowledge of the readers was manipulated. The results of both series of experiments converged: Inference behavior depends on the availability of world knowledge. This can be accommodated nicely in the memory-based processing framework.

Inferences about *unfamiliar* causal relations are not made during reading. This is the case even if the presence of a conjunction signals the inference to be made. However, these inferences are made if required by the reader's goal. Two types of goal have been investigated. goals defined in terms of a specific topic that the reader should pay attention to and goals defined in terms of the demands of the task, for example, a question-answering task or a verification task. The explanation of the effect of topic-goal is not that the goal activated the causal relations that have to be inferred, because these relations were not familiar. The explanation of the effect of both kinds of goal is that they urge the reader to process the information in the texts more deeply. Inferences about *familiar* causal relations are made during reading. But making these inferences requires the presence of a causal conjunction.

The inference behavior of experts and nonexperts confirms these results. We first investigated the knowledge representation of experts and nonexperts in economics and identified relations between economic concepts that were part of the knowledge representation of experts but not of nonexperts. Experts made the inferences about these causal relations during reading, although nonexperts did not. Again, the nonexperts did make the inference when they were requested to do so in a verification task. Interestingly, the experts made the inference both during reading and during the verification task after reading. This means that experts, when asked to verify a statement in their expertise domain, are extra motivated to process the information thoroughly and to make the inference. The effect of the explicit information, diagnostic for an inference, was stronger in delayed verification than in immediate verification. This suggests that inferred information decays over time.

Can we account for these results in a computational model? The answer is no, because we don't have an implementation of the economic knowledge of experts and nonexperts. However, our distributed situation space model can simulate knowledge-based inferences and explain a number of phenomena that we observed in the experiments. The effects of the reading goal, defined in terms of instructed task, can be explained in terms of the depth of processing parameter. Increasing its value leads to slower reading and more inferencing. The same is true for the effect of the conjunction, although there is no mechanism yet for restricting the effect to the clauses connected by the conjunction. The fact that the explicit information speeds up the reading time for the target sentence for experts and not for nonexperts can be accommodated in the DSS framework by the fact that the relation between two situations in the model is strengthened for experts and not for the nonexperts, since the two states are not connected for the nonexperts. This same difference in knowledge representation in the model can explain the shorter reading time for a *because* sentence by the experts than by the nonexperts.

The present chapter highlights the importance of the reader's knowledge for inference processes and illustrates how current computational models fall short in this respect. Although the explanation of the experimental findings described here requires a further elaboration of the DSS model so as to include a very large knowledge base that can be accessed in a cognitive plausible way, the model can in principle simulate causal inference processes and explain a number of findings of discourse processing studies.

REFERENCES

Albrecht, J. E., & O'Brien, E. J. (1993). Updating a mental model: maintaining both local and global coherence. *Journal of Experimental Psychology: Learning, Memory, and Cognition, 19,* 1061–70.

Andrews, M., Frank, S. L., & Vigliocco, G. (in press). Reconciling embodied and distributional accounts of meaning in language. *Topics in Cognitive Science.*

Charniak, E. (1977). A framed PAINTING: the representation of a commonsense knowledge fragment. *Cognitive Science, 1,* 355–94.

Cook, A. E., Limber, J. E., & O'Brien, E. J. (2001). Situation-based context and the availability of predictive inferences. *Journal of Memory and Language, 44,* 220–34.

Cozijn, R., Commandeur, E., Vonk, W., & Noordman, L. G. M. (2011). The time course of the use of implicit causality information in the processing of pronouns: a visual world paradigm study. *Journal of Memory and Language, 64*(4), 381–403.

Cozijn, R., Noordman, L. G. M., & Vonk, W. (2011). Propositional integration and world-knowledge inference: processes in understanding *because* sentences. *Discourse Processes, 48*(7), 474–500.

Frank, S. L., Koppen, M., Noordman, L. G. M., & Vonk, W. (2003). Modeling knowledge-based inferences in story comprehension. *Cognitive Science, 27,* 875–910.

(2007). Coherence-driven resolution of referential ambiguity: a computational model. *Memory & Cognition, 35,* 1307–22.

(2008). World knowledge in computational models of discourse comprehension. *Discourse Processes, 45,* 429–63.

Gerrig, R. J., & McKoon, G. (1998). The readiness is all: the functionality of memory-based text processing. *Discourse Processes, 26,* 67–86.

Gerrig, R. J., & O'Brien, E. J. (2005). The scope of memory-based processing. *Discourse Processes, 39,* 225–42.

Glenberg, A. M., & Robertson, D. A. (2000). Symbol grounding and meaning: a comparison of high-dimensional and embodied theories of meaning. *Journal of Memory and Language, 43,* 379–401.

Golden, R. M., & Rumelhart, D. E. (1993). A parallel distributed processing model of story comprehension and recall. *Discourse Processes, 16,* 203–37.

Graesser, A. C., & Clark, L. F. (1985). *Structures and Procedures of Implicit Knowledge.* Norwood: Ablex.

Graesser, A. C., Singer, M., & Trabasso, T. (1994). Constructing inferences during narrative text comprehension. *Psychological Review, 101,* 371–95.

Grefenstette, E., & Sadrzadeh, M. (2011). Experimental support for a categorical compositional distributional model of meaning. In *Proceedings of the 2011 Conference on Empirical Methods in Natural Language Processing* (pp. 1394–1404). Edinburgh, UK: Association for Computational Linguistics.

Kant, E. (2004). *Kritiek van de zuivere rede* (J. Veenbaas & W. Visser, Trans.). (*Original work, Kritik der reinen Vernunft [Critique of Pure Reason], published in 1781*). Amsterdam: Boom.

Keefe, D. E., & McDaniel, M. A. (1993). The time course and durability of predictive inferences. *Journal of Memory and Language, 32,* 446–63.

Kintsch, W. (1988). The role of knowledge in discourse comprehension: a construction-integration model. *Psychological Review, 95,* 163–82.

(2001). Predication. *Cognitive Science, 25,* 173–202.

Kintsch, W., & Mangalath, P. (2011). The construction of meaning. *Topics in Cognitive Science, 3,* 346–70.

Kintsch, W., & Van Dijk, T. A. (1978). Toward a model of text comprehension and production. *Psychological Review, 85,* 363–94.

Landauer, T. K., & Dumais, S. T. (1997). A solution to Plato's problem: the latent semantic analysis theory of acquisition, induction, and representation of knowledge. *Psychological Review, 104,* 211–40.

Levinson, S. C. (1983). *Pragmatics.* Cambridge: Cambridge University Press.

Lund, K., & Burgess, C. (1996). Producing high-dimensional semantic spaces from lexical co-occurrence. *Behavior Research Methods, Instruments, & Computers, 28,* 203–8.

McKoon, G., & Ratcliff, R. (1992). Inference during reading. *Psychological Review*, *99*, 440–66.

Mitchell, J., & Lapata, M. (2010). Composition in distributional models of semantics. *Cognitive Science*, *34*, 1388–1429.

Mueller, E. T. (2004). Understanding script-based stories using commonsense reasoning. *Cognitive Systems Research*, *5*, 307–340.

(2007). Modelling space and time in narratives about restaurants. *Literary and Linguistic Computing*, *22*, 67–84.

Mulder, G., & Sanders, T. J. M. (2012). Causal coherence relations and levels of discourse representation. *Discourse Processes*, *49*, 501–22.

Myers, J. L., & O'Brien, E. J. (1998). Accessing the discourse representation during reading. *Discourse Processes*, *26*, 131–57.

Myers, J. L., O'Brien, E. J., Albrecht, J. E., & Mason, R. A. (1994). Maintaining global coherence. *Journal of Experimental Psychology: Learning, Memory, and Cognition*, *20*, 876–86.

Myers, J. L., Shinjo, M., & Duffy, S. A. (1987). Degree of causal relatedness and memory. *Journal of Memory and Language*, *26*, 453–65.

Noordman, L. G. M. (2005). *Taal en Kennis. [Language and Cognition]*. Valedictory lecture. Tilburg University.

Noordman, L. G. M., & Vonk, W. (1992). Readers' knowledge and the control of inferences in reading. *Language and Cognitive Processes*, *7*, 373–91.

(in press). Inferences in discourse, psychology of. In J. D. Wright (ed.), *International Encyclopedia of the Social and Behavioral Sciences* (2nd ed.). Amsterdam: Elsevier.

Noordman, L. G. M., Vonk, W., & Kempff, H. J. (1992). Causal inferences during the reading of expository texts. *Journal of Memory and Language*, *31*, 573–90.

Noordman, L. G. M., Vonk, W., & Simons, W. H. G. (2000). Knowledge representation in the domain of economics. In L. Lundquist & R. J. Jarvella (eds.), *Language, Text, and Knowledge: Mental Models of Expert Communication* (pp. 235–60). Berlin/New York: Mouton de Gruyter.

O'Brien, E. J. (1995). Automatic components of discourse comprehension. In R. F. Lorch & E. J. O'Brien (eds.), *Sources of Coherence in Reading* (pp. 159–76). Mahwah, NJ: Erlbaum.

Padó, U., Crocker, M. W., & Keller, F. (2009). A probabilistic model of semantic plausibility in sentence processing. *Cognitive Science*, *33*, 794–838.

Ratcliff, R. (1978). A theory of memory retrieval. *Psychological Review*, *85*, 59–108.

Schank, R. C., & Abelson, R. P. (1977). *Scripts, Plans, Goals, and Understanding*. Mahwah, NJ: Erlbaum.

Simons, W. H. G. (1993). *De regulering van inferenties door de kennis van de lezer [The control of inferences by the knowledge of the reader]*. Doctoral dissertation, University of Nijmegen.

Singer, M. (1994). Discourse inference processes. In M. A. Gernsbacher (ed.), *Handbook of Psycholinguistics* (pp. 479–516). San Diego: Academic Press.

(2007). Inference processes in discourse comprehension. In M. G. Gaskell (ed.), *The Oxford Handbook of Psycholinguistics* (pp. 343–59). Oxford University Press.

Singer, M., & O'Connell, G. (2003). Robust inference processes in expository text comprehension. *European Journal of Cognitive Psychology*, *15*, 607–31.

Van den Broek, P. (1994). Comprehension and memory of narrative texts: inferences and coherence. In M. A. Gernsbacher (ed.), *Handbook of Psycholinguistics* (pp. 539–88). San Diego, CA: Academic Press.

Van den Broek, P., Risden, K., Fletcher, C. R., & Thurlow, R. (1996). A "landscape" view of reading: fluctuating patterns of activation and the construction of a stable memory representation. In B. K. Britton & A. C. Graesser (eds.), *Models of Understanding Text* (pp. 165–87). Mahwah, NJ: Erlbaum.

Van Dijk, T. A., & Kintsch, W. (1983). *Strategies of Discourse Comprehension*. New York: Academic Press.

Vonk, W., & Noordman, L. G. M. (1990). On the control of inferences in text understanding. In D. A. Balota, G. B. Flores d'Arcais, & K. Rayner (eds.), *Comprehension Processes in Reading* (pp. 447–64). Mahwah, NJ: Erlbaum.

(2001). Inferences in discourse, psychology of. In N. J. Smelser & P. B. Baltes (eds.), *International Encyclopedia of the Social and Behavioral Sciences* (pp. 7427–32). Amsterdam: Elsevier.

13 Constructing inferences in naturalistic reading contexts

Arthur C. Graesser, Haiying Li, and Shi Feng

Twenty-five years ago my colleagues and I (the first author of this chapter) were in an intense debate over what inferences are generated during text comprehension. It was a lively debate. At the one end there was the *minimalist* position that predicted the only inferences that were encoded were those that were activated quickly by associations in long-term memory and those that were triggered by obstacles in text cohesion that forced more deliberate thought (McKoon and Ratcliff, 1992). At the other end was the *promiscuous* position, typically by researchers outside of psychology (ranging from literature to computer science) that postulated that a very large and unconstrained set of inferences were generated by virtue of background knowledge and experiences. My research team advocated an intermediate *constructionist* position (Graesser, Singer, and Trabasso, 1994; Singer, Graesser, and Trabasso, 1994) that attempted to predict what subset of inferences are generated on the basis of what we know about social, discourse, and cognitive mechanisms. These mechanisms stretched beyond the memory-based models of the minimalist position and into concerns of the goals and emotions of people and the explanations of events that occur in our everyday worlds. A book edited by Graesser and Bower (1990) articulated the various theoretical positions, methods to study inference generation, and of course empirical data.

A flurry of models and empirical findings evolved in the 1990s in an effort to pin down what inferences were generated under what conditions. The models also aspired to achieve more general goals of specifying the discourse representations that are encoded during comprehension, the processes of generating these representations, and performance on different tasks. The research efforts were captured in several edited volumes from the mid to late 1990s that covered psychological research on text comprehension, inference generation, coherence, and other components of deeper levels of understanding (Britton and Graesser, 1996; Goldman, Graesser, and van den Broek, 1999; Goldman and van Oostendorp, 1999; Lorch and O'Brien, 1995; Weaver, Mannes, and

Fletcher, 1995; Zwaan and van Oostendorp, 1993). Below are a sample of these models and their signature claims.

1. *Construction-integration model* (Kintsch, 1998). Comprehension is guided by the bottom-up activation of knowledge in long-term memory from textual input and contents in working memory (the *construction* phase), followed by the integration of activated ideas in working memory (the *integration* phase). As each sentence or clause in a text is comprehended, there is a construction phase followed by an integration phase.
2. *Structure building framework* (Gernsbacher, 1990). Information structures are built during comprehension but cohesion gaps force the reader to build new structures. Inferences are needed to conceptually relate structures that are weakly related.
3. *Memory-resonance models* (Cook, Halleran, and O'Brien, 1998; Myers and O'Brien, 1998; O'Brien, Rizzella, Albrecht, and Halleran, 1998). Inferences are generated to the extent that there is a resonance between world knowledge and text cues plus contents of working memory.
4. *Event indexing model* (Zwaan, Magliano, and Graesser, 1995; Zwaan and Radvansky, 1998). Inferences are generated when there is a break in causal, intentional (goals), spatial, and/or temporal cohesion.
5. *Landscape model* (van den Broek, Risden, Fletcher, and Thurlow, 1996). Inferences are activated by text and world knowledge to establish referential and causal cohesion.
6. *Embodied and indexical models* (Glenberg, 1997; Glenberg and Robertson, 1999). Inferences are needed to elaborate the perceptions, actions, and emotions of characters in the situation model.

It appeared that each research team had its own sketch of inference mechanisms as they attempted to sort out the contributions of text characteristics, world knowledge, working memory, comprehension strategies, and task constraints.

In the midst of this blossoming of models and empirical work on inferences and discourse representations in the late 1990s, an unexpected series of events unfolded that shined the spotlight on studies of inference generation and text comprehension in the national arena. There was substantial funding behind the momentum. The Institute of Education Sciences of the U.S. Department of Education was launched at the beginning of the new millennium. Substantial funding was influenced by some research panel reports that emphasized the need to better understand comprehension mechanisms (such as the *Reading for Understanding* report of the National Research Council; Snow, 2002) and the need to better understand learning at deeper levels of mastery (Brans-ford, Brown, and Cocking, 2000). The National Science Foundation and the Office of Naval Research had a series of interdisciplinary initia-tives that focused on the learning sciences, discourse comprehension, automated natural language processing, intelligent tutoring systems, and other computer technologies that promote deeper learning, comprehen-sion, problem solving, and reasoning. Revolutionary advances in com-puter science, computational linguistics, and information retrieval changed the landscape of research avenues for some of us who had been investigating discourse comprehension. For the first time in history, we could get electronic access to a large repository of thousands (if not millions) of documents for computer analyses. We could analyze the texts with lexicons, syntactic parsers, and semantic analyzers developed in computational linguistics (Jurafsky and Martin, 2008) and statistical models of world knowledge (Landauer, McNamara, Dennis, and Kintsch, 2007). The world had changed.

These trends fundamentally changed the direction of research for many of us. Our focus shifted from systematic experimental studies designed to discriminate models of comprehension (including infer-ences) to more applied but equally scientific directions. By the year 2000, the research teams at the University of Memphis were building automated computer systems with conversational agents (talking heads), such as AutoTutor and iSTART, that helped students better understand science texts by holding conversations in natural language (Graesser, Jeon, and Dufty, 2008; Graesser, Lu, Jackson, Mitchell, Ventura, Olney, and Louwerse, 2004a; Graesser and Lehman, 2012; McNamara, O'Reilly, Best, and Ozuru, 2006). Developing such systems required an interdisciplinary intersection of computer science, psychology, educa-tion, and linguistics. We were building automated text analysis systems, such as Coh-Metrix, that analyzed discourse automatically at multiple levels: words, syntax, discourse cohesion, and genre (Graesser, McNa-mara, and Kulikowich, 2011; Graesser, McNamara, Louwerse, and Cai, 2004b; McNamara, Graesser, McCarthy, and Cai, 2014). We were using eye-tracking methodologies to analyze college students' comprehension of naturalistic materials, such as illustrated texts from Maccauly's (1988) *The Way Things Work* (Graesser, Lu, Olde, Cooper-Pye, and Whitten, 2005) and survey questions on the U.S. Census (Graesser, Cai, Louwerse, and Daniel, 2006). Our research world was shifting from the tight experimental paradigms that investigated *textoids* (texts created by experimental psychologists and linguists) and short discourse seg-ments to automated systems, complex learning, and lengthy naturalistic texts. Some of our colleagues may have viewed us as going down the primrose path, but others viewed our efforts as having a good balance between science in the lab and science in the real world.

This chapter has two major goals. Our first goal is to articulate the constructionist model of inference generation (Graesser et al., 1994) and to reflect on where it stands today, over two decades later. We will particularly focus on its three distinctive components: reader goals, coherence, and explanation. These three components are receiving considerable research attention today, just as they did decades ago. Our second goal is to briefly identify some ways that automated computer analyses can help researchers solve some of the theoretical and empirical challenges in investigations of inferences during comprehension.

The constructionist model: what does it claim and where does it stand today?

The constructionist model of Graesser et al. (1994) was originally designed to account for the inferences that readers generate during narrative comprehension. Readers generally have a sufficient body of experiences and background world knowledge to understand the episodes and supporting content of narrative texts, so many inferences are expected to be constructed (Graesser, 1981; Hiebert and Mesmer, 2013). The model was extended to science texts (Graesser and Bertus, 1998; Millis and Graesser, 1994) with some modest success, but inferences are limited because of the lack of background knowledge on most science topics. As with virtually all other psychological models of inference generation, the constructionist model assumes that readers have a rich background of declarative and experiential world knowledge in long-term memory that is activated during comprehension and that is recruited to fill in inferences. The model also assumes, along with other models, that there is a working memory that holds a limited amount of information and a discourse focus that holds prominent words or ideas in the mind's eye.

Nevertheless, memory activations are not sufficient according to the constructionist model. Comprehension also is to some extent directed and strategic. The distinctive strategies of this model are reflected in its three principal assumptions: reader goals, coherence, and explanation. The *reader goal* assumption states that readers attend to content in the text that is relevant to the goals of the reader. For example, advertisements in a newspaper are written and read for very different purposes than factual news reports. The *coherence* assumption states that readers attempt to construct meaning representations that are coherent at both local and global levels. Cohesion gaps in the text will stimulate the reader to think actively, generate inferences, and reinterpret the text in an effort to fill in, repair, or acknowledge the cohesion gap. The *explanation* assumption states that good readers tend to generate explanations of *why* events and actions in the text occur, *why* states exist, and *why* the author bothers expressing particular ideas. Why-questions encourage analysis of goals or plans of characters, of causal mechanisms, of justifications of claims, and other deeper levels of understanding.

The constructionist model set the bar higher on what it means to comprehend text than the minimalist position, memory-based models, and the construction integration model. It also was more attentive to the social, biological, and developmental worlds of humans. The constructionist model emphasized that people are trying to achieve goals, are experiencing emotions when the goals are blocked versus achieved, are explaining what is happening in the world to ensure survival and satisfaction, and are sometimes wanting to be entertained. However, the constructionist model was limited by the fact that the deeper inferences relied so much on world knowledge, and also the fact that the reader's goals were potentially so ad hoc that a science could never emerge from the reader-goal assumption. This raises the question of where the science is, the question to which we turn.

Reader goal assumption

This assumption is trivial and nonscientific if the underlying claim is that readers generate inferences that address their goals. The obvious prediction would be that explicit information and inferences that are relevant to a person's goals would have a privileged status compared to irrelevancies. If we take orienting questions as a type of goal for reading, then eye-tracking studies confirm that relevant information is inspected more thoroughly than irrelevant information (Graesser and Lehman, 2012; Lewis and Mensink, 2012; McCrudden, Schraw, and Kambe, 2005; Reynolds and Anderson, 1982; Rothkopf and Billington, 1979; Wiley, Goldman, Graesser, Sanchez, Ash, and Hemmerich, 2009) and inferences follow this direction as well (Graesser, Baggett, and Williams, 1996; Narvaez, van den Broek, and Ruiz, 1999). Such results confirm theory and intuitions. Although that is the case, the claim lacks teeth unless there are systematic mechanisms that generate the goals and questions. A theory of goal and question generation is needed before this claim is theoretically interesting. We contend that two mechanisms are at the heart of generating questions and goals: cognitive disequilibrium and genre. We believe that these two mechanisms will fortify the constructionist theory's reader goal assumption over and above the ad hoc and circular prediction that inferences are generated if they are relevant to the idiosyncratic goals of the reader.

A cognitive disequilibrium framework has been sketched to integrate a number of psychological processes: confusion (and other learning-centered emotions), question asking (inquiry), deliberative thought, inferences, and deeper learning. Cognitive disequilibrium is a state that occurs when people face obstacles to goals, interruptions, contradictions, incongruities, anomalies, impasses, uncertainty, and salient contrasts (Barth and Funke, 2010; D'Mello and Graesser, 2012; Festinger, 1957; Graesser, Lu, Olde, Cooper-Pye, and Witten, 2005). Initially the person experiences various emotions when beset with cognitive disequilibrium, but notably confusion, frustration, surprise, or curiosity (D'Mello and Graesser, 2012; D'Mello, Lehman, Pekrun, and Graesser, 2014; Graesser and D'Mello, 2012; Lehman, D'Mello, and Graesser, 2012). This elicits question asking and other forms of inquiry (Graesser, Lu et al., 2005; Graesser and McMahen, 1993; Otero and Graesser, 2001), such as social interaction, physical exploration of the environment, the monitoring of focal attention, and inference generation. Why does the impasse occur? What can be done? The person engages in inference generation, problem solving, reasoning, and other thoughtful cognitive activities in an attempt to resolve the impasse and restore cognitive equilibrium.

Cohesion breaks, contradictions, and misinformation trigger such questions and inferences during text comprehension for proficient readers. Discourse processing studies have confirmed that additional time for inference generation and elaboration occurs when an event, action, or state in the text contradicts earlier information (Blanc, Kendeou, van den Broek, and Brouillet, 2008; Cook et al., 1998; Hyona, Lorch, and Rinck, 2003; Myers and O'Brien, 1998; Myers, O'Brien, Albrecht, and Mason, 1994; O'Brien et al., 1998) or when the text statement is incompatible with prior knowledge of a reader (Maier and Richter, 2013; van Oostendorp, 2003; Rapp, 2008). This mechanism is also compatible with the coherence assumption.

The cognitive disequilibrium construct would ideally extend to the reading of multiple texts. That is, readers would discover when the claims or inferences in different texts are compatible (drawing a generalization) or incompatible (creating cognitive disequilibrium). Researchers have recently investigated comparisons among texts in multiple documents when processing the plausibility of a claim (Braasch, Rouet, Vibert, and Britt, 2012; Bråten and Strømsø, 2006; Britt and Rouet, 2012; Goldman, Braasch, Wiley, Graesser, and Brodowinska, 2012; Perfetti, Rouet, and Britt, 1999; Stadtler, Scharrer, Brummernhenrich, and Bromme, 2013; Wiley et al., 2009). Many readers have difficulty integrating content from multiple documents and often miss contradictory information. This may change if students are trained to take a more critical stance and to acquire a more fine-tuned palate on comparison of meanings among different texts (called intertextuality). Contradictions in text and conversation are most likely to be detected when they are contiguous in time, discourse, and working memory.

Text genre is the other component that gives the reader goal assumption some teeth in making discriminating predictions. There are salient questions that are associated with different text genres and these questions go a long way in predicting the inferences that readers generate (Graesser and Lehman, 2012). In a narrative text, the relevant questions during the setting are who?, what?, where?, and when? but the questions shift to why? and so what? when the plot occurs. In persuasive texts, the underlying questions are what does the writer believe?, why is the writer telling me this?, what is the argument?, and do I agree with the writer? When the text has the function of giving directions to a destination (i.e., instructions in a map to a party), the relevant questions are where is the destination? and how do I get there? When the text is a procedure or recipe, the questions are how do I enact the procedure?, what can go wrong?, and how do I know if I succeed? A text on purchasing a car would have questions such as, how is car X similar or different from car B? A text in a claim of an evidence frame would have questions such as what is the claim? How does X support the claim? Why do people doubt the claim? There are, of course, other questions for other genres. We propose that there are a limited number of genres in a culture, there are distinctive questions associated with each genre, and these questions drive the goals and inferences that readers encode during comprehension. These hypotheses are, of course, quite plausible, but empirical evidence is needed to support them.

Coherence and explanation assumptions

The constructionist model offered some discriminating predictions about the classes of inferences that are consistently, if not automatically and unconsciously, encoded during comprehension. Table 13.1 lists the predictions for twelve categories of inferences and the status of whether the inference is generated. Of course, any of these inferences could be generated if the reader adopts idiosyncratic goals that target a particular class of inferences (e.g., the reader is tracking the personality of one of the characters) or if the inference is highly activated by idiosyncratic prior experiences (e.g., the reader's occupation matches that of a particular

Table 13.1 *Inference classes and their status of being generated during comprehension according to the constructionist model of Graesser, Singer, and Trabasso (1994)*

	Inference category	Description of inference	Constructed during comprehension?
1	Referential	A word/phrase is referentially linked to a previous element or constituent in the text	Yes
2	Causal antecedent	The inference is on a causal chain between the current explicit action/event/state and the previous passage context	Yes
3	Causal consequence	The inference is on a forecasted causal chain into the future, including events and new plans of characters	No
4	Character emotional reaction	The inference is an emotion experienced by a character directly caused by an event or action	Yes
5	Superordinate goals	The inference is a goal that motivates a character's intentional action	Yes
6	Subordinate goal	The inference is a plan or action that specifies how a character's action is achieved	No
7	Instrument	The inference is an object, part of the body, or resource used when a character performs an action	No
8	Subcategory of noun	The inference is a subcategory or exemplar of an explicit noun	No
9	States of people and objects	Inferences about static properties of characters, objects, and spatial layout	No
10	Thematic	The main point or moral of the text	Yes
11	Author's intent	The inference is the author's motive in writing or attitude	No
12	Emotion of reader	The inference is the emotion that the reader is expected to experience	No

character). The predictions in Table 13.1 reflect the coherence and explanation assumptions of the constructionist model.

Table 13.1 specifies that only five out of the twelve classes of inferences are encoded during comprehension. The referential (class 1) and causal antecedent inferences (class 2) are constructed by virtue of the coherence assumption. The causal antecedent (class 2), character emotional reactions (class 4), superordinate goals (class 5), and thematic inferences (class 10) are constructed by virtue of the explanation assumption. The latter are answers to why questions:

Why did the event occur? (class 2, causal antecedent)
Why did the character do something? (class 5, superordinate goal)
Why did the author write this? (class 10, thematic)

The emotional reactions (class 4) are constructed by virtue of the intuition that emotional reactions of characters (e.g., happiness, anger, fear)
are motivated by the goals of other characters who try to elicit the
emotions or by the author trying to have an emotional impact.

The remaining classes of inferences are not predicted to be routinely
generated during the comprehension of narrative texts. Some are mere
elaborations of nouns (classes 8 and 9) and character actions (classes
6 and 7) that are not sufficiently constrained by context. Causal consequences were not generated because most predictions about the future
plot do not end up being correct because they are insufficiently constrained by prior context (Graesser, 1981). The author's intent (class 11)
and emotions of the reader (class 12) tap the communicative exchange
between the author and reader, once again being insufficiently constrained by context. To most readers, the author is invisible.

It is noteworthy that other models of inference generation make rather
different predictions than the constructionist model, although there
is some overlap in the predictions. The minimalist position predicts
classes 1 and 2, but not 3 through 12. Interestingly, nine of twelve of
the predictions overlap between the constructionist and minimalist positions. The embodiment and indexical position predict that the manner
in which actions are executed are generated during comprehension (e.g.,
the style and path in which a gangster drives to the hideout in a mystery),
but that is irrelevant information according to the constructionist model.
It is difficult to know how many of the twelve predictions match with the
constructionist model because the embodiment and indexical hypothesis
are silent on so many predictions. Quite clearly, it is difficult to compare
the models when the scope and decisiveness of the predictions vary.

There are challenges in comparing models when the models are pro-
gressively more statistical and complex. The construction-integration
model (Kintsch, 1998) and the landscape model (van den Broek et al.,
1996) are the most quantitatively sophisticated models for comparison.
They have a suite of parameters in the models that generate the activation
levels of potential inferences at various points in time as texts are read,
sentence by sentence. That quantitative infrastructure presents a foundation for generating quantitative predictions, but the downside is that
the predictions are dependent on the parameters and any judgments that
the human modelers incorporate in the formulas. These limitations
compromise the decisiveness of predictions. To compare models, a

researcher would need to model the degree to which a set of inferences $(I_1, I_2, \ldots I_n)$ had corresponding encoding values $(A_1, A_2, \ldots A_n)$ that fit a set of performance measures on the inferences $(M_1, M_2, \ldots M_n)$, such as word naming latencies or recall proportions. The predictions of each model would need to be compared on an even playing field. A large space of parameters would need to be tried out to give each model its fair test. Such endeavors require quite a bit of work. The bar may simply be too high.

One criticism of the constructionist theory is that it gave discrete predictions of what inference classes were versus were not generated rather than giving a continuous set of values. Our reply has always been that our critics are correct, but we were at a pre-paradigmatic stage of research when we were trying to get an approximate handle on prospects of likely inferences. We were never extremely worried about this criticism because there is a long history of comparisons between discrete and continuous models in mathematics and computational sciences. Models in the two traditions are essentially interchangeable. One can test a discrete model in which inferences are encoded if they are activated to the point of meeting a distribution of thresholds, the researcher can vary the thresholds and inspect the output. Interpreting such data is comparable to interpreting the activation values of a continuous model.

One of the luxuries of developing a model is that you have the opportunity to be its most incisive critic. Doubts about our constructionist theory arose in our research teams at the turn of the millennium. The doubts were not prompted by details of experimental findings or quantitative modeling fits, both of which could be salvaged by creative interpretations of the data. There were two major sources of doubts. The first doubt and worry is that our findings were restricted to narrative texts and could not scale up to other text genres. For example, the minimalist position trumped the constructionist position when we investigated expository texts on physics (Graesser, D'Mello, Hu, Cai, Olney, and Morgan, 2012; VanLehn, Graesser, Jackson, Jordan, Olney, and Rose, 2007) and computer literacy (Graesser et al., 2004a). In essence, when students read textbooks on these subject matters and were later given tests on inferences, the performance on such tests were no different between a condition in which college students read the text and a condition when they did nothing. As another example, the embodiment and indexical model (Glenberg, 1997; Glenberg and Robertson, 1999) was likely to trump the constructionist position when the comprehender had to understand directions to execute a procedure, assemble a piece of equipment, or understand the directions to a destination. Subordinate goals (class 6), instruments (class 7), and visual-spatial states (class 9) were likely to play a more salient role in these contexts. We could, of course, salvage the constructionist model by appealing to reader goals, but that would open the door to an endless array of ad hoc predictions. We fundamentally recognized the importance of text genre and that the constructionist model could not explain the differences among genre.

These concerns never led us to doubt the prominence of coherence and explanation in the inference mechanism, however. Coherence has a robust impact on constraining what inferences are encoded versus merely activated (Kintsch, 1998). Causal explanations play a fundamental role in constraining the inferences that are generated during comprehension (Briner, Virtue, and Kurby, in review; Graesser and Bertus, 1998; Millis and Graesser, 1994; Singer, Andruslak, Reisdorf, and Black, 1992; van den Broek et al., 1996; van den Broek, Rapp, and Kendeou, 2005; Zwaan and Radvansky, 1998) and that inoculate the reader from accepting and remembering false claims in texts (Kendeou, Smith, and O'Brien, 2013). Coherence and explanation continue to be accepted as powerful constructs in contemporary research in discourse psychology.

The second doubt arose when we considered scaling up our findings to the real world. The NRC *Reading for Understanding* report (Snow, 2002) emphasized the importance of considering the texts, tasks, and reader in a sociological context when improving reading comprehension. Unfortunately, we found our field of discourse processing in need of improvement in considering these components. There needed to be better understanding of the variability of texts, tasks, readers, and sociological context. Our approach to this challenge was to develop technologies to help us analyze the landscape.

Language and discourse technology

This is a unique point in history because there is widespread access to hundreds of computer tools that analyze specific texts and large text corpora. Advances in computational linguistics (Jurafsky and Martin, 2008), statistical representations of world knowledge (Landauer et al., 2007), and corpus analyses (Biber, Conrad, and Reppen, 1998) have allowed us to analyze texts on objective criteria and thereby provide a broader and more precise analysis of text characteristics.

Our research team has devoted considerable effort in using technologies to analyze characteristics of texts and to develop tasks (interventions) that promote both learning and assessment of comprehension. This section provides highlights of these two efforts. Although our efforts have implications for scaling readers on various abilities and for automatically analyzing sociocultural contexts, these aspects will not be addressed in this chapter.

Automated scaling of texts on multiple levels of language and discourse

We developed Coh-Metrix to scale texts on hundreds of dimensions of language and discourse (Graesser et al., 2004b; Graesser et al., 2011; McNamara et al., 2014). The original purpose of the Coh-Metrix project was to concentrate on the cohesion of the textbase, the coherence of the situation model, and the discourse genre because those levels needed a more precise specification. However, we quickly discovered the need to also measure texts on characteristics of words and sentence syntax. Two versions of Coh-Metrix are available for the public for free on the web: The original version with over 100 measures (www.cohmetrix.com) and a version with a handful of major dimensions called the *Text Easability Assessor* (http://tea.cohmetrix.com).

The original version of Coh-Metrix had nearly a thousand measures, 100 of which were put on the website for colleagues to use. However, we were encouraged by researchers and practitioners to simplify the analysis and converge on a smaller number of factors. Therefore, a principal components analysis was performed on 37,520 texts to identify central constructs of text complexity (Graesser et al., 2011). The PCA resulted in eight dimensions that accounted for 67 percent of the variance in variations among texts. The top five of these dimensions were incorporated in TEA-Coh-Metrix. The five dimensions of TEA-Coh-Metrix have also been validated in a comprehensive analysis of texts in the Common Core of the National Governors Association (2010, www.corestandards.org) and various high-stakes assessments in the United States (Nelson, Perfetti, Liben, and Liben, 2012). The five major dimensions are listed and defined below.

1. **Narrativity.** Narrative text tells a story with characters, events, places, and things that are familiar to the reader. Narrative is closely affiliated with everyday oral conversation.
2. **Referential cohesion**. High cohesion texts contain words and ideas that overlap across sentences and the entire text, forming threads that connect the explicit text together for the reader.
3. **Situation model cohesion.** Causal, intentional, and temporal connectives help the reader to form a more coherent and deeper understanding of the text.
4. **Syntactic simplicity**. Sentences with few words and simple, familiar syntactic structures are easier to process and understand. Complex sentences have structurally embedded syntax.
5. **Word concreteness**. Concrete words evoke mental images and are more meaningful to the reader than abstract words.

Each of the five dimensions above is expressed in terms of ease of comprehension. Text complexity is defined as the opposite of ease, so principal component scores are reversed in measures of text complexity.

The five Coh-Metrix dimensions have been correlated with unidimensional metrics of text complexity, such as Flesh-Kincaid, Degrees of Reading Power (DRP), and Lexiles. If we use grade level and text genre (i.e., narrative versus informational texts) as a yardstick, several trends support the claim that researchers should consider multiple levels and resist the temptation to settle for a single dimension of text complexity (Graesser and Li, 2013; Graesser et al., 2011). For example, narrativity and syntactic simplicity robustly decrease as a function of grade level, and word concreteness moderately decreases also. However, the correlation between grade level and cohesion is extremely small and sometimes not statistically significant. Apparently, cohesion is not on the radar of the standard readability metrics, even though discourse processing researchers have established that cohesion is an important predictor of reading time and comprehension (Goldman et al., 1999; Lorch and O'Brien, 1995; McNamara, Louwerse, McCarthy, and Graesser, 2010). There were also trade offs among the different levels as we correlated the texts in different age groups and genres. For example, informational texts (non-narratives) typically are on topics that are less familiar to readers. These informational texts tend to have higher referential cohesion and simpler syntax than the narrative texts, perhaps because good writers compensate for the difficulty of the subject matter. Narrative texts tend to occur at earlier grade levels whereas informational texts occur at later grade levels. Therefore, any analysis of texts at different grade levels needs to understand the trade-offs among narrativity, cohesion, and syntax.

Coh-Metrix is a useful tool to sort out complex interactions among text constraints and data reported in laboratory experiments. As one example, McNamara et al.(2010) analyzed the stimulus materials of experimental studies in discourse processing that investigated the impact of text coherence/cohesion on measures such as reading time and recall. The researchers manipulated text cohesion by adding connectives or referring expressions to explicitly bridge text constituents rather than relying on the readers to fill in the connections inferentially. It is conceivable that there can be trade-offs in such manipulations. For example, adding connectives to link sentences can perhaps help cohesion, but it can also add to comprehension difficulty by virtue of sentence length and syntactic complexity. Replacing pronouns with nouns and rich referring expressions can perhaps help cohesion, but it adds to difficulty by lowering word frequency (i.e., nouns are less frequent than pronouns) and increasing noun-phrase density (i.e., with adjective modifiers). Coh-Metrix allowed us to measure the impact of text manipulations on multiple levels of language/discourse and to track the fallout of such manipulations. We contend that these objective metrics from Coh-Metrix should be routinely used in experimental investigations of inferences in discourse.

Another example of the utility of Coh-Metrix to discourse researchers is to compare experimental texts to the norms of texts in different genres, such as narrative, science, social studies, and so forth (Graesser et al., 2011; McNamara et al., 2014). A researcher would expect a large number of inferences to be generated in narrative texts with high-frequency words, but fewer inferences in science texts with a technical vocabulary. Coh-Metrix can be used to assess texts in experiments to judge whether readers are likely to draw inferences and to confirm that texts are in particular genres (e.g., see Eason, Goldberg, Young, Geist, and Cutting, 2012).

It is beyond the scope of this chapter to describe the computational linguistics modules that were incorporated in the Coh-Metrix tool. This information is provided in other reports (Graesser et al., 2004b, McNamara et al., 2014) and there is a help system in the web facility. However, Table 13.2 presents a sample of example measures that went into analyzing texts at multiple levels of language and discourse, namely words, syntax, textbase referential cohesion, situation model coherence, and genre (Graesser and McNamara, 2011).

Technologies that promote learning and assessment of comprehension

Learning from texts for school and lifelong learning is one of the many authentic tasks to consider as one moves out of the experimental lab into the real world. This has been the direction of the research teams in Memphis during the last two decades. More specifically, we have investigated inferences during comprehension, reasoning, and problem-solving activities that are associated with learning difficult subject matters, such as computer literacy, physics, biology, and scientific methods. Computer technologies have been developed to (1) track inferences, comprehension, and other psychological states while studying the material and (2) provide interventions to facilitate comprehension and learning of the difficult subject matter.

Coupling reading times with text difficulty. One simple technology collects self-paced reading times while students read texts and compares these times with the text difficulty metrics provided by Coh-Metrix

Table 13.2 *Example Coh-Metrix measures and indices*

Level or class	Measure (index)
Words	Frequency, concreteness, imagery, age of acquisition, part of speech, content words, pronouns, negations, connectives (different categories), logical operators, polysemy, hypernym/hyponym (reflects abstractness); these counts per 1,000 words.
Syntax	Syntactic complexity (words per noun phrase, words before main verb of main clause).
Referential textbase cohesion	Cohesion of adjacent sentences as measured by overlapping nouns, pronouns, meaning stems (lemma, morpheme). Proportion of content words that overlap. Cohesion of all pairs of sentences in a paragraph.
Situation model cohesion	Cohesion of adjacent sentences with respect to causality, intentionality, temporality, spatiality, and latent semantic analysis (LSA). Cohesion among all sentences in paragraph and between paragraphs via LSA. Given versus new content.
Genre and rhetoric	Type of genre (narrative, science, other). Topic sentencehood.
Other	Flesch-Kincaid grade level, type token ration, syllables per word, words per sentence, sentences and paragraphs per 1,000 words.

(Vega, Feng, Lehman, Graesser, and D'Mello, 2013). Screens of text of approximately 100 words are scaled on Flesch-Kincaid scores and various dimensions of Coh-Metrix, based on the norms collected from 37,520 texts that are representative of the texts that college students experience throughout their lifetimes (Graesser et al., 2011; McNamara et al., 2014). Engagement during reading is manifested by a close correspondence between the self-paced reading times of screens of text (converted to z-scores for each individual reader) and the difficulty of the texts on the various metrics (converted to z-scores based on the TASA norms). An engaged reader should speed up on easy text and slow down on difficult text. Low engagement with the text is manifested by a decoupling between the time spent reading and the text difficulty profile (Franklin, Smallwood, and Schooler, 2011; Vega et al., 2013). More specifically, this decoupling may be explained by either mind wandering (Feng, D'Mello, and Graesser, 2013) or by thoughtful reflection about difficult ideas expressed in the text. For example, good comprehenders are expected to slow down and reason when they encounter contradictions between two or more ideas in the text (Baker, 1985; O'Brien et al., 1998) or by claims in the text that clash with world knowledge (Kendeou, Papadopoulos, and Spanoudis, 2012; Rapp, 2008). Reading times that are much higher than the projections of the Coh-Metrix metrics at these points of contradictions or inconsistencies in the text would be signals of deep comprehension whereas reading times shorter than the projections would be signals of shallow comprehension.

Tracking correct inferences and misconceptions from natural language. Automated essay scoring has now reached a level of accuracy such that the scoring of many classes of written essays is as accurate as expert human raters (Attali and Burstein, 2006; Graesser and McNamara, 2012; Landauer, Laham, and Foltz, 2003; Shermis, Burstein, Higgins, and Zechner, 2010). These systems have had exact agreements with humans on a five-point scale as high as the mid-1880s, adjacent agreements (i.e., within two points on the scale) in the upper mid-1990s, and correlations as high as the mid-1980s. These performance measures are slightly higher than agreement between trained human raters. The Intelligent Essay Assessor (Landauer et al., 2003) analyzes the words in the essay with latent semantic analysis (LSA, Landauer et al., 2007) as well as sequences of words with an n-gram analysis (e.g., word pairs, word triplets). The algorithm computes the similarity of the words and word sequences between a new essay and the essays associated with each level of a scoring scale.

LSA is an important method of computing the conceptual similarity between words, sentences, paragraphs, or essays because it considers implicit knowledge. It is a mathematical, statistical technique for representing knowledge about words and the world on the basis of a large corpus of texts that attempts to capture the knowledge of a typical human. The central intuition of LSA is that the meaning of a word W is reflected in the company of other words that surround word W in naturalistic documents (imagine 37,520 texts and 11 million words). Two words are similar in meaning to the extent that they share similar surrounding words. For example, the word "cup" is highly associated with words in the same functional context, such as *glass, liquid, pour, handle, coffee,* and *heat.* These are not synonyms or antonyms that would occur in a dictionary or thesaurus. LSA uses a statistical technique that condenses a very large corpus of texts to 100–500 statistical dimensions (Landauer et al., 2007). The conceptual similarity between any two text excerpts (e.g., word, clause, sentence, entire essay) is computed as the geometric cosine between the values and weighted dimensions of the two text excerpts. The value of the cosine typically varies from approximately 0 to 1.

The accuracy of scoring short verbal responses has also improved with advances in computational linguistics and statistical representations of world knowledge such as LSA. Short verbal responses by students can vary from one word to a few sentences. In all of these automated assessments, the verbal input of the student is compared with an expected answer. The expected answer may be a word, a set of alternative words, a sentence, a set of sentences, or a pattern of symbolic expressions (Cai, Graesser, Forsyth, Burkett, Millis, Wallace, Halpern, and Butler, 2011; Leacock and Chodorow, 2003; Magliano and Graesser, 2012). The expected answer may be either correct (called an expectation) or incorrect (a bug or misconception). It may be either an explicit sentence in the text or an inference. A semantic or conceptual match is computed between the student input and anticipated answers, with match scores that vary between 0 and 1. Matches to single words are not particularly challenging, whereas matches to more complex expressions are computed by a variety of models. Technologies such as C-Rater developed at Educational Testing System (Leacock and Chodorow, 2003) score answers to short-answer questions that extend beyond single words. AutoTutor (Graesser et al., 2012) and Operation ARA (Cai et al., 2011) track the verbalizations of students over many conversational turns with conversational computer agents (as discussed below) and compare this student input with sentential expectations (either inferences or explicit sentences in a text). The performance of these systems can be quite impressive. For example, Cai et al. (2011) analyzed the student responses in conversational turns in Operation ARA, comparing student verbal responses and expectations. The match scores of trained judges correlated 0.69, whereas the match scores between the computer scores and human judges was 0.67. The Cai et al. algorithm used a combination of LSA and regular expressions (see Jurafsky and Martin, 2008 for a definition of regular expressions).

Tracking comprehension strategies. It is possible to track inferences and strategies during comprehension from verbal protocols while students comprehend text (Kurby and Zachs, 2013; Magliano, Trabasso, and Graesser, 1999; Millis and Magliano, 2003). For example, the Reading Strategy Assessment Tool (RSAT) was developed to identify the comprehension strategies that are manifested in think-aloud protocols that students type in (or say aloud) while reading texts (Magliano, Millis, Levinstein, and Boonthum, 2011; Millis and Magliano, 2003). One important comprehension strategy measured by RSAT is to identify content that reflects causal connections or *bridges* between clauses in the text. RSAT distinguishes between local and distal bridges. Local bridges occur between the target sentence and the immediately prior sentence. Distal bridges occur between the target sentences and sentences located two or more sentences back. Skilled readers are more likely to make distal bridges, whereas less-skilled readers tend to focus more on the immediate context surrounding each sentence (Coté, Goldman, and Saul, 1998). Another type of strategy is *elaboration*. Elaborative inferences are constructed in a fashion that caters to the constraints of the text but also recruits relevant world knowledge (McNamara and Magliano, 2009). Unlike bridges, elaborations do not connect sentences. A third strategy is *paraphrasing*. The student articulates explicit text information but in slightly different words. There is some evidence that the amount of paraphrasing in verbal protocols is negatively correlated with comprehension, whereas bridging and elaborating is positively correlated (Magliano and Millis, 2003). The match scores that accumulate in the think-aloud protocols allow the RSAT analyzer to infer the strategies of the reader.

Tracking affective states. Automated technologies are capable of tracking emotions and other affective states when reading technical texts (Calvo and D'Mello, 2010; D'Mello, Dowell, and Graesser, 2012) and when being tutored by humans or computers (D'Mello and Graesser, 2010; Graesser and D'Mello, 2012). The common affective states during learning are boredom, engagement/flow, frustration, confusion, delight, and surprise in a wide range of learning environments (Baker, D'Mello, Rodrigo, and Graesser, 2010; D'Mello and Graesser, 2012; Graesser and D'Mello, 2012). The learning centered affective state that best predicts learning at deeper levels is confusion, a cognitive-affective state associated with thought and deliberation (D'Mello and Graesser, 2012; D'Mello, Lehman, et al., 2014; Lehman et al., 2013). Confusion can be detected automatically by the patterns in tutorial dialog, body posture, and facial movements (D'Mello and Graesser, 2010) in addition to the decoupling profiles of reading time discussed above. Good comprehenders are expected to exhibit signals of confusion when encountering contradictions and false claims during reading (Lehman et al., 2013), whereas these signals should be less prevalent for poor comprehenders.

Conversational pedagogical agents. Research teams at the University of Memphis have developed and tested conversational pedagogical agents (talking heads) to improve learning of technical material on subject matters in science, technology, engineering, and mathematics (STEM). It is difficult for students to generate inferences while reading and studying texts in these STEM areas so the pedagogical agents scaffold them to promote deeper comprehension and learning. As discussed earlier, students acquire explicit information when reading texts on computer literacy, physics, and research methods, but their performance on inference questions is no different from when they read nothing (Graesser et al., 2004a; VanLehn et al., 2007). Learning environments with pedagogical agents have been developed to serve as substitutes for humans who range in expertise from peers to subject matter experts with training in tutoring (Graesser, Conley, and Olney, 2012).

Pedagogical agents can be designed to perform a large range of tasks that human tutors and peers can do. Agents can guide the interaction with the learner, tutor them with dialogs in natural language, instruct the learner what to do next, and interact with other agents to model ideal behavior, strategies, reflections, and social interactions. Some agents generate speech, gestures, facial expressions, and body movements in ways similar to people, as exemplified by Betty's Brain (Biswas, Jeong, Kinnebrew, Sulcer, and Roscoe, 2010), Tactical Language and Culture System (Johnson and Valente, 2008), iSTART (McNamara, Boonthum, Levinstein, and Millis, 2007; McNamara et al., 2006), Crystal Island (Rowe, Shores, Mott, and Lester, 2010), and My Science Tutor (Ward, Cole, Bolaños, Buchenroth-Martin, Svirsky, Van Vuuren, Weston, Zheng, and Becker, 2011). Systems such as AutoTutor and Why-Atlas can interpret the natural language of the human when it is generated in spoken or typed channels and can respond adaptively to what the student expresses (Graesser et al., 2012; D'Mello, Dowell, and Graesser, 2011; VanLehn et al., 2007). These agent-based systems have frequently demonstrated value in improving students' learning and motivation (Graesser et al., 2012; VanLehn, 2011), but it is beyond the scope of this chapter to review the broad body of research on agents in learning environments.

Training reading strategies with agents. Pedagogical agents can be used to directly train students how to implement comprehension strategies, including inferences. iSTART (Interactive Strategy Trainer for Active Reading and Thinking) is one of these systems that has successfully improved comprehension strategies (McNamara, O'Reilly, Rowe, Boonthum, and Levinstein, 2007; McNamara et al., 2006). The iSTART trainer is designed to help students become deeper text comprehenders by constructing self-explanations of the text. The construction of self-explanations during reading is known to facilitate deep comprehension when there is some context-sensitive feedback on the explanations that are produced (Chi, de Leeuw, Chiu, and LaVancher, 1994; McNamara, 2004). The iSTART interventions focus on five reading strategies that are designed to enhance self-explanations, construction of inferences, and interpreting the explicit text: *monitoring comprehension* (i.e., recognizing comprehension failures and the need for remedial strategies), *paraphrasing* explicit text, making *bridging inferences* between the current sentence and prior text, making *predictions* about the subsequent text, and *elaborating* the text with links to what the reader already knows. The accuracy of applying these inferential and metacognitive skills is measured and tracked throughout the tutorial session.

Groups of agents scaffold these strategies in three phases of iSTART training. In an Introduction Module, an instructor and two student agents collaboratively describe self-explanation strategies with each other. In a Demonstration Module, two agents in a trialog demonstrate the use of self-explanation in the context of a science passage and then the student identifies the strategies being used. The accuracy of the students' identification of the correct strategy exhibited by the student agent serves as a measure of understanding the inference and metacognitive strategies. In a final Practice phase, an agent coaches and provides feedback to the student one-to-one while the student practices self-explanation reading strategies. For particular sentences in a text, the agent reads the sentence and asks the student to self-explain it by typing a self-explanation. The iSTART system then attempts to interpret the student's contributions, gives feedback, and asks the student to modify unsatisfactory self-explanations.

Training metacognition and self-regulated learning with agents. MetaTutor trains students on thirteen strategies that are theoretically important for self-regulated learning (Azevedo, Moos, Johnson, and Chauncey, 2010). The process of self-regulated learning (SRL) involves the learners' constructing a plan, monitoring metacognitive activities, implementing learning strategies, and reflecting on their progress and achievements. Inferences are required in all of these processes. The MetaTutor system has a main agent (Gavin) that coordinates the overall learning environment and three satellite agents that handle three phases of SRL: planning, monitoring, and applying learning strategies. Each of these phases can be decomposed further, under the guidance of the assigned conversational agent. For example, metacognitive monitoring is decomposed into judgments of learning, feeling of knowing, content evaluation, monitoring the adequacy of a strategy, and monitoring progress toward goals. Learning strategies include searching for relevant information in a goal-directed fashion, taking notes, drawing tables or diagrams, rereading, elaborating the material, and coordinating information sources (text and diagrams). Each of these metacognitive and SRL skills have associated measures that are based on the student's actions, decisions, ratings, and verbal input. The frequency and accuracy of each measured skill is collected throughout the tutoring session and hopefully increases as a function of direct training.

Trialogs in scientific reasoning. Trialogs involve two agents interacting with the human learner. The agents can take on different roles, such as tutor and student or two peer students. These trialogs can be implemented in conjunction with the human reading texts. Our research team has conducted several studies with trialogs in the context of critiquing case studies of scientific research with respect to scientific methodology. The design of the case studies and trialog critiques were adapted from an educational game called Operation ARIES! (Forsyth, Graesser, Pavlik, Cai, Butler, Halpern, and Millis, 2013; Millis, Forsyth, Butler, Wallace, Graesser, and Halpern, 2011), which was subsequently commercialized by Pearson Education as Operation ARA (Halpern, Millis, Graesser, Butler, Forsyth, and Cai, 2012). Players learn how to critically evaluate research they read in magazines and newspapers. A series of cases were presented to the student that described experiments that have a number of flaws with respect to scientific methodology. For example, one case study described a new pill that purportedly helps people lose weight, but the sample size was small and there was no control group. The goal of the participants in the trialog is to identify the flaws and express them in natural language. The game was designed to teach high school or college students how to apply the principles of good methodology critically in scientific investigations (e.g., the need for control groups, adequate samples of observations, operational definitions, differentiating correlation from causation, etc.).These activities require inferences and reasoning in addition to the interpretation of explicit text.

A series of studies were conducted that planted false information and contradictions in the trialogs as case studies were critiqued (D'Mello et al., 2014; Lehman et al., 2012; 2013). We attempted to induce cognitive disequilibrium by manipulating whether the tutor agent and the student agent contradicted each other during the trialog and expressed points that are incorrect. Each case study had a description of a research study that was to be critiqued during the trialogs. Then the tutor agent and student agent engaged in a short exchange about (1) whether there was a flaw in the study and (2) which part of the study was flawed if there was a flaw. In the True-True control condition, the tutor agent expressed a correct assertion and the student agent agreed with the tutor. In the True-False condition, the tutor expressed a correct assertion but the student agent disagreed by expressing an incorrect assertion. In the False-True condition, it was the student agent who provided the correct assertion and the tutor agent who disagreed. In the False-False condition, the tutor agent and student agent agreed about an incorrect assertion. The human student was asked to intervene after particular points of possible contradiction in the conversation. For example, the agents turned to the human and asked, "Do you agree with Chris [student agent] that the control group in this study was flawed?" The human's response was coded as correct if he or she agreed with the agent who had made the correct assertion about the flaw of the study. If the human experienced uncertainty and was confused, this should be reflected in the incorrectness and/or uncertainty of his or her answer. This uncertainty would ideally stimulate thinking and learning.

The data indeed confirmed that the contradictions and false information had an impact on the human's answers to these yes or no questions immediately following a contradiction. The proportion of correct student responses showed the following order: True-True > True-False > False-True > False-False conditions. These findings indicated that learners were occasionally confused when both agents agreed and were correct (True-True, no contradiction), became more confused when there was a contradiction between the two agents (True-False or False-True), and were either confused or simply accepted the incorrect information when the agents incorrectly agreed (False-False). Confusion was best operationally defined as occurring if both (1) the student manifested uncertainty/incorrectness in their decisions when asked by the agents and (2) the student either reported being confused or the computer automatically detected confusion (D'Mello and Graesser, 2010; Graesser and D'Mello, 2012). Interestingly, the results of these studies revealed that contradictions, confusion, and uncertainty caused more learning at deeper levels of mastery, as reflected in a delayed test on scientific reasoning and far-transfer case studies. There may be a causal relationship between contradictions (and the associated cognitive disequilibrium) and deep learning, with confusion playing either a mediating, moderating, or causal role in the process.

There was a need for the two agents to contradict each other directly in a conversation before the humans experienced an appreciable amount of uncertainty and confusion. We suspect that the contradiction would need to be contiguous in time before the contradiction would be detected. That is, the contradiction is likely to be missed if one agent makes a claim and then another agent makes a contradictory claim ten minutes later. This is compatible with research in text comprehension that has shown that the contradictory claims must be co-present in working memory before they get noticed unless there is a high amount of world knowledge. It is also compatible with the observation that it is difficult for many students to integrate information from multiple texts and spot contradictions (Bråten, Strømsø, and Britt, 2009; Britt and Aglinskas, 2002; Goldman et al., 2012; Rouet, 2006) unless there is a high amount of world knowledge. A strategic attempt to integrate information from multiple texts would be needed to draw such connections unless the person is fortified with sufficient subject matter knowledge (Goldman et al., 2012; Graesser, Wiley, Goldman, O'Reilly, Jeon, and McDaniel, 2007; Wiley et al., 2009).

Closing comments

Research on inference generation has evolved considerably since we started conducting laboratory studies on short texts three decades ago. Discourse psychologists have a better understanding of the types of inferences that are routinely generated while comprehending different types of texts and of the psychological mechanisms that generate such inferences. All of the models postulate that subject matter knowledge and memory robustly guide these processes. However, such knowledge and memory are not enough. Competent readers in the twenty-first century also need strategies of language comprehension, discourse, critical thinking, and self-regulated learning. The three signature assumptions of the constructionist model, namely, reader goals, coherence, and explanation, will no doubt be important components of the manifold of strategies.

Acknowledgments

This research was supported by the National Science Foundation (0834847, 0918409, 0904909, 1108845) and the Institute of Education Sciences (R305G020018, R305H050169, R305B070349, R305A080589, R305A100875, R305C120001). Any opinions, findings, and conclusions or recommendations expressed in this material are those of the authors and do not necessarily reflect the views of NSF and IES.

REFERENCES

Attali, Y., & Burstein, J. (2006). Automated essay scoring with e-rater R V.2. *Journal of Technology, Learning and Assessment*, 4, 1–30.

Azevedo, R., Moos, D., Johnson, A., & Chauncey, A. (2010). Measuring cognitive and metacognitive regulatory processes used during hypermedia learning: issues and challenges. *Educational Psychologist*, 45, 210–23.

Baker, L. (1985). Differences in standards used by college students to evaluate their comprehension of expository prose. *Reading Research Quarterly*, 20, 298–313.

Baker, R. S., D'Mello, S. K., Rodrigo, M. T., & Graesser, A. C. (2010). Better to be frustrated than bored: the incidence, persistence, and impact of learners' cognitive-affective states during interactions with three different computer-based learning environments. *International Journal of Human-Computer Studies*, 68, 223–41.

Barth, C. M., & Funke, J. (2010). Negative affective environments improve complex solving performance. *Cognition and Emotion*, 24, 1259–68.

Biber, D., Conrad, S., & Reppen, R. (1998). *Corpus Linguistics: Investigating Language Structure and Use*. Cambridge University Press.

Biswas, G., Jeong, H., Kinnebrew, J., Sulcer, B., & Roscoe, R. (2010). Measuring self-regulated learning skills through social interactions in a teachable agent environment. *Research and Practice in Technology-Enhanced Learning*, 5, 123–52.

Blanc, N., Kendeou, P., van den Broek, P., & Brouillet, D. (2008). Updating situation models during reading of news reports: evidence from empirical data and simulations. *Discourse Processes*, 45, 103–21.

Braasch, J. L., Rouet, J. F., Vibert, N., & Britt, M. A. (2012). Readers' use of source information in text comprehension. *Memory & Cognition*, 40, 450–65.

Bransford, J. D., Brown, A. L., & Cocking, R. R. (eds.). (2000). *How People Learn* (expanded edn.). Washington, DC: National Academy Press.

Bråten, I., Strømsø, H. I., & Britt, M. A. (2009). Trust matters: examining the role of source evaluation in students' construction of meaning within and across multiple texts. *Reading Research Quarterly*, 44, 6–28.

Bråten, I., & Strømsø, H. (2006). Constructing meaning from multiple information sources as a function of personal epistemology. *Information Design Journal*, 14, 56–67.

Briner, S. W., Virtue, S., & Kurby, C. A. (in review). Forward and backward causal relations in narrative text. *Discourse Processes*.

Britt, M. A., & Aglinskas, C. (2002). Improving students' ability to identify and use source information. *Cognition and Instruction*, 20, 485–522.

Britt, M. A., & Rouet, J. F. (2012). Learning with multiple documents: component skills and their acquisition. In M. J. Lawson & J. R. Kirby (eds.), *The Quality of Learning: Dispositions, Instruction, and Mental Structures* (pp. 385–404). Cambridge University Press.

Britton, B. K., & Graesser, A. C. (1996) (eds.). *Models of Understanding Text*. Mahwah, NJ: Erlbaum.

Cai, Z., Graesser, A. C., Forsyth, C., Burkett, C., Millis, K., Wallace, P., Halpern, D., & Butler, H. (2011). Trialog in ARIES: user input assessment in an intelligent tutoring system. In W. Chen & S. Li (eds.), *Proceedings of the Third IEEE International Conference on Intelligent Computing and Intelligent Systems* (pp. 429–33). Guangzhou: IEEE Press.

Calvo, R. A., & D'Mello, S. K. (2010). Affect detection: an interdisciplinary review of models, methods, and their applications. *IEEE Transactions on Affective Computing*, 1, 18–37.

Chi, M. T. H., de Leeuw, N., Chiu, M., & LaVancher, C. (1994). Eliciting self-explanations improves understanding. *Cognitive Science*, 18, 439–77.

Cook, A. E., Halleran, J. G., & O'Brien, E. J. (1998). What is readily available during reading? A memory-based view of text processing. *Discourse Processes*, 26(2–3), 109–29.

Coté, N., Goldman, S. R., & Saul, E. U. (1998). Students making sense of informational text: relations between processing and representation. *Discourse Processes*, 25, 1–53.

D'Mello, S. K., Dowell, N., & Graesser, A. C. (2011). Does it really matter whether students' contributions are spoken versus typed in an intelligent tutoring system with natural language? *Journal of Experimental Psychology: Applied*, 17, 1–17.

(2012). Unimodal and multimodal human perception of naturalistic non-basic affective states during human-computer interactions. *IEEE Transactions on Affective Computing*, 4, 452–65.

D'Mello, S. K., & Graesser, A. C. (2010). Multimodal semi-automated affect detection from conversational cues, gross body language, and facial features. *User Modeling and User-adapted Interaction*, 20, 147–87.

(2012). Dynamics of affective states during complex learning. *Learning and Instruction*, 22, 145–57.

(in press). Confusion. In R. Pekrun & L. Linnenbrink-Garcia (eds.), *Handbook of Emotions and Education*. New York: Taylor & Francis.

D'Mello, S., Lehman, B., Pekrun, R., & Graesser, A. C. (2014). Confusion can be beneficial for learning. *Learning and Instruction*, 29, 153–70.

Eason, S. H., Goldberg, L. F., Young, K. M., Geist, M. C., & Cutting, L. E. (2012). Reader–text interactions: how differential text and question types influence cognitive skills needed for reading comprehension. *Journal of Educational Psychology*, 104, 515–28.

Feng, S., D'Mello, S. K., & Graesser, A. (2013). Mind wandering while reading easy and difficult texts, *Psychonomic Bulletin & Review*, 20, 586–92.

Festinger, L. (1957). *A Theory of Cognitive Dissonance*. Stanford, CA: Stanford University Press.

Forsyth, C. M., Graesser, A. C. Pavlik, P., Cai, Z., Butler, H., Halpern, D.F., & Millis, K. (2013). Operation ARIES! methods, mystery and mixed models: discourse features predict affect in a serious game. *Journal of Educational Data Mining*, 5, 147–89.

Franklin, M. S., Smallwood, J., & Schooler, J. W. (2011). Catching the mind in flight: using behavioral indices to detect mind wandering in real time. *Psychonomic Bulletin & Review*, 18, 992–97.

Gernsbacher, M. A. (ed.). (1990). *Language Comprehension as Structure Building*. Mahwah, NJ: Erlbaum.

Glenberg, A. M. (1997). What memory is for. *Behavior and Brain Sciences*, 20, 1–55.

Glenberg, A. M., & Robertson, D. A. (1999). Indexical understanding of instructions. *Discourse Processes*, 28, 1–26.

Goldman, S. R., Braasch, J. L. G., Wiley, J., Graesser, A. C., & Brodowinska, K. (2012). Comprehending and learning from internet sources: processing patterns of better and poorer learners. *Reading Research Quarterly*, 47, 356–81.

Goldman, S. R., Graesser, A. C., & van den Broek, P. W. (1999). Reflections. In S. R. Goldman, A. C. Graesser, & P. W. van den Broek (eds.), *Narrative Comprehension, Causality, and Coherence: Essays in Honor of Tom Trabasso* (pp. 1–15). Mahwah, NJ: Erlbaum.

Goldman, S. R., & van Oostendorp, H. (1999). Conclusions, conundrums and challenges for the future. In H. van Oostendorp & S. R. Goldman (eds.), *The Construction of Mental Representations during Reading* (pp. 367–76). Mahwah, NJ: Erlbaum.

Graesser, A. C. (1981). *Prose Comprehension beyond the Word*. New York: Springer-Verlag.

Graesser, A. C., Baggett, W. B., & Williams, K. (1996). Question-driven explanatory reasoning. *Applied Cognitive Psychology*, *10*, 17–31.

Graesser, A. C., & Bertus, E. L. (1998). The construction of causal inferences while reading expository texts on science and technology. *Scientific Studies of Reading*, *2*, 247–69.

Graesser, A. C., & Bower, G. H. (eds.). (1990). *The Psychology of Learning and Motivation: Inferences and Text Comprehension*. New York: Academic Press.

Graesser, A. C., Cai, Z., Louwerse, M. M., & Daniel, F. (2006). Question understanding aid (QUAID): a web facility that tests question comprehensibility. *Public Opinion Quarterly*, *70*(1), 3–22.

Graesser, A. C., Conley, M., & Olney, A. (2012). Intelligent tutoring systems. In K. R. Harris, S. Graham, and T. Urdan (eds.), *APA Educational Psychology Handbook: Vol. III. Applications to Learning and Teaching* (pp. 451–73). Washington, DC: American Psychological Association.

Graesser, A. C., & D'Mello, S. (2012). Emotions during the learning of difficult material. In B. Ross (eds.), *The Psychology of Learning and Motivation*, Vol. *LVII* (183–225). New York: Elsevier.

Graesser, A. C., D'Mello, S. K., Hu. X., Cai, Z., Olney, A., & Morgan, B. (2012). AutoTutor. In P. McCarthy and C. Boonthum-Denecke (eds.), *Applied Natural Language Processing: Identification, Investigation, and Resolution* (pp. 169–87). Hershey, PA: IGI Global.

Graesser, A. C., Jeon, M., & Dufty, D. (2008). Agent technologies designed to facilitate interactive knowledge construction. *Discourse Processes*, *45*, 298–322.

Graesser, A. C., & Lehman, B. (2012). Questions drive comprehension of text and multimedia. In M. T. McCrudden, J. Magliano, & G. Schraw (eds.), *Text Relevance and Learning from Text* (pp. 53–74). Greenwich, CT: Information Age Publishing.

Graesser, A. C., & Li, H. (2013). How might comprehension deficits be explained by the constraints of text and multilevel discourse processes? In B. Miller, L. E. Cutting, & P. McCardle (eds.), *Unraveling Reading Comprehension: Behavioral, Neurobiological, and Genetic Components* (pp. 33–42). Baltimore: Paul Brooks Publishing.

Graesser, A. C., Lu, S., Jackson, G. T., Mitchell, H., Ventura, M., Olney, A., & Louwerse, M. M. (2004a). AutoTutor: a tutor with dialogue in natural language. *Behavioral Research Methods, Instruments, and Computers*, *36*, 180–93.

Graesser, A. C., Lu, S., Olde, B. A., Cooper-Pye, E., & Whitten, S. (2005). Question asking and eye tracking during cognitive disequilibrium: comprehending illustrated texts on devices when the devices break down. *Memory & Cognition*, *33*, 1235–47.

Graesser, A. C., & McMahen, C. L. (1993). Anomalous information triggers questions when adults solve problems and comprehend stories. *Journal of Educational Psychology*, *85*, 136–51.

Graesser, A. C., & McNamara, D. S. (2011). Computational analyses of multilevel discourse comprehension. *Topics in Cognitive Science*, *3*, 371–98.

(2012). Automated analysis of essays and open-ended verbal responses. In H. Cooper, P. M. Camic, D. L. Long, A. T. Panter, D. Rindskopf, & K. J. Sher (eds.), *APA Handbook of Research Methods in Psychology, Vol. I: Foundations, Planning, Measures, and Psychometrics* (pp. 307–25). Washington, DC: American Psychological Association.

Graesser, A. C., McNamara, D. S., & Kulikowich, J. (2011). Coh-Metrix: providing multilevel analyses of text characteristics. *Educational Researcher, 40*, 223–34.

Graesser, A. C., McNamara, D. S., Louwerse, M. M., & Cai, Z. (2004b). Coh-Metrix: analysis of text on cohesion and language. *Behavioral Research Methods, Instruments, and Computers, 36*, 193–202.

Graesser, A. C., Singer, M., & Trabasso, T (1994). Constructing inferences during narrative text comprehension. *Psychological Review, 101*, 371–95.

Graesser, A. C., Wiley, J., Goldman, S. R., O'Reilly, T., Jeon, M., & McDaniel, B. (2007). SEEK Web tutor: fostering a critical stance while exploring the causes of volcanic eruption. *Metacognition and Learning, 2*, 89–105.

Halpern, D. F., Millis, K., Graesser, A. C., Butler, H., Forsyth, C., & Cai, Z. (2012). Operation ARA: a computerized learning game that teaches critical thinking and scientific reasoning. *Thinking Skills and Creativity, 7*, 93–100.

Hiebert, E. H., & Mesmer, H. A. E. (2013). Upping the ante of text complexity in the Common Core State Standards examining its potential impact on young readers. *Educational Researcher, 42*, 44–51.

Hyönä, J., Lorch, R. F., Jr., & Rinck, M. (2003). Eye movement measures to study global text processing. In J. Hyönä, R. Radach, & H. Deubel (eds.), *The Mind's Eye: Cognitive and Applied Aspects of Eye Movement Research* (pp. 313–34). Amsterdam: Elsevier.

Johnson, L. W., & Valente, A. (2008). Tactical language and culture training systems: using artificial intelligence to teach foreign languages and cultures. In M. Goker & K. Haigh (eds.) *Proceedings of the Twentieth Conference on Innovative Applications of Artificial Intelligence* (pp. 1632–39). Palo Alto, CA: AAAI Press.

Jurafsky, D., & Martin, J. H. (2008). *Speech and Language Processing: An Introduction to Natural Language Processing, Computational Linguistics, and Speech Recognition*. Upper Saddle River, NJ: Prentice Hall.

Kendeou, P., Papadopoulos, T. C., & Spanoudis, G. (2012). Processing demands of reading comprehension tests in young readers. *Learning and Instruction, 22*, 354–67.

Kendeou, P., Smith, E. R., & O'Brien, E. J. (2013). Updating during reading comprehension: Why causality matters. *Journal of Experimental Psychology: Learning, Memory, and Cognition, 39*, 854–65.

Kintsch, W. (1998). *Comprehension: A Paradigm for Cognition*. Cambridge University Press.

Kurby, C. A., & Zacks, J. M. (2013). The activation of modality-specific representations during discourse processing. *Brain and Language, 126*, 338–49.

Landauer, T. K., Laham, R. D., & Foltz, P. W. (2003). Automated scoring and annotation of essays with the intelligent essay assessor. In M. Shermis & J.

Bernstein (eds.). *Automated Essay Scoring: A Cross-disciplinary Perspective.* Mahwah, NJ: Erlbaum.

Landauer, T., McNamara, D. S., Dennis, S., & Kintsch, W. (eds.). (2007). *Handbook of Latent Semantic Analysis.* Mahwah, NJ: Erlbaum.

Leacock, C., & Chodorow, M. (2003). C-rater: automated scoring of short-answer questions. *Computers and the Humanities, 37,* 389–405.

Lehman, B., D'Mello, S. K., & Graesser, A. C. (2012). Confusion and complex learning during interactions with computer learning environments. *Internet and Higher Education, 15,* 184–94.

Lehman, B., D'Mello, S. K., Strain, A., Mills, C., Gross, M., Dobbins, A., Wallace, P., Millis, K., & Graesser, A. C. (2013). Inducing and tracking confusion with contradictions during complex learning. *International Journal of Artificial Intelligence in Education, 22,* 85–105.

Lewis, M. R., & Mensink, M. C. (2012). Prereading questions and online text comprehension. *Discourse Processes, 49,* 367–90.

Lorch, R. F., Jr, & O'Brien, E. J. (eds.). (1995). *Sources of Coherence in Reading.* Mahwah, NJ: Erlbaum.

Macaulay, D. (1988). *The Way Things Work.* Boston: Houghton Mifflin.

Magliano, J. P., & Graesser, A. C. (2012). Computer-based assessment of student constructed responses. *Behavioral Research Methods, 44,* 608–21.

Magliano, J. P., & Millis, K. K. (2003). Assessing reading skill with a think-aloud procedure and latent semantic analysis. *Cognition and Instruction, 21,* 251–83.

Magliano, J. P., Millis, K. K., Levinstein, I., & Boonthum, C. (2011). Assessing comprehension during reading with the reading strategy assessment Tool (RSAT). *Metacognition and Learning, 6,* 131–54.

Magliano, J. P., Trabasso, T., & Graesser, A. C. (1999). Strategic processing during comprehension. *Journal of Educational Psychology, 91,* 615–29.

Maier, J., & Richter, T. (2013). Text belief consistency effects in the comprehension of multiple texts with conflicting information. *Cognition and Instruction, 31,* 151–75.

McCrudden, M. T., Schraw, G., & Kambe, G. (2005). The effect of relevance instructions on reading time and learning. *Journal of Educational Psychology, 97,* 88–102.

McKoon, G., & Ratcliff, R. (1992). Spreading activation versus compound cue accounts of priming: mediated priming revisited. *Journal of Experimental Psychology: Learning, Memory, and Cognition, 18,* 1155–72.

McNamara, D. S. (2004). SERT: Self-explanation reading training. *Discourse Processes, 38,* 1–30.

McNamara, D. S., Boonthum, C., Levinstein, I. B., & Millis, K. (2007). Evaluating self-explanations in iSTART: comparing word-based and LSA algorithms. In Landauer, T., D.S. McNamara, S. Dennis, & W. Kintsch (eds.), *Handbook of Latent Semantic Analysis* (pp. 227–41). Mahwah, NJ: Erlbaum.

McNamara, D. S., Graesser, A. C., McCarthy, P. M., & Cai, Z. (2014). *Automated Evaluation of Text and Discourse with Coh-Metrix.* Cambridge University Press.

McNamara, D. S., Louwerse, M. M., McCarthy, P. M., & Graesser, A. C. (2010). Coh-Metrix: capturing linguistic features of cohesion. *Discourse Processes*, *47*, 292–330.

McNamara, D. S., & Magliano, J. (2009). Toward a comprehensive model of comprehension. In B. Ross (ed.), *The Psychology of Learning and Motivation* (pp. 297–383). Oxford: Elsevier.

McNamara, D. S., O'Reilly, T., Best, R., & Ozuru, Y. (2006). Improving adolescent students' reading comprehension with iSTART. *Journal of Educational Computing Research*, *34*, 147–71.

McNamara, D. S., O'Reilly, T., Rowe, M., Boonthum, C., & Levinstein, I. B. (2007). iSTART: a web-based tutor that teaches self-explanation and metacognitive reading strategies. 3In D. S. McNamara (ed.), *Reading Comprehension Strategies: Theories, Interventions, and Technologies* (pp. 397–421). Mahwah, NJ: Erlbaum.

Millis, K., Forsyth, C., Butler, H., Wallace, P., Graesser, A. C., & Halpern, D. (2011). Operation ARIES! A serious game for teaching scientific inquiry. In M. Ma, A. Oikonomou, & J. Lakhmi (eds.), *Serious Games and Edutainment Applications* (pp. 169–96). London: Springer-Verlag.

Millis, K., & Graesser, A. C. (1994). The time-course of constructing knowledge-based inferences for scientific texts. *Journal of Memory and Language*, *33*, 583–99.

Myers, J. L., & O'Brien, E. J. (1998). Accessing the discourse representation during reading. *Discourse Processes*, *26*, 131–57.

Myers, J. L., O'Brien, E. J., Albrecht, J. E., & Mason, R. A. (1994). Maintaining global coherence during reading. *Journal of Experimental Psychology: Learning, Memory, and Cognition*, *20*, 876–86.

Narvaez, D., van den Broek, P., & Ruiz, A. B. (1999). The influence of reading purpose on inference generation and comprehension in reading. *Journal of Educational Psychology*, *91*, 488–96.

Nelson, J., Perfetti, C., Liben, D., & Liben, M. (2012). *Measures of Text Difficulty: Testing Their Predictive Value for Grade Levels and Student Performance*. New York: Student Achievement Partners.

O'Brien, E. J., Rizzella, M. L., Albrecht, J. E., & Halleran, J. G. (1998). Updating a situation model: a memory-based text processing view. *Journal of Experimental Psychology: Learning, Memory, and Cognition*, *24*, 1200–10.

Otero, J., & Graesser, A. C. (2001). PREG: elements of a model of question asking. *Cognition and Instruction*, *19*, 143–75.

Perfetti, C. A., Rouet, J. F., & Britt, M. A. (1999). Toward a theory of documents representation. In H. van Oostendorp & S. R. Goldman (eds.), *The Construction of Mental Representations during Reading* (pp. 99–122). Mahwah, NJ: Erlbaum.

Rapp, D. N. (2008). How do readers handle incorrect information during reading? *Memory & Cognition*, *36*, 688–701.

Reynolds, R. E., & Anderson, R. C. (1982). Influence of questions on the allocation of attention during reading. *Journal of Educational Psychology*, *74*, 623–32.

Rothkopf, E. Z., & Billington, M. J. (1979). Goal-guided learning from text: inferring a descriptive processing model from inspection times and eye movements. *Journal of Educational Psychology, 71,* 310–27.

Rouet, J. (2006). *The Skills of Document Use: From Text Comprehension to Web-based Learning.* Mahwah, NJ: Erlbaum.

Rowe, J., Shores, L., Mott B., & Lester, J. (2010). Integrating learning and engagement in narrative-centered learning environments. In V. Aleven, J. Kay, & J. Mostow (eds.), *Proceedings of the Tenth International Conference on Intelligent Tutoring Systems* (pp. 166–77). Pittsburgh, PA.

Shermis, M. D., Burstein, J., Higgins, D., & Zechner, K. (2010). Automated essay scoring: writing assessment and instruction. In E. Baker, B. McGaw, & N. S. Petersen (eds.), *International Encyclopedia of Education* (pp. 20–26). Oxford: Elsevier.

Singer, M., Andruslak, P., Reisdorf, P., & Black, N. L. (1992). Individual differences in bridging inference processes. *Memory & Cognition, 20,* 539–48.

Singer, M., Graesser, A. C., & Trabasso, T. (1994). Minimal or global inference during reading. *Journal of Memory and Language, 33,* 421–41.

Snow, C. (2002). *Reading for Understanding: Toward an R&D Program in Reading Comprehension.* Santa Monica, CA: RAND Corporation.

Stadtler, M., Scharrer, L., Brummernhenrich, B., & Bromme, R. (2013). Dealing with uncertainty: readers' memory for and use of conflicting information from science texts as function of presentation format and source expertise. *Cognition and Instruction, 31,* 130–50.

Van den Broek, P., Rapp, D. N., & Kendeou, P. (2005). Integrating memory-based and constructionist processes in accounts of reading comprehension. *Discourse Processes, 39,* 299–316.

Van den Broek, P., Risden, K., Fletcher, C. R., & Thurlow, R. (1996). A "landscape" view of reading: fluctuating patterns of activation and the construction of a stable memory representation. In B. K. Britton & A. C. Graesser (eds.), *Models of Understanding Text* (pp. 165–87). Mahwah, NJ: Erlbaum.

VanLehn, K. (2011). The relative effectiveness of human tutoring, intelligent tutoring systems and other tutoring systems. *Educational Psychologist, 46,* 4, 197–221.

VanLehn, K., Graesser, A. C., Jackson, G. T., Jordan, P., Olney, A., & Rose, C. P. (2007). When are tutorial dialogues more effective than reading? *Cognitive Science, 31,* 3–62.

Van Oostendorp, H. (ed.). (2003). *Cognition in a Digital World.* Mahwah, NJ: Erlbaum.

Vega, B., Feng, S., Lehman, B., Graesser, A., & D'Mello, S. (2013). Reading into the text: investigating the influence of text complexity on cognitive engagement. In S. K. D'Mello, R. A. Calvo, & A. Olney (eds.), *Proceedings of the Sixth International Conference on Educational Data Mining* (pp. 296–99).

Ward, W., Cole, R., Bolaños, D., Buchenroth-Martin, C., Svirsky, E., Van Vuuren, S. Weston, T., Zheng, J., & Becker, L. (2011). My science tutor:

a conversational multimedia virtual tutor for elementary school science. *ACM Transactions of Speech and Language Processing*, *13*, 4–16.

Weaver, C. A., Mannes, S., & Fletcher, C. R. (eds.). (1995). *Discourse Comprehension: Strategies and Processing Revisited*. Mahwah, NJ: Erlbaum.

Wiley, J., Goldman, S. R., Graesser, A. C., Sanchez, C. A., Ash, I. K., & Hemmerich, J. A. (2009). Source evaluation, comprehension, and learning in Internet science inquiry tasks. *American Educational Research Journal*, *46*, 1060–106.

Zwaan, R. A., Magliano, J. P., & Graesser, A. C. (1995). Dimensions of situation model construction in narrative comprehension. *Journal of Experimental Psychology: Learning, Memory, and Cognition*, *21*, 386–97.

Zwaan, R. A., & Radvansky, G. A. (1998). Situation models in language comprehension and memory. *Psychological Bulletin*, *123*, 162–85.

Zwaan, R. A., & van Oostendorp, H. (1993). Do readers construct spatial representations in naturalistic story comprehension? *Discourse Processes*, *16*, 125–43.

14   Inference generation during online study and multimedia learning

Kirsten R. Butcher and Sarah Davies

Many studies investigating inference generation have studied comprehension of single texts, often consisting of short passages or paragraphs (e.g., Cook, Limber, and O'Brien, 2001; Klin, Guzmán, and Levine, 1999; McKoon and Ratcliff, 1992; Narvaez, van den Broek, and Ruiz, 1999; Singer, Andrusiak, Reisdorf, and Black, 1992; Singer and Ritchot, 1996; Vidal-Abarca, Martínez, and Gilabert, 2000; Wiley and Myers, 2003). Thus, much of what we know about inferential processing during comprehension has been observed as learners read (in its entirety) a single text from start to finish. However, modern learning opportunities overwhelmingly occur in online environments where the materials bear little resemblance to experimental texts used in comprehension studies. Indeed, some research has found that students' use of non-Internet resources accounts for less than 2 percent of student academic searches (Graham and Metaxas, 2003). When working in these online environments, students rarely (if ever) will encounter learning materials that share the simple, structured characteristics of traditional texts. Unlike traditional text materials, online learning materials are dynamic, diverse, and integrative, allowing nearly infinite learning paths through a variety of complex representations. Students may fail to finish some (or most) of the resources they choose to begin reading, especially if hyperlinks are included throughout the text – as is typical in online materials. In addition to text, students likely will encounter pictures, diagrams, animations, videos, simulations, or any combination of these as they learn online. Students also may encounter large amounts of commercial content or information with doubtful veracity or dubious origins, all of which complicate the comprehension task in an online environment.

Even if we restrict our focus to accurate, relevant, and trustworthy online content available to a learner – thereby ignoring demands associated with assessing the relevance and source of online content (cf., Bråten, Strømsø, and Salmerón, 2011) – learners face a complicated challenge in integrating and understanding the variety of materials they encounter. As others have noted (e.g., Lynch, 2008), many students fail to recognize the fundamental difference between finding information online and learning from it in meaningful ways. Understanding meaningful learning in online contexts requires a better understanding of when and how inference making occurs with the complex, varied, and potentially disjointed materials that comprehenders encounter in digital environments. In this chapter, we synthesize relevant research related to inference generation during online study and multimedia learning, considering what currently is known about the conditions under which inference generation is supported or suppressed in various digital contexts with wide-ranging materials.

Multimedia materials for learning

Increasingly, text encountered in online contexts is embedded within multimedia materials. Multimedia materials can be defined simply as materials that include both verbal and visual content (Mayer, 2001), and early research on multimedia learning focused mainly on text combined with (static or animated) illustrations (e.g., Mayer, 1989; Mayer, Bove, Bryman, Mars, and Tapangco, 1996; Mayer and Gallini, 1990). However, text in online resources now often is coupled with a large variety of more complex visual materials that include photographs, diagrams, charts, graphs, interactive models, simulations, and 3D graphics. The term "multimedia" is used to refer broadly to these types of digital and interactive content, but more structured classification quickly becomes unwieldy because many online materials include multiple forms of visual and verbal media. For example, a website may contain text content, static diagrams, animations, a video, and several photographs. Accordingly, it is most practical to consider multimedia to encompass a category of learning materials with highly varied forms and combinations of visual, verbal, and interactive components.

As may be expected because of the variety and complexity of multimedia materials, research on multimedia learning only has begun to understand the processes by which learners comprehend available multimedia components during learning. Thus, direct evidence as to inference generation that occurs during multimedia learning (i.e., as multimedia materials are being processed) is somewhat limited. Few studies of multimedia learning have measured inference generation as the comprehension task unfolds with text and visual materials (e.g., Ainsworth and Loizou, 2003; Butcher, 2006; Cromley, Snyder-Hogan, and Luciw-Dubas, 2010; Lewalter, 2003); this is in direct contrast to comprehension studies of text, which have frequently employed measures that capture inference generation as it occurs during comprehension (e.g.,

Albrecht and Myers, 1995; Albrecht and O'Brien, 1993; Cook et al., 2001; Lea, 1995; McKoon and Ratcliff, 1992; Myers, Cook, Kambe, Mason, and O'Brien, 2000; Singer et al., 1992; Wiley and Myers, 2003). It should be noted that measures of real-time inference generation often are called "online" measures in the text comprehension literature, but we will avoid using this term to prevent confusion related to Internet or Web resources as online content.

In the absence of a large number of converging studies testing real-time comprehension processes during multimedia learning, examining the types of knowledge developed during multimedia learning using a well-known model of comprehension – the construction-integration (CI) model (Kintsch, 1988; van Dijk and Kintsch, 1983) – provides implicit evidence of inferences that occur as the result of comprehension. Analyzing the multimedia learning research from this perspective allows us to identify an initial set of factors that influence high-level processing of online and multimedia materials.

The construction-integration model applied to multimedia learning

The CI model (Kintsch, 1988; van Dijk and Kintsch, 1983) posits that representations at three levels of knowledge are formed during text comprehension: the surface level, the textbase, and the situation model. The surface-level representation contains the specific words and syntax of the learning materials, but this representation rarely is retained except in specialized cases where recall must be precise (e.g., memorizing a poem). The textbase represents the meaning of the text but does not extend beyond the information contained in the text. That is, the textbase faithfully encodes the content of a text in a way that facilitates later recall of text propositions. The situation model is a representation (i.e., mental model) of the situation described in the learning materials and, by definition, is a result of inferential processing (Kintsch, 1998). The situation model drives student performance on measures of deeper learning and understanding from text content (Kintsch, 1986).

The textbase and situation model representations both can be formed during a comprehension episode, but different cognitive processes are associated with the development of each one (for a discussion, see Butcher and Kintsch, 2012), as evidenced by think-aloud data (e.g., Ainsworth and Loizou, 2003; Butcher, 2006; 2010; Cromley et al., 2010; Lewalter, 2003; Wolfe and Goldman, 2005). Paraphrases – utterances in which learners summarize or repeat the gist of texts – are the most commonly generated type of utterance when students learn with print materials (Wolfe and Goldman, 2005), as well as with multimedia (Butcher, 2006) and visual representations (Lewalter, 2003). Because paraphrasing focuses on encoding text (or multimedia) content, paraphrasing behaviors support the development of a textbase representation. Accordingly, paraphrasing activities support recall performance but not performance on transfer tasks or reasoning problems (Wolfe and Goldman, 2005).

Generative inferences can be tracked during think alouds via utterances that create new knowledge during learning; these inferences may be formed by integrating text content with prior knowledge or connecting parts of a text or presentation in a way that was not provided in the learning materials (Butcher, 2006; Wolfe and Goldman, 2005). Inferences are associated with development of a situation model (Butcher, 2006; Kintsch, 1986, 1998; Wolfe and Goldman, 2005) and, as a result, facilitate performance on assessments requiring transfer, application, or extension of the learned information (Butcher, 2006; 2010; Butcher and Chi, 2006; Kintsch, 1986).

The CI model forms a useful basis for generating hypotheses about learning with hypertext (Salmerón, Cañas, Kintsch, and Fajardo, 2005; Salmerón, Kintsch, and Cañas, 2006) as well as for analyzing the depth of processing involved in multimedia learning (Butcher, 2006; 2010), online search (Butcher, Bhushan, and Sumner, 2006), and self-regulated learning with online resources (Butcher and Sumner, 2011). Because inference generation facilitates the development of a situation model, knowledge outcomes that show deeper understanding demonstrate that inference generation occurred as the result of comprehension. Thus, comparing the outcomes of multimedia learning with different materials and different contexts allows us to synthesize diverse research and to derive an initial understanding of when inference generation is facilitated during modern (online) learning opportunities.

In the remainder of this article, we first discuss what is known about inference generation during online and multimedia learning. We then discuss potential factors influencing inference generation that occurs as the result of online and multimedia learning by analyzing knowledge outcomes from studies that do not measure comprehension processes directly but use assessments that target the situation model.

Comprehension processes in learning with online and multimedia resources

When considering online and multimedia materials that learners may encounter on the World Wide Web, the challenges of comprehension are exacerbated when compared to learning with a single, static text. An initial challenge to understanding inference generation during online study is the iterative and interconnected nature of text that is read online. Links between different online resources mean that learners may read a wide range of materials in virtually limitless possible orders. Thus, readers must infer and integrate across multiple documents during online comprehension. The processing of multiple texts has been addressed by the documents model (Perfetti, Rouet, and Britt, 1999), which builds upon the CI model. The documents model comprises two models: the situations model, in which the situation model developed for several individual texts are integrated into a general understanding across the texts, and the intertext model, which represents meta-level information about each text (e.g., source, bias) as well as potential relationships between texts (e.g., conflicting content). The situations model and the intertext model assuredly are involved in learning with multiple, online texts as they describe the processes by which a single mental representation is formed as readers comprehend multiple sources of information. As such, it is reasonable to assume that the comprehension processes involved in learning with online texts (i.e., hypertext without added multimedia components) are not much different than the comprehension processes involved in learning with multiple print documents. However, few online resources contain only text, making it highly unlikely that online learners will be working across multiple resources without encountering additional multimedia elements.

The comprehension task assuredly is complicated when multiple resources include representations other than text. Theories of multimedia learning assume that learners must integrate across visual and verbal representations (Heiser and Tversky, 2006; Mayer, 2001; Schnotz and Bannert, 2003), but some research has found that students find it difficult to connect multiple representations of information during learning (Ainsworth, Bibby, and Wood, 2002), even when prompted to do so (Seufert, 2003). Thus, learning materials that include visual (e.g., diagrams or animations) and verbal (e.g., text) sources of information may pose special comprehension challenges.

Although online and multimedia learning operates on more varied materials than those that have been studied in "pure" text comprehension research, the available evidence demonstrates that the same underlying comprehension processes tend to be involved regardless of whether students are learning from a single text, multiple texts, or text with visual representations (e.g., Butcher, 2006; Wolfe and Goldman, 2005). Butcher (2006) coded learners' utterances during multimedia learning according to text comprehension processes (i.e., paraphrases, elaboration, monitoring, and inferences) and found over 95 percent of learners' total utterances could be reliably coded using these categories. Wolfe and Goldman (2005) found that students engaged in similar cognitive processes when working with multiple-versus single-text resources, but with added processing of the connections between the texts when multiple texts were used. The fact that Wolfe and Goldman's (2005) learners generated inferences that connected multiple texts and resources provides specific evidence of the inferential processing necessary to construct the intertext model and the situations model predicted by Perfetti et al.'s (1999) documents model theory. It also provides some preliminary evidence regarding the nature of inferential processing for multiple documents as following the inferential processes involved in single-text comprehension. In Wolfe and Goldman (2005), students working with multiple resources generated the same types of inferences as in single-text comprehension (i.e., those that connected current text information with prior knowledge and with prior text information) but also went on to generate inferences that connected the current text content with other texts – consistent with development of an intertext model – and with the contents of visual representations (i.e., a time line and a map) – consistent with the development of a situations model. These results also offer evidence that development of a situations model can involve integration across multiple media (in this case, a text, a time line, and a map).

Notably, Wolfe and Goldman (2005) found that generation of each type of connecting inference (i.e., inferences that linked different materials) was positively correlated with students' reasoning scores. The extent to which processing multiple documents may spur the generation of additional inferences needed to connect across documents may help explain why research generally shows that reading from multiple texts enriches students' understanding of a situation or topic (for a discussion, see Rouet, 2006). Additional cross-documents inferences may lead to the development of a richer and more complex documents model, which then facilitates reasoning and knowledge application. In online learning, where students encounter many different texts and forms of visual content, the degree to which learners can generate inferences that will serve to connect multiple forms of representations is likely to have a strong impact on their eventual understanding. Interestingly, the mere presence of visual representations may be sufficient to bias comprehension processes toward inference generation, especially those inferences that integrate the information encountered during learning.

Visual representations increase inference generation

As noted earlier in this chapter, unlike studies of text comprehension, only a few studies have assessed students' real-time comprehension processes as they learn with *multimedia* materials (Ainsworth and Loizou, 2003; Butcher, 2006; Cromley et al., 2010; Lewalter, 2003). Although studies that examine comprehension processes as they occur during multimedia learning are not common, the available evidence so far leads to a consistent conclusion: learning with visual representations (rather than text alone) increases inference generation and leads to improved mental models and understanding (Ainsworth and Loizou, 2003; Butcher, 2006; Cromley et al., 2010). The extent to which inference generation is supported by the presence of visual material during a learning opportunity may provide a cognitive rationale for the multi-media effect (e.g., Mayer, 1997; Mayer, 2001), which refers to repeated research evidence demonstrating that learning with words *and* pictures promotes deeper understanding than learning with words alone (for a discussion, see Butcher, in press). If the presence of visual representations promotes inference generation during a comprehension episode, we would expect students learning with multimedia (text and visual) content to form better (i.e., richer and more coherent) situation models from which inferences can be drawn following comprehension, leading to improved performance on assessments of deep understanding (e.g., mental model assessments or transfer tasks).

The positive effects of visual representations on inference generation during comprehension appear to be quite robust, given that studies have found increased inference generation with different forms of multimedia and when learners with differing prior knowledge work with multimedia materials (Ainsworth and Loizou, 2003; Butcher, 2006; 2010; Cromley et al., 2010; Lewalter, 2003). Butcher (2006, Experiment 2) examined college students' comprehension processes using think alouds as students learned with online materials that consisted of text alone or text plus static diagrams. Results demonstrated that the addition of static diagrams to the text had a significant positive effect on students' generation of inferences as they moved through the multimedia materials, but had no discernible effect on the frequency with which other comprehension processes (i.e., paraphrasing, elaboration, or monitoring) occurred during learning. Students who saw the diagrams in particular generated a significantly higher number of inferences that integrated information across the learning materials compared to students who saw text alone. It is important to note that the diagrams in this research were designed to depict text content about a scientific topic (the heart and circulatory system) but were not specifically designed to prompt inferences or connections during learning. Thus, the nature of diagrammatic processing appears to be, at least partially, inferential.

Rather than studying the impact of adding diagrams to a text in a digital multimedia environment, Ainsworth and Loizou (2003) studied comprehension processes via think alouds when college students learned with a paper packet containing static diagrams or text alone. They found differences only in the generation of utterances that reflected an inference about the goal or purpose of an action (coded as "goal-driven explanations") – students who learned with diagrams generated significantly more goal-driven inferences than students who learned with text. Correspondingly, at posttest, students in the diagram condition earned significantly higher scores on a measure of knowledge inference. Cromley et al. (2010) found similar results when studying the think alouds generated by higher-knowledge students reading authentic study materials (i.e., biology majors reading a biology textbook): students generated a significantly higher percentage of inferences when processing diagrams as opposed to reading text.

Together, the studies described in this section provide converging evidence that processing diagrammatic representations promotes more frequent inference generation than processing text alone. Diagrammatic processing appears to be, to some extent, inherently inferential. However, as discussed in the next section, this does not mean that simply adding diagrams to text is a sure-fire method to ensure that learners engage in sufficient levels of inference generation during comprehension.

Limitations to visually supported inference generation

Although inferential processing appears to be an inherent component of diagram comprehension, inference generation during diagram comprehension still is observed at far lower levels than processes such as paraphrasing or rereading (Butcher, 2006; Cromley et al., 2010). Moreover, learners often do not spontaneously attend to visual content when it is coupled with text information. During textbook reading, researchers have found that students frequently skip or superficially skim diagrams (e.g., Cromley et al., 2010). Recent work using eye-tracking methodology to measure the allocation of attention to text and images during multimedia instruction confirms that learners primarily focus on text content during available study time (Schmidt-Weigand, Kohnert, and Glowalla, 2010; Schwonke, Berthold, and Renkl, 2009); even when additional study time is provided, learners only occasionally devote this time to the inspection of visual elements (Schmidt-Weigand et al., 2010).

When asked to verbalize their thinking during a video replay of fixations gathered during eye tracking (i.e., retrospective reporting), students do not articulate an understanding of why multiple representations should be processed (Schwonke et al., 2009). Thus, many learners may strategically ignore the very representations that would enhance their ultimate learning outcomes.

It is possible that individuals learn to ignore visual content of learning materials in purposeful and strategic ways due to prior experience with commercial textbooks; despite comprising a large amount of available space in textbooks, diagrams and illustrations in these sources have been found to consist primarily of decorational or example images that do not add useful information for comprehension (Levin and Mayer, 1993; Mayer, 1993). Accordingly, students may ignore visual content as an adaptive strategy developed during early textbook learning; during subsequent learning opportunities, they may not distinguish between different forms of visual representations (e.g., diagrams vs. decorational images) nor recognize the importance or utility of diagrams in well-designed educational materials.

If students have learned to ignore visuals based on their previous experiences with textbooks, one question is whether unfamiliar visuals to which students are more likely to attend – particularly animations that draw learner attention via dynamic movement – will promote greater inference generation than static visuals. Because the dynamic movement depicted in animated visuals tends to demonstrate causal behaviors in a system, it also would be logical to assume that animations may increase inference generation by making dynamic behaviors visible and, therefore, available to high-level processing. However, evidence so far suggests that adding dynamic features to a multimedia presentation offers no processing benefits beyond those of static images and, moreover, that students have difficulty drawing inferences from animated content (Lewalter, 2003).

The lack of differences in cognitive processing occurring with dynamic versus static content may reflect an inherent difficulty in processing dynamic content: even expert meteorologists examining dynamic weather phenomena choose to view and analyze static images when given an option between static and dynamic visualizations (Bogacz and Trafton, 2005). Further, experts infer large numbers of dynamic behaviors from static displays (Bogacz and Trafton, 2005). Findings with novice learners have shown that students can learn more from static versus animated images when students are able to mentally animate the static content (Hegarty, Kriz, and Cate, 2003). Together, these studies demonstrate that the degree of processing facilitated by a visual representation is a central consideration in determining its potential utility.

To effectively process animated – or even complex static – content, learners may need support in attending to relevant aspects of the display. Novice learners find it especially difficult to distinguish between relevant and irrelevant components of animated displays because visually salient information often is not of central conceptual importance (Lowe, 1999; 2003). Thus, studies of multimedia learning have explored the use of embedded visual cues to direct students' attention to diagrams and animations as they learn (e.g., Bartholomé and Bromme, 2009; Butcher and Aleven, 2013; de Koning, Tabbers, Rikers, and Paas, 2009; 2010a; 2010b; Jamet, 2014; Jamet, Gavota, and Quaireau, 2008). A key question is what form of processing these visual cues may foster; that is, does using visual cues to guide learner attention during multimedia learning facilitate inference generation?

Impact of visual cues on inferential processes during multimedia learning

Visual cues have been implemented frequently as a perceptual strategy to guide learner attention during multimedia comprehension (de Koning et al., 2009). Visual cues can take a number of formats, including highlighting of key content (Bartholomé and Bromme, 2009; Butcher and Aleven, 2013; Jamet, 2014; Jamet et al., 2008), color coding (Ferrara and Butcher, 2011; Ozcelik, Arslan-Ari, and Cagiltay, 2010; Ozcelik, Karakus, Kursun, and Cagiltay, 2009), increasing brightness (also referred to as "spotlighting") of relevant features (de Koning et al., 2010a; 2010b), increasing the size of relevant components (Amadieu, Mariné, and Laimay, 2011; Ferrara and Butcher, 2011), using arrows to signal temporal sequence of a system (Heiser and Tversky, 2006), or including animated agents that point out relevant visual features (e.g., Craig, Gholson, and Driscoll, 2002). Although research has shown positive benefits of cueing for retention of knowledge (for a discussion, see de Koning et al., 2009), results have been mixed for assessments – such as transfer tests – that would indicate that inferences have been made as the result of comprehension. For example, although Jamet (2014) found that colored highlights helped to guide learners' attention (as assessed by eye-tracking fixations), this guidance facilitated recall but not transfer performance. In contrast, de Koning, Tabbers, Rikers, and Paas (2007) found that highlighting key visual features during a multimedia presentation facilitated improved transfer performance in a rather robust way: students who viewed cued animations performed better not only on transfer questions targeting cued content but also on transfer questions targeting information that was not cued.

It is difficult to reconcile discrepant results of cueing on inference generation at this point, but existing research provides some tentative conclusions and suggests a few directions for additional research. Existing studies are consistent in demonstrating (via fixations during eye tracking) that visual cues are effective in guiding attention to key elements during multimedia learning (de Koning et al., 2010a; Ozcelik et al., 2009; Ozcelik et al., 2010). Furthermore, guiding attention may serve to reduce cognitive demands on visual search during multimedia learning (Amadieu et al., 2011), thus freeing cognitive resources to be allocated to inference generation as multimedia materials are processed. This possibility has been supported by one study that used think alouds to assess cognitive processing as students worked with animated multimedia (de Koning et al., 2010b). In de Koning et al.'s (2010b) research, students who viewed cued animations were more likely to generate correct inferences than students who viewed uncued animations, even though the groups did not differ in the number of paraphrases generated during study. As may be expected given the cued animations' impact on inference generation, students who viewed the cued animations also scored better than students who viewed the uncued animations on knowledge assessments targeting inference and transfer. However, providing cues that lead to efficient visual search does not always result in better performance on measures of transfer, with some research showing no effect (Kriz and Hegarty, 2007; Ozcelik et al., 2010) or a negative effect (Bartholomé and Bromme, 2009; Butcher and Aleven, 2013; Ozcelik et al., 2009) on measures of deeper understanding (e.g., transfer tests or mental model tasks). These results have led some researchers to argue that visual features that improve the external display of multimedia do not necessarily optimize processing (de Koning et al., 2010a; Kriz and Hegarty, 2007).

Understanding when cueing leads to effective inference generation during multimedia learning will require more studies that directly measure the impact of different cues on the inferences that are generated as comprehension ensues. Studies also will need to vary the complexity of the multimedia materials and the prior knowledge of learners in systematic ways, as the difficulty of visual search within complex representations can be expected to influence the degree to which attentional guidance is necessary or helpful to comprehenders.

Recent evidence suggests the impact of inference generation on multimedia learning may be more closely tied to the type of inferences that are generated during comprehension rather than the overall amount of inference generation that is observed (de Koning et al., 2010b). Think-aloud data from de Koning et al.'s (2010b) work showed that students who learned with cued animations generated fewer than half the number of possible inferences that could be made from the provided animations. Despite these seemingly "impoverished" levels of inference generation with cued animations, participants in this condition scored similarly on inference and transfer assessments to participants who were provided with *all possible* inferences via instructional explanations. Thus, in some cases, visual cueing may promote generation of key inferences that are necessary to construct richer and more accurate mental models from which correct inferences can be drawn. In other words, a select number of inferences generated during comprehension may improve the inferences that can be made as a result of comprehension (and that ultimately drive knowledge outcomes). This possibility is consistent with research on the visual mental models that students construct when reading a text; when students fail to make key inferences and (consequently) construct an inaccurate mental model early during text reading, the inaccurate mental models persist throughout the learning episode and impair performance on posttest measures of inference and understanding (Butcher and Chi, 2006).

More work is needed to understand when and how cues and other types of multimedia features will generate specific, key inferences necessary for mental model construction. As discussed later in this chapter, a growing body of literature demonstrates that the addition of interactive features that mimic or scaffold inferential processes have shown promise in promoting meaningful understanding of multimedia and digital content (Bodemer, Ploetzner, Bruchmüller, and Hacker, 2005; Bodemer, Ploetzner, Feuerlein, and Spada, 2004; Butcher and Aleven, 2013; Evans and Gibbons, 2007). However, it also is possible that simply providing more integrated external displays – where visual and verbal content are tightly linked – may spur key inferences that connect information in each format, leading to more coherent mental models that support subsequent inferencing.

Supporting inference generation via integrated visual-verbal materials

When multimedia materials contain visual and verbal content, developing a coherent mental model requires integrating information from both sources. Eye-tracking research has found that more integrative patterns of eye movements – that is, eye movements that transition between text and relevant components of a diagram – facilitate knowledge transfer (Johnson and Mayer, 2012; Mason, Tornatora, and Pluchino, 2013). This may help explain why research on multimedia learning frequently has found that students who learn with materials in which text is nearby or embedded within visual representations demonstrate better performance on knowledge measures that require inference generation (e.g., Kalyuga, Chandler, and Sweller, 1998; Mayer, 1989; Mayer, Steinhoff, Bowers, and Mars, 1995); in multimedia learning, this effect is commonly referred to as the contiguity effect (Mayer, 2001; 2005).

The potential importance of making inferences that link verbal information with visual representations processing also may help explain why multimedia learning studies often show a modality effect such that students perform better on transfer tasks when visual content is accompanied by audio narration rather than written text (for discussions of the modality effect, see Ginns, 2005; Mayer, 2001; 2005). By removing the need to locate written text content when switching between verbal and visual information, mixed modality materials (i.e., narration with diagrams or animations) may facilitate inferential processing that connects verbal and visual content by allowing the learner to continuously focus on the visual representation as relevant verbal information is provided. Similarly, providing animated or video content with verbal information can facilitate performance on transfer tasks (Schüler, Scheiter, and Gerjets, 2013) and increase inferential processing during multimedia learning (Tibus, Heier, and Schwan, 2013), but the cognitive demands associated with drawing inferences from visual materials that are transient in nature nevertheless can prevent development of a coherent mental model (Tibus et al., 2013).

Together, these results suggest that the "passive" support for inference generation offered by combining visual and verbal content in close physical and/or temporal proximity may be limited to situations where few other demands are placed on the learner. This possibility is supported by recent evidence showing that transfer tests that require inference generation fail to demonstrate differences between written and audio text accompanying animations when longer (more authentic) texts are used (e.g., Schüler et al., 2013) or when learners have limited prior knowledge in the domain of study (e.g., Scheiter, Schüler, Gerjets, Huk, and Hesse, 2014). Similarly, placing text and visual representations in close physical proximity has failed to improve performance on transfer tasks when multimedia materials are complex (Florax and Ploetzner, 2010; Ozcelik and Acarturk, 2011). Implicit support for making inferences may not be sufficient when materials are complex or otherwise demanding; in these cases, representations or materials that influence learners' behaviors and, consequently, their active processing of multimedia content may be required to support inference generation.

Facilitating inference generation via learner behaviors and interactions

Promoting inferential processing via graphical overviews

Most of the multimedia research discussed previously in this chapter has used visual materials that convey information via iconic representations (e.g., Ainsworth and Loizou, 2003; Butcher, 2006; Florax and Ploetzner, 2010; Lowe, 1999; Mayer and Anderson, 1992). Iconic representations depict one or more aspects of an object's visual appearance such as shape, structure, size, or layout; diagrams and animations are common examples of iconic representations. However, multimedia materials also can use visual representations to communicate high-level relationships between concepts, as in the case of graphical overviews. Typically, graphical overviews take the form of a node-link diagram, where text describing concepts or ideas is depicted in nodes that are spatially organized and linked to show their causal or conceptual relationships. The spatial organization of a graphical overview may take several different forms: for example, *network* overviews use complex visuospatial organization to depict important relationships between ideas (e.g., Amadieu, Tricot, and Mariné, 2009; Butcher et al., 2006; de Jong and van der Hulst, 2002; Salmerón, Gil, Bråten, and Strømsø, 2010); *hierarchical* overviews use linear branching to communicate an overview of text structure (e.g., Amadieu et al., 2009; Salmerón, Baccino, Cañas, Madrid, and Fajardo, 2009); and, *outline* overviews (e.g., Davies, Butcher, and Stevens, 2013; Schnotz and Heiß, 2009) highlight important points linearly without explicitly representing the relationships between them. In the research literature, graphical overviews have been used to depict causal relationships within a single document (e.g., McCrudden, Schraw, and Lehman, 2009) and conceptual relationships across hypertexts covering a single topic (e.g., Salmerón et al., 2009), as well as conceptual relationships across a collection of (many) online resources covering multiple topics within a domain (e.g., Butcher et al., 2006).

Static versions of graphical overviews (i.e., graphical overviews that do not offer interactive features) have been found to facilitate better knowledge transfer than reading a text twice (McCrudden et al., 2009). Evidence from hypertext learning research suggests that this benefit may be due to the graphical overview's support for inferential processes that integrate information as study materials are encountered: presenting a graphical overview to students before working with hypertext materials improved their performance on inference questions but presenting it after hypertext learning diminished performance (Salmerón et al., 2009). Thus, graphical overviews may be successful in providing a knowledge organization that facilitates inference generation by making it easier to integrate and connect materials as they are processed.

Making relationships between hypertext documents clear is one successful strategy to reduce navigational disorientation that is a significant barrier to online learning (e.g., Rouet, 2006) and may provide support for effective navigation behaviors to lead to inference generation (Salmerón et al., 2010). Salmerón et al. (2010) found that following hypertext links in an order driven by conceptual coherence as opposed to personal interest was a significant predictor of students' inference scores but not scores on a test of recall. This confirms prior work demonstrating that the number of links that readers visit when working with online hypertexts influences textbase development, whereas the order in which links are visited affects situation model development (Salmerón et al., 2005). However, the impact of navigation behaviors on inferential processing also interacts with prior knowledge. Students with lower prior knowledge were found to score better on an inference assessment when hypertext links were followed in a coherent order, but high knowledge participants achieved better inference scores when following a low-coherence order of links (Salmerón et al., 2005). Navigating hypertext in a manner that results in low-coherence between links may promote generative processing for higher-knowledge learners in a way that is too taxing for lower-knowledge learners.

Although the aforementioned studies in this section have shown that the use of graphical overviews can support inference generation when students are learning from hypertext documents that encompass a single topic or overall text, less is known about how conceptual overviews might influence inference generation when students learn from multiple, independent online resources. Previous work found that using a graphic organizer to access online resources prompted students to spend more time processing the conceptual content of multimedia materials than when they located online content using keyword searches, but this work did not specifically examine whether the additional domain-focused processing resulted in inference generation (Butcher et al., 2006). More recent work has indicated that the complexity of a graphical overview that is used to access online content can play an important role in whether or not successful inference generation is supported (Davies et al., 2013).

Davies et al. (2013) asked students with low prior knowledge to use either a complex network graphical overview or text-based outline as they learned from a large collection of online digital resources. The graphical overview and the outline differed in their visuospatial organization, but the text in both representations was identical. The graphical overview and the outline both structured navigation to online multimedia content: students clicked on a text concept in either representation to access a list of hyperlinks that provided access to relevant, online resources. Students were randomly assigned to either the graphical overview or outline condition and were asked to learn as much as possible about the domain in general (plate tectonics) as well as the relationships between important ideas within the domain. Following learning, situation model development was assessed using items that required inferences about the application of domain concepts to new situations and about the relationships between domain concepts. Davies et al. (2013) hypothesized that the conceptual relationships depicted in the graphical overview would promote inference generation – particularly inferences that integrated domain ideas during learning – leading to better performance on inferential assessment items. However, results showed the opposite pattern. Students who learned with the graphical overviews made more erroneous inferences when explaining relationships between domain concepts and students who learned with the outline overviews scored better on items that required inferences about the application of domain concepts to new situations.

Davies et al.'s (2013) findings suggest that the design of a graphical overview may play a strong role in the quality of inferences that students generate as they learn from a set of independent online materials. Although the graphical overview in Davies et al.'s (2013) research made relationships between concepts explicit, complex interrelationships between the depicted nodes may have obscured a clear route through domain content (de Jong and van der Hulst, 2002). For students with low prior knowledge, the more straightforward and linearly organized outline view may have been more effective in supporting inferential processes because its visual layout encouraged a structured sequence through domain content (see also de Jong and van der Hulst, 2002). With strong navigational support, students may be able to devote more processing resources to making inferences about conceptual relationships across online materials.

Another way to structure online navigation may be to provide visual cues that guide students' interactions with more complex graphical overviews. Providing visual highlights in a graphical overview has been found to be an effective method to guide sequential exploration of content according to domain concepts, resulting in a more structured knowledge organization (de Jong and van der Hulst, 2002). Other research confirms the potential benefit of visual cues to structure navigational sequences. Both color-coding and size-scaling can be used effectively to cue student processing of key domain concepts within network organizers, resulting in better knowledge integration (Ferrara and Butcher, 2011). Guiding learners along an optimal conceptual path via their online navigation may encourage them to make inferences that integrate knowledge as they move from one online resource to another. However, more research that examines real-time comprehension processes during online navigation and learning will be needed to fully understand these effects.

To this point in the chapter, scaffolds and strategies to facilitate inferential processing during online and multimedia learning mainly have focused on making learners' processing more effective as they move within and across online and multimedia content. However, increasing evidence suggests that placing additional (and more difficult) processing demands on learners can facilitate inference generation if the demands are implemented in strategic ways.

Promoting inference generation via strategic processing of multimedia content

In digital environments, learning can be facilitated by systems that increase processing demands by requiring students to interact with multimedia content in ways that spur inferential processing. For example, providing students with visual and verbal information sources that are initially separated but must be integrated via a drag-and-drop interface has been shown to facilitate deeper understanding of complex multimedia than when processing demands are removed by providing students with a preintegrated multimedia representation (Bodemer et al., 2004). Similarly, requiring students to actively integrate visual and verbal information sources before using simulations and dynamic visualizations promotes more systematic and goal-oriented exploration (Bodemer et al., 2005). Even with paper-based multimedia workbooks, requiring high school students to generate text that is integrated into diagrams has been found to foster inference making during learning (Cromley et al., 2013). Each of these studies requires that students infer relevant connections between visual features and verbal content. Requiring the learner to create an integrated visual-verbal representation encourages these connective inferences, resulting in a more coherent mental model that can guide subsequent learning.

As computational power increases, there is growing interest in creating interactive, online learning environments that are customized to individual students and their existing prior knowledge (e.g., Butcher and Sumner, 2011). An existing example of interactive and personalized learning interfaces is found in Intelligent Tutoring Systems (ITS). ITS are digital environments that scaffold student activities to assess and promote learning (Corbett, Koedinger, and Anderson, 1997). Model-tracing tutors are a particular form of ITS that compare step-by-step student inputs during problem solving against a model of expert knowledge. By identifying the students' solution paths within a very large problem space, model-tracing tutors can identify students' knowledge needs and select targeted practice and support for an individual student (Corbett et al., 1997; Corbett, McLaughlin, and Scarpinatto, 2000).

Although ITS have been found to be effective for improving students' problem-solving performance in digital environments (Anderson, Corbett, Koedinger, and Pelletier, 1995; Koedinger, Anderson, Hadley, and Mark, 1997), it sometimes is difficult to ensure that students are engaged in deep, inferential processes as they learn with these systems (Aleven, Koedinger, Sinclair, and Snyder, 1998). Students frequently apply low-level strategies to problem solving in ITS, for example, using a formula without consideration of its relevance or guessing an answer (Aleven and Koedinger, 2002; Aleven et al., 1998). When students use shallow problem-solving strategies, they fail to engage in the inferential processes necessary to connect specific instantiations of problems with larger domain concepts. Although students rarely make these connections spontaneously, they represent the most effective forms of self-explanation that students can deploy to promote deep understanding (Chi, Bassok, Lewis, Reimann, and Glaser, 1989; Renkl, 1997). Thus, a key question is how features of online environments can be leveraged to promote this type of deep, inferential processing. Developing such features is analogous to manipulations in which text is inserted in a written document to spur causal inferences (Vidal-Abarca et al., 2000), only these technologies spur inferential processing by inserting prompts or controls for user actions rather than additional text.

Aleven and Koedinger (2002) found that requiring students to identify the mathematical principles relevant to specific problem-solving steps in an intelligent tutoring system for geometry led to increases in students' conceptual understanding and knowledge transfer. In this case, students explicitly connected verbal concepts (in the form of written domain principles) to numerically and visually represented problem components. Subsequent work (Butcher and Aleven, 2008; 2010) explored the possibility that implicit support for visual-verbal integration would facilitate the development of meaningful domain understanding. These studies showed that requiring students to input numerical answers and mathematical principles directly into a visual diagram improved subsequent knowledge application and transfer, leading to the conclusion that technology-supported interactions that require deployment of inferential processes can promote deeper learning (Butcher and Aleven, 2008; 2010). However, findings did not explicitly demonstrate that inference generation was promoted when using the interactive diagrams.

In recent research, Butcher and Davies (in preparation) explored whether interactive diagrams promoted increased inference generation as students learned to solve problems in an intelligent tutoring system: the Geometry Cognitive Tutor. In the control version of the Geometry Cognitive Tutor, students used a basic version of diagram interaction; students interacted with geometry diagrams by clicking on missing values as they solved the problem (see Butcher and Aleven, 2008; 2010). In the treatment condition, students used interactive diagrams that were designed to link visual features to conceptual principles (see Butcher and Aleven, 2013, Experiment 3). After making an error, students could not proceed until they had correctly identified the geometry principle needed to solve the current step of the problem and had highlighted specific (visual) diagram features relevant to using that (verbally expressed) domain principle. This "highlighting" form of interaction was designed to facilitate integration of visual and verbal information in a manner that mimicked the inferential processes that connect specific instantiations of problems with larger domain concepts during successful self-explanation (Chi et al., 1989; Renkl, 1997).

Think-aloud data was collected and analyzed to understand students' cognitive processes as they worked in their randomly assigned tutor condition. We were particularly interested in two categories of utterances: inferential reasoning about geometry principles and/or the problem situation and students' narration of their problem-solving processes. Inferential reasoning was coded for utterances in which the students reasoned about diagram features, geometry principles, problem features, or the relationships between them; inferential reasoning reflected processing that went beyond the information present in the problem or on the screen. For example, "This line here must be the transversal because it connects two parallel lines to create these angles." Process narration was coded for utterances in which the students described problem-solving actions without justification or explanation; process narrations are low-level utterances that describe problem-solving activities but fail to connect a conceptual explanation to actions. These narrative utterances often included naming diagram angles, describing mathematical operations, or stating numerical answers. For example, "So, it's going to be 61.1 plus 43.1, which makes 104.2 my answer." Although process narration may describe the computational procedures necessary to calculate a correct answer, they do not show (observable) evidence of inference generation.

Results demonstrated that interactive diagram highlighting facilitated inferential processing significantly more than the basic diagram inter-action in the control condition. Furthermore, students who were prompted to highlight specific, principle-relevant diagram features as related to (verbally expressed) domain principles produced fewer low-level process narrations, and fewer low-level narrations were correlated with higher performance on posttest transfer items. These findings pro-vide direct evidence that increasing processing demands via visual inter-actions can reduce shallow processing and increase deep, inferential reasoning during problem solving. Although more research is needed to fully understand when and how inferences can be supported in com-plex, personalized multimedia systems, this research offers preliminary evidence that, if they are strategically designed, interactive features of next-generation educational technologies can successfully change the patterns of cognitive processing in which students engage as they learn.

Conclusions

Although traditional text materials, online hypertext, and multimedia materials differ greatly in the amounts of information and in the variety of representations that come into play during a comprehension episode, the importance of inference generation for deep understanding and eventual knowledge remains constant. Mental models of to-be-learned content are formed via integrative and inferential processing regardless of the representation types that must be integrated. This chapter has focused on the impact of different external supports and features in facilitating inference generation during online and multimedia learning. However, it is important to keep in mind that learners' prior knowledge, comprehension task and goals, learned comprehension strategies, and exposure to instruction all are also important to understanding how and why a particular learner is successful or unsuccessful with a set of learn-ing materials. In contemporary situations, the vast likelihood is that these materials are digital in nature – almost certainly consisting of some combination of hypertext and multimedia. Thus, understanding what factors promote inference generation with these materials is critical to understanding when deep learning will be achieved by modern learners.

When learning with hypertext that includes multiple online resources, coherence across digital materials is central to supporting inference generation. Such coherence can be supported by exposing learners to a graphical overview that structures their navigation through the learning space, allowing greater opportunities for learners to make (correct) infer-ences that bridge across multiple resources. Similarly, inference generation occurs during multimedia learning when learners process relevant verbal and visual content in close succession. This integrative processing can be facilitated by creating multimedia presentations that closely integrate verbal and visual information or requiring learners to engage in behaviors that generate connections between related information sources. Although mixed results have been achieved with visual cues and other passive supports, features that prompt or require active processing have shown potential for robust effects.

As online and multimedia learning becomes increasingly central to students' learning experiences, additional interactions for promoting active integration of information and strategic inference generation should be explored. More research that directly assesses the impact of multimedia features on cognitive comprehension processes is needed, so that a clearer picture will emerge regarding multimedia features that are necessary and sufficient to facilitate inference generation. Moreover, we need to understand more about the relationships between inference generation, mental model development, and knowledge transfer to effectively design cognitive scaffolds and interactions that result not only in inference generation during learning, but also in effective and long lasting understanding of domain materials.

REFERENCES

Ainsworth, S., Bibby, P., & Wood, D. (2002). Examining the effects of different multiple representational systems in learning primary mathematics. *Journal of the Learning Sciences, 11*(1), 25–61.

Ainsworth, S., & Loizou, A. T. (2003). The effects of self-explaining when learning with text or diagrams. *Cognitive Science, 27,* 669–81.

Albrecht, J. E., & Myers, J. L. (1995). Role of context in accessing distant information during reading. *Journal of Experimental Psychology: Learning, Memory, and Cognition, 21*(6), 1459–68.

Albrecht, J. E., & O'Brien, E. J. (1993). Updating a mental model: maintaining both local and global coherence. *Journal of Experimental Psychology. Learning, Memory, and Cognition, 19*(5), 1061–70.

Aleven, V., & Koedinger, K. R. (2002). An effective metacognitive strategy: learning by doing and explaining with a computer-based Cognitive Tutor. *Cognitive Science, 26*(2), 147–79.

Aleven, V., Koedinger, K. R., Sinclair, H. C., & Snyder, J. (1998). Combatting shallow learning in a tutor for geometry problem solving. In B. P. Goettl, H. M. Halff, C. L. Redfield, & V. J. Shute (eds.), *Intelligent Tutoring Systems, Fourth International Conference, ITS '98. Lecture Notes in Computer Science 1452* (pp. 364–73). Berlin: Springer Verlag.

Amadieu, F., Mariné, C., & Laimay, C. (2011). The attention-guiding effect and cognitive load in the comprehension of animations. *Computers in Human Behavior, 27*(1), 36–40.

Amadieu, F., Tricot, A., & Mariné, C. (2009). Prior knowledge in learning from a nonlinear electronic document: disorientation and coherence of the reading sequences. *Computers in Human Behavior*, *25*, 381–8.

Anderson, J. R., Corbett, A. T., Koedinger, K. R., & Pelletier, R. (1995). Cognitive tutors: lessons learned. *Journal of the Learning Sciences*, *4*(2), 167–207.

Bartholomé, T., & Bromme, R. (2009). Coherence formation when learning from text and pictures: what kind of support for whom? *Journal of Educational Psychology*, *101*(2), 282–93.

Bodemer, D., Ploetzner, R., Bruchmüller, K., & Hacker, S. (2005). Supporting learning with interactive multimedia through active integration of representations. *Instructional Science*, *33*, 73–5.

Bodemer, D., Ploetzner, R., Feuerlein, I., & Spada, H. (2004). The active integration of information during learning with dynamic and interactive visualisations. *Learning and Instruction*, *14*, 325–41.

Bogacz, S., & Trafton, J. G. (2005). Understanding dynamic and static displays: using images to reason dynamically. *Cognitive Systems Research*, *6*(4), 312–9.

Bråten, I., Strømsø, H. I., & Salmerón, L. (2011). Trust and mistrust when students read multiple information sources about climate change. *Learning & Instruction*, *21*(2), 180–92.

Butcher, K. R. (2006). Learning from text with diagrams: promoting mental model development and inference generation. *Journal of Educational Psychology*, *98*(1), 182–97.

(2010). How diagram interaction supports learning: evidence from think alouds during intelligent tutoring. In A. Goel, M. Jamnik, & N. H. Narayanan (eds.), *Diagrammatic Representation and Inference: Lecture Notes in Computer Science, Volume 6170* (pp. 295–7). Berlin/Heidelberg: Springer.

(in press). The multimedia principle. In R. E. Mayer (ed.), *Cambridge Handbook of Multimedia Learning* (2nd ed.) Cambridge University Press.

Butcher, K. R., & Aleven, V. (2008). Diagram interaction during intelligent tutoring in geometry: support for knowledge retention and deep understanding. In B. C. Love, K. McRae, & V. M. Sloutsky (eds.), *Proceedings of the 30th Annual Conference of the Cognitive Science Society* (pp. 1736–41). Austin, TX: Cognitive Science Society.

(2010). Learning during intelligent tutoring: when do integrated visual-verbal representations improve student outcomes? In S. Ohlsson & R. Catrambone (eds.), *Proceedings of the 32nd Annual Conference of the Cognitive Science Society* (pp. 2888–93). Austin, TX: Cognitive Science Society.

(2013). Using student interactions to foster rule-diagram mapping during problem solving in an intelligent tutoring system. *Journal of Educational Psychology*, *105*(4), 988–1009.

Butcher, K. R., Bhushan, S., & Sumner, T. (2006). Multimedia displays for conceptual search processes: information seeking with strand maps. *ACM Multimedia Systems Journal*, *11*(3), 236–48.

Butcher, K. R., & Chi, M. T. H. (2006). *How Can Diagrams Scaffold Text Comprehension?* Paper presented at the EARLI SIG2 Conference, August 30–September 1, 2006, Nottingham, UK.

Butcher, K. R., & Davies, S. (in preparation). Cognitive processes during diagram interaction in an intelligent tutoring system.

Butcher, K. R., & Kintsch, W. (2012). Text comprehension and discourse processing. In A. F. Healy & R. W. Proctor (eds.), *Handbook of Psychology, Vol. IV: Experimental Psychology* (2nd. ed.). Hoboken, NJ: Wiley.

Butcher, K. R., & Sumner, T. (2011). Self-directed learning and the sensemaking paradox. *Human Computer Interaction*, *26*(1), 123–59.

Chi, M. T. H., Bassok, M., Lewis, M. W., Reimann, P., & Glaser, R. (1989). Self-explanations: how students study and use examples in learning to solve problems. *Cognitive Science*, *13*(2), 145–82.

Cook, A. E., Limber, J. E., & O'Brien, E. J. (2001). Situation-based context and the availability of predictive inferences. *Journal of Memory and Language*, *44*(2), 220–34.

Corbett, A. T., Koedinger, K. R., & Anderson, J. R. (1997). Intelligent tutoring systems. In M. Helander, T. K. Landauer, & P. Prabhu (eds.), *Handbook of Human-Computer Interaction* (2nd ed.) (pp. 849–74). Amsterdam: Elsevier Science.

Corbett, A. T., McLaughlin, M., & Scarpinatto, K. C. (2000). Modeling student knowledge: cognitive tutors in high school and college. *User Modeling and User-Adapted Interaction*, *10*(2/3), 81–108.

Craig, S. D., Gholson, B., & Driscoll, D. M. (2002). Animated pedagogical agents in multimedia educational environments: effects of agent properties, picture features, and redundancy. *Journal of Educational Psychology*, *94*(2), 428–34.

Cromley, J. G., Bergey, B. W., Fitzhugh, S., Newcombe, N., Wills, T. W., Shipley, T. F., & Tanaka, J. C. (2013). Effects of three diagram instruction methods on transfer of diagram comprehension skills: the critical role of inference while learning. *Learning and Instruction*, *26*(0), 45–58.

Cromley, J. G., Snyder-Hogan, L. E., & Luciw-Dubas, U. A. (2010). Cognitive activities in complex science text and diagrams. *Contemporary Educational Psychology*, *35*, 59–74.

Davies, S., Butcher, K. R., & Stevens, C. (2013). Self-regulated learning with graphical overviews: when spatial information detracts from learning. In M. Knauff, M. Pauen, N. Sebanz, & I. Wachsmuth (eds.), *Proceedings of the 35th Annual Conference of the Cognitive Science Society* (pp. 2136–41). Austin, TX: Cognitive Science Society.

De Jong, T., & van der Hulst, A. (2002). The effects of graphical overviews on knowledge acquisition in hypertext. *Journal of Computer Assisted Learning*, *18*(2), 219–31.

De Koning, B. B., Tabbers, H. K., Rikers, R. M. J. P., & Paas, F. (2007). Attention cueing as a means to enhance learning from an animation. *Applied Cognitive Psychology*, *21*(6), 731–746.

(2009). Towards a framework for attention cueing in instructional animations: guidelines for research and design. *Educational Psychology Review*, *21*(2), 113–40.

(2010a). Attention guidance in learning from a complex animation: seeing is understanding? *Learning and Instruction*, 20(2), 111–22.

(2010b). Learning by generating vs. receiving instructional explanations: two approaches to enhance attention cueing in animations. *Computers & Education*, 55(2), 681–91.

Evans, C., & Gibbons, N. J. (2007). The interactivity effect in multimedia learning. *Computers & Education*, 49(4), 1147–60.

Ferrara, L., & Butcher, K. (2011). Visualizing feedback: using graphical cues to promote self-regulated learning. In L. Carlson, C. Hölscher, & T. Shipley (eds.), *Proceedings of the Thirty-third Annual Conference of the Cognitive Science Society*. Boston: Cognitive Science Society.

Florax, M., & Ploetzner, R. (2010). What contributes to the split-attention effect? The role of text segmentation, picture labelling, and spatial proximity. *Learning and Instruction*, 20(3), 216–24.

Ginns, P. (2005). Meta-analysis of the modality effect. *Learning and Instruction*, 15(4), 313–31.

Graham, L., & Metaxas, P. T. (2003). Of course it's true; I saw it on the Internet! *Communications of the ACM*, 46(5), 71–5.

Hegarty, M., Kriz, S., & Cate, C. (2003). The roles of mental animations and external animations in understanding mechanical systems. *Cognition and Instruction*, 21(4), 325–60.

Heiser, J., & Tversky, B. (2006). Arrows in comprehending and producing mechanical diagrams. *Cognitive Science*, 30(3), 581–92.

Jamet, E. (2014). An eye-tracking study of cueing effects in multimedia learning. *Computers in Human Behavior*, 32(0), 47–53.

Jamet, E., Gavota, M., & Quaireau, C. (2008). Attention guiding in multimedia learning. *Learning and Instruction*, 18(2), 135–45.

Johnson, C. I., & Mayer, R. E. (2012). An eye movement analysis of the spatial contiguity effect in multimedia learning. *Journal of Experimental Psychology: Applied*, 18(2), 178–91.

Kalyuga, S., Chandler, P., & Sweller, J. (1998). Levels of expertise and instructional design. *Human Factors*, 40, 1–17.

Kintsch, W. (1986). Learning from text. *Cognition and Instruction*, 3(2), 87–108.

(1988). The role of knowledge in discourse comprehension: a construction-integration model. *Psychological Review*, 95(2), 163–82.

(1998). *Comprehension: A Paradigm for Cognition*. Cambridge University Press.

Klin, C. M., Guzmán, A. E., & Levine, W. H. (1999). Prevalence and persistence of predictive inferences. *Journal of Memory and Language*, 40(4), 593–604.

Koedinger, K. R., Anderson, J. R., Hadley, W. H., & Mark, M. A. (1997). Intelligent tutoring goes to school in the big city. *International Journal of Artificial Intelligence in Education*, 8, 30–43.

Kriz, S., & Hegarty, M. (2007). Top-down and bottom-up influences on learning from animations. *International Journal of Human-Computer Studies*, 65(11),

Lea, R. B. (1995). Online evidence for elaborative logical inferences in text. *Journal of Experimental Psychology: Learning, Memory, and Cognition*, 21(6), 1469–82.

Levin, J. R., & Mayer, R. E. (1993). Understanding illustrations in text. In B. K. Britton, A. Woodward, & M. Binkley (eds.), *Learning from Textbooks: Theory and Practice* (pp. 95–114). Mahwah, NJ: Erlbaum.

Lewalter, D. (2003). Cognitive strategies for learning from static and dynamic visuals. *Learning & Instruction, 13*, 177–89.

Lowe, R. K. (1999). Extracting information from an animation during complex visual learning. *European Journal of Psychology of Education, 14*(2), 225–44.

  (2003). Animation and learning: selective processing of information in dynamic graphics. *Learning and Instruction, 13*, 157–76.

Lynch, C. (2008). Digital libraries, learning communities, and open education. In T. Iiyoshi & M. S. V. Kumar (eds.), *Opening Up Education* (pp. 105–18). Cambridge, MA: MIT Press.

Mason, L., Tornatora, M. C., & Pluchino, P. (2013). Do fourth graders integrate text and picture in processing and learning from an illustrated science text? Evidence from eye-movement patterns. *Computers & Education, 60*(1), 95–109.

Mayer, R. E. (1989). Systematic thinking fostered by illustrations in scientific text. *Journal of Educational Psychology, 81*(2), 240–46.

  (1993). Illustrations that instruct. In R. Glaser (ed.), *Advances in Instructional Psychology* (Vol. *V*, pp. 253–84). Mahwah, NJ: Erlbaum.

  (1997). Multimedia learning: are we asking the right questions? *Educational Psychologist, 32*(1), 1–19.

  (2001). *Multimedia Learning.* New York: Cambridge University Press.

  (2005). *Cambridge Handbook of Multimedia Learning.* New York: Cambridge University Press.

Mayer, R. E., & Anderson, R. B. (1992). The instructive animation: helping students build connections between words and pictures in multimedia learning. *Journal of Educational Psychology, 84*, 444–52.

Mayer, R. E., Bove, W., Bryman, A., Mars, R., & Tapangco, L. (1996). When less is more: meaningful learning from visual and verbal summaries of science textbook lessons. *Journal of Educational Psychology, 88*(1), 64–73.

Mayer, R. E., & Gallini, J. (1990). When is an illustration worth ten thousand words? *Journal of Educational Psychology, 82*, 715–26.

Mayer, R. E., Steinhoff, K., Bowers, G., & Mars, R. (1995). A generative theory of textbook design: using annotated illustrations to foster meaningful learning of science text. *Educational Technology Research and Development, 43*(1), 31–43.

McCrudden, M. T., Schraw, G., & Lehman, S. (2009). The use of adjunct displays to facilitate comprehension of causal relationships in expository text. *Instructional Science, 37*(1), 65–86.

McKoon, G., & Ratcliff, R. (1992). Inference during reading. *Psychological Review, 99*(3), 440–66.

Myers, J. L., Cook, A. E., Kambe, G., Mason, R. A., & O'Brien, E. J. (2000). Semantic and episodic effects on bridging inferences. *Discourse Processes, 29*(3), 179–99.

Narvaez, D., van den Broek, P., & Ruiz, A. B. (1999). The influence of reading purpose on inference generation and comprehension in reading. *Journal of Educational Psychology, 91*(3), 488–96.

Ozcelik, E., & Acarturk, C. (2011). Reducing the spatial distance between printed and online information sources by means of mobile technology enhances learning: using 2D barcodes. *Computers & Education, 57*(3), 2077–85.

Ozcelik, E., Arslan-Ari, I., & Cagiltay, K. (2010). Why does signaling enhance multimedia learning? Evidence from eye movements. *Computers in Human Behavior, 26*(1), 110–17.

Ozcelik, E., Karakus, T., Kursun, E., & Cagiltay, K. (2009). An eye-tracking study of how color coding affects multimedia learning. *Computers & Education, 53*(2), 445–53.

Perfetti, C. A., Rouet, J.-F., & Britt, M. A. (1999). Toward a theory of documents representation. In H. van Oostendorp & S. Goldman (eds.), *The Construction of Mental Representations during Reading* (pp. 99–122). Mahwah, NJ: Erlbaum.

Renkl, A. (1997). Learning from worked-out examples: a study on individual differences. *Cognitive Science, 21*, 1–29.

Rouet, J.-F. (2006). *The Skills of Document Use: From Text Comprehension to Web-based Learning.* Mahwah, NJ: Erlbaum.

Salmerón, L., Baccino, T., Cañas, J. J., Madrid, R. I., & Fajardo, I. (2009). Do graphical overviews facilitate or hinder comprehension in hypertext? *Computers & Education, 53*(4), 1308–19.

Salmerón, L., Cañas, J. J., Kintsch, W., & Fajardo, I. (2005). Reading strategies and hypertext comprehension. *Discourse Processes, 40*(3), 171–91.

Salmerón, L., Gil, L., Bråten, I., & Strømsø, H. I. (2010). Comprehension effects of signalling relationships between documents in search engines. *Computers in Human Behavior, 26*(2), 419–26.

Salmerón, L., Kintsch, W., & Cañas, J. J. (2006). Coherence or interest as basis for improving hypertext comprehension. *Information Design Journal, 14*(1), 45–55.

Scheiter, K., Schüler, A., Gerjets, P., Huk, T., & Hesse, F. W. (2014). Extending multimedia research: how do prerequisite knowledge and reading comprehension affect learning from text and pictures. *Computers in Human Behavior, 31*(0), 73–84.

Schmidt-Weigand, F., Kohnert, A., & Glowalla, U. (2010). A closer look at split visual attention in system- and self-paced instruction in multimedia learning. *Learning and Instruction, 20*(2), 100–10.

Schnotz, W., & Bannert, M. (2003). Construction and interference in learning from multiple representation. *Learning & Instruction, 13*(2), 141–56.

Schnotz, W., & Heiß, A. (2009). Semantic scaffolds in hypermedia learning environments. *Computers in Human Behavior, 25*(2), 371–80.

Schüler, A., Scheiter, K., & Gerjets, P. (2013). Is spoken text always better? Investigating the modality and redundancy effect with longer text presentation. *Computers in Human Behavior, 29*(4), 1590–1601.

Schwonke, R., Berthold, K., & Renkl, A. (2009). How multiple external representations are used and how they can be made more useful. *Applied Cognitive Psychology, 23*(9), 1227–43.

Seufert, T. (2003). Supporting coherence formation in learning from multiple representations. *Learning & Instruction, 13,* 227–37.

Singer, M., Andrusiak, P., Reisdorf, P., & Black, N. L. (1992). Individual differences in bridging inference processes. *Memory & Cognition, 20*(5), 539–48.

Singer, M., & Ritchot, K. F. (1996). The role of working memory capacity and knowledge access in text inference processing. *Memory & Cognition, 24,* 733–43.

Tibus, M., Heier, A., & Schwan, S. (2013). Do films make you learn? Inference processes in expository film comprehension. *Journal of Educational Psychology, 105*(2), 329–40.

van Dijk, T. A., & Kintsch, W. (1983). *Strategies of Discourse Comprehension.* New York: Academic Press.

Vidal-Abarca, E., Martínez, G., & Gilabert, R. (2000). Two procedures to improve instructional text: Effects on memory and learning. *Journal of Educational Psychology, 92*(1), 107–16.

Wiley, J., & Myers, J. L. (2003). Availability and accessibility of information and causal inferences from scientific text. *Discourse Processes, 36*(2), 109–29.

Wolfe, M. B., & Goldman, S. R. (2005). Relations between adolescents' text processing and reasoning. *Cognition and Instruction, 23*(4), 467–502.

15   What about expository text?

Robert F. Lorch Jr.

There is a long history of research on text processing in psychology, but developments in the 1970s gave the field theoretical focus and momentum. Kintsch and van Dijk (1978) provided the first comprehensive theory of how readers construct a representation from a text as they read. Their theory was extremely influential for several reasons: It provided a clear statement of the nature of the representation of text content, along with a procedure for deriving such a representation for a text. It proposed a process model to explain how readers build a mental representation as they read, and it linked the hypothesized processes to readers' abilities to remember text content. Importantly, the process model was firmly founded on well-established cognitive constructs (e.g., a limited-capacity working memory). Interestingly, the text materials used to illustrate and test the principles of the theory were predominantly examples of expository text. Before long, however, text researchers narrowed their attention to the representation and processing of narrative texts.

The focus on narrative came about in large part because of the work of Trabasso and his colleagues (Trabasso, Secco, and van den Broek, 1984). This work gave a definition of causality and an objective procedure for analyzing causal relations among events in narrative. Subsequent empirical work (Trabasso and van den Broek, 1985; Trabasso, van den Broek and Suh, 1989) provided convincing demonstrations of the validity of the proposed causal network representations of narrative. As attention turned from explaining memory for text to researching the online processing underlying text comprehension, causal network analyses were useful in specifying connections (i.e., inferences) that readers should identify in order to construct a causally coherent representation of the events in a narrative. Because researchers had a reasonably good understanding of what it meant to comprehend narrative, narratives provided a tractable domain in which to study the online processes underlying comprehension. It soon became apparent that inferential processes played a central role in text comprehension.

The chapters in this book document the state of theory and research on the types of inferences that readers make and the conditions under which they make them. In the following section, I will summarize our current understanding of the nature of inferencing in narrative processing. Next, I will ask how well that model explains what we know about the nature of inferencing in processing of expository text. Finally, I will discuss several reasons why our understanding of inferential processing during reading is limited by the fact that virtually all of our knowledge of inference making is based on the study of narrative processing. I will argue that study of the processing of expository texts promises to greatly broaden our understanding of inferential processing.

The modal model of inference making during the processing of narratives

Narrative is a very attractive genre for research on text-processing because its structure is relatively simple and relatively well understood. Globally, narratives have a goal-outcome structure (Trabasso et al., 1984, Trabasso and van den Broek, 1985). Characters have goals that motivate their thoughts and actions. To the extent that there are multiple characters with possibly conflicting goals and there are obstacles to those goals, stories can vary in complexity and interest value. But the goal-outcome structure is the basic organizing principle of narrative.

Locally, narratives also have a simple structure in that the events of a narrative are predominantly causally related (Trabasso and Suh, 1993; Trabasso et al., 1989). Characters' goals motivate chains of causally connected events that lead to outcomes. In addition, other types of relations may be important in a narrative. Descriptions of locations may emphasize spatial relations (Radvansky, 2009; Morrow, Greenspan, and Bower, 1987). Temporal relations among events may be important in some narratives (Magliano, Miller, and Zwaan, 2001; Radvansky, Zwaan, Federico, and Franklin, 1998). From this perspective, "comprehension" is thought of as the construction of a coherent representation that captures the relations among the events in the narrative (van den Broek, Bohn-Gettler, Kendeou, Carlson, and White, 2011; van den Broek, Risden, and Husebye-Hartmann, 1995; Zwaan, Magliano, and Graesser, 1995).

The process of comprehending a narrative is conceptualized as one of systematically updating a model of the situation communicated in the narrative (Glenberg, Meyer, and Lindem, 1987; Zwaan et al., 1995; Zwaan and Radvansky, 1998). There is theoretical consensus on the broad outlines of the processing involved. As a reader attends to the content of a sentence, a fast, passive search process accesses related information in the reader's text representation and background knowledge. This process has variously been described as a "construction" process (Kintsch, 1988), a resonance process (McKoon and Ratcliff, 1992; O'Brien, 1995), and an activation process (van den Broek, Young, Tzeng, and Linderholm, 1998). The resonance/activation process is "dumb" in the sense that information in the reader's memory will be accessed based only on factors such as featural overlap with, or strength of association to, concepts in focus (O'Brien and Albrecht, 1991; O'Brien, Albrecht, Hakala, and Rizzella, 1995; O'Brien, Cook, and Guéraud, 2010). Access to potentially relevant information must be followed by the selection and evaluation of information that resolves how the focal event should be integrated into the representation under construction (Cook and O'Brien, 2014). This selection and evaluation process is less well-specified than the resonance process, but is generally described as a constraint satisfaction process that is sensitive to converging sources of evidence for the same interpretation (Kintsch, 1988).

The well-investigated resonance process accounts for monitoring of coherence at both the local, sentence-to-sentence level and at more global levels of narrative structure. When a sentence is read, the resonance process quickly identifies relations between the focal event and preceding story events and related prior knowledge (Albrecht and O'Brien, 1993; Myers and O'Brien, 1998). If the resonance process uncovers prior information in the narrative or in the reader's background knowledge that is inconsistent with the focal event, the inconsistency is an obstacle to the process of integration so it must be resolved and processing is temporarily disrupted (Albrecht and O'Brien, 1993; Trabasso and Suh, 1993). Also, if the resonance process fails to access information relevant to the integration of the focal event, processing is again disrupted to repair the gap in the reader's mental representation.

Critically, the stories that have typically been investigated in the narrative literature have been simple in structure and minimal in their demands on comprehension. The great majority of studies use stories that are short (i.e., fifteen sentences or less) and based on activities that are very familiar to the audience of college readers. This means that participants in the studies can be expected to have all of the requisite prior knowledge needed to make the routine inferences demanded by the texts. Thus, even when processing disruptions occur, they tend to be minor. Under these circumstances, a passive process of resonance plus integration provides a sufficient account of inferencing during reading of narrative. However, it is important to emphasize that this is not the typical situation in everyday reading experience. Rather, it is common for a reader to be lacking some knowledge that is assumed by the author, especially when the reading material consists of textbooks. It is therefore not surprising that once we step outside the limited domain in which we have studied inferential processes, we quickly encounter evidence that our model of inferential processing may need considerable elaboration.

Inference making during the processing of expository texts

The cognitive literature on inferences during reading of expository texts is very small. The handful of available studies has investigated reading of texts on scientific topics. Texts vary in structure and content across the studies but are consistently short, ranging from just two sentences long (Singer, Harkness, and Stewart, 1997) to a maximum of only ten sentences long (Noordman, Vonk, and Kempf, 1992; Singer et al., 1997). Some of the studies presented texts sentence-by-sentence (Noordman et al., 1992; Singer et al., 1997; Wiley and Myers, 2003) and others used RSVP presentation of individual words (Millis and Graesser, 1994). The occurrence of inferences has been assessed by effects on reading time (Noordman et al., 1992; Wiley and Myers, 2003), effects on time to verify statements (Noordman et al., 1992), and effects on time to make lexical decisions on probe words (Millis and Graesser, 1994). Given that there have been so few studies and that the materials and procedures have been varied, it is not possible to derive any definitive conclusions from the literature. However, there are hints that inferences are not reliably generated during the processing of scientific texts.

The literature on processing of narrative repeatedly affirms that college readers make causal bridging inferences when reading (Graesser, Singer, and Trabasso, 1994). The literature on processing of scientific texts suggests that college readers make causal bridging inferences under some circumstances but not others. College readers have been found to make bridging inferences when reading simple scientific texts on relatively familiar topics (Millis and Graesser, 1994; Singer et al., 1997, Experiments 2 and 4). However, they fail to make such inferences when reading challenging texts (Noordman et al., 1992, Experiments 1 and 2; Singer et al., 1997, Experiment 1) unless they are given a reading goal that specifically encourages inferencing (Noordman et al., 1992, Experiments 4 and 5). In addition, college readers make causal bridging inferences when reading texts in which a sentence designed to probe for an inference immediately follows the two premise sentences supporting the inference (Wiley and Myers, 2003). However, college readers fail to make the same inference if a single filler sentence is inserted between the second of two premises and the probe sentence. In short, the tentative conclusion indicated by the available studies is that causal bridging inferences during reading of brief scientific texts are not very robust, in contrast to causal bridging inferences during the reading of narrative texts.

There is an extensive literature on the influence of commonly held misconceptions on learning from science texts. This literature has not focused on online processing, in general, or inferential processing, in particular; however, the findings from this literature raise questions about how prior knowledge is accessed during reading. The literature on scientific misconceptions consistently shows that readers often fail to correct their misconceptions after reading a text that provides a correct explanation of the relevant scientific phenomenon (e.g., Kendeou and van den Broek, 2005). As an example, students who believe that seasonal temperature variations are due to corresponding seasonal variations in the distance of the earth from the sun are *not* likely to revise that belief simply by reading a text that explains seasonal temperature variations as due to the tilt of the earth's axis. The reason that students fail to revise their misconceptions appears to be that they do not make the connection between their prior misconception and the explanation given in the text (van den Broek and Kendeou, 2008). According to a resonance model of inferencing, it would be expected that obviously related prior knowledge would be routinely accessed while reading such a text. That does not seem to be the case: If the misconception is not directly and explicitly addressed, students are unlikely to update their understanding. However, if the author of the scientific text calls attention to the frequently held misconception and explicitly refutes it, then students who subscribe to the misconception are much more likely to attend to the correct explanation and revise their understanding (Kendeou and van den Broek, 2007).

Although the simple resonance model cannot explain these results, Kendeou and O'Brien (2014; Kendeou, Walsh, Smith, and O'Brien, 2014) have provided a straightforward elaboration of the resonance model that can. The KReC model emphasizes the importance of co-activation as a condition for the revision of prior knowledge when information is encountered that calls for such revision. The model does not assume that relevant prior knowledge will be automatically activated when relevant new information is read; rather, the relation between the prior knowledge and the new information must be made explicit for the inconsistent information to be co-activated in memory. Only then will the reader be in a position to revise a prior misconception.

Four reasons to study inference making in the context of expository text

Research on inference making during reading of narrative suggests that inferences are readily made because of a passive, undirected, dumb resonance process that quickly finds potential connections between the event currently in focus and prior textual context. As portrayed in the narrative literature, the resonance process is always active, providing the foundation for inferential processing during reading. As such, we would expect the process to operate the same way independently of genre. However, the little bit of research that has been conducted on the processing of exposition indicates that an account of inference making during reading may require considerable elaboration of our current model. There are at least four reasons to expect that inference making in the context of exposition is more complicated than inference making in the context of narrative.

Less sufficient prior knowledge. Many researchers have pointed out that readers' prior knowledge is sufficient to support most inferences that are required by the types of simple narratives that have been studied in the literature (Gilabert, Martinez, and Vidal-Abarca, 2005; McNamara, Kintsch, Songer, and Kintsch, 1996). The stories that researchers have typically constructed are based on situations that are highly familiar to college readers. In contrast, the purpose of much exposition is to inform so it is assumed that readers' background knowledge is lacking to some degree. Consider the example of texts on scientific topics. The topics of science texts are often relatively unfamiliar to college readers. In fact, as already noted, it is not uncommon for college readers to have incorrect beliefs on science topics that may actually interfere with their attempts to understand a text they are given to read.

The likelihood that college readers have limited prior knowledge about a science topic means they may struggle with aspects of text processing that are taken for granted in the context of narrative. For example, whereas resolving anaphoric references is rarely an obstacle to comprehension of narratives, this basic requirement for constructing a coherent text representation is not always accomplished in as routine a fashion for many expository texts. Readers will fail to recognize instances of coreference if they are unfamiliar with alternative ways of referring to the same concept. That is the likely explanation of the finding that memory for text content is improved if a history text is revised to make coreferential relations more explicit (Britton and Gulgoz, 1991). Similarly, bridging inferences are regularly required and routinely made during the reading of narratives because they often depend on general world knowledge about common human interactions (Graesser et al., 1994). In contrast, bridging inferences in science texts sometimes rely on knowledge that is stated earlier in the text but may not have been fully understood by the reader. Or the bridging inferences may depend on access to background knowledge that many readers do not possess.

Authors of texts on complex topics such as those addressed in science face a difficult challenge in determining how much background knowledge to assume on the part of their audiences. At any point where an author overestimates a reader's prior knowledge, the resonance process will be insufficient to resolve how the event or concept currently in the reader's focus relates to previous information in the text. The result will be a gap in the reader's representation unless the reader expends additional effort to resolve the problem. We will return to this point shortly.

The greater complexity of expository text. A second reason to anticipate a need to elaborate our model of inference making is that exposition is a much more complex genre than narrative in several respects. "Exposition" is really a collection of distinguishable subtypes of texts. There are systematic differences between expository texts in different substantive domains (e.g., history vs. science). There are differences between texts constructed for different audiences (e.g., newspaper articles, magazine articles, textbooks) and for different purposes (e.g., a textbook designed to support teaching, a magazine article designed to inform in an entertaining fashion). Further, the structure of each subtype of exposition is less familiar to readers than narrative. The variation in expository text structures and their relative unfamiliarity alone probably make expository texts more challenging than narrative. However, even if we restrict ourselves to a particular type of exposition (e.g., science texts) it is quickly apparent that expository texts are more complex than narratives in both their global and local structures.

At a global level, exposition is often composed of distinct substructures corresponding to different types of information the author wishes to communicate (Meyer, 1975). At a local level and correlated with the distinguishable substructures, a range of relations may exist among concepts and events described in exposition. One common substructure in a science text is associated with the description of entities. For example, an introductory neuroscience text will contain a chapter on neuroanatomy that describes the different regions of the brain and their functions. Such a description will likely be built heavily on referential and spatial relations.

Another common substructure in science texts is associated with the description of processes. For example, a neuroscience text will somewhere contain a description of neurotransmission. That description will be built largely on temporal and causal relations; these relations explain the chain of events beginning with an input being processed by the first cell and ending with an account of how processing in the first cell is transmitted to the next cell in the chain.

Science texts are also likely to contain sections that have a compare-and-contrast structure. For example, a physics text describing the properties of light might compare and contrast a wave theory with a particle theory of light. The relations involved in representing parallel accounts of a common phenomenon can be very complex. Points of comparison between competing theories may be at the level of how two alternative theories explain a particular phenomenon. A deep understanding of the differences between the two theories may involve "running" the two mental models to identify distinguishable predictions of the two alternative theories.

Other substructures may occur. For example, a taxonomy has a hierarchical organization based on logical principles that may refer to comparisons of properties of the entities occupying the taxonomy. The point is that expository texts, in general, and science texts, in particular, are complexly structured. There is no single global structure common to all instances of the genre; rather, a variety of global structures are encountered in exposition – often within a single text (Meyer, 1975). Associated with the variability in global structures is variability in the types of relations among the elements of exposition. In addition to coreference and causal relations, spatial, temporal, and logical relations are frequently important in expository texts. Further, whereas relations in narratives are often one-to-one (e.g., a goal motivates and action; an action leads to another action; an action leads to an outcome) or, sometimes multiple-to-one (e.g., a combination of events leads to some outcome), relations in science texts are often more complicated. For example, it is common that a co-occurrence of events is necessary to cause some outcome (e.g., the right combination of elements in the right environment in order for some reaction to occur) or for antecedents to have several possible consequences. In other words, narrative comprehension as it has been studied in the literature involves the construction of a simple situation model whereas comprehension of exposition often involves the construction of a complex situation model. The greater complexity of exposition may well translate into more complex inferential processing.

A greater role for strategic processing. The dual challenges of inadequate background knowledge and greater complexity of content suggest a third reason that our model of inference making will need to be elaborated as we investigate processing of exposition. Namely, memory-based processing will often need to be supplemented by strategic processing (Hyöna, Lorch, and Kaakinen, 2002; Linderholm and van den Broek, 2002; van den Broek, Lorch, Linderholm, and Gustafson, 2001; Wiley, Ash, Sanchez, and Jaeger, 2011). This suggestion is supported by Noordman et al.'s (1992) finding that readers make logical inferences while reading short science texts only when they are given task instructions that focus them on monitoring the logic of the text.

If a reader does not possess the knowledge needed to bridge the gap between two events in a biological process that is being described in a text, then the resonance process will fail and the reader will need to resolve the incoherence in some more strategic way. A motivated reader might generate a hypothesis about the nature of the relation and look for evidence elsewhere in the text to verify or disconfirm the hypothesis. Or the reader might consult an external source (e.g., Wikipedia, a classmate, the teacher).

In the case of a complex concept, a reader's working memory capacity may be overwhelmed by the amount of information to be integrated to construct an adequate mental model based on the text content. In such circumstances, readers need strategies for systematically building a situation model. For example, understanding how the tilt of the earth contributes to seasonal temperature variations in the northern hemisphere involves the integration of a great deal of information. The reader must know that the earth's axis is tilted. The reader must understand that the tilt of the axis means that the angle at which the sun's rays hit the earth's axis changes systematically as the earth orbits the sun. The reader must understand why differences in the angle of the sun's rays will translate into temperature differences. The reader must also understand the tilt of the axis is toward the sun during the summer (in the northern hemisphere) and away from the sun during the winter. Figuring out and integrating these components of an explanation of seasonal temperature variation might be accomplished by visualizing the tilted earth orbiting the sun across the course of a year; that is, mentally "running" a model or actually simulating the process with concrete objects.

In these examples, strategic inference making takes on the qualities of reasoning and problem solving. In the case of a highly motivated reader determined to develop a deep understanding of a complex topic, the reader is put in the position of constructing a *possible* understanding of the topic. Such a mental model would presumably be tagged as uncertain and therefore open to likely revision. The reader must be prepared to test the mental model against new information and revise the model as needed.

A greater role for metacomprehension skills. Comprehending exposition is often more difficult than comprehending narrative. In fact, what it means to "comprehend" a text seems more complicated in the context of exposition than in the context of narrative. It is common for researchers to define comprehension of narrative as the construction of a coherent representation (e.g., van den Broek et al., 1995). This definition may be adequate for narrative because it is unlikely that readers will make errors in identifying the appropriate connections for a narrative text. That is, if they construct a coherent representation, it is likely to be the representation the author intended to communicate. An implication of this analysis is that the task of monitoring ongoing comprehension is relatively straightforward for narrative: As long as a reader is able to determine the referential and causal relations of the current story event to previous story events, the reader is probably constructing an adequate understanding of the story.

The situation for exposition is not as simple (Wiley and Sanchez, 2010). The situation model that must be constructed from processing a science text may be very complex and the reader's prior knowledge may be insufficient to passively fill the gaps in the exposition. As discussed, this requires a greater role for strategic processing – problem solving and reasoning to generate inferences to construct a possible understanding. In this scenario, even if the reader is able to construct a coherent representation, there is no guarantee that the representation accurately captures the information the author intended to communicate. The implications of this perspective are that (1) readers must be more self-motivated to understand exposition than to understand narrative, and (2) the task of monitoring comprehension is more challenging and more important in the case of expository text.

With respect to self-motivation, readers may opt out of the goal of developing a deep understanding when confronted with a difficult text. Rather than exerting the effort to construct a situation model that integrates the information in the text with background knowledge on the topic, the reader might construct only a textbase representation that emphasizes the maintenance of referential coherence. By adopting such a lenient standard of coherence (van den Broek et al., 1995), the reader minimizes effort albeit at the cost of deep understanding. Any teacher can attest that this is a common strategy adopted by students.

At the other extreme, readers may aim for deep understanding. This goal commits them to strict standards of coherence and a correspondingly close monitoring of their ongoing attempts at comprehension. With respect to standards of coherence, readers must commit to constructing a representation that accurately captures the author's intended communication. This means that readers must represent all of the types of relations appropriate to the topic; in other words, they must monitor referential, causal, logical, temporal, and spatial coherence (Zwaan et al., 1995). As I have discussed, a complex topic may require extensive strategic processing if the reader is to construct an accurate situation model of the topic. This means that a reader's efforts are fallible and the reader must be sensitive to the possibility of mistakes in understanding. Close monitoring of comprehension efforts should alert readers when there are coherence gaps or unsatisfactory coherence resolutions in their representations (e.g., "I get that the angle at which the sun's rays hit the atmosphere affects the temperature of the atmosphere, but I don't understand why."). In addition, readers must be alert to the implications of new information for the validity of the situation model they have built at a given point during reading. That is, even if a reader has built a situation model that is coherent and plausible based on the information presented, the reader must continue to evaluate and update the model as new information is encountered during reading. In this perspective, inferences are hypotheses that may need to be revised or replaced as new information requires.

Conclusion

We know a lot about inferential processing in a very constrained domain. When we switch our attention from simple narratives to exposition as potentially complex as science texts, we realize that comprehension is more difficult and inferencing surely becomes more effortful and possibly less successful at resolving gaps and inconsistencies in readers' understandings. With narrative, we are in the world of inferencing in the service of comprehension; with exposition, we enter the world of inferencing in the service of learning.

This book celebrates the culmination of twenty-five years of progress in understanding how readers make inferences when reading narrative. I hope it also serves to encourage us to expand our horizons and take on the challenge of understanding how readers make inferences when reading exposition.

REFERENCES

Albrecht, J. E., & O'Brien, E. J. (1993). Updating a mental model: maintaining both local and global coherence. *Journal of Experimental Psychology: Learning, Memory, and Cognition, 19*, 1061–70.

Cook, A. E., & O'Brien, E. J. (2014). Knowledge activation, integration, and validation during narrative text comprehension. *Discourse Processes, 51*, 26–49.

Gilabert, R., Martinez, R., & Vidal-Abarca, E. (2005).Some good texts are always better: text revision to foster inferences of readers with high and low prior background knowledge. *Learning and Instruction, 15*, 45–68.

Glenberg, A. M., Meyer, M., and Lindem, K. (1987). Mental models contribute to foregrounding during text comprehension. *Journal of Memory and Language*, *26*, 69–83.

Graesser, A. C., Singer, M., & Trabasso, T. (1994). Constructing inferences during narrative text comprehension. *Psychological Review*, *101*(3), 371–95.

Hyönä, J., Lorch, R. F., Jr., & Kaakinen, J. K. (2002). Individual differences in reading to summarize expository text: evidence from eye fixation patterns. *Journal of Educational Psychology*, *94*, 44–55.

Kendeou, P., & O'Brien, E. J. (2014). Knowledge revision: processes and mechanisms. In D. N. Rapp & J. L. G. Braasch (eds.), *Processing Inaccurate Information: Theoretical and Applied Perspectives from Cognitive Science and the Educational Sciences* (pp.353–77). Cambridge, MA: MIT Press.

Kendeou, P., Walsh, E., Smith, E. R., & O'Brien, E. J. (2014). Knowledge revision processes in refutation texts. *Discourse Processes*.

Kendeou, P., & van den Broek, P. (2005). The effects of readers' misconceptions on comprehension of scientific text. *Journal of Educational Psychology*, *97*, 235–45.

  (2007). Interactions between prior knowledge and text structure during comprehension of scientific texts. *Memory & Cognition*, *35*, 1567–77.

Kintsch, W. (1988). The role of knowledge in discourse comprehension: a construction–integration model. *Psychological Review*, *95*, 163–82.

Kintsch, W., & van Dijk, T.A. (1978). Towards a model of text comprehension and production. *Psychological Review*, *85*, 363–94.

Linderholm, T., & van den Broek, P. (2002). The effects of reading purpose and working memory capacity on the processing of expository text. *Journal of Educational Psychology*, *94*, 778–84.

Magliano, J.P., Miller, J., & Zwaan. R.A. (2001). Indexing space and time in film understanding. *Applied Cognitive Psychology*, *15*, 533–45.

McKoon, G., & Ratcliff, R. (1992). Inference during reading. *Psychological Review*, *99*(3), 440–66.

McNamara, D. S., Kintsch, E., Songer, N. B., & Kintsch, W. (1996). Are good texts always better? Interactions of text coherence, background knowledge, and levels of understanding in learning from text. *Cognition and Instruction*, *14*(1), 1–43.

Meyer, B. J. F. (1975). *The Organization of Prose and Its Effect on Memory*. Amsterdam: North-Holland.

Millis, K. K., & Graesser, A. C. (1994). The time-course of constructing knowledge-based inferences for scientific texts. *Journal of Memory and Language*, *33*(5), 583–99.

Morrow, D.G., Greenspan, S.I., & Bower, G.H. (1987). Accessibility and situation models in narrative comprehension. *Journal of Memory and Language*, *26*, 165–87.

Myers, J. L., & O'Brien, E. J. (1998). Accessing the discourse representation during reading. *Discourse Processes*, *26*, 131–57.

Noordman. L., Vonk, W., & Kempf, H. (1992). Causal inferences during reading of expository texts. *Journal of Memory and Language*, *31*, 573–90.

O'Brien, E. J. (1995). Automatic components of discourse comprehension. In R. F. Lorch & E. J. O'Brien (eds.), *Sources of Coherence in Reading* (pp. 159–76). Mahwah, NJ: Erlbaum.

O'Brien, E. J., & Albrecht, J. E. (1991). The role of context in accessing antecedents in text. *Journal of Experimental Psychology: Learning, Memory, and Cognition, 17*(1), 94–102.

O'Brien, E. J., Albrecht, J. E., Hakala, C. M., & Rizzella, M. L. (1995). Activation and suppression of antecedents during reinstatement. *Journal of Experimental Psychology: Learning, Memory, and Cognition, 21*(3), 626–34.

O'Brien, E. J., Cook, A. E., & Guéraud, S. (2010). Accessibility of outdated information. *Journal of Experimental Psychology: Learning, Memory, and Cognition, 36*, 979–91.

Radvansky, G. A. (2009). Spatial directions and situation model organization. *Memory & Cognition, 37*, 796–806.

Radvansky, G. A., Zwaan, R. A., Federico, T., & Franklin, N. (1998). Retrieval from temporally organized situation models. *Journal of Experimental Psychology: Learning, Memory, and Cognition, 24*, 1224–37.

Singer, M., Harkness, D., & Stewart, S. T. (1997). Constructing inferences in expository text comprehension, *Discourse Processes, 24*, 198–228.

Trabasso, T., Secco, T., & van den Broek, P. W. (1984). Causal cohesion and story coherence. In H. Mandl, N. L. Stein, & T. Trabasso (eds.), *Learning and Comprehension of Text* (pp. 83–111). Mahwah, NJ: Erlbaum.

Trabasso, T., & Suh, S. (1993). Understanding text: achieving explanatory coherence through online inferences and mental operations in working memory. *Discourse Processes, 16*, 3–34.

Trabasso, T., & van den Broek, P. W. (1985). Causal thinking and the representation of narrative events. *Journal of Memory and Language, 24*, 612–30.

Trabasso, T., van den Broek, P. W., & Suh, S. Y. (1989) Logical necessity and transitivity of causal relations in stories. *Discourse Processes, 12*, 1–25.

Van den Broek, P., Bohn-Gettler, C. M., Kendeou, P., Carlson, S., & White, M. J. (2011). When a reader meets a text: the role of standards of coherence in reading comprehension. In M. T. McCrudden, J. Magliano, & G. Schraw (eds.), *Relevance Instructions and Goal-focusing in Text Learning*. Greenwich, CT: Information Age Publishing.

Van den Broek, P., & Kendeou, P. (2008). Cognitive processes in comprehension of science texts: The role of co-activation in confronting misconceptions. *Applied Cognitive Psychology, 22*, 335–51.

Van den Broek, P., Lorch, R. F., Linderholm, T., & Gustafson, M. (2001). The effects of readers' goals on inference generation and memory for texts. *Memory & Cognition, 29*, 1081–7.

Van den Broek, P., Risden, K., & Husebye-Hartmann, E. (1995). The role of readers' standards for coherence in the generation of inference during reading. In R. F. Lorch & E. J. O'Brien (eds.), *Sources of Coherence in Reading* (pp. 353–73). Mahwah, NJ: Erlbaum.

Van den Broek, P., Young, M., Tzeng, Y., & Linderholm, T. (1998). The landscape model of reading: Inferences and the online construction of a memory representation. In H. van Oostendorp, & S. R. Goldman (eds.), *The Construction of Mental Representations during Reading* (pp. 71–98). Mahwah, NJ: Erlbaum.

Wiley, J., Ash, I. K., Sanchez, C. A., & Jaeger, A. (2011). Clarifying goals of reading for understanding from expository science text. In M. T. McCrudden, J. P. Magliano, & G. Schraw (eds.), *Text Relevance and Learning from Text* (pp. 353–74). Charlotte, NC: Information Age Publishing.

Wiley, J., & Myers, J. L. (2003). Availability and accessibility of information and causal inferences from scientific text. *Discourse Processes, 36,* 109–29.

Wiley, J., & Sanchez, C. A. (2010). Constraints on learning from expository science texts. In N. L. Stein & S. Raudenbush (eds.), *Developmental Cognitive Science Goes to School* (pp. 45–58). New York: Routledge.

Zwaan, R. A., Magliano, J. P., & Graesser, A. C. (1995). Dimensions of situation model construction in narrative comprehension. *Journal of Experimental Psychology: Learning, Memory, and Cognition, 21,* 386–97.

Zwaan, R. A., & Radvansky, G. A. (1998). Situation models in language comprehension and memory. *Psychological Bulletin, 123,* 162–185.

16   The role of inferences in narrative experiences

Richard J. Gerrig and William G. Wenzel

Readers' narrative experiences are anything but passive. Consider a moment from the suspense novel *A Wanted Man* (Child, 2012). The hero, Jack Reacher, has been systematically working his way through a fortresslike structure, eliminating his enemies. He finally arrives at a room that contains the person he is trying to rescue, Don McQueen. He finds McQueen tied to a chair (p. 385):

> There was a man behind the chair.
> The man behind the chair had a gun to McQueen's head.
> The man behind the chair was Alan King.
> Living and breathing.
> Alive again.

It seems very likely that readers would become cognitively and emotionally engaged as these sentences unfold. McQueen has a gun to his head. "Oh no!" Alan King is alive. "How could that be?" The words of the text create an opportunity for readers to have a vivid and intense narrative experience.

The goal of this chapter is to explore the foundational role that inferences play to provide readers with experiences of this sort. We will focus on two phenomena. The first is exemplified by readers' impulse to encode mental contents such as "Oh no!" when they learn that McQueen has a gun to his head. We call such mental contents *participatory responses*: They represent the types of responses people would encode if the events were unfolding before them in real life (Gerrig, 1993; Gerrig and Jacovina, 2009). We will describe how the products of inferential processes lay the groundwork for a variety of participatory responses. Our second phenomenon is the *mystery*, exemplified by the puzzle provided at the end of this excerpt from *A Wanted Man*. Given strong evidence provided previously in the novel, how is it possible that Alan King is alive? This moment scratches the surface of the types of mystery with which texts are rife (Gerrig, Love, and McKoon, 2009; Love, McKoon, and Gerrig, 2010). We will consider how inferential processes help call readers' attention to various mysteries and how those processes enable readers to engage with those mysteries.

In this chapter, we use the term "inference" to refer to information that was not explicitly stated in a text that becomes part of readers' discourse representations (cf. McKoon and Ratcliff, 1992). We also refer to "inferential processes" that give rise to inferences. Much research has tried to discriminate between those inferences that arise automatically and those that are the products of readers' strategic effort (for a review, see McNamara and Magliano, 2009). We will provide examples to illustrate the importance of both automatic and strategic inferences for readers' narrative experiences. In addition, we illustrate how individual differences in readers' automatic inferences as well as their strategic effort may yield quite distinctive narrative experiences. Note, also, that we intend our analyses to extend to the full range of circumstances in which people experience narratives (i.e., as viewers of films, television productions, live performances, and advertisements, as addressees for conversational stories, and so on). Although we use the term "readers" for most of this chapter, we intend that term as shorthand to refer to people's roles as experiencers of narratives across the full range of contexts.

An important goal of this chapter is to illustrate reciprocity between cognitive science theories and real-world narratives. On some occasions, we use the products of psychological research to consider why authors are able to achieve certain effects. We suggest that basic cognitive processes allow narratives to take particular forms. On other occasions, we look to real-world narratives to expand the scope of cognitive science inquiry. We suggest that authors achieve effects that should be accommodated within theories of narrative processing. To illustrate this reciprocity between research and reality, we provide a series of examples from real-world narratives.

We devote the major sections of the chapter to participatory responses and narrative mysteries. Within those two topics, we discuss particular types of inferences (i.e., anaphoric and predictive inferences) as well as cognitive processes that underlie readers' experiences of those types of inferences. For each major topic, we also discuss individual differences among readers that may allow their narrative experiences to diverge.

We begin now with a discussion of the importance of inferences for participatory responses.

Participatory responses

In an early scene in the Hitchcock (1964) film *Marnie*, Marnie has robbed an office safe and is trying to leave a building without getting caught. She sees a cleaning lady through a glass partition. Marnie is worried that the cleaning lady will hear her walking by. To make her footfalls less audible, Marnie removes her high-heel shoes and puts them in the pockets of her jacket. But the shoes begin to slip out. To make this fact salient to viewers, Hitchcock intercuts close-ups of the slipping shoes with wider shots of an unaware Marnie. And then a shoe falls!

This moment from *Marnie* provides viewers with an optimal opportunity to encode participatory responses. To demonstrate that viewers avail themselves of such opportunities, Bezdek, Foy, and Gerrig (2013) had participants watch four brief excerpts from suspenseful movies. The participants were asked to think aloud as they watched the excerpts. Here is a sample of participants' responses to the scene with Marnie's shoes:

1. a. One of the shoes is probably going to fall out.
    b. Oh, this sucks... it's gonna fall.
    c. I feel like the shoe is going to fall off... shoe's going to fall out of her pocket 'cause she put it in her pocket and it's going to fall out and make a noise and then the janitor will know that she was trying to run

2. a. That's what I thought she should do, she should take her shoes off so no one hears her. She's probably going to slip on the water or her shoe's going to drop. Good one ... she should've held them.
    b. Oh that's cool ... OH NO THE SHOE ... the freakin' shoe. Why did she have to put it in her pocket; why couldn't she just hold the shoe?
    c. The shoe's going to fall out your pocket – just hold them. Told you your shoe's going to fall out your pocket. Your shoe's going to fall out your pocket ... there it goes ... ha!

The responses in (1a–c) demonstrate that viewers were quite likely to encode a pair of inferences: First, given the accumulating evidence, they inferred that the shoes were likely to fall; second, they inferred that, when the shoes fell, they were likely to make enough noise to alert the cleaning lady to Marnie's presence. The responses in (2a–c) show how some viewers integrated participatory responses into statements of those inferences. For example, the viewer in (2c) offered advice to Marnie ("Your shoe's going to fall out your pocket") and then enjoyed the fact that the advice was correct ("ha!"). Viewers' experiences of Marnie provide strong confirmation for our main contention that inferences often provide a foundation for participatory responses. Some viewers not only looked into the future, but they also used their precognition to attempt to direct Marnie's actions and to evaluate those actions once they occurred.

Bezdek et al. (2013) used the thoughts viewers articulated as they watched the film excerpts to define a taxonomy of participatory responses. Bezdek et al. were careful to differentiate between inferences and participatory responses. They specified that participatory responses did not add information to the viewers' mental model of the narrative. Rather, they were the products of viewers' emotional engagement. Table 16.1 presents the final taxonomy. The table indicates the many ways in which readers participate as they experience narratives. Responses (2a–c) illustrate several of the categories. The critical claim is that readers inevitably encode these types of mental contents, even when they are not specifically prompted to make their private thoughts public.

In the sections that follow, we will not attempt to specify exactly what types of participatory responses are likely to occur at particular narrative

Table 16.1 *Taxonomy of participatory responses (Bezdek, Foy, and Gerrig, 2013)*

Category	Definition	Examples
Emotional	Emotional responses as if the events were occurring in real life	"Oh my god!" "Oh no!"
Problem-solving instruction	Directly instructing a character to carry out a particular action to accomplish a goal	"Just do it!" "Get out of there!"
Problem-solving assertion	Suggesting a particular course of action without directly addressing a character	"He should run faster." "He better not go upstairs."
Replotting	Undoing an event or outcome	"He should've just moved away from the door right away." "He should've tried to hide behind a seat or somebody."
Outcome preference	Expressing a preference for a specific outcome	"He's leading him right into a trap, I hope." "I hope there's no one in the house."
Self-projection	Describing how the viewer would feel or act in a situation	"If people were onto me I wouldn't keep turning around like that." "I would leave and not go up there."
Positive character evaluation	Positive judgment of characters' actions	"Smart idea!" "Good job."
Negative character evaluation	Negative judgment of characters' actions	"That's stupid." "They're just dumb."

junctures. Rather, our goal is to demonstrate how the inferences that readers encode are necessary to create the contexts in which readers may experience any number of participatory responses. We consider readers' anaphoric inferences, their predictive inferences, and their preferences. We conclude the section by considering why, as a function of their participatory responses, readers may have greatly different narrative experiences.

Anaphoric inferences

As narratives unfold in time, readers must make connections between the present and the past. For example, readers of *The Dogs of Rome* (Fitzgerald, 2010) will miss the grave implications of the arrival of an "old man with no ears" (p. 364) if they are unable to make a link to a moment earlier in the text that involved an "older man": "Where his ears should have been were two crumpled pieces of pink flesh that resembled the @ of an email address" (p. 247). As in this case, the connection of present to past is achieved by an *anaphor*, a word or phrase that refers to a concept earlier in the text. Anaphors range from minimally specific pronouns (e.g., I, she, it) to more content-full expressions such as "old man with no ears." The inferential processes readers use to link anaphors to their referents have been the subject of a good deal of theoretical and empirical work (e.g., Gerrig and McKoon, 2001; Klin, Guzmán, Weingartner, and Ralano, 2006; Love and McKoon, 2010; McKoon and Ratcliff, 1980; O'Brien, Raney, Albrecht, and Rayner, 1997). Here, we focus not on the processes that give rise to anaphoric inferences but on their consequences for participatory responses.

Let's consider an example of how anaphoric inferences create a context for participatory responses. Early in the novel *The Trinity Six* (Cumming, 2011), Grek (who is working to protect a secret that is at the heart of the book) has entered a writer's workplace with a vial of the liquid form of "sodium fluoracetate": a poison "commonly used ... to control the spread of rats in sewers" (p. 33). Grek picks up a half-finished bottle of Evian, and pours the colorless poison "into the water, and sealed the cap." Grek succeeds at killing his prey. Somewhat later in the text, another killer contemplates the same method of execution (p. 174):

Just as Alexander Grek had broken into [Charlotte Berg's] office, [Doronin] would access Meisner's apartment, add 10mg of sodium fluoracetate to the bottle of water which Meisner kept by his bed, and return to London on the next scheduled flight from Tegel.

In this case, the author has provided an abundance of memory cues to make it easy for readers to make the connection between the actions

Doronin plans and Grek's earlier success. Because most readers likely wish Doronin to fail, this efficient evocation of the earlier episode immediately creates a context for participatory responses.

A bit later in the novel, matters become even more intense. The novel's hero, Edward Gaddis, has a girlfriend, Holly, who has gotten out of bed because she "needed a glass of water" (p. 204). Now, the anaphoric inference from water to water creates intense feelings of urgency. Those feelings only grow when Holly proceeds to pour "herself a glass of water from a bottle in the fridge" (p. 206). If readers have made the connection, it's hard to imagine they won't encode participatory responses in the realm of "Don't drink the water!" What makes this moment even more intense is that Gaddis and Holly have no idea that anyone's water has been poisoned (i.e., they think that Grek's victim died of natural causes). As Holly pours her glass from the bottle and drinks the water ("the entire glass, like a cure for a hangover," p. 206), she has no idea that her life could be in peril. Again, it seems reasonable to imagine that responsible readers will do their best to provide Holly with some kind of mental warning.

We have started with this example of an anaphoric inference because, to a large extent, these sorts of inferences seem particularly unglamorous. Researchers often tout them as the types of inferences that readers must draw to ensure that they have had coherent narrative experiences (e.g., O'Brien et al., 1997). That is the spirit in which we glossed the "old man with no ears." However, as we have just seen, anaphoric inferences often connect readers to past moments in a narrative that have consequences for the readers' emotional engagement. Such is also the case for the "old man with no ears." His reappearance signals to readers that an act of revenge may be near at hand. Thus, a focus on participatory responses suggests that theories of narrative might consider not just when and how readers encode anaphoric inferences but, also, what ensues once they do so.

Predictive inferences

In the last section, we suggested that readers would feel a sense of urgency when Holly poured herself a glass of water. Readers' anaphoric inference gave them the idea that the water might be poisoned. However, the urgency also arises because readers likely encoded *predictive inferences* about what would happen were Holly to drink the water. We also saw in the example from *Marnie* that people are often prepared to look into the future. Still, note how much there is for *Marnie* viewers to do in this moment:

3.   a. Viewers must infer that the shoes will fall.
        b. They must infer, should the shoes fall, how much noise they will
           make when they hit the ground.
        c. They must infer how audible that amount of noise is likely to be,
           given the film's indication of other noise in the environment.
        d. They must infer, based on those considerations, how likely it is that
           the cleaning woman will be able to hear that noise.
        e. They must infer whether, having heard the noise, the cleaning lady is
           likely to orient toward the noise in a way that will lead her to see
           Marnie.

Each of these inferences, and smaller gradations within them, could
provide the context for readers' participatory responses.

As we noted earlier, researchers have often tried to discriminate automatic from strategic inferences. This quest has been particularly active
with respect to the study of predictive inferences (for a review, see
McKoon and Ratcliff, 2013). Taken together, the data support a theoretical approach called *memory-based processing* (Gerrig and O'Brien,
2005; McKoon and Ratcliff, 1992). The major claim of memory-based
processing is that, through a memory process known as *resonance*,
"incoming text information – as well as information already residing in
working memory – serves as a signal to all of long-term memory, including both the inactive portion of the discourse representation as well as
general world knowledge" (Gerrig and O'Brien, 2005, p. 229). If the
products of resonance are sufficiently constrained by the discourse context, readers will encode reasonably specific predictions through automatic processes. For example, when participants in a study conducted by
Lassonde and O'Brien (2009) read a story that emphasized the soft,
unblemished metal on a brand new car, they were likely to encode the
specific inference "dent" rather than the more general inference
"damage" when a rock hit the car door.

Still, with respect to participatory responses, what matters most is that
automatic processes often lead to some indication of the emotional
valence of what lies in the future. Consider this sentence from a classic
experiment (McKoon and Ratcliff, 1986):

4.   The director and cameraman were ready to shoot close-ups when
        suddenly the actress fell from the 14th story.

If readers engage strategic reflection on this scenario, they should
conclude that the actress is likely to die. However, McKoon and Ratcliff
(1986) demonstrated that readers' automatic inference is no more
specific than "something bad will happen" (see also McKoon and
Ratcliff, 2013). It is unlikely that readers will have any long-term
memory representations that are exactly about actresses falling from

14th floors and dying. If they did, the resonance process could find those traces, and yield the specific inference "die." However, for most readers, the resonance process will yield a mix of representations of various falls from various heights. What the majority of those traces will have in common is an outcome that was "something bad." An inference with only that specificity should be sufficient to prompt participatory responses. Any indication of what may lie in the future may prompt readers to yield a minimal response ("Oh no!" or "Yeah!"). Meanwhile, even such minimal participatory responses could create a context in which readers would begin to expend strategic effort to look into the future. Thus, *Marnie* viewers may be prompted by their sense of foreboding to contemplate the series of inferences we laid out in (3a–e). (We assume that readers will have insufficient life experiences to make all these inferences automatically.) In addition, as predictive inferences become more specific (through automatic or strategic processes), participatory responses are also likely to accrue more content. However, the important conclusion here is that predictive inferences provide an immediate trigger for participatory responses.

Readers' preferences

As readers experience narratives, they have ample opportunities to express preferences for how various aspects of the story should unfold. For example, the viewers who responded to the moment in which Marnie removed her shoes largely seemed to express the preference that she pass by the cleaning lady undetected. That preference is interesting, in part, because Marnie appears to have just robbed a safe. Apparently, readers' preferences are not always informed by their moral values (see Gerrig, 2005; Smith, 2011)! In any case, readers quite generally appear to root for one narrative outcome over another. They also may encode preferences with respect to characters' particular actions. For example, in *A Moment in the Sun* (Sayles, 2011), a black character, Dorsey, must decide whether to vote in the face of violent opposition from the white inhabitants of Wilmington, North Carolina. Dorsey debates with his wife, Jessie, about what he ought to do: "If it make you think better of me, Jessie, I am willing to suffer the consequences" (p. 458). It's hard to imagine reading this scene without encoding a preference on Dorsey's behalf. As a final example, readers may weigh in on the wisdom of characters' goals. Thus, in the novel *When Tito Loved Clara* (Michaud, 2011), Tito has the explicit goal of trying to win Clara back. Readers are likely to have mental opinions about the prudence of that goal.

In each of these cases, readers' preferences are likely the product of inferential processes. We will make this point more concretely in the context of research that demonstrated how readers' preferences for particular outcomes structure their narrative experiences. Rapp and Gerrig (2002; see also Rapp and Gerrig, 2006) asked participants to read brief stories that ended with a time shift of either a minute or an hour. For example, in one story Jerry is a college freshman. He studies all night for a chemistry final because it would determine his final grade. Jerry sleeps through his alarm clock and rushes to the testing room in his pajamas, hoping he will not be too late. The two versions of the story, continued in this way:

5.   a. A minute later, the professor announced that the test was over and
             collected the exams.
          b. An hour later, the professor announced that the test was over and
             collected the exams.

   Then, one of two outcomes occurred:

6.   a. Jerry wouldn't pass the chemistry course.
          b. Jerry managed to pass the course.

In the experiment, participants read one of four versions of each story that provided outcomes that were either consistent or inconsistent with the time that had passed. Participants took reliably longer to read and understand sentences when the outcome mismatched the time interval (e.g., when Jerry passed the course even though he arrived at the classroom only a minute before the end of the exam). This effect relies on readers' drawing appropriate inferences about what actions, given a particular scenario, could possibly transpire in a minute versus an hour as well as the consequences of those actions.

   In a second experiment, Rapp and Gerrig added additional material into the stories that they intended as prompts for readers to encode preferences:

7.   a. Jerry had worked hard and studied intensely to do well in school,
             even hiring a tutor to prepare for his tests.
          b. Jerry figured he'd cram for his final exams and simply copy from the
             other students if he didn't know the answers.

Through a norming procedure, Rapp and Gerrig ensured that (7a) produced (in most readers) a preference that Jerry pass the course, whereas (7b) produced a contrary preference. We suggest that these preferences relied on readers' past experiences in the world. In particular, the textual information should resonate through readers' long-term memory to yield some collection of memory representations that refer to people's behavior with respect to exams. Readers may minimally infer that a character is a "good guy" or a "bad guy," or some more specific inference may emerge. Those inferences provide a context for readers to experience preferences.

When, in Rapp and Gerrig's experiment, participants read stories that induced outcome preferences, their reading times still showed an overall impact of the duration of time that had passed. They still understood, for example, that Jerry was unlikely to pass the course if the professor collected the exams after only a minute. However, readers' preferences also wielded an impact: Overall, reading times were shorter when the outcome matched the preferences and longer when the outcome mismatched. Thus, it took participants longer to read "Jerry managed to pass the course" when they wished that circumstances were otherwise. These results illustrate the interplay between inferences and participatory responses. Again, an inference (perhaps, "Jerry is a good guy") creates the context for a preference ("I want Jerry to pass his course"). These results also suggest why theories of narrative should be broader than their traditional scope (for a review of traditional theories, see McNamara and Magliano, 2009). Without consideration of readers' preferences, it would not be possible to make accurate predictions of why readers respond to the stories' outcomes as they do.

Individual differences

In this section, we have argued that readers' inferences create contexts that give rise to participatory responses. Against that background, we'd expect different readers to encode different inferences and, as a consequence, produce different participatory responses. Some individual differences in the inferences readers encode will arise as a product of the expertise they bring to particular domains (e.g., Fincher-Kiefer, Post, Greene, and Voss, 1988; Griffin, Jee, and Wiley, 2009; Spilich, Vesonder, Chiesi, and Voss, 1979). For example, one classic study demonstrated the importance of readers' knowledge by having participants listen to a half-inning of a fictional baseball game (Spilich et al., 1979). Participants who were high in baseball knowledge showed better recall memory for important features of the game, such as how runners advanced. High-knowledge individuals were also more likely to produce accounts of the game that included elaborations of the original text.

We can apply such results in the context of participatory responses. Consider a moment from *The Art of Fielding* (Harbach, 2011) in which

Mike Schwartz, the catcher for the Westish Harpooners, gets into an argument with an umpire about a bad call at home plate (pp. 162–3). Readers who have relatively little baseball knowledge may have a sense of foreboding. Readers with more baseball experience will likely be able to predict the probable outcome as Schwartz escalates his rhetoric (p. 163):

"Stand up and talk to me like a man," Schwartz said.
"Watch yourself."
"You watch yourself. You blew the call and you know it."

Given their ability to make concrete predictions based on Schwartz's behavior, we might expect that readers with greater baseball knowledge will encode participatory responses that are both more urgent and more specific. If, in fact, those readers encode warnings, such as "You're going to be ejected," those warnings will be in vain.

Readers' differing responses to another moment in *The Art of Fielding* may arise from other sources than expertise. Henry Skrimshander, the Harpooner's star shortstop, has played a devastatingly awful game. As a consequence, he wishes to resign from the team. The coach attempts to change Henry's mind: "You're not quitting anything. In fact, you're unsuspended, effective immediately. Practice starts in fifteen minutes. Go get dressed" (p. 366). This context provides readers with an opportunity to weigh in on Henry's decision. Should he, in fact, quit or should he accede to the coach's admonition that he suit up for practice? It seems quite likely that readers' responses to this moment will be quite variable, with respect to the mental advice they offer to Henry. Earlier, we briefly described how readers' preferences arise as a product of their memory representations. In the current context, it becomes important that each reader has representations of a unique set of life experiences. Based on those unique sets, individual readers are likely to define a dimension of responses that varies from an intense preference that Henry quit to an intense preference that he stay on the team. In the novel, Henry makes his decision. That creates a second opportunity for readers to bring their own life experiences to bear. Readers' responses are likely to populate a dimension from "good decision!" to "bad decision!"

This example from *The Art of Fielding* illustrates how easily and substantially readers' experiences of the same narrative might diverge. Suppose one reader, Ann, wishes for Henry to stay on the team whereas another, Bob, wishes for him to quit. Suppose Henry decides to stay on the team. After Henry makes this decision, Ann and Bob will be in quite different psychological states. Ann is likely to read the rest of the novel with an eye to supporting her belief that Henry's decision was prudent; Bob is likely to be seeking evidence that Henry was unwise.

In fact, Jacovina and Gerrig (2010) demonstrated that readers' individual responses to characters' decisions affected their experience of narrative outcomes. Jacovina and Gerrig asked participants to read a series of brief stories that arrived at everyday dilemmas. They chose dilemmas for which they could reasonably expect their college-age participants to have abundant expertise. For example, in one story, a character named David must decide whether to wear casual or formal garb to his niece's sweet sixteen party. When each story arrived at the character's decision point, participants gave explicit ratings of which decision they favored and with what strength (i.e., "Definitely choose ... ," "Probably choose ... ," and "No preference"). The stories continued with the characters making their decisions (e.g., David chose his attire). Finally, the stories ended with outcomes that cast light on the decision (e.g., "He saw that with a few exceptions, they were formally dressed," or "He saw that with a few exceptions, they all dressed casual"). Participants' reading times for these outcomes depended on their particular preferences. Suppose the story concluded with "He saw that with a few exceptions, they all dressed casual." The participants who preferred that David wear casual attire took less time to read that sentence than the participants who preferred that David be more formal. Thus, participants' own preferences determined whether the stories had endings that were easy or hard for them to understand.

These results indicate how easily and definitively readers' experiences of the same narrative may diverge. Different life experiences may yield different inferences. Those inferences may yield different participatory responses. Given this accumulation of differences, it becomes easy to understand why people, after comparing notes with their peers, might hardly believe that they've read the same novel or viewed the same movie.

We turn now to a consideration of how mysteries affect readers' narrative experiences.

Mysteries

We opened this chapter with an intriguing moment from *A Wanted Man* (Child, 2012): Jack Reacher has discovered Alan King, to be "alive again" (p. 385). This moment provides an engaging example of a narrative mystery – an instance in which a text establishes a gap between what the narrator knows and what the reader knows (see Gerrig, Love, and McKoon, 2009). In fact, on this definition, every text provides an infinite number of mysteries. Consider another sentence from the same scene:

"The man behind the chair had a gun to McQueen's head." Readers could cause themselves to ask any number of questions:

8.   a. What type of chair?
        b. How far behind the chair was the man standing?
        c. What type of gun was he holding?
        d. How close, exactly, was the gun to McQueen's head?
        e. What part of McQueen's head?

It seems unlikely that ordinary readers would expend much effort to encode or resolve most of these questions. This moment from *A Wanted Man* both allows us to assert that mysteries have an impact on readers' narratives experiences and to ask, "Which mysteries?"

This question provides an interesting parallel to the study of inferences. Theorists of text processing recognized, early and often, that every text permits an unlimited number of inferences (e.g., Rieger, 1975). Consider all the inferences readers could potentially attempt with respect to the properties of the chair to which McQueen has been bound. Given the forward motion of this text, readers would likely have no motivation to encode these inferences. In fact, most research on inferences has focused on determining exactly which inferences readers do actually encode (for a review, see McNamara and Magliano, 2009). With respect to mysteries, the initial question becomes, when do mysteries have an impact on readers' narrative experiences? In that context, a second question immediately presents itself: What impact does a particular mystery have?

Before we move on, we want to make some observations to ensure that our use of the concept of mystery is clear (cf. Gerrig et al., 2009). To begin, we stress that mysteries occur in all narrative works, irrespective of genre. In fact, authors of literary fiction often deform the time line of their narratives to highlight gaps between what the narrator, characters, and readers know. Such is the case, for example, in *When Tito Loved Clara* (Michaud, 2011), in which an essential mystery is why and how Clara disappeared from Tito's life. We also emphasize that mysteries have different scope within readers' narrative experiences. Some mysteries are, in a sense, the official topic of an entire narrative. Thus, readers of *Stagestruck* (Lovesey, 2011) understand that the novel largely centers on the mystery of who put a caustic substance into the makeup of an actress of dubious talent. Other mysteries occur with far less warning, as when Alan King suddenly turns up (apparently) alive again. Some mysteries endure over long durations. For example, in *A Moment in the Sun* (Sayles, 2011), the text raises the possibility that Niles Manigault has been killed (p. 911):

The pain is worse than Niles has imagined, the first blow snapping his collarbone close to the neck and twisting as it rends him apart, and he hears something like the bellowing of a mule before the white light –

His fate is revealed twenty-six pages later (on p. 937). Other mysteries are resolved almost instantly. To solve the mystery of Alan King, the reader need only turn the page. Some mysteries will never be resolved. What exactly befell Tony Soprano at the end of the television series *The Sopranos*? We offer these observations to reinforce the claim that an understanding of readers' responses to mysteries should figure as an important element of a comprehensive account of narrative processing.

We also wish to note the relationship between this concept of a narrative mystery and the affective response of suspense. Not all mysteries will involve suspense: Uncertainty is a necessary but not a sufficient condition to give readers an experience of suspense. For example, Ortony, Clore, and Collins (1988) argued that suspense requires "a Hope emotion and a Fear emotion" (p. 131) in the context of uncertainty between two (or more) outcomes. Thus, readers who hope that the odious Niles Manigault is dead, but fear that he may not be, will experience suspense until the matter is settled. Some mysteries will not generate suspense because they do not have sufficient focus (i.e., an explicit contrast between outcomes) that allows readers to develop their preferences. Other mysteries will not generate suspense because readers are largely indifferent between two outcomes, even if they have sufficient focus. Thus, readers experience suspense for the subset of mysteries that have particular formal properties. That subset may be different for different readers.

In this section, we will demonstrate the importance of inferential processes to address the questions of when and how readers' narrative experiences are affected by mysteries. We will suggest, in particular, that inferential processes both help call readers' attention to mysteries and also often provide the substance of readers' responses. We will begin by reviewing research that demonstrates the impact of a particular type of mystery. Then we broaden our scope to engage, once again, with the topics of anaphoric and predictive inferences. Finally, we consider how mysteries often engage processes of convergent and divergent thinking.

The impact of small mysteries

Consider this moment from *The Dogs of Rome* (Fitzgerald, 2010), in which Alec Blume, a chief commissioner on the Roman police force, learns that a large number of people have been walking around, compromising a crime scene (p. 13):

"What people?"

"D'Amico was here. Then he went, only to be replaced by the Holy Ghost, of all people."

In this excerpt, both "D'Amico" and the "Holy Ghost" are new to the narrative, but they are introduced in a fashion that suggests Blume will know who they are. Gerrig, Love, and McKoon (2009; see also Love et al., 2010) characterized this exact sort of situation as a "small mystery" – one in which readers have a strong expectation that the identity and importance of these characters will soon be revealed.

Gerrig et al. (2009) conducted a series of experiments to demonstrate that mysteries of this sort have an impact on readers' narrative experiences. They suggested that characters (such as D'Amico) remain relatively accessible in readers' discourse representations until a narrative establishes how a character will function within a particular world. Consider this brief story (p. 152):

9.   Anton was getting course credit doing volunteer work. Every evening, without fail, he wore a jacket and tie to work in an office for three hours. A co-worker named Jeremy asked Anton why he'd gotten involved. Anton said, "If I work for Lawrence, it will count for my major." Jeremy replied, "It's important to get a solid education."

Gerrig et al. called a character such as Lawrence a *focal character*. In this version of the story, the focal character's function within the narrative world presents a small mystery. A different version of the story resolved that function:

10.   Anton said, "If I work for the senator, Lawrence, it will count for my major."

Ordinarily, we expect that, as readers make their way through a narrative, new information will displace old information in working memory. However, Gerrig et al. predicted that, when characters' functions remain unresolved, their accessibility in readers' discourse representations will be less likely to fade. To test this prediction, Gerrig et al. asked participants to read stories one line at the time. At some point, the story was interrupted by a test word. Participants attempted to respond as quickly as possible whether that word had appeared in the previous part of the story. Gerrig et al. demonstrated that participants found it easier to indicate, for example, that Lawrence had appeared in the story when Lawrence's role remained unresolved. Additional experiments showed that this small mystery had a broad impact on readers' narrative experiences. For example, when the focal character's role remained unresolved, participants processing of information was disrupted downstream from the point at which the story introduced the mystery. Participants also had worse memory for story information that followed the introduction of a focal character when the mystery remained unresolved (Love et al., 2010).

These experiments demonstrate why a consideration of mysteries must be a component of a comprehensive theory of narrative experiences. In the next sections, we review the importance of inferential processes with respect to readers' responses to mysteries.

Anaphoric and predictive inferences

We saw earlier how anaphoric inferences create a context for participatory responses. These same inferences may draw readers' attention to mysteries. Recall our example from *The Trinity Six*, in which Holly has poured herself a glass of water. Inferential processes will lead readers back to the earlier, poisoned water. A mystery is whether this water is poisoned as well. The mystery arises as readers contemplate whether the connection between the two instances of *water* is superficial, or has deeper causal implications. We see a similar example in the novel *When Tito Loved Clara* (Michaud, 2011). Tito Moreno works for a moving company. He has been alerted by a customer that, during a move, an item of great sentimental value has gone missing (p. 117):

The bangle. A gold bangle. It was in the top drawer of my bureau and now it's not there.

Tito promises to make a sincere effort to find the bangle. The bangle weighs heavily on his thoughts because the customer who lost it, Mrs. Almonte, was a major figure in the life of Clara Lugo, Tito's lost love. Tito believes that a character named Raúl may have stolen the bangle. He tracks Raúl from New York City to a house in suburban New Jersey (p. 132):

A minivan was now in the driveway of the house across the street. The engine cut off and a chubby, brown-skinned girl [Deysei] in overalls and short sleeves walked from the car toward the front of the house. On her arm – *son of a bitch* – was what looked from this distance to be a gold bangle. But he didn't have time to dwell on that, because the driver's side door slammed and, around the back of the minivan, here came Clara.

Readers will, no doubt, make the connection between this gold bangle and the one that Tito seeks to find. However, that link provides at least two layers of mystery. On their own behalf, readers may wonder if, in fact, this is the same bangle. If they conclude that the bangle on Deysei's arm is the very same bangle, they will have to wonder how it came into her possession. Meanwhile, readers may also try to represent how, in the same moment, Tito will experience both the question of the bangle and other mysteries. For example, readers know why Tito's search for the bangle has led him to Clara – but Tito does not. Tito still has many pieces to fit together. These examples generate a more general conclusion about anaphoric inferences. Each time inferential processes yield a link of apparent identity from a current element of a narrative to some past element, readers are faced with a mystery: Is the identity valid?

Predictive inferences also often call readers' attention to mysteries. Recall our example from *Marnie*. As the viewers reported their thoughts, almost all of them made some mention of the inference that the shoes were going to fall (Bezdek et al., 2013). Some viewers also added material that indicated that they'd noted some mysteries that would follow as a consequence:

11.   a. She dropped the shoe in the . . . okay, I find it hard to believe that the cleaning lady's not going to hear the shoe drop and turn around.
       b. How'd she not even notice that? She must be like a deaf old woman.
       c. Of course that woman mopping wouldn't hear. That woman's crazy thinking that she's going to make noise with just a shoe.

Note that the viewer in (11b) has found her way to the correct solution (i.e., the cleaning woman is, in fact, hearing impaired) whereas the viewer in (11c) reaches a conclusion that may be valid but isn't the one that Hitchcock, apparently, intended.

We also reviewed evidence earlier suggesting that readers may not encode specific expectations. Thus, people may read "The director and cameraman were ready to shoot close-ups when suddenly the actress fell from the 14th story" and encode an inference akin to "Something bad will happen." Circumstances of this sort immediately present the mystery, "Exactly what bad thing *did* happen?" Thus, this one-sentence story presents a rather powerful cliffhanger. The cliffhanger is not present in the text. Rather, readers' predictive inferences, however lacking in specificity, help them find their way to the mystery that makes the moment suspenseful.

Of course, the tradition for cliffhangers, and mysteries more generally, is that authors often make readers wait to learn an outcome. In the next section, we consider the types of activities in which readers may engage while authors make them wait.

Convergent and divergent thinking

The research on small mysteries provided a concrete demonstration of the capacity of mysteries to draw readers' mental resources. In this section, we review circumstances in which readers might be inclined to take a voluntary pause, as they experience a narrative, to engage in particular types of thinking that will give rise to inferences. In particular, we focus on the types of thinking that have been associated with creativity, *convergent thinking* and *divergent thinking* (Eysenck, 2003; Guilford, 1959). Convergent thinking helps people to fuse ideas, pull concepts together, and find solutions to problems with one well-defined answer. By contrast, divergent thinking is responsible for novelty and allows people to form many solutions to problems with ill-defined answers. Both types of thinking are relevant to readers' experience of mysteries.

Consider the classic genre mystery. Earlier, we alluded to *Stagestruck* (Lovesey, 2011). As the novel unfolds, a police detective named Peter Diamond leads a team of officers who are tasked with discovering who it was that laced an actress's makeup with a caustic substance. Readers have the opportunity to use their convergent thinking skills to draw their own inferences about the identity of the guilty party. The author (mostly) plays fair, so that attentive readers could gather together various clues so that their inferences converge on the right solution. Part of the readers' fun is pitting their own convergent thinking ability against Diamond's and his colleagues.

Still, we emphasize that readers' opportunities to engage in convergent thinking do not just arise in particular genres. Consider a compelling mystery that arises in the literary novel, *The Family Fang* (Wilson, 2011): Are Caleb and Camille Fang (the parents of the family Fang) dead? This is a good moment for convergent thinking, because clues push in opposite directions. The official, Officer Dunham, who contacts the children, Annie and Buster, believes the Fang parents are, in fact, dead (pp. 155–6):

There is a significant amount of blood around the car, there are signs of a struggle, and we have been dealing with similar incidents occurring at rests stops around this area for the past nine months. I don't want to alarm you, but there have been four incidents in East Tennessee involving rest-stop abductions, all ending in homicides.

The children believe that this is an elaborate performance piece by their artist parents. They marshal evidence that a disappearance of this sort would be consistent with their parents' past art practice. Readers have the opportunity to determine, for themselves, how they believe the pieces fit together. Readers' convergent thinking may, in addition, be influenced by an aesthetic question: Will the novel be more interesting if the parents are dead or alive?

Narratives also provide readers with abundant opportunities to engage in divergent thinking. Consider another moment from *A Wanted Man*

(Child, 2012). Along with two partners, Jack Reacher is moving stealthily across a piece of land that they believe is a farm. They begin to sense *something* in the distance (p. 345):

> And then they saw it. Maybe the greater proximity did the trick, or maybe the wind moved the cloud and threw a couple of extra moon beams down to earth. Or maybe both.
>   It wasn't a farm.

The mystery here is clear: If "it" wasn't a farm, what was it? The scene provides an optimal prompt for divergent thinking. The classic laboratory measure of divergent thinking is the Alternate Uses Task (AUT; Guilford, 1967). For this task, participants must generate many uses for common objects, such as a brick, newspaper, or paper clip. Novelty is measured by the originality of an idea in a given sample of responses. This moment from *A Wanted Man* provides readers with the opportunity to generate ideas for what "it" might be. In a sense, they are testing their own ingenuity against the author's creativity. Readers are likely to be most impressed when the author provides an answer to, in this case, "not a farm" that eludes their own divergent thinking.

Readers also have opportunities to engage in both convergent and divergent thinking when characters are faced with dilemmas. For example, in *Hell & Gone* (Swierczynski, 2011), Charlie Hardie has been sent to a prison that is far below ground, with its one exit welded shut. To add to his misery, the prison has a "death mechanism" (p. 74) that will call everyone (prisoners and guards) should anyone try to escape. The novel provides abundant prompts for readers to make mental attempts to help Charlie find his way out of this very locked room. Reasonable ideas are regularly thwarted.

Readers' unsuccessful attempts to aid Charlie should increase their feelings of suspense. Consider research by Gerrig and Bernardo (1994) that demonstrated how suspense varied with the apparent elimination of solutions to characters' dilemmas. In one experiment, Gerrig and Bernardo created a story about James Bond. In the story, Bond had a confrontation with a villain, Le Chiffre, and Le Chiffre's henchmen. During a scuffle, Bond moved his fountain pen deeper into his breast pocket, as if to indicate that the pen had some problem-solving significance for escape. At the end of the *pen-removed* version of the story, the villain searched Bond and confiscated the pen. At the end of the *not-removed* version, Bond retained his pen. Participants who read the pen-removed version reported higher levels of suspense than those who read the not-removed version. When faced with the removal of the pen, we suggest that readers engaged in a brief bit of divergent thinking. By convincing themselves that the pen provided *some* solution for Bond, readers also likely convinced themselves that, by virtues of the pen's removal, Bond's options had been narrowed. Readers' strategic use of their own inferential processes caused them to experience the scenario as more suspenseful.

But will all readers have undertaken this mental effort? In our final section, we turn to individual differences with respect to convergent and divergent thinking.

Individual differences

We have suggested that readers have ample opportunities to engage strategic effort to address narrative mysteries. They may encode inferences as the products of either convergent or divergent thinking. Within the territory we have outlined, there is abundant room for readers' efforts to bring about radically different experiences. Here, we provide a sketch of relevant individual differences.

To begin, people differ in their ability to engage in convergent and divergent thinking (Hennessey and Amabile, 2010). For example, researchers often measure convergent thinking using the Remote Associates Test (RAT; Mednick, 1962). The test challenges participants to find a single word that connects three other words. Thus, a participant might see "land," "hand," and "house." The word that connects them is "farm." In one study using the RAT, college students attempted to solve twenty-five problems (Smith, Huber, and Vul, 2013). Their performance ranged from 16 percent to 68 percent correct. We suggest that such individual differences would likely also have an impact on readers' ability to piece together the clues to generate a solution to a mystery. Similarly, individual differences in divergent thinking could affect the quantity or quality of mental assistance readers are able to give when characters are imperiled. Recall the research we just reviewed that demonstrated readers' role in their experiences of suspense (Gerrig and Bernardo, 1994). Individual differences in divergent thinking may affect the extent to which readers experience suspense.

Readers' narrative experiences will also differ as a function of their motivation to engage in either convergent or divergent thinking. Recall the moment from *A Wanted Man*, in which the text reads, "It wasn't a farm" (Child, 2012, p. 345). Readers will choose how much effort they wish to expend, in the moment, to infer what the not-farm could be. Some readers will likely take up the author's invitation to engage in creative thought whereas others will likely immediately choose to turn the page. Similarly, some readers of *Stagestruck* (Lovesey, 2011) will labor to infer the perpetrator of the assault against the actress (and other crimes that follow), whereas others will cede full responsibility to the detective, Peter Diamond, to unmask the villain(s). Individual readers' motivation may be influenced by their *self-efficacy for creativity* (e.g., Carmeli and Schaubroeck, 2007; Choi, 2004; Tierney and Farmer, 2002). Generally speaking, self-efficacy is people's belief that they can perform adequately in a particular situation (Bandura, 1997). Creative self-efficacy is people's particular belief that they can perform well on a creative task. Self-efficacy has a positive relationship with creative performance (e.g., Carmeli and Schaubroeck, 2007; Choi, 2004). Readers may not specifically think of narrative experiences as a domain in which they need to exercise creative thinking. Still, some readers are likely to have developed a sense of themselves as being, for example, good at solving (genre) mysteries. A history of perceived successes would lead to a type of self-efficacy that would likely affect both the types of narratives readers would choose to consume and the mental effort they would expend once they have begun to experience those narratives.

Readers' narrative experiences will also differ as a function of the products of their convergent and divergent thinking. Recall *The Family Fang* (Wilson, 2011), in which readers face the mystery of whether Caleb and Camille Fang are actually dead. Some readers will use convergent thinking processes to infer that the Fangs are, in fact, dead, whereas other readers will infer that they are still alive. In the face of those inferences, readers' experiences will radically diverge. Each type of reader (i.e., dead or alive), will evaluate subsequent events in a different light. They must determine how new evidence supports or challenges their initial inference. And, of course, one group of readers will be wrong. The novel's resolution will play out quite differently, once again, as a function of individual differences in the products of convergent thinking.

Conclusions

In this chapter, we have discussed two pervasive elements of readers' narrative experiences: Their encoding of participatory responses and their engagement with mysteries. In each case, we have suggested how inferences often create a context for these phenomena to wield an impact. Inferences often lead readers to encode participatory responses. Inferences help readers recognize when a mystery is present; readers engage the inferential processes of convergent and divergent thinking to address those mysteries. Although we have discussed participatory responses and mysteries separately, we hope it has become clear that they often emerge at the same moments, and intensify people's experiences: At the same time viewers engage mental effort to prevent Marnie from letting her shoe drop, they are contemplating the mystery of what might happen if and when it does. This moment obtains much of its vigor from the foundation of viewers' inferences.

REFERENCES

Bandura, A. (1997). *Self-efficacy: The Exercise of Control.* New York: Freeman.

Bezdek, M. A., Foy, J. E., & Gerrig, R. J. (2013). "Run for it!": Viewers' participatory responses to film narratives. *Psychology of Aesthetics, Creativity, and the Arts, 7,* 409–16.

Carmeli, A., & Schaubroeck, J. (2007). The influence of leaders' and other referents' normative expectations on individual involvement in creative work. *The Leadership Quarterly, 18,* 35–48.

Child, I. (2012). *A Wanted Man.* New York: Delacorte Press.

Choi, J. N. (2004). Individual and contextual predictors of creative performance: the mediating role of psychological processes. *Creativity Research Journal, 16,* 187–99.

Cumming, C. (2011). *The Trinity Six.* New York: St. Martin's Press.

Eysenck, H. J. (2003). Creativity, personality, and the convergent-divergent continuum. In M. A. Runco (ed.), *Critical Creative Processes* (pp. 95–114).

Fincher-Kiefer, R., Post, T. A., Greene, T. R., & Voss, J. F. (1988). On the role of prior knowledge and task demands in the processing of text. *Journal of Memory and Language, 27,* 416–28.

Fitzgerald, C. (2010). *The Dogs of Rome.* New York: Bloomsbury USA.

Gerrig, R.J. (1993). *Experiencing Narrative Worlds.* New Haven, CT: Yale University Press.

(2005). Moral judgments in narrative contexts. *The Behavioral and Brain Sciences, 28,* 550.

Gerrig, R. J., & Bernardo, A. B. I. (1994). Readers as problem-solvers in the experience of suspense. *Poetics, 22,* 459–72.

Gerrig, R. J., & Jacovina, M. E. (2009). Reader participation in the experience of narrative. In B. H. Ross (ed.), *The Psychology of Learning and Motivation* (Vol. *LI,* pp. 223–54). Burlington, MA: Academic Press.

Gerrig, R. J., Love, J., & McKoon, G. (2009) Waiting for Brandon: how readers respond to small mysteries. *Journal of Memory and Language, 60,* 144–53.

Gerrig, R. J., & McKoon, G. (2001). Memory processes and experiential continuity. *Psychological Science, 12,* 81–5.

Gerrig, R. J., & O'Brien, E. J. (2005). The scope of memory-based processing. *Discourse Processes, 39,* 225–42.

Griffin, T. D., Jee, B. D., & Wiley, J. (2009). The effects of domain knowledge on metacomprehension accuracy. *Memory & Cognition, 37,* 1001–13.

Guilford, J. P. (1959). Traits of creativity. In H. H. Anderson (ed.), *Creativity and Its Cultivation* (pp. 142–61). New York: Harper.

(1967). *The Nature of Human Intelligence.* New York: McGraw-Hill.

Harbach, C. (2011). *The Art of Fielding.* New York: Little, Brown and Company.

Hennessey, B. A., & Amabile, T. M. (2010). Creativity. *Annual Review of Psychology, 61,* 569–98.

Hitchcock, A. (Producer/Director). (1964). *Marnie [Motion picture]*. United States: Universal Pictures.

Jacovina, M. E., & Gerrig, R. J. (2010) How readers experience characters' decisions. *Memory & Cognition, 38*, 753–61.

Klin, C. M., Guzmán, A. E., Weingartner, K. W., & Ralano, A. S. (2006). When anaphor resolution fails: partial encoding of anaphoric inferences. *Journal of Memory and Language, 54*, 131–43.

Lassonde, K. A., & O'Brien, E. J. (2009). Contextual specificity in the activation of predictive inferences. *Discourse Processes, 46*, 426–38.

Love, J., & McKoon, G. (2011). Rules of engagement: incomplete and complete pronoun resolution. *Journal of Experimental Psychology: Learning, Memory, and Cognition, 37*, 874–87.

Love, J., McKoon, G., & Gerrig, R. J. (2010). Searching for Judy: how small mysteries affect narrative processes and memory. *Journal of Experimental Psychology: Learning, Memory, and Cognition, 36*, 790–6.

Lovesey, P. (2011). *Stagestruck*. New York: Soho Crime.

McKoon, G., & Ratcliff, R. (1980). The comprehension processes and memory structures involved in anaphoric reference. *Journal of Verbal Learning and Verbal Behavior, 19*, 668–682.

(1986). Inferences about predictable events. *Journal of Experimental Psychology: Learning, Memory, and Cognition, 12*, 82–91.

(1992). Inference during reading. *Psychological Review, 99*, 440–66.

(2013). Aging and predicting inferences: a diffusion model analysis. *Journal of Memory and Language, 68*, 240–54.

McNamara, D. S., & Magliano, J. (2009). Toward a comprehensive model of comprehension. In B. H. Ross (ed.), *The Psychology of Learning and Motivation* (Vol. LI, pp. 298–384). Burlington, MA: Academic Press.

Mednick, S.A. (1962). The associative basis of the creative process. *Psychological Review, 69*, 220–32.

Michaud, J. (2011). *When Tito Loved Clara*. Chapel Hill, NC: Algonquin Books of Chapel Hill.

O'Brien, E. J., Raney, G. E., Albrecht, J. E., & Rayner, K. (1997). Processes involved in the resolution of explicit anaphors. *Discourse Processes, 23*, 1–24.

Ortony, A., Clore, G., & Collins, A. (1988). *The Cognitive Structure of Emotions*. Cambridge University Press.

Rapp, D. N., & Gerrig, R. J. (2002). Readers' reality-driven and plot-driven analyses in narrative comprehension. *Memory & Cognition, 30*, 779–88.

(2006). Predilections for narrative outcomes: the impact of story contexts and reader preferences. *Journal of Memory and Language, 54*, 54–67.

Rieger, C. J. (1975). Conceptual memory and inference. In R. C. Schank (ed.), *Conceptual Information Processing* (pp. 157–288). New York: Elsevier.

Sayles, J. (2011). *A Moment in the Sun*. San Francisco: McSweeney's Books.

Smith, K. A., Huber, D. E., & Vul, E. (2013). Multiply-constrained semantic search in the Remote Associates Test. *Cognition, 128*, 64–75.

Smith, M. (2011). Just what is it that makes Tony Soprano such an appealing, attractive murderer? In W. E. Jones & S. Vice (eds.), *Ethics at the Cinema* (pp. 66–90). Oxford University Press.

Spilich, G. J., Vesonder, G. T., Chiesi, H. L., & Voss, J. F. (1979). Text processing of domain-related information for individuals with high and low domain knowledge. *Journal of Verbal Learning & Verbal Behavior, 18,* 275–90.

Swierczynski, D. (2011). *Hell & Gone.* New York: Little, Brown and Company.

Tierney, P., & Farmer, S. M. (2002). Creative self-efficacy: its potential antecedents and relationship to creative performance. *Academy of Management Journal, 45,* 1137–48.

Wilson, K. (2011). *The Family Fang.* New York: Ecco.

17 Interpretive inferences in literature

*Susan R. Goldman, Kathryn S. McCarthy, and
Candice Burkett*

Acknowledgments

We gratefully acknowledge the important contributions to our thinking about literary interpretation made by members of the Project READI Literature Team, in particular Carol Lee, Sarah Levine, and Joseph Magliano. Other members of the Literature Team include ourselves, Stephen Briner, Jessica Chambers, Rick Coppolla, Julia Emig, Angela Fortune, MariAnne George, Allison Hall, Courtney Milligan, Teresa Sosa, and Mary Pat Sullivan. Project READI (Reading, Evidence, Argumentation in Disciplinary Instruction) is a multi-institution collaboration to improve complex comprehension of multiple forms of text in literature, history, and science. It is supported by the Institute of Education Sciences, U.S. Department of Education, through Grant R305F100007 to University of Illinois at Chicago. The opinions expressed are those of the authors and do not represent views of the Institute or the U.S. Department of Education.

In this chapter we address the kinds of inferences that are made when people read literary texts. Literary texts may include a variety of genres, including narratives, science fiction, folk tales, fables, poetry, songs, and historical fiction. Distinctions between literary and "nonliterary" texts may seem obvious. Indeed, there is general consensus that literary texts afford a displacement of meaning (Scholes, 1977, cited in Levine, 2013) or "duplicity of code." Schraw (1997) characterized literary texts as "narratives that are richly symbolic and include both an interpretable surface meaning and one or more coherent subtexts (i.e., implicit thematic interpretations that run parallel to the explicit surface-level meaning of the text)" (p. 436). In fact, clear distinctions are difficult to make, partly because such distinctions depend upon assumptions about whether meaning is "in the text," "in the author," "in the reader," in the "transaction between reader and text" (Rosenblatt, 1978; 1994), or in the interaction of reader, text, and task, situated in a social and cognitive context (RAND Report, 2002).

Different assumptions about the "locus" of meaning are reflected in differences among psychological theories of meaning as well as among movements within literary and rhetorical theory (Fish, 1980; Rabinowitz, 1987; Scholes, 1985). For example, if it is assumed that meaning is in the text, then it ought to be possible to identify features that differentiate literary texts that have a "duplicity" of meaning from nonliterary texts that do not. If meaning is in the author, then knowing whether the author intended a surface meaning and a subtext would be the key to defining whether a text is literary or not. If in the reader, then whether a text is literary or not depends on whether the reader derives a surface meaning and a subtext. And so on for the other assumptions about meaning. This seems an untenable way to distinguish between literary and nonliterary texts, and it should not be surprising that scholars have not agreed on a specific definition of what constitutes a literary text.

From our perspective, we think it is more productive to take a situated approach and distinguish among occasions or comprehension situations where readers are more likely to adopt a literal stance toward text and those where they are more likely to adopt an interpretive stance (cf. Langer, 2010). A literal stance orients readers to constructing what the text *says* based on the propositions and connections among them in the text, using prior knowledge to the extent necessary to create a coherent representation of the situation referenced by the text. An interpretive stance orients readers to what the text *means* beyond the situation of the specific text and depends on integrating what the text says with prior knowledge of a variety of sorts, including knowledge of motivated human action, text genres and their characteristics, plot structures, character types, moral and philosophical systems, and pragmatic aspects of the communicative event. A situated approach is consistent with assumptions that comprehension is a constructive process reflecting interactions among reader, text, and task occurring in a particular sociocultural context. Particular constellations of values on these dimensions in a particular reading situation affect the likelihood that readers go beyond taking a literal stance toward text to embrace an interpretive stance (cf. Goldman, 1997; 2004). To return to the idea of duplicity of code, a literal stance orients the reader to Schraw's (1997) surface meaning and an interpretive stance to the subtext(s). We assume that a literal stance leads to readers constructing some representation of what the text says as a "prerequisite" to adopting an interpretive stance. Furthermore, whether readers adopt an interpretive stance is probabilistic and depends on readers' interpretations of their tasks and what they require. Readers' task interpretations and their requirements, in turn, depend on readers' prior knowledge of the world, the domain, text genre, and communicative intent of authors and readers as well as their standards of coherence (e.g., Goldman, Varma, and Coté, 1996; Graesser, Olde, and Klettke, 2002; Graesser, Louwerse, McNamara, Olney, Cai, and Mitchell, 2007; Graesser, Singer, and Trabasso, 1994; Kintsch, 1988; 1998; Kintsch and van Dijk, 1978; van den Broek, Lorch, Linderholm, and Gustafson, 2001; van Dijk and Kintsch, 1983).

Other chapters in this volume focus on inferential processes involved in constructing what the text says – with the anaphoric, predictive, causal, and elaborative inferences that build a coherent model of the situation depicted in the text. Our concern in this chapter is with the kinds of inferences and processes involved in taking an interpretive stance. Specifically, we focus on the inferential processes needed to construct coherent subtexts, the knowledge needed to engage in these processes, and the implications for the types of interpretations and representations that result from adopting an interpretive stance.

The interpretive stance highlights aspects of narrative text comprehension and representation that have not received a great deal of attention over the past twenty-five years in discourse psychology: theme, emotional response of readers, author intent, and how that intent is communicated through character choice, plot structure, and the specific words and sentence structures that comprise the actual text (Graesser et al., 2002; Hillocks and Ludlow, 1984; Rabinowitz, 1987). This is somewhat understandable in the context of experimental designs that require clear operational definitions of variables, the need for control over potentially confounding variables, and the desire to have multiple observations of the "same" phenomenon so that any effects are not attributable to a specific text. At the same time, it is ironic, given the historical context of work in discourse psychology on narrative. In 1975, Rumelhart proposed grammatical systems for describing the syntactic and semantic structure of stories that originated in the oral tradition, such as fairy tales and fables (Rumelhart, 1975). Interest was in understanding how the structure of stories and variations in story structure impacted memory (e.g., Mandler and Johnson, 1977; Rumelhart, 1975; Stein and Glenn, 1979). Specifically, departures from canonical structures led to poorer memory for what had been presented but the "distortions" tended toward the canonical form (Mandler and Goodman, 1982). These findings hearkened back to the seminal work of Bartlett (1932) on reconstructive memory. Bartlett found that when people recalled stories that followed culturally unfamiliar semantic and structural conventions, they reconstructed the story to reflect culturally familiar stories. He dubbed this "effort after meaning" and used it to argue for the active role of prior knowledge in shaping people's memory for events. In the

1970s, during the "early days" of the cognitive revolution, Bartlett's earlier work on reconstructive memory and the postulation of schema as organizing structures for knowledge took on substantial importance as evidence for claims about the active role of the learner in cognitive approaches to memory and learning.[1]

Although Bartlett's (1932) and earlier work on story comprehension was less concerned with interpretive stances than with literal memory for stories, the legacy of comprehenders as actively seeking meaning and using prior knowledge to do so may be seen as fundamental to modern discourse psychology's interests in inferential processes writ large. Ironically, in their desire to control for extraneous variables and produce multiple examples of stories that conformed to a particular semantic or syntactic structure, discourse researchers moved away from authentic literature and began creating "textoids" in which variables of interest could be manipulated and therefore put to experimental test. Much of the inference literature has relied on these types of "texts." As a result there is a plethora of work on inferences during the construction of literal meaning and much less on inferences and reasoning involved in an interpretive stance.

The chapter is organized into three sections and concluding comments. In the first section, we discuss comprehension processes and the inferences involved in constructing mental representations of what a text says as well as what it means. In the second section, we review research that describes the ways in which literary experts make sense of texts and how their approaches contrast to those of novices. We highlight the types of knowledge that come into play in adopting an interpretive stance. The third section reports on two studies that we have conducted as exploratory investigations into the circumstances that promote an interpretive stance in literary novices. In the concluding section, we discuss ways in which existing models of comprehension and representations of texts need to be expanded to more appropriately and completely account for the processing implied in an interpretive stance toward text and the representations that result.

Inferential processes and the interpretive stance

The representations that result from adopting a literal stance correspond to textbase and situation model levels as described and characterized in contemporary theories of discourse comprehension and representation

---

[1] This was against a backdrop of the learner as passive recipient of information based in behaviorist learning theories.

(Kintsch, 1994; 1988; 1998; van Dijk and Kintsch, 1983). Textbase representations reflect information that was explicit in the text or can be inferred with minimal use of prior knowledge. These inferences tend to be local and are sometimes triggered by a single word or clause and sentences that occur over relatively short stretches of text (Graesser et al., 1994; Graesser et al., 2007). The textbase typically captures the characters, events, objects, settings, and emotions to the degree that they are explicit in the text. The situation model goes beyond what is explicit in the text itself to elaborate the textbase so that a coherent representation of the situation referenced in the text can be constructed. Several types of explanatory inferences contribute to the formation of a situation model but they are all relatively local. These inferences establish what happened and why, who was involved, and basic motives for characters' actions and emotions. They are important to both plot and character coherence in the context of the story world (Graesser et al., 1994).

An interpretive stance generally involves moving beyond the specific text or situation and relies on explanatory inferences that operate at more global levels. For example, thematic interpretive inferences encompass longer stretches of text – sometimes the entire narrative. They provide an organizing concept, schema, or framework that expresses the point or moral of the story (Graesser et al., 2007; Vipond and Hunt, 1984). Thematic interpretive inferences often take a general characteristic of motivated action and use it to explain the characters and events in the context of the specific narrative. They may be stated in terms of the specific events in the story or they may be stated as generalizations about the world writ large (Kurtz and Schober, 2001). For example, in Aesop's fable in Box 17.1 "The Dog and His Shadow" the statement "The dog was greedy because he tried to get a bigger piece of meat and so he lost everything" is an explanatory thematic inference that ties a general concept, *greed*, to a statement about the specific character and events in the story. In contrast, the thematic interpretive inference "Greedy people

---

Box 17.1   The Dog and the Shadow

A dog, crossing a bridge over a stream with a piece of flesh in his mouth, saw his own shadow in the water and took it for that of another dog, with a piece of meat double his own in size. He immediately let go of his own, and fiercely attacked the other dog to get his larger piece from him. He thus lost both: that which he grasped at in the water, because it was a shadow; and his own, because the stream swept it away. www.aesopfables.com/cgi/aesop1.cgi?1&TheDogandtheShadow Dec 1, 2013.

risk losing everything" is stated as a general truism about human behavior. Thematic inferences – whether specific or more abstracted – are akin to "morals of the story" as in this and other Aesop's fables. They often rely on religious, philosophical, or experiential knowledge bases and may constitute a commonsense theory of human action (e.g., Heider, 1958). Thematic interpretive inferences may serve to connect to other stories with similar themes. Such a mechanism would allow readers to form categories of stories that deal with similar themes. This may be particularly useful as readers begin to identify commonalities in the human experience and criteria for recognizing new instances of situations that reflect the operation of particular themes (cf. Smith, 1991).

Thematic generalizations abstracted away from the story to the world outside the story *and* connected to reasoning about how the author conveyed the message are designated as *author generalizations* (Hillocks and Ludlow, 1984). They reflect readers' interpretations of the message the author intended to communicate in the particular literary work and tie the interpretations to those aspects of the text that readers are using as evidence for the author's message. Author generalizations are therefore linked to a specific situation model and use evidence from the text itself, often specific patterns of language usage or rhetorical devices. In addition, author generalizations may also be a mechanism by which readers develop author schemas that represent characteristic style, craft, rhetorical devices, plot lines, and so forth of specific authors. Such schemas would be built up through reading multiple works and perhaps rereading previously read works by a specific author. Such author schema might then, in turn, lead to predictions and expectations when reading additional works by particular authors. For example, across a number of O. Henry short stories, readers might come to anticipate an unexpected twist at the end of a story. Author schema are not typically mentioned as part of a situation model representation for single texts. However, in the context of models of multiple document comprehension in history and science, several researchers highlight the importance of representing sourcing information, including the author (Goldman, 2004; Perfetti et al., 1999; Rouet, 2006; Rouet and Britt, 2011).

In summary, a literal stance involves inferences that establish a textbase and situation model that reflects a coherent representation of what the text says and the situation referenced by the text. Such inferences create connections from sentence-to-sentence and from episode-to-episode. The information needed to make these inferences is largely contained within the text and everyday knowledge of motivated action. These inferences help establish the basics of the actors/characters, events, and goals of the story. It is these kinds of inferences that have been the subject of much of the discourse comprehension research on situation models for narratives. An interpretive stance involves inferences that build from and go beyond the world of the text. That is, the interpretive stance draws on the literal, but generalizes from it with inferential reasoning that connects or associates the literal with more general tendencies of, or generalizations about, human nature and life's principles that seem to govern the way the world operates (e.g., Don't be greedy or you might lose what you have; The world isn't always fair; Good things happen to bad people; If you are bossy, people won't listen to you or like you; Do unto others as you would have them do unto you). These types of interpretive inferences may serve as "higher-order" organizational structures and provide a basis for creating intertextual connections in that they could be linked to both specific situation models of stories from which they were abstracted as well as to new situation models formed when reading additional stories either by the same or by different authors.

In the next section, we consider empirical evidence regarding interpretive inferences. Much of this work has been conducted in the context of contrastive expert–novice studies.

Adopting an interpretive stance: studies of experts

One way in which researchers have validated the existence of an interpretive stance is through research on expertise in the literary domain. There are several seminal studies that reflect discourse researchers' efforts to explore this issue. We highlight two that are representative of the findings regarding expertise.

Graves and Frederiksen (1991) used a think-aloud methodology and compared experts' (two English department senior faculty) and novices' (undergraduates enrolled in a literature course) descriptions of a piece of literature. Participants read an excerpt (780 words) from *The Color Purple* by Alice Walker that consisted mostly of Black English Vernacular dialogue between characters. Participants were asked to read the excerpt one sentence at a time and comment on its content and style. Graves and Frederiksen analyzed the comments with respect to whether they repeated or paraphrased the text (text-based) or were situational and high-level inferences that reflected use of the text and/or prior knowledge (text-derived). Comments in their category of text-derived align with what we referred to previously as interpretive inferences. Comments were also coded with respect to the unit of text referenced: linguistic (e.g., lexical, syntactic, topical), conceptual propositional content (e.g., propositional meaning, coherence relations, logical relations), conceptual frame (e.g., description of character or setting, narrative actions, dialogue, goals and plans). Finally, comments were coded for what Graves and Frederiksen referred to as the discourse perspective. This analysis basically captured whether the comment described something about the text only or about the text plus reference to the author, the text plus reference to the reader, or the text plus reference to an author/reader relationship.

Results revealed multiple differences between experts and novices. First, novices' comments were overwhelmingly text-based whereas experts' comments were text-derived inferences. There were also several differences in the types of units referenced in the comments. Experts commented more on syntactic features whereas novices commented more on lexical/morphological structures (i.e., spellings or words). Experts made inferences about the narrative structure and functions of the dialogue, using the text to support their inferences, whereas novices tended to repeat the narrative events or what characters had said. Experts, but not novices, also commented on the author's use of language (e.g., "There is a deliberate manipulation of the syntax"), the impact of the style of writing on the reader (e.g., "The lack of standard punctuation makes this difficult for the reader"), and the author's intentional use of a specific style for purposes of engaging the reader (e.g., "It's a self-conscious effort to do a kind of stream-of-consciousness style which is, of course, deliberately elliptical and telegraphic and invited the reader to fill in all the deleted syntax, punctuation, etc.").

Overall, Graves and Frederiksen (1991) provided evidence that experts used the text to derive inferences about the larger meaning of the situation depicted in the text. In contrast, novices were focused almost exclusively on the textbase; that is, they focused on what the text explicitly said about an event and dialogue sequence. Equally significant is that experts considered how the author used language – the role of deliberate syntactic, semantic, and discourse choices – to engage the reader. This study thus provides evidence for the claims made by literary theorists that authors assume a set of conventions that readers will rely on in interpreting literary works (e.g., Rabinowitz, 1987). Similar differences between experts and novices have been found for poetry genre (e.g., Peskin, 1998; Warren, 2011).

However, what is not clear is how widely held these conventions are. That is, is knowledge of these conventions one of the distinguishing characteristics of literary expertise and a type of knowledge that the average reader does not have? Or are these conventions and their importance to an interpretive stance simply more explicit to literary experts than to novices? In either case, it seems likely that these knowledge differences could impact interpretations of the actual task instructions, leading experts to make a different set of assumptions about what the task requires than novices. For example, literary experts might see the task as requiring detailed examination of the text and interpretations of the author's message, whereas novices see the task as being more constrained, for example, to figuring out the action sequence. Of course, in addition to knowledge of shared conventions, literary experts also have far greater knowledge of a range of literary works, movements, and authors, than do novices. Thus, the foregoing analysis is just one of several possible explanations for the expert–novice differences observed by Graves and Frederiksen (1991).

There is also the possibility that literary experts are simply better text comprehenders than novices. However, the results of a second comparative study suggest that expert-novice differences for literary texts are specific to that genre and not due to some more generalized differences in text comprehension. Zeitz (1994) compared the memory and reasoning performance for three text genres of literary experts (graduate students in English) to two groups of literary novices – engineering graduate students and third-year high school students. Each participant read a poem, a short story, and a scientific expository passage and completed recall and recognition memory tasks as well as interpretation and reasoning tasks.

With respect to memory tasks in the Zeitz (1994) study, for gist recall of the poem the English graduate students outperformed the other two groups; however, for gist recall of the science text, engineering graduate students outperformed the English and high school students. A recognition memory task for plot statements and for inferences that were based on several sentences for the short story indicated poorer overall performance by the high-school students but an interaction for the two groups of graduate students: Performance of the two groups of graduate students was equivalent on the plot statements but English graduate students outperformed the engineering graduate students on the inference statements. The patterns of results on the memory tasks thus indicate that the "advantage" for the literary experts is restricted to literary genres and measures that reflect an interpretive stance. A similar conclusion applies to performance on the reasoning measures.

Zeitz (1994) carried out extensive analyses of a variety of characteristics of the responses to the reasoning tasks to establish that literary novices were working with more basic-level representations of the literary texts than were literary experts. As in Graves and Frederiksen (1991), literary experts drew on derived representations that reflected interpretative inferences based on the presented texts. However, for the science texts, literary experts worked with more basic-level representations and their performance was similar to that of the engineering graduate students. That is, literary experts adopted an interpretive stance only for the literary texts, demonstrating domain-specificity in contrast to some more generalized skill. For example, one set of results supporting this conclusion concerned whether the topic sentences were facts (literal information from the texts), interpretations (inferences using prior knowledge), or other. English students produced more interpretive sentences than engineering students, particularly for the literary texts. A content analysis of the topic sentences also indicated that all three groups showed similar content types for the science text, but for the literary texts the English students focused on language and theme whereas the other two groups concentrated on characters and events. Differences between the English and engineering graduate students were replicated in the argument structure of essays that were written for the literary texts. (Essays were not written for the science text.) English students had more sophisticated arguments that asserted more claims for which relevant evidence was provided than did the other two groups.

These two seminal studies of expert–novice differences in the processing of literary texts indicate that literary experts are more likely to adopt an interpretive stance; Zeitz's (1994) work further established that the greater likelihood of literary experts adopting an interpretive stance was specific to literary texts. Both of the studies reviewed here indicate that experts have a well-developed knowledge base relevant to literary interpretation, similar to experts in other domains (cf. Chi, Feltovich, and Glaser, 1981). Theory and empirical data indicate that there are at least two critical, epistemological components of literary experts' knowledge bases: (1) literary texts are indirect and contain both a surface and a deeper meaning (Carlsen, 1981; Purves 1971; Schmidt, 1982; Scholes, 1985; Schraw, 1997; Zeitz, 1994); and (2) authors are purposeful in constructing a surface text that uses conventions for providing clues to deeper meaning (Rabinowitz, 1987; Schmidt, 1982). In other words, literary experts' interpretive stance constitutes an "effort after meaning" that includes an orientation to discover conventionalized textual features and use them to construct multiple meanings that are abstracted away from the specific characters, events, and situations depicted in the surface text (Schmidt, 1982). They endeavor, as Vipond and Hunt (1984) put it, to determine the point of the text. Of course, there may be more than one intended message (Classen, 2012; Gibbs, 2011), and readers may not agree with one another on the inferences they make about an author's point. Indeed, disagreements regarding the "point" of a literary piece often set the stage for literary argument.

There has been a fair bit of speculation about the second aspect of an expert's knowledge, namely the nature of the conventions that authors assume are shared by their readers. Perhaps one of the most well-developed proposals is that of Rabinowitz (1987), who posited that authors count on their readers' awareness and use of narrative conventions. He casts these conventions as four major types of rules: rules of notice, rules of signification, rules of configuration, and rules of coherence. Rules of notice direct readers to pay attention to and prioritize some details, characters, objects, or events over others. Rules of notice – really more heuristics than rules – suggest the potential importance of elements that, for example, appear in privileged positions in a text (e.g., in titles, in first or last sentences of a text), are semantically or syntactically stressed, are repeated frequently, are described in great detail although seemingly obscure or mundane, or that are unexpected or create breaks in the continuity of a text. Referring back to the Aesop's fable shown in Box 17.1, "dog" and "shadow" appear in the title. This positioning heightens expectations that these are key to interpreting the fable, although by no means ensures it. Rules of signification help the reader figure out how to make sense of things that we notice. Often this involves considering nonliteral, metaphorical, symbolic, satirical, or ironic meanings. For example, Appendix A contains an adapted version of a short story by James Hanley titled "The Butterfly" that we used in one of the studies we discuss subsequently. However, there are no butterflies in the story; only a caterpillar that gets killed before it turns into a butterfly. That there are no butterflies in the story but that it is the title might suggest that there is some symbolic significance to the butterfly and may lead the reader to consider what that might be. Rules of configuration help organize initially disparate symbolic elements into recognizable plot or thematic patterns (e.g., the love triangle, the triumph of good over evil) and provide a basis for predictions and expectations. Rules of coherence provide us with ways to reconcile apparent disjunctures and inconsistencies in expectations through metaphor, irony, or through a reframing in which they make sense. This process often points to potential moral, political, or philosophical messages of the text. Rabinowitz (1987) distinguishes configuration and coherence with respect to the questions they address and when they operate: Rules of configuration operate during reading and address "the question, 'How will this in all probability work out?'" whereas rules of coherence operate once we have finished reading and allow us to answer the question, "Given how it worked out, how can I account for these particular elements?" (p. 112).

From a processing perspective, the four types of rules operate inter-actively and iteratively as readers construct representations of literary text. Studies of literary experts provide evidence that they are explicitly engaging these rules during reading, and after reading when asked to provide or evaluate interpretations (Graves and Frederiksen, 1991; Peskin, 1998; Warren, 2011; Zeitz, 1994). Indeed, Warren (2011) reported that literary experts who read poetry outside of their expertise area indicated the need to know more about the common conventions, stylistic choices, and common themes of particular authors before they could provide informed interpretations of their work. In contrast, the performance of novices suggests that they adopt a literal stance only. The absence of evidence for an interpretive stance in novices could reflect lack of the knowledge that supports the kinds of inferences experts make or it could reflect differences in how they interpret task instructions in these experimental situations. In other words, the research to date does not allow us to determine what knowledge novices do have that would support the adoption of an interpretive stance and abstractions from the specific story world created in a literary text.

Other research indicates that even preschool and elementary school-aged children engage in metaphorical thinking and that they "get the point" of Aesop's fables (e.g., Goldman, Reyes, and Varnhagen, 1984; Johnson and Goldman, 1987; Winner, 1988). Lee's work on cultural modeling (Lee, 2001; 2007) also indicates that high school students have a wealth of strategies for recognizing figurative and symbolic meaning in song lyrics, films, and other forms of popular culture texts. However, they are not explicitly aware of how they know what they know. Cultural modeling is an instructional process for making those strategies explicit as a first step to building on them in adopting an interpretive stance toward the literary canon of school.

In an effort to better elucidate how literary novices approach the processing of literary texts and their assumptions about task-appropriate responses given particular instructions, in the next section we discuss findings from several studies that explore these issues. Specifically, we discuss studies that were designed to investigate literary novices' "sense making" for literary texts under different task conditions. Variations among task conditions were expected to differentially encourage or bias an interpretive stance. In some cases, the variations were in the text genre; in other cases, the variations were in the task instructions; and in still others, the variations were in the directness of the request for interpretations.

When do novices adopt an interpretive stance?

In the context Project READI, a large multi-institutional collaboration designed to examine evidence-based argumentation in literature, science, and history, we have conducted a number of exploratory and descriptive studies to attempt to elucidate the processes and resulting understandings that "literary novices" construct. Our goal in conducting this research has been to ascertain how these individuals "make sense" of literary texts and the effects of different tasks on the likelihood that performance reflects an interpretive stance. In this chapter, we discuss only the performance of undergraduates.

The first study we describe examined essays produced in response to specific questions that differed in terms of the bias they were intended to create toward an interpretive stance versus a literal stance. The second set of studies used think-aloud methodology to tap into processes of comprehension during initial reading followed by specific question prompts. The findings we report are consistent with the contrastive studies discussed in the second part of the chapter (e.g., Graves and Frederiksen, 1991; Zeitz, 1994); literary novices rarely adopt an interpretive stance. However, the findings we report here also provide some initial evidence that when explicitly prompted for interpretations of literary texts, these novices demonstrate evidence of at least early forms of the knowledge of conventions and inference strategies that literary experts provide.

Study 1: task instructions that promote an interpretive stance

In one of our initial studies (McCarthy and Goldman, under revision), undergraduates (n = 114) read the short story "Harrison Bergeron" by Kurt Vonnegut (1968). The story relates a dystopian future where the government imposes handicapping devices on everyone so that they are "all equal." When a young man, Harrison Bergeron, rebels by removing his handicapping, he is murdered. His parents witness this event, but their handicaps prevent them from realizing that the government has killed their son. The story was read under one of four task instruction conditions. These conditions were designed to encourage a focus on either plot, theme, or interpretation. A fourth condition left the focus intentionally ambiguous. Table 17.1 provides the specific wording of the task instructions in each of these conditions. Essays were written with the text present. None of these undergraduates had taken more than two semesters of college-level English courses.

Essays were analyzed with respect to the number of clauses they contained. We sought to characterize the content of the essays with respect to the degree to which they reflected a literal stance, an interpretive stance, or both. Accordingly, we categorized each clause as reflecting

Table 17.1 *Four essay-writing instructions used in Harrison Bergeron study*

Condition	Essay writing instruction
Plot	What happened in this story? Use evidence from the text to support your claims.
Theme	Discuss the theme of the text using evidence from the story.
Argument	Critics often claim that this short-story is a political satire warning us of the dangers of letting "Big Brother" get out of control whereas others believe it is a story about human potential. Which do you think is the better interpretation? Use evidence from the text to support your claims.
Ambiguous	What is this story about? Use evidence from the text to support your claims.

one of the following: Verbatim copy of presented text; Paraphrase of presented text; Connection among ideas explicit in the text (text-based inferences); and inferences that were derived from the text but that went beyond what was stated to posit some form of message, symbolic meaning, moral, or generalization about the human condition (global/thematic inferences). The difference between text-based and global/thematic inferences corresponds to the distinctions discussed earlier in this chapter regarding the kinds of inferences reflective of literal versus interpretive stances. Verbatim, paraphrase, and text-based inferences were taken as indicative of a literal stance toward the text; global/thematic inferences were taken as indicative of an interpretive stance toward the text.

Consistent with predictions, participants in the plot instruction wrote essays that reflected a literal stance toward the text whereas those in the argument and Theme conditions wrote essays that reflected an interpretive stance. Table 17.2 provides the evidence for this claim, displaying the mean number of clauses per essay for each condition, the mean proportion of inferences to total clauses, and the mean proportion of global/thematic inferences to total inferences. Although essays were longest in the Plot condition, only about one-fourth of the clauses were inferences, and of the inferences only 8 percent were global. In other words, essays in this condition predominantly consisted of verbatim or paraphrased parts of the presented text. In contrast, in the Argument condition, almost 70 percent of the clauses were inferences, and of these, 55 percent were global/thematic. The trend for the Theme condition is similar to that of the Argument condition. The lower portion of Box 17.2 provides representative essays from the Argument condition. Interestingly, participants in the ambiguous condition included a higher proportion of inferences than in the Plot condition, but of these inferences, almost 80 percent were text-based inferences.

Table 17.2 *Length and composition of essays produced in the four task instruction conditions for Harrison Bergeron*

Task instruction condition	Total clauses		Proportion of inference clauses to total clauses		Proportion of global inference clauses to total inferences	
	M	*SD*	*M*	*SD*	*M*	*SD*
Plot	22.16	5.48	0.26	0.18	0.08	0.17
Ambiguous	17.64	7.56	0.49	0.21	0.21	0.21
Argument	14.32	5.81	0.69	0.21	0.55	0.29
Theme	12.08	3.49	0.56	0.22	0.65	0.24

These data indicate that with instructions that reflect a more interpretive bent, participants were more likely to include interpretive statements in their essays than when the instructions emphasized what happened in the story. Box 17.2 provides representative essays produced by a subject in the Plot condition, and two essays produced by subjects in the Argument condition, the first choosing the Big Brother interpretation and the second the human potential interpretation. In addition to the obvious length differences, the Plot condition essay recounts the gist of the events in the story and gives us no information about the reader's response to it or what the reader thinks it means. In contrast, the essays from the Argument condition say very little about the actual story events. Rather, they focus on providing evidence for the interpretation they favor. When they reference the story, they are selective and incorporate events that illustrate a claim they are making about the interpretation they chose.

The results of this study indicate that "literary novices" do make inferences related to moral, philosophical principles and can organize their reasoning in support of an interpretive claim. However, they only performed in this way under certain instructional conditions that directed them to this type of response. When the prompt was ambiguous and used the more neutral language "What was this story about?" responses tended toward the literal to a greater degree than toward the interpretive. We hypothesize that literary novices adopt this literalist stance as the "default" mode of response, whereas literary experts take the interpretive stance as the default mode of response. These "defaults" may be related to differences between literary expert and novices in their standards of coherence for literary texts, with experts defining standards that encompass interpretive inferences whereas the standards of literary novices are at the situation model level only (cf. van den Broek, Bohn-Gettler, Kendeou, Carlson, and White, 2011).

Box 17.2   Representative essays for each condition

PLOT CONDITION

Basically what occurs is that we have jumped into the future. Everyone is equal by giving them handicaps or changing their appearance. There are 2 main characters named George and Hazel who are watching the t.v. At first the t.v. show ballerinas, which of some of them have handicaps. Hazel talks to George about how beautiful the ballerinas danced. Then all of a sudden there is a news flash about a man who escaped from jail. They showed this boy at 7 feet tall and he also had many handicaps. A little bit after this the boy named Harrison Bergeron burst into the studio and called himself the emporer [sic] and took all of his handicaps off. He then found his empress in one of the head ballerinas and rips her handicaps off as well. He then says to her, "Shall we show the people the meaning of the word dance?" He tells the musicians to play and also takes their handicaps off. While the emperor and empress are dancing the handicap general busts in and kills them with a 12 gauge. Then the screen goes blank. George walks back in the room and sees Hazel crying. He asks her why she is crying and she replies something happened on the tv.

She couldn't remember then it ended.

ARGUMENT CONDITION

Big brother

I believe that this is a story about letting "Big Brother" get out of control. The fact that in the first sentences it brings up God, law, and equality almost sets the idea that this is a political message. The story talks about George being "required by law" to wear the transmitter at all times. This is an example of government interference with people's individuality. The fact that people in this story are actually being "dumbed down" by the government and the fact that they are afraid to rebel, shows a government that is in all control. I view the handicap weights around there [sic] necks as a metaphor for, government pressure on their shoulders. I also think this story is showing us through Harrison that people have the power to rise up, but are constrained by government power.

HUMAN POTENTIAL

I think it's more so a story of human potential. As time progresses human advancement and technology continue to grow and develop and would be no surprise if this day were to come about. I believe society is often so intent to try to control mankind and life that the well-being and ending effect are often not the first thought. This story displays that through the idea of making everyone equal in each way. It is an unrealistic idea and is more prone to result in a less well-off society. It's good to have some people better than others in some way because it drives people to work hard to try

Box 17.2   *(cont.)*

to become better. If everyone is the same it gives no room for creativity or change and unintentionally may cue the demise of civilization. Human potential wouldn't exist if everyone were prohibited from having their own ideas. This story shows that with such unbearable control there is a high likelihood of revolt and would most likely result in return to the way society was before the change.

Study 2: spontaneous and prompted processing as sources of evidence for an interpretive stance

The findings of the task manipulation study were based on an off-line essay product and did not tap the online processes in which readers engaged during reading and writing of the essay. The second study we report used think-aloud methodology as a window into the kinds of spontaneous processing in which undergraduates engaged while reading a short story. The think aloud was followed by a series of specific questions that asked for a summary of the story, and whether and what symbols participants noticed in the story. Responses were oral and the story was present throughout the think-aloud and question-answering portions of the study.

In this study, twenty undergraduates read an adapted version of the short story *Butterfly* by James Hanley (991 words) and another twenty read *Eleven* by Sandra Cisneros (1,266 words) (see Appendix A). They received instructions to read out loud and say what they were thinking at the end of each sentence. After reading, participants were asked to summarize the story and to answer a series of questions, two of which specifically probed for symbol identification and interpretation.

1 Symbol identification prompt: Sometimes stories have symbols or ideas, events, objects, or characters in them that actually stand for something else. Now I would like you to look carefully through the story you just read and tell me where that might be going on in this story. What makes you think that?
2 Symbol interpretation prompt: **Butterfly:** What does the caterpillar mean in the story? **Eleven:** What does the sweater mean in the story?

Think-aloud statements were parsed and coded for type of processing including elaborations, paraphrases, evaluations, comprehension problems, and successes (Wolfe and Goldman, 2005). Additionally, think-aloud statements were coded for mention of symbols or other rhetorical devices and for interpretative inferences. Interpretive inferences were categorized as thematic if they referenced specifics of the story or meaning of a symbol in the story context, or as global if they were stated more generally. If think-aloud statements mentioned the author or rules of notice, this was also noted. Summaries were scored with respect to whether they "retold" the story or elaborated upon it.

Responses to the Symbols Identification prompt were categorized by the symbol named and whether the reasons provided reflected thematic or global inferences. Similarly, responses to the second prompt were coded as thematic or global using the same criteria as described for the think-aloud inferences. Examples of thematic and global inferences are provided in Table 17.3.

The types of processing activities that occurred during the think alouds indicated that approximately 60 percent of the statements for each story were elaborations, with the majority being self-explanations. Approximately 20 percent were paraphrases and less than 5 percent were reports of comprehension problems. This profile is consistent with prior reports of the kinds of processing in which students engage when reading short narratives (Magliano and Millis, 2003).

Consistent with the findings of Graves and Frederiksen (1991) and Zeitz (1994), and with the Plot and Ambiguous conditions of our Task Manipulation study, there was little evidence of spontaneous interpretive inferencing unless participants were specifically prompted. Less than 1 percent of the statements made during the think aloud were interpretations. Figure 17.1 indicates that the majority of participants failed to make any interpretive inferences in the think aloud during their initial reading, and interpretations were virtually nonexistent in the summaries. However, when prompted to identify symbols, over 70 percent of the participants explained the basis for their identification with interpretive inferences. Finally, when provided with a symbol and asked to interpret it, all subjects provided an interpretive inference.

A content analysis of the symbols named suggests that these literary novices were guided by at least some of the conventions reflected in Rabinowitz's (1987) rules of notice. That is, when specifically asked if they had noticed any symbols in the story, nearly all participants (90 percent for "The Butterfly" and 95 percent for "Eleven") provided a candidate symbol, and these converged on a small set of concepts in each story. Figure 17.2 provides the data.

Interestingly, in responding to the second part of the symbol identification prompt, participants did not voice rules of notice; that is, they did not make statements such as "Butterfly is a symbol because it is the title." Rather, they discussed the interpretive meaning of the named symbol in

Table 17.3 *Examples of responses classified as thematic or global interpretive inferences*

Type of interpretive inference	Butterfly	Eleven
Thematic	I think the caterpillar reflected Cassidy's situation. The caterpillar was his [Cassidy's] best friend and gateway into the world. The caterpillar – I thought that was Cassidy. Like a caterpillar is a –pretty much an insect and it turns out into a beautiful butterfly so right now Cassidy is growing – he's being morphed into something else and later on when he's an adult he'll become a wise one. The caterpillar symbolizes happiness and hope for Cassidy. I think it signified the life that Cassidy wanted to have and that he is being deprived of.	The sweater would be a symbol of her bad birthday turning eleven. I think the red sweater was kinda maybe symbolizing her growing up and having to deal with things that might make her feel uncomfortable, and she just has to deal with it even though it's a day like her birthday and kind of ruining it. The sweater I have a feeling was her becoming eleven, her maturing and, uh, she wasn't ready for it. This story is about the oppression of the main character. The sweater was, by her putting on the sweater she's physically giving up to the teacher. I think that saying 102 – I think that could be a symbol for [what] she wants to be – not just older in number, but have more experience and be wiser. I think it means that she just wants to – like push away this year basically – like she doesn't want to be eleven she's pushing that away.
Global	Kids have a hope like growing up but sometimes it gets crushed. The caterpillar represents growing up. Caterpillar represents freedom. I think the caterpillar is just like a stage in either like, well, like it's life and it symbolizes for like people's life where you're like starting to grow.	I guess as you get older you kind of get away from cake but it still makes you realize that it's your birthday. So in a sense age is only a number; you're as old as you feel you are. (Sweater) It's a symbol of power. This story is about how people have to struggle for power in the face of oppression. You still have to move on and just get over and go on with life. I think it's just the feeling of wanting to just give up and maybe just run away from everything and, but you can't like you have to address it and you can try to get it away, but still no matter what you do it's still yours.

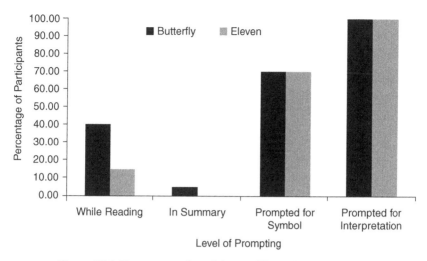

Figure 17.1 Percentage of participants (N = 20) who made interpretive statements during specific phases of the study.

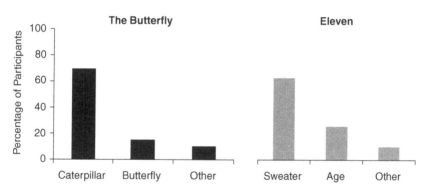

Figure 17.2 Percentage of participants identifying indicated concepts as symbols.

the story (thematic interpretation) or with respect to the world outside the story (global interpretation). The percentages for each type of interpretive inference provided as a reason for identifying particular symbols within each story are shown in columns 2 and 4 in Table 17.4. Furthermore, when specifically provided with a symbol (caterpillar for "The Butterfly" and sweater for "Eleven"), all participants provided interpretive inferences. Thus, when the question identified a symbol for participants and asked them what it meant in the story, everyone

Table 17.4 *Percentages of interpretive inferences for "The Butterfly" and "Eleven"*

	Butterfly		Eleven	
Interpretive statements	Prompted for symbol[a]	Prompted for interpretation	Prompted for symbol[a]	Prompted for interpretation
Thematic	76.47	38.10	66.67	54.55
Global	23.53	61.90	33.33	45.45

[a] Percentages are based on a total of seventeen statements from fourteen participants for "The Butterfly" and eighteen statements from fourteen participants for "Eleven."

discussed the meaning conveyed by the symbol. Indeed, for "The Butterfly" there was a tendency to state these as more general messages beyond the world of the story (e.g., caterpillar: *transformation stands for freedom*).

The results of this study indicate that during initial processing of these stories, participants were focused largely on constructing a coherent textbase and situation model that reflected a coherent plot. Explanatory inferences filled in gaps needed to connect the events of the story. It was not until they were subsequently prompted to think about symbolic interpretation of characters, objects, and events in the story that participants showed any evidence that they were able to process the information at that level. Responses to the prompts indicated that they were indeed able to identify symbols and reason about their meaning, suggesting that they do indeed have at least some knowledge of literary conventions that signal important elements of a text, however tacit this may be. What novices may be less aware of is that authors use these conventions to convey their message and that complete representations of literary texts include connections to themes and universals about the human condition such as are reflected in what we call here global interpretive inferences.

Concluding comments

Overall, results of our initial studies into literary interpretation on the part of "literary novices" suggest that undergraduate literary novices have some knowledge of the conventions that authors assume in their readers and that literary experts make explicit when asked to respond to a literary text. That this knowledge only begins to appear in novices when they are specifically prompted suggests that they may have a different understanding of what it means to comprehend a literary text than do experts. As van den Broek, Goldman and colleagues have suggested (Goldman et al., 1996; van den Broek et al., 2001; van den Broek et al., 2011), these differences in what it means to comprehend may be reflected in the standards of coherence that literary experts apply when reading text they define as literature. Literary novices, on the other hand, may hold the same standards of coherence for literature as they do for other texts and may be "content" with a coherent representation of the basic plot elements. Alternatively, literary novices may, in some sense, know that comprehension of literary texts includes arriving at some message or point beyond the plot and characters, but they may be less apt to or able than experts to process at these multiple levels on initial passes through literary texts. Indeed, one aspect of literary text processing that may be overlooked in empirical studies of literature is the need to revisit a text multiple times to *really* get the point and be able to access and organize attended- to elements of text into meaningful patterns that convey the subtext or duplicity of meaning that is said to distinguish literary text from nonliterary. The findings we presented in this chapter, along with other emerging research of ours and others, suggests that there are productive starting points for enhancing "text comprehension instruction" to build on the nascent literary bent we have begun to explore in novices.

However, as we argued earlier in this chapter, rather than characterizing the texts as literary or nonliterary, it seems more productive to focus on the conditions that support adopting interpretive stances, as well as literal, toward texts. Adopting an interpretive stance fosters attention beyond the semantic and syntactic to the prosodic and pragmatic aspects of texts because all of these have potential significance for interpretative inferences that build toward the point or message of a particular literary work. Representing these aspects of meaning implies augmenting theories of single-text comprehension that posit largely semantic situation models and giving serious attention to how information about language use, theme, and author are represented not only with respect to the specific text in which they occur but to the formation of interpretive frameworks that are useful across multiple literary texts. What is needed is a literary instantiation of intertextual representational models analogous to those proposed for other disciplinary domains (e.g., Goldman, 2004; Goldman and Bloome, 2005; Perfetti, Rouet, and Britt, 1999; Rouet 2006; Rouet and Britt, 2011). "Nodes" in literary intertextual models would capture knowledge of genres within, for example, the narrative genre (e.g., tragedy or satire) and the various character and plot types that constitute them as well as themes specific to individual texts and their abstraction to principles of motivated human action, and universals of the human condition.

REFERENCES

Bartlett, F. C. (1932). *Remembering: A Study in Experimental and Social Psychology*. Cambridge University Press.

Carlsen, G. R. (1981). Literature isn't supposed to be realistic. *English Journal*, *70*, 8–10.

Chi, M. T. H., Feltovich, P. J., & Glaser, R. (1981). Categorization and representation of physics problems by experts and novices. *Cognitive Science*, *5*, 121–52.

Claassen, E. (2012). *Author Representation in Literary Reading*. Utrecht, Netherlands: John Benjamins.

Fish, S. (1980). *Is There a Text in This Class? The Authority of Interpretive Communities*. London: Harvard University Press.

Gibbs, R. (2001). Authorial intentions in text understanding. *Discourse Processes*, *32*, 73–80.

Goldman, S. R. (1997). Learning from text: reflections on the past and suggestions for the future. *Discourse Processes*, *23*, 357–98.

  Cognitive aspects of constructing meaning through and across multiple texts. In N. Shuart-Faris & D. Bloome (eds.), *Uses of Intertextuality in Classroom and Educational Research* (pp. 317–51). Greenwich, CT: Information Age.

Goldman, S. R., & Bloome, D. M. (2005). Learning to construct and integrate. In A. F. Healy (ed.), *Experimental Cognitive Psychology and Its Applications: Festshrift in Honor of Lyle Bourne, Walter Kintsch, and Thomas Landauer* (pp. 169–82). Washington, DC: American Psychological Association.

Goldman, S. R. Reyes, M., & Varnhagen, C. K. (1984). Understanding fables in first and second languages. *Bilingual Research Journal*, *8*, 35–66.

Goldman, S. R., Varma, S., & Coté, N. (1996). Extending capacity-constrained construction integration: toward "smarter" and flexible models of text comprehension. In B. K. Britton & A. C. Graesser (eds.), *Models of Text Comprehension* (pp. 73–113). Mahwah, NJ: Erlbaum.

Graesser, A. C., Olde, B., & Klettke, B. (2002). How does the mind construct and represent stories? In M. C. Green, J. J. Strange, & T. C, Brock (eds.) *Narrative Impact: Social and Cognitive Foundations* (pp. 229–62). Mahwah, NJ: Erlbaum.

Graesser, A. C., Louwerse, M. M., McNamara, D. S., Olney, A., Cai, Z., & Mitchell, H. H. (2007). Inference generation and cohesion in the construction of situation models: some connections with computational linguistics. In F. Schmalhofer & C. A. Perfetti (eds.), *Higher Level Language Processes in the Brain* (pp. 289–310). Mahwah, NJ: Erlbaum.

Graesser, A. C., Singer, M., & Trabasso, T. (1994). Constructing inferences during narrative text comprehension. *Psychological Review*, *101*, 371–95.

Graves, B., & Frederiksen, C. H. (1991). Literary expertise in the description of fictional narrative. *Poetics*, *20*, 1–26.

Heider, F. (1958). *The Psychology of Interpersonal Relations*. Mahwah, NJ: Erlbaum.

Hillocks, G., & Ludlow, L. H. (1984). A taxonomy of skills in reading and interpreting fiction. *American Educational Research Journal*, *21*, 7–24.

Johnson, D. F., & Goldman, S. R. (1987). Children's recognition and use of rules of moral conduct in stories. *The American Journal of Psychology, 100,* 205–24.

Kintsch, W. (1994). Text comprehension, memory, and learning. *American Psychologist, 49*(4), 294–303.

(1998). *Comprehension: A Paradigm for Cognition.* Cambridge University Press.

Kintsch, W., & van Dijk, T. A. (1978). Toward a model of text comprehension and production. *Psychological Review, 85,* 363–94.

Kurtz, V., & Schober, M. F. (2001). Readers' varying interpretations of theme in short fiction. *Poetics, 29,* 139–66.

Langer, J. A. (2010). *Envisioning Literature: Literary Understanding and Literature Instruction,* 2nd edn. New York: Teachers College Press.

Lee, C. D. (2001). Is October Brown Chinese? A cultural modeling activity system for underachieving students. *American Educational Research Journal,38*(1), 97–141.

(2007). *Culture, Literacy, and Learning: Taking Bloom in the Midst of the Whirlwind.* New York: Teachers College Press.

Levine, S. R. (2013). Making interpretation visible with an affect-based strategy, (unpublished doctoral dissertation). Northwestern University, Evanston, IL.

Magliano, J. P , & Millis, K. K. (2003). Assessing reading skill with a think-aloud procedure. *Cognition and Instruction. 21,* 251 83.

Mandler, J. M., & Goodman, M. S. (1982). On the psychological validity of story structure. *Journal of Verbal Learning and Verbal Behavior, 21,* 507–23.

Mandler, J. M., & Johnson, N. S. (1977). Remembrance of things parsed: story structure and recall. *Cognitive Psychology, 9,* 111–51.

McCarthy, K. S., & Goldman, S. R. (in press). Comprehension of short stories: effect of task instruction on literary interpretation. *Discourse Processes.*

Perfetti, C. A., Rouet, J. F., & Britt, M. A. (1999). Toward a theory of documents representation. In H. van Oostendorp & S. R. Goldman (eds.), *The Construction of Mental Representations during Reading* (pp. 99–122). Mahwah, NJ: Erlbaum.

Peskin, J. (1998). Constructing meaning when reading poetry: an expert-novice study. *Cognition and Instruction, 16,* 135–263.

Purves, A. (1971). Evaluation of learning in literature. In B. S. Bloom, J. T. Hastings, & G. Madaus (eds.), *Handbook on Formative and Summative Evaluation of Student Learning* (pp. 697–766). New York: McGraw-Hill.

Rabinowitz, P. (1987). *Before Reading: Narrative Conventions and the Politics of Interpretation.* Ohio State University Press.

RAND Reading Study Group (2002). *Reading for Understanding: Toward an R&D Program in reading comprehension.* Santa Monica, CA: Rand Education. Also available at www.rand.org/multi/achievementforall/reading/

Rosenblatt, L. (1994). The transactional theory of reading and writing. In R. B. Ruddell, M. R. Ruddell, & H. Singer (eds.), *Theoretical Models and Processes of Reading* (4th edn., pp. 1057–92). Newark, DE: International Reading Association.

Rouet, J. F. (2006). *The Skills of Document Use: From Text Comprehension to Web-based Learning.* Mahwah, NJ: Erlbaum.

Rouet, J. F., & Britt, M. A. (2011). Relevance processes in multiple document comprehension. In M. T. McCrudden, J. P. Magliano, & G. Schraw (eds.), *Text Relevance and Learning from Text* (pp. 19–52). Greenwich, CT: Information Age Publishing.

Rumelhart, D. E. (1975). Notes on a schema for stories. In D. Bobrow & A. Collins (eds.), *Representation and Understanding: Studies in Cognitive Science*. New York: Academic Press.

Schmidt, S. J. (1982). *Foundations of the Empirical Study of Literature*. Hamburg: Buske.

Scholes, R. (1985). *Textual Power: Literary Theory and the Teaching of English*. New Haven, CT: Yale University Press.

Schraw, G. (1997). Situational interest in literary text. *Contemporary Educational Psychology, 22*, 436–56.

Smith, M. (1991). *Understanding Unreliable Narrators: Reading between the Lines in the Literature Classroom*. Urbana, IL: National Council of Teachers of English.

Stein N. L., & Glenn, C. G. (1979). An analysis of story comprehension in elementary school children. In R. Freedle (ed.), *Discourse Processing: Multidisciplinary Perspectives*. Norwood, NJ: Ablex.

Van den Broek, P., Bohn-Gettler, C. M., Kendeou, P., Carlson, S., & White, M. K. (2011). When a reader meets a text. In M. T. McCrudden, J. P. Magliano, & G. Schraw (eds.), *Text Relevance and Learning from Text* (pp. 123–39). Greenwich, CT: Information Age Publishing.

Van den Broek, P., Lorch, R. F., Linderholm, T., & Gustafson, M. (2001). The effect of readers' goals on inference generation and memory for texts. *Memory & Cognition, 29*, 1081–7.

Van Dijk, T. A., & Kintsch, W. (1983). *Strategies of Discourse Comprehension*. New York: Academic Press.

Vipond, D., & Hunt, R. A. (1984). Point-driven understanding: pragmatic and cognitive dimensions of literary reading. *Poetics, 13*, 261–77.

Vonnegut, K. 1968. Harrison Bergeron. In *Welcome to the Monkey House* (pp. 7–13). New York: Delacorte.

Warren, J. E. (2011). "Generic" and "specific" expertise in English: an expert/novice study in poetry interpretation and academic argument. *Cognition and Instruction, 29*, 349–74.

Winner, E. (1988). *The Point of Words: Children's Understanding of Metaphor and Irony*. Cambridge: Harvard University Press.

Wolfe, M. B., & Goldman, S. R. (2005). Relationships between adolescents' text processing and reasoning. *Cognition and Instruction, 23*, 467–502.

Zeitz, C. M. (1994). Expert-novice differences in memory, abstraction, and reasoning in the domain of literature. *Cognition and Instruction, 4*, 277–312.

Appendix A Stories used in Study 2:
"The Butterfly" and "Eleven"

By James Hanley

The Butterfly

Brother Timothy's robes made a strange noise as he strode up and down the passage. The priest's face was red, his mouth twitched, and his fingers pulled nervously at the buttons upon his robe. One could see at a glance that he was angry. He muttered to himself, staring at a strong wooden door before him.

He simply could not understand the boy. Every time the name Cassidy came into his mind, the blood mounted to his forehead. It was the boy's silence that was the enraging thing, his silence! And what was even worse was how happy the boy seemed. Curse him for his silence and happiness. The boy must have no conscience at all.

Brother Timothy stopped and stared at the wooden door. He listened. Not a sound. The boy might be standing behind it now, maybe thinking that he would be let out. Brother Timothy laughed then. That boy would not be let out until he explained himself, until he broke his silence. How to break it down then? Yes, one must try to think.

The priest drew a key from his pocket, opened the door and went inside. The boy was sitting on the bed. He looked up at the Brother, but something in the other's glance made him hurriedly drop his eyes again.

"Well, Cassidy," said Brother Timothy, "Have you come to your senses yet?" The veins in his neck stood out. The silence galled him. "Answer me, I tell you!" he shouted. But Cassidy did not speak.

"Look at me! Yesterday you missed mass, you and this other child Byrne. Did you ask permission to miss mass? Why were you truant? Why are you so unlike the others? And this silence! I will not stand it. You have the devil in you; it's he who has trapped your tongue. But I'll break you. Do you hear me? I ask you for the last time, why did you skip mass?"

Cassidy, a boy of twelve, looked up at the Brother. His lips moved, but he made no sound.

In fury, Brother Timothy struck him across the face.

Then Cassidy said slowly, "Brother Timothy, I told you yesterday."

"You are determined then. Fine. You will remain here, and out of this room you will not go until you open that mouth of yours. And when you have explained to me you will go to confession, and you will confess." The priest strode out of the room.

The door banged, the key turned.

In the morning when the boy woke the sun was streaming through the window. It filled him with an intense longing for the open air, to be free of this room, free of the sound of those well-known footsteps, from the sight of that face, which mirrored rage and defeat.

Cassidy reflected that he meant no harm. He had simply gone into the forest, had become absorbed in the strange life that abounded in the hedges and ditches, and had not heard the bell. And here he was stuck in this musty room for two days because he would not explain. "But I have explained," he kept saying to himself. "I have explained."

From his pocket he took a cardboard box pinned with air-holes. He removed the lid. Slowly a green caterpillar crept out and along his finger. Cassidy watched its slow graceful movements down his hand. He lowered his head and stared hard at it. What a lovely green it was. And one day it would turn into a beautiful butterfly. How marvelous. He stroked it gently with his finger. The sun came out, it poured through the window, filled the room, and the green caterpillar was bathed in the light.

"I think I'll call you Xavier," he said to the insect, and smiled. For two whole days he had had it in the cardboard box. It made him happy knowing it was there, in the room with him. It made him forget Brother Timothy, forget many things. He knew he would be happy while he had the green caterpillar. If it could speak, he would explain to it why he was kept in the stuffy room by Brother Timothy. Perhaps this green caterpillar did know, perhaps it looked at him.

Cassidy heard footsteps in the corridor. A moment later the door opened and Brother Timothy stepped into the room.

"Well, Cassidy," he said. "Have you come to your senses?" But the boy appeared not to hear him. He was standing with his back to the Brother, the sunlight on his face, and he was gently laying the caterpillar on a bit of moss in the cardboard box.

"Cassidy!" roared the man behind him, and the boy turned round. "What have you there?"

"Nothing – I mean – Brother Timothy, it's a –"

"What! And this is how you spend your time. Aren't you sorry for your sin?"

"Sin? Brother Timothy, I – I mean, it's only a little caterpillar."

If silence had been poisonous, this was worse. "Is this how you think upon your conscience? Is this how you think out your explanation? Outrageous, boy! Give me that at once."

"But it's only a caterpillar, Brother Timothy, a little green one. Soon it'll be a butterfly. It's so green and soft, and it crawls up my finger just like it knew me. Please, Brother – I – while I was sitting here all by myself it made me happy, I liked having it, I –"

"How dare you!" Brother Timothy grabbed the box and turned out the caterpillar. It fell to the floor and slowly began to crawl.

"You have no right to skip mass and you have no right to be happy or anything else. Do you hear me?" and with a quick movement of his broad foot Brother Timothy trod on the insect and crushed out its life. Cassidy looked up at the Brother. Then he burst into tears.

Eleven

By Sandra Cisneros

What they don't understand about birthdays and what they never tell you is that when you're eleven, you're also ten, and nine, and eight, and seven, and six, and five, and four, and three, and two, and one. And when you wake up on your eleventh birthday you expect to feel eleven, but you don't. You open your eyes and everything's just like yesterday, only it's today. And you don't feel eleven at all. You feel like you're still ten. And you are – underneath the year that makes you eleven.

Like some days you might say something stupid, and that's the part of you that's still ten. Or maybe some days you might need to sit on your mama's lap because you're scared, and that's the part of you that's five. And maybe one day when you're all grown up maybe you will need to cry like if you're three, and that's okay. That's what I tell Mama when she's sad and needs to cry. Maybe she's feeling three.

Because the way you grow old is kind of like an onion or like the rings inside a tree trunk or like my little wooden dolls that fit one inside the other, each year inside the next one. That's how being eleven years old is.

You don't feel eleven. Not right away. It takes a few days, weeks even, sometimes even months before you say eleven when they ask you. And you don't feel smart eleven, not until you're almost twelve. That's the way it is.

Only today I wish I didn't have only eleven years rattling inside me like pennies in a tin Band-Aid box. Today I wish I was one hundred and two instead of eleven because if I was one hundred and two I'd have known what to say when Mrs. Price put the red sweater on my desk. I would've known how to tell her it wasn't mine instead of just sitting there with that look on my face and nothing coming out of my mouth.

"Whose is this?" Mrs. Price says, and she holds the red sweater up in the air for all the class to see. "Whose? It's been sitting in the coatroom for a month."

"Not mine," says everybody. "Not me."

"It has to belong to somebody," Mrs. Price keeps saying, but nobody can remember. It's an ugly sweater with red plastic buttons and a collar and sleeves all stretched out like you could use it for a jump rope. It's maybe a thousand years old and even if it belonged to me I wouldn't say so.

Maybe because I'm skinny, maybe because she doesn't' like me, that stupid Sylvia Saldivar says, "I think it belongs to Rachel." An ugly sweater like that, all raggedy and old, but Mrs. Price believes her. Mrs. Price takes the sweater and puts it right on my desk, but when I open my mouth nothing comes out.

"That's not, I don't, you're not ... Not mine," I finally say in a little voice that was maybe me when I was four.

"Of course It's yours," Mrs. Price says. "I remember you wearing it once."

Because she's older and the teacher, she's right and I'm not.

Not mine, not mine, not mine, but Mrs. Price is already turning to page thirty-two, and math problem number four. I don't know why but all of a sudden I'm feeling sick inside, like the part of me that's three wants to come out of my eyes, only I squeeze them shut tight and bite down on my teeth real hard and try to remember today I am eleven, eleven. Mama is making a cake for me tonight, and when Papa comes home everybody will sing Happy birthday, happy birthday to you.

But when the sick feeling goes away and I open my eyes, the red sweater's still sitting there like a big red mountain. I move the red sweater to the corner of my desk with my ruler. I move my pencil and books and eraser as far from it as possible. I even move my chair a little to the right. Not mine, not mine, not mine.

In my head I'm thinking how long till lunchtime, how long till I can take the red sweater and throw it over the school yard fence, or even leave it hanging on a parking meter, or bunch it up into a little ball and toss it in the alley. Except when math period ends Mrs. Price says loud and in front of everybody, "Now Rachel, that's enough," because she sees I've shoved the red sweater to the tippy-tip corner of my desk and it's hanging all over the edge like a waterfall, but I don't care.

"Rachel," Mrs. Price says. She says it like she's getting mad. "You put that sweater on right now and no more nonsense."

"But it's not – "

"Now!" Mrs. Price says.

This is when I wish I wasn't eleven, because all the years inside of me – ten, nine, eight, seven, six, five, four, three, two and one – are pushing at the back of my eyes when I put one arm through one sleeve of the sweater that smells like cottage cheese, and then the other arm through the other and stand there with my arms apart like if the sweater hurts me and it does, all itchy and full of germs that aren't even mine.

That's when everything I've been holding in since this morning, since when Mrs. Price put the sweater on my desk, finally lets go, and all of a sudden I'm crying in front of everybody. I wish I was invisible but I'm not. I'm eleven and it's my birthday today and I'm crying like I'm three in front of everybody. I put my head down on the desk and bury my face in my stupid clown-sweater arms. My face all hot and spit coming out of my mouth because I can't stop the little animal noises from coming out of me, until there aren't any more tears left in my eyes, and it's just my body shaking like when you have the hiccups, and my whole head hurts like when you drink milk too fast.

But the worst part is right before the bell rings for lunch. That stupid Phyllis Lopez, who is even dumber than Sylvia Saldivar, says she remembers the red sweater is hers! I take it off right away and give it to her, only Mrs. Price pretends like everything's okay.

Today I'm eleven. There's cake Mama's making for tonight, and when Papa comes home from work we'll eat it. There'll be candles and presents and everybody will sing Happy birthday, happy birthday to you, Rachel, only it's too late.

I'm eleven today. I'm eleven, ten, nine, eight, seven, six, five, four, three, two, and one, but I wish I was one hundred and two. I wish I was anything but eleven, because I want today to be far away already, far away like a runaway balloon, like a tiny o in the sky, so tiny-tiny you have to close your eyes to see it.

Index

Lightning Source UK Ltd.
Milton Keynes UK
UKOW06n1936050416

271630UK00003B/57/P